D0151390

Fourth Edition

The Counterterrorism Handbook

Tactics, Procedures, and Techniques

CRC SERIES IN
**PRACTICAL ASPECTS OF CRIMINAL
AND FORENSIC INVESTIGATIONS**

VERNON J. GEBERTH, BBA, MPS, FBINA *Series Editor*

Investigating Computer Crime
Franklin Clark and Ken Diliberto

Practical Homicide Investigation Checklist and Field Guide
Vernon J. Geberth

Practical Aspects of Munchausen by Proxy and Munchausen Syndrome Investigation
Kathryn Artingstall

Quantitative-Qualitative Friction Ridge Analysis: An Introduction to Basic and Advanced Ridgeology
David R. Ashbaugh

Practical Criminal Investigations in Correctional Facilities
William R. Bell

Officer-Involved Shootings and Use of Force: Practical Investigative Techniques, Second Edition
David E. Hatch

Sex-Related Homicide and Death Investigation: Practical and Clinical Perspectives, Second Edition
Vernon J. Geberth

Global Drug Enforcement: Practical Investigative Techniques
Gregory D. Lee

Practical Investigation of Sex Crimes: A Strategic and Operational Approach
Thomas P. Carney

Principles of Bloodstain Pattern Analysis: Theory and Practice
Stuart James, Paul Kish, and T. Paulette Sutton

Cold Case Homicides: Practical Investigative Techniques
Richard H. Walton

Practical Crime Scene Processing and Investigation
Ross M. Gardner

Practical Bomb Scene Investigation
James T. Thurman

Practical Analysis and Reconstruction of Shooting Incidents
Edward E. Hueske

Tire Tread and Tire Track Evidence: Recovery and Forensic Examination
William J. Bodziak

Bloodstain Pattern Analysis: With an Introduction to Crime Scene Reconstruction, Third Edition
Tom Bevel and Ross M. Gardner

Serial Violence: Analysis of Modus Operandi and Signature Characteristics of Killers
Robert D. Keppel and William J. Birnes

Practical Crime Scene Analysis and Reconstruction
Ross M. Gardner

Fourth Edition

The Counterterrorism Handbook

Tactics, Procedures, and Techniques

Frank Bolz, Jr., Kenneth J. Dudonis, David P. Schulz

CRC Press
Taylor & Francis Group
Boca Raton   London   New York

CRC Press is an imprint of the
Taylor & Francis Group, an **informa** business

CRC Press
Taylor & Francis Group
6000 Broken Sound Parkway NW, Suite 300
Boca Raton, FL 33487-2742

Printed in the United States of America on acid-free paper
10 9 8 7 6 5 4 3 2 1

International Standard Book Number: 978-1-4398-4670-4 (Hardback)

Library of Congress Cataloging-in-Publication Data

Bolz, Frank, 1930-
  The counterterrorism handbook : tactics, procedures, and techniques / Frank Bolz Jr., Kenneth J. Dudonis, and David P. Schulz. -- 4th ed.
  p. cm. -- (CRC series in practical aspects of criminal and forensic investigations ; 54)
  Includes bibliographical references and index.
  ISBN 978-1-4398-4670-4
  1. Terrorism--Prevention. I. Dudonis, Kenneth J. II. Schulz, David P. III. Title. IV. Series.

HV6431.B65 2011
363.325'16--dc22   2011000832

Visit the Taylor & Francis Web site at
http://www.taylorandfrancis.com

and the CRC Press Web site at
http://www.crcpress.com

To all the law enforcement officers and armed forces personnel who are on the front lines in the War on Terrorism, and to all the victims of terrorism of all kinds in all places.

Table of Contents

Series Note

This textbook is part of a series entitled "Practical Aspects of Criminal and Forensic Investigations." This series was created by Vernon J. Geberth, a retired New York City Police Department Lieutenant Commander, who is an author, educator, and consultant on homicide and forensic investigations.

This series has been designed to provide contemporary, comprehensive, and pragmatic information to the practitioner involved in criminal and forensic investigations by authors who are nationally recognized experts in their respective fields.

Foreword

Terrorism is a form of warfare that relies principally upon fear to deliver its message. The target of the violence often goes beyond the immediate victim. Its ultimate goal is theatrical, the Broadway of villainous acts. This holds especially true today with television news programs broadcasting images of a terrorist event even before senior officials have had time to assess the situation. This, together with the advent of cell phones, has led to just-in-time decision making, a new phenomenon in managing a crisis.

In recent years, we have witnessed a staccato succession of bombings, assassinations, and hostage-taking incidents, with every new threat spawning a new countermeasure and every new countermeasure resulting in new threats. While terrorists are unlikely to give up the truck bombs or spectacular suicide missions that afford them instant gratification and notoriety, a new cadre of terrorists exists that may look to nontraditional tactics and weapons. The young terrorist of today is often Internet savvy and well educated, bringing a whole new level of sophistication to the table. Computers and wireless communication are increasingly being used for planning terrorist activity, recruiting, and fundraising. And, while terrorists can afford the latest technological equipment, law enforcement and other officials more often than not find themselves lagging behind, making it difficult for them to keep up with the terrorists.

Further complicating terrorism warfare calibrations is the possibility that cyberattacks against critical infrastructures may be used as a force multiplier to extend the deadliness of an incident. Furthermore, the target of the attack, the critical infrastructure, currently is owned and operated primarily by the private sector, bringing a whole new group of players into the counterterrorism game.

In contrast with the period of the Cold War when terrorist groups were predominantly politically motivated, the most prominent groups today carry a religious banner. This makes them especially dangerous, for the only entity they need to justify their actions to is God, in whose name they carry out the violence. Politically motivated groups traditionally looked for targets of symbolic value: a soldier, a government official, etc. Religious groups, on the other hand, feel that any mode of attacking the infidel is legitimate, even if it means killing innocent civilians. Anyone, anywhere, anytime can become a target.

What we end up with is an unholy marriage between advances in technology and indiscriminate targeting, an extremely lethal combination. Many experts in the emerging field of counterterrorism refuse to believe that terrorism will escalate to a level involving weapons of mass destruction (WMD), even though the technology and expertise are readily available. This holds true despite the sarin gas attack in Tokyo subways in March 1995 by the religious cult Aum Shinrikyo that killed 12 people and injured thousands of others; it is often regarded as an anomaly — even by the Japanese.

The question is not so much whether or not there is a real probability of a terrorist incident involving WMD, but whether one can afford not to be prepared. The consequences of any incident involving WMD are so devastating that even if there is only an infinitesimal chance of one occurring, the framework has to be in place to swiftly and efficiently deal with the crisis.

So far, the United States' counterterrorism strategy, while impressive in appearance and number of acronyms, could in fact be a recipe for disaster should another grievous terrorist attack occur on American soil. The byzantine bureaucracy comprising the U.S. response, for example, could easily result in a delay in the deployment of the right tools to a local community dealing with an attack never before envisaged by its citizens.

The Counterterrorism Handbook is among the first serious efforts to lay out a comprehensive strategy of how to deal with a whole gamut of possible terrorist incidents in language that a first responder (policeman, fireman, medic, etc.) can understand. The book covers everything from bombings and hostage-taking to nuclear terrorism and what needs to be done before, during, and after an event. The handbook combines what needs to be minimally understood about counterterrorism by the Washington-level policymaker, while at the same time helping first responders who are planning to cope with what must at least initially seem like an overwhelming attack.

The book makes clear that the only way to effectively deal with terrorism is to have a thorough understanding of its present-day characteristics — who is involved and what weapons and tactics they are likely to use. The players on the counterterrorism team need to take stock of what is in their toolkits; what works and what doesn't work; and what new capabilities need to be developed in order to face not only today's terrorist, but tomorrow's as well.

The authors of *The Counterterrorism Handbook*, Frank Bolz, Kenneth Dudonis, and David Schulz, each bring to the table unique insights and real-world experience based on years in the counterterrorism field. Their hands-on knowledge of the topic infuses the book with a down-to-earth practicality often missing from other counterterrorism studies. This book is a must read for anyone who may need to cope with a serious terrorist attack on U.S. soil.

Dr. Robert Kupperman*
Stephanie Lanz

---

* Robert Harris Kupperman died November 24, 2006. He served with the Center for Strategic and International Studies, and among the books he wrote or coauthored was *Final Warning: Averting Disaster in the New Age of Terrorism*. While with the federal government, he was executive director of the Office of Emergency Preparedness and worked with the U.S. Arms Control and Disarmament Agency, where he assisted in the creation of the Cabinet Committee to Combat Terrorism.

Preface

This book represents the results of our experiences with the tactics, procedures, and techniques that date to the dawn of the modern era of terrorism. Its serial reincarnations demonstrate that even as the actors and their stage and sets may change, the principles of combating terrorism have not.

Acknowledgments

We thank our families who sustained us—Ruth, Carol, and Dorothy—and the folks at P.J. Clarke's who put up with our meetings. Special thanks to Vernon Geberth and to the bomb technicians, investigators, tactical personnel, and hostage negotiators for professional assistance. We gratefully acknowledge Neil Monaco, New York Police Department Bomb Squad (Retired); Detective John Breslin (Retired); Special Agent James Lyons; Lt. Frank Guerra, SIS, Inc.; J. Christopher Ronay, president of the Institute of Makers of Explosives; Dr. Harvey Schlossberg; the late Lt. Justin McGarvey, NYPD, for his unique contribution to the NYPD's hostage negotiating program; Bert Solivan, vice president of news information, Fox News Channel; Joseph Conley, FBI (Retired); Brian Jenkins, formerly of the Rand Institute and Kroll Associates, and Prof. Dorothy M. Schulz, John Jay College of Criminal Justice (City University of New York), for her invaluable assistance and contacts in a variety of fields. For the fourth edition, we also acknowledge the assistance of Lt. Jack Cambria, commanding officer of the NYPD hostage negotiating team and Det. Sgt. Wallace Ziens, NYPD (Retired).

Introduction

President George W. Bush in 2001 told the American people that the war on terror would be unlike any other war in our history. Since 9/11 that prediction has certainly come to pass, as we face global jihad that has yet to be defeated. The war against radical Islam must be taken seriously by the leaders of the United States and its citizens to ensure the national security of the United States, the American families, and the democratic values for which we stand. The issue of international and domestic security is the foremost challenge. This battle, which we all must fight and understand, is based on protecting the values and traditions of America that are the foundation of our society and the free democratic world.

America is a nation at war externally and internally and requires a unique awareness of the people and the elected and appointed leaders. We are in a global war just as (or maybe more) threatening and deadly as the war against Nazi Germany, communism, or the Imperial Army of Japan. The best way to plan the future is to understand the world as it is in order to make plans and take action against those threats that we face. There is no substitute for victory, and hope is not a strategy.

The authors of *The Counterterrorism Handbook* each bring unique qualifications and experiences to this study and a blueprint for success that is espoused. It is extremely important to develop an intense understanding of the strategy, tactics, and techniques required to deal and meet with contemporary terrorism and global jihad head-on. The book makes vividly clear the profiles and characteristics of modern-day terror cells and organizations that conduct terror operations.

To win this war, we must meld all elements of national power in a determined and relentless campaign to defeat the enemies that we face across the globe and within and without our borders. The Mexican border, the southern border, is as much a threat as the global jihad. It is a new reality that leaders, civilian agencies, and soldiers must be well trained for this new type of warfare. For any war, as Carl von Clausewitz, the nineteenth century German military theorist, pointed out, it is essential to understand "the kind of war on which [we] are embarking." Although the fundamental nature of war is constant, its methods and techniques constantly change to reflect the operational capabilities at hand. The United States is driving a rapid evolution in the methods and techniques of war. Operations are dependent on good operational intelligence.

This book is a must read for anyone involved in a leadership position at any level of federal, state, or local government, or at a private organization involved in the support of war on terror operations.

Paul E. Vallely, MG, U.S. Army (Ret.)
Chairman, Stand Up America

Terrorism
An Overview

1

New Game

Terrorism is a political act, though its use and processes have very specific, horrific components and consequences. In this country terror is perhaps no longer perceived to be the same thing it was in the years immediately following the events of September 11, 2001—events that tragically introduced international terrorism to the American public. Terrorism on American soil was not new, since political activists, extremists, and radicals had used bombs, kidnapping, hijackings, and hostage taking as tactics in campaigns to press their points of view into the public awareness. But foreign terrorists striking on the American mainland had a devastating effect physically, psychologically, and emotionally that, a decade later, still inhabits the nation's psyche. Governments—federal, state, and local—continue to struggle to reduce the anxiety levels among the general public. In addition, private sector security has never been so finely tuned.

The last two decades of the twentieth century saw the rise of extreme Islamic radicalism to levels that threaten regimes throughout the Muslim world, as well as nations throughout Asia, Europe, much of Africa, and North America. Terrorist attacks carried out by Islamic terrorist groups have risen not only in number, but also in level of violence. The United States, which had largely been free of confrontations with Islamic terrorism, received its first taste in 1993, with a truck bomb attack on the World Trade Center in New York City, the same target leveled in the aerial assault on September 11, 2001. The earlier incident was largely disregarded at the highest levels of our government, perhaps considered aberrant and amateurish, and it went largely unacknowledged. In the years up to the first World Trade Center attack, there were a number on incidents against Americans and American interests perpetrated, or believed to have been perpetrated, by Islamic radicals. But these were largely confined to the Middle East and adjacent territories. More recently, however, the United States has been engaged in hot wars in Iraq and Afghanistan. The war in Iraq quickly went from a classic military operation into an insurgency—though the "rebels" were mostly from outside Iraq—with the improvised explosive device a weapon of choice. The incursion by American forces into these countries further fanned the flames of radical Islam.

Terrorist activities on American soil by foreigners were a lightly regarded threat in large part because it was believed that there was not a critical mass of immigrant population through which terrorists could establish a support infrastructure. This has all changed with the influx of a large number of Middle Eastern immigrants at the end of the twentieth century and in the early years of the twenty-first century. The great majority of these immigrants follow the Islamic faith in a peaceful manner, but some do not. This has raised concern among many in the law enforcement and intelligence communities, but the level of their concern has not always been shared by those in other areas of government, particularly at the federal level, such as the Department of State, to name one.

Global War on Terrorism

A decade has passed since the devastating attack on the World Trade Center in New York City. The counterterrorism response that was formulated precipitated a bold and rapid reaction to what is still called the war on terrorism. It began in October 2001, when President George W. Bush told the American people, "The attack took place on the American soil, but it was an attack on the heart and soul of the civilized world. And the world has come together to fight a new and different war, the first, and we hope the only one, of the twenty-first century. A war against all those who seek to export terror and a war against the governments that support or shelter them."[1] This war is being waged not only by the military, but also by numerous law enforcement and intelligence agencies around the globe. Inevitably, there are arguments as to whether bullets or diplomats are the way to address the problem. The answer is not easy—force must be met with force—but we still need the cooperation of the governments in countries where terrorists operate.

After 9/11, the United States and a number of allies began implementing policies that would take the war to the terrorists on multiple fronts and in multiple ways. The battle to destroy terrorism, or at least control it, involves diplomatic, financial, military, and traditional law enforcement strategies and tactics. In an effort to thwart future terrorist attacks, New York City launched a number of initiatives, including the placement of police detectives in selected overseas locations to interact with their counterparts in the gathering of intelligence information. In this way information that is useful to New York's safety can be transmitted directly without being first filtered through federal intelligence agencies.

After three decades of intensive activity by Islamic radicals who were increasing attacks in both number and audacity against civilized countries and their worldwide interests, the civilized world struck back. Led by the United States in the wake of 9/11, the fight was brought to the enemy, through the Taliban and al Qaeda operations in Afghanistan and the removal of Saddam Hussein's regime in Iraq. Initially more than 170 nations participated in the war on terrorism by actively pursuing terrorists within their borders, freezing funds of terrorist support networks, and providing military assistance. Enthusiasm, both at home and abroad, ebbs and flows, but yet the war against terrorism continues.

On the domestic front, the creation of the cabinet-level Department of Homeland Security (DHS) brought together virtually all the federal agencies directly involved with the war on terror. The enactment of the USA Patriot Act codified many existing practices and extended them to uses specific to both preventing and fighting terrorism.

The creation of the DHS represents one of the most sweeping restructurings of the U.S. government in the nation's history. The speed with which the department came into existence in the wake of 9/11 is almost as dramatic as the tasks assigned to the department. Though something of an unwieldy superagency, DHS now includes Customs and Border Protection (CBP), the Federal Emergency Management Agency (FEMA), the Transportation Security Administration (TSA), U.S. Citizenship and Immigration Services (USCIS), the Coast Guard, U.S. Immigration and Customs Enforcement (ICE), and the Secret Service among its constituent agencies. On a day-to-day basis, none of the department's responsibilities stray from the primary reason for its creation: to prevent terrorist attacks by reducing the nation's vulnerability to terrorism, to minimize the damage that might occur in the event of terrorist attacks, and to assist in the recovery from attacks that might have occurred. Under DHS, there are more than a hundred joint terrorism task forces around the country, 70% of them created since 9/11, with more than 600 state and local agencies and 50 different federal agencies participating. Their efforts are coordinated by the National Joint Terrorism Task Force.

Though much has been made of the differences between the Bush and the Obama administrations' respective approaches to counterterrorism, the differences are more of style and rhetoric than substance. The Obama administration has largely followed the groundwork developed by its predecessor, but has adopted new language and moved to treat some incidents as criminal acts rather than part of a terror war.

Meaning of Terrorism

The word *terror* derives from the Latin word *terrere*, meaning "to frighten." The word and its derivatives have been applied in a variety of contexts—from a sobriquet for a vicious despot (as in Ivan the Terrible), to eras of violent political turbulence (as in the Reign of Terror during the French Revolution), to the sporadic outbursts of violence the world knows today as international terrorism. Violence is not the key characteristic, however, since such violent confrontations as World Wars I and II are not considered terrorism. Rather than being an end in itself, violence is a means to instill fear into, i.e., to terrify, whole populations.

Instilling fear can be purposeful for criminal or political ends that are malevolent in nature, yet populations can be frightened without terrorism being involved; for example, the cause may be disease, such as the West Nile-type avian virus that plagued sections of the United States, the "mad cow" virus that struck England and parts of Europe and North America, the spread of autoimmune deficiency syndrome (AIDS) through many countries south of the equator, the severe acute respiratory syndrome (SARS) outbreak in China, and the deadly Ebola epidemics in sub-Saharan Africa in the late 1990s and early twenty-first century, to name just a few. There are those who believe that the outbreaks of these diseases were not entirely natural but were intentionally spread by human intervention; if true, they would be acts of bioterrorism.

The intention of all terrorists is to instill fear in the population at large. With the bombings of the resort hotels and night clubs in Bali, the attacks in Mumbai, the bombings of transportation facilities in Spain and London, and of course, the attacks of 9/11, such fear has been greatly elevated both in the United States and around the world. For terrorists, there is a common motivation to the specific acts that they perpetrate, and frequently in today's world it is the advancement of radical Islam. Because there are common elements to terrorism, counterterrorism has a foundation on which to base defensive strategies and tactics. Anything that can be done to reduce fear and anxiety among the general population is an effective defense against terrorism.

What Is Terrorism?

The modern godfather of urban terrorism and author of the *Minimanual of the Urban Guerrilla*, Carlos Marighella, defined terrorism as action: "It is an action that the urban guerilla must execute with the greatest of cold-bloodedness, calmness and decisions."[2] No police officers, legislatures, or philosophers could better describe the essence of terrorism: attacks that are ruthless in nature and calculated in their impact on society at large.

On a more scholarly level, Brian Jenkins of the Rand Corporation described terrorism as "the calculated use of violence to attain goals that are political, religious or ideological in nature. Terrorism is a criminal act that is often symbolic in nature and intended to influence an audience beyond the immediate victims."[3]

On the political level, the U.S. Department of State acknowledges that there are a range of definitions for terrorism, influenced particularly by the definer's perspective on any given conflict or group. A middle-of-the-road definition that initially surfaced in the mid-1980s and has retained currency says it best: "Terrorism is a premeditated, politically motivated violence perpetrated against non-combat targets by substantial groups of clandestine state agents, usually intended to influence an audience."[4] Since 9/11, we have come to recognize, however, that all terrorists are not state agents; they may be adherents of groups of organizations that often act with the assistance of state agents.

In the past, the lack of a working definition of *terrorism* presented a serious problem when terrorists were apprehended and brought to trial. Terrorism itself was, for the most part, not prohibited by law, although the planting of explosive devices, kidnapping, arson, robbery, taking hostages, hijacking planes, conspiring to commit illegal acts, and similar activities were prohibited by federal, state, and local laws. The result was that in court, terrorists argued they were being persecuted for supporting certain political or religious beliefs, and that the proceeding was a political trial rather than a criminal case. Arguments continue on how to adjudicate criminal acts committed in a terrorism context. The Obama administration has been particularly riven by internal debate over whether such actions should be handled by civilian courts or through military tribunals.

Terrorism is included in many parts of the U.S. legal code, but definitions and context vary. Some of these uses include:

- International terrorism: Terrorism involving citizens or territory of more than one county.
- Terrorism: Premeditated, politically motivated violence perpetrated against noncombatant targets by substantial groups or clandestine agents.
- Terrorist group: A group that has significant subgroups that practice international terrorism.
- Terrorist territory: An area in a country or countries used by a terrorist or terrorist organization to carry out terrorist activities, including training, fund-raising, financing, and recruitment; or as a transit point, in which the government(s) expressly consents to, or with knowledge, allows, tolerates, or disregards such use of its territory.

With the USA Patriot Act and related legislation, Congress has addressed terrorism at the federal level, and many states and even some municipalities have followed suit. The USA Patriot Act, for instance, provides specific authority to seize assets used by terrorists or in support of the commission of terrorist acts, thus depriving terrorists of the use of these assets, including funds. There have also been questions, not all of them fully resolved legally, as to whether individuals apprehended in the war on terrorism are "enemy combatants" who may be tried by military tribunals.

Like the creation of the DHS, the USA Patriot Act, formally named the United and Strengthening America by Providing Appropriate Tools Required to Intercept and Obstruct Terrorism Act, was signed into law in the wake of 9/11. It was adopted on October 26, 2001, less than two months after it was initially proposed by the Department of Justice attorneys, and made permanent, with a few modifications, five years later. It is intended, in the words of the law, to provide the government with "resources necessary to disrupt, weaken, thwart, and eliminate the infrastructure of terrorist organizations, to prevent and thwart terrorist attacks, and to punish perpetrators of terrorist acts."[5] Despite these national security aims, it is one of the most controversial pieces of domestic legislation that has become law in the past three decades.

Many groups, foremost among them civil libertarians, are concerned about the expansion of information that the law makes available to law enforcement. The law expands the methods permitted for collection of personal data and for sharing that data among law enforcement and investigative agencies. This is particularly true surrounding investigations in which foreign intelligence information is sought even when it is not a primary purpose of the investigation. The USA Patriot Act also broadens the use of a number of traditional surveillance techniques and permits the expanded use of wiretaps for certain types on investigations, most of which involve, primarily, federal law enforcement agencies rather than local police. Provisions of the law have been, and will continue to be, tested in a number of court cases around the country. It remains to be seen what impact various sections of the law will have as the courts decide on their constitutionality and the part they will play in the long and ongoing fight against terrorism.

Brief History of Terrorism

International terrorism, though it has intensified in the twenty-first century, is not a new phenomenon. Political betrayal, treachery, deceit, and violence have been around as long as humans have formed themselves into political groups. Ancient texts such as the Bible, the *Iliad*, and the *Odyssey*, and Egyptian hieroglyphics and letters inscribed in cuneiform on clay tablets have related specific details about such occurrences in the eastern Mediterranean. The act of murder for political ends, a major component of terrorism, was raised to a fine art by a small group of Ismali Shiite Muslims late in the eleventh century, under the direction of Hassam-I Sabbah. His followers, who came to be known as Assassins, were a small fundamentalist religious sect engaged in numerous confrontations with other Shiites and the more dominant Sunni Muslims of the Fatimid dynasty. In the world of Islam, the demarcation between secular and religious authority is blurred so that a religious dispute may equally be viewed as political, and vice versa.

In addition to their name and legacy of terrorism, the Assassins have also been credited with precipitating the invention of chain-mail body armor as protection against dagger attacks. These loyal followers of Sabbah and his successors were known as *fedai*, or faithful, and as *fadayeen*, men of sacrifice.

As religious and domestically political as their motives usually were, the Assassins were not above engaging in terrorism on behalf of others, including, according to some accounts, Richard the Lion-Hearted (King Richard III of England) while he was engaged in one of his crusades to the Holy land. The Christian religious group Order of the Knights Templar was said to have adopted the Assassins' system of military organization.

The Assassins were also trained to participate in suicide missions. They were often paid in advance so they could give the money to their families. The only success was the death of the target, whether or not it cost the life of the individual assassin. The Assassins eventually fell prey to internal squabbles and internecine disputes and were effectively neutralized as a political power by the middle of the thirteenth century, but managed to remain cohesive enough to resurface in the 1830s and again in the 1940s as foes of the Shah of Iran.

Although the Assassins were the most notorious group of historical terrorists, there have been many others, including the celebrated Guy Fawkes, bomber of the English Parliament (who nonetheless is viewed by others as a fighter against oppression). The Barbary pirates of North Africa in the eighteenth and nineteenth centuries made their living kidnapping citizens of other countries and holding them for ransom. This activity led to the founding of another Christian religious group, the Redemptionist Order, whose members often acted as intermediaries between the states of the Barbary Coast and the foreign governments whose citizens were being held hostage.

Terrorism in the United Kingdom

In 1605, the Gunpowder Plot involved a group with Guy Fawkes at the center that planned to kill King James I at the opening session of Parliament. The plan failed when one of the plotters advised a relative not to attend Parliament that day. Terrorism was also prominent in England during the nineteenth century when Irish rebels launched what became known as the Fenian Dynamite Campaign from the mid-1860s until 1885, in which prisons, Scotland Yard, London Bridge, the House of Commons, and the Tower of London became bomb targets. The 75 years from the middle of the nineteenth century until World War I was an active period for nationalists and rebels who employed terrorist acts in their campaign against the British, including a bombing campaign in London that diminished as World War II heated up. Sporadic bomb attacks occurred in the last three decades of the twentieth century as terrorists adopted the status of Northern Ireland as their cause. The turn of the twenty-first century saw the rise of Islamic terrorists in Great Britain, with bomb attacks on the London transit system and multiple other plots that were foiled by authorities or otherwise failed in execution. Many of the Islamic radicals involved in these incidents were born in Britain, a vestige of Britain's imperial heritage as a colonial power in regions that are today referred to as the Muslim world.

Modern Terrorist Groups

In the Middle East, the rise of Islamic fundamentalism in the modern era can be traced to the Muslim Brotherhood, founded in 1928 by Hassen al-Banna, a schoolteacher who preached for Sharia law. A militant wing known as the secret apparateur was formed, and in 1948 some of the Brotherhood members assassinated Egypt's prime minister. A short time later, alleged government agents killed Hassen al-Banna. In the early 1950s the Brotherhood was accused in some 750 cases of arson, mostly in Cairo. The targets were mainly nightclubs, theaters, hotels, and restaurants frequented by the British and other Westerners, including tourists, in an effort to end the secular lifestyle. In 1954, after the attempt on the life of Gamal Nassar, a crackdown on the Brotherhood was carried out. After Nassar's ousting, Anwar Sadat became president and eased the restrictions on the Brotherhood, but he also fell from favor when he signed a peace accord with Israel. He was assassinated on October 6, 1981, by members of the violent Tanzim al-Jihad.

The Brotherhood has spawned or inspired a number of ideological terrorist groups, such as al Qaeda, Hamas, and Jamaat-al-Islamiyya, to mention a few. In addition, the second in command to Osama bin Laden, Ayman al-Zawahiri, was a former member of the Egyptian Brotherhood.

During the 1960s, 1970s, and 1980s, radical Islamic terror groups increased in number and strength throughout the Middle East and also spread into Europe. This coincided with a number of terrorist groups espousing a Marxist-Leninist philosophy. These groups, the most notable of which included the Baader-Mienhof Gang (later Red Army Faction) in Germany and the Red Brigades in Italy, which kidnapped and later killed Aldo Moro, a former prime minister of Italy, would operate well into the 1980s. It was reported that a conclave of terrorists occurred in 1983 in Benghazi, Libya, when Muamar Khaddafy brought together more than a thousand representatives from such disparate organizations as the Palestine Liberation Army, Abu Nidal, the Irish Republican Army (IRA), the Puerto Rican independence group FALN, the Black Liberation Army, the American Indian Movement, the Nation of Islam, and several unaffiliated freelance terrorists, to further push their terrorist campaign against the West.

There were also a number of nationalistic groups that engaged in major acts of terrorism. One of the more well-known groups was the Euskadi ta Askatasuna (ETA), a Basque separatist group that operates throughout Spain and is still very much alive today. The Provisional Irish Republican Army, which was still active in the early 2000s in Ireland, Northern Ireland, and England, carried out a number of devastating bomb attacks around Great Britain and particularly in London. Armenian nationalist causes have also given rise to a number of terrorist groups going back to 1890 with the Armenian Revolutionary Faction, a group seeking autonomy for Armenia from the Ottoman Empire. More recently, the Armenian Secret Army for the Liberation of Armenia was active from the mid-1970s well into the 1980s, using as a rationale the massacre of Armenians by Turkey in the early 1900s. The group launched a number of bomb attacks across Europe, mainly in Turkey and France.

The Balkans have long been a hotbed of terrorist activity, from the days of the Black Hand, to the assassination of Archduke Franz Ferdinand that touched off World War I, through the cowardly Croatian terrorist who hijacked TWA flight 355 en route to Chicago from JFK airport. A New York City Police Department Bomb Squad officer was killed in an attempt to disarm an improvised explosive device (IED) left in a locker at Grand Central Terminal by the hijackers.

In the United States, in the early decades of the twentieth century anarchists operating under the banner of the Black Hand preyed on newly arrived immigrants, especially on the Lower East Side of Manhattan. Their tactics of selective assassinations with guns and bombs proved extremely effective for a short period of time.

Many Third World leaders of Africa, the Middle East, the Caribbean, and the Pacific Rim engaged in activities that could be described as terrorism against colonial governments prior to their countries gaining independence. In the post–World War II period, the Middle East became a particular focal point of wars of liberation, or terrorist insurrection, depending upon political perspective. In an area called Palestine, Zionists popularly called the Stern Gang and Irgun fought the British rulers for a state in the traditional Jewish homeland. When Israel was created and became an independent state in 1948, many Arab and Islamic residents of the immediate area settled outside the borders and began demanding a fully independent Palestinian state, a demand that continues to this time and reinforces how the designation *terrorism* or *terrorists* can be seen differently from opposite sides of an issue.

In the United States, the war in Vietnam and opposition to it was a springboard for launching a wave of domestic terrorism unparalleled in this country's history. Such groups as the Weather Underground, the New World Liberation Front, and groups with similar antiwar, antiestablishment, and anarchist sympathies spawned bombing campaigns, armed robberies to finance their activities, and other criminal acts. The attention drawn by these groups to various causes encouraged political radicals of other stripes, spanning the political spectrum from the Puerto Rican national group FALN to the Black Panthers to the anti-Castro Cuban group Omega-7, to engage in increasingly violent activities.

Such domestic terrorism waned following the end of the Vietnam War, only to yield to a new breed of domestic terrorists that included antiabortionists, environmental extremists, and such radicals as Aryan Nation members, survivalists, and militia groups. Among the more notorious of these was Timothy McVeigh, who carried out the bombing of a federal office building in Oklahoma City, Oklahoma, in 1995. Another such terrorist, Eric Rudolf, a loner with an antiabortion and antigay agenda, carried out a series of bombings; the most well known was at an Olympic venue in Atlanta, Georgia, in 1996.

Terrorism as a Political Statement

One argument often advanced by radical apologists is that the judgment of terrorists' actions is purely subjective, so that one man's terrorist is another man's patriot and revolutionary leader. In recent times, this view has been articulated by the Baader-Meinhof partisans in the Red Army Faction, the West German terrorist group, when one of its members declared that George Washington was a terrorist. More pointedly, in early 2001, German Foreign Minister Joschka Fischer, a member of the Green Party and part of Chancellor Gerhard Schroder's government alliance, admitted he had participated in terrorist activity in his youth, including incidents that resulted in the deaths of hostages. In a court trial, however, he swore he had never been a member of the Red Army Faction.

Many modern terrorists believe that they will not see their goals achieved during their lifetimes, and so they view their activities as the base or building blocks of greater movements yet to come. These individuals, even when imprisoned, will use any and every opportunity to further their goals by recruiting, training, and indoctrinating new members, in addition to keeping existing members in line.

Examining, analyzing, and critiquing such philosophical arguments goes beyond the scope of the book. It is important to note, however, that almost every terrorist group espouses a noble or at least rational or justifiable cause. The truth is, however, that the terrorists may be merely a group of common criminals using their stated cause as a smokescreen or front for nefarious activities. Alternatively, a group may have legitimate origins as a political or activist organization but have since degenerated into terrorist activity. On rare occasions, they may actually be a group of dedicated people acting on behalf of a legitimate cause against oppression or repression, but engaged in terrorist activity nonetheless.

Regardless of which type of group is involved, terrorist activities are all the same. The bombings, hostage takings, kidnappings, or other types of illegal behavior all present the same problems and challenges to law enforcement and private security personnel.

The Nature of Terrorism

Brian Jenkins of the Rand Corporation has said terrorism is "the use or threatened use of force designed to bring about political change,"[6] while the Federal Bureau of Investigation (FBI) has defined terrorism as "the unlawful use of force or violence against persons or property to intimidate or coerce a government, the civilian population, or any segment thereof, in furtherance of political or social objectives."[7] In the twenty-first century, the once driving forces of terrorism—Marxist-Leninism or Maoism, or both—have largely been replaced by fundamentalist Islamic radicalism on the world stage. Yet Jenkins's observation remains valid that the three most serious conflicts that fall short of nuclear confrontation are:

1. Conventional warfare
2. Guerrilla or insurgency warfare
3. International terrorism

In the first two types of conflict, noncombatants are usually able to distinguish themselves from the combatants. This is not to say that noncombatants are never killed, because they are, whether through inadvertent collateral damage or at times when insurgents use noncombatant civilians and their houses or other structures as cover. These casualties are usually isolated or unusual incidents because in both guerrilla and conventional warfare the major focus of killing is one armed force against another. Conflicts can be either high intensity or low intensity in nature, such as the vast majority of combat taking place in Third World areas of the globe and the few confrontations in industrial nations of the world. Battlegrounds range from erstwhile socialist republics of the old Soviet Union, to former colonies of European imperial powers and areas where age-old ethnic hatreds still exist, to territories where drug trafficking is rampant.

However, the exploitation of noncombatants (i.e., their suffering and death) is the essence of international terrorism. Because of the covert nature of the activity, terrorist attacks can be carried out by a small cohort of operatives who receive financial and logistical support from radical political and activist organizations, which can, and do, include governments of rogue nations. Political, ethnic, religious, fraternal, and other activist organizations may be suspected of acting in support of terrorist goals, even if not actually fostering and furthering these goals.

In many terrorist acts, individuals and groups only loosely connected or ostensibly unconnected to the terrorist operatives perform support functions, such as arranging financial assistance; providing travel documents, safe houses, and ground transportation as required; and providing alibis or other cover. Today we see major terrorist operations being funded not only by sympathetic state sponsors and wealthy ideologues, but also by legitimate business networks and so-called charitable funds that raise funds specifically to finance terrorist operations. Osama bin Laden built his al Qaeda organization with his personal wealth, donations from sympathetic family members and other wealthy individuals, and through the cash flow of business fronts engaged in legal activities.

The U.S. Department of Defense (DOD) has described terrorism as a phenomenon in transition and has indicated that the nature of the terrorist threat has changed dramatically. The DOD attributes the change to five factors:

1. Collapse of the Soviet Union spawning insurgent nationalist groups
2. Changing motivations of terrorists and emergence of radical Islamic fundamentalism
3. Proliferation in technologies in the production of weapons of mass destruction
4. Increased access to information and communication technologies
5. Accelerated centralization of vital components of the national infrastructure, which has increased vulnerability to terrorist attack

Much of the thrust on international terrorism has been, and will continue to be, directed toward the United States, American targets abroad, and U.S. allies on a global scale. As seen in the 9/11 attacks, there is almost no limit to the imagination used in designing an assault. Attacks will continue to be directed toward high-profile targets that may be difficult to defend, such as landmark buildings and national icons. On the other hand, the most hard core of the terrorist groups, such as al Qaeda, will continue to tackle high-security targets, such as airports, airplanes, and airline facilities, on which they seem to have a particular fixation. And most likely, they will be concentrated in urban locations, perpetrated by those acting on behalf of religious and ethnic causes and, as in the past, political points of view.

Characteristics of Terrorism

Terrorist groups are becoming tougher, more resilient, and more difficult to defeat. In addition, terror attacks are becoming more sophisticated and deadly.

Terrorist groups evolve and adapt in response to the ever-changing tactics of law enforcement and intelligence agencies working to defeat them. Terrorist groups are organized in many different ways, including the traditional pyramidal power chart with a leader or small clique at the top and ever-widening tiers of authority moving down the chain of command. Various other configurations for depicting the organization of terrorist groups include circles, squares, and bull's-eye target designs. Anarchist groups claim to be leaderless. With that possible exception, one thing all groups have in common is a hard-core leadership, surrounded by active and loyal cadre, and then, moving farther from the center, a broader group of active supporters, and outside that, an even broader level of passive support.

In the shifting nature of terrorist groups—or at least the vocal justifications they provide for their actions—religion and ethnicity have equaled or surpassed politics as the driving force behind their stated goals. Hiding behind the shield of accepted religious organizations (or ethnic societies or political activist associations), support groups are free to operate with virtual impunity in most parts of the world and particularly in Western democracies. In addition to fund-raising, religious and ethnic groups provide cover for covert activities of more militant representatives of terrorist organizations. This has become evident since 9/11 in tracing the preincident activities of the perpetrators of the attacks and their supporters, where Islamic mosques in North America and Europe were the sites of fund-raising and recruiting activities. There is ample evidence of training camps organized for terrorist recruits, Islamic radicals in particular, being conducted in Afghanistan, Pakistan, Yemen, and Lebanon, to name a few countries where these camps have been reported.

Actions and characteristics of terrorist groups do change over time. For example, kneecapping was used as a signal or scar to demonstrate the wide reach of a terrorist organization during the 1970s and 1980s. In Italy, terrorists shot the victim in the knee; in Ireland, an electric drill was used to mutilate the knee. In either case, victims walking around for the remainder of their lives with a limp were a constant reminder to the populace of terrorist power and omnipresence in the region. In Africa, terrorists use a machete to chop the hand(s) of victims, even children, to accomplish a similar effect on villagers and urban dwellers alike. Today, Islamic terrorist groups enforce their warped beliefs by beheading selected captured enemies who oppose their views.

Financial Terrorism

Money laundering can lead to financial terrorism or at least financing terrorism, and many well-known financial institutions have had officers involved in moving money in and out of offshore banks. Some manipulations and movement of money are done for the purposes of avoiding taxes or legal restrictions and regulations, but often, and this is what makes the movement of funds money laundering, the machinations are performed to legitimize ill-gotten funds of illegal businesses, criminals, and terrorists. Major financial institutions and even governments of both large and small countries have been brought down as a result of money manipulations. There are recurring attempts or at least reports of attempts at large-scale counterfeiting of U.S. and other Western currencies by rogue states, terrorists, and criminal organizations. The USA Patriot Act and other legislation dealing with the use of otherwise legitimate international financial dealings for terrorist purposes were highlighted by President Bush in November 2001 when he said, "We put the world's financial institutions on notice: If you do business with terrorists, if you support them or sponsor them, you will not do business with the United States of America."[8]

Even with these strong words, little can be done about funding terrorism with legitimately gained funds. For example, the United States continues to rely on foreign oil, a good portion of which comes from the Middle East, Saudi Arabia in particular. It is strongly suspected that a substantial amount of oil profit is funneled through various organizations and eventually into the hands of terrorist organizations. Since the liberation of Iraq and the reestablishment of the oil industry, it is estimated that a substantial amount of oil is redirected to the black market, and eventually into insurgent operations.

According to Loretta Napoleoni, the Italian economist who tracks terrorist financing, the Taliban and al Qaeda gain funds from rogue economies located within the so-called tribal belt of Pakistan in South America. Centered in the city of Quetta, and similar to its New World counterpart in Ciudad del Este in South America, markets thrive on trade in counterfeit luxury goods and stolen merchandise, as well as drugs and smuggled arms.

The following are among the tools used to monitor financial activities:

1. The Terrorist Finance Tracking Program, under the aegis of the Treasury Department, works to identify foreign terrorist groups, assesses their funding sources and fund-raising methods, and provides information to law enforcement agencies as to how the funds are moved about.
2. Operation Green Quest is a Customs Service-led multiagency initiative involving investigators from the Internal Revenue Service, the Treasury's Office of Financial Assets Control, and the FBI who target sources of funding for terrorist groups.
3. The Financial Action Task Force, with representatives from 35 different countries, oversees and reviews money laundering and terrorist financing techniques and countermeasures. The aim is to identify,

disrupt, and dismantle the financial operations of charities and non-governmental organizations associated with Osama bin Laden and al Qaeda, as well as other terrorist organizations.

Early in the war on terrorism, the United States shut down al-Barakaat and al-Tawa, both of which were important financial conduits for al Qaeda and Osama bin Laden. In addition, in the United States, the Holy Land Foundation for Relief and Development was closed for activities that included funneling money to the Palestinian group Hamas.

Narcoterrorism is a specific type of financial terrorism that is so named because it relies on the profits from illegal narcotics trade to finance various terrorist activities around the world. Unlike most terrorism, it is not based on any ideology, but is strictly profit driven. A classic example of this was found in South America, where a substantial amount of profits from drug dealing were used to support the Revolutionary Armed Forces of Columbia, a Marxist insurgent group known by its acronym FARC. Drug profits from the Far East, primarily involving Afghanistan and Myanmar, have supported al Qaeda and other Muslim terrorist groups. Although most of the drugs filtering into the United States come from South America and Mexico, with Far Eastern poppies primarily supplying European drug markets, the intertwining of profits and support for terrorist activities makes the location where the supplies end up less important than the vast amount of money the supplies generate.

The source countries for drug products share in common weak state authorities that are often corrupt or considered illegitimate by the general population. The poorer the population, the more likely they are to turn to drug crops, where profits greatly exceed those that could be derived from any legitimate agriculture or subsistence farming. Just as drug distribution sources led to the creation of such drug millionaires as Colombian cocaine baron Pablo Escobar in the 1980s, and more recent examples among Mexican drug cartels, those same sources have been tapped by terrorist groups to amass cash that can be used to pay for terrorist activities. It is extremely difficult for local police to stem such activity. Most cases must be made at the federal level, where agents may rely on a variety of federal drug, racketeering, and money laundering laws.

Terrorist Actions

By definition, terrorists espouse a philosophical, religious, or political basis for their actions, and thus they have strategic goals to achieve. The methods by which these goals are reached, or at least approached, are the tactics of terrorists. By and large, these tactics are designed to gain as much media attention as possible through intimidation and fear, while at the same time enhancing the group's stature in its theater of political operation. Bomb attacks, hostage taking, hijacking, kidnapping, and similar types of assaults have been the traditional tactics of terrorists. Domestic terrorists, the so-called New Age terrorists of the twenty-first century, have to some extent taken a step backward from the violent confrontational tendencies of their predecessors. The Weather Underground, the FALN, and similar "bombing groups" have faded into history. The new groups now engage in such activities as arson, vandalism, and theft in the conduct of their ecoterrorism, bioterrorism, animal rights terrorism, and cyberterrorism. On the other hand, American jihadists tend to favor bombs, armed assaults, and similar confrontational tactics.

The bomb remains the weapon of choice among terrorists on the international level, both for the anonymity it affords operatives and the amount of media attention an explosion garners. This latter point is still valid, even in light of the relatively quick apprehension and trials, dating back to the 1995 Oklahoma City and 1993 World Trade Center bombings, and internationally, the Madrid train bombing early in 2004. There has, however, been less success against the frequent bomb attacks in Iraq and Afghanistan as al Qaeda and various insurgent groups try to maintain control over the civilian population. The success, where it has occurred, in apprehending the individuals and breaking up the groups of terrorist cells responsible for these actions has been attributed to more sophisticated investigative techniques, coupled with an increase in intelligence operations, particularly on the transborder international level.

The four types of bomb attacks are:

1. Antipersonnel
2. Symbolic target
3. Selected target
4. Sustained or prolonged campaign

Antipersonnel attacks include targeted individuals as well as improvised explosive devices (IEDs) placed in areas with a high population density that can be expected to produce a high casualty rate. At the other end of the spectrum are bomb attacks directed at individuals, such as those of the "Unabomber," Theodore Kaczynski, with his mail bombs, or Eric Rudolph, known as the abortion clinic bomber, who used strategically placed IEDs in attacking his targets. The devices used can be as simple as a pipe bomb, a parcel or letter bomb, or a vehicle rigged with explosives designed to detonate by some action of the intended driver/victim or by remote control. Vehicles can also be filled with explosives and driven to the attack site, sometimes by a driver prepared to commit suicide to ensure the bomb is delivered. Total disregard for human life, including the perpetrator's, is a common element in this type of terrorist action. Bombs directed at specific individuals, such as politicians, businessmen, celebrities, etc., are typically referred to as assassinations or assassination attempts.

Symbolic target attacks are generally carried out against government buildings, military installations, facilities of selected corporate enterprises, or historic or iconic landmarks. The devices used in these attacks are usually placed at a time or a location in which casualties could be expected to be at a minimum, although this circumstance cannot be guaranteed to terrorists or would-be terrorists. Symbolic bomb attacks are sometimes preceded by a warning call that may be construed as an effort to reduce casualties, although it also serves as a claim for credit by the perpetrating group. In recent years, the use of warning calls has waned and has been replaced by a certain group claiming credit for the attack by a notification to a news organization or a posting on the Internet after the attack is completed. Diligent security measures, call tracing techniques, voice identification technology, and rapid response by law enforcement may have also contributed to the waning use of warning calls. Also helping to reduce the number of bomb attacks against the symbolic targets are the widespread increases in physical security and the additional use of bomb detection equipment, walk-through metal detectors and other sensors, and use of explosive-sniffing canines.

Selected target attackers aim at a specific facility or group of individuals in order to accommodate a belief or political ideology. The attack may be part of a series of actions against a government, a governmental agency or private enterprise, its buildings, property, or personnel, or all of them. Many international terrorist groups, particularly Islamic groups terrorizing Israel, the Jewish Diaspora, and Western sympathizers, are examples of selected target attacks, as are antiglobalists attacking such iconic American symbols as Coca-Cola bottling plants or McDonalds restaurants.

Sustained or prolonged campaigns are designed to draw attention to a particular cause or target, such as the release of imprisoned comrades of the perpetrating group or operatives of a terrorist group, or even "political prisoners" believed to be sympathetic to the terrorists' cause or aims. Some classic examples of this type of activity include the Real IRA attacks against Britain for an independent Northern Ireland, most of the Palestinian attacks against Israel, and the al Qaeda campaign against the United States, "the Great Satan." The FALN and Weather Underground bombing campaigns during the 1970s are domestic examples of this type of attack.

Other Terrorist Actions

Hostage taking, warehousing of hostages, and other incidents involving hostages are tactics that may be used by terrorists to attempt to coerce governments or private companies to act in a certain fashion, desist from certain actions, or modify a specific point or subject. Such was the case on October 23, 2002, when Chechen terrorists took over an entire theater in Moscow and held the audience hostage. A rescue attempt by Russia proved to be a disaster, seeing some 120 of the hostages dying during it. Two years later, on September 1, 2004, Chechen and Ingush terrorists occupied a Russian school in Beslan in the North Caucus region, taking hundreds of school-children hostage in the process. Again, the rescue attempt turned into a disaster. These are extreme examples of hostage taking. More commonly, criminals may use hostages to abet their escape during the commission of a crime interrupted by the police; emotionally disturbed persons may use hostages in times of rage or in domestic disputes. Although there is a distinction between hostage taking and kidnapping, both are used by terrorists in political contexts to elicit behavior modification or change of heart on the part of governments or private entities. The distinction between hostage taking and kidnapping is, in the simplest terms, knowledge of where the victims are being held. Both are used to raise a group's profile and to garner media exposure. Kidnappings, in particular, are also used to raise funds via ransom payments. A dramatic example of this occurred in 2000, when a terrorist from the Abu Sayyaf Group (ASG) kidnapped a group of tourists from a resort in Indonesia and removed them to the ASG camp located in the Philippines. Police freed the abducted tourists, including two Americans, several months later. This did not stop the ASG from continuing to kidnap foreigners and wealthy businessmen to extort funds. Terrorists, including narcoterrorists in South America and Islamic fundamentalists in Egypt, have in the past used the kidnapping of tourists to elicit ransoms.

Aircraft hijackings of the type we witnessed throughout the 1970s and 1980s, in which aircraft are left intact and passengers held as hostages, have all but disappeared due to the enhanced security procedures that have been implemented in major airports around the globe. Nonetheless, the potential obviously exists for this type of action to occur, even in the age of heightened security precautions.

The threatened use of weapons of mass destruction by terrorists is still very real. These types of attacks might take the form of "dirty bombs" using toxic biological agents such as anthrax or chemicals such as ricin, as well as nuclear material to attack crowds of people or even entire cities. While threat levels have been heightened, actual use of such weapons has been limited and contained within a very small number of sophisticated and well-organized terror groups.

Intimidation and Threats

The "chatter," or terrorist operatives communicating about activity in the works or in the planning stage, has virtually vanished from the 24/7 news cycle. It was different in the immediate aftermath of 9/11, when it seemed every alert or warning issued by government agencies was based on "increased chatter" picked up by intelligence operatives monitoring terrorist activity or at key communication listening posts. In truth, much of the chatter was rife with misinformation or false threats.

As far as furthering terrorist aims, however, destructive and violent action is itself a potent weapon, and there are a number of different forms these threats may take:

1. The bomb threat is still the most useful tool to harass or intimidate, particularly when privately owned facilities or industrial installations are involved. It is also a weapon against specialized targets, such as schools, abortion clinics, airlines, and similar facilities and operations. A bomb threat, especially one handled improperly, can cause as much disruption as an explosive device that is actually planted. The use of bomb threats is particularly successful in the aftermath of an actual terrorist attack, at a time when public awareness and apprehension are intensified. In a classic example, a bomb threat was uncovered in February 2003, based upon information provided by an al Qaeda operative captured during Operation Enduring Freedom in Afghanistan. The captive indicated al Qaeda intended to use a dirty bomb against an unspecified target, resulting in the national terror threat level being raised to orange. The information about the dirty bomb proved to be false, whether by design or the captive's intent to curry favor with his captors, but the incident caused heightened anxiety levels throughout the United States and Western Europe.

2. Scare or hoax bombs are simulated, improvised explosive devices that can cause an even longer disruption of operations than the use of an anonymous bomb threat because a search must be conducted and an evacuation ordered once the device is discovered. These devices must be treated as though they contain actual explosives, until they can be verified as otherwise by qualified bomb technicians.

3. Environmental and public service threats can generate widespread disruption and unrest, particularly on a short-term basis. In recent years, the threat of biological and chemical agents in this type of attack has increased greatly in the wake of a successful sarin gas attack on the Tokyo subway system in 1995 by the group Aum Shinrikyo. Threats of this nature have also included contaminating sources of public drinking water, attacks against electrical grids (i.e., power lines, transformers, generating plants, etc.), and disrupting mass transit systems. Also included are hacking attacks on computers supporting any of these utilities and installations.

4. Expropriation and extortion encompass everything from armed robbery to coerced protection money used to fund an organization and its terrorist activity. This funding may include purchasing arms, renting and maintaining safe houses, obtaining transportation, receiving advanced terrorist training, or paying day-to-day living expenses. In his tract on urban guerillas, Carlos Marighella, a South American terrorist of the 1960s, recommends such illegal activities because they are the "expropriation of wealth of the principle enemies of the people."[9] Such activity is more common outside the United States, particularly in Latin America. Domestically, however, one of the most spectacular terrorist acts of expropriation took place on October 21, 1981, in Nanuet, New York, when members of several different terrorist groups acting under the umbrella of the Armed Revolutionary Task Force bungled an armored car robbery. They killed one guard and two police officers at a roadblock in their subsequent escape attempt. Members of the gang were identified with such terrorist groups as the Weather Underground, the Black Liberation Army, the May 19th Communist Coalition, and the Republik of New Afrika. Expropriation is still a very viable weapon in the arsenal of a terrorist organization.

5. The disruption of legitimate government operations is of paramount importance to a terrorist organization. With radical Islam, any influence by a Western power on the Middle East is an affront. One example: During the latter stages of Operation Iraqi Freedom, and particularly during the country's transition from American administration to Iraqi self-rule, terrorists were actively trying to undermine the effort. In Iraq, there was a series of kidnappings of foreign nationals—both Americans and others whose governments were allies of the United States. The kidnapped victims were threatened with death unless their governments ended their roles in Iraq. Most were subsequently executed, but one Filipino was spared when the Philippine government promised to withdraw its troops from Iraq. Similarly, in Spain in 2004 Moroccans associated with al Qaeda bombed commuter trains near Madrid three days before national elections. The attack was credited with influencing the election so the candidate who opposed Spain's support of the United States in Iraq was elected.

6. Other criminal activities include almost anything that generates funds or furthers the aim of the terrorist organizations, or both. Drug trafficking is a major source of income, with virtually every major terrorist organization engaged in some sort of drug business either directly or by providing security and performing other services for smugglers and traffickers. In the past, the more

prominent groups involved in drug trafficking were the FARC in Colombia (where two IRA terrorists were apprehended along with members of FARC) and the Tamil Tigers in Sri Lanka. It appears now that al Qaeda operatives in the Middle East, Western Asia, and parts of Africa are also involved in the drug trade in the form of supplying poppies that eventually become heroin or opium. These poppies are grown in the Taliban-controlled areas of Afghanistan. Support groups abetting the 9/11 terrorists were said to have raised money by bootlegging cigarettes from low-tax states to high-tax urban areas.

7. Sabotage and subversive acts may not be immediately recognized as terrorist acts when they first occur. These actions involve the blockading of military installations and damage of property, looting during street demonstrations, civil disobedience by disrupting transportation systems or government operations, and other actions carried out under the banner of "protest." These acts of selective indignation and "spontaneous" expressions of protected speech are often initiated by well-intentioned, legitimate organizations that are undermined by terrorist-supported groups. One example: The February 15, 2003, demonstrations protesting the military effort that resulted in the liberation of Iraq, the toppling of Saddam Hussein, and the ending of the Baathist reign in Iraq were orchestrated by an organization calling itself Not in Our Name. Realizing it had been undermined and used as a cover for nefarious intent, the organization ended its operations in the spring of 2009. There are many such groups that have been spawned by old-school Marxist-Leninist thinkers who use such issues as climate change, the petroleum industry, and financial institutions to foment protests and propagate an anti-American message. Some of this activity is carried out by anarchist groups, many of which may also voice support for Palestinian terrorists operating in the Middle East.

Acts of sabotage are intentional destruction of property and disruption of an industrial or governmental operation by means other than an explosive device. These include break-ins or other illegal entries designed to harass or intimidate the owners or occupants of the premises. Computer hacking, electronic attacks against a website, and disruption of network servers or other communications are other examples of sabotage, as are simple arson and various attacks staged by ecoterrorists, animal rights activists, and antiabortion extremists. More traditional incidents include damaging power transmission lines and oil pipelines.

Subversion is a systemic attempt to undermine a society. The ultimate objective is the total collapse of the state as a result of bringing its governing administration into disrepute, causing a loss of confidence in the ruling establishment's institutions and government and provoking a breakdown of law and order.

Disinformation and Propaganda

Misinformation, disinformation, propaganda, and media manipulation are not always clearly defined as terrorist activities, although these actions certainly must be included as tactics employed by terrorist organizations and their support apparatus. In his guerilla warfare treatise, Carlos Marighella recommends these tactics as part of what he called a war of nerves. Such actions include using the telephone and mail to announce false clues to the government and police, letting false plans fall into the hands of the police to divert their attention, planting rumors, and exploiting by every means possible the corruption, errors, and failures of government. Contemporary followers of Marighella's advice are finding new methods virtually every day to use cell phones, the Internet, social media, and other electronic communications to advance their agendas. Even knowing that law enforcement agencies may be monitoring the airwaves allows operatives the opportunities to provide misinformation and false leads.

Assassination

Assassination is a specialized form of assault that has been proven to be a very effective terrorist tool. It is the ultimate weapon of intimidation against target communities. These attacks are designed to gain maximum media attention as well as to have a major psychological impact on the organization the victim represented. Frequently, political leaders and their military or police officials will react to an assassination with a wave of repression aimed at the general population, which usually works to further the terrorists' aims. Assassination is a tactic that has been recently used by such groups as the separatist Basque movement, ETA, in Spain; the FARC narcoterrorist rebels in Colombia; and the various Islamic groups in the Middle East.

In January 2010, in the United Arab Emirates, the Hamas military commander Mahmoud al Mabhouh was assassinated. It was suspected that this was carried out by more than a dozen covert operatives of Israel's intelligence agency, the Mossad. Security videos at airports and hotels indicated that the persons responsible for the action had fake or stolen passports and stolen identities. Some countries whose passports were used made vocal outcries, even to the extent of expelling Israeli diplomats for a time. Whether or not the expected results were accomplished remains to be seen. Sometimes assassinations have more immediate effects with the desired outcome. One such example is the shooting of Archduke Franz Ferdinand of Austria and his wife on June 28, 1914, in Sarajevo, Bosnia. This was carried out by a group of Bosnia Serbs. Within a month, the Great War, as World War I was then called, started.

Endnotes

1. *President Bush's Opening Statement*, articles.orlandosentinel.com/2001-10-12/ new, viewed March 29, 2011.
2. *Minimanual of the Urban Guerilla*, Carlos Marighella, New World Liberation Front, 1970.
3. As introduced to the U.S. Senate by Senator Abraham Ribicoff of Connecticut on October 25, 1977, and as indicated in *On Domestic Terrorism*, a publication of the National Governors Association, Emergency Preparedness Project, Center for Policy Research, Washington, DC, May 1979.
4. *Pattern of Global Terrorism*—1984, U.S. Department of State, cover statement, Washington, DC, 1985.
5. Strategic Plan for Fiscal Years 2001–2006, Washington, D.C., U.S. Department of Justice, 2001 (Patriot Act).
6. Defining Terrorism, drstevebest.org, viewed March 29, 2011.
7. 28 Code of Federal Regulations (C.F.R.) Sec. 0.85.
8. The HSBC Monitor, householdwatch.com/Arizona/php, viewed March 30, 2011.
9. Minimanual of the Urban Guerilla, Carlos Marighella, New World Liberation Front, 1970.

Common Elements of Terrorism

2

Purpose of Terrorism

Terrorism for political purposes is usually a form of theater, and as such there are a number of elements that are almost universally present in modern terrorist actions:

1. The use of violence to persuade, where bombings or other attacks are employed to "make a point" with target victims. The target victims are not necessarily those who are injured or killed. Rather, the attack may have been carried out to influence a government, or a group of governments, or private entities to take a certain course of action or perhaps to terminate a course of action.

2. Selection of targets and victims for maximum propaganda value. This means choosing targets and victims to ensure the heaviest possible media coverage. This, of course, has been magnified over the years, first with the advent of 24-hour cable television news programming, then with web-based news, and today with social media supplementing official reports; events are reported by live coverage and are shown repeatedly. The 9/11 attack on the World Trade Center was viewed live by millions of people, especially as the second plane crashed into the South Tower, as all the major networks and cable news channels keyed on the event. The story dominated the airwaves for months, certainly surpassing any prior or subsequent terrorist attack anywhere in the world.

3. The use of unprovoked attacks. This encompasses just about all terrorist attacks; because they were "provoked" is only the misguided and convoluted rationale offered by terrorists themselves.

4. Maximum publicity at minimum risk. This is the principle behind many terrorist actions, particularly those involving explosive devices. Today, bombings typically generate a good deal of news coverage. The amount of coverage will be determined in part by the size of the bomb, but more so by target selection, especially if a symbolic or iconic location is involved. The use of sophisticated timer-power units will ensure a fair amount of lead time for the bomber to escape detection, unless a suicide bombing is effected. Moving up the list of

favored terrorist activities, kidnapping or assaults and assassinations may generate greater or prolonged publicity, although at greater personal risk for the perpetrators. An example of this is the case of *Wall Street Journal* reporter Daniel Pearl, who was kidnapped and assassinated in Pakistan by Islamic extremists in February 2002. The publicity generated by this case most likely influenced a rash of terrorist kidnappings and assassinations in 2003 and 2004 in Iraq and Saudi Arabia, where non-Arabs were beheaded by fundamentalist Islamic groups. There is something of a cyclical pattern to terrorist activities, so that if, for instance, there has been a rash of kidnappings, the public may become somewhat inured, and subsequent abductions may not generate the same amount or intensity of news coverage and public reaction. Bombings or hijackings, just because they have been less frequent during the same period, may generate more publicity than another kidnapping. A change in tactics, then, would produce more coverage than another kidnapping. Terrorists always want to remain in the forefront, so they will switch tactics in order to maximize publicity.

5. Use of surprise to circumvent countermeasures. This is one way terrorists try to attack a hardened target. Even with enhanced security personnel, detection devices, and increased perimeter security, the element of surprise can be employed to undermine the hardware and overwhelm the human factor in a fortified security system. Time is the terrorist's best friend and is frequently used to conduct in-depth surveillance and reconnaissance. Even a well-protected and hardened target will experience slackened security measures during long periods of terrorist inactivity. The 9/11 attacks came at a time when, over more than a dozen years, airplane hijackings had been reduced to near zero after a spate of such incidents in the 1970s and 1980s. Unless a suicide attack is planned, and sometimes even for a suicide attack, terrorists will wait to strike when security is relaxed.

6. Threats, harassment, and violence. These are tools terrorists use to create an atmosphere of fear. On occasion, terrorists have planted a number of small bombs or incendiary devices in public places, such as department stores and movie theaters. In recent years, pro-Islamic terrorists in Egypt have attacked groups of tourists visiting the pyramids and other monuments. To the public, there is no rhyme or reason for these terrorist acts, but the mere threat of more attacks is enough to create a climate of fear.

7. Disregarding women and children as victims, often to the extent that locations with innocent victims are selected specifically to heighten the outrage and fear at the boldness of the terrorist actions. This is yet another tactic to garner wider publicity and media coverage, as

negative as it may be, of the suffering and death of the noncombatants. This characteristic differentiates the terrorist from a soldier or guerrilla fighter. A soldier fights with the authority of the government for the protection of that government. A guerrilla wages the same kind of warfare as the soldier in technique and code of behavior; i.e., women and children are not specifically targeted. A terrorist, on the other hand, will focus on women and children specifically just to create a higher atmosphere of fear. Rape has also been used frequently as a terrorist tactic, not only to specifically impregnate women, but also to totally demoralize men who cannot defend the women from such acts. Thus, the ethnic cleansing evidenced in Bosnia and Kosovo as well as Rwanda and the Republic of the Congo in the 1990s crossed the line from warfare to terrorism by military units. Similarly, roving bands of terrorist Muslims have been tolerated by the Sudanese government in the decimation of fellow Muslims who were black in the Darfur region of the country.

8. Propaganda used to maximize the effects of violence, particularly for economic or political goals. To carry out an operation without getting any publicity from the action would be wasteful to a terrorist's cause. Thus, in 1972 the group Black September selected the Olympic Games in Munich as its venue to maximize the news coverage of the event. From that point, many international terrorist groups have mimicked the staging of spectacular assaults and attacks in an effort to both garner worldwide attention and further economic goals. On August 7, 1998, one of the reasons the U.S. Embassy in Nairobi, Kenya, may have been selected as a target was that the American ambassador was a woman, and thus the attack would generate more publicity. From a political standpoint, a group wants to show that it is a viable organization, a power to be reckoned with, and a force to be feared. On an economic level, the terrorist organization demonstrates to sympathetic governments and others who support radical organizations that it too is worthy of funding and support. Even when terrorists do not publicly claim responsibility for an attack, many leave a signature or obvious clues during the action.

9. Loyalty to themselves or kindred groups. This is a common element of terrorist groups, existing among Armenians, Croatians, Kurds, Tamils, and Basques, to name a few. With these and similar groups, the loyalty is so intense—*distorted* is not too strong a word—that the more radical elements of an otherwise peaceful movement will commit unspeakable criminal acts on behalf of that loyalty and associated cause. For the most part, however, second- and third-generation terrorists have diminished loyalty to the original cause, and the sense of pride associated with it, and a reduced vision of the original goal.

Many of them engage in terrorism as a form of gratification and perpetuate criminal activity as an end in itself. They have thus become nihilistic and interested primarily in financial remuneration for themselves. Terrorism during the 1960s and 1970s was carried out, for the most part, by college-age individuals and educated political activists. Now, much of the terrorism is driven by religious zealots and ethnocentric radicals, many of whom are very young and poorly educated.

Modern Terrorist Groups

Terrorist groups come in virtually every size, shape, and political color, but the major ones operating today can be grouped under a few major headings, with some actually fitting more than one category:

Religious groups. In today's world of terrorist activity, Islamic fundamentalists have grabbed most of the attention, following a long tradition in which religion has been a motivating factor, or at least a stated justification, for organized groups to commit terrorist acts. Whether of leftist or rightist political persuasions, religion has been behind such groups as the Irish Republican Army, antiabortion militants, the Jewish Defense League, and many of the Muslim groups operating in and around the Middle East. As have the groups preceding them, several Islamic groups have spread beyond their original theater of operations to foment terrorist activity from the Americas to the Philippines. Such organizations as Hamas, the Iranian Mujahedin-e-Khalq (MEK), and various incarnations and subgroups of al Qaeda have been active in Western Europe, particularly Great Britain, and the United States.

Minority nationalist groups. Often styled as freedom fighters, these groups depend for support on the sympathy of ethnic, religious, or linguistic minorities in conflict with the dominant culture, community, or political power. Groups in this category, although levels of activity ebb and flow, include the organization now called the Real Irish Republican Army, the Basque nationalist movement (ETA is the acronym in the Basque language), the Tamil Tigers in Sri Lanka, and numerous others less well known outside their home territories. Nationalists in Chechnya have carried out terrorist acts against Russia, as have nationalist groups in other former republics that once were part of the Soviet Union. In addition, there are many indigenous peoples' movements that have surfaced in different parts of the world, particularly in Latin America, such as those in some southern Mexican states.

Marxist revolutionary groups. These groups have been on the wane since the collapse of the Soviet Union, which in turn led to losing financial support from Cuba, although Venezuela, under Hugo Chavez, has shown a readiness to step into this space. There are some groups still spouting Marxist rhetoric that lingered on afterward, such as the Shining Path in Peru or the Tamil Tigers in Sri Lanka, although the Tigers fall into the nationalist category also. Historically, some of the more infamous Marxist terrorist groups were the Weather Underground in the United States, the Red Brigade in Italy, Action Directe in France, the Red Army Faction in Germany (West Germany when it was a divided country), and the Combatant Cells in Belgium.

Anarchist groups. They have no particular political orientation or bias other than an antiestablishment sentiment. What started largely as a European phenomenon with a history dating back to the nineteenth century, anarchism has had somewhat of a revival among groups opposed to globalization. In recent years, this has been demonstrated by the "smash it up, bring it down" mentality evidenced during the World Trade Organization meeting in Seattle, Washington, in 1999, and subsequent meetings in both Europe and the United States. Individual anarchist organizations have in the past usually been short lived due to the fact there was no real central theme for their existence. Today in the world of social media, instant communication among like-minded people can rally vast crowds in a flash, and in fact, they are sometimes referred to as flash crowds or demonstrations.

Neo-fascist right-wing extremists. Only a minimal threat in Europe, they have nonetheless persisted and even grown in number in the United States since the end of World War II. The recent rise has been fueled by Christian extremists, white supremacists, and antifederal government activists. The traditional groups, including Aryan Nation, Posse Comitatus Committee, and Ku Klux Klan, have been joined by various looser-knit groups using the word *militia* in their names—hence the frequent use of the phrase "militia movement" to describe these right-wing groups. Their influence was demonstrated during the trial and conviction of Timothy McVeigh, the man executed June 11, 2001, for the bomb attack on the Alfred P. Murrah Federal Building in Oklahoma City on April 19, 1995. The Jewish Defense Organization is also classified as a right-wing group. A group called the Hutarees surfaced in Michigan in 2008, and nine members were arrested in March 2010. Spouting some religious trappings, the group had targeted police officers at the local, state, and federal levels, as well as members of the U.S. armed forces as members of a brotherhood supporting the antichrist, who should be killed.

Pathological groups/pathological individuals. These individuals or small cult-like groups are driven by a psychological need to make a particular statement or to manipulate people. Many of these operate in relative obscurity, surfacing often in a violent or spectacular manner. Pathological activities include the multiyear bombing campaign of Unabomber Theodore Kaczynski, which was driven by his rabid concern for the military-industrial society and its possible effect on the future of the world, and the radical Japanese cult/terrorist group Aum Shrinrikyo, which released sarin gas in an attack against the Tokyo subway system. This terrorist category encompasses single-issue groups and includes antiabortionists, animal rights terrorists such as those steered by People for the Ethical Treatment of Animals and the Animal Liberation Front, and antidevelopment groups such as the Earth Liberation Front.

Ideological mercenaries. They include individuals and groups who share a common faith and commitment to worldwide revolution (as opposed to several individual revolutions in many places). There are a number of organizations that follow the New World Order philosophy, while the Japanese Red Army was one group practicing mercenary terrorism in the past. More recently, former members of the Irish Republican Army traveled to Colombia to assist FARC (Revolutionary Armed Forces of Colombia) in its terrorist activities, although it is somewhat difficult to discern whether these individuals are driven more by the monetary rewards than by the beliefs that they espouse.

Why Terrorists Succeed

Terrorists have experienced a number of tactical successes for a variety of reasons, some of which are controllable and some of which are not, particularly in open and democratic societies. Factors aiding terrorists fall into six areas:

1. Mobility
2. Communications
3. Security
4. Democratic legal systems
5. Access to arms
6. Vulnerability of targets

Mobility

Terrorists enjoy the same freedom of movement in a country as do law-abiding citizens of those countries. When traveling internationally, terrorists have the protection of passports and other documents, often forged or obtained illegally, and even possibly diplomatic passports provided by a sympathetic state. The ease with which terrorists can move about the world was brought to light in an extraordinary fashion on Christmas Day 2009. Umar Farouk Abdulmutallab, a Nigerian-born terrorist who had more red flags raised than seen in a communist May Day parade, managed to fly aboard an American airliner without being intercepted or detained. His name was on several terrorist watch lists. His own father told U.S. authorities that he was a radicalized Muslim bent on carrying out a terrorist mission. He purchased an international airline ticket with cash and was not carrying or checking any luggage. In addition, he traveled from a politically sensitive nation and was allowed to board the aircraft unchallenged. It was only good fortune that the explosive device he had secreted in his underwear failed to function as designed. In the years since 9/11 and the subsequent enhanced security measures, it is still easy for those bent on attacking a U.S. target to get where they want to go almost unimpeded. In developed countries, high-speed highway systems and internal rail and air networks allow terrorists and their supporters to operate over long distances, commuting to the scene of an attack and given avenues of escape.

In Russia, in the years after the fall of the communist regime and collapse of the Soviet Union, there was a relaxation of totalitarian controls over civilians, which also allowed terrorism to flourish. Ethnic terrorist groups from the newly autonomous states were able to easily travel and penetrate Russian security to carry out bomb and hostage-taking activities. These acts, along with nonterrorist criminal activity, have played havoc with the Russian economy. It is suspected that organized crime gangs and terrorists have collaborated in attempting to obtain and sell nuclear technology and stolen nuclear materials and weapons to foreign radical groups and rogue nations. The new borderless European Union enhances mobility for terrorists engaged in such activity. Above all, mobility aids terrorists in avoiding detection.

Communications

Major mobility and communications go hand in hand, and communication technology has evolved so rapidly that its potential, for good or evil, has not been fully realized. Everyday communication technology is sufficient to enable a terrorist organization to easily plan attacks on multiple targets over a wide geographic area—worldwide, in fact. Operatives can communicate and coordinate whether they are around the corner or around the globe. The al Qaeda organization has used cell phone communication extensively in planning such attacks in New York and Washington, D.C. Although much of this communication "chatter" is monitored by intelligence agencies, use of coded conversations and sanitized messages is a viable method of conducting business. In addition, Internet communications and social media further allow terrorist groups to decentralize their organizations, making them harder to identify, observe, infiltrate, and monitor.

Communications technology allows terrorists to tactically maintain contact with each other in the field during assaults and attacks, as demonstrated with the assault in Mumbai and at the various anarchist rampages whenever a group of world leaders convene at summits.

Security

Security is a prime concern of terrorists. Having learned from past mistakes and mistakes of others, they know that loose operating procedures make apprehension and prosecution much easier. A large, loosely run operation can be infiltrated by undercover law enforcement agents relatively simply. It was once said, only half in jest, that in the waning days of the Weather Underground movement there were more law enforcement agents in the organization than there were Weathermen. In an effort to maintain the highest level of operational security, successful terrorist organizations have long directives detailing policies and procedures regarding security. Whether the organization is run from a single safe house or a mountain base camp, the terrorist organizations can be very difficult to infiltrate by law enforcement operatives. One of the things that surfaced during the court trials of al Qaeda members involved in the U.S. Embassy bombings in East Africa was the group's training manual, seized in a raid on an apartment in Manchester, England. The manual included advice that cells should be used in establishing a security plan. A cell must be:

1. Realistic and based on fact, so it will be credible to the enemy before and after the work.
2. Coordinated, integrated, cohesive, and accurate, without any gaps, to provide the enemy the impression of a continuous linked chain of events.
3. Simple, so that the members can assimilate it.
4. Creative.
5. Flexible.
6. Secretive.

From documents retrieved at the Manchester location as well as from a variety of other locations and groups, the following security measures were stressed, starting with the conduct of meetings. Meetings can be stationary, where three or more members convene, or mobile, where two members meet. Security measures prior to a stationary meeting include:

1. Specifying the time of a meeting in such a way as to not raise suspicions because of the members' movements.
2. Minimizing the time between notifying members of the meeting and the meeting itself.
3. Securing the meeting place and routes to the location by assigning members to monitor the site before and during the meeting, staying in cell phone communication en route to the meeting, placing a member close to the nearest enemy security point (i.e., police station or post) to communicate signs of security movement, and positioning an armed guard to stop any attack and allow members to escape.

Suggestions for security procedures while traveling to a meeting include:

1. Ensure that the enemy is not behind an individual while en route to the meeting.
2. Do not head directly to the meeting location but go through secondary places.
3. Travel individually, not in groups.
4. Members' clothing and general appearance should be suitable for the location of the meeting.
5. Alight from public transportation away from the meeting place and walk; if driving a car, park in a secure location some distance from the meeting place and walk. Distances in either case should be sufficient to maneuver quickly if a "tail" is suspected.
6. Verify that proper cover is established for any documents being carried, including identification.
7. If armed, make sure that the weapon is in good working order.

The advice continues for meeting sites, so that in the case of stationary meetings, the location should be in the middle of a group of houses, not at either end, and there should be several routes to the location, which should also have multiple entrances/exits, making it more difficult to surround the location and facilitating fast escapes. Leave behind no traces of a group meeting, including trash. For mobile meetings, the location should be at or near the intersection of several roads, and the site should be away from places where security or police congregate, such as coffee shops. Times and places of meetings should be rotated frequently, and members should have personal documentation to support agreed on cover. When a meeting concludes, members should leave individually or in pairs, heading in various directions and not discussing what went on at the meeting.

Information gleaned from various terrorists' manuals provides the basis for many of the security and operational guidelines used today. Some additional general points are as follows:

1. Punctuality is important since tardiness risks exposure of all members.
2. Prudence and discretion are necessary in conversation during the meeting since "walls have ears"; thus, euphemisms and generalities are preferred to specifics, and radio, television, or music should be on constantly at high levels to frustrate eavesdropping.
3. Sufficient observers should be placed along routes to, as well as at, the meeting site to be on the alert for surveillance or unusual security and police activity.
4. Meetings should never be discussed in public or on cell phones used in public places, and members should not acknowledge each other upon chance meetings in public.
5. If members are detained or arrested, they should demand prisoner-at-war status and provide no information whatsoever.

Universally, the fear of infiltration is paramount with a group's security. Virtually every terrorist group regards infiltrators as greater enemies than whatever group is the professed "enemy" the terrorists are fighting.

Democratic Legal System

The laws of a country and its system and procedures for safeguarding the rights of its citizens are perverted by terrorists in order to help them achieve success in undermining that country. The need for court approval to obtain certain types of evidence or employ certain types of investigative techniques leads to long, time-consuming investigations in which every policy and procedure must be meticulously observed, lest the letter of the law not be followed, even if the spirit had not been violated. Once apprehension has been effected, civil rights guarantees and procedures make for long-drawn-out and costly trials. There is almost no reason why terrorists, actual or suspected, would want a speedy trial, because time works only in their favor as memories get hazy, people get bored, and witnesses and other key figures become sick or die. In addition, even when they are incarcerated, terrorists may continue to espouse their radical views, or at least complain about their treatment, to receptive media outlets. Legal maneuvering by defense attorneys and long delays prior to the start of trials allow for the public's interest in the progress of the events to wane, while at the same time they allow the terrorist to rally support. The trials themselves are often used as stages from which the terrorists can spout propagandistic rhetoric.

In differentiating itself from the policies of President Bush, the Obama administration had considered but didn't hold the trials of "high value" terrorists in civilian courts in New York City or other large cities, rather than at a secure venue at Guantanamo Bay Naval Base in Cuba. This not only opens the door for sensitive materials and intelligence techniques to be made public, but also would provide a stage for defendants and their supporters to vent against the United States and its policies for sympathetic audiences, both domestic and overseas.

Access to Arms

With the advances in weapon technology, terrorists have a wide variety of sophisticated weaponry with which to work, particularly when explosives are involved. The miniaturization of electronic components and circuitry in time-delay and detonating systems, along with the use of plastic explosives and the ease of improvising highly concentrated toxic substances, makes construction of sophisticated improvised explosive devices frighteningly possible. The collapse of the Soviet Union in the late twentieth century and the fall of Saddam Hussein's regime witnessed a dispersal of a variety of weapons that contributed to the arming of a number of terrorist and insurgent groups. In addition to the illegal arms market that surfaced in the former Soviet republics, rogue nations in places like the Horn of Africa allow for an almost endless supply of explosives and small arms weapons. State-of-the-art weapons are readily available on the open market for use not only by terrorist organizations, but also by paramilitary groups involved in both low-intensity conflicts and narcoterrorist operations.

Of particular concern within the intelligence communities are the small, tactical nuclear weapons, popularly referred to as "suitcase nukes," that may have gone missing with the fall of the Soviet Union and dissolution of its satellite states and political bloc.

Vulnerability of Targets

It was not too many years ago that there was an almost endless list and variety of high-profile targets available for terrorists to attack. Since the 9/11 attacks, however, national security agencies have sounded the alarm regarding the potential for other large-scale terrorist attacks, and many have listened. The result has been an enhanced effort to harden high-profile potential targets, particularly government buildings and public facilities. The result has been that the al Qaeda network, other jihad groups, and terrorists of various persuasions have focused on carrying out attacks on "softer" targets, usually located in urban areas and those particularly identified with Christian, Jewish, or Western religious, economic, and human interests. Other targets that have become popular with Islamic terrorists are tourist areas, such as the attacks we saw on the Mumbai and Bali hotels. Another target has been expatriate workers in Iraq, Saudi Arabia, the Philippines, and Malaysia. Oil field workers, mining officials, and other North American and European foreigners have also been taken hostage, killed, or both in some areas of Latin America.

Private corporations, their facilities and their workers, are particularly vulnerable since there are frequently multiple locations and bottom-line issues with which to contend. Because security is not revenue generating, it is presumed to have a low priority in many companies. During periods of high terrorist activity, security is typically enhanced; when the threat subsides, so does security awareness relating to terrorist threats. This point is not lost in planning sessions by terrorist operatives. They would rather attack a location with a lower degree of preparedness than a tight or hardened target. Given that, the security practitioner and law enforcement planner should always remember that, as 9/11 demonstrated, and as repeatedly said throughout this book, a determined foe, with time and study, can attack virtually any target with a reasonable chance of success.

Counterterrorist Response

The United States has dramatically enhanced its counterterrorist response capability since the tragic events of 9/11 in order to address the widening threat of global terrorism reaching domestic targets and U.S. interests abroad. The president sets the overall policy for counterterrorism, with the assistance of a special coordinating committee of the National Security Council. Presidential Directive 39, entitled *United States Policy on Counterterrorism*, and enhanced by Presidential Directive 62, recognizes that there must be rapid and decisive capability in defeating terrorism. In general, the policy spells out the need to protect U.S. citizens, arrest terrorists, respond to sponsors of terrorism, and provide assistance to the victims. The problems encountered in combating global terrorism are too complex to expect a single agency to deal with them successfully, as acknowledged when President George W. Bush declared the war on terrorism in the wake of the 9/11 attacks and established the Department of Homeland Security (DHS). In organizing the response to terrorism, the effort is divided into two broad phases: the crisis, or preincident phase, and the consequence, or postincident phase.

Major points of U.S. counterterrorism policy include:

1. Make no concessions to terrorists and strike no deals.
2. Bring terrorists to justice for their crimes.
3. Isolate and apply pressure on the states that sponsor terrorism to force them to change their behavior.
4. Bolster the counterterrorism capabilities of those countries that work with the United States and that require assistance.

After 9/11, the counterterrorism response was given top priority by President Bush. Up and down the chain of law enforcement, intelligence, and military communities, roles were greatly enhanced and the various agencies were grouped within the newly created Department of Homeland Security. With the election of Barack Obama in 2008, terrorism rhetoric was toned down—the phrase "war on terror" was eliminated from official use—but most of the initiatives begun during the Bush years have continued under the Obama administration.

The Secret Service has the most defined role in protecting government officials from terrorist attacks, with particular responsibility for the president and vice president and their families, as well as selected other individuals, including presidential candidates, the president-elect and vice-president elect, and selected other senior government officials. The Secret Service and the U.S. Department of State share responsibility for protecting heads of foreign states and other international dignitaries visiting the United States. As a practical matter, these federal agencies coordinate efforts with local law enforcement departments, particularly on such matters as crowd and traffic control, building security, and uniformed police presences.

The response to a terrorist action is addressed on three discrete levels:

1. Local. In a terrorist attack, such as a bombing or the taking of hostages, the first responders are typically local public safety and medical personnel. Unless the attack has occurred in a major municipality, local assets are usually not sufficient to meet the emergency, particularly when weapons of mass destruction are used. Even when local first responders take the lead, however, as happened on 9/11, federal agencies respond within a matter of hours.
2. State. If local authorities require help in responding to major terrorist activity, assistance can be requested through a state Office of Emergency Services, or similar agency. The state's substantially greater resources, including selected elements of the National Guard, can readily be dispatched to the affected area or location. In addition, the state government is a quick conduit for federal assistance as required. This may include the use of U.S military units when

National Guard units do not have the assets, expertise, or manpower to respond adequately.

3. Federal. The DHS develops and coordinates the implementation of a comprehensive national strategy to secure the country from terrorist threats and attacks. The DHS coordinates the executive branch's efforts to detect, prepare for, prevent, protect against, respond to, and recover from terrorist's attacks within the boundaries of the United States. The attorney general has responsibility for ensuring the development and implementation of policies directed at preventing terrorist acts directed at the United States. Traditionally, the Federal Bureau of Investigation (FBI) has been the lead agency in executing the federal response to terrorist incidents. The FBI designates an on-the-scene commander to coordinate the federal response with state and local authorities until such time as the Federal Emergency Management Agency is ready to provide support. In an incident where weapons of mass destruction are used, the response capability of rescue and medical units may be impaired. In extraordinary cases, active military units garrisoned in the vicinity of the incident may be called upon for immediate deployment in order to save lives, prevent human suffering, and assist in protecting physical property.

Internationally, the U.S. Department of State has increased its assistance to cooperating nations in their efforts to combat terrorism. Such assistance includes financial support and training and intelligence sharing. The Central Intelligence Agency also plays a major role in combating international terrorism through its proactive intelligence gathering and interaction with government and nongovernment agencies and organizations.

Weapons of Mass Destruction

Perhaps the greatest challenge facing counterterrorist efforts is the potential use of weapons of mass production, whether nuclear, biological, or chemical. Previously, nuclear attack was considered the most destructive form a terrorist attack could take, but now there has been increased sophistication in the development of other types of weapons that can cause widespread death, suffering, and destruction. The threat of attack by rogue states' biological or chemical weapons has brought the specter of state-sponsored terrorism to new heights. There is the potential for rogue nations to arm their own operatives with these weapons, as well as to supply terrorist groups elsewhere. The most publicized use of a chemical weapon in a terrorist attack was by a Japanese religious cult, which on March 20, 1995, unleashed sarin gas in the Tokyo subway system. Saddam Hussein used chemical agents to kill Kurds on more than one occasion—March 16, 1988, was the deadliest—during his brutal regime as the leader of Iraq. More terrifying, in many ways, was the rash of incidents involving anthrax in the days and weeks after 9/11, with letters mailed to politicians and media outlets.

To combat future incidents, the role of the military has been greatly enhanced, as has that of other agencies. The U.S. Postal Service, for example, has developed a program to deliver emergency medical supplies to neighborhoods that might be subjected to a biochemical or low-level radiation attack. In addition, civilian support teams have been organized within the National Guard structure to help communities form a response effort in the event of a biological or chemical attack. Members of the FBI and of specialized units of the Marine Corps have been trained to respond and render assistance to local first responders in such incidents. New York City, as do other large metropolitan areas, maintains mobile monitors designed to detect a variety of radiological, chemical, or biological indicators.

In an effort to deal with such threats, the FBI operates the National Domestic Preparedness Office (NDPO), which acts as a clearinghouse on weapons of mass destruction for federal, state, and local authorities. The NDPO facilitates and coordinates efforts of various government agencies in providing the emergency response community with detection, protection, analysis, and decontamination equipment, as needed, in dealing with weapons of mass destruction.

Role of the Military

Since the attacks of 9/11, the Department of Defense has been assigned a much greater role than previously in dealing with terrorist attacks, on both U.S. and foreign soil and at sea. Special operation commands were engaged in destroying remnants of Taliban and al Qaeda organizations in Afghanistan and Pakistan, and in assisting Philippine forces in combating terrorists of that country. A unit called Task Force 121, a highly classified special operations group built around U.S. Army forces, was assigned the mission of tracking down Osama bin Laden and, subsequently, Saddam Hussein. The streamlined unit acts against "high-value targets" and is not restricted by traditional bounds governing conventional forces. In addition, the U.S. military plays an important role in gathering intelligence and providing logistical support to other agencies engaged in counterterrorism.

On the domestic front, the use of the military for combating terrorism remains a controversial issue, much of it coming as a result of the events surrounding the siege and destruction of the Branch Davidian compound outside Waco, Texas, on April 19, 1993. It was reported that U.S. Army personnel were present as observers and perhaps advisors because military vehicles were used in the siege. If the Army personnel had taken a more active role, it would have been a violation of law.

The attack of 9/11 and the anthrax incidents that occurred shortly afterward require that the military take an active role in the domestic war on terrorism. For instance, the Air Force provided combat air patrols over certain major population centers; the Navy has increased offshore patrolling. Military aircraft still scramble to address any reported suspicious or disruptive behavior aboard U.S. domestic airlines. All branches of the military have enhanced their counterterrorism capabilities, particularly in dealing with weapons of mass destruction.

National concerns over the U.S. military in civilian law enforcement have a long history and became an issue as early as 1876, during allegations of violence and stuffed ballot boxes during the election contest involving Republican Rutherford B. Hayes and Democrat Samuel Tilden. President Ulysses S. Grant sent troops to a number of polling places in several southern states to maintain order, but Democrats alleged that the action was really an attempt to fix the election for Hayes. The presidential election of 1876 was as controversial as, if not more than, the 2000 contest between Republican George W. Bush and Democrat Al Gore. The election went to Hayes when a special panel established to oversee the count awarded one more electoral vote to Hayes than to Tilden.

In 1878, as an aftermath of the resultant controversy, and over the veto of President Hayes, a Democratic-led Congress passed the Posse Comitatus Act (PCA), which banned the use of the army for domestic law enforcement unless specifically authorized by the Constitution or an act of Congress. Since then, until recently, the law has been interpreted as a virtual ban on the use of military for domestic law enforcement. The only branch of service that is exempt is the Coast Guard, which is considered a civilian law enforcement agency except during the times of declared warfare.

Even the military presence at the 2002 Winter Olympics in Salt Lake City, Utah, in the event of a terrorist attack, was criticized by many as a direct violation of the PCA. Although the military had been used in the past in some law enforcement situations, including to assist in federal desegregation efforts in the 1950s, in the antidrug efforts in the 1980s, and to aid local police and National Guard units during the Los Angeles riots of 1992, it has been primarily in response to 9/11 that the provisions of the act have been questioned. Despite the initial flurry of attention to the act, though, military leaders support the provisions and have not been eager to become involved in local law enforcement. Therefore, it does not appear that the act will be altered unless additional acts of international terrorism occur on U.S. soil.

Homeland Defense

In an effort to secure our homeland, critical pieces of legislation were enacted to improve the nation's response to terrorism threats. Some of these initiatives are:

Homeland Security Act of 2002
USA Patriot Act 2002, renewed in 2006
Aviation and Transportation Security Act of 2001
Public Health Security and Bioterrorism and Response Act of 2002
Enhanced Border Security and Visa Entry Reform Act of 2002
Maritime Transportation Act of 2002

In an effort to better protect the United States from terrorism, President George W. Bush created the DHS and named former governor Tom Ridge as its first director to organize the new organization, largely cobbled together from existing administrations, agencies, offices, and bureaus that had been part of other federal departments. The mission statement says the department is designed primarily to prevent terrorist attacks within U.S. borders, to reduce the country's vulnerability to terrorism, to minimize damage, and to facilitate appropriate response and recovery efforts when attacks do occur. The basic strategy includes four major points:

1. Enhance analytic capabilities of the FBI.
2. Initiate a new information analysis and infrastructure protection division.
3. Implement a homeland security advisory system.
4. Utilize dual-use analysis to assess attack threats.

Ridge served as secretary of Homeland Security until 2005 and was succeeded by Michal Chertoff, who served until President Barak Obama appointed Janet Napolitano to head the agency, which since its creation has met with mixed reviews. DHS includes 22 major federal agencies, and to critics, this is much too large to manage effectively. One of the constituent agencies that has come under particular criticism is the Transportation Safety Administration, which was faulted in the incident involving Umar Farouk Abdulmutallab, who flew from Europe to Detroit on Christmas Day 2009 with explosives secreted in his underwear. TSA is also responsible for maintaining "no fly" lists, which have become a source of public ridicule since the agency is secretive about where, why, when, or how names are entered on the list, and provides even less information when individuals seek an explanation after being barred from a flight.

Implementation of Homeland Security

DHS was created by the largest reorganization of the national government in history and the most substantial shuffle of federal agencies since the National Security Act of 1947 in the post-World War II Cold War era. The department now encompasses more than 200,000 employees. DHS's responsibilities include:

1. Securing the nation's borders, ports, transportation, and other critical infrastructure components
2. Enhancing intelligence analysis from diverse sources
3. Coordinating, with state and local governments as well as private industry, the dissemination of terrorist threat information
4. Managing federal response activities and helping equip first responders
5. Reducing duplicate or redundant management functions in order to put more security operatives in the field

Organizing Homeland Security

The secretary of homeland security is responsible for carrying out the directives of the president with regard to defending the United States against terrorist attacks. Two agencies that report directly to the secretary are the Secret Service and the U.S. Coast Guard. The Secret Service remained intact during its transfer from the Treasury Department and still has the primary mission of protecting the president and other government leaders, as well as tracking down currency counterfeiters. The Coast Guard, which had previously been moved from the Treasury Department to the Department of Transportation, was moved again, to the DHS, and also remained largely intact in the reorganization and retained its responsibility of securing the nation's ports and waterways. The Coast Guard also maintained its independent identity as a military operation under the leadership of the commandant of the Coast Guard. In keeping with existing law, the Coast Guard can operate as an element of the Department of the Navy upon a declaration of war by the direction of the president.

Border and Transportation Security

In order to better secure and control the country's borders after the 9/11 attacks, security was enhanced in a number of areas, including document security; tracking, monitoring, and interdicting suspected terrorists; port security; aviation security; protecting critical infrastructure; and cyberse-curity. While many of these efforts rely on individual federal law enforcers taking a more active role in screening individuals at U.S. borders, they are augmented by a variety of activities to harness technology to monitor the physical borders and those passing through them. This has been something of a trial-and-error process, and since the implementation of these processes, some have been successfully put into effect while others have fallen seriously short.

Document security has been addressed through the development of new tamper-resistant visas and more stringent review of the application process. Although physical changes have been implemented, the process by which these documents are processed and approved is still suspect. Individuals on a number of watch lists have managed to gain U.S. entry documentation. One example is the case of the Christmas Day underwear bomber, Umar Farouk Adbulmutallab, who obtained a visa to enter the United States. There are ongoing discussions about enhancing travel documents to include biometric identifiers similar to those used at a number of private companies to monitor access to their facilities. These include such things as face recognition, scans of an eye's iris, skin recognition systems, and thumb or finger prints, but none have been implemented.

In addition, the Department of State initiated the Terrorist Interdiction Program in countries that are at high risk for terrorist transit, using a data-base system that enables officials to track those who attempt to enter or leave the United States. There is also a Student and Visitors Exchange to track for-eign students entering the United States and verify that they are enrolled in and attending classes, although many institutions of higher learning are failing to cooperate.

Port security enhancement includes establishing new procedures for tar-geting high-risk cargo prior to its being loaded onto container ships heading to U.S. ports. The Coast Guard requires ports, vessels, and facilities to per-form security assessments and develop plans to address security deficiencies. Port security was considered to be serious enough to emerge as an issue dur-ing the 2004 election campaign when Democrat John Kerry noted that the vast majority of containers that enter the United States on seagoing freight vessels did not receive any type of human oversight at any time during the trip from the original port to the United States.

Aviation security enhancement included the formation of the Transportation Security Administration (TSA), which was charged with the responsibility of securing airports and aircraft, including overseeing screen-ing functions. The TSA was created in November 2001 under the Aviation and Security Transportation Security Act as an agency within the U.S. Department of Transportation, and was moved to the DHS in early 2003. It is responsible for all civilian aviation security, a responsibility that was previously assigned to the Federal Aviation Administration. TSA is responsible for such visible functions as airport passenger and baggage screening, and less public functions, such as upgrading preemployment policies and training of TSA and private security screeners. Most law enforcement or security professionals with airports in their jurisdiction have interacted with TSA's airport security directors or their staffs, who are mandated to act as liaisons between airport personnel and law enforcement and first responder agencies. Many of these directors have prior police experience, although some are specialists from various sectors of the aviation industry. The TSA security director is considered the lead employee in assessing airport security and in implementing the Federal Security Crisis Management Response Plan, which is designed to aid coordination among airport personnel, air carrier managers, and first responders to any real or potential terrorist threats. Local law enforcement managers should be aware of emergency plans at airports within their jurisdictions, inquire about the 24-hour intelligence watch that the TSA maintains to alert airline industry professionals to threats to the transportation environment, and familiarize themselves with new rules pertaining to the arming of certain airline pilots.

The Federal Air Marshal program was developed in response to airplane hijackings to Cuba in the 1960s, and enhanced when hijackings by international terrorists increased during the 1970s and 1980s. Air marshals operate in plain clothes, traveling as ordinary passengers, but are armed and authorized to take passengers into custody if they are found to be creating a disturbance. Air marshals were involved in the incident of the Christmas Day underwear bomber in 2009. Other in-flight security measures, such as restricting access to the cockpit on commercial passenger flights and more stringent federal laws protecting flight crews, were put into effect following the 9/11 attacks involving hijacked airplanes. The TSA has also conducted tests of passenger and baggage screening at selected train stations. Although this has received far less publicity than airport security, the potential number of passengers is actually far greater, and law enforcement officials with test sites in their communities should be aware of the potential for false threats from inconvenienced members of the public or potential traffic delays in and around train stations selected as test sites. On a local front, a number of law enforcement agencies have implemented similar programs on mass transit systems in their communities, perhaps the most notable being random search points set up in the New York City subway system.

Emergency Preparedness and Response

Emergency preparedness and response includes overseeing domestic preparedness training and coordinating government disaster response. The

Federal Emergency Management Agency is the central unit of this component, administering grant programs for firefighters, law enforcement, and other first responders and emergency services that had previously been under the auspices of other departments, such as the Department of Health and Human Services and the Department of Justice. Chemical, biological, radiological, and nuclear response assets and the Domestic Employee Support Team were consolidated from a variety of agencies. The Federal Law Enforcement Training Center in Glynco, Georgia, is now part of the Department of Homeland Security.

Science and Technology

Science and technology units lead the effort to prepare for and respond to terrorist threats involving weapons of mass destruction, including agroterrorism. Activities include encouraging research and development of improved security systems to diminish the threat of nuclear materials entering the country, as well as enhancing detection methods of chemical and bioterror materials. Among the facilities involved in this area are the Plum Island Animal Disease Center, which had been part of the Department of Agriculture; the Civilian Biodefense Research programs, formally part of the Department of Health and Human Services; the National Chemical and Biological Warfare Defense Analysis programs from the Department of Defense; and the Lawrence Livermore National Laboratory, which had been part of the Department of Energy.

Information and Infrastructure Protection

Information and infrastructure protection involves interacting with other agencies regarding threats to homeland security. Among the units that had been involved in these areas prior to coming under the DHS umbrella are the Critical Infrastructure Assurance Office, National Communication System, National Infrastructure Protection System, Federal Computer Incident Response Center, and National Infrastructure Simulation and Analysis Center. This is an important area in which law enforcement, private security professionals, and other first responders need to become familiar. The specific mandate of this section of the DHS is to activate effective first responses to terrorist attacks. A number of training programs to enhance skills and coordination of the first responders have been designed. There are also moves toward creation of a comprehensive national incident management system that will streamline federal procedures and attempt to create interoperable communications to enable a seamless response among the many different agencies that may be called upon during a disaster.

Task Force Initiatives

The Joint Bank Robbery Task Force was formed during the 1970s to combat a growing problem of bank robberies plaguing the nation. To attack the problem, the FBI and the New York City Police Department (NYPD) formed a joint bank robbery task force that combined seasoned NYPD detectives, who possessed "street smarts," with special agents, who were unencumbered by jurisdictional boundaries. The success of the program led to the formation of the NYPD/FBI Joint Terrorist Task Force to combat domestic terrorism as perpetrated by the Puerto Rican FALN, anti-Castro group Omega-7, and remnants of the Weather Underground. The Joint Terrorism Task Force was strengthened and enhanced after 9/11, and the concept was extended to other parts of the country. More than 100 task forces were added to the armamentarium. The task forces, roughly one in each federal judicial district, are part of a national effort to coordinate dissemination of information and develop investigative and prosecutorial strategies throughout the country. Part of their mission is to act as an informational pipeline between local law enforcement and federal agencies. They also assist in coordinating a response to terrorist incidents if and when they do occur.

Local Law Enforcement Capabilities

In hostage or barricade situations, the local police department's guidelines are the basic operational procedures in the early stages of such terrorist activities. Information in this book may be able to assist as a tool for preparing an outline for forming those procedures, or in guiding actions in situations not directly covered by established procedures. In bombing incidents, unless intelligence provides foreknowledge, local police will be dealing with a suspected bomb or a consequence investigation. In this day and age, a federal response will also be initiated almost automatically to assist the local law enforcement community. In both instances, however, good liaison with the private sector on the part of local police and, conversely, good cooperation by private industry with local police will have the effect of hardening the target against terrorist activity.

Today, nearly all major police departments and smaller agencies have hostage and barricade situation procedures in place. Past events, even nonterrorist incidents such as the shootings at Columbine High School in Littleton, Colorado, the Virginia Tech massacre, and the sniper attacks in and around

Washington, D.C., including nearby areas of Maryland and Virginia, illustrated the need for cooperative training among police agencies responding to a mutual aid call. The techniques that local law enforcement uses in responding to such a situation could just as easily be used during the opening stages of a terrorist attack, investigation, or both. How the first responding officers establish contact, seal off the affected area, conduct an evacuation, and protect the crime scene will greatly influence how the incident is played out.

Local Significance

An important component of counterterrorism is intelligence gathering. Much of the intelligence is not difficult to find, although assessing its importance and significance can be. One area in which this is especially true involves the names of people, locations of places, and lists of dates that have significance locally.

For example, in Seattle, early December dates have special significance because that was when, in 1999, demonstrators disrupted a major conference on world trade. April 19 is the date of the conflagration at the Branch Davidian compound outside Waco, Texas, and the bombing of the Murrah Federal Building in Oklahoma City two years later.

In coastal areas, dates of whale migration could bring about activity by radical environmental groups. Dates of uprisings and revolutions "in the old country" may have symbolic importance to ethnic or national groups living in a community.

There are many dates marked by terrorists that transcend local importance. May 19, for example, has double significance: it is the birthday of both Ho Chi Minh, who led North Vietnam during its war with South Vietnam, and Malcolm X, the Black Muslim. November 6 marks the date of the birth of Mohammed the Prophet, founder of Islam, while four days later, November 10, the U.S. Marine Corps celebrates its birthday. Any of these, and numerous other dates, could elicit terrorist actions in an effort to garner publicity on a significant occasion.

Although in recent past terrorist attacks, significant dates have diminished in importance, this is not to say that terrorists have abandoned that tactic. It well may be that a "lone wolf" attacker will use a date to make a statement or mark the date with an action, such as Timothy McVeigh did in 1995.

Private Sector Cooperation

In order to harden a potential target against terrorist attacks, a good deal of cooperation is required between private industry and law enforcement. The contacts by the private sector should also extend to emergency service agencies as well as state and federal agencies. As a matter of practical fact, in some areas, the security force of a private company may be significantly larger than the local police force. Many of the railroads are privately owned, but have sworn officers with multistate commissions, giving them wider jurisdictions than municipal, county, and state police. Private industry has been a frequent supporter and sponsor of training programs that involve local and state agencies in a variety of emergency response scenarios. This cooperation may extend to allowing facilities to be used in practice drills for first responders.

The private sector has also contributed toward the purchase of specialized equipment for emergency services or law enforcement agencies for which no municipal funds have been budgeted. Such purchases have included tactical robots for remote entry in bomb and hostage situations, as well as state-of-the-art bomb suits for explosive disposal personnel. Privately supported police foundations in a number of areas have provided funds for the purchase and training of horses for mounted units; dogs for bomb, search and rescue, and narcotic detection; and similar expenditures.

Another positive aspect of security cooperation between public and private sectors involves local police specialists advising about private security guidelines and training for various emergency situations, so that the private security personnel can properly set the stage should such an incident occur.

Terror Defense Planning

3

Introduction to Risk Assessment

In today's world of high-stakes terrorism, there are few individuals or organizations in either the private sector or law enforcement that will question the need for planning in order to meet the threat of terrorism. The events of 9/11, the London transit bombings, and the Mumbai attacks, and even such unsuccessful attempts as the Christmas Day "underwear" bomber in 2009 and the Times Square car bomber less than six months later, have demonstrated that the tactics of terrorists know no bounds and out-of-the box planning is now the rule rather than the exception. In fact, there is no other area in which there is a greater need for cooperation among federal, state, and local law enforcement and the private sector than terrorism defense. In the pre-9/11 days, when questions arose, they were generally about costs and potential benefits resulting from these expenditures. In the aftermath of 9/11, questions of cost have been put aside, but as we move on from 9/11 and terrorist attacks diminish or the perceived threat subsides, budget issues are again being raised—in times of financial downturn when money is tight. History shows, unfortunately, that security operations are frequently the first to feel the budget axe. It must be remembered, however, that the moral obligation to protect people's lives cannot be evaluated in dollars. For law enforcement's consideration, there is a legal obligation to protect lives. It is the foundation of the police mandate. On the part of the private sector, the obligation can be derived from what the courts have called "foreseeability" in vicarious liability suits. In this light we can ill afford to let our guard down.

Thus, in the private sector, an incident such as hostage taking could be considered a foreseeable occurrence under the vicarious liability statutes and case law, particularly if the company is doing business with a country or group that has been or is known to be a focal point of terrorist activity. In effect, such a company can be foreseen to be a potential target of violent action, and therefore operate under a legal obligation to protect its employees and property, and perhaps even its customers. Although terrorists are the most identifiable source of such violent action, disgruntled employees are also potential perpetrators of violence, as are common criminals. Courts have held companies liable for failure to react appropriately when such incidents occur.

The preincident plan is a guide to dealing with terrorist threats on a pragmatic level. Whether developed by a law enforcement agency, by private security personnel, or ideally, through a joint effort between the two, a preincident defense plan is a living—rather than an archival—document. It must be reviewed periodically and updated or altered as necessary. Terrorist defense planning can be divided into three component areas:

1. Preincident
2. Incident
3. Postincident

Preincident planning involves all the planning, anticipation, and "what if" modeling and intelligence gathering that can be done in advance. With today's "outside the box" thinking a must, cooperation between police and the private sector is especially crucial, since information and intelligence can be shared and the most efficient use of resources can be made.

Incident planning involves the development of a course of action in the event of terrorist activity, or if suspected or potential terrorist action occurs or is even threatened. Again, communication between the private sector company or organization that may be a target and the public safety community is essential.

Postincident, or consequence, planning is concerned with handling events in the aftermath of a bomb threat, explosion, hostage taking, kidnapping, or other attack, and deals with emergencies, physical damage, any possible collateral damage, and the need to get operations back to normal as quickly and safely as possible. During this period, continued cooperation between the private and public sectors is still essential. It should be noted in today's tense environment that many companies maintain disaster recovery plans that will enable minimal operations to be relocated to a satellite location within a short period, even before addressing long-term effects of an attack.

Security Advisory System

In the wake of the 9/11 attacks and subsequent war on terrorism, the Department of Homeland Security (DHS) inaugurated a comprehensive security advisory system in order to clarify and simplify ways to alert both law enforcement and the public in general. The system was scrapped early in 2011, even before the government had settled on a new method of alerting the public about heightened threat levels due to terrorist activity. After several months, however, the new color-free National Terrorism Advisory System (NTAS) was unveiled. Ironically, Russia began developing a color-coded terror alert system after a terrorist attack at the Moscow airport in January 2011 killed 36 people. The U.S. color-coded system provided guidance for protective measures to be employed when specific information to a particular sector or geographic region was received.

Replacing the old green (lowest threat level)-blue-yellow-orange-red (highest) alert level is one that is more black and white, though those designations are not actually being used. The new two-tiered system advises of either an "elevated threat," which warns of a credible terrorist threat against the United States or an "imminent threat" warning of a credible, specific and impending terrorist threat against the U.S.

In explaining the reasons for instituting a new security advisory system, DHS noted the terrorist threat facing the country has evolved significantly over the 10 years after the color-coded system was adopted. In the current environment DHS felt the best security strategy is one that counts on the American public as a key partner in securing the country. In essence, the idea is to provide just enough specific information about the impending threat to alert the public but not so much information that it makes it harder for law enforcement and counterterrorism officials to perform their duties.

The new system was developed through a collaboration of federal state, local, tribal and private sector representatives. Under NTAS, which is pronounced as N-TAS, DHS will coordinate with other federal agencies and organizations to issue detailed alerts to the public when intelligence is received about a credible terrorist threat. The NTAS alerts are designed to provide a concise summary of the potential threat, including geographic region, mode of transportation or critical infrastructure potentially affected by the threat, actions being taken to ensure public safety, and recommended steps that individuals, communities, businesses and governments can take to help prevent, mitigate, or respond to the threat.

The alerts will also include a clear statement on the nature of the threat. Depending upon the nature of the threat, the alerts could be sent to various law enforcement agencies, distributed to the businesses and industries in the private sector most likely to be affected, or issued more broadly to the public through official channels, the media and social media as well. NTAS alerts and posters will also be displayed in places such as transit hubs, airports and government buildings, among others. In some cases, the alerts might be for a specific geographical area, such as New York City, Washington, D.C., or Southern California, or the alert might specify an industry or sector of the economy, such as hotels or sports stadiums, or retailing or banking.

The new alert system encourages the public to report suspicious activity by suggesting steps individuals and communities can take, including precautionary and preparedness measures for themselves and their families. The NTAS initiative recommends that individuals should report suspicious activity to local law enforcement authorities. The "If you see something, say something" campaign will continue and encourages all citizens to be vigilant for indicators of potential terrorist activity, and to follow NTAS alerts for information about threats in specific places and about individuals exhibiting certain types of suspicious activity.

DHS introduced the NTAS system in order to provide more information to the public, even though some law enforcement officials felt that making too much information available might complicate intelligence gathering on the plot and plotters or even cause the operation to be abandoned before arrests could be made. In any case, the alerts would remain in effect for no longer than two weeks unless additional intelligence dictated extensions. The responsibility for raising the alerts falls on the Secretary of Homeland Security but only after conferring with a panel of national security and intelligence agencies.

Structuring a Preincident Plan

Preincident planning involves preparing for an occurrence that everyone hopes will never come to pass. The planning process is complex, involving information gathering (intelligence), risk analysis, organization, training, determining logistical needs, and purchasing necessary supplies and equipment required to handle an extraordinary event. What is the purpose of planning? First, it establishes the amount or level of potential risk to which a community, corporation, government entity, property, building, or other facility, or an individual executive or group of individuals, may be exposed vis-à-vis terrorist operatives.

Once the risk is assessed, policies must be in place to implement and adhere to procedures. It should be remembered, and this is a point we make frequently, such a plan is a living document and must be updated and revised as circumstances change. Such circumstance include, but are not limited to, remodeling or other changes to physical facilities; changes in personnel, particularly those named in the document, even by position or title; and changes in external political, economic, and international events.

The incident segment of a defense plan is in reality an operations manual for handling the initial phases of a terrorist attack of any nature. It should explain what actions are to be taken, when they should be taken, who should take them, and how these actions should be carried out. Even in the chaos of the World Trade Center disaster, the presence of a basic recovery plan allowed core businesses to maintain at least some level of business services. The collapse of the Twin Towers, accompanied by an extraordinary loss of life among the senior ranks of the emergency service personnel, especially within the New York Fire Department, revealed serious flaws in the planning process. A number of postincident reports severely criticized the placement of the command in such close proximity to the scene of potential, and as it turned out literally, disaster.

Postincident activity should include everything required to assist representatives of authorized agencies who may investigate the incident, as well as to restore the location to a point at which normal operations may resume. Postincident planning also involves metrics for assessing the long-term effects of the incident and provides a method for evaluating the strengths and weaknesses of the defense response so everyone can be better prepared should there be another incident. In this "lessons learned" phase, it is important to include all levels of participants so all points of view can be taken into consideration. In the case of the World Trade Center attack, the devastation was so great that some small companies never recovered, and even larger firms that lost hundreds of employees suffered the consequences for years afterward.

Information Gathering

Although this might seem contradictory, information gathering with regard to terrorist operations is at once the easiest and most difficult of tasks. It is easy because much of this information already exists—in files, letters, official documents, records of municipal and other government agencies, libraries, computer and Internet databases, and similar sources. The difficult part of information gathering is that there is no certainty as to what kind of information will be most helpful. Likewise, there are no guidelines for how much information is enough. One thing is certain; new information will be flowing constantly, altering previous assumptions and conclusions, as well as opening whole new areas of concern. In today's world there are many options— from televisions to the Internet to mobile communication devices—in order to follow global events. The advent and advancements in reporting from all locations around the world give real-time information to law enforcement and security professionals.

There are a host of resources at the disposal of the security professional, including specialized repositories on everything from terrorist activity to security hardware. The Internet has made such information easily available to the security profession, although the same information is also accessible to terrorist operatives. Some of the sources are subscription oriented, but a great many are free, including GlobalSecurity.org, which offers comprehensive information on military and terrorism subjects, including ongoing and past military and counterterrorist operations. There also are a variety of other websites that provide information on biological and chemical agents and various weapons of mass destruction.

In addition to the privately administered websites, the government has a number of sites that provide terrorism information, including one at the Centers for Disease Control and Prevention, which also provides information on diseases and biological agents. Other federal agencies, including the Federal Emergency Management Agency (FEMA), DHS, and the Department of State, as well as many states and educational institutions, maintain websites that provide security practitioners with useful information on counterterrorism-related issues. This method of gaining information, coupled with a strong liaison with law enforcement on the local and federal levels, should provide any security practitioner with a handle on what to do.

A word of caution: Information overload can easily occur, so the appropriate level of data gathering, in both amount and periodical updates, should be ascertained early in the process. For the most part, private security does not require the amount and depth of information that the law enforcement community requires. On the other hand, corporate security officials may require more geographically focused data, particularly when foreign operations are involved, than would a local police department. As the 9/11 and later investigations revealed, however, terrorist cells can be located almost anywhere in the country or in the world. In any event, there is a tendency to gather so much information that it can be difficult to process and properly evaluate—almost to the point of rendering it worthless. There is also the problem of organizing and retrieving information when it is needed in a timely fashion.

Whatever the sources, and however the data are collected, there are three general categories of information: targets, target profiles, and terrorists.

Targets

Information on who and what can be targets is subdivided into two categories. The first type of target involves primarily physical facilities; not only those located in the United States, but also American-related facilities anywhere around the world. The second type of target is personnel; individuals who may make useful kidnapping or hostage victims to terrorists. Once targets are identified, information should be assembled that covers the type or types of facilities and individuals and what it would take to reestablish operations after an emergency situation.

Whether target identification information is being gathered on behalf of a municipality, a quasi-public corporation, or a private company, the data are simply an enumeration of assets, including human resources, buildings and real estate, inventory, other physical assets, and intangibles, such as goodwill, name recognition, and publicity value. In other words, a target is anything or anybody that could be burned, bombed, stolen, damaged, contaminated, taken over, occupied, kidnapped, or held hostage. All of these potential targets should be listed (or inventoried) and major characteristics identified. Individuals have personnel files with home addresses, medical histories, dependents' names, and names of next of kin. Buildings have blueprints, floor plans, and drawings of electrical and heating, ventilation, and air conditioning (HVAC) systems, as well as fire alarm and other security systems. Vehicles have operating and repair manuals. Real estate has descriptions and dimensions in the deed and title files. All this information must be gathered so it can be assessed, filed, updated, copied, stored, or handled by whatever policy is decided upon during the risk analysis phase. Target identification should include rankings of vulnerability and information on what it would take to get the entity up and running again after an emergency situation. Needless to say, all information on targets should be given the highest security priority, and should be backed up with copies off premises, but in a relatively easy to access location.

Target Profiles

This refers to subjective information dealing with people's perceptions of all the identified potential targets. Much of target profiling is based upon not only analyzing the current trends of bomb attacks, but also reviewing attacks that occurred several years prior. If a municipality is involved in compiling a possible list of targets, obviously the city or town hall is included, but so should be all schools because of their high profile for media interest. The same goes for law enforcement facilities, which have prime symbolic value, particularly for right-wing terrorists. If corporate targets are included, considerations include evaluation of the company's image within the local community, the country, and perhaps even the world. Who are the company's suppliers, customers, investors, and perhaps primarily, what is the company's product or service?

Individuals in the company should be evaluated for their symbolic or strategic importance as a target. Corporations may have to think of ancillary targets that may have an impact on their ability to operate and how well they provide security for their operations. For instance, an electric utility may provide excellent security for corporate headquarters and the main generating plants, but leave the substations, service trucks, payment stations, and transmission lines with minimal protection. Even if the decision is made not to protect the miles of transmission lines, a cost analysis should be made by all parties concerned in order to justify that decision.

Almost anything can be attacked, and many of the targets selected by terrorists can be classified as "soft," that is, any target that may be frequented by the public and receive no special security protection. In attacking these types of targets, the terrorists seek not to disrupt a key installation, but to kill as many people as possible. This will give the perception that a terrorist group is operating "under the radar" and can strike with impunity.

In devising a target profile, it is imperative to include the quality of responding emergency services: the local police, fire, medical, and other emergency agencies. Questions should cover whether the response teams are volunteers or professionals, and if there are specialists such as bomb technicians or hostage negotiators included in the first responder teams. If not, how long will it take to have them on the scene? What is the response time for emergency situations? What are the cooperative arrangements, if any, with agencies that provide support or supplemental backup? Are local hospital facilities adequate to handle mass casualties, and if not, how fast can that type of medical assistance be available? How long does it take local power and gas companies to respond to emergencies? These subjective and qualitative questions will help in evaluating the risk potential for possible terrorist targets.

Terrorists

The old adage about knowing your enemy comes into play here. Much information regarding local and regional threats must obviously come from local law enforcement as well as state and federal sources, but a surprisingly large amount can also be gleaned from professional security bulletins, archival resources and databases, newsletters, and even well-circulated publications found in any large library. Today the Internet is probably the main source of gathering information. It allows access to a variety of government and private resources, including the DHS, Federal Bureau of Investigation (FBI), Department of State, and Central Intelligence Agency, to name just a few. There are also helpful sites by such organizations as Global Security, STRATFOR Global Intelligence, and for statistics, the Global Terrorism Database, as well as many other similar groups.

Almost all the foreign news organizations maintain websites, many of them in English or with an English version available, providing wider coverage on far-away political unrest that may affect overseas operations. One such source is Al Jazeera, the main media outlet for radical Islamic groups operating in the Middle East, including al Qaeda and Osama bin Laden. Terrorist groups or their sympathizers may also maintain websites, providing clues to current activities and specific references to the enemy of their cause and plans for future demonstrations and actions. The Earth Liberation Front and the Animal Liberation Front are two of many domestic radical and anarchist groups maintaining active websites.

Radical, anarchist, and terrorist groups often disseminate tracts and manifestos during quiet periods, when they may be engaged in proselytizing. For security professionals in the private sector, questions to be asked of local law enforcement officials are the same questions they should be asking themselves. What are the current trends in terrorism, and how will they affect the security professional's operation? Which, if any, terrorist or radical groups are active in the region? Terrorists and radical groups come in a wide variety of political and activist stripes and ethnic backgrounds. Just because a group is not currently on the front page or evening news does not mean that it is not capable of perpetrating a terrorist act.

Local law enforcement personnel should be aware of militant groups, political cadres, or ethnic populations that have a manifest interest in the political conflict that may be occurring in their former homeland. A relatively easy tactic in information gathering on groups that might cause problems is to monitor the protest letters received from a particular group or individuals associated with them. Almost every radical group within and outside the United States started out as a concerned citizens organization that was subsequently radicalized or spawned radical splinter groups.

The all-important information gathering process of terrorist defense planning can be likened to collecting jigsaw puzzle pieces from an almost infinite variety of sources while not knowing how many pieces there are supposed to be or whether they fit one, two, or several different puzzles. And no one provides a picture of the finished puzzle either.

Target Analysis

One of the more difficult challenges facing defense planners is accurately assessing the likelihood of any particular person, piece of property, or service becoming the target of a terrorist attack. Overestimating the threat potential means wasting dollars, personnel time, and effort. On the other hand, underestimating the threat could result in physical injury or death, as well as millions of dollars in damages, ransoms, or liability judgments. The failure of the intelligence agencies to detect the 9/11 attack drew much attention—most of it viewed with perfect 20/20 hindsight—but whatever led up to the attack, the assault itself was so far outside of contemporary thinking that it is no surprise that everyone was caught by surprise. But 9/11 was not only an intelligence failure; it was also the result of policy failures over several years involving numerous areas of government operations. Even in the aftermath of 9/11, for example, Secretary of Transportation Norman Mineta would not authorize racial or ethnic profiling in airport security checks. This was despite the observation by the National Commission on Terrorist Attacks upon the United States that "the enemy rallies strong support in the Arab and Muslim world."[1]

Target or threat analysis includes not only the likelihood of becoming a target, but also whether or not offered defenses are sufficient to discourage potential attacks or protect individuals and organizations in liability suits.

Many terrorist attacks today, especially in the international arena, are directed at U.S. government facilities, but U.S. private sector organizations sustain the largest number of attacks, even if they are not of the same magnitude as those against official government facilities. Based upon data from the Terrorist Threat Integration Center, now known as the National Counterterrorism Center (NCTC), which was established in January 2003 and includes elements from the CIA, FBI, and DHS, the U.S. State Department said there were 82 anti-U.S. terrorist attacks in 2003, up slightly from 77 attacks in 2002.

Terrorist incidents worldwide and the number of deaths attributed to terrorist activity declined from their high points in 2006 and 2007 to approximately 11,000 incidents in 83 countries during 2009. These affected more than 58,000 victims, including 15,000 fatalities, according to NCTC. The Near East and South Asia were the locations of nearly two-thirds of the 234 high-casualty attacks, defined as causing 10 or more deaths. Attacks in Afghanistan were almost double the number in 2008, and terrorist attacks increased in Pakistan for the third year in a row. Though terrorist attacks in Iraq continue to decline, over in the five years from 2005 to 2009, Iraq has seen more terrorist activity and deaths resulting from terrorism than any other country. This does not include attacks against U.S. military units in Afghanistan and Iraq, since these are directed toward combatants and thus, by definition, are not terrorist attacks.

"Islamic extremists conducted several attacks in the United States, including two that resulted in fatalities," the NCTC report states. "These attacks represent the most significant activity by such extremists in the United States since 2001."

In East Asia and the Pacific, terrorist attacks declined 16 percent between 2008 and 2009, due mostly to decreased activity in the Philippines. Terrorist attacks increased 19 percent in Africa, with nearly 700 of the reported 850 incidents occurring in either Somalia or the Democratic Republic of the Congo. Fatalities resulting from these attacks rose to 250.[2]

In conducting an analysis, security practitioners should be thinking about domestic and international terrorists, whether right wing, left wing, or unknown orientation. Any business entity outlined below should consider these concepts and determine where they fit into the equation:

1. Any business or organization that has an operation or facility in a politically sensitive country.
2. A company heavily involved in the military-industrial complex. This could include any company or subcontractor with a defense contract and anyone supplying goods and services, or both, to the defense sector of the economy.
3. Financial institutions, especially those involved in financing (or cosponsoring with the government) programs that are antithetical to the aims of various terrorist organizations and their causes, for example, a bank holding government-backed loans to countries where terrorist organizations are active.
4. Businesses that are working with advanced technologies, particularly if they are weapons oriented, defense systems oriented, or both.
5. Companies involved in the processing or use of petrochemicals or other environmentally sensitive products. This is especially applicable in South America, where oil pipelines and refinery operations are located in remote regions.
6. Utilities, particularly those whose service disruption would have a dramatic impact on the public.
7. Companies with manufacturing operations in the Third World or developing countries, especially where low wage rates could leave the companies open to charges of exploitation.
8. Companies with operations in politically sensitive countries: traditionally Israel, Sri Lanka, Spain (particularly the Basque areas), and current hot spots, such as the former socialist republics of Central Asia, anywhere in the Middle East including the Arabian Peninsula, the Philippines, Pakistan, Malaysia, the Venezuela-Colombia region, Kenya, and Zimbabwe. Terrorist activity is fluid and subject to ebbs and flows, and thus can crop up almost anywhere, or recur after years of relative calm.
9. Companies that by virtue of ever-changing political winds may find themselves on the wrong side of emotional political issues. These include, but are not limited to, forest production companies (particularly true of rain forest products), makers of abortion or birth control products, researchers who use live animals in their testing process, researchers or agribusinesses involved in genetically modified foodstuffs, consumer product manufacturers, food processors, real estate developers, and manufacturers or users of nuclear power products.
10. Corporations that, because of their size, history, marketplace, dominance, or status as cultural icons, have become symbolic of the United States, capitalism, or both, such as Coca-Cola, McDonalds Corp., Microsoft, IBM, and virtually any international commercial bank.

Law enforcement officials with companies or organizations located in their jurisdictions that may be potential terrorist targets should ask questions such as the following:

1. Has the company or organization ever been the target of a terrorist attack?
2. Has the company's or organization's name ever been mentioned in a derogatory manner in any radical oratory, literature, website, online chat room, or other communication medium? This includes whether the company has been the target of demonstrations locally or at facilities outside the local jurisdiction.
3. Is the entity in any way affiliated with a company or organization that would have answered in the affirmative to either of the first two questions?
4. Does the company supply raw materials, packaging, or any other goods or services to such companies or organizations?
5. Does the company or organization receive materials from or ship goods to or through "sensitive" countries or territories?

The challenge in target analysis is to look at an operation through a microscope, noting suppliers, customers, distribution networks, end users, financial supporters, and even public statements and personal politics of leading officials. If an organization is defensive enough, it will be able to surmise, even in the unlikeliest scenarios, who might want to mount an attack.

While many terrorist and radical groups are well known, there are many others whose presence is virtually unknown and whose grievances are unaired. There are feuds that blow hot and cold over incidents that may seen inconsequential, or even resolved, to the mainstream population, but which burn in the memories of small cliques that used them to justify violent actions. Witness the decades-old, if not centuries-old, animosity between Catholics and Protestants in Northern Ireland; Armenians and Turks; Turks and Greeks in Cyprus; virtually every ethnic and religious group in the Balkans; the Tamils and the Sinhalese; and the Muslims, Sikhs, and Hindus in South Asia; to name just a few. Thus, the key component in determining who may pose a terrorist threat to a company, or organization, or locality, is identifying anyone who may be able to conjure grievances, however far-fetched or historically remote they may seem.

Organization

The organization of a preincident or defense plan for a large exposed company is not an easy task to accomplish. It requires the assignment of authority and responsibility for everybody, from the highest level of management down to the rank and file, who must know whose orders to follow. There are probably more roadblocks when trying to put a crisis management team into place than in opening a new road. The prime components of organizing are establishing levels of responsibility and structuring a chain of command for the team. Individuals assigned to decision-making positions in any defense plan structure should be chosen for their ability to act under pressure. Bureaucrats, drones, slow but steady functionaries, or impulsive hunch players should be passed over in favor of those who possess the ability to keep their wits about them in difficult circumstances. The difficulty in this selection is that private industry allows little opportunity for observing individuals in stressful situations that will allow for evaluation. Finding such individuals is, of course, the best-case scenario, and reality may precipitate deviations from the ideal. To overcome this problem, many companies and other organizations are turning to former counterterrorism operatives to assist them during the planning process—sometimes as part of a full-time security team.

Any organization, whether a law enforcement agency, private company, or public institution such as a school or hospital, has established lines of authority and a chain of command for normal day-to-day operations. These individuals may be adequate for the daily operations of a business, but in an emergency situation precipitated by a terrorist attack may require special operating rules. A terrorist defense plan could well call for a variation in the routine and a crisis team taking over control from the usual hierarchy. Such a change could include transferring the seat of power from the chief administrator's office to a command center that is better protected, has more space, or better and secure communications. This would operate until the arrival of first responders and follow-up public safety officials, who will then assume command of the situation.

The structure of the chain of command—with lines of communications as short and direct as possible—can take many forms, depending upon the nature of the target and type of emergency. More important than how the chain of command is structured is the fact that such a chain has been planned, exists, is in place, and everyone is aware of it. The changeover to crisis management can be made rapidly and orderly as long as everyone knows who is in charge and who has what authority and what responsibilities. Only then can the challenge of dealing with, and resolving, the emergency conditions proceed with any reasonable expectations of success.

Defining levels of responsibility is an important component in the chain of command. Each person in a decision-making or leadership role should be aware of, and well schooled in, his or her responsibilities and extent of authority. The limits of that authority must also be well understood. Training for those individuals should include drills and quizzes as to who must make what decisions, as well as "what if" modeling in hypothetical situations.

In addition to individuals being fully aware of their roles, responsibilities should be spelled out in writing in the defense plan, so that the operation can proceed accordingly even if key personnel have been replaced over time. The organization of a well-defined and thoroughly schooled crisis team is required until public safety units arrive. In some cases, especially in rural areas or smaller communities, this may take longer than in more urban locations. Some elements of crisis teams may be in place, such as a first aid squad or fire brigade, especially in large manufacturing operations. Other teams that should be formed, if they are not already in place, are an evacuation team, which, as we will see later, is not the same group as the wardens who conduct drills; a bomb search team; and a consequence management unit to aid in such things as medical emergencies, evaluating the condition of the area where the incident occurred, and assisting authorities with their investigations. There should also be a risk assessment team that meets to assist in creating and maintaining the defense plan, as well as evaluating threats and situations as they arise.

In organizing a crisis team and its subunits, every attempt should be made to eliminate overlap of duties among members. In the event of an actual emergency, it is likely that each individual would be occupied with specified tasks and unable to handle multiple assignments. The amount of personnel available may be a limiting factor, but eliminating overlap as much as possible should be part of the initial planning considerations.

In evaluating potential team members, maintenance staff and building engineers are especially helpful because of their knowledge of the facilities, layouts, and heating, air conditioning, and ventilation systems. There is a distinction to be made between maintenance people and janitorial or cleanup crews. Janitorial staff is often composed of part-time or contract employees with minimal skills, responsibilities, and perhaps even language comprehension, and thus may not be the best choices for important responsibilities during an emergency.

The composition of an "action team," defined as the staff responsible for evacuation, search, etc., should include supervisory and management personnel. People in position of authority are more likely to be listened to in times of emergency. As a practical matter, more wardens will probably be needed for an evacuation team than, say, a search team, since every staircase and exit must be covered during an evacuation. Evacuation personnel will report to the same location each and every drill, or in the event of an actual emergency. This means that those employees who are on the premises every day, all day, are preferred for such assignments.

Training

"How you train is how you play" is an old adage among sports coaches and managers. The same philosophy can be applied to training in a terrorist pre-incident plan. Responsibilities must be communicated to all participants at all levels of involvement, since these people are members of a coordinated unit in which teamwork is required. The foundation for coordinated teamwork is through understanding of individual assignments. Training of some of the specialized teams used in crises can be accomplished without the necessity of outside assistance; however, local and state police agencies as well as specialized security professionals can better provide assistance in conducting the training.

Training sessions should include a complete explanation of the defense plan, the theory involved, and the detailed application in order to provide operational flavor to all those involved. The classroom sessions should be followed by tests and drills of each aspect or phase of the plan, which should then be critiqued so alterations can be made accordingly. Finally, a full-scale crisis simulation should be conducted.

Once the simulation has been conducted and evaluated, regular testing of plan components should be scheduled, at least as regularly as fire drills. A full-scale mock crisis drill should be conducted annually, at the minimum, unless local conditions dictate greater frequency.

Perhaps the biggest deficiency in terrorist defense planning and crisis management comes in the area of replacing and training personnel. When a plan is adopted initially, there usually is sufficient enthusiasm and commitment to ensure well-trained teams. As individuals are promoted, transferred, or replaced within the organization, large gaps can develop in the defense plan's organization or personnel. Familiarizing newcomers with their responsibilities in the plan and regular simulations of crises and disasters—even just selected phases of the whole plan—is simply good management. Such drills not only school newcomers, but also reacquaint experienced personnel with their roles and duties. The whole effort presents opportunities for reviewing the plan, and altering or updating where required.

The planning and training is a difficult sell to management, especially in times of cost control initiatives. However, management would be remiss, perhaps even in a legal sense, to completely ignore the situation, dismissing such a possibility on the premise of its unlikeliness to occur.

Terrorist Tactics

To establish a meaningful defense plan requires knowledge of what types of action you will be defending against. The four most important tactical operations involving terrorists are, in the general order of relative frequency:

1. Bombings
2. Assassinations and assaults
3. Kidnappings
4. Hostage taking, skyjacking, and barricade situations

Bombings are the most frequent, accounting for the great majority of terrorist-related violence. Currently the suicide bomber is the terrorist weapon of choice, especially among the Islamic terror groups operating in the Middle East, South Asia, and Pacific Rim regions. Another popular bomb choice is the massive vehicle-borne explosive device, which usually results in a large number of casualties. In recent attacks, vehicle-borne IEDs were used in conjunction with armed assaults on nearby targets.

Although skyjackings and hostage takings are now relatively infrequent, when successfully conducted they are the most spectacular in terms of garnering publicity for terrorist groups. More recently, these actions have targeted a number of aircraft to be taken simultaneously with the intention of destroying them in mid-flight. Fortunately, almost all of these plots were thwarted through various intelligence sources.

Assassinations and assaults tend to be more selective in order to include a particular individual, especially a political or media celebrity, the better for the terrorists to make a statement. A case in point was the January 23, 2002, kidnapping of *Wall Street Journalist* Daniel Pearl by al Qaeda terrorists in Karachi, Pakistan. Nine days later he was beheaded and dismembered. His remains were recovered from a shallow grave outside Karachi. This attack reinforced the savagery Islamic terrorists are willing to perpetrate in the name of their cause. In Spain, Euskadi ta Askatasuna, ETA or Basque Fatherland and Liberty, Somalian pirates and the al Shabaab radicals, and many similar nationalist groups around the world use assassination of political adversaries or notable persons as a favored terror tactic.

The practice of mass kidnappings and the "warehousing" of hostages, as was seen in Lebanon during the 1980s, has waned in the twenty-first century, but remains in the terrorist arsenal. Iraq over the years has seen more than its share of terrorist acts—although a war zone to some degree, terrorism flourishes. Government officials have been kidnapped by Islamic fundamentalists, as have businessmen, journalists, and their families.

Hostage taking, skyjacking, and barricade situations were among the incidents by well-trained multinational hijack teams during the 1970s and 1980s. This type of coordinated team attack continues to occur, but with assault as the primary tactic, such as in Peru, where Shining Path terrorists assaulted the Japanese ambassador's residence in Lima late in 1996 and held hostages for several days.

More recently, the Mumbai attack of December 2, 2008, demonstrated the more organized terror tactics being implemented. More training programs in the use of weapons and explosives are being presented to young militants at hidden camps in the Middle East and Pakistan. Young, disillusioned men and women from many countries, including the United States, seek out these training facilities run by radical Islamic terrorists. It has been reported that some rogue governments may also be involved in supporting these camps.

Islamic terrorists have demonstrated persistence in attacking targets associated with U.S., Christian, and Jewish interests. The assailants generally mount attacks against soft targets—tourist attractions, reception halls, shopping areas, and similar locations frequented by the general public—which have minimal security coverage. Such apparently "out of nowhere" assaults are designed to keep law enforcement officials and counterterrorist operatives off balance. In selecting these targets, in-depth surveillance and long periods of preparation are not required. These types of attacks, such as the attacks in Mumbai, Bali, and other similar targets resulting in heavy casualties, are sure to attract mass media attention.

In addition to conducting actual assaults, some terrorist groups engage in a campaign of sophisticated misinformation. Time and time again, intelligence agencies intercept or receive "credible" information on forthcoming terrorist activities that fail to materialize. As in almost all conflicts, the era immediately after 9/11 saw an all too frequent response to increased "chatter" attributed to radical elements. In almost all cases nothing was actually carried out.

The resulting implementation of heavy security measures eventually eroded the public's confidence in the veracity of such intelligence and subsequent terror alerts. This ultimately led to a general scaling back of terror alerts, and thus reduced the misinformation tactic of the terrorists. In general, the tactics terrorists employ can best be described as fluid, taking whatever shape fits a particular organization's tactical plan at any given time. Depending upon the sophistication of the group, it will adopt tactics that the members feel comfortable carrying out, which generally leads to going more and more to the soft target. Whatever form the terrorist attacks take, a favorite tactic is to use multiple coincidental events in an effort to separate the defense's resources. The countertactic is to try to sever the terrorist lines of communication, thus dividing and eventually conquering. Although the geography, location, type of tactic, and time involved may change, the terror remains the same.

The Suburban Threat

Without a doubt, urban areas offer a host of targets that should be more tantalizing to the terrorist than those found in the suburbs. What do the suburbs have to offer? The most tantalizing targets of all: shopping malls and airports. Generally speaking, the mall may fall into the category of a soft target and airports as "hard" targets. Although since the 9/11 attack many large shopping centers have hardened the target with door barriers, additional CCTV, and additional security, they can still be attacked rather easily. Parking lots can be a critical area for vehicle-borne bombs and are very difficult to secure.

In addition to the threat of attack against the malls, banks offer a perception of an "easy hit" by radicals looking for an opportunity to expropriate funds necessary required for their operations. Suburban banks offer opportunities for easier escape with probably less security.

Even more disturbing are the number of radical cells, of both the right and left, as well as radical Islamic schools located in suburban areas. For example, in December 2009 five men from a Virginia suburb of Washington, D.C., were arrested in Pakistan, looking to join an Islamic terrorist group. There were also a number of Islamic schools, such as the Islamic Saudi Academy located in Fairfax County, that had been under congressional scrutiny for their radical teachings.

Risk Analysis

Target analysis was discussed earlier, with guidelines for assessing whether or not a potential target is, in fact, a likely target. In risk analysis, an attempt is made to evaluate that likelihood and assign a degree of risk to it. The questions asked are more detailed, the modeling more complex, the analysis more sophisticated, and the conclusions more serious.

Risk, of course, is inherent to life. The danger could be presented by natural disasters, such as hurricanes, earthquakes, tsunamis, or volcanic eruptions, or by industrial accidents, such as occurred in Bhopal in India or at Chernobyl in the Ukraine (which was finally shut down in 2000). Danger can also come in the form of criminal acts, such as bomb threats, espionage, sabotage, kidnapping, or murder.

Risk analysis is a survey to ascertain how high the probability is of one of these dangers occurring, how well the organization could respond should the threat become a reality, and how well the organization can carry on once that reality materializes. Inherent to the analysis is the identification of the vulnerabilities and threats that go along with the risk.

In the course of the analysis, one of the things to be determined is the extent of the organization's exposure, which could materially contribute to loss or damage in the event of a terrorist attack. Thus, a branch office or nonessential satellite facility is more susceptible to attack than the central office. Similarly, a police call box or temporary post is more vulnerable than headquarters or the communications center. In the private sector, a chain of retail stores exposes a company to more risk than does a manufacturing operation concentrated in a single location. Other factors in the risk analysis equation include considerations as to what can cause injury to employees and, in the event injuries are sustained, how well the organization could continue to function.

Risk exposure considerations that could affect the smooth operation of the organization include those involving persons—from the chief at the top down to the lowest-level employee. If the top administrator is kidnapped, killed, or otherwise harmed, the unique service the chief contributes would be gone. In the private sector, the price of a company's stock could be affected, and its national or international standing or operational effectiveness might be jeopardized. This is exactly what happened in 1986 when George Besse of Renault automobile works was assassinated by Action Directe terrorists. Not only were the day-to-day workings of the company disrupted, but a proposed merger with American Motors Corporation was imperiled.

Even in situations in which an entry-level employee is threatened or harmed, the organization's perceived lack of sensitivity could bring about labor problems or a loss of public confidence in the organization.

Risk can be described in terms of its potential for occurrence and its capacity for loss. Risk measurement and quantification use any number of economic equations and mathematical models. Equations include weighted factors, such as loss of individual life, substantial interruption of the individual's activity, moderate interruption of the individual's activity, or little or no interruptions. The amount of interruption may be indeterminable. One such risk analysis formula reads:

$$L = D + R + I - IC^3$$

Here, L is loss, D is direct cost, R is replacement cost, I is indirect cost, and IC is insurance compensation. This equation deals strictly with the dollars and cents of risk, although thorough analysis is required to put a figure on the indirect and replacement costs, as well as to factor in the cost of insurance premiums over time.

Risk Avoidance

When risk directly affects individuals, i.e., the likelihood that an individual would be killed, harmed, or taken captive, the subject of risk avoidance must be raised. In its simplest form, risk avoidance means identifying risks and neutralizing or eliminating the hazards creating the risks. For example, if there is a geographical area where kidnappings are very common, increased training for law enforcement officers may cut down the risk by neutralizing the hazard. Perhaps the training can be underwritten by a local company whose executives would be likely targets of kidnappers. A most recent example involves three American activists who traveled to Iraq and decided to hike in mountains on the Iraq-Iran border in the summer of 2009, even after being warned of danger by local inhabitants. The three may or may not have wandered into Iran, but in any event, they were taken into custody and charged with spying. They were held 13 months before just one was released in September 2010. It is obvious that the three put themselves into harm's way unnecessarily. Their actions precipitated an international incident that easily could have been avoided.

Another common method of reducing risk is hardening the target, that is, making the target less vulnerable to attack, or reducing the likelihood of a successful attack. Although risk can rarely be eliminated totally, it can be reduced. Egress and ingress can be controlled in buildings and other locations, protective barriers can be used and perimeters bolstered to segregate areas to which outsiders and the public have access, detection devices can be employed, and for individuals considered high-risk targets, defensive behavioral techniques can be implemented.

In the bluntest terms, an organization is trying to make sure that if a terrorist group is going to mount an attack, it does so against some other organization. Preventing a terrorist attack may be impossible; shifting the focus of that attack is attainable.

Hostage/Kidnap Defense

Individuals likely to become targets of terrorist activities include people of high wealth or status, travelers to politically unstable areas of the world, and particularly, corporate executives and overseas employees. Individuals in these latter two groups are at even higher risk if they are associated with companies that have a poor corporate image vis-à-vis terrorist groups, or if they trade with the "wrong" countries or are on the "wrong" side in an internal political dispute. Other persons with above-average chances of becoming hostages or kidnap victims are employees of noncorporate American organizations, such as schools, charities, foundations, and the U.S. government, as well as U.S. citizens living abroad for whatever reason. Perhaps the most exposed are members of the media reporting from the hot spots around the globe. A prime example, but unfortunately not the only one, is Daniel Pearl, kidnapped and killed in Pakistan. Another is Steve Centanni of Fox News Channel, who was taken by Palestinian extremists in Gaza. In that instance, Centanni and his cameraman were released a couple of weeks later.

Just being aware of these risk categories is the first step in an individual's defense plan to avoid being taken captive. Traveling is one of the highest-risk activities for individuals who are potential terrorist targets. Defensive travel tactics include:

1. Taking direct flights on U.S. carriers
2. Checking in early and proceeding immediately to the secure area, being mindful to sit away from lockers, plate glass windows, or anything else that a bomb could turn into shrapnel
3. If a foreign airline must be taken, using carriers from neutral countries, those with a reputation for high security, or both
4. Avoiding aisle seats and those facing bulkheads, since they have greater visibility and accessibility to terrorist hijackers who roam the aisles

These are just a few major actions that can assist a traveler in avoiding trouble.

Endnotes

1. *The 9/11 Commission Report*, Final Report of the National Commission on Terrorist Attacks upon the United States, W.W. Norton & Company, New York, 2004, p. xvi.
2. National Counterterrorism Center, *2009 Report on Terrorism*, Washington, D.C.
3. *The Executive Protection Manual*, Paul Short and James Deiber, MTI Teleprograms, Sheila Park, IL, 1980.

Bomb Defense Planning
4

Bomb Incidents

The improvised explosive device has been a favorite weapon of terrorists since the invention of explosive powder. Today's terrorists and their weapon of choice have evolved from the simplistic approach of Guy Fawkes and his Gunpowder Plot of 1605 to the sophisticated IEDs used by Islamic and other terrorists today. With global availability of a wide variety of explosives, IEDs present great danger and concern to both law enforcement and the private security community. A major reason bombs, including firebombings, currently enjoy particular favor among terrorists is because of the 24/7 global media coverage of such events. Bomb incidents fall into three general categories:

1. Bomb threat
2. Suspicious package or actual explosive device
3. Explosion

The most difficult of the three to deal with in terms of planning and developing procedures for a bomb defense plan is the bomb threat. The threat embraces so many variables that there is virtually no guaranteed defense against it. More often than not, the intended target will receive notification that a bomb or explosive has been planted, with the intended target or victim then reporting it to a law enforcement agency. It is difficult to access the risk of a bomb threat, especially in today's charged atmosphere. Overreaction can be expensive, disruptive, and play right into the hands of those responsible for making the threat. Underreacting, however, can be even more costly in terms of time, money, and worse, human life.

Dealing with suspicious packages or actual explosive devices in a defense plan will limit options to the civilian community, but the procedures developed should be much more concrete and specific. It makes no difference, in fact, whether a suspicious package turns out to be an ineffective but dangerous practical joke, an innocent misplaced personal item, or a live device, since once a package—be it a box, briefcase, backpack, pocketbook, or other kind of container—is deemed suspicious, it should be treated as though it were an explosive device. At this point, public safety officials assume responsibility and trained bomb technicians take over.

There are very few *always* prescribed in this book, and not many more *nevers*. However, one of the *nevers* is never touch a suspicious package unless you have been fully trained or are a certified bomb technician. An untrained individual, even a sworn law enforcement officer, a civilian security worker, or former member of the military, should never be allowed to handle or move a suspicious package. The determination of whether a suspicious package is an explosive device and the removal and disposal of such explosive devices are jobs for authorized and qualified bomb technicians, whether they are from the local law enforcement agency, or from county, state, or federal agencies, or even the military.

Planning and crisis response in the event of an explosion are the same whether the explosion is accidental or bomb related. Only after the determination has been made whether or not an explosion was accidental or intentional do the procedures vary. The use of weapons of mass destruction other than explosives, such as biological or chemical agents, requires different procedures, as discussed in Chapter 8.

The Bomb Threat

A bomb threat can be delivered in a number of ways and for a variety of reasons. In the past, it was often a means of claiming responsibility for a particular action by a terrorist or radical organization. The notification could be made by telephone, mailed notes, or hand-delivered messages to news media, proclamations secreted in public areas such as bus stop shelters, or messages scrawled on restroom mirrors in the targeted premise, or even veiled or overt references posted on the Internet. A number of bomb threats that target commercial travel have been left scrawled in rest rooms both aboard aircraft and in terminal restrooms.

Although threats may be communicated in a number of ways, the most commonly employed medium by far is the phone, which affords the caller a great deal of anonymity. Although public pay phones have virtually disappeared from the streets and other public places, throwaway cell phones are used to thwart caller identification. Even though the bomb threat is a tactic that has been employed by terrorists and radicals in the past, the fact is that bomb threats are more often perpetrated by nonterrorists and pranksters. These would be the threats received from individuals who want to disrupt activities at the target or who seek the thrill of precipitating an emergency response to the threat. The number of terrorist bombings in the United States has decreased in recent years, but the threat of bombings is still a major concern of law enforcement agencies and of facilities managers in both the private and public sectors.

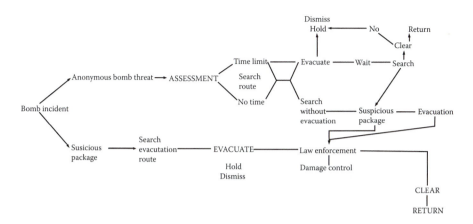

Figure 4.1 Bomb incident flowchart. The course of actions can differ whether a bomb threat is involved or whether a suspicious package has been found.

Work locations, shopping centers, schools, theaters, arenas and stadiums, and centers of public transportation, such as airports, train depots, and bus stations, are favorite targets of bomb threats because of the considerable amount of disruption and media attention they could generate. Even in instances where no explosives have actually been placed, the threat alone becomes an instrument of harassment and disruption (Figure 4.1). A single telephone call can result in the evacuation of thousands of people from a named target location.

In 1985, the Toronto, Canada, subway system was severely disrupted when a bomb threat was received. It was purported that an Armenian terrorist organization had placed a bomb in the system to protest the Canadian government's refusal to release several Armenians being held in connection with an earlier hostage situation at the Turkish Consulate. The threat, although real and believable, produced no explosive device. Ten years later, however, a radical terrorist group in Japan released sarin gas in the Tokyo subway system that killed a dozen people and severely injured scores of others. In this case, the Aum Shinrikyo group did not bother to issue a warning before the coordinated attacks.

Statistically speaking, any given bomb threat is probably the work of a prankster, an emotionally disturbed person, someone looking for thrills or sexual fulfillment, or someone seeking revenge for some real or imagined grievance. However, and this is an important consideration, any given bomb threat may also be the real thing. The caller may in fact have actual knowledge that an explosive device or some other weapon of mass destruction has been placed, or will be placed, at the announced location, and for whatever reason wants to share that information.

No threats should be taken lightly. Threats should, however, be evaluated in the context in which they are made so that appropriate responses can be implemented.

Rationale of Bomb Threats

As already noted, most bomb threats are made when the caller knows that the threat is a hoax and that no actual device has been placed. For whatever reason, the caller wishes to disrupt the intended target. Not only is this the most common type of incident, but it is the most successful, for by its very nature it achieves the desired results of disruption and excitement. In this type of threat, the offender usually is not apprehended or successfully prosecuted. Like actual makers of bombs, threat makers and their rationales are limited only by their imagination.

Typical situations involve employees looking for a day off work, students seeking to avoid exams, dismissed employees getting even, jilted lovers striking back, family disputes spilling over into the workplace, or pure pranksters and thrill seekers with no discernable motivation. One sinister motivation behind a bogus bomb threat is a terrorist group testing the system in terms of response times of emergency personnel or the response of the targeted location.

There are other instances of bomb threats in which the caller has a serious purpose. The threat maker may want to bring media attention to a particular cause or ensure that his or her organization gets proper credit for the disruption that the threat caused. In utilizing the preincident call when a device has actually been planted, the organization or individual is ensuring the proper group gets the media exposure that is so important to terrorist causes. In many instances, a follow-up communication may be transmitted, expounding the aims, goals, and philosophy of the organization responsible. Numerous Internet sites are maintained by support groups or sympathizers of radical causes that also carry the terrorists' message.

There may be other reasons why warning calls are made in cases in which actual devices have been planted. It may be that the caller has had pangs of conscience or is having second thoughts about going through with the act. Perhaps this person never thought a real bomb would be planted and now wants to distance himself or herself from the action.

Another rationale for the warning call may be to shift responsibility for any deaths or injuries away from the bombers and onto the police or the organization against which the attack is directed. This may be an attempt to build an affirmative defense in the event of apprehension. Those responsible for the incident may say something to the effect of: "We gave fair warning to the police or intended target; the only reason people were killed or injured was because the police or the target, or both, failed to take proper action."

A Note of Warning

Terrorism is in reality a macabre form of theater, and in that context, there is a long tradition among terrorists and radicals to espouse theories and threats to the rest of the world through written word, audio or videotapes, and websites.

The current Islamic terrorist campaign against the United States and other Western nations can be traced to a fatwa that was issued by Osama bin Laden, at the time a little-known terrorist. The document, titled "Declaration of War against Americans Occupying the Land of the Two Holy Places,"[1] was first published in an Arabic language London newspaper in August 1996. This was followed up by another issued on February 23, 1998. This document was faxed to the Arabic newspaper *al-Quds al-Arabi* and was signed by five individuals identifying themselves as Osama bin Laden, Ayman al-Zawahiri, Ahmed Refai Taha, Mir Mamaz, and Fuzul Rahman. The group identified themselves as belonging to the World Islamic Front for Jihad against Jews and Crusaders. In this "holy order," Osama bin Laden commanded his followers to wage war against those he considered unholy. He began the threatening document by presenting an indictment of the United States and its citizens and addressed his followers: "We issue the following fatwa to all Muslims. The ruling to kill Americans and their allies—civilian and military—is an individual duty for every American Muslim who can do it in any country in which it is possible to do it, in order to liberate the al-Asqa Mosque and the holy mosque from their grip." The fatwa continues, "We ... with God's help ... call on every Muslim who believes in God and wishes to be rewarded to comply with God's order to kill the Americans and plunder their money wherever and whenever they find it. We also call Muslim ulema, leaders, youths and soldiers to launch the raid on Satan's U.S. troops and the devil's supporters allying with them, and to displace those who are behind them so that they learn a lesson."[2]

In an entirely different vein, warnings of a fashion came in the voluminous creeds of Theodore Kaczynski, known as the Unabomber. He began a 16-bomb, 17-year reign of terror that killed 3 people and injured 23. Kaczynski targeted those whom he believed contributed to the erosion of human freedoms through modern technology that required large-scale organizations. After sending letters to a number of victims, he drafted a rambling 35,000-word document called the "Industrial Society and Its Future." On September 19, 1995, the *New York Times* and *Washington Post* published the Unabomber's so-called manifesto. Kaczynski's brother then recognized the writings as his brother's and alerted authorities, leading to the Unabomber's apprehension.

Not all threats are serious or come from international criminals. In the mid-1980s, a communiqué was issued by a "revolutionary anti-imperialist organization" carrying out "armed attacks on military, police and governmental installations/personnel and on death merchants, both military contractors and corporations engaged in oppression of the people and exploitation of our resources." This communiqué, delivered to several news organizations, said the group was going to use bombs and explosive devices in attacking intended targets. It continued, "It is not the intention of the United Freedom Front to hurt innocent civilians and workers and it has been our procedure, where applicable, to give *sufficient warning* [emphasis in the original] for evacuation of buildings and to use other methods to minimize the chances of personal injury."[3] The message detailed how evacuation plans should be drawn up and employed whenever a bomb threat was made. In addition, it also advised against touching suspicious packages once a threat had been received.

Though generally falling into the pattern of tactics and activities espoused by such terrorist theorists as Carlos Marighella, author of the *Minimanual of the Urban Terrorist*, this communication is unique because it strongly appears to have been designed to establish a defense against the organization being held accountable for injury or death resulting from one of its attacks.

In practice, the UFF did employ a warning call prior to most of its attacks. It also used surveillance of the target to make sure that the warning message was acted upon. The group also called a third party with a warning call when members of the group felt that the target might not have received its warning call or was not acting upon it seriously. In one particular case, when a UFF caller indicated that a bomb would go off in 30 minutes and no apparent response was taking place, a second call was placed to reinforce the warning call and note that only 15 minutes were left before detonation.

There are variations of the preexplosion warning, and on occasion, calls are made with prerecorded messages to reduce the effectiveness of any voice identification techniques that may be employed. In recent years, the Internet has brought dramatic changes. There are a number of websites dedicated to hate that espouse philosophies from every political angle imaginable, and with chat rooms to rally the faithful and perhaps recruit the curious. On occasion, serious threats are buried in the countless lines of text, but are noticed and reported to authorities. One such incident occurred in January 2003, when a high school student noted that a Columbine-type incident would occur at 11:18 a.m., with a specific date but no location other than a New York State school. Officials locked down the system for several hours.

Warning or Hoax?

When an individual makes a call with the knowledge that a bomb has been (or will be) placed, this should be considered a viable warning call. When a person makes a call knowing full well that no device is present, this should be considered a bomb threat or hoax. Unfortunately, it is not easy to distinguish between the two until after the following actions have occurred:

1. The bomb explodes.
2. A search is conducted and a bomb is found.
3. A suspicious package is located that may or may not be associated with the warning/hoax.
4. A thorough search is conducted and nothing of an unusual nature is found.

To the law enforcement official, public safety officer, or private security practitioner, distinguishing a threat from a warning call is one of the most difficult determinations to make. There is no easy answer to the dilemma. To best be prepared to address the problem, a risk profile must be developed in preincident planning, whether in the public or private sector, and a thorough risk assessment survey made of the affected area or facility.

While the vast majority of bomb threats turn out to be hoaxes, the fact that a bomb was not planted does not automatically rule out the possibility of terrorist involvement. The group may be using the bomb threat as a tool, not only of disruption, but also for surveillance and intelligence gathering concerning the target's preparedness for a bomb attack. It was believed that the Irish Republican Army (IRA), for example, once developed a means of incorporating a code word in its warning calls to verify the validity of the call. Members could make a number of validated calls that turned out to be hoaxes, before conducting an actual attack. And this was, in fact, something the IRA did on numerous occasions.

In handling hoaxes—or to be exact, bomb threats that may be hoaxes—experience has taught that there are some behavioral and psychological characteristics common to typical hoaxers. A risk profile based on these characteristics may be developed, as we will discuss later. Often, however, it is as much circumstances that create hoaxers as it is any particular predisposition to this type of behavior. An important factor, one that could play a role in the continuation of a hoax problem, is the reaction of the management of a targeted facility. Overreaction will almost invariably result in the escalation of these types of calls.

In truth, most nonterrorist bomb threat hoaxers do not realize the seriousness of their actions, especially in terms of lost production time and injuries that could occur during an unnecessary evacuation. It is analogous to children being unaware of the possible consequence of transmitting a false fire alarm. In the wake of 9/11, lawmakers throughout the country recognized the seriousness of making these types of crank calls. In many states and under certain conditions under federal statutes, making a false threat is now considered a felony.

Taking a Bomb Threat Call

On the outside chance that a person making a bomb threat is willing to communicate that to the person receiving the call, there are a series of "preferred practices" that have been developed by law enforcement authorities. In a perfect world, individuals responsible for taking phone calls from the general public should have a "bomb call" checklist available to them. If a formal checklist is not available, the individual should write down all the information on a piece of paper while it is still fresh in his or her mind. The information should include:

- Attempt to keep the caller on the line as long as possible.
- Ascertain where the bomb is located, what it looks like, and what time it will detonate.
- Try to estimate sex, age, race, etc., of the caller or any accents or other distinct characteristics in the voice.
- Obtain a description of any background noises, such as traffic, radio, laughter, music, or similar sounds.
- Find out why the call is being placed.

After the call is ended, the person receiving the call should notify the proper authorities within the organization, who should then call the police or the organization's security staff. The information should not be shared with nonsecurity personnel because this could trigger a panic reaction and precipitate an uncontrolled evacuation.

The first responding unit should remember not to transmit over the radio within 300 feet of the targeted building and not to block any egress points with emergency vehicles. Once on the scene, officers should locate the individual who received the call and, as with any witness to a crime, isolate that individual from others. If there was no checklist completed, the officer should gather the information regarding the call from the person who received the call. If warranted, notify a supervisor to respond to the location.

The person responsible for security at the facility receiving the call should be consulted as to whether any other threats had been received previously, and whether there are any individuals who may be suspected of making the threat or threats.

Among the responders, the ranking person on the scene should make sure that additional responding units do not cluster and block access to other emergency vehicles, such as fire and medical, should the need arise. If possible, these vehicles should be staged some 900 feet away and upwind from the site.

Once all information is gathered regarding the threat, the management of the affected facility and ranking law enforcement should confer, with the ultimate decision of whether to evacuate at this time being the call of management. Although in real-life situations public safety officials may feel that a life-threatening situation is present and on their authority order the premises evacuated, this is an iffy call.

Bomb Threat Decision Making

When a bomb threat is received, regardless of the medium, decision-making boils down to two options: stay or go. If stay is the decision, what should be done to protect the facility and its occupants? Bomb threats can come from virtually any quarter. All bomb threats (even anonymous threats) must be treated as the real thing until determined otherwise. There are certain parameters or risk profiles that can assist in assessing the likelihood of a bomb threat being serious or frivolous. Much of the work in determining a credibility index, however, must be completed prior to the threat being received. This reinforces the need for preincident planning.

In developing a risk profile of a potential target, there are several points to be considered:

1. How tight is security at the target, particularly with respect to a potential bomb attack? That is, is there sufficient security engaged in perimeter defense, especially at points of entry with regard to the placement of IEDs within the facility?
2. What is the target's previous experience with bomb threats or bomb attacks, or both?
3. What is the current climate of terrorist or radical activity? Has there been an incident that could inspire copycat activity? This is especially true if the target is engaged in a business or activity that may inflame a radical cause.
4. Does the warning call fit any of the known methods of terrorist activity currently or in the recent past? Is this intelligence up-to-date and reliable? Does the verbiage fit any prior legitimate bomb threats?
5. Is the target involved in protracted labor contract negotiations, or has it been involved in a labor-management confrontation in the recent past?
6. To whom was the threatening call made, and what was the exact wording of the message? Did the caller indicate knowledge of the threatened area? Was the call directed at a particular individual within the facility, with whom the caller may have had a grievance or disagreement?

7. Evaluate distinctive traits in the caller's voice or speech mannerisms: Was the speech slurred? Did it contain accents, stutters, or other speech impediments? Was the caller rambling or excessive, to the point of indicating alcohol or drug influences?
8. Has any employee of the target recently been discharged or disciplined to the extent that it might precipitate a bomb threat? Has an employee exhibited bizarre or irrational behavior that may precipitate such a call?
9. Could the organization that is targeted have caused the alienation of a consumer, member of the public, a special interest group, or radical organization?

Consider how specific the wording of the threat is. The general rule to follow is that the more specific the details, even if they are excessive, the greater the need to take the caller seriously. If a person is malicious enough to place an explosive device, or even threaten placement of such a device, there is no guarantee that he or she will be telling the truth about the time or place a bomb will explode. Yet the caller may be telling the truth. Both possibilities must be considered.

Bomb threats, even obvious hoaxes, cannot be totally ignored. If nothing else, a violation of law has been committed by the mere fact of a threat being made. In addition, if there is a series of calls or a pattern of harassment, serious criminal charges may be lodged when the callers are apprehended. In all cases, in addition to reporting the threat to the appropriate law enforcement agency, a search of the affected area should be conducted. The various search options are discussed later.

Evacuation Options

When a bomb incident results in evacuation of a building or other specific area, tight control must be exercised during the procedures. While a fire evacuation (drill or actual) must be orderly and speedy, a bomb evacuation must be more controlled, yet as quick as possible, to reduce risk of injury in the event of a premature detonation.

There are three options in handling a bomb threat:

1. Evacuation
2. Partial evacuation of the affected area
3. No evacuation

Which option is employed will depend upon the tactical demands of the situation, including the size of the suspected device. A suspected letter bomb, for example, may require the evacuation of only the immediate area from where the package or letter is located, and not the entire facility. In other situations, a suspected device may be found in a location that does not allow for a complete evacuation to proceed safely. That is, its placement is in such a location that people might be required to pass in close proximity to the suspected package. Perhaps in another scenario the caller may have indicated that only a certain area of the building has been targeted. In some situations, a full evacuation may not be prudent, such as in a high-rise building where people may have to be evacuated upward from the area rather than descending a stairway past the floor where the suspected device is located.

The size of the device will certainly dictate the distance that will be required for safe removal of the facility's occupants. In addition, construction, age of the building, and building materials utilized must also be considered in how an evacuation may proceed. And in truth, there are not answers to all possibilities. There were no warnings given to either the 1993 bombing at the World Trade Center (WTC) in New York City or that of the Murrah Federal Building in Oklahoma City two years later, and certainly none in the 9/11 attacks. Even if there had been advanced notice, in all likelihood there would not have been time for a full and complete evacuation, and given the power of the explosives used and the resulting damage, there could have been more death and injuries to hundreds of people exiting the building.

A bomb threat evacuation must be treated much differently than a fire evacuation. For one, the primary evacuation routes should be searched prior to ordering an evacuation to ensure the route is clear of any suspected items. Also, the evacuees must be removed a distance sufficient to ensure they will not be injured by blast effects or fragmentation in the event of detonation. Some of the most powerful bombs used in terrorist attacks have been delivered in vehicles parked outside the target, thus damaging not only the intended building or facility, but also the immediate vicinity.

Spreading the order to evacuate in the face of a bomb threat should be given over the public address system, if one is available. The use of fire alarms is not recommended to give notice to evacuate for a bomb threat, since fire alarms elicit an automatic response and do not allow for a controlled evacuation. Additionally, when dealing with explosive devices, doors and windows should be left open in order to ventilate the area. An explosion follows the path of least resistance and open doors and windows will allow the explosive force to vent, and thus somewhat reduce the amount of damage from the blast. In fire drills, doors and windows are usually closed to reduce drafts and the amount of oxygen available to feed the fire. Another reason for not using the fire alarm is that occupants of the building may assume there is an unannounced fire drill and, without the presence of smoke or fire, linger about or ignore the alarm altogether.

Evacuation Procedure Overview

Once an evacuation plan has been formulated, it is important that drills are conducted on a regular basis in order to see whether or not the written plan is viable. There are not many security or safety directors who have responsibility for a building or facility the size of the WTC before it was destroyed in the 9/11 attacks. The time required to evacuate most buildings is much less than the four hours that was required to evacuate the 50,000 people from the WTC towers following the 1993 bombing that occurred in the garage of the complex. The 9/11 Commission took note of this fact and indicated that it was an unacceptable amount of time. The commission reported that the WTC's owner, the Port Authority of New York and New Jersey, had conducted evacuation drills prior to 9/11 that were thought by some observers to be effective, while other experts felt that they were perfunctory and did not fully engage the participants. Fire wardens in the building had complained that many people did not participate or were uncooperative because they were too busy, and even those who did participate were inattentive. It was further noted that there never was a full-scale evacuation test of the WTC buildings, creating an unknown for a reasonable expectation of the time it would take to evacuate the buildings. One positive note was the Wall Street firm of Morgan Stanley had its own plan of evacuation and employees had practiced the recommended procedures. Copies of the plan were given to each employee for both home and office. This preparation later proved invaluable.

In designing an evacuation plan, both partial and full evacuations should be considered. As previously indicated, anticipated or designated evacuation routes must be searched prior to giving the order to evacuate. Keep in mind that in many buildings and locations there are many possible evacuation routes that may be used, making it a time-consuming effort to search each one individually, even with sufficient personnel available. In order to reduce preevacuation search time, specific bomb evacuation routes should be predetermined and searched immediately upon receipt of a bomb threat, even before the decision has been made whether or not to evacuate. Then, should the evacuation order be given, the escape routes will be clear for safe passage.

To reinforce the importance of searching the evacuation route, bear in mind that a number of terrorist organizations that were operating in the United States in the last third of the twentieth century used fire stairwells as prime locations for their planted explosive devices. Fire stairs were used because of their accessibility and lack of traffic during normal business hours, thus lessening the chance of an IED being discovered.

Damage control in a bomb incident differs from that used during a fire. As mentioned, during a fire, the usual procedure is to shut windows and doors to reduce oxygen that could feed the fire. With bombs, it is desirable to ventilate the explosion. Also with bombs, lights, electrical devices, and office equipment should be turned off. If there is time, gas and fuel lines should be shut down or closed off.

Even when an evacuation has been initiated, it may be necessary to maintain a minimum workforce at a location in order to continue essential services. Contingency plans of high-risk companies and agencies should be reviewed and updated on a regular basis so that minimum operating requirements can be met with maximum automation. In some instances, remote or off-site backup systems may be employed on a short-term basis to maintain essential operations.

To facilitate safe and orderly evacuations, an evacuation warden should be appointed, much in the same way a fire warden functions. The two responsibilities may be held by one and the same person. The primary function of an evacuation warden is to ensure that all people are removed from the affected area as quickly as possible. It is preferable to have supervisory or management personnel selected as wardens because they command respect and possess enough authority to have their instructions carried out without argument. In addition, such personnel are more likely to have better knowledge of who is assigned where and be familiar with the physical layout of the facility, thus ensuring that all employees are accounted for.

The number of evacuation wardens needed depends upon the size and layout of the areas that would be affected and the number of people occupying these spaces at any one time. In cases in which a number of wardens are required, an evacuation team coordinator should be designated. All those actually carrying out evacuation duties must be under the coordinator's direction. The coordinator need not be a member of the risk assessment team because the evacuation is primarily a mechanical function, but should have sufficient authority to make things work effectively.

Putting Out the Message

A major consideration before initiating an evacuation order is how to get that evacuation order to the population of the building without creating panic, yet at the same time communicating the need for immediate compliance. The best and most efficient way to give an evacuation order is by utilizing an internal communication system, such as a public address system. Prior to the general announcement, an internal alert, via e-mail or other medium, can be sent to only evacuation wardens, then followed by messages over the public address system, universal intercom, or an emergency loudspeaker network. The idea is to initiate immediate compliance, but without creating panic. In utilizing the internal communication system, it would be best to have a recorded and previously scripted message designed to create the least amount of alarm among the building occupants.

As a backup to e-mail, a coded system, which should be confidential, could be used to alert key personnel of the need to effect a successful search or evacuation. This prerecorded message should be prepared with the assistance of individuals trained in communications, so that confusion and potential misunderstandings are eliminated. The correct terminology must be used to reduce fear and anxiety. Keep the evacuation message simple, bilingual, in a medium for the visually or hearing impaired, if necessary, and make sure it reaches everybody in the building.

The importance of internal communications and the need for backup plans were highlighted by the 9/11 Commission, which was very critical of the WTC communication system in both the 1993 bombing incident and the 9/11 attacks. Although much of the communication was disabled in the aftermath of the crashes, landlines were still functioning. However, they were soon overloaded with traffic, as was wireless communication when transmission capabilities were damaged, with loss of antennas on the buildings' roofs. Once evacuated, employees must be accounted for. Following the WTC evacuations on 9/11, this was the task that took several days to accomplish even on a preliminary level. Naturally the size and scope of the WTC evacuation was an extreme event in the world of security, but it is a textbook lesson to be studied by security practitioners when developing communication systems.

Planning Issues

Even in terms of security plans, physical changes in the building are often overlooked. New interior walls are constructed, staircases are added or removed, doors and windows are blocked off, and similar alterations are made that can make a defense plan obsolete very quickly. A tragic example occurred on October 18, 2007, when a fire occurred during the demolition of the Deutsche Bank, which was heavily damaged in the 9/11 attack in New York City. In that fire, two firemen were killed and scores of others injured battling the fire. It was later discovered that the floor plans used by the fire department to fight the fire were obsolete.

More than once, investigators conducting postblast investigations, especially in larger building complexes, have been forced to conduct searches or postblast investigations using floor plans or other mechanical drawings that were several years out of date. It is important to make sure the building engineer or facility manager has on hand floor plans; structural drawings; heating, ventilation, and air conditioning drawings; and design plans for remodeled or reconstructed sections of the building. Copies of all of these drawings should be maintained in a secure off-site location in the event it is not possible to retrieve working copies from the affected facility. Even with such drawings in hand, building engineers and maintenance personnel should be made available to investigators to lend technical assistance if an attack has occurred.

Continuity of effort, training, and current information are vital if a defense plan is to be worth the time, money, and effort spent on it. Since private security practitioners are more concerned with such day-to-day matters as employee screening, loss prevention, access control, and perimeter security than with potential terrorist attacks, it is up to the public safety officials to reinforce the message that preparation is also needed to defend against bomb attacks, firebombs, hostage takings, and kidnappings.

As discussed previously, the vast majority of bomb threats turn out to be hoaxes. However, if a company receives a series of threats that turn out to be hoaxes, police officers should work with the company's professionals to channel the energies of the internal security force into addressing the problem, whether it be a disgruntled employee, a prankster, or—just maybe—a terrorist.

Threats cannot be ignored. Yet some threats need to be taken more seriously than others. It is the responsibility of the police, working with a company's risk assessment team, to develop guidelines and procedures on how seriously each threat should be taken.

Bomb Threats and the Police

In general, the police department has the responsibility in responding to bomb incidents for protection of life and property. In the initial stages of a bomb threat, the role of the police, fire department personnel, or other public safety officials is primarily just that. In the past, a bomb threat hoax was dealt with as a harassment situation or perhaps causing a public nuisance, depending upon circumstances and local statutes. In a world where there is a war on terror, these types of incidents are looked upon as something much more serious and call for a more robust response by law enforcement.

In a situation where an actual device or a suspicious package has been located, the police role becomes much more defined, for it now requires more extensive action due to its escalating into something far more serious. On-site security or facility management and first-arriving law enforcement and emergency personnel should confer in an effort to determine whether the seriousness of the threat requires an evacuation of the premises.

If there is a prepared evacuation or overall security plan that includes designated search and evacuation teams, law enforcement officials may allow these individuals to conduct the search with their assistance. The police should be prepared to take over in the event a device or suspicious package is found, or if there is an explosion. Even if there is no defense plan, in a bomb threat only, the law enforcement officials should leave the evacuation decision to management of the facility after strongly advising the senior decision maker of the degree of gravity of the situation. An explanation of the reasons for a controlled evacuation should be made, along with the ramifications of other options. The law enforcement officer must realize, as should management personnel, that it is better to err on the side of caution than to act hastily and precipitate unnecessary concern or injury.

The Bomb: Terrorist Weapon of Choice

Over the last several years, the total number of bombings in the United States has decreased significantly, although internationally large and spectacular bomb attacks continue.

Terrorists commit bombings for a number of reasons:

1. To gain media attention, particularly if the target is highly visible or symbolic and the attack is spectacular.
2. Bombing is the most cost-effective and efficient way to attack a facility.
3. A bombing mission can be accomplished with a small number of persons.
4. There is a minimal risk of bombers being detected or apprehended, and in the case of a suicide bomber, being stopped.
5. Bombing is inexpensive compared to alternatives, like a long-term kidnapping or hostage-taking event.
6. A campaign of random bombings makes a considerable impact on the population, because more people fear a bomb attack than being kidnapped or taken hostage.
7. Explosives are readily available through theft, sympathetic supporters, or purchase. In addition, explosives can be constructed through the use of legitimately purchased chemicals, fertilizers, and other material.

In mounting a bomb campaign, or even a single bombing incident, terrorists undertake a great deal of reconnaissance and typically select whichever target looks most vulnerable but still holds some symbolic or publicity value. The target need not be a corporate headquarters or a major facility, but could be a satellite, subsidiary, or temporary operation. The impact will be the same. The attack on the *USS Cole* in Yemen in October 2000 was carried out in the water with explosives loaded onto rubber rafts to assist the ship while docking, and carried the same weight as if it occurred on U.S. soil.

On the other hand, terrorists also look for factors that may frustrate or defeat security efforts and make plans accordingly. Thus, terrorists who hijack or attempt to bomb aircraft in flight will, if passenger screening is enhanced to a great degree, move their attack to the terminal area, where passengers, family, and friends can be assaulted. When access to the terminal is tightened, the logical target will be the outer perimeter, such as a passenger drop-off area or parking lot. Downtown airline ticket offices or airport transportation vehicles have also been chosen. Rocket grenade launchers have been used against some organizations, further removing terrorist operatives from the scene of the attack. Like water, terrorists follow the path of least resistance.

Types of Bombers

There are four types of bombers:

1. Amateur
2. Professional
3. Psychopathic
4. Suicidal

Amateur bombers can best be described as experimenters. For the most part, the devices amateurs construct are usually crude and unsophisticated, but some can be quite sophisticated. They are usually delivered against targets of inconsequential value or targets of opportunity, meaning those with low levels of security awareness located in remote areas. Many amateurs begin in their youth, experimenting with fireworks in various combinations and devising explosive devices fashioned with material found in school chemistry labs, the laundry room, and the garden shed.

Amateur devices may have sophisticated firing mechanisms that challenge the builder's ingenuity but ordinarily employ only a small amount of main charge explosive, which is usually a propellant explosive, such as smokeless powder, black powder, or common fireworks powder. What these substances have in common is that they are relatively easy to obtain. In many instances, the amateur bomber may be a copycat bomber, such as a teenager looking for excitement or an attention-seeking individual. Many individuals who fall into this category fail to venture beyond it.

Professional bombers, whether a terrorist, or a mercenary who constructs explosive devices and causes the bombing for profit, or an operative in an organized crime syndicate, are distinguished from amateurs by the higher quality of their operational techniques. The professional will build devices that are more sophisticated and conduct a detailed reconnaissance, including the use of strict timetables that are an integral part of the operation. The placement of the device is done to ensure inflicting maximum damage on the intended target. With time and study, the professional bomber can attack almost any target, using devices that are sufficiently sophisticated to exact a considerable toll.

Psychopathic bombers—it can be argued that any person who places an improvised explosive device in a location where it will result in death, injury, or a great deal of destruction is to some degree mentally ill—commit these acts for a perverse pleasure or to avenge an alleged (perhaps real) wrong festering in their own minds. Two individuals who fall into this category are Theodore Kaczynski, the Unabomber, and George Metesky, known as the Mad Bomber. Metesky terrorized New York City for 16 years with a 33-bomb campaign during the 1940s and 1950s. Although his bombs were not large or powerful, he planted his devices in very public locations such as Radio City Music Hall, the New York Public Library, and subway trains. Kaczynski railed against modern technology, while Metesky, who died in a mental institution, was avenging a workplace injury.

Suicide bombers have emerged as a major attack weapon in the arsenal of Islamic terrorist groups in recent years. Little in the way of scientific study has been done on the training and motivation of suicide bombers, though speculation leads to parallels with the kamikaze bombers employed by Japan during World War II. Prior to the war in Iraq, most suicide bomb attacks had been attributed to the Hamas organization, carried out against Israeli and Western targets. Today the suicide bomber is a weapon for virtually all radical Islamic terrorist groups. The attacks are perpetrated by a shahid, or martyr, apparently carrying out a religious mission after having been ensured that eternal life in paradise and the chance to see Allah's face await him or her upon completion of the mission.

The early profile devised for a suicide bomber was that it was a male, between the ages of 18 and 27, high school educated at most, from a poor family, and a student of fundamentalist beliefs. But now that profile has been challenged with the emergence of female suicide bombers, including as many as two dozen Chechen female suicide bombers, known as the Black Widows, who have attacked numerous Russian targets in the last decade. Suicide attacks can be delivered by either a person on foot or vehicle-borne IEDs, such as trucks, vans, cars, and even bicycles. The largest IED to date was delivered by an Islamic suicide bomber against the U.S. Marine Corps barracks in Beirut, Lebanon. It is estimated that the exploded device was the equivalent of about 15,000 pounds of high explosives. In a more recent suicide bombing, that of the naval destroyer *USS Cole* in Aden Harbor, Yemen, in October 2000, the bombers employed a Zodiac-motorized raft carrying a charge that was estimated at approximately 400 pounds of high explosives.

Motivation of Bombers

There are a variety of motivations for persons who construct and plant IEDs:

1. Ideological bombings may be carried out on behalf of, or in defense of, a wide range of political and philosophical beliefs, from the extreme left wing to the radical right wing, and all sorts of permutations in between. Ideological bombers are generally professional bombers motivated by radical politics, racial or ethnic hatred, religious, environmental, or ecological fanaticism, or even a distorted fondness for animals. The bombing itself may be a gesture of protest or a purely symbolic attack.

2. Experimental motivation is common among youthful offenders and immature adults. The experimental bomber is drawn by the excitement and noise created by the explosion, curiosity as to whether the device will actually work, what the results of an explosion will be, and the thrill of seeing an explosion as a reward for the efforts involved. Bombers motivated by experimentation are usually amateurs, although they may eventually develop into terrorists or other types of bombers.

3. Vandalism, destruction for the sake of destruction, is particularly common at times of the year when fireworks are readily available and can be used in bomb making. Alcohol and drug use may also be involved. Targets of these bombers tend to be small, such as mailboxes and store windows, but public, so the handiwork can be observed. Vandals will tend to use larger fireworks devices joined together to fashion pipe bombs and similar devices. As with experimentation bombers, they are usually amateurs, often youthful offenders or immature adults.

4. Profit bombings occur for either direct or indirect monetary gain. The largest number of profit bombings is associated with organized crime operatives extorting money by intimidating or denying businesses associated with the wrong side in a power struggle. Profit bombers can also be employed by terrorists or radical organizations that lack the expertise to carry out a particular action. A mercenary carrying out the wishes of a client in bombing a target for insurance fraud purposes is also included in this category. Insurance may also be a profit factor in bomb attacks on commercial airliners. In addition, there is arson by bombing and the use of bombs to cover up robbery or burglary, all of which are profit motivated.

5. Emotional release bombings are usually associated with psychopathic bombers seeking to let go of real or imagined frustrations. The Unabomber falls into this category because of his pathological hatred of technology. There are cases of bombers who have had a love-hate relationship with someone associated with the target. Jealousy and revenge on the part of a dysfunctional family or a jilted lover would fall into this category. The bombs in these cases range from the extreme of antipersonnel devices to small charges used to harass the target by causing minor property damage.

6. Revenge bombings are closely associated with emotional release. The revenge bomber is motivated by earlier transgressions, real or imagined, committed by the intended target. Many psychopathic bombers are motivated by revenge.

7. Recognition bombings often overlap with other motivation categories, particularly emotional release. The bomber seeking recognition will place a device in a location where he or she can discover it and thus be recognized for performing a heroic act. What is so dangerous about this type of motivation is that the target is being attacked from within, often by an employee who is bored or wants attention for himself or herself in the hope of achieving public honor or advancement. A classic case of motivation occurred during the 1984 summer Olympic Games in Los Angeles, when a municipal police officer who was in trouble with his superiors used the ploy in an attempt to work his way back into their good graces. He planted an explosive device on one of the buses carrying Olympic athletes from a politically sensitive nation. He then called in a bomb threat, located the bomb himself, and became the hero of the day. Twelve years later, during the Olympic Games in Atlanta, a warning call involved an improvised explosive device that was actually detonated. Perhaps because of the Los Angeles incident, authorities and news media were quick to accuse, falsely as it turned out, a temporary security guard named Richard Jewell of planting the device. It was not Jewell who planted the bomb, but rather right-wing extremist Eric Rudolph.

Endnotes

1. Terrorism/International/Fatwa.1996, www.pbs.org/newshour (accessed March 15, 2011).
2. Terorism/International/Fatwa.1998, www.pbs.org/newshour (accessed March 15, 2011).
3. The UFF routinely notified authorities of its bombing attempts, a tactic noted by Bruce Hoffman, *Terrorism in the United States and the Potential Threat to Nuclear Facilities* (Santa Monica, CA: The Rand Corporation, January 1986), and Harvey W. Kushner, "United Freedom Front," in *Encyclopedia of Terrorism*, Thousand Oaks, CA: Sage, 2005, p. 381.

Hostage Situations

5

A Rare Occurrence

The cop on the street never knows, or at least almost never knows, if when he or she responds to a call it will result in a hostage situation. The call could be a robbery in progress, a domestic dispute, or a person with a gun. Each of these, or any one of a number of other so-called routine incidents, could wind up in a hostage situation.

With improved communications systems and deployment techniques, the very fact that officers are able to respond quickly may precipitate a hostage situation. There have been many occasions in which officers have responded to robbery calls only to find the robbers still inside the store. With escape blocked, it is not inconceivable that clerks or customers could be taken hostage. However, there are appropriate response tactics, which if employed properly, could preclude such hostage taking or at least minimize the chances of it happening.

Who Takes Hostages?

Persons who take hostages, whether in the course of a well-planned, well-thought-out action or a spur-of-the-moment reaction, can be divided into four categories:

1. Professional criminals
2. Inadequate personalities
3. Loose groups, such as prison inmates
4. Structured groups, such as terrorists

Professional criminals make their livings (full- or part-time) by robbery, burglary, and similar illegal activity. When they take a hostage, it means that the job has gone wrong. Usually the crime in progress is a felony and the criminal takes a hostage or hostages in order to escape. For the police, the professional criminal is, in the first moments of confrontation, the most dangerous type of hostage taker. There is an initial period of panic that generates a fight-or-flight reaction, so called because the instinct of cornered animals is to either flee or turn and attack. In humans, the fight-or-flight reaction is that brief time during which the trapped person most wants to strike out at or flee from whatever is causing the panic. In this case, it is the police.

The police tactic here is to carefully contain the professional criminal in the smallest practical area and give him time to think, rationalize, and generally consider all the options regarding the situation in which he finds himself. In containing the professional criminal, the officers should find good cover that affords sufficient protection. Cover is not the same as concealment, since a curtain or cardboard box can conceal but not afford much protection. We discuss the differences of cover vs. concealment elsewhere. After the panic reaction period has subsided, usually in 10 to 30 minutes, the professional criminal becomes the easiest type of hostage taker with whom the police deal. This is because as a professional, the criminal realizes he has nothing to gain from keeping the hostages, much less harming or killing one of them.

The *inadequate personality* is an individual who police officers in the street may refer to as a psycho. The more delicate designation is inadequate personality or emotionally disturbed person. This individual is a self-professed loner and loser for whom nothing goes right, and who the whole world is against. He wants to get attention, and taking someone hostage is just the way to do it. The last thing this type of hostage taker wants is escape. He wants to keep the incident going because he is enjoying it. Newspaper and broadcast reporters have repeatedly established contact with such hostage takers, provided a public forum for them, and incidentally, almost invariably prolonged an agonizing incident for the hostages.

Loose groups, such as prison inmates, also have attracting attention as their primary intent. They may not even know what their actual wants are, but they will demand things such as better food, conjugal visits, and improved recreational facilities. The loose group (this term is used because inmates usually are not organized into a tightly knit unit) is unique among hostage takers. Accordingly, the strategy in dealing with them is different. Rather than stretching out time as a tactic, it is appropriate early on in the incident, during that period called a window of time, to use a show of force. This use of force can break down the least adequate of the hostage takers involved in the loose group.

Since most prison takeovers are spontaneous, this early show of force can be effective. However, if there is information or other suspicions that it is a carefully planned takeover, the show-of-force tactic should be abandoned, lest it result in immediate harm to the hostages. In addition, even if a prison takeover is spontaneous and hostages are involved, if the appropriate show of force is not effected almost immediately, that window of time is closed and the use of force no longer appropriate or effective. In this event, it is best to resort to using time and delaying tactics because in reality the hostage takers become a group of inadequate personalities. When in doubt, use time.

Terrorists who engage in hostage taking, and this includes hijacking, are employing a tactic used primarily as a propaganda tool to maximize the effect of violence for political or economic gains. The selection of targets and victims is made with the aim of eliciting the maximum propaganda value from the incident. These incidents may be immediate reactions to world events, or an eruption in a long-standing feud or continuing animosity. Often, it is impossible to discern the motivation behind a particular hostage-taking incident.

Terrorists, particularly in hostage situations, will often use multiple incidents in an effort to separate and disperse law enforcement resources. The primary defensive tactic is to cut the terrorists' lines of communication while the police maintain and improve their own.

Terrorists engage in both kidnappings and hostage takings. Remember, the difference is that in hostage takings there is a confrontation; in kidnappings the perpetrators have mobility and anonymity unless they announce and identify themselves. Piracy, a related activity, is discussed in Chapter 7.

Panic Reaction

One element that is common to almost all hostage-taking situations is the panic reaction, that period early in the incident in which the fight-or-flight quandary arises in the perpetrators. This panic is dangerous to the hostage taker, the hostage, and especially to the police officers who respond to the incident. More police officers are killed during the panic reaction than at any other time during a hostage situation, or other confrontation, for that matter.

Those first few minutes, which may last up to a half hour, after the hostages have been taken and the perpetrator or perpetrators are consolidating power, are the most dangerous. It is during this time period when hostage takers are most likely to kill someone. It could be a security guard, one of the hostages trying to flee or not responding quickly enough to an order, or one of the responding police officers. An effective example of a panic reaction, one that did not even include a hostage situation, involved a group of adherents of a Caribbean religious sect and a city marshal in New York City. A marshal in New York City performs a number of civil functions, including serving eviction notices. It is not uncommon for breaches of the peace to occur during this service, so police officers sometimes accompany marshals on their rounds. The marshal can serve the eviction notice in one of three ways: by handing it to the person, affixing it to the door of the premises, or slipping it under the door. If a police officer is present, this is noted in a memo book as evidence that the notice has been served. In this particular instance, the officer with the city marshal—it may have been the end of a long day of serving many notices—grew somewhat lax in procedures. When he knocked on the door of the premises where the group was living, a voice demanded, "Who's there?"

The officer, standing directly in front of the door, responded, "Police." It was the last word he would ever utter; for unbeknownst to him, the occupants had created a bomb factory inside the dwelling. When the person behind the door heard the word *police*, he panicked and sent a shotgun blast through the door, killing the police officer.

This was a classic panic reaction. All the person behind the door had to do was ask the officer what he wanted. The officer, in turn, would have said something about an eviction notice, and the occupant could have told him to slip it under the door. The incident would have ended there. Instead, one officer was shot and killed. A gun battle ensued, with a number of the occupants killed or wounded and the rest taken into custody.

Panic reaction results in the deaths of more police officers than any other facet of a hostage situation. Officers finding themselves in such a situation should step back, behind cover to protect themselves, so as not to return fire until they are absolutely certain of target identification. This reduces the risk of some innocent person being hit by gunshots.

There is good reason for police to avoid confrontation with hostage takers during the period when there could be a panic reaction. If a person were killed during the initial takeover or during its earliest stages, it would be ascribed to panic reaction. Although inexcusable from a legal or moral standpoint, it would be understandable. In contrast is the killing of a hostage later in the incident, after communication has been established. If a person were killed on a deadline or to otherwise show the hostage taker's resolve, this would be neither excusable nor understandable.

Suicide by Cop

Though the phenomenon known as suicide by cop is not necessarily new, it has been occurring with greater frequency, while at the same time being affected more dramatically. An incident that occurred a few years ago is illustrative. Two individuals, Keith FOU Haggler and Kate FOU Haggler, were members of a very small and extreme religious group in which each person took the name *FOU* (Father of Us) as a middle name. The pair hijacked a bus in Jasper, Arkansas, to create a confrontation with the responding law enforcement officers. After a period of give-and-take with a negotiator from the sheriff's department, they agreed to release about 20 hostages in exchange for an interview with a television news camera crew. During that interview they indicated that part of their religious belief, which was from the Bible's Book of Revelation, was that they should be killed (by the police) so they could lie in state on the father's land and on the third day rise from the dead and walk upon the earth. In their interview with the television crew, they indicated that after the interview they would release the remaining hostages and then would exit the bus and approach the police. They stated that they would point their guns at the police in a threatening manner and that the police would have to shoot them. Having been made aware of their plan to bait the police into this incident, the sheriff decided he would use a sharp-shooter with good cover to only wound the male by shooting him in the shoulder to disarm him. When the two armed subjects came out of the bus, they approached the police. After moving up about 20 feet, they went down on their knees and started to creep toward the police, pointing their guns in that direction. When the sharpshooter fired, the bullet struck the male in the right shoulder. He turned, and the two perpetrators turned their guns on each other, with the female shooting the male and then turning the pistol on herself. Their plan was to have the police do it for them. But this time, it didn't work.

On November 14, 1997, the most classic of suicide by cop rituals took place. A 19-year-old college student, who had amassed a series of gambling debts on the World Series totaling about $6,000, would carry this out. Apparently this debt, though his family was not without means, was too much for him to bear. He was greatly depressed. On that Friday, he told his best friend that he wanted to drive into something. He talked about suicide. That evening he purchased a toy gun and a sheriff's badge for $1.97 at a local drugstore. At about 10:20 p.m. on a dark and rain-swept Long Island parkway, the young man drove his 1998 Honda Accord in a very fast and erratic manner. He was weaving in and out of traffic, sideswiping and sometimes pushing other cars. He exited the parkway, then turned and reentered. Various calls from cell phones were made to the 911 operator reporting this violent auto behavior. At about 10:35 p.m., the Honda sped past a police patrol car. The officer gave chase with lights and siren. The Honda pulled onto the shoulder, with the patrol car in a position behind it. The young man jumped out of his car and started waving his arms. The officer told the youth to get back into his car. The youth continued to approach, and as he reached the grill of the patrol car, he pulled the silver toy pistol from his waistband and pointed it at the cop. The officer retreated behind his vehicle and called for backup. He continued to yell at the youth, "Drop the weapon! Drop the weapon!" An officer responding to the backup call arrived on the service road, saw the youth pointing the gun at the first officer, and he too yelled at the youth to drop the gun. The youth turned and pointed the gun at the second officer, who was out in the open. He leveled the gun with two hands. Upon seeing this and believing that the officer was in mortal danger, the first officer opened fire. The second officer, hearing the shots and believing they were coming from the youth, also opened fire. Approximately 10 rounds were fired at the subject, who was hit by at least one of the bullets. As he fell, the silver plastic toy gun fell from his hand to the ground. Upon further investigation, the officer found a handwritten envelope on the passenger seat addressed "To the officer who shot me." Inside the envelope, there was a handwritten letter that read:

> Officer,
> It was a plan. I'm sorry to get you involved. I just needed to die. Please send my letters and break the news slowly to my family and let them know I had to do this. And that I love them very much. I'm sorry for getting you involved. Please remember that this was all my doing. You had no way of knowing.
>
> **(Signed by the youth)**

These two officers became victims of this troubled young man. Fortunately, his letter did give them some understanding of how they were used, helping them alleviate some of the guilt that is usually heaped upon officers involved in the shooting of a civilian. Many times officers are not so fortunate. They are saddled with the "if only, if only" syndrome, becoming victims (often without any support) because of their involvement in suicide by cop.

It has been estimated that as many as 30% of the persons killed by police are, in fact, victim-precipitated homicides. A thesis was prepared in 1996 by a Canadian police officer, John Parent, at Simon Fraser University in Burnaby, British Columbia, entitled "The Phenomenon of Victim-Precipitated Homicide." In it, Parent said that suicide by such traditional methods as leaping off a tall building or off a bridge required commitment of the victim. In suicide by cop, the hard part is done for the victim by the police.

Why Hostages Are Taken

One of the principles of hostage negotiating is the assumption that the hostage has no value to the hostage taker other than the audience the incident can create. In the case of the professional criminal, hostages are seen as a possible means of escape from a difficult situation. Inadequate personalities use hostages as a means of getting attention. People will start talking to them, asking what's wrong. A disgruntled or dismissed employee then has the opportunity to air grievances in public. A jilted lover may want to prove his love is greater, and somehow feels that by taking his ex-girlfriend hostage, he is expressing that love for all to see. For prisoners, hostages are used to give inmates the power to negotiate with prison officials. Terrorists use hostages to get the widest possible media coverage.

In all cases, however, the hostage takers want to extract something from the authorities or the outside world. They cannot get what they want from the hostages, so it is not the hostages themselves who are the important factor; they merely allow the hostage taker to make an announcement. This announcement may take the form of a telephone call to the police or news media by the perpetrator, or it could be a shouted warning to passersby, or even gunshots fired into the air. If a bad guy took a hostage and no one knew, what would the hostage taker accomplish? Even if he had all of his windows booby-trapped or had a well-written note or a prepared statement to make to the media, these preparations would be meaningless if no one was aware of the situation.

Of course, police must respond in order to protect the life of that hostage. You can't take a chance on what might happen if the police did not respond or, upon arriving, saying to the hostage taker, "good luck," and then leaving for lunch or some other assignment.

The Magic Triangle

For an organization to function, it needs manpower and money. In order to obtain money, manpower is needed. And to obtain manpower, the public must be made aware of the organization. Media attention is required. Whether the organization is a group of terrorists, the Girl Scouts of America, a business corporation, or the Federal Bureau of Investigation (FBI), it utilizes the media-manpower-money triangle. In each case, the organization will create attention or generate media coverage, or both. The private business may call it a publicity stunt: the Girl Scouts will promote a story about a kid who sold thousands of boxes of cookies, the FBI might engage in some high-profile action against organized crime, and terrorists will take some well-chosen hostages or maybe bomb a few specially selected targets.

In each case, the media exposure leads directly to either more money or more recruits, usually both. The organization then has enough manpower and money to continue its operations. The concept of the magic triangle was developed many years ago in response to the activities of the Popular Front for the Liberation of Palestine (PFLP), sometimes referred to by its acronym in French, PLFP. In the late 1960s and early 1970s, many of these self-styled Palestinian freedom fighter groups were receiving funds from the moderate Arab countries, such as Saudi Arabia, the United Arab Emirates, and similar nations. This was not so much out of any ideological agreement or particular desire to fund terrorists activities per se, but rather it was a form of protection payment for the Palestinians to keep their operations—and inevitable Israeli reprisals—out of those countries (Figure 5.1).

The PFLP was among the groups receiving such tribute. The situation took a dramatic turn on Hijack Sunday, September 6, 1970, when the organization hijacked four aircraft and successfully brought three of them to Dawson

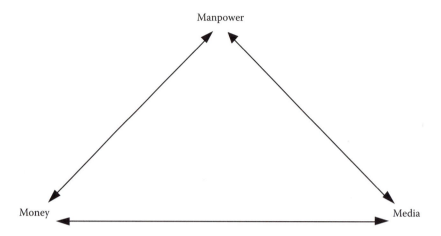

Figure 5.1 The magic triangle: A successful terrorist group—as with any business, organization, or government—relies on dynamic interaction among three essential elements: manpower, money, and communications media.

Field, an airstrip in what is now the country of Jordan. The runway had been built by the British during World War II and had been largely unused since then. The planes, American, French, and Swiss airliners, were brought to this field, and all the passengers released except those who were Israeli or who had Jewish-sounding names. On the sixth day following Hijack Sunday, all three airliners were blown up.

The big problem for the PFLP, however, was that Jordan's King Hussein was very much angered that these planes were brought into his sovereign territory without his knowledge or permission. He sent the Jordanian army against the Palestinians, with the result that during the month of September 1970, the PFLP sustained more casualties than it had while fighting Israel during the entire previous decade. There were more than 3,400 PFLP troops killed and nearly 11,000 wounded. For the PFLP, that month became known as Black September, and an organization called Black September came into existence.

Following September 1970, the PFLP did not receive much money in the way of tribute. Not only had the organization lost manpower in its battle with the Jordanian army, but it had also lost face. There was a downward spiral: the loss of face led to the loss of money, which in turn meant new members could not be recruited to replace those lost during Black September. The PFLP was forced to do something spectacular to get manpower, which would enable them to get more money, which would then allow them to get on with their avowed purpose of liberating Palestine from Israeli occupation.

The organization known as Black September, with its affiliation to the PFLP, staged a hostage-taking incident during the Olympic Games in Munich, West Germany, in September 1972. Its hostages were athletes and coaches of the Israeli national team. By carrying out the operation during the Olympic Games, Black September had some 3,000 international newspaper, magazine, radio, and television reporters detail its actions and send its messages around the world. Almost immediately, other Arabs wanted to join the group, the kind of organization that could pull off something so daring and spectacular. As the ranks of Black September/PFLP swelled, those countries that had cut back or ceased paying tribute began to rethink their decisions. Black September was again in the position to extort money to finance its operations.

The media-manpower-money magic triangle helps explain why terrorists engage in activities such as hostage takings, bombings, and kidnappings. Once it became known that these were the favored activities of terrorists, law enforcement and defense agencies in the free world were able to begin developing countermeasures and tactics to reduce their adversaries' effectiveness.

Munich, 1972

When the Olympic Games were held in Munich in 1972, one of the thoughts uppermost in the German planners' minds was that these games were going to be a showcase for peace. This would be in marked contrast to the militarism that permeated the Nazi-orchestrated Berlin Olympics of 1936, the last time the summer games were held on German soil. Whereas Adolf Hitler wanted to parade his master race philosophy for the world to see, the Munich Olympics were to demonstrate how much West Germany had distanced itself from Nazism since the end of World War II.

This was the atmosphere that confronted the terrorists of Black September as they plotted their strategy to secure worldwide recognition with the speed of satellite transmission. Just before dawn on September 5, 1972—the eleventh day of Olympic competition and almost exactly two years to the day after the start of the Black September debacle in Jordan—six young Arab men scaled a chain-link fence to gain entry to the Olympic Village apartment complex that housed athletes, coaches, and trainers.

The six met up with two comrades who had been working in the village since before the Olympics had begun. They had managed to duplicate a key to the front door of the building in which 21 members of the Israeli men's team were staying on the lower floors. The terrorists were dressed like athletes, complete with small equipment bags; however, instead of holding shoes, towels, and athletic gear, the bags were filled with Soviet-made automatic weapons, including hand grenades and combat rifles. Apparently, the plan was to capture all 21 Israeli men without firing a shot, and then demand that Israel release Arab terrorists being held prisoner in exchange for the Israeli hostages.

For all their careful planning, the Arabs found things going wrong almost from the start. The front door key failed to work immediately, with the resulting commotion awakening a sleeping Israeli who was able to shout warnings when the Arabs finally did make it inside. Another Israeli arriving back in his quarters in the wee hours of the morning was shot and killed, as was another who attacked the terrorists with a kitchen knife. The Arabs wound up with nine hostages, two dead bodies, and because shots had been fired and several Israelis had escaped, the local police were alerted to what was taking place.

Within a half hour or so, Manfred Schreiber, who held the dual role of Munich police commissioner and head of the Olympic security forces, had ordered all roads leading to the site closed to traffic. He arrived at the scene shortly afterward, but the terrorists had already begun to make their demands known in the form of a note passed through a window. The Arabs wanted Israel to release some 230 terrorists from prison, and also demanded that West Germany free five members of the left-wing terrorist group the Baader-Meinhof Gang. The note was signed "Black September."

The first thing that was apparent to Schreiber was that the local police were really just middlemen, because only the government of Israel could adequately respond to the terrorist demands. His own government officials in Bonn were involved not only with regard to the release of the Baader-Meinhof Gang members, but also in conducting diplomatic discussions with Israel, whose prime minister, Golda Meir, had stated previously that her government would never negotiate with terrorists. Schreiber's channel of communications with higher officials was Bruno Merk, the interior minister of Bavaria, the region in which Munich is located.

The Arabs holding the Israeli hostages announced the first of many deadlines: if the State of Israel did not respond positively to its demand by 9 a.m., a hostage would be killed. About 15 minutes prior to the deadline, a group approached the terrorist leader, Mohammed Mahmud Essafadi, with an offer: Interior Minister Merk; Walter Trager, head of the West German Olympic Committee; A. D. Touney, the Egyptian mayor of the Olympic Village; Hans-Dietrich Genscher, the West German federal interior minister; and former Munich mayor Jochen Vogel would trade places with the Israeli hostages. It was an offer that would be repeated several times, and each time Essafadi would reject it.

Touney, the Egyptian, did ask Essafadi for a six-hour extension of the deadline, maintaining that the Israelis had not had sufficient time to study the names on the list of prisoners whose releases were being demanded. Essafadi granted a three-hour extension.

While West German Chancellor Willy Brandt consulted via telephone with Israel's Meir, at 9:10 a.m., 10 minutes after the original deadline, the Arabs passed another note with several demands and assertions. The first demand was that the police allow the terrorists to move the hostages to another location within the Olympic Village. Another demand was that three planes be readied for takeoffs at various times to different, unspecified locations. The note asserted that if any trickery was attempted, the hostages would be killed, that the noon deadline was absolute, and that other terrorists in unnamed locations were prepared to act if the more than 230 terrorists were not released from prison.

Shortly afterward, the Arabs verbally demanded that police officers who had taken up forward positions be pulled back because they were "spying from behind pillars." Schreiber ordered six officers to retreat. As the noon deadline approached, Touney, accompanied by Mohamed Khadif, the chief administrator of the Arab League in Germany, and two others approached Essafadi to ask for more time, claiming communications problems between Germany and Israel. Essafadi, with a grenade in each hand and a lieutenant identified only as Tony at his side, listened to the group. Khadif told the terrorists they could have safe passage out of Germany and a large sum of money as ransom, but that Israel was likely to release only some, perhaps as few as 10, prisoners. Essafadi responded that he was not interested in money, but in the release of all of his comrades. He also pushed the deadline back to 1 p.m., but noted that if Israel had not acted by then, two hostages would be killed.

Noting Israel's reluctance to negotiate or apparently make any concessions, Schreiber told the Israeli ambassador to West Germany, who was at the scene, that there was little choice but to try to free the hostages by force. Schreiber also offered his opinion that this would likely lead to the death of most, if not all, of the hostages and most of the terrorists. As 1 p.m. neared, Schreiber and Merk were able to extract another two-hour extension of the deadline. As 3 p.m. approached, Genscher led another group to speak with Essafadi and conceded that a final decision was not likely to be forthcoming from the Israelis, who were still debating the issue. He also let it be known that Germany was not pleased with the way the Israelis were responding to the situation. Genscher asked whether there was a demand that perhaps the Germans themselves could satisfy. Essafadi then asked for two airplanes to transport the terrorists and hostages to Egypt. He added that the captives would be killed if the 230 prisoners whose releases had been demanded were not waiting for them in Cairo.

A seasoned politician adept at making deals, Genscher complained that two planes seemed extravagant and would present tremendous logistical problems. Soon Essafadi agreed that one plane would be enough and, not coincidentally, that the deadline would be pushed back another two hours to allow time to arrange for the plane.

It was the Germans' turn to make a demand, asking for proof that the hostages were still alive. First one, then another was trotted out. However, when the Arabs were asked to produce all the hostages, Essafadi was enraged. "You're trying to trick us," he shouted. "Your soldiers have surrounded the building and they're getting ready to attack us. Take a good look at that Jew! If you do not immediately order your men away, we will shoot him down where he is before your eyes and throw his corpse to you. And in another five minutes, two more hostages will be shot right on the spot where you are standing."

Schreiber, not certain that the riflemen had actually been spotted but also unwilling to call the terrorist's bluff, had no choice but to pull back his troops. Essafadi then agreed to allow Genscher to go inside the quarters to see the Israeli hostages. What he saw were nine hostages bound in groups of three, two sitting on separate beds and the third on chairs. In the middle was the bloody body of one of the Israelis slain hours before. A coach of the Israeli shooting team acted as spokesman, saying that morale was high and that no one would object to going to Cairo if the Israeli government gave assurances that the released prisoners would be waiting for them.

With a 7 p.m. deadline approaching, Genscher again asked for more time, claiming that it was difficult to find a volunteer crew to fly a plane to Egypt. Essafadi, whose men had been listening to newscasts reporting that Israel steadfastly refused to negotiate, demanded to know whether this was true. No, he was told, this was merely idle speculation on the part of the media. Another two-hour extension was granted, but Essafadi let it be known that he was in the mood for no more delays.

Schreiber, for one, believed him and tried to formulate a plan of action. The Egyptians, meanwhile, let officials in Bonn know that they were unwilling participants in this drama and their cooperation could not be counted on for anything. It then became apparent that, given Israeli intransigence and Egyptian reluctance to help, the hostages could not be allowed to leave Germany. An assault would have to be mounted.

Schreiber had four options: he could attack the terrorists where they were; he could assault them in the underground passageway as they transported the hostages to the waiting helicopters that would take them to the airport; he could attack as they boarded the helicopters; or he could mount the assault at the airstrip as they transferred from the helicopters to the aircraft. The airstrip was an abandoned military airfield located at Furstenfeldbruck outside of Munich. The second and fourth options seemed to hold the most promise of success, while exposing police and bystanders to the least risk; however, when the terrorists rejected the underground walk and demanded a bus be provided to take them to the helicopters, there was but a single course of action left.

In planning the ambush at the airport, Schreiber and his top aide, Georg Wolf, were (17 hours after the incident had begun) still uncertain how many terrorists were involved. Their best count was five individuals. Accordingly, five sharpshooters were ordered into position at Furstenfeldbruck. With Schreiber at the Olympic Village and Wolf at the airstrip, Schreiber was surprised to see 17 passengers board the helicopters. If there were nine hostages, that meant there were eight terrorists. Three more sharpshooters would be needed, but they never materialized since the information was never communicated to Wolf.

A dummy Lufthansa Boeing 727 had been set up at Furstenfeldbruck, and as a defensive, last-ditch measure, Schreiber and Wolf had placed eight police officers aboard dressed as flight attendants and crew members. The cops were none too happy about the setup, feeling that the dummy plane would not fool anyone and that they would be overwhelmed by the superior firepower the terrorists possessed. The lieutenant in charge of the eight-person contingent was not in radio contact with his superiors, so there was little he could do to allay his officers' fears. Why there was no radio contact has never been fully explained—it could have been a malfunction, a communications line may have been severed, or no radios, in fact, may have been issued—but eventually the whole group, including the lieutenant, abandoned the plan before the helicopters arrived.

Schreiber knew the assault would have to come when the terrorists and hostages alighted from the helicopters. Leaving six terrorists to guard the nine hostages and the two two-man helicopter crews, Essafadi and one other terrorist approached the plane to inspect it. As they walked back toward the helicopters, Schreiber noted for the first time that all the terrorists were not accompanied by hostages. Feeling this was the best opportunity he would get, and hoping that the action would shock the others into submission, he ordered his five sharpshooters to open fire on the two terrorists. The first round of fire missed.

Schreiber was later able to explain that by law and tradition, West German police were not trained to shoot to kill, but were taught to fire only at extremities. This, coupled with a long, tiring day, he surmised, contributed to the inaccuracy. It also led to a gun battle in which all nine hostages were killed, five terrorists died, and a German police officer in the tower next to Schreiber was fatally wounded.

The Munich Olympics hostage incident provides a touchstone for the handling of subsequent terrorist hostage takings. A major question raised was why the Olympic Village, as controlled an environment as it was, was so susceptible to attack in the face of threats and forewarnings. Another question: Were all avenues of peaceful resolution explored before force was employed? Tactically, were the police adequately prepared when they finally did mount an attempt to rescue the hostages? Last, but not least, would the outcome have been different if the Israeli government had given Schreiber some latitude to negotiate?

In addition to these questions, there are three things that very obviously did go wrong and that serve as points to be expanded upon later. First, there was a lack of complete intelligence; the number of terrorists involved was not known until just before the shooting started. Second, there was a definite lack of communication, for whatever reason. Third, there was no discipline of firepower; the sharpshooters were given "shooter's prerogative" rather than specific targets.

Deadlines

In the years since Munich, very few hostages have been killed by their captors outside of the initial stages of the incident, when the fight-or-flight panic reaction occurs. In other words, there have been very few cases of hostages being killed on deadline. The best way to deal with a deadline is to seemingly ignore it. That is, do not be pressured by a deadline and do not call attention to it. The tactic is to talk the perpetrator or perpetrators through the deadline and not refer to it at all. If they bring it up, the negotiator can be reassuring and say that the demands, whatever they may be, are being worked on, but that these things take time. Then change the subject.

Calling attention to a deadline may precipitate an action that otherwise might not be taken. The hostage taker will want to prove that he has power by firing a shot, or hurting someone, or both. In fact, one theory holds that if a perpetrator kills a hostage outside of the initial stages of a hostage incident, this evinces a depraved mind. The individual involved is a psychopath or sociopathic personality who, if he kills once, will kill again. Negotiations, in this case, would probably prove fruitless, and a more parochial method of hostage recovery would best be attempted, even though direct assault, for example, is extremely risky and dangerous.

These are hostage incidents where there is a confrontation between the hostage takers and authorities. The hostage takings so publicized in Iraq in 2004 were really kidnappings, in which the abductors had anonymity (unless they chose to identify themselves) and mobility, where they could move the victim or victims from place to place. In kidnap situations, as discussed in more detail in Chapter 6, many times the perpetrators dig the holes and buy the quicklime even before the victim is snatched. The demands in Iraq were political in nature, and in order to shock people, the abductors killed to get others to adhere to their demands. As hard-hearted as it may seem, standing fast will, in the long run, save lives, even as difficult as that may be for the families of the persons used as "examples" by the kidnappers. If the perpetrators don't succeed with their demands, the killing will stop and they will go on to something else, like bombing, to get attention for their cause.

Killing on Deadline

In all of the incidents around the world involving terrorist hijackings and hostage situations, there have been so few people killed on deadline that it is possible to track almost all of them. The ones that stand out most, in chronological order, are the hijacking of a British Overseas Air Corporation (BOAC; the forerunner of British Airways) airliner, the take-over of the Iranian Embassy in London, the hijacking of a Dutch train by South Moluccans, and the killing of a U.S. sailor on a TWA flight hijacked to Iran in 1985.

The BOAC incident occurred in 1970 when an airliner was hijacked en route from Frankfurt in what was then West Germany to London. The jet was taken to Tunisia, where it was allowed to land at an airstrip in the desert. It was so hot that even on television one could see the heat rising over the desert floor. The Arab hijackers had made many demands and set various deadlines that had come and gone, and come and gone. Late in the afternoon of the first day that the hostages were held, the terrorists brought a man to the door of the plane, put a gun to his head, shot him, and dumped his body on the tarmac. A few minutes later, two men in white coats came out of the crowd with a stretcher, picked up the body, and took it away. It was somewhat surprising that troops didn't go in, because the hypothesis is that if a hostage is killed after the panic fight-or-flight reaction subsides, there could be more killing and the authorities might as well try to save as many hostages as possible by mounting an immediate assault. This is considered a preferable alternative to not acting at all and watching the hostages die one by one. The following day, however, all the hostages aboard the British airliner were set free and the terrorists accepted passage to another country.

Moluccans are people from islands popularly called the Spice Islands in what is now the country of Indonesia, but which at one time was a posses-sion of the Netherlands and part of the Dutch East Indies. In the war for Indonesian independence fought after World War II, the Moluccans were on the side of the Dutch. When Indonesia gained independence, the Dutch government offered the Moluccans refuge in the Netherlands. Over the years, however, the Moluccans were not assimilated into Dutch society and became ghettoized. There was chronic unemployment among them, and many subsisted solely by virtue of the government dole. As with many immi-grant peoples, the elders spoke fondly and longingly of the old country while ignoring the political and economic realities of what was happening back home. The younger generation, hearing only good things about a homeland most of them had never seen, was more disgruntled and rebellious than their parents and grandparents. They resorted to terrorism, which included the hijacking of a train in Bellen. When these young Moluccans took over the train, a motorman was killed at the outset in the takeover (during the period of panic reaction), which is different, psychologically, from killing on a dead-line once the hostage taking has been accomplished. Unexpectedly, however, on the second day of the incident, the Moluccans killed a man and dumped his body out of the back of the train. Again, for whatever reason, the police failed to intervene. The incident continued another 12 days (December 2–14, 1975) before the Moluccans surrendered without another person being shot or killed.

The Iranian Embassy in London is located in an area known as Prince's Gate. It was here, on April 30, 1980, at a time when several Americans were being held hostage in the U.S. Embassy in Teheran, the capital of Iran, that six dissident Iranians stormed the embassy and took a number of hostages. On May 5, the sixth day of the incident, and after several deadlines had come and gone with scant attention paid to them, the terrorists brought a man to the front of the building, put a gun to his head, shot him, and rolled the body down the stairs. Within two hours, a team of commandos from the British Special Air Service went in on a direct assault, killing five of the terrorists and capturing one. One member of the assault team was wounded, but none of the hostages were hurt.

Other deadline killings include a case in which a Kuwaiti airliner was hijacked to Teheran in late 1985, and while on the ground there, two Americans were beaten and killed on a deadline. In addition to this, there was also the hijacking of TWA Flight 847 in 1985, in which U.S. Navy diver Robert Dean Stethem was beaten and killed and his body mutilated.

Evaluation

If a person is killed during a panic reaction, the hypothesis says that fruitful negotiation can still be conducted. If a hostage is killed otherwise, it is presumed the terrorist is deranged and could kill again. Careful analysis of the deadline killings, however, adds a modification to the hypothesis. In the incident involving the British airliner taken to Tunisia, all of the hostages on the plane were British, with the exception of one German man. At the time the hijackers effected their takeover, the German was, to put it bluntly, roaring drunk according to other passengers who were interviewed after the ordeal. Not only was the German drunk, but they said that he was loud and arrogant. There was also some indication that he might have made what appeared to be homosexual advances toward one or more of the terrorists. It was the German who was killed, and at least some of the surviving hostages said they felt he virtually committed suicide behaving in the manner he did.

On the train in Bellen, it was the second day of the hijacking and nothing was going right for the Moluccans. Almost anything that could go wrong did. One of the hostages was a man named Hans Prinz, who was called "the doctor" because he dispensed the medical supplies and prescriptions sent to the hostages. Afterward, Prinz described the man who was killed by the Moluccans as difficult and a troublemaker who was making things uncomfortable for everyone. When he was killed, Prinz added, nobody seemed to mind too much. He, too, apparently contributed to his own demise.

At Prince's Gate, when terrorists stormed the Iranian Embassy, they made statements about having purified themselves, how they were going to paradise, and how they were prepared to meet Allah. One of the employees of the embassy told the terrorists that he, too, was prepared to meet Allah and that, in fact, he was more deserving than they to go to paradise and see Allah. Six days later they accommodated him. The lack of hostage deaths during the police assault at Prince's Gate is attributable to the superior intelligence gathered during the long incident.

In the Kuwaiti airliner case, the only contribution the two victims made to their own demise was that they were Americans traveling on official passports. In the case of TWA Flight 847, Robert Dean Stethem was military, traveling on a military ID rather than a passport. When one of the hijackers asked about Stethem, a flight attendant replied that Stethem was from New Jersey and that he was a sailor or, in German, *bei der Marine dienen*, which means to serve in the navy. The Lebanon-based hijackers may have thought Stethem was one of the U.S. Marines stationed in Beirut, or perhaps associated him with the battleship *New Jersey* that had bombarded the city, reportedly killing relatives of one of the hijackers.

In each of these cases, the victims contributed to their demise either actively, as in the first three examples, or passively, as in the cases of the American diplomats and the serviceman. These killings did not preclude negotiations, however. So the hypothesis about killing after the fight-or-flight stage has to be softened to include the fact that the victim could somehow contribute to his or her own demise. This places an even greater emphasis on the need for timely, accurate intelligence. The effort has to be raised to the nth degree. This is easy enough to recognize and acknowledge, but extremely difficult to accomplish because each hostage situation comes with its own unique set of circumstances. Still, every effort must be made because, for example, if a hostage tried to disarm a perpetrator and was killed in the ensuing ruckus, that would not evince a depraved mind. This would be no time to go in on an assault. Remember, an assault is a very dangerous act, bringing death—both potentially and statistically—to hostages, perpetrators, and the assault team alike.

Responsibilities of the First Responding Officers

In most cases, the cop on the street learns of a hostage situation when the perpetrator or perpetrators announce that hostages have been taken. This is often accomplished by the firing of shots. Then come the demands to be satisfied in return for the safety of the hostages. The first duty of the responding officers—whether advised by gunshots, announcement, or other communications that this is, indeed, a hostage situation—is to take cover and protect themselves while assessing the situation. Only then can aid and assistance be offered to the innocent person or persons being held hostage.

There have been times when an officer has responded to a man with a gun report that could have been a hostage incident but in reality was just a barricade situation. Occasionally, an officer might ask, "Have you got anybody in there with you?" The perpetrator might decide it is to his advantage to answer in the affirmative. All this does is make things unnecessarily complicated for the police. The appropriate procedure is not to make any suggestions about hostages. Don't put any ideas into anybody's head. Let the perpetrator do the talking (Figure 5.2).

The hostage taker should be confined to the smallest area practicable, preferably without a face-to-face confrontation. If possible, the perpetrator should be locked in, i.e., by chocking the door or blocking it with a desk or other heavy, but movable, object. The physical blocking of an escape route precludes what is called a push-out by the perpetrator, in which he uses the hostage as a shield to effect a getaway while challenging the police to take a chance with the hostage's life.

The underlying assumption in hostage situations is that human life is the most important thing of all, much more so than apprehending the hostage taker. In certain circumstances, then, it may be more prudent to let the perpetrator and hostage go in a push-out. For example, if the perpetrator has a weapon cocked at the body of the hostage, even a well-placed shot may kill the perpetrator but still cause a reflex muscle reaction sufficient to fire the weapon and kill the hostage. A not-so-well-placed shot could kill the hostage rather than the hostage taker. The only thing worse than the perpetrator killing the hostage would be the police killing the hostage, from both moral and liability standpoints.

The second duty is to call for backup. In many instances, if the initial report were a man with a gun or other serious felony, backup would be on the way. When radioing or calling in, the officer should mention the weapon or weapons involved and where the danger zone lies, so that other responding officers do not blunder into the line of fire while responding to the scene. There was an incident in the late 1970s in Ottawa, Ontario, Canada, that illustrates the importance of identifying streets and directions within the danger zone, the location of the perpetrator within the building, weapons involved, and if possible, what precipitated the incident.

In this case, constables had attempted to serve a warrant on a man who responded by firing shots. He took refuge on the widow's walk of the house involved, which afforded him a 360° view of the neighborhood. Armed with a rifle and afforded this vantage point, he was able to observe the responding

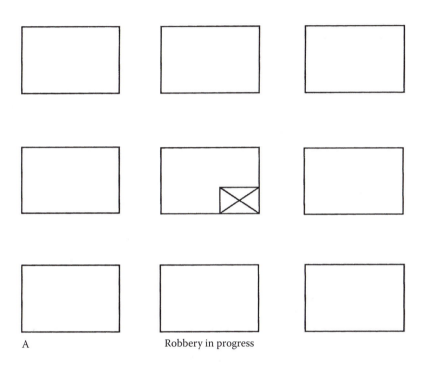

A   Robbery in progress

Figure 5.2A First response: The report of a robbery in progress. (A) triggers the response of patrol cars. (*continued*)

officers, who were unaware of his location. He managed to wound four different officers responding from four different directions. Although in this incident every direction was fraught with danger, in most incidents there are safe routes to the scene. It is imperative, then, to provide such information as the size and shape of the danger zone and the type of weapons (i.e., rifles, handguns, knife, or bomb) to the radio dispatcher.

The Mobilization Point

If circumstances permit, the responding officer can indicate a mobilization point at the scene so backup can head there and be afforded some

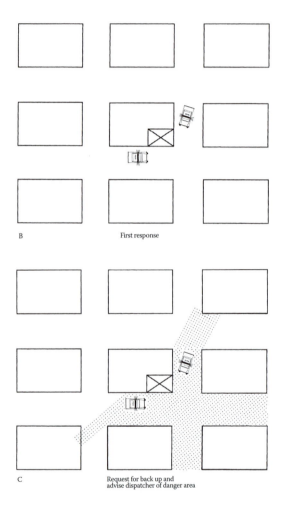

Figure 5.2B (*continued*) Which in turn advise the radio dispatcher of the nature of the danger area while requesting backup support (C).

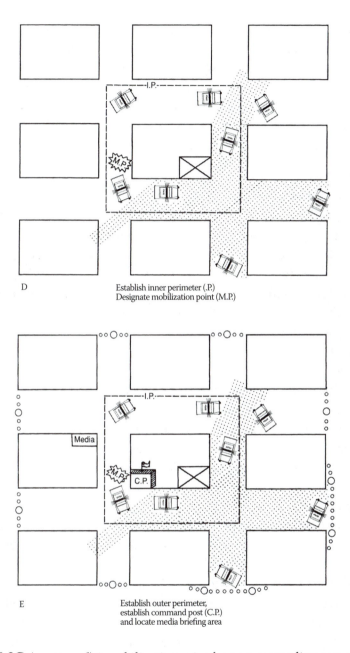

D Establish inner perimeter (.P.)
Designate mobilization point (M.P.)

E Establish outer perimeter,
establish command post (C.P.)
and locate media briefing area

Figure 5.2C (*continued*) A mobilization point for next-responding cars and personnel is established within an inner perimeter around the area (D). Access to the inner perimeter is extremely limited, while an outer perimeter is established to allow some access by the media and others (E).

protection. The mobilization point should be close enough for the convenience of responding officers, but out of the perpetrator's view so he can't see the response. If the response is large, or the perpetrator perceives it to be, it might elicit a panic reaction and he might strike out at the police or one of the hostages. Be mindful of the possibility of video surveillance cameras, both government and private systems. The perpetrator may have access and be able to view the deployment of responders.

Location of the Mobilization Point

There are some important reasons for selecting a concealed location for the mobilization point. For one, the hostage taker should not be aware of who is, or is not, responding. Keeping this information from the perpetrator is a psychological tactic and becomes a psychological weapon. Imagination will be stimulated, and he may think there are more police present than there really are. On the other hand, if he sees the force being assembled and all the cars coming and going, this might induce a panic reaction, fight or flight, which could result in violence, either internal or external. Internalized violence is suicide; externalized is homicide. In either case, it is not the outcome the police should want to precipitate.

One of the best illustrations of the value of concealment in hostage situations, although not a terrorist incident, occurred in DeKalb County, just outside Atlanta, Georgia. A man had kidnapped two babies of his common-law wife and told her that if she didn't come to his place by 5 p.m., he would kill her babies and himself. She called the police, who rushed to the scene. They used a shopping center parking lot as a mobilization point. The only problem was, unbeknownst to them, it was in full view from a window to which the man had access. The woman had also neglected to tell police about the 5 p.m. deadline. Tactical units began to arrive shortly before five; the SWAT team was on hand in full gear. They moved forward to take up assigned positions closer to the apartment complex. It was about 4:50 p.m. by this time, and the perpetrator apparently misperceived the intentions of the police. He must have thought they were mounting an assault. He fired a couple of shots at the police, which had no effect, then put one into the heads of each of the babies and one shot into his own head. Newspaper photographs and television footage of police officers carrying out the dead babies were graphic portrayals of the tragic consequences of lack of concealment.

Decision Makers

Once backup arrives and a decision maker is on the scene, the command post can be established. The question always arises, "Can a chief negotiate?" Certainly, but should a chief negotiate? In almost all cases, probably not. It is impossible to be both a negotiator and in command of the situation. These are two hats that cannot be worn by one person. This may pose problems in smaller communities and in places where sheriffs and chiefs are elected or on tenuous appointment. It would probably be better if these individuals didn't show up at all; however, if they must be there, it is imperative that they turn over some of the reins to subordinates and rely on the advice of their experts. They may still be the top decision makers, but there is no way they should handle the negotiations themselves. The actual mechanics and outlines of authority can vary. This is not as important as everyone knowing exactly who is in charge, and who has what responsibilities and what delegated authority. The decision maker, commander if you will, at the scene must establish the lines of authority and how the lines of communications are organized. Three foundation stones upon which to build the successful handling of a hostage situation are the ICD building blocks: intelligence, communications, and discipline of firepower.

Evacuation

Once backup arrives, evacuation of the area can begin. Evacuation should be conducted for two reasons: first, so innocent people don't get hurt, and second, so no additional hostages can be taken. The evacuation process may have to be delicately handled because people may not want to leave their homes or offices. Local laws vary as to what police may or may not be able to do other than through the power of persuasion. Forcible evacuation could result in lawsuits, so more often than not, officers must cajole and coax people out of the area. Most people will cooperate, especially if they are faced with the possibility of a group of terrorists roaming through a building or marauding around a neighborhood accumulating hostages. Evacuation should be orderly, with all people accounted for and listed by office or street address or some other logical manner. The evacuees should be taken to a safe place so they don't mill around or be tempted to reenter, but also so they can be interrogated and perhaps provide some intelligence about the hostages and how the situation developed. Care should be taken during the evacuation because perpetrators or perhaps accomplices and lookouts may be exiting the scene. In more than one instance, criminals were shooed away by overzealous officers clearing an area of civilians. It is important to discern whether the incident is a hostage situation or just an individual who has barricaded himself or herself.

A barricade situation does not have the same urgency. In fact, there is no urgency at all. Hypothetically, the perpetrator could be kept isolated for weeks if necessary. In a hostage situation, however, there is a greater urgency because of the concern for the safety of the hostages. When innocent people are taken hostage, the police are expected to take greater risks and chances in attempting to rescue them. If there is any doubt as to whether or not there are hostages, then police must assume there is a hostage until it is proven otherwise.

Keeping Track of People

An example that illustrates the importance of accounting for everyone involved in an evacuation is demonstrated by firefighters who routinely search a burning building. Although it is dangerous, the firefighters look for people who may be trapped by fire, were overcome by smoke, or who are otherwise still in the building. In this particular instance, police and firefighters were working together at the scene of a warehouse fire. At one point a lone fireman, burnt and injured, stumbled out of the building. Two police officers came to his assistance and sent him to the hospital in an ambulance. No fire department personnel were notified. A short time later, a fire lieutenant and three firefighters exited the building. When they counted noses, they realized one of their members was missing and assumed he was still inside the burning building. Intent on finding him, they reentered the building, only to be trapped inside when the structure collapsed. All four were killed.

As a result of this tragedy, police department rules require that no firefighters be removed from the scene of a fire without permission of the fire chief at the scene. The same care and caution must be exercised when building searches and evacuations are conducted in hostage situations.

Start Intelligence Gathering

As more backup arrives, some of the officers can be gathering intelligence. Remember the ICD building blocks:

1. Intelligence
2. Communication
3. Discipline of firepower

The intelligence gathering begins with trying to find out exactly what is taking place. This information should be communicated as quickly, as concisely, and as accurately as possible to the communications or radio dispatcher, who in turn can relay it to other responding officers and supervisors. There will be a constant demand on the officers to brief and update the others who are responding. More importantly, they are going to be asked repeatedly to brief responding higher-ranking officers, who will then brief other responding officers. Later, we will explore methods of quick information transfer in the form of time bar charts.

Inner Perimeter

Once the evacuation is completed, or at least in its final stages, a perimeter must be established. This inner perimeter should be free of anybody who does not have a need to be there. Establishing this inner perimeter makes it easier to identify the principals involved, and to maintain control of the perpetrators and the situation. The area should be defined by police. It is not always feasible to rope off or tape off the area, but the reference should be transmitted to all at the scene. The area and its reference points should also be recorded at the command post so later arrivals can be briefed.

Police positions within the inner perimeter should be taken by officers wearing bullet-resistant garments, and carrying appropriate weaponry and sufficient communications equipment on the designated or tactical channel. If a mobilization point was not established earlier, or if the first mobilization point was not in the best of locations, this would be the time to designate a more suitable location to which manpower and equipment can respond. The mobilization point should be convenient, but it should also be concealed, situated in such a way that the perpetrator cannot observe the assembling officers and equipment.

Tactical Units

Tactical units are dispatched and deployed to replace the backup officers who responded initially and helped establish the inner perimeter. This is, of course, assuming the department is large enough to have the luxury of specialized units. When this change is made, the officers who initially responded and have been replaced should report to the command post, where they can be debriefed as rapidly as is practical, so as much information as possible can be gleaned and disseminated quickly. This will supplement and confirm other intelligence reports and pinpoint areas of uncertainty, such as the number of hostages, number of hostage takers, types of weapons, etc. If, for example, there are reports of sighting seven people in garments of seven different colors, this could be any combination of perpetrators and hostages, but there can be reasonable certainty that seven people are involved, unless there is reason to believe that a deliberate attempt to mislead and confuse is being made.

Communications

In addition to intelligence, the other touchstones of a hostage incident procedure plan are communication and discipline of firepower. As early as possible, a communications frequency should be established on which all communications related to the particular incident will be carried. In jurisdictions that have several frequencies, one may already be designated for emergency or tactical use. In those areas where a good deal of interaction exists between different agencies, a networking frequency may be employed. Often there is one frequency, usually statewide, that is used as a repeater system that permits police agencies throughout the state to be on one frequency should they have to interact and work on an incident together.

There have been disastrous situations, such as the one that occurred in New Orleans in 1973, in which a number of police agencies were involved in a hostage situation. In this case, there was no common communication frequency among the three different police agencies responding. Although they tried to cooperate, they started shooting at each other because one group was unaware of the location of another agency in the building. Several officers were wounded or killed, many by friendly fire, some by their own ricocheting bullets.

To ensure that there is a thorough understanding of communications, one of the things to be considered is the nuance of language. This will be covered later.

First Response Review

The duties and responsibilities of the first officers on the scene are:

1. Gather cursory information as quickly as possible on what is taking place.
2. Call for backup.
3. Evacuate the area in an orderly fashion.
4. Communicate intelligence as rapidly and as accurately as possible, noting the safest approach routes.
5. Establish a mobilization point.
6. As backup arrives, establish an inner perimeter.
7. Upon being relieved, become an intelligence source.

For the initial responding officer, there is no urgent need to begin negotiations or even to converse with the perpetrator. Doing so, in fact, may lead to some problems. Deadlines may be set and the hostage taker's clock may start ticking before reinforcements arrive on the scene, a negotiator is available, tactical people are in place, and commanders are on hand to make decisions. Certainly the best course of action for the first responding officer is to wait until a trained negotiator is on the scene. A second problem that could develop if negotiations are begun prematurely is that the perpetrator may not be confined to the smallest possible area. This can be done only when containment units are in place. If the hostage taker has mobility, negotiations will not be fruitful.

Summary

There are four types of hostage takers:

1. Professional criminals who are interrupted or trapped during the commission of another crime
2. Inadequate personalities, persons with psychological problems who want to air some grievance or otherwise attract attention to themselves
3. Loose-knit groups, such as prison or jail inmates
4. Tight-knit and well-organized groups, such as terrorists

Hostages are taken because they provide the hostage taker with a bargaining chip or a forum for making a statement. Terrorists use hijacking and hostage taking as a means of gathering publicity and wide media exposure, which in turn help them attract new recruits to their organizations and raise funds for their causes. The interconnected relationship of money, manpower, and media is called the magic triangle.

While there may be persons killed during the initial stages of a hostage-taking incident, it is rare that anyone is harmed once the hostage takers have established control. In fact, if a hostage is killed after the initial takeover and period of power consolidation, it evinces depraved minds on the part of the perpetrators. If they killed once, they could kill again. However, if there are mitigating circumstances indicating that the killed hostages might have contributed to their own demise, this, in turn, lessens the probability that the perpetrators are depraved.

The first officers responding to a crime scene involving the taking of hostages have a number of duties and responsibilities. The one thing they should not do, however, is begin negotiations with hostage takers unless this is unavoidable. The commanding officers at a hostage-taking incident should not participate directly in the negotiating. The negotiator's job is to establish a relationship with and communicate with the hostage taker; the commander's job is to maintain control of the situation and make decisions involving all of the police personnel at the scene of the incident. The key elements to a successful resolution of a hostage incident are summarized in the acronym ICD: intelligence, communication, and discipline of firepower.

Though the principles here are basic and still totally relevant, technology has advanced exponentially. One of the most significant in intelligence gathering is IBM and Dimension Data's contribution to the Real time Crime Centers (RTCC) for the New York and Houston police departments. Data are used from criminal, parole and probation records, local crime complaints, arrests summonses, 911 and 311 calls, 30 million criminal records and 33 billion public records. It is staffed and available for inquiries 24/7. Before negotiators get to the scene of a hostage situation, the information about the location and persons involved may be made available. This blended with current interviews of witnesses and family of the perpetrator and victims enhances the life saving efforts of the police.

Kidnapping

6

Kidnapping as a Weapon

Kidnapping is another favored weapon in the arsenal of terrorists. The crime can be used as a fund-raising device in the form of ransom payment, for extortion by trading the release of the victim for some specific goal or action, or simply as a publicity event to thrust the kidnappers' organization and cause into the headlines and onto television screens. Kidnapping has been especially favored by terrorist groups in Italy, Ireland, Central and South America, and the Middle East. Second-generation terrorist groups also tend to make frequent use of kidnapping. These are groups that may trace their origins to political causes or ethnic or national freedom efforts, but have since lost their ideological orientation—though not necessarily the rhetoric—and have become merely self-indulgent criminal terrorists.

In Colombia, narcoterrorist gangs have been engaging in wholesale kidnapping, seizing large numbers of victims from the same company or group of companies. After certain sums are paid, a few victims are released and more ransom demanded. In Africa, large numbers of United Nations personnel have been captured and held for ransom by rebel forces. Ransom demands include everything from supplies to the removal of United Nations troops from a certain territory. In India, a nationally popular film actor was kidnapped by a dissident group in order to force the government to yield to its demands.

More recently, the Mexican drug cartels have been engaging in kidnapping and abductions of police officers and politicians or their families. Some of this activity has extended into the United States. Phoenix, Arizona, has been hit with low-level victims being targeted. The police have established kidnap incident teams that respond to the large number of incidents. There were 368 reported kidnappings in 2008, but the number has tapered off since then.

Risks Involved

Kidnapping falls somewhere between bombs/bombing incidents and hijacking/hostage taking in the degree of risk involved for the perpetrators.

Terrorists planting bombs, because of the availability of inexpensive timing or delay devices, run very little risk of being identified or apprehended. Hostage taking or hijacking, on the other hand, is an action designed to precipitate a confrontation during which the terrorists will identify their cause and organization. It is also likely that each member will be identified individually.

This was demonstrated most dramatically on September 13, 1987, when the Federal Bureau of Investigation (FBI), after extensive investigation, was able to identify a Lebanese man, Fawaz Youonis, who was involved in a Jordanian hijacking incident in which two Americans were killed. On the promise of women and drugs, he was lured to an undercover U.S. ship in international waters in the Mediterranean in what is popularly referred to as a sting operation. He was arrested and brought to the United States to stand trial. He was convicted and sentenced to 30 years. This confirms the operational belief that those involved in hijacking and hostage incidents run a good chance of being captured or apprehended, if the incident comes to a peaceful conclusion, and wounded or killed, if it comes to a violent end.

The risk for victims is the opposite. Hostage victims are rarely killed by the perpetrators because they have more value alive than dead. Kidnappers, on the other hand, often intend to kill their victims from the outset, having dug the hole or bought the quicklime even before abducting the unfortunate victim.

Differences between Hostage Taking and Kidnapping

It is important that persons working with or within the criminal justice system are able to distinguish between hostage taking and kidnapping. Kidnapping is the surreptitious taking and holding of a person or persons for the purpose of achieving some personal or organizational gain. In the case of terrorists, that gain may be strictly monetary, or it could be to force some course of action or to obstruct some course of action on the part of a government, a governmental agency, a private corporation, or some other group or organization. In all instances, a secondary goal of the terrorists is to attract media and public attention to themselves.

Kidnapping exposes the terrorists to a lesser risk, primarily because this type of incident lacks the confrontational aspects of hostage situations. The kidnappers have mobility and anonymity unless they choose to make their identities known. Except for the ransom note, telephone call, e-mail, or other electronic communication, no one has any idea who or where the perpetrators are. Neither is there any way of knowing, in fact, whether or not they actually have the victim. For this reason, the kidnap victim is always in very grave danger.

Also, it is not unusual for a successful kidnap investigation to grow into a hostage situation before the incident is concluded. This is exactly what happened in Ireland when members of the Irish Republican Army kidnapped Jennifer Guinness of the Guinness brewery family in April 1986. Police tracked the culprits to a cottage in the countryside where they were holding the woman. Once the location of the victim and the perpetrator became known, it was obviously possible for a confrontation to take place between the perpetrators and the law enforcement investigators. In hindsight, the agencies investigating the abduction should have notified their tactical units during the early stages of the investigation, because it appeared that apprehension or confrontation was an inevitable consequence. This information should have been communicated to the tactical commander, which would have helped him or her move personnel to more practical or convenient locations. These locations, of course, should have been clandestine enough that they did not call attention to the number of armed personnel being assembled. The heiress was released April 8, 1986, following the siege. We discuss more on the differences between a hostage victim and a kidnap victim in Chapter 12.

In spite of media and popular use of the word *hostage* to describe various foreign nationals, and sometimes fellow citizens, abducted in Lebanon, Colombia, and other nations around the world, these incidents are more often kidnappings. This is because there is no confrontation between authorities and abductors. A kidnap victim is held hostage. The difference lies in knowing the whereabouts of the perpetrators and their victim in the latter instances, and their unknown whereabouts in the former.

Uses of Kidnapping

Kidnapping, like bombing, is often used to make a statement or register a protest. The victim may be symbolic (i.e., associated with a government, corporation, or organization that is somehow associated with the wrong side of the kidnappers' cause), or the victim may be virtually unknown to the public but still valuable to a government, corporation, or other organization, and thus might have a high ransom value.

It is difficult to determine why kidnapping has not been used to a very great extent by terrorists and radicals operating inside the United States. Most likely, U.S. terrorists have alternative means of achieving publicity aims and raising funds. In addition, the mystique of the FBI's success in tracking down kidnappers may serve as a deterrent.

Members of the media, long believing they were considered neutral, because that is how they are treated in the United States and a few other countries, have become targets. In the years since 9/11, the media have been suffering the devastation of having to list the ever-growing number of casualties.

In European, Middle Eastern, Latin American, and Pacific Rim countries, kidnapping may be a more popular terrorist tactic because there are fewer publicity opportunities for terrorists to call attention to themselves. As for fund-raising, banks in most countries are much more security conscious than in the United States, where the banks are very consumer oriented and emphasize customer service over security. In addition, outside the United States, relatively fewer opportunities exist to rob armored cars or retail establishments with large amounts of cash.

Types of Kidnappers

Kidnappers can be grouped into four categories:

1. Criminal
2. Professional
3. Political (including post-Cold War)
4. Abduction/domestic spousal confrontation or emotionally disturbed persons

Criminal Kidnappings

Criminal kidnappings are committed by persons attempting a one-shot effort at extracting a large sum of money from the family, friends, associates, or employer of a wealthy or well-connected individual. Kidnappings falling into this category include the Lindbergh baby in the mid-1930s; the December 1968 case involving Barbara Mackle, daughter of a wealthy Florida real estate developer; the 1973 abduction of Reg Murphy, the publisher of the *Atlanta Constitution* newspaper; the 1978 incident involving an entire bus full of schoolchildren in Chowchilla, California; the January 1987 case of Stephen Small, the heir to a publishing fortune in the Midwest; cases in 1992 involving the abduction of a 10-year-old girl by a child molester on Long Island; and the kidnappings of Exxon oil executive Sidney J. Reso in New Jersey in 1992 and wealthy clothing manufacturer Harvey Weinstein in Queens, New York, in 1993.

All of these were kidnappings motivated by criminal intent and perpetrated by amateur criminals. There are those who believe the Lindbergh baby was dead by the time he left his parents' yard, or not long afterward. Barbara Mackle, abducted from her college dormitory, was buried in a box two feet below ground level, given two ventilation pipes, a small amount of water, and a small, battery-operated fan. Acting on a tip, authorities located and rescued her after more than three days. The California schoolchildren were buried in a truck trailer. Only because the bus driver was able to dig his way out were the children rescued and the perpetrators apprehended. Stephen Small was not so fortunate, for although his kidnappers provided air vents, water, and a light, he was dead by the time police got to him.

In a more recent case, on April 29, 1992, Sidney Reso was kidnapped from his car while still in the driveway of his home, by a former police officer who was working in a security position at Exxon, Arthur Seale, and his wife, Irene (Jackie) Seale. This was done after a tremendous amount of research into the habits of the victim. Reso was subdued and immediately placed in a large wooden box that had been constructed just for this purpose. The box was loaded into a rented van. Reso was held in that box, aboveground, at Secure Storage, a self-store facility, until May 3, 1992, when he was found dead by the kidnappers when they came to feed him. They buried his body in a shallow grave. They could have walked away with almost complete certainty of not being detected or apprehended. Instead, their greed for the ransom contributed to their apprehension by the FBI. They were eventually convicted and incarcerated.

On August 4, 1993, Harvey Weinstein, a well-liked maker of men's formal wear, was kidnapped as he left the diner where he ate breakfast every day. A few weeks prior to the incident, two brothers, one a former employee of Weinstein's, had found a sump manhole in a secluded area off a parkway along the Hudson River in New York City. After finding the location, they decided to undertake a kidnapping and selected Weinstein. He would be held there undiscovered for almost two weeks. During the ransom drop, the perpetrators were apprehended and the detectives, who had been given the approximate location, spent a considerable amount of time before locating the victim, tired, but alive and well. Weinstein, a former Marine who fought at Iwo Jima in World War II, was recovered from the hole by two detectives. All he did was ask them for a cigarette. Weinstein died May 13, 2007, at the age of 82. One of the kidnappers, Aurelina Leonard, who made many of the ransom calls, was paroled in 2011 after serving the minimum time of her 18-years-to-life sentence.

From December 29, 1992, through early January 1993 on New York's Long Island, pedophile John Esposito held a 10-year-old girl prisoner. He had constructed a virtual prison cell under his driveway with an entry shaft through a closet that was so secretive the police, executing search warrants, missed the entrance on two occasions. When the pedophile was arrested as a material witness and incarcerated, he told his lawyer (who was about to leave on vacation) that he had the child secreted in the cell. He realized the child might die of starvation. Esposito would eventually lead the police to the location and unlock the mysterious entrance of rugs, linoleum, cement cover, and block and tackle. The girl was alive and well.

The common trait in all these cases is that the perpetrators have the option of producing the victim if they have to in order to provide the veracity to their claims, or to walk away from the whole incident if they get cold feet or the police investigation gets too close for comfort. There have been a number of long-term abductions of young, and some prepubescent, girls:

Elizabeth Smart

On June 5, 2002, late at night, 14-year-old Elizabeth Smart was kidnapped from her bedroom, in Salt Lake City, Utah, which she shared with her younger sister, Mary Katherine. The perpetrator, Brian Mitchell, took her to a wooded area some distance from her home, where he and his female companion, Wanda Ileen Barzee, had been camping. Barzee informed Elizabeth that Mitchell, a self-described profit called Emmanuel, would take her as his second wife. She stripped Elizabeth and had her put on a robe of sorts. It was later learned that Mitchell was one of many homeless people that the Smart family had been trying to help by giving them day work at their home from time to time.

When the younger sister was initially interviewed by the police, her description and information did not seem credible (perhaps she was still in a state of shock), and she was not considered a good witness. After a few months, the younger daughter told her family that she had heard the voice of the abductor before. She said it sounded like "Emmanuel," who worked at the house. The family had Mary Katherine describe the abductor to a sketch artist they had hired. With the aid of *America's Most Wanted*, the sketch was made public. Mitchell was spotted by a person who recognized him from the sketch on TV about 18 miles from the Smart residence. There were two females with Mitchell. When police responded and interviewed Mitchell and the females, they were able to identify Elizabeth, even though she had been made to wear a red wig and sunglasses, and was now affected by the Stockholm syndrome. From this example we can see that follow-up interviews are very important.

Jaycee Lee Dugard

On June 10, 1991, at South Lake Tahoe, California, Carl Probyn, the stepfather of 11-year-old Jaycee Lee Dugard, observed a gray car make a U-turn at the school bus stop within sight of her home, where Jaycee was waiting. A woman forced Jaycee in the car and it drove off. Probyn grabbed a bicycle and gave chase but was unable to catch up and lost sight of the vehicle. Within hours of the abduction the media swamped the area. Local volunteers searched the area and took part in various fund-raisers over the following weeks, to cover the cost of photos and posters of Jaycee. The National Center for Missing and Exploited Children and other agencies offered assistance. Weeks went into months, then years. The story was covered many times by *America's Most Wanted*. Initially both Probyn, the stepfather, and Jaycee's biological father were acknowledged suspects, but both were cleared. The marriage of Probyn to Jaycee's mother fell victim to the abduction as well.

Phillip Craig Garrido, a convicted sex offender who had served time for kidnapping and rape, with his wife, Nancy Garrido, abducted Jaycee using the car described by the stepfather. In a previous case, Garrido had been evaluated as a "sexual deviant" by a court-ordered examination. He was on probation at various times during the more than 18 years that this event lasted. At one point he was returned to prison for a parole violation for five months in 1993. During that time, apparently Nancy Garrido guarded Jaycee. The young girl was held prisoner at the Garridos' home in Antioch, California, in the rear yard. The yard had a high privacy fence, large trees, and there were outbuildings in the back with a lot of "junk" strewn around. There were tarpaulins and a makeshift shower and toilet, covered by tarps as well. One of the outbuildings was soundproofed. It had been used by Garrido as a recording studio. During her captivity, Jaycee was raped at various times. Jaycee had two daughters from these encounters. One was born in August 1994 and the second in November 1997. Both children were delivered without outside medical assistance. Neither Jaycee nor her two children had ever seen a doctor or attended school. During the early period of captivity they had little interaction with people in the outside world. Later, after the children were born, there were many times where Jaycee did have interaction with people in the outside world, even, at one time, working in the Garridos' business office.

During the time of Jaycee's captivity, there were a number of occasions where the authorities responding to the Garrido house missed opportunities that might have led to her being found there.

On August 24, 2009, when Phillip Garrido showed up at the University of California, Berkley with the two children, asking permission to distribute religious pamphlets, the official became suspicious of the situation and told him to return the next day to speak with someone who could grant permission. A campus police officer did a background check on Garrido and sat in on the meeting. She noticed the odd behavior of the girls. Notification was made to the parole office. A home visit was made by the parole officers, and they brought Garrido to their office. There, he told the PO that the two girls were daughters of a relative and that he had permission to be with them. Though they had a prohibition of him being with children, they didn't violate him. They told him to report to the officer the next day. He showed up with his wife, Nancy, and Jaycee, whom he introduced as "Alyssa." The girls who were at Berkley with Garrido were there too, calling Garrido "Daddy."

During the interview, Alyssa (Jaycee) said that she was the girls' mother. After a series of false statements by Jaycee, Phillip Garrido, and Nancy Garrido, during which time Jaycee was particularly evasive, questions remained. It was only after detectives broke Phillip Garrido's story that Jaycee finally admitted her identity and that she was kidnapped and raped. This was an extreme example of the Stockholm syndrome. Jaycee's two daughters, fathered by Garrido, also had problems, because Garrido was the only father they had ever known. Jaycee has custody of the two girls.

In July 2010, the State of California granted a $20 million settlement to Jaycee Lee Dugard for her claims of the state's lapses in dealing with her kidnapper.

Elisabeth Fritzi

These weird cases are not limited to the United States. The Elisabeth Fritzi case is about a father sexually abusing one of his daughters. In Amstetten, Austria, near Vienna, Josef Fritzi started abusing his 11-year-old daughter. After she ran away from home, she was found and returned to her parents. The mother, Rosemarie, was never aware of the abuse. In August 1984, Josef lured his now 17-year-old daughter into the basement of their home on a ruse. There he drugged her and started a captivity that lasted 24 years in a custom-made secret dungeon that Josef had constructed secretly under their home. During this time he raped her and fathered seven children. Elisabeth and three children lived in these sparse living quarters. One child had died, and the other three were taken into the household as foundlings. After 24 years, when one of the children in the dungeon became ill, Elisabeth convinced her father to take the child to the hospital. That started the events that led to the police discovering what had taken place. Josef Fritzi pleaded guilty during the fourth day of his trial.

In each of these cases there may have been opportunities that were missed by the authorities, whether it be reinterviews, enlarged canvasses, or greater background checks.

Professional Kidnappings

Professional kidnappings are carried out by a more or less organized group that uses kidnapping as a source of revenue. The Mafia in Sicily and other parts of Italy, guerrilla groups in Latin America, and the Irish Republican Army have all operated in this way. Quite often the victims are employed by or are principals of large, usually foreign, corporations; they are kidnapped in the hope that the company will pay a huge ransom. One American oil company did pay $14 million to ransom one of its executives who was kidnapped in Latin America. One of the distinguishing characteristics of a professional kidnapping is that the victim is almost always returned alive. As professionals, these kidnappers expect to keep doing business and maintain their credibility by releasing victims in exchange for ransom. Professional operatives do not always limit their activities to people, abducting and holding for ransom everything from valuable racehorses to priceless artwork.

Among the areas where professional kidnapping is prevalent is the island of Sardinia off the west coast of Italy. Here the per capita rate of kidnapping was once the highest in the world. Criminal groups in Sardinia research the financial resources of potential victims, and ransom demands are scaled according to the family's ability to pay. The amount is high enough to make the enterprise worthwhile, but still low enough that the family has little trouble meeting the demand. If there is an initial resistance to meeting the demand, a finger or ear of the victim may be severed and sent to the family as an inducement to pay the ransom.

A curious side effect of the success of the Sardinian kidnappers and the political kidnappings of the Red Brigade in the 1970s and 1980s was that the Mafia became active in trying to organize the kidnapping industry on mainland Italy by streamlining procedures and codifying behavior.

By the end of 2009 and into 2010, Phoenix, Arizona, was plagued with a tremendous increase in kidnappings. Some were calling Phoenix the new kidnapping capital of the world. These crimes were fueled by Mexican drug and immigrant-smuggling gangs. The Phoenix Police Department had to establish additional kidnap investigative teams to keep up with the influx of the reported kidnappings. No doubt, many more incidents have gone unreported, especially by illegal immigrants who may have been victimized.

Political Kidnappings

Political kidnappings are designed to create incidents that put pressure on governments or political parties, and are usually conducted by terrorist gangs adept at exploiting the accompanying media coverage. The kidnappings can be accomplished with either long-term or short-term gains in mind. In Madras, India, on August 3, 2000, there was a political kidnapping of the popular film star Rajkumar by Tamil kidnappers who were led by a man named Veerappan. In addition to demands for amnesty and $12 million, the abductors also included political demands, such as referring territorial disputes involving Tamil Nadu to the International Court of Justice and making Tamil the sole language used in schools in the Indian state of Tamil Nadu.

Long-term kidnapping has been used to a large extent by Islamic fundamentalists in Lebanon, who have at various times kidnapped American, British, French, and West German nationals and held them for long periods of time, stockpiling them, so to speak, to be used as bargaining chips at some future time. It has been reported that Libyan leader Muamar Khaddafy attempted to buy kidnap victims from Lebanese-based terrorists. Most victims of political kidnappings have been released in order to effect specific propaganda ends, although a number have been killed for the same purpose.

Short-term political kidnappings include such notorious crimes as the abduction and murder of Italian politician Aldo Moro by the Red Brigade; the kidnapping and killing of Hans-Martin Schleyer, head of the West German Federation of Industries, by the Baader-Meinhof Gang; and the kidnapping of U.S. Army General William Dozier in Italy.

The Moro kidnapping was a classic terrorist operation. Moro was head of the ruling political party in Italy and in line to possibly become president of the country. On March 16, 1978, after Moro attended Mass as usual, he was sitting in the back of his limousine reading a newspaper en route to Parliament. His driver and bodyguard were in the front seat, while an Alfa Romeo with three security agents followed. As described in the book *Political Terrorism:*[1]

> Just before crossing the Via Stresa, a white Fiat sedan with diplomatic license plates cut in front of Moro's car, forcing the driver to brake hard. His escort car ran into the back of his car. The passengers in the white Fiat leaped out of their car as if to see whether their car had been damaged, then drew pistols and shot Moro's driver and bodyguard, killing both instantly. Four men in Alitalia uniforms, who were standing on the corner as if waiting for a bus, now drew automatic weapons from their flight bags and fired at the Alfa Romeo, killing all three policemen. Moro was dragged from his car, unharmed, and thrust into a waiting blue Fiat. A blonde woman wearing a scarf and a man had been watching the operation with interest. Now they climbed into a car and smoothly formed part of the convoy of three escape vehicles. The entire episode took 30 seconds.
>
> A few minutes later, a woman standing on her balcony overlooking Via Casale de Bustis, a road barred to general traffic, watched as two cream Fiats with a blue Fiat in between, paused at the padlocked chain while a blonde woman calmly cut the chain with long-handled clippers and returned to her car. That was the last ever seen of Aldo Moro alive.
>
> … That morning false bomb reports had diverted police to Fiumicino airport and the Piazza Cavour; the telephone system of Monte Mario was mysteriously put out of action for fifteen minutes after the attack; the man who sold flowers at the intersection where the kidnapping took place had wakened that morning to find the four tires of his small station wagon slashed and had not come to work; the diplomatic license plates of the decoy car were found to have been stolen from the Venezuelan embassy over a year before; and the getaway cars were equipped with police sirens.

Although Moro was held for 54 days and wrote more than 50 letters during his captivity before being killed, the terrorists failed in their goal of preventing the trial of 49 members of the Red Brigade and winning their release from jail. Likewise, the abduction and murder of Hans-Martin Schleyer failed to win terrorists what they said was their stated goal: the release of jailed members of the Baader-Meinhof Gang.

The General William Dozier kidnapping proceeded even worse, as far as the terrorists were concerned, for he was rescued, somewhat beleaguered but otherwise unharmed, mainly through the cooperation of various Italian police agencies and U.S. Armed Forces intelligence units. (One of the reasons kidnapping occurred with such frequency in Italy during the 1970s and 1980s was the organizational chaos created by interagency squabbles among various units handling the Red Brigade, as well as other terrorists and kidnappings. It is a negative case in point on the importance of preincident interagency liaison.) The treatment of General Dozier offers another insight into what terrorist kidnappers will do to a political victim. During his incarceration, the general was kept in a tent that had been pitched inside an apartment, all in an effort to disorient him. He was also forced to wear headphones, through which loud music was blasted at all times, so he would be unable to pick up ambient sounds that might help him identify his location or his captors.

Domestic Spousal Confrontation/Emotionally Disturbed Persons

Disputes involving spouses sometimes escalate into kidnappings. Statistical data indicate that there have been more than 3,000 cases of parental kidnapping of children when the other spouse was awarded legal custody. In some instances, the marriage is between persons of significantly different cultures with conflicts and difficulties exacerbating normal marital differences. Often children in such cases are removed from one country to another. In many cases, there are no reciprocal agreements and marital disputes are considered so low level in importance as to be lost in diplomatic channels.

Abductions of infants from hospital maternity wards are most often carried out by persons with an emotional disturbance, such as a woman who either never had a child or had a child who died. The motivation in these cases may be understandable, but the action is still illegal. The importance of websites, such as that of the National Center for Missing and Exploited Children or the FBI's list at http://fbi.gov.mostwant/kidnap/kidmiss.htm, can be useful tools in kidnapping incidents. In one recent incident, while looking at a website that displayed photos of missing or exploited children, a teenage boy saw his own picture. That would eventually lead to the arrest of the only mother he had ever known.

There also have been an increasing number of kidnappings of babies from the wombs of pregnant women. After killing the woman, the assailant, usually another woman, cuts the baby from the mother in a crude Caesarean procedure.

Post-Cold War Political Kidnapping

For a long time, political kidnapping was mainly a Latin American phenomenon, with a few isolated incidents in Europe. Colombian terrorists were among the most adept. When selecting targets, they would conduct thorough financial analyses and background checks of potential victims and their connections, family or business. They would look not only at banking information, but also check tax returns to determine the amount of ransom to be demanded. By the 1990s, with increased interest by tourists and businesses in Asian and Pacific Rim countries, kidnapping became a means to support the political aims of new dissident groups. Many of these groups were comprised of former military people and so-called freedom fighters who were no longer able to make a living or support their families. Other kidnappers were members of radical religious groups or rebel factions looking to have colleagues released from jails and prisons.

In the Pacific Rim area, groups like Abu Sayyaf have conducted "group kidnappings" in an effort not only to discredit or embarrass the Philippine government, but also to finance their own political enterprise. One of the most notable cases involved an American couple from Kansas. Martin and Gracia Burnham were missionaries in the area.

In May 2001, they were celebrating their eighteenth wedding anniversary at Dos Palmas, a resort in the southern Philippines. They were abducted with a group of other people in a boat and landed five days later on the island of Basilan. During the course of many months of captivity in the steaming jungles, life was very difficult and primitive. They were forced to endure long marches and to dodge bullets during gun battles between their captors and government troops trying to rescue them.

During the course of this ordeal the Abu Sayyaf would release videos of the Burnhams and others. This apparently was done to demonstrate their power and confirm the holding of their hostages. Some of the hostages were released over the weeks and months of the prolonged incident. The kidnappers made contact with members of the Burnham family via hostages who were released after their families had paid ransoms. Church friends and relatives of the Burnhams in Kansas raised monies that Martin Burnham's father would pay in March 2002. It was reported that $300,000 was paid, but the Burnhams were not released. A representative of Abu Sayyaf said the monies had gone to a rival group and demanded another $200,000.

On June 7, 2002, Philippine military units on a rescue mission engaged the kidnappers in a firefight. During that rescue, Martin Burnham and another hostage, a Filipino nurse, were killed. Gracia Burnham was seriously wounded, but recovered and returned home to the United States.

Other political kidnappings include a rash of abductions of multinational oil workers from rigs in the Nigerian delta in Africa. These kidnappings have been carried out by Nigerians who maintain that the government is not letting the general population share in the riches being pumped out of the Nigerian oil fields. Islamic fundamentalists have used similar tactics in the Middle East, kidnapping foreign workers and demanding ransom or some political actions by foreign governments.

An ever-continuing conflict exists between the Chechen leaders and the government of Russia. In addition to forays by Chechen rebels, or freedom fighters, depending upon one's perspective, into Russia itself to carry out suicide bombings and killings, they have stormed a border village, killing nine Russian border guards. In this same raid, they entered a hospital and took a large number of patients and workers hostage. Similar incidents, though usually on a smaller scale, continue to the present.

Kidnapping during and after the U.S. Operation in Iraq

"Where there is no order, there is no law," the saying goes. In the months after official hostilities ended in Iraq in 2003, and continuing on a smaller scale after authority was returned to Iraqis themselves days before the June 30, 2004, deadline the U.S. government had set for itself, there was a good deal of disorder as criminal and insurgent elements of the population utilized kidnapping to terrorize the nation and countries around the world. At its height, Iraqi police estimated that there was an onslaught of child kidnapping, at a rate of one child per day in and around Baghdad. Most of the victims were children of middle-class or affluent families. Exact figures are unavailable, often because the snatches were not reported to the newly established police organizations. The population, accustomed to tribal justice, distrusted the new Western-style law enforcement. They were afraid that during a rescue attempt their loved ones might be killed either by the kidnappers or accidentally by the would-be rescuers. The United States continues to supply local police with training and equipment to deal with this criminal activity.

Private Industry's Role in Combating Kidnapping

Private industry and private security companies can play major roles in effectively combating terrorist activity with regard to kidnapping. The single most important responsibility is to train executives and other key or sensitive individuals in the corporation about how to avoid becoming a kidnap or hostage victim. This falls under the larger umbrella of hardening the target, as discussed earlier.

A second major important consideration is the formation of a crisis management team (CMT) that includes not only terrorist-related incidents, but also other crises, such as natural disasters and industrial accidents. Although there may be some overlapping, it does not mean that the same individuals will bear the same responsibilities in each category. For example, in a kidnapping, many decisions will have to be made based on little information or fragmented information at best, rather than the usual detailed analysis.

There are many private organizations, such as insurance companies, that hire specialists to negotiate ransom prices down. Control Risks and Risks International are two such companies, in addition to the Ackerman Group, Kroll Associates, and the Pinkerton Group. There are also many other businesses and individuals who serve as crisis managers. These private sources, who charge substantial fees, nevertheless have ever-growing client lists, in part because their analyses can be more blunt than those of government agencies, like the State Department, for example. Government agencies, admittedly or not, are influenced by treaties or trade agreements, or both, and may hesitate to publicize dangers for Americans traveling or working in certain countries or regions. The common experience has been that terrorist kidnappers will ask for the moon, but they are willing and fully expect to negotiate down from there. The official policy of the U.S. government is that it will not negotiate with terrorists; however, in diplomatic language, talking is not the same thing as negotiating. Neither will the U.S. government pay ransoms, but it may very well assist a family in paying ransom. An incorrect way of dealing with kidnappers was carried out by a Canadian businessman in 1999, when he actually exchanged himself for an employee who was being held by a South American gang.

The running of training exercises or role-playing "games," conducted by either in-house security staff or contracted professional kidnap organizations, will assist the CMT in decision making in the event of a real crisis or kidnapping. In addition, the lessons learned may assist in avoiding or at least mitigating any possible litigation from affected employees or families should any unforeseen tragedy take place.

The Police Role in Kidnappings

When a kidnapping is reported, it is preferred that marked police cars or police officers in uniform not respond. Kidnappers usually include in their ransom demand a warning not to notify the police. Well-organized kidnappers have had homes and businesses under surveillance just to see whether the police have been called. Such surveillance is more likely to occur when terrorists are involved, because those groups are more likely to have a bigger and better organized cadre than most amateurs perpetrating a criminal kidnapping.

Noting the exact time of a ransom call can be important. Sometimes the local phone company can "dump" its billing computer, although this can be expensive, and go backward from the telephone on which the ransom call or other communication was received in order to determine where the incoming call originated. Wireless providers may also be able to ascertain the identity of the cell phone from which the call was made. Follow-up investigation may allow the locations of that cell phone to be determined. However, many perpetrators resort to the use of prepaid, throwaway devices.

In dealing with kidnappers or hostage takers, there is a significant difference between being the individual cop and being the government. It is unimportant if an individual police officer is embarrassed, but it is a major concern should the embarrassment be upon the government of the United States or Germany or Colombia or any other country. Police in countries where there is a national police force have to balance compassion and strength when dealing with their own citizens. Civil rights must be respected, even if the individual is rebellious or a notorious criminal. In dealing with outside terrorists or those who would tear down the country, however, a harsher stance must be taken, with appropriate precautions, so the government does not appear to be repressive. The objective is to avoid being pushed into an extreme position, as urban guerrillas have been counseled to do. This is precisely what Carlos Marighella indicated in his *Minimanual of the Urban Guerrilla*.

Police Response to Residence or Workplace of Victim

Who the first responders will be may very well depend on how the report of the incident comes to the attention of law enforcement. Most persons will just call 911 or some other emergency number, and in the panic and excitement may not indicate correctly the description and extent of the crime. It is important that dispatchers are trained and aware not to send uniformed members to the location if it appears to be a kidnapping. If the call comes from a business executive or a family member who has been briefed on the potential vulnerability of the victim, it should be directed to the unit designated to handle kidnap investigation. The designated investigators will be mindful of their response procedures. That is why it is important for agencies to designate who will be responsible for a kidnap investigation, preincident, before it occurs.

Many corporations have security or public safety departments headed by former law enforcement personnel. Many times, depending upon the affiliation, the notification will be to their respective "alma maters," with the ex-FBI agent contacting the FBI and a former state or municipal police officer contacting his or her former local agency. This is why it is important to have preincident liaisons between the various agencies.

Many hostage and crisis negotiating teams or units have affiliated themselves in statewide associations, allowing for interagency communication on an informal but effective level. The infrequency of kidnappings and often the lack of specific units to investigate them do not lend themselves to the same type of organizations as negotiators have formed. The benefits of reaching out by investigators to their counterparts in other agencies are immeasurable.

The initial actions of the kidnap response team to the residence or workplace of the kidnap victim will set the pace and may very well affect the outcome of the investigation and the safe recovery of the victim. Many such victims come from affluent or influential families, or both. It is not uncommon for the responding officers to be somewhat in awe of the people and the opulent surroundings of their homes or offices. When the officers arrive on the scene, they must have a take-charge attitude as well as compassion. With the use of checklists to cover the various procedures to follow and tasks to be accomplished, the officers will not have time to be bullied or overly impressed by the principals. While it is natural to have compassion for a mother or father who seems to have lost a child, later investigation may implicate either or both as suspects. However, there may be other instances where the victims come from less affluent backgrounds and live or work in less luxurious circumstances, or come with questionable backgrounds, i.e., drug dealing, gambling, etc. These families, too, must be accorded proper and effective service.

When responding to either the residence or the workplace of the victim, the response team should have unmarked and otherwise nondescript vehicles. If none are available, the response team should park at some distance from the location and walk, to not raise suspicions of accomplices who may be keeping an eye on the location. Of course, the geography of the location will affect how the residence or workplace location is approached.

Family or Friend Response to the Kidnap/Extortion Threat

It is not unreasonable for the family, friends, or associates of a kidnap victim to request verification that the person is actually being held. More often than not, this request will be met. When the first report of kidnapping reaches the business associates, family, and friends of the victim, there is a sense of disbelief, quickly followed by fear and panic. These are part of the tactics kidnappers employ. They want a quick, emotional response to their demands. The first realization should be, however, that it is quite possible the victim is already dead. Or, if no request is made for verification, the victim may be killed as a matter of convenience. It is always wise to request to speak to the victim. Any pretext is acceptable, including the guise that it is assurance that ransom payments will be made to the correct individuals. In addition to verifying that the victim is being held and is still alive, speaking on the telephone helps keep the line of communication open longer, which may prove useful in a subsequent investigation. Even when verification is accomplished with videotape, a live video or video clip, or a picture via a disposable or stolen cell phone, where the victim holds up a newspaper to indicate the date, various opportunities present themselves for the gathering of information, as well as evidence for future prosecution.

The decision whether or not to pay ransom is strictly up to the family, business, or to whomever the demand has been made. Neither the local police nor the FBI will advise one way or the other. If the decision to pay is made, however, most law enforcement agencies will do what they can to assist in accumulating the funds and dropping off the ransom payment. If a large sum of money is involved, be mindful that the perpetrators or some independent criminal might rob the people moving or holding the ransom. In the case of Exxon executive Sidney Reso, the oil company had actually delivered $18.5 million in cash to his home. After it had been there almost a day, someone called attention to the lack of security for such a large sum, and eventually an FBI team was assigned to protect it.

In international kidnappings, terrorist or otherwise, it is the policy of the U.S. government not to pay ransom to anyone. There have been instances, however, when unofficial logistical assistance has been rendered by government agencies.

From time to time, some countries have acquiesced to kidnappers' ransom demands, be it money or some other action or inaction. In July 2004, the Philippine government acquiesced to demands by Islamic fundamentalist kidnappers in Iraq holding a civilian Filipino worker by withdrawing its troops supporting the U.S.-led effort to restore self-government to the country.

During February and March 2003, there were a number of kidnapping incidents in the Sahara Desert involving more than 30 European tourists. In August of that year, 14 tourists were released by their captors, said to be members of an Algerian Islamic organization. Nine of those were German citizens. After their release they were asked by the German Foreign Ministry to pay various amounts of money, ranging from €1,000 to €2,000 to help defray the cost of their rescue. It was reported that Germany had paid a ransom for the hostages. This is something the government has refused to confirm or deny.

A spokesperson for the Foreign Ministry told a news agency that it had always been understood that the former hostages would have to pay something toward the cost of their rescue. The onus seemed to be placed on the hostages, and it was suggested that the tourists should have informed the authorities of their planned route before they set out without guides. Rainer Bracht, a former hostage, put it very clearly in an interview with the German media: "If I was taken captive on a tram in Bremen, I wouldn't have to pay for my rescue."

"Do Not Contact the Police"

A warning is often given, along with the ransom demand, not to contact the police. Unfortunately, there is no guarantee the kidnappers will not harm the victim even if the police are not contacted. A case in point: In April 1984, a successful young New York restaurateur named Ernesto Castro was kidnapped. Later, he telephoned his family and said to his brother Benny, "They have kidnapped me, they want ransom." At this juncture another voice broke in and said, "thirty thousand," and specified a drop site. The second voice warned, "The money, no cops, or your brother will be killed." Brother Benny made the drop without notifying the police. As instructed, he waited at a nearby pay telephone. After five hours and no contact, he gave up; 48 hours later, the police notified Benny that they had found Ernesto's body with two bullet wounds in the head.

When kidnappers initiate contact, whether a ransom demand or other demands are made, there are procedures that, if followed, can be helpful to investigators. These include:

1. Note the exact time, or the time as close as possible, that the notification is made and whether it is by telephone or a hand-delivered communiqué.
2. Request to speak to the victim or ask for some other verification to ensure that there is no hoax involved.
3. If the notification is made via telephone, note as much information as possible, i.e., the exact wording of the message, the tone, pitch, and other qualities of the caller's voice, including accent, speech impediment, or other distinguishing characteristics, as well as background noises, such as car, train, or plane sounds, or bells, whistles, machinery, etc. At the very least, such information could help pinpoint the telephone location or locations from which the call or calls were made.

McKidnapping

McKidnapping, a play on the name of the McDonald's fast food chain, is a term that has been coined to describe the fast, quick score that kidnappers are often trying to accomplish. The *modus operendi*, or MO, is to grab someone off the street, usually in an affluent area, or from an expensive vehicle, usually during the daytime (during hours that banks are open). The kidnappers contact the family and demand a fast $5,000 or $10,000. The exchange is also made quickly, and the victim is usually released unharmed. Again, the cooperation, compliance, and safe recovery of the victim are most important.

Good postincident investigation and debriefing will assist in the apprehension of the perpetrators.

Hoax

A bogus kidnapping can be carried out by strangers or by members of the alleged victim's family. Devious persons may attempt to make a quick score if they know a prominent or key individual (i.e., a prime target) will be out of touch for a relatively long period of time, be it six to eight hours or one or two days. One such hoax was perpetrated by the niece of a wealthy banker and her ne'er-do-well boyfriend, who knew that the aunt had changed plans for the day and was not in a position to inform her husband or other relatives. The niece and her boyfriend then called the bank and demanded a substantial ransom, but an amount that was small enough for the bank to have on hand in cash. The bank's director of security had good preincident liaison with the local kidnap task force, and the two perpetrators were apprehended before the aunt returned home.

Another kidnap hoax involved a young boy named Etan Patz, who had disappeared from his New York City home. On the third anniversary of his disappearance, a call was made to the Patz home saying "information about the disappearance" of the boy could be had in return for a payoff. The kidnap task force was mobilized and in a short time apprehended the would-be extortionist, who had no information at all concerning the whereabouts of the boy. To this day, decades after young Patz's disappearance, there has been no evidence that he is dead or that he is still alive. However, a sex offender who was in prison allegedly told another inmate that he killed Etan. The family sued civilly for wrongful death. Because the offender refused to testify, the court awarded for the plaintiff. This was a closure of sorts for the family.

Prevention Tactics

The most important factor in combating kidnapping and extortion is prevention. Obviously, if a person is not abducted, the family or company need not be concerned about meeting ransom demands. By the same token, if a company's products are secure, tamperproof, and never adulterated, there is little need to worry about extortion threats.

A key to personal kidnap prevention is awareness—awareness of physical surroundings, whether on the road or at home. All too often, when a person (who by nature of occupation, nationality, or business affiliation) is a potential target of terrorist action, he or she still remains oblivious to danger signs. When traveling abroad, it would be wise to check into the possibility of local political unrest, or perhaps dates and anniversaries that are of significance to political minorities. As with virtually everything in the area of security and defense, there are no 100% guarantees that anything anyone does can prevent a kidnapping or hostage situation. Individuals who consider themselves targets or who are associated with target organizations can vary daily routines so that predictability cannot be used to the terrorists' advantage. When traveling, direct flights are preferred to those with stopovers or a change of planes. U.S. airlines are the preferred carriers, other than on flights to the Middle East, where the more secure airlines tend to be El Al and those from neutral first world nations. However, since 9/11 and the subsequent hostilities in Afghanistan and Iraq, many nations, especially those that are part of the coalition forces, have become targets of internal and international violence. The March 11, 2004, train bombings in Madrid are said to have affected the Spanish national elections held three days after the explosions. The incumbent government, which had supported the United States in its Middle East efforts, was voted out of office in favor of an administration pledged to withdraw Spanish troops from Iraq.

Once in the plane, a window seat in the middle of the cabin will insulate the occupant both physically and psychologically from terrorists during a hijacking. Aisle seats, bulkhead seats, and those in the front and back of the plane provide the perpetrators with a direct line of sight and provide easy access should they want to make an example of someone.

Many individuals, corporate executives or otherwise, upon accepting a high-risk position, should take the time to prepare a personal profile folder containing information that could assist authorities in verifying an alleged or reported kidnapping. The folder should include a photograph, a biography, telephone numbers, a medical and dental history, optical prescriptions, information on club and organization memberships, and similar information that could help prove positive identification.

It is equally important for a person in a high-risk position to prepare his or her family for the possibility of a kidnapping. Terrorists, who are seeking publicity as much as anything else, have made the media, particularly television, an integral part of their planning, strategy, and tactics. There is no question that in some instances, the kidnappers had done research into potential victims' families to determine whether they would be effective in pressuring the victims' employers or the government to comply with the demands of the captors. Terrorists will also callously manipulate a victim's family and associates by using them to deliver messages or lobby on behalf of the demands. Terrorists, through the wording of their messages, also will try to divide public opinion, so that whatever course of action the authorities take, a significant portion of the public will be opposed to it.

In a kidnap situation, unlike a hostage situation, time is on the terrorists' side. With a small group of loyal operatives in on the act, there is little chance of the perpetrators being apprehended. This is not withstanding the limited success the Philippine national police and military have had. Much of their success, however, is due to the nature of their adversaries. Often the military will conduct excursions into rebel-held locations where it is usually, often correctly, presumed the victims are being held, but sometimes accidentally coming across them.

What the Individual Can Do

As explained previously, high-risk individuals should prepare a personal profile. It should include sensitive information on how and where the individual can be contacted to minimize the possibility of a hoax being perpetrated. Obviously, it is very important that the profile folders be sealed and secured, to be opened only if the individual becomes a kidnap or hostage victim. If the individual leaves the company, the file should be returned, still sealed and unopened. In addition, the person's residence should be equipped with as many security devices as practical, given the degree of risk and the funds available for preventive measures. Telephone procedures should be instituted to establish a pattern of check-ins and verifications. Codes should be employed, but they must be kept simple enough for family members to understand.

Despite whatever preventive measures are taken, an abduction could still occur. In order to minimize day-to-day complications for a kidnap or hostage victim's family while they go through the ordeal of waiting for the return of a loved one, there are a number of things that can be arranged ahead of time. These include:

1. Make all checking, savings, and other bank accounts joint accounts.
2. Draw up a checklist of all bills that must be paid regularly, whether weekly, monthly, quarterly, or annually.
3. Arrange to have salary deposited directly to the bank to facilitate the family's ability to carry on.
4. Execute a power of attorney to a dependable relative in the event both husband and wife are taken.
5. Maintain a backup supply of prescription drugs, eyeglasses, and other medical or personal effects that may be needed on short notice.

Journalists Do Not Have Exemptions

In January 2002 Daniel Pearl, a journalist for the *Wall Street Journal*, was the Southeast Asia bureau chief. He was stationed in Mumbai (Bombay), India. From that location he reported on the war on terrorism for the *Wall Street*

Journal. On some occasions he would travel into Pakistan as well. On January 23, 2002, after a series of e-mails with a "source," later to be identified as Ahmed Omar Saeed, Pearl set out to meet him. Saeed was to have had some information about Richard Reid, the "shoe bomber" then in U.S. custody. On December 22, 2001, Reid had attempted to bring down American Airlines Flight 63 from Paris to Miami with an improvised explosive device he had secreted in one of his shoes (Figure 6.1). When he tried to light the fuse, he was disarmed and held by fellow passengers until the plane landed safely.

Pearl was kidnapped by a militant group that called itself the National Movement for the Restoration of Pakistan Sovereignty (NMRPS). Using e-mails, the group made various demands on the United States that included, among other things, the release of all Pakistani detainees from Guantanamo Bay, Cuba, and shipment of F-16 jet fighters that they said were paid for but never delivered to Pakistan.

A few days later, photos of a handcuffed Pearl were sent to authorities with a daily newspaper in the picture to indicate the date. Despite pleas from Pearl's wife and the editors at the *Wall Street Journal*, six days later the journalist was killed. On February 21, 2002, a 3½-minute videotape of

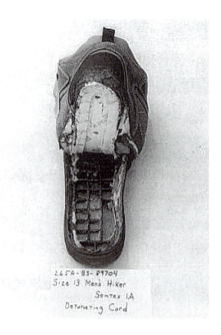

Figure 6.1 Handout photo released Friday afternoon, January 17, 2003, by federal prosecutors in Boston, showing the shoe bomb found worn by British citizen Richard C. Reid aboard American Airlines Flight 63 in December 2001. Reid was stopped in his effort to detonate the shoe bomb by the flight crew and passengers. The explosive Semtex and detonating cord are seen in the lower heel area. (AP Photo/U.S. Attorney Boston handout.)

his murder was released. It had the ominous title *The Slaughter of the Spy Journalist, the Jew Daniel Pearl*. The tape opened with Pearl stating the demands of the people holding him. It had many scenes depicting various occasions and images, including dead persons said to be Muslims, and President George W. Bush with Israeli Prime Minister Ariel Sharon. The tape later showed Pearl, bare chested, with his throat slit. The vicious tape then showed a man decapitating the journalist. In attempts to professionally edit the tape, various images were superimposed over the dead reporter's head being held by the hair. The tape ended with the previously stated printed demands scrolling over the last image of the head of Pearl. He was confirmed to be dead after the government authorities obtained the video.

The video was sent to the governments of the United States and Pakistan. It was also placed on a website that terrorist organizations use to recruit new terrorists. The video was picked up by the U.S. media. CBS broadcast portions of the tape, leaving out the actual death scenes, an action for which it received great criticism from the State Department and from the Pearl family. The Pearl Foundation, started after the abduction and death of Daniel Pearl, expressed concern that by broadcasting the tape, the media were playing into the hands of the terrorists, putting forth their propaganda, saying that the tape had been prepared for just that reason. English translation of the text shown on the videotape read:

NATIONAL MOVEMENT FOR THE RESTORATION OF PAKISTAN SOVEREIGNTY (NMRPS)
We still demand the following:

The immediate release of U.S. held prisoners in Guantinamo [*sic*] Bay, Cuba.
The return of Pakistani prisoners to Pakistan.
The immediate end of U.S. presence in Pakistan.
The delivery of F-16 planes that Pakistan had paid for and never reieved [*sic*]

We asure [*sic*] Americans that they shall never be safe on the Muslim Land of Pakistan. And if our demands are not met this scene shall be repeated again and again.... (End of Text).

When it comes to international terrorism, reporters and journalists do not have the neutrality they often receive from domestic criminal elements. They are "fair game" to get the terrorists' messages across. In Operation Iraqi Freedom, journalists became the targets of some terrorists. Hotels where reporters stayed were shelled or bombed. Even on assignments on the streets, they came under fire.

Many reporters were embedded with military units in Iraq and Afghanistan. They saw, reported on, and were involved in combat situations, including taking gunfire and exploding IEDs. Many received wounds, and some even died in their assignments. A large number of reporters and correspondents have experienced posttraumatic stress disorder (PTSD). Psychiatrist Frank Ochberg, MD—a contributor to this book—is involved in the study and treatment of members of the media who are experiencing PTSD.

What the Family Can Do

An individual who is deemed to be a potential high-risk kidnapping or hostage victim should make an agreement with immediate family members to accept the support of the employer, close friends, and other relatives. This may even include a promise by the family to return home immediately in the event of an abduction overseas. Such an arrangement will provide some comfort for the captive, who then will need to be concerned only with his or her own survival. The family should observe basic security procedures traveling to and from their residence. Telephone service should be switched to unlisted numbers to lessen the number of crank or harassing calls. Travel plans should be kept confidential. The family should consider who would be the best family spokesperson, though the company, if the kidnapping is business related, will usually have a person assigned to deal with the media. However, their interests, at times, may seem to be in conflict with the family's concerns.

One Man's Ordeal

A classic example of how one high-risk individual hardened the target, was still kidnapped, but managed to survive the ordeal involves Sir Geoffrey Jackson, the British ambassador to Uruguay, who was kidnapped January 8, 1971.

As recounted in his book *Surviving the Long Night*, Sir Geoffrey was aware that he and his embassy were under covert surveillance by persons later identified as Tupamaros, the Marxist guerrillas active in Uruguay at the time.[2] Jackson began taking precautions to protect himself and his family. He varied his daily routine, taking different routes to work and using a number of vehicles. Although he was eventually taken, his efforts did force the terrorists to use more time, manpower, money, and vehicles than they had originally planned. A less well-financed group might have abandoned the effort. Realizing he was a high-risk target, Sir Geoffrey had also arranged with his wife to pack two suitcases, one for herself and one for him, which should be left in the foyer of their residence and used in the event he were kidnapped. Lady Jackson was to leave the country immediately for the United Kingdom and then proceed to their cottage in the country. Knowing she would comply, Jackson was relieved of any concern for his wife, and he was able to concentrate on his own situation and how to survive it.

What the Corporation Can Do

A company with even the slightest possibility of being a terrorist target should develop an internal policy on kidnapping. The policy should include the creation of a crisis management team (CMT) and provide for alternate members in the event of emergencies involving permanent members. By virtue of their key decision-making positions within the company, the CMT should contain the chief executive officers, the chief financial officer, and the heads of the legal and security departments. Among the CMT's considerations should be:

1. Who should be given protection? Be mindful that every employee is important. Which executives should be given what kind of protection, and to what level does family coverage extend?
2. Who should determine when to implement the CMT plan? The major consideration here is whether or not a hoax is involved.
3. The establishment of awareness conferences for executives and their families, to explain the company's policies. This will also provide an opportunity to define the reasons for requests for biographical profiles, pictures, etc.
4. Whether or not to provide assistance in securing offices, residences, and vehicles.
5. Establishing support procedures for families should an abduction take place.
6. How and for what time period salary should continue to be paid in the event of a prolonged kidnapping or hostage incident.
7. Determining that the company does, in fact, have the authority to pay ransom, vis-à-vis stockholders and the Internal Revenue Service, as well as guidelines for when, where, and how much ransom will be paid.
8. Developing a plan for securing the actual funds and paying a ransom.
9. Establishing liaisons with federal, state, local, and foreign authorities who may become involved in the event of a kidnapping.
10. If the abduction takes place outside the United States, a local negotiating team (LNT) would be onsite, maintaining close communication with the CMT at its base. The LNT should be made up of those who know the local people, laws, and customs. This might be where professional kidnap negotiators work from as well.

These are but a few points to be addressed by the CMT. The use of pre-incident role-playing will give members the opportunity to make mistakes in order to see who might function better in specific roles. It also provides a forum to examine the actions, or inaction, that might become the crux of future litigation should an incident ever occur.

On Becoming a Victim

Certainly the best tactic to employ upon becoming a kidnap victim or a hostage is to be well coached in the preincident psychological preparations discussed in defense planning earlier. Should a person not have the advantage of that training, the first thing to do is control fear and anxiety levels. The word *hope* has been developed into a mnemonic aid for the four attributes most helpful to a captive: humor, optimism, patience, and energy. Another strength captives must have is courage, the courage to maintain self-respect even when terrorist captors try to torment and demoralize their victims.

Endnotes

1. *Political Terrorism*, Vol. 2, 1974–1978, Lester A. Sobel, Facts on File, New York, 1978, pp. 209–215.
2. *Surviving the Long Night*, Sir Geoffrey Jackson, Vanguard Press, New York, 1974.

Terrorism on Public Transportation

7

DOROTHY MOSES SCHULZ*

Overview

Acts of terrorism can take place anywhere. Just as there are many types of terrorists and many types of tactics that terrorists can use to achieve their aims, there are also different locations that will factor into the terrorists' plans.

Transportation facilities provide terrorists with perfect locations for achieving the aims of making their causes known and creating fear throughout the world. In the United States, the primary focus of antiterrorism activities surrounding transportation has centered on airports and planes, but these are not the only modes of transportation that have been sites for terrorist activities. In fact, throughout the world, ground transportation—primarily trains, subways, and buses—has been the primary target of both international and domestic terrorists. Waterborne terrorism, whether through destruction of a vessel, extortion or kidnapping after a vessel's hostile takeover, or piracy, is a less common concern of domestic responders than land-based terrorism, but as recent events have shown, a single incident can change the focus of antiterrorism activities virtually overnight.

Whether trains, planes, buses, boats, or ferries, public transit provides terrorists with the opportunity to involve large numbers of innocent bystanders in their activities and to achieve the large audience they desire. Depending upon the type of transit target, these facilities provide opportunities for

* Dorothy Moses Schulz, PhD, a professor of police studies at John Jay College of Criminal Justice (CUNY), retired as a captain from the Metro-North Commuter Railroad Police Department. Her assignments included commanding officer of New York's Grand Central Terminal. She was the principal investigator on two Transportation Research Board studies, *Guidelines for the Effective Use of Uniformed Transit Police and Security Personnel* (Final Report, May 1997) and *Video Surveillance Uses by Rail Transit Agencies* (2011). A contributor to the Transit Cooperative Research Program (TCRP) report on *Making Transportation Tunnels Safe and Secure* (2006), she has published and spoken widely on historical and current issues in railroad/transit policing. Dr. Schulz has worked with the U.S. Federal Transit Administration (FTA) developing security policies for existing transit systems and those in development and has consulted with transit agencies to assist them in complying with federal safety and security regulations.

placing explosive devices, committing arson, taking hostages, or kidnapping crew members or passengers.

While flying planes into the World Trade Center towers on September 11, 2001, may have had a more dramatic impact than exploding a bomb in either New York City's Pennsylvania Station or Grand Central Terminal during the morning rush hour, the number of fatalities in either train station would have exceeded the number of 9/11 fatalities by the thousands. A similar attack on any subway platform in downtown Chicago, Boston, Cleveland, Philadelphia, or Washington, D.C., would also have resulted in a greater number of fatalities. Yet the United States has escaped the level of violence on ground transportation that other countries have seen. One explanation is simply that public transit is less fully woven into the fabric of everyday life here. First responders can be thankful for this, because the complexities of responding to a terrorist incident are multiplied when moving vehicles traveling through overlapping jurisdictions become the sites of criminal activity.

The size of the nation's transit network can overwhelm those unfamiliar with it. There are more than 7,000 miles of transit line, more than 113,000 miles of railroad (generally freight tracks over which few, if any, passenger trains travel), 26,000 miles of navigable waterway, and an additional 4 million miles of roadway. More than 6,000 transit agencies move more than 14 million people to work each day; in 2009, this translated into more than 10 billion transit trips. And about 350,000 people work directly for public transit agencies, which vary in size from small, rural systems that operate a handful of buses daily to Boston's approximately 1,000 buses and New York's almost 6,000 buses. In addition to each vehicle having the potential to become a terrorist target, each station, shelter, garage, or storage facility is also a potential target of terrorists and criminals alike.

Where Are Terrorists Likely to Strike?

According to a report issued in 2002 by the General Accounting Office (GOA), *Mass Transit: Challenges in Securing Transit Systems* (GAO Report 02-1075T), buses, tourist buses, and bus terminals were the most common targets (41% buses, 5% tourist buses, and 8% terminals). Other targets, in the order in which they were attacked, were subways and trains and subway and train stations (22 and 10%, respectively), train tracks (8%), bridges and tunnels (1%), and other (5%). A longer-range study, this one covering events from 1920 to 2000, reported similar findings; although over this 80-year period, subways, trains, rails, and subway and train stations accounted for a larger percentage of targets, buses, tour buses, school buses, and bus terminals together made up 47% of the targets.[1]

Answering the question of how secure our passenger and transit infra-structure is, another report noted that almost one-third of the world's terror-ist attacks had been aimed at public transportation facilities.[2]

This has important implications for first responders. Attacks on transit systems have received widespread publicity around the world, but most have focused on rail transit. This may encourage police and fire officials in the United States, where many jurisdictions have no rail systems, to misunder-stand the vulnerability of buses, which are far more common throughout the world.

A study by the RAND Corporation calculated that from 1995 to 2005 there were more than 250 terrorist attacks throughout the world against trains and rail facilities, resulting in about 900 deaths and 6,000+ inju-ries.[3] Of these, relatively few occurred in the United States; five were recorded during the early 1990s. In 1992, someone left a hand grenade on a Chicago railroad station platform. In December 1994, six days apart, two bombs went off on the New York City subway system. The first explo-sion injured two people; the second injured the bomber. In 1995, a token booth clerk in the New York subway was set on fire and severely burned (but this was most likely not terrorism related). Two years later, in 1997, a plot to bomb the Atlantic Avenue subway and Long Island Railroad stations in Brooklyn, New York, was prevented with the capture of two Palestinian men who were charged with federal conspiracy and weapons charges. One was convicted and sentenced to life in prison; the other was acquitted of all but charges of immigration fraud and was sentenced to three years in prison.

The Port Authority Trans Hudson (PATH) rail line connecting New Jersey and New York has suffered most at the hands of terrorists. The 9/11 attacks on the World Trade Center put one of PATH's two main tunnels out of service, and PATH experienced minor damage in the 1993 WTC bombing. During the 9/11 attacks, three New York City subway lines suffered damage, although none were the terrorists' direct targets. Ironically, on the day of the WTC attacks, the Port Authority Transit Corp., which operates a tran-sit line between Philadelphia and its New Jersey suburbs, was conducting a drill involving a terrorist bomb under City Hall in Camden, New Jersey. As the real attack occurred, the drill was cancelled so the agency could pro-vide transportation for those leaving Philadelphia and fill gaps in New Jersey Transit's suspended service throughout the state.

Knowing where terrorists might strike is only part of the intelligence gathering. Knowing *how* they might strike is equally important. Although analysts are aware that terrorist groups are constantly testing new weap-ons and delivery systems, as with all crimes, analysis of past events plays a large part in designing countermeasures. Terrorists' tactics have changed surprisingly little during that time. Technology has not so much changed the tactics as made them more efficient.

In the 80-year period from 1920 to 2000, the major terrorist tactic against transportation targets has been bombings (60%). No other tactic except ambushes/assaults has exceeded 10%. Other methods of attack, listed by Brian M. Jenkins and Larry N. Gersten in their order of use, have included standoffs (9%), hijackings and hostage situations (5%), mechanical sabotage (5%), grenades and bombs thrown at equipment (4%), bomb threats (4%), arson (3%), and a handful of miscellaneous other tactics.[1]

Transit as a Target—Vulnerable and Attractive

What makes transit so attractive to terrorists? The answer goes directly to the heart of the aims of terrorists. What better place to achieve maximum publicity and maximum casualities of innocent people? What better way to create mass fear while at the same time affecting commerce and industry?

The characteristics that make transit systems vulnerable are the same characteristics that make them easy to use. They are far more difficult to control than airports and air traffic. Public transit systems are:

- Naturally open and accessible, with multiple access and exit points. Anyone can get on a bus or railcar at any station and may exit virtually anywhere along the transit route.
- Used by people of all ages and races, making it difficult to determine who "belongs" or "fits in." They are points of congregation for young people, idle people, and homeless people.
- Used for purposes other than travel. Particularly in downtown areas, transit stations are often urban malls; people come to browse, shop, dine, and people-watch. Sometimes they come to escape uncomfortable weather conditions.
- Predictable. Transit vehicles travel in predictable paths at predictable times and are rarely accompanied by police or security personnel.

For these reasons, transit facilities are attractive to both international and domestic terrorist groups, although not always for the same reasons. Large, iconic train stations are more likely to be targeted by international terrorists seeking to cause multiple deaths and injuries of innocent bystanders. They have symbolic value and are often landmarks located in a city's commercial district.

Although a small bus or rail facility may be attractive to international terrorists, either could appeal to local activist groups. In such situations, members of the group are more likely to vandalize a location rather than detonate an explosive device. They may cause trains to run late by mass tres-passing on the tracks or preventing buses from leaving the garage, or they may picket or distribute leaflets at major stops along the route.

The anonymity of a transit facility adds to its attractiveness. Except in the case of intentional public protests, terrorists are unlikely to be observed by anyone who will become suspicious of their activities. Terrorists—similar to many other types of criminals—may enter unobserved, commit their ille-gal act, and make their getaway stealthily.

Their getaway is aided by the ease of crossing political, and therefore law enforcement, boundaries. For example, a thief may get on a bus in Eastern Village, pilfer the purse of a woman sitting next to him, and exit the bus in Western Village. The victim may not notice her wallet missing until she attempts to purchase something when she gets off the bus. Similarly, a ter-rorist may get on a bus in Eastern Village and also exit in Western Village, this time leaving behind a suspicious package set to detonate in 30 minutes, assured that the explosion will take place in yet a third community. Such a case occurred in the New York–New Jersey metropolitan area years before terrorism was a common topic. Shortly before Thanksgiving 1994, dozens of New Jersey commuters shared a bus into New York's Port Authority Bus Terminal with a pipe bomb that was found by the driver in the vehicle's over-head luggage rack. A second bomb was later found on the same bus by the same driver; the first bomb was not live, but the second one was.

The problems this presents to initial responders and postevent investigative personnel are obvious. Attempts to organize an immediate response may be fur-ther complicated by the variety of policing arrangements that exist within the transit industry. Many agencies, particularly highly vulnerable bus-only systems, may have no staffs assigned solely to security tasks. If an incident occurs on a bus or is observed along the route by an operator, he or she contacts the transit agency dispatcher, who in turn contacts the local police. All follow-up activities and inci-dent reporting in these situations are the responsibility of the local police.

Overlapping Jurisdictions Complicate Response Efforts

The number of agencies responsible for securing transit facilities, as well as the vagaries of their arrangements, complicates policing strategies. With the exception of Canada, which has far fewer transit systems but which also relies on the individual agencies to patrol their facilities, most other nations assign transit patrol and investigation to their national police force or to a transit-specific force with nationwide jurisdiction, or they develop a more fully defined relationship between national and local levels, including dedi-cated transit forces.

While Amtrak, the nation's only national rail system, has its own nation- ally recognized police force, it has no responsibility for transit areas through which it does not travel. National, in this case, means only that its officers may be stationed anywhere in the nation. Many freight railroads' police, although employed by private companies, have full police authority in all states through which their railroad travels. Like transit police, though, they obtain their status by state statute. While the geographic authority of rail- road or transit police often exceeds that of local police, they must be granted such authority by each state through which their system travels.

Large rail systems have full-service police departments, but bus agencies do not. Bus systems with their own police are part of what are called multi- modal transit systems, which mean the agency includes a variety of types of transportation, generally buses and rail or ferries and rail. The two largest independent transit police agencies are both in the New York metropolitan area and are responsible for facilities in two states. The Port Authority of New York and New Jersey (PANY&NJ) employs more than 2,000 law enforcement officers who work in the New York–New Jersey airports, bridges, and tun- nels, and the Port Authority Trans Hudson (PATH) rail line. New York– Connecticut's Metropolitan Transportation Authority (MTA) employs more than 600 officers. Like PANY&NJ officers, MTA police are scattered through the two states, with the largest numbers located in New York City. Amtrak has about 500 officers, most assigned in the Northeast Corridor (defined as between Washington, D.C. and Boston). From here the sizes of transit police agencies drop considerably; a few have about 200 officers, but most have fewer than 100.

Many agencies do not have their own police departments. Some, like both the New York City Transit Authority and the Chicago Transit Authority, rely on transit divisions located within the municipal police department. Other agencies rely on members of the local police department or county sheriff's office for regular, nonemergency patrol coverage or for response to incidents. Generally, similar to New York and Chicago, this means that a certain number of officers are assigned to the transit unit or bureau, often under the command of a mid-level supervisor (generally a sergeant, lieuten- ant, or captain).

Some jurisdictions have very formal arrangements. In areas where sher- iffs' offices are heavily involved in contract policing, such as Los Angeles County, the arrangement is covered by a contract similar to those with cit- ies and towns. In these situations, in addition to patrol coverage, the transit agency is entitled to specialized services such as use of canine officers, or evidence or bomb technicians as needed.

If you are in a jurisdiction that relies on contract policing and your agency is not the designated police provider, it is important to be aware of who has primary jurisdiction for the transit agency and to have had made plans for emergency response coordination. In contract policing situations, the amount of control the transit agency retains over the officers assigned to the system may differ and should be clarified with the transit agency and the contract police department. This may be covered by formal memoranda of understanding (MOUs) or regional compacts, or the local procedure may be simply that the first agency on the scene or the largest agency in the area takes control until more formal arrangements are made.

There are also areas where the policing arrangements are quite fluid. Very little is prearranged. This exists particularly with small bus systems; should there be a need for law enforcement, the local police are contacted and respond much as they would to any other business or residence in their jurisdiction.

Some transit agencies employ few, if any, sworn police officers, but employ either contract security personnel or proprietary (employed directly by the agency being secured) security officers. Depending on local options, in some jurisdictions, such as Miami, Florida, and Denver, Colorado, these officers carry firearms and at first glance cannot be distinguished from sworn police officers. Their level of legal authority may also differ, depending on local licensing regulations. At the opposite end of the spectrum, some security officers may be authorized to act solely as "eyes and ears," with no authority to intervene even in a violent confrontation occurring in their presence. The viability of this type of patrol was called into question, though, in early 2010, when a 15-year-old girl was attacked by other teens in the Seattle Downtown Transit Tunnel while security officers who lacked any authority to separate the combatants stood by. When responding to a transit-related incident, it is beneficial for first responders to have an awareness of the limitations placed on security personnel who may have observed or intervened in an incident.

Just as some agencies have no police, a few rely on more than one police department, including sometimes all those whose jurisdiction they travel through. In these situations, each local police, fire, or emergency medical agency responds to calls or events in its city or town, and the adjacent providers do the same. The Altamont Commuter Express (ACE) in California, for example, which has no police department of its own, relies on nine separate police agencies. In addition to the local departments whose jurisdictions it travels through, ACE also coordinates with Amtrak and Union Pacific Railroad police officers. Valley Metro Rail, operating in the cities of Phoenix, Tempe, and Mesa, also has a shared-responsibility arrangement to secure its transit system. Although each of the three cities supports the system by responding to calls for service in their individual jurisdictions, only Phoenix has a dedicated transit bureau. Tempe and Mesa use the same vendor to provide contract security officers.

In emergencies such as derailments, fires or explosive detonations, or accidents that result in fatalities, state and federal investigative agencies may also respond to the incident. Knowing who is responsible for these activities prior to the emergency is vital to prevent any misunderstandings that can result in loss of time in handling an emergency and in ill-will among responding agency personnel.

A Brief Case Study—Washington, D.C. Metro Incident

A bomb plot involving the Washington, D.C., subway system, known locally as Metro, involved a lone-wolf terrorist, in this case a 34-year-old naturalized U.S. citizen originally from Pakistan. Although Farooque Ahmed of suburban Virginia had planned to detonate bombs in at least four Metro stations, at the time of his arrest by the FBI the public was assured that the transit system was never in danger. The reason? As with a number of American-born terrorists whose plots have been foiled in recent years, his co-conspirators were all FBI agents. In these cases, FBI officials rarely describe exactly how they came to identify the would-be bombers beyond mentioning tips that came from identified sources.

In this plot, Ahmed hoped to bomb stations that were adjacent to military locations, including the Pentagon City, Courthouse, and Crystal City stations. Aware of the flow of commuter traffic, he told the undercover agent he believed to be a fellow terrorist that attacking the stops between 4 and 5 p.m., the start of the evening rush hour, would assure the largest number of casualties. Although it could not be determined whether he had specifically watched the periodic baggage screening activities at some of the stations, he also is alleged to have suggested that using rolling suitcases would be better than backpacks, the common method of choice for many transit facility bombers around the world.

While both the FBI and the Metro Transit Police assured residents that the transit system was never in danger, this incident called into question the value of a number of countermeasures that have become common in transit system protection. Despite the popularity of programs urging members of the public to report any suspicious activities they observe, Ahmed tracked ridership in his stations of choice and had also recorded videos and sketched diagrams of the locations, all unnoticed by patrons or police.

Because of FBI involvement throughout the case, Ahmed was arraigned on federal charges brought by the U.S. Attorney for the Eastern District of Virginia, rather than by local authorities. Despite these minor differences, though, Ahmed is one of a number of defendants charged in the past few years who have launched terror plots that may seem amateurish but could easily have resulted in the deaths of hundreds of people and the destruction of portions of the nation's critical infrastructure.

This case also underscores the difficulty police face in such cases. A year earlier Metro police arrested a homeless man accused of making bomb threat calls from at least five Metro stations over a six-month period. Although he, too, faced federal charges for making threats and conveying false information using fire and explosives, these crimes were more akin to the types of nonterrorist threats that transit facilities are faced with on a regular basis.

Terrorists and Criminals Ride the Rails

Crimes against railroads have a long history in the United States, although far more often associated with robberies than with terror-inspired violence. Almost anyone who has ever watched a movie or television program set in the American West has observed a train robbery in progress. Whether Old West robberies or modern terrorism, though, crimes against railroads often occur in remote locations, involve overlapping police jurisdictions, and are often unsolved.

Each of these factors came into play when Amtrak's Sunset Limited was derailed on October 9, 1995, in Hyder, Arizona, about 59 miles southwest of Phoenix, on an isolated portion of track owned by the Southern Pacific Railway (SP). The train carried 248 passengers and a crew of 20; the derailment caused 65 injuries and the death of one employee. Property damage was estimated at close to $3 million. The crime was committed by removing spikes from the rails and other acts of vandalism, including disabling the signal system. Because no other train had passed over the tracks for 18 hours, it was impossible to determine the exact time of the crime. This made it difficult to pinpoint whether anything or anyone suspicious had been observed, although the remoteness of the location might have made such identification unlikely under any circumstances.

All evidence, including notes found at the scene, indicated an intentional derailment that has been attributed to a group called "Sons of the Gestapo," presumably a white supremacy group. But authors who have written about hobos who illegally ride freight trains believe anger at railroad police or fights among the hobo groups are also possible causes. Regardless, despite the involvement of hundreds of police officers from railroad, local, state, and federal agencies, including more than 150 FBI agents, the crime has never been solved.

Whether the act was the work of domestic terrorists (as the notes indicate), international terrorists using the notes as a cover, disgruntled employees, or persecuted hobos may never be known. What can be learned, though, is that anyone with the knowledge, time, and willingness to violate federal and state laws may be able to derail, disable, or wreck a passenger or freight train and stands a good chance of being successful and, under certain circumstances, a fairly good chance of remaining at large.

Amid various acts of sabotage and vandalism, one case sticks out for its similarity to the Sunset Limited derailment. In 1939, in another case that was never solved, a passenger train was derailed in a remote area of Nevada. Again, spikes had been removed from the tracks and wires cut that would have warned the engineer of a problem. The train jumped the tracks, killing 24 people and injuring more than 100 others.

More recently, in August 1992, two U.S. Coast Guardsmen were arrested and pled guilty to intentionally derailing the Amtrak Colonial in Newport News, Virginia, by cutting a switch padlock that resulted in altering the track alignment. Although no one was killed, the perpetrators received sentences of almost 20 years in federal prison.

The vast majority of terrorist incidents involving railroads occur on passenger trains or in stations; generally they have centered on explosive devices meant to incur a large number of casualties as well as to obtain worldwide publicity for the terrorists' causes. The large number of casualties alone can guarantee the type of media coverage terrorists crave, but the photos of mangled railcars, often accompanied by photos of covered bodies laid out along the tracks, can be counted on to keep the story in the public's eye for days. The accompanying disruption to daily commerce provides the additional benefit to terrorists of hampering economic activity in the immediate area, and often for hundreds of miles along the right-of-way.

Freight Trains Are Also Targets

Freight trains have also been victimized by sabotage. While these events will likely result in far fewer deaths because only a handful of crew members will be on the trains, they are one method of targeting commerce. If a derailed train happens to be carrying flammable materials or chemicals or other hazardous cargo, the explosion and fire may cause evacuation for miles and halt rail traffic until the wreck can be removed and the tracks reconstructed.

In February 1996, sabotage was suspected but never proven in the wreck of a runaway Burlington Northern Santa Fe (BNSF) freight train in St. Paul, Minnesota, that resulted in a train traveling 50 miles an hour striking several parked locomotives in a Canadian Pacific Railroad yard, setting off a chain accident that in turn derailed more than 40 cars and 6 locomotives, and destroyed a one-story office building, but caused no fatalities.

Disruption of freight traffic is likely to have a greater economic impact than incidents involving passenger trains, but is also likely to result in few fatalities and in less publicity. Yet freight trains are more vulnerable to attack than passenger trains carrying commuters in high-density areas. Like Amtrak, freight trains travel long distances over remote parts of the country. Some are over 100 cars long, accompanied by a handful of crew who are at the front of the train or, on railroads that still use cabooses, at the end.

Even if every railcar carried an observer, without electronic protection along the tracks, a saboteur could easily vandalize the track or signal system long before the train was due. Yards are similarly vulnerable; they are generally not well lit, and their 24-hour operation makes them difficult to secure. Due to the danger of moving trains, railroad companies discourage outsiders, even emergency responders, from entering unannounced and without railroad personnel to guide them.

The need for multiagency coordination is not solely in response to terrorist activity. Other criminals also benefit from the overlapping jurisdictions and anonymity provided by the railroad. Trespassers are common and may cause damage inadvertently. Despite reckless endangerment and criminal mischief laws in all states, many people consider shooting at moving trains or throwing rocks to be sport. The increases in thefts of materials often found in rail yards and at rail construction sites, particularly copper wire, wood, and equipment such as bulldozers, raise the question of whether these are simply thefts or are parts of plans to use the materials in terrorist activities.

The paths that criminals have been able to carve out on the railroads are indications of the possibilities that exist for terrorists to do the same and the problems faced by those trying to thwart them. In July 1999, after spending considerable time on the FBI's list of Ten Most Wanted Fugitives, Angel Maturina Reséndiz turned himself into the Texas Rangers at the urging of his sister. He had been the target of a nationwide search involving numerous police agencies.

Reséndiz, who for most of the hunt was known as "The Railroad Killer," a drifter who was believed to have entered the United States illegally in 1976, had for years ridden freight trains between Mexico, the United States, and Canada. Although he had been stopped a number of times by railroad police and possibly by Border Patrol agents, as one of the approximately 100,000 freight hoppers stopped annually, he managed to evade being deported or was able to return quite easily. At the time of his arrest he was believed to have killed as many as 15 people in five states, including Florida, Kentucky, Texas, Georgia, and Illinois. Many of his female victims had also been raped. He was found guilty of murder of one Texas victim in 2000 by a Houston jury and executed at the Huntsville, Texas, prison in 2006.

While some might believe that the ease with which Reséndiz moved across three countries for more than two decades using 30 or more aliases could not be duplicated today, many law enforcement professionals would disagree. Could a lone terrorist or a small cell of terrorists do the same, possibly setting off small fires or explosions rather than committing individual murders and rapes? The answer is unknown.

International Rail Transit Terrorism

Prior to 9/11, most of what American law enforcement agencies knew about transit terrorism came from abroad, largely from the British experience with Irish Republican Army (IRA) threats against and actual bombings of the London Underground.

Less well known, France has witnessed considerable transit terrorism. In July 1995, Paris was the scene of a bombing in an underground station. The bomb exploded in the sixth car of an eight-car, double-decked train entering a major station during the evening rush hour; seven people were killed and 80 injured. Based on existing emergency plans, the Paris Fire Brigade arrived within seven minutes and set up a command post in a nearby café. Three hours after the attack all the dead and injured had been removed; normal service was resumed by 5:30 a.m. the next morning. The philosophy behind the rapid return to service is that the more quickly the scene is restored to normal, the less the terrorists benefit from continuing press coverage.

But two additional bombings occurred in Paris shortly after this event. On October 6 a bomb exploded outside a subway station entrance, injuring 13 people, and on October 17 a subway car was bombed at Orsay Museum station by the Armed Islamic Group (GIA), injuring more than 24 people.

Events in France reinforce the difficulty of separating terrorism from less politically motivated crimes. When French police discovered a bomb in 2004 under a section of track between Paris and Limoges, they were following information from a group identified as AZF. Although they were unfamiliar with this group, subsequent investigation revealed that some of its members had been involved in extortion attempts and had threatened to detonate 10 bombs after neither the nation's president nor the interior minister responded to their demands.

England has often been viewed as the major locale of transit-related terrorism. But despite the extraordinarily high level of fears of IRA attacks on Great Britain's rail system, the attacks have been less frequent and resulted in fewer fatalities than many presume to have occurred. While there have been many real attacks, the IRA also developed the technique of falsely reporting events. While these false warnings may have minimized civilian casualties, they kept the fear level high, wasted police resources, and undermined government attempts to assure the public of the safety of the transit system.

Great Britain is also known worldwide for its widespread use of video surveillance throughout the country, and particularly in the Underground, where it was installed primarily as a safety and crowd control mechanism after a major fire in 1987 that resulted in 31 fatalities at the King's Cross Station. By 2005, more than 6,000 cameras had been installed throughout the 275-station system. Somewhat eerily, despite surveillance, on July 7, 2005, suicide bombers were able to bomb the same King's Cross Station and a bus, killing 52 people and wounding more than 700.

Often compared to 9/11 and referred to similarly as 7/7 throughout the United Kingdom, the July 7 bombing was carried out by 4 young men who claimed an association with al Qaeda; they were quickly identified based partially on images of them entering a train station about 50 miles north of London at about 7:20 a.m. on the day of the attacks.

In another instance of a copycat crime, on July 21, terrorists planted three bombs on the subway and on another London bus. Despite the surveillance network and the additional police presence, this attack was thwarted only because the devices failed to detonate. This copycat bombing differed from the IRA hoaxes. In this instance, as in Madrid a year earlier, the attempts shortly after the actual bombing were intended to succeed rather than to keep the fear level high and to cause disruption rather than casualties.

The London and Madrid bombings have a number of common elements. Madrid was the scene of rail violence on March 11, 2004, when several massive explosions occurred on four commuter trains. Spain, like Great Britain, has witnessed considerable terrorist activity, primarily at the hands of the Basque independence organization, ETA. Just as Great Britain was initially prepared to attribute the London explosions to the IRA, Spain initially suspected the ETA of having caused the attack, which was quickly determined to have been carried out by Moroccan-based al Qaeda operatives. The well-coordinated attack involved 10 devices that were detonated on four separate commuter rail line trains running into central Madrid. Occurring during the morning rush hour, the attacks killed almost 200 people and injured more than 1,600. Reinforcing the copycat phenomenon, less than a month later a similar device was found under the tracks of a different commuter line into Madrid.

The persistent danger posed by conflicts between adjacent nations is illustrated by India and Pakistan. India especially has been the site of a number of major rail terrorist events. In their research into international terrorism, Brian M. Jenkins and Larry N. Gersten found that between July 1997 and December 2000, nearly 200 people in the two countries were killed during attacks on surface transit systems. The two nations ranked first (India) and third (Pakistan) in total fatalities. The carnage was more disproportionate over a longer period of time; between 1920 and 2000, the two nations accounted for the majority of fatalities, ranking one and two. India's 640 fatalities were far greater than all others listed; Pakistan recorded 274 deaths, while the third nation, Algeria, saw 250 people killed during transit attacks.[1]

A few examples will suffice; in 2002 a Muslim bomber attacked a trainload of Hindus, burning 58 people—mostly women and children—to death. More than 180 people were killed in 2006 in Mumbai (Bombay), and less than a year later, in February 2007, two bombs ripped through a passenger train traveling from India to Pakistan, killing 68 people. On May 28, 2010, a Mumbai-bound passenger train collided with a freight train after someone sabotaged tracks in West Bengal, resulting in more than 70 deaths and more than 100 injuries. The same suspects were implicated in an attack a week earlier that involved blowing up a bus carrying civilians and police officers. Although a Maoist group was blamed for the crash, within days the Communist Party of India said it was not involved, although India has continued to view the Maoists as the most likely perpetrators.

Chechen Separatists Target the Moscow Subway System

Since 1997, Russia has witnessed numerous terrorist events, many linked to Chechen separatists and many aimed at the Moscow subway system. The system carries an average of 8.6 million riders daily. As the world's largest subway system, it is a highly attractive target.

Although bombs have been the tactic of choice, the system was also victimized by a copycat threat to release sarin gas in 1998 on the third anniversary of the Tokyo attack. That threat passed without incident, as did numerous bomb threats made against Moscow and St. Petersburg stations for many years. Because of the passenger density, and the reality of constant political unrest, threats are taken seriously and result in considerable disruption even when unfounded. Many of the threats have been real. In 1996 a bomb in a subway car killed four people. Four years later, another bomb placed in a Moscow underpass leading from the railway station at Pushkin Square to the street killed and injured a total of about 100 people. This case is yet another instance of the possible overlap of crime and terrorism; although Chechen separatists were blamed, some police officials suspected that the bombing may have been a turf war between criminal gangs or rival businessmen.

But the suicide bombing on February 4, 2004, was clearly terrorist inspired. About 40 people were killed and many others wounded when a bomb that was the equivalent of 11 pounds of TNT that had been hidden in a backpack detonated in a crowded subway train traveling toward the center of Moscow. As in so many transit emergencies, there were problems opening the train car doors. The evacuations of more than 700 people from two stations were complicated by many riders having walked through tunnels once they were able to pry open the train doors. Street-level congestion, including emergency but also other vehicles, caused additional evacuation problems.

Six months later another suicide bomber killed at least 10 people and injured more than 50 others when she set off a bomb outside a Moscow subway station. Although this incident did not occur during rush hour, the surrounding area was busy with shoppers and those enjoying the last days of summer vacation. The event was noteworthy because it introduced the idea that women might also be bombers, complicating efforts to identify suspicious persons or activities. The 29-year-old Chechen bomber was the sister of another woman who was suspected of detonating a bomb on one of the two Russian planes that had been blown up a week earlier.

These women terrorists from the North Caucasus became known in Russia as the Black Widows. The name played on what was believed to be a desire to avenge deaths of their husbands or other relatives at the hands of Russian security forces. Despite widespread interest in women terrorists, the Black Widows had faded from view until March 29, 2010, when twin bombs that killed 40 subway riders were attributed to two women, a 28-year-old teacher from Dagestan, a predominantly Muslim region of southern Russia, who was the wife of an extremist leader, and a 17-year-old woman from the same region. Five months later, five men believed to have played a role in sending the women to Moscow were killed in a shootout with Russian security forces in Dagestan.

Not all the attacks have been in Moscow. In 1993, an attack on a commuter rail train by Chechens resulted in 45 deaths and 165 injuries. In 2007 a bomb set adjacent to railroad tracks derailed a passenger train traveling between Moscow and St. Petersburg. Although there were no fatalities, many were injured and the busy rail line was shut down. Two years later a similar bombing of a train traveling the same route resulted in 28 deaths.

Gas and Arson Attacks

While bombs have been the weapons of choice for terrorists attacking public transit systems, they have not been the only means of attack. Two events in Asia—one in Korea and the other in Japan—are reminders that gas and fire can be particularly deadly in the confined boundaries of a subway station or tunnel.

The sarin gas attack in the Kasumigaseki subway station in Tokyo, Japan, in 1995 is an example of a politically motivated crime that resulted in relatively few fatalities but maximum exposure for the attackers. Only 12 people died, in large part because the five canisters released by members of the Aum Shinrikyo religious sect contained highly diluted sarin. But as many as 6,000 people were believed to have been exposed to the chemical gas. As described elsewhere, the attack occurred at the height of the morning rush hour on trains that are often so crowded that it is virtually impossible for passengers to move.

The police headquarters and other government buildings aboveground were the cult's actual targets, but their selection of the transit system as the locale in which to release the gas illustrates the type of problems faced by responders. Train dispatchers, unaware of what had occurred, allowed trains to continuing moving—one train made five stops after the sarin was released, spreading the gas to each of those stations.

A major finding of the postevent review was the lack of coordination among police and other authorities. Despite the proximity of police headquarters directly above the station, there was little knowledge of the location. Also reinforcing the importance of including area hospitals in emergency planning, hospitals turned away victims or failed to admit them in a timely manner. The analysis resulted in steps that have become commonplace in the intervening years; namely, the transit system removed trash cans to prevent placement of bombs or other explosives, added patrols by police and security officers, installed surveillance cameras, and introduced crime prevention announcements reminding passengers to report suspicious persons and objects.

The sarin gas attack is also an example of how criminals with no political agenda learn from more sophisticated terrorists. Two years and many after-action reports later, a gang of pickpockets was able to spray tear gas in a commuter train, injuring 65 people, including two undercover police officers. The gang had been observed stealing a purse; when the police tried to apprehend them, they sprayed the gas. Fearing another sarin attack, passengers panicked, which allowed the thieves to escape. Only one of the four was later arrested.

An arson fire in a subway station in Daegu (Taegu), Korea, in early 2003 resulted in close to 200 fatalities and an equal number of persons injured or missing when a mentally unstable passenger who was trying to commit suicide threw flammable liquid inside a subway car carrying 600 people. Despite the attempts of passengers to detain the suspect, he was able to flee just as the train burst into flames. Indicative of problems that can occur in such situations, the fire was fueled by the train's vinyl seats and flammable floor tiles and windows. Response to a circuit breaker fire on a Bay Area Rapid Transit (BART) train in 1979 that occurred while the train was about two miles into the Transbay Tunnel was also complicated by toxic materials that led to combustion of the train's seats, as well as from a second train that had been permitted to proceed into the tunnel even though a smoke condition had been reported.

An important lesson from these events is the need to immediately stop the train. In Korea, a train traveling in the opposite direction entered the same tunnel as the burning train. When the second train stopped in the tunnel, its driver removed the master control key, trapping passengers inside as the cars filled with smoke and fumes from the burning train. As has occurred more often with the availability of cell phones, friends and families reported receiving phone calls from trapped victims even before emergency responders could get to the scene.

The response delays pinpoint the types of problems that responders face during transit emergencies, particularly when they occur in tunnels. In addition to a faulty emergency communications network within the subway system, the electrical system failed, shutting off all emergency lighting and ventilation. Other miscommunications stemmed from inadequate emergency evacuation procedures and confusion over halting train traffic below ground level and vehicular traffic above.

Although less common on trains than on buses, hijackings of trains have occurred. The most publicized of these events occurred in 1975, when a group that called itself the Free South Moluccan Youths seized a passenger train in the Netherlands. After a number of the hostages escaped, the terrorists used those left behind as collateral in their demands for a bus to the Amsterdam airport and a plane to fly them to an unknown destination. They also later added to their demands the release of five Moluccans in Dutch prisons. After a 12-day standoff, the hijackers surrendered. After trial each was sentenced to 14 years in prison.

Buses—Mobile Explosives and Hostage Sites

Probably no single country is as closely associated with suicide bomb attacks on its bus system as Israel. A 14-page list of major terrorist attacks in Israel published by the Anti-Defamation League covering October 2001 to September 2010 has 36 separate incidents that took place either on buses, at bus stops, or at central bus stations in major cities.[4] Although there has been a diminution of the attacks in recent years, their frequency in the early years of the twenty-first century made riding buses a particularly dangerous activity. One observer noted 10 attacks in the month of September 2000. Many of the attacks followed a pattern of occurring on Fridays or Mondays because the terrorists were aware that many Israeli soldiers rode the buses on those days because they were permitted to leave base to go home on Fridays and return on either Sunday or Monday morning. A typical attack occurred, for instance, on a Sunday in August 2002; nine people were killed and more than 40 injured in a suicide bombing for which Hamas claimed responsibility.

According to the online *Counter Terror Gazette*, at the height of the second Palestinian intifada between 2001 and 2004, more than 20 bus-related attacks killed more than 200 civilians, or more than 25% of the civilian deaths attributed to the conflict.[5] Israel is a physically small nation about the size of New Jersey, where buses are a popular mode of both local and intercity transportation. More than a million passengers ride buses daily, making buses an efficient way to kill a large number of people. The goal of maximum casualties is reinforced by shopping malls and outdoor markets forming the next largest locations of bombings. These bombings rarely involve hijacking or any attempts at hostage taking. A suicide bomber—although in some instances in shopping areas the bombers have attempted to flee—need only be successful in entering the bus or standing near a bus shelter while detonating the explosives. The most recent attack, in March 2011, followed a similar pattern except that it occurred in the middle of the week. In this incident, a bomb exploded at a crowded bus stop near Jerusalem's main station. The blast killed one woman and injured more than 20 people. Although a number of Palestinian groups praised the bombing, none took immediate responsibility for the attack. Israel's much smaller rail system has also been the scene of terrorist bombings, although these have been less successful than the many bus attacks.

As with the man rail terrorist incidents in India and Pakistan, these two countries have also been the scenes of numerous bus bombings; in 1987 two bus-related bombings occurred in Pakistan within five weeks of each other. The first took place on the same date a bomb exploded on a railroad platform and at a taxi stand. In later attacks that year, again within weeks of one another, five people were killed and 16 injured when a bomb detonated at a bus station in Rawalpendi; Afghans were suspected. A bomb also exploded at the main bus terminal in Peshawar about one month later, and another at the same bus terminal another month later, the last one resulting in one death and 19 injuries.

India's bus bombings have been attributed to a number of local separatist groups, including, in 1991, the United Liberation Front of Assam, and throughout the 1990s to Sikh militants and independence advocates. In China, various Muslim separatists have also been responsible for a number of bus bombings. In Turkey, members of the Kurdish Workers Party and of the Dev Sol (Revolutionary Left) terrorist group have attacked both buses and trains.

Over the years, many bus ambushes may have been less terrorist events than simply economic crimes. Many nations in Asia and South America have reported bandit ambushes on buses. While some of these have resulted in deaths of passengers and have been credited to groups that may have had political motives, many appear to have been the modern equivalent of train robberies. Bandits generally robbed passengers and permitted the buses to continue traveling. A number of bus-related incidents have targeted tourists rather than nationals, indicating a desire by the terrorist group to undercut the host country's economic viability as a destination that outsiders would consider visiting. Such events have occurred in Ski Lanka, Kenya, and South Africa. The Thai government has also received extortionist threats against buses carrying international tourists. In Egypt, Muslim fundamentalists have attacked a number of tour buses.

A recent example of events that take place on buses that can have international ramifications occurred in the summer of 2010 in the Philippines, where a siege of a bus carrying a Hong Kong tour group resulted in the deaths of 8 members of the group and friction between the two countries. In this situation, as in many that involve public transit, the deaths occurred during a standoff between the hostage taker, identified as an armed former police officer who was demanding his job back, and the local police.

Situations where the transit venue is merely a stage for local dispute can be among the most dangerous because the hostage taker is more emotional than in an organized attack, and the response may be equally disorganized. In a textbook example of how not to set up a hostage command post, the Manila police director took direct command and set up his command post in a restaurant that lacked a television or any equipment with which to communicate with the hostage taker. Postincident analysis pointed to some of the deaths having been caused by police gunfire rather than by the hostage taker. It was also estimated that the deaths could cost the Philippines about $70 million in losses by keeping tourists from Hong Kong and China away.

In the United States, incidents of what could be termed bus hijackings or bus kidnappings have generally involved disgruntled employees or, more commonly, emotionally disturbed persons. In some of these cases, the perpetrators have wanted to make their real or imagined grievances known to the public, but many cases have involved individuals with a fascination for buses who have simply entered bus garages as trespassers and driven the buses out of the garages. An example of this occurred in the fall of 2010, when a well-known individual fascinated with both buses and trains simply drove a bus out of an unlocked depot in Hoboken, New Jersey, across the Hudson River, into Manhattan. Upon surrendering to police, he claimed to have stolen as many as 150 buses from the same depot and to have driven them as far as North Carolina before returning them without ever being challenged.

While this is a transit-related incident, it was only the suspect's interest in buses that prevented him from taking a truck or a motor vehicle from a similarly unlocked facility. The potential for far greater danger is obvious: the entire facility could be destroyed, individual buses could be rigged with explosives to be used as weapons, or individuals disguised as legitimate drivers could hijack a busload of patrons.

Instances of hijacking or rigging an occupied bus with explosives are rare. Many bus systems in the United States have installed surveillance cameras onboard. Although intended primarily to deter vandalism and assaults against operators, the presence of video recording is generally well publicized and may deter hijackers or terrorists. Currently, funding for additional surveillance is available from the Department of Homeland Security (DHS). As with its funding of surveillance in rail stations and, to a lesser degree, on transit vehicles, these are projects where crime prevention and terrorist deterrence are seen as having a considerable overlap. In one such case, Portland, Oregon, arson investigators in 2006 released tape taken from a bus to help identify a man who was photographed planting a pipe bomb and then leaving the bus.

The advent of global positioning technology has made it easier for transit systems to track buses along their routes. Seen primarily as a customer service to enable riders to estimate a bus's time of arrival, these tracking systems also provide security assistance. Cell phone and WiFi tracking systems, which also were developed primarily to meet the communications needs of passengers, are also viewed as crime and terrorist prevention tools.

Waterborne Terrorism

Terrorism on water has primarily involved attempting to blow up a ship, or its cargo, or to take the ship, its cargo, crew, or passengers as hostages. In that regard, it is closer to bus incidents, but on water rather than on land. Generally, the difference between piracy and waterborne terrorism pertains more to motives than to tactics. Historically, although piracy often contained a political rationale, the primary motive was money. Today this distinction has been blurred.

Attacks and Hijackings

The most remembered water-based terrorist events that involved U.S. citizens could not have been more different; one involved the hijacking of a civilian vessel in which the United States was not the primary target of the attack, and the other the bombing of the *USS Cole*, a naval destroyer, as it was being refueled in Yemen, in which the United States was the obvious target.

Although it occurred a long time ago, the *Achillo Lauro* incident seems to have occurred even earlier than 1985. In retrospect, the nation was naïve about terrorism. In the intervening years, many incidents have been labeled by observers as the start of the era of terrorism; to many of these observers, the *Achillo Lauro* must be included in that listing. In October 1985, 4 Palestinian militants who were part of the Palestine Liberation Front (PLO) seized the Italian cruise liner just outside of Port Said, Egypt. More than 400 vacationing passengers were held hostage; it was later learned that the British and American passengers had been separated from the others. What was known immediately was that an elderly, wheelchair-bound Jewish passenger from New York, Leon Klinghoffer, after having been separated from his wife, was killed and thrown overboard.

As the hostage situation continued, the hijackers demanded the release of 50 Palestinian prisoners being held in Israel. Other than the death of an American citizen, the United States was very much a bystander to the original events, which ended two days later when the ship docked in Cairo after Abu Abbas, the PLO leader, negotiated its exchange for passage to Tunis for himself and his cohorts. Although U.S. fighter planes intercepted the plane and forced it to land in Sicily, the Italian government refused to turn Abbas and two of his associates over to the U.S. Marines. Although he was eventually tried in absentia, Abbas was never imprisoned or otherwise held accountable for the events.

Fifteen years later, in October 2000, two suicide bombers in a small rubber boat floated next to the *USS Cole* and blew a hole in its side in the port of Aden, Yemen. Seventeen sailors were killed and another 39 wounded. The blast, although technically unsolved, has been attributed by most observers to al Qaeda. For many it was their first exposure to what has since become one of the best-known terrorist organizations in the world, responsible for the September 11, 2001, attacks and numerous others targeting a variety of transit facilities around the world.

The attack was as unsophisticated as it was lethal. The naval destroyer was in port to refuel and few security precautions had been taken. The two men in the small craft waved up at the sailors on deck and detonated their cargo of explosives. The men, presumed to have died, were never seen again. Despite the work of a large number of U.S. civilian and military investigators, who received little cooperation from Yemeni officials, the official investigation was for all practical purposes discontinued in the summer of 2001, although Yemeni officials claimed in 2002 to be investigating a suspect who blew himself up before he could be arrested. The *USS Cole* underwent more than $250 million in repairs; it was deemed seaworthy three days before the 9/11 terrorist attacks.

Piracy—Updating an Old Crime to New Purposes

Piracy has traditionally been defined as the taking of persons or property by force or threat on water, whether rivers, lakes, seas, or oceans. During biblical times the amphoras of oil and spices were the loot taken by marauding thieves. Ships have changed from oar-manned, to sail, to steam, to newer power sources, but the practice of piracy remains. Like the train robbers of the Old West, piracy and pirates have been glamorized by countless authors and Hollywood producers, who depicted them as swashbuckling heroes, but in fact they were and continue to be thieves and murderers.

In the sixteenth and seventeenth centuries, trade from Europe to the New World was particularly harassed. Pirates were captured and "hung from the yardarm" or taken back to Europe for trial and more formalized hanging. From the late eighteenth century until the early nineteenth century, various Muslim mini-state leaders along the North African Barbary Coast engaged in piracy as well as slave trade. They were quite successful in demanding tribute from the European countries that sailed the Mediterranean, as well as from the United States, in part because it was deemed cheaper to pay than to fight.

In the United States, Thomas Jefferson opposed paying tribute and, upon being elected president, refused to meet the demands. Tripoli's Pasha declared war on the United States, and on February 16, 1804, an important battle against the Barbary Pirates was led by Lt. Stephen Decatur. His men captured a small Tripolian ketch, which he would use to retrieve the *USS Philadelphia*, which had been captured months before when it went aground while patrolling the harbor at Tripoli. After neutralizing the Tripolian sailors on board, he and his men set the *Philadelphia* afire, depriving the pirates of the prize. Two months later, another important battle was fought to free the prisoners in the city of Derne, Tripoli (now Libya), and depose the Pasha. John Eaton, an American accompanied by Marine Lt. Presley O'Bannon and seven Marines, took a group of 500 Arab and Greek mercenaries across the desert from Egypt and eventually secured the release of all the prisoners. This battle formed the basis of the words "to the shores of Tripoli" that are included in the Marine Corps Hymn.

Piracy has occurred wherever there is water for ships to traverse. Until recently, most reported acts of piracy were found in the China Seas, the Malacca Straits, and the Philippines, with smaller incidents occurring in the Caribbean and along the west coast of South America. Today the greatest number of ship hijackings and ransom transactions are taking place off the Horn of Africa, primarily in the Gulf of Aden, the Indian Ocean, and further south, toward the Seychelles Islands. This is the path of merchant shipping traffic transiting the Suez Canal, in both directions. These crimes are being carried out mostly by young Somalians, with at least some of the proceeds going to terrorists affiliated with al-Shabaab, a group patterned after al Qaeda.

One theory is that the reason for the country's involvement in piracy is its lack of a functioning government, in large part a product of its history. In the late nineteenth century, when European colonialism came to Africa, the northern part of Somalia, Somaliland, was ruled by the British, while the main part of Somalia was ruled by the Italians. This colonial period mirrored precolonial times, when five principal clans held the country together, but just as easily drove it apart. When colonial rule ended in the 1960s, Somaliland had a more formal government structure than southern Somalia. The ensuing civil war that began in 1991 included a number of battles. In the October 1993 Battle of Mogadishu (called the first battle), United Nations forces were pitted against Somali militia fighters, with support from civilians who were loyal to the warlord Aidid. This battle, a strategic victory for the militia and a tragic situation for U.S. forces, was depicted in the book and motion picture *Black Hawk Down*.

The civil war continued, and by 2006, after the second Battle of Mogadishu, the government was almost nonexistent, a problem that persists despite the efforts of the Transitional Federal Government. It was in this context, with no official Somali Coast Guard, that various foreign commercial fishing fleets began harvesting huge catches from Somali waters. Fishing by local Somali fishermen was severely diminished, which devastated their livelihood as well as the nation's weak economy. In anger, some fishermen attacked smaller foreign boats and took what they could. Success led to increased hijackings and escalated demands, as the ransoms became an economic windfall.

As the ransom money started arriving, sometimes dropped by parachute to the ships being held, the organized criminal element moved in. They supplied the pirates with newer and more powerful weapons, technology, and ransom collection procedures, and reportedly began using countries like Lebanon to arrange money exchanges.

It has been reported that certain communities in Somalia have become boomtowns, not unlike the gold rush days of the American and Canadian West in the 1890s. Young men who were drawn into the piracy operations now have money and power—including women, large homes, and expensive cars. Their lives are not unlike the drug cartel operators in Latin America.

Somali pirates captured 45 ships in 2009 and 49 vessels in 2010, sometimes killing crew members in the process. The rest of the crew and the ships were taken ashore and held for ransom. To increase their range of operations, the pirates use skiffs to speed off shore, hijack local ocean-going fishing boats and then head out to sea to overtake merchant ships. The U.S. Navy has been part of an international force assembled to protect ships navigating the Horn of Africa and the Indian Ocean and have occasionally captured pirates. In November 2010, five Somali pirates were found guilty of attacking the Navy warship U.S.S. Nicholas. At a trial in Norfolk, Virginia, the five were found guilty. It was the first piracy conviction in the U.S. in 190 years. In February, 2011, another pirate, Abduwali Abdukhadir Muse, was tried for hijacking the Maersk Alabama and holding its captain, Richard Phillips, and crew hostage. He was convicted and sentenced to 33 years in prison.

These trials and lengthy prison sentences do not seem to have had any immediate impact on piracy. In late February 2011, within days of Abdukhadir Muse being sentenced, Somali pirates fatally shot four unarmed Americans who had been sailing their 58-foot sloop on an around-the-world cruise, distributing Bibles at a number of the ports they visited. The victims, two retired couples who had been seized in the Arabian Sea after leaving a group that sailed together for protection, were killed as the U.S. Navy was attempting to bargain for their freedom. Following the shooting, Navy SEALs captured 13 of the 19 pirates who took part in the hijacking. Two pirates were found dead on the Americans' boat and two were already in U.S. custody. After the pirates were turned over to the FBI, 14 of them were indicted in Norfolk, Va., on multiple charges of piracy, kidnapping and firearms use. Americans are not the only targets; a pirate who had kidnapped a Danish family in February 2011 offered a month later to let all but the 13-year old daughter go free if the family allowed her to remain behind and marry the pirate instead of paying the $5 million ransom he had originally demanded. The family—father, mother, two teen-aged sons, and the daughter—were kidnapped along with two crew members as they sailed their yacht about 350 miles off the Somali coast.

Conclusion

All modes of transportation have been attractive targets to terrorists; this is unlikely to change. Despite the difficulties in protecting facilities that are widely used and highly accessible, a number of techniques have been developed. These are discussed in Chapter 13.

Endnotes

1. Peter Guerrero, Director, Physical Infrastructure Issues, Government Accountability Office. Statement in Testimony before the Subcommittee on Banking, Housing, and Urban Affairs, U.S. Senate, Sept. 18, 2002; Brian M. Jenkins and Larry N. Gersten. *Protecting Public Transportation against Terrorism and Serious Crime: Continuing Research on Best Security Practices.* MTI Report 01-07. San Jose, CA: Mineta Transportation Institute, 2001.
2. Senate Committee on Governmental Affairs. *Riding the Rails: How Secure Is Our Passenger and Transit Infrastructure?* 107th Congress, 1st sess., 2001, S. Hrg. 107-311.
3. Dorothy M. Schulz and Susan Gilbert. *Video Surveillance Uses by Rail Transit Agencies.* Washington, D.C.: Transit Cooperative Research Program, in press.
4. Anti-Defamation League. Major Terrorist Attacks in Israel. www.adl.org/israel_attacks.asp (accessed October 31, 2010).
5. Israeli Bus Bomb Attacks. *Counter Terror Gazette*, August 17, 2010. ct-gazette.com/.../Israeli-bus-bomb atta.... (accessed October 31, 2010).

Weapons of Mass Destruction

8

A Long History

The use of biological and chemical weapons in warfare and criminal acts has a long history and predates modern science, the Industrial Revolution, and even the Renaissance. In ancient Greece, the Spartans used toxic sulfur fumes against their enemies. Even before that, Assyrians in the sixth century B.C. used grain mold ergot to poison the wells of their enemies. In Greece, Solon, the archon of Athens, used the herb hellebore, whose roots and leaves are poisonous, in the siege of Krissa. In Mesopotamia in the third century, the inhabitants of Hatra dropped clay pots filled with poisonous scorpions on the heads of the invading Romans. Though the practice of throwing dead animals or other noxious material into fortified positions certainly predates them, the Tartars in 1346 catapulted bodies of comrades who died of the plague into a settlement of Western traders at Kaffa in the Crimea. Some historians believe the survivors of this attack carried the plague, called the Black Death, with them when they returned to Italy. Spanish conquistadors used germ warfare, unintentionally or otherwise, in wiping out populations as they forged through the Americas. In 1763, in an effort to quell Pontiac's Rebellion during the French and Indian Wars, British General Jeffery Amherst was said to have ordered the use of smallpox blankets against Indians allied with the French. The use of disease-bearing blankets and clothing remained a frontier-clearing tactic through most of the nineteenth century.

The major milestone, and perhaps birthplace of the concept of weapons of mass destruction (WMD), came during the Great War of 1914–1918. As World War I settled into static trench warfare where gains were measured in yards rather than in miles, military leaders on both sides scrambled for methods for gaining a breakthrough. Then on April 22, 1915, at the Belgian town of Ypres, a new horror was unleashed on the world. On a beautiful spring day, with a slight breeze blowing toward the Allied trenches occupied by French colonial troops, the soldiers were alerted to a hissing sound that was emanating from the German trenches. The French troops watched with curiosity as a greenish yellow fog rolled toward them, coming in low, barely head high. By the time the cloud of gas completely enveloped the trench line, thousands of men were retching uncontrollably and some were already dead.

The Germans had unleashed a lethal cloud of chlorine gas that incapacitated thousands of French colonial troops.

Following the war, as a direct result of liberal use of gas, not to mention the horrific injuries and death that it caused, most nations of the world adopted the Geneva Protocol, which outlawed the use of chemical and biological weapons in warfare, but did not ban the development of such weapons. Although the United States did not ratify the treaty, a "no-first-use policy" has been in place from the beginning. Like America, Japan declined to adopt the Geneva Protocol. In the 1930s, after its invasion of the Asian mainland, Japan established a biological weapons research facility near Harbin, Manchuria, that included experiments on prisoners of war, resulting in as many as 3,000 human deaths. By the end of World War II, the Japanese had produced more than 4½ kilos[1] of anthrax for use in fragmentation bombs. The United States also had biological and chemical weapons research programs throughout the war until 1969, when President Richard M. Nixon put an end to the research. All of the U.S. biological and chemical weapons were subsequently destroyed.

The use of chemical weapons by Iraq against their Kurdish people within its borders shocked the civilized world. In March 1988, the Iraqi army, under orders from Saddam Hussein, unleashed an artillery barrage using nerve gas shells against the Kurdish town of Halabja in northeastern Iraq. The attack killed an estimated 5,000 people. Now, after decades of these weapons being dedicated to military use, the specter of their being used by terrorists is all too real. The Japanese terrorist group Aum Shinrikyo launched a sarin gas attack on an unsuspecting civilian population in a time of peace. In addition, there is the threat of the al Qaeda terrorist network, as well as others, gathering the necessary material to make a "dirty nuke" weapon.

The attack of September 11, 2001, rewrote the book on how law enforcement views the terrorist threat, especially in dealing with the potential use of WMD that may fall into the hands of a more determined terrorist organization. The "out of the box" planning and execution of the attack on the World Trade Center in New York and the U.S. Defense Department headquarters at the Pentagon shocked every counterterrorist planner and practitioner, bar none. The hijacking of aircraft has always been a key concern of government and airline security, but the simultaneous taking of four commercial airliners and mounting a suicide attack on the Pentagon and World Trade Center was certainly not in any terrorist defense playbook.

As always, the emphasis must be placed on deterrence, detection, and apprehension of terrorists. It is more important that any defensive measures put into place should be well thought out and not a knee-jerk reaction to major terrorist actions. Though Saddam Hussein had used chemical weapons and boasted of stockpiling WMDs, there were no massive caches of such weapons discovered in Iraq. Still, the threat of biological or chemical weapons of these types—or the knowledge and plans for creating them—falling into the hands of terrorists is still a real possibility.

Definition of Weapons of Mass Destruction

The term *weapons of mass destruction* encompasses a broad array of weapons, including conventional, biological, chemical, radiological, nuclear, or other such advanced weapons. Their broad-sweeping intended effect is to inflict widespread casualties and/or physical destruction.

The Threat Today

In recent decades, international terrorists have employed tactics and operations that have increased in complexity and scope. Still, the great majority of terrorist attacks involve placing explosive devices outside a building in the dead of the night or suicide bombers carrying explosives on their person or using large vehicle-borne improvised explosive devices (VBIEDs). But the suicide bomb attacks as carried out on September 11, 2001, broke the bounds in which security planning had been carried out. A number of terrorist organizations, especially those of a radical Islamic bent, are now believed to be exploring the use of new and deadlier methods with which to kill innocent victims. The use of chemical and biological agents as WMD can now also be included as a viable terrorist option.

Biological and chemical agent weapons, in what was once an option limited to the military of a very select group of nations, now fall into the arsenal of the terrorist. Many of these chemical and biological agents can be manufactured or obtained by a determined group of terrorists or an individual. The anthrax attack that came on the heels of 9/11 made the threat a reality. The case remains unsolved, although officially the suspected source is believed to be domestic rather than foreign. But the question asked by many was: Is this the work of an Islamic radical group, such as al Qaeda, a right-wing domestic operation, or simply the work of a demented mind? A case in point is the Arkansas farmer who was arrested in 1995 for having 130 grams of the deadly biological agent ricin in his possession. If released into the atmosphere in a weaponized form, this amount had the potential to kill thousands of people. The individual who was arrested in this case committed suicide in his jail cell. In a much lower-profile incident in July 2004, ground-up castor beans and trace amounts of ricin were found in jars of baby food sold in a southern California supermarket.

Closely following on the heels of the 9/11 attack, a series of anthrax-laced letters were delivered through the U.S. Postal Service that ultimately resulted in the deaths of five individuals, all U.S. citizens. With this attack, new ground was broken and the public in both this country and allied nations was thrown into a state of panic and concern about their vulnerability to attacks of WMD. In addition to biological and chemical attacks, the use of a nuclear weapon against domestic targets is also very much a concern, as witnessed by fear generated by the arrest of Jose Padilla, the so-called dirty bomber at O'Hare Airport in Chicago on May 8, 2002. For the most part, chemical and biological agents, or at least the building blocks to create them, are fairly easy to obtain through a number of venues by almost any fairly sophisticated and organized terrorist group.

Nuclear material, however is somewhat more difficult, but not impossible, to obtain. Not only can raw nuclear-grade materials be obtained, but complete nuclear warheads are said to be available for purchase on the underground for the right price. Since the breakup of the Soviet Union in the 1990s, intelligence reports indicate that a number of nuclear warheads are unaccounted for and may have fallen into the hands of underworld criminals and black marketers. Complicating the matter is that many of the now-independent former socialist republics laid claim to assets of the Soviet Union, including weapon factories and the military equipment located within their borders. This included nuclear material for power usage as well as weapons and materials used in their manufacture. As newly created and independent countries, many were desperately short of hard currency, and such nuclear material would be viewed as a valuable commodity by a major terrorist organization or rogue nation.

Even though the public fixation of a biological or chemical attack being imminent has died down considerably, the threat is still very real. The stronger Iran becomes and as long as al Qaeda and other Islamic terrorist groups with philosophical, if not operational, ties to it stay active, the threat remains.

Aum Shinrikyo Incident

Human destruction and fanatical cults have a long association, through mass suicides or episodes that result in the death of others. In 1978, a messianic Jim Jones convinced followers to commit suicide in a jungle encampment called Jonestown in Guyana. More than 900 of them did, including adults who fed poison-laced Kool-Aid to their children. At the end of the twentieth century, a group of nearly 40 individuals belonging to a cult called Heaven's Gate committed suicide in a misguided effort to rendezvous with an alien spacecraft they thought would appear in the wake of the Hale-Bopp Comet passing close to Earth. These inner-directed killings were horrific on one level, but what happened in Tokyo in 1995 prompted new cause for concern by counterterrorism planners dealing with the potential use of WMD.

The Aum Shinrikyo cult was unknown to the general public, especially outside Japan. The leader of the group was a half-blind former acupuncturist named Shoko Ashara who turned to religion and mysticism. He was born in 1955 as Shoko Matsumoto. At one point he owned a folk medicine shop before traveling to Tibet to study Buddhism and Hinduism. In 1984 he founded the Aum Shinsen Club, recruiting 15 original followers. Within a few years the organization had grown to 1,300 members. There was international growth as well, particularly in the Soviet Union and, following its collapse, Russia and the other newly independent republics. The ranks swelled with tens of thousands of new members. The organization later changed its name to Aum Shinrikyo, or the "Supreme Truth," with Ashara now considered as god by his followers. At its peak, the movement counted almost 40,000 members in six countries.

Ashara's aim soon became the overthrow of the Japanese government. In order to neutralize the nation's leaders, he planned to attack key points of the Japanese government's operations. The group first experimented with a wide range of chemical agents, including a number of variants of nerve agents such as sarin, tabun, soman, and VX. In addition, they explored using hydrogen cyanide and possibly phosgene and mustard agents. Aum Shinrikyo finally settled upon sarin, primarily because it is relatively easy to manufacture.

The sarin gas to be used in the attacks was manufactured by cult members in Kamikuishiki, Japan. During this growth period, the group's extreme radical views came to the attention of law enforcement officials. It also became known that the sect was manufacturing sarin gas. Although the group was responsible for a number of accidental spills that affected nearby areas, and despite their suspected experimentation with chemical agents, local officials took no action because they determined up to that point the group had violated no existing laws. This neutralized law enforcement's efforts to control the group's activity. The Aum Shinrikyo group made several attempts to use chemical weapons on selected targets, first targeting rival religious and cult leaders. The cult launched its first successful attack at Matsumoto against an apartment complex as the occupants were asleep. The attack occurred on the morning of July 27, 1994, when sarin gas was released using a truck-mounted dispersal system located outside the complex. The gas traveled into the open windows of the building, and before long there were seven dead and 600 others sickened. The attack was launched with the intent of assassinating several judges who were about to hand down a ruling in a land dispute that the cult felt would be injurious to its members.

Although the Japanese police launched a massive investigation, they had little success in tracing the chemical agent to Aum Shinrikyo. It was later learned that the group had been testing their sarin on animals in Western Australia and the attack at Matsumoto was the testing ground for a weapon that they had been working on for years.

As the police continued to investigate the group's activity, members launched another attack on March 20, 1995. This attack was made against the Tokyo subway system at the height of rush hour. Aum Shinrikyo members produced approximately seven liters of high-grade sarin for the attack. The attack was well planned, and targeted the five different train lines that merged at the Kasumigaseki station, which was located closest to the Tokyo police headquarters. The attackers hoped that releasing the gas on these trains would kill those who worked in police headquarters and other government buildings located in the area. The sarin was packaged in plastic bags and activated by a cult member who punctured the bags with an umbrella. Although sarin is an extremely deadly gas and caused close to 6,000 injuries of various degrees, only 12 people died. This was attributed to the fact that the chemical was only 35% pure, as well as to the efficiency of the air-filtering systems in the subway.

The hospitals treated the attack victims with drug inhibitors and antidotes, mostly atropine and two-pan chloride. Due to the short supply of these drugs, only the most severe cases were able to be treated with the antidote serum. The typical sarin poisoning symptoms are convulsion, vomiting, loss of balance, double vision, and slurred speech.

Shortly after the attack, the police raided a number of Aum Shinrikyo locations and seized a large amount of chemicals that can be used in the manufacture of sarin, mustard gas, VX, and other biological agents. Besides manufacturing gas, the group also attempted to manufacture assault rifles based on the design of the Russian-made AK-47.

Since the Supreme Truth came to the attention of the Japanese law enforcement community, more than 400 of its members have been arrested over the years. Of those arrested, 100 have been convicted of crimes ranging from attempted murder to wiretapping, kidnapping, and possession of illegal weapons. There were 14 cult members arrested in connection with the subway attack. Of the five members who actually took part in the attack, four were given death sentences and one member was given a life sentence.

U.S. Anthrax Attack

On September 28, 2001, a 38-year-old assistant to NBC TV newscaster Tom Brokaw noticed a lesion on her cheek and sought medical assistance at a local hospital. Within two weeks, the woman's sores were diagnosed as a cutaneous, or skin, form of anthrax. In short order, news surfaced about other anthrax-laced letters sent to the headquarters of major television networks, the *New York Post* newspaper, New York Governor George Pataki's office, and that of Senator Tom Daschle, Democratic party leader in the

U.S. Senate. The Morgan postal service center in New York City was shut down for several days, while the Brentwood postal facility in Washington, D.C., was shut down for a lengthy period of time. One of the first places where anthrax-laced mail was confirmed was the headquarters of American Media, Inc. in Boca Raton, Florida. In addition, a number of other mail handling facilities were contaminated to varying degrees by tainted letters or packages through them.

Five people would die from exposure to anthrax. All would die of the inhalation type of infection. Almost a dozen others were infected with both inhalation and skin versions of the disease. These incidents triggered massive law enforcement investigations. Coming so close on the heels of the 9/11 terrorist attacks, a panic reaction hit hundreds of thousands Americans. The FBI investigated a number of suspects, or at least persons of interest. One in particular, Stephen Hatfill, came to the forefront after the FBI raided his home and went so far as to drain a pond looking for evidence, but the cases remain unsolved for the longest time. Periodically the subject resurfaced in the news and Hatfill later sued the Department of Justice, FBI's parent agency, and was awarded $2.8 million and an annuity of $150,000 for 20 years. Later, on August 1, 2008, a Dr. Bruce Ivins, another person of interest looked at by the FBI, committed suicide. After that the FBI conveniently declared the cases officially closed.

Even with the closure of the 2001 incidents, a number of "white powder" cases have cropped up in the ensuing years. Because anthrax spores can easily spread throughout an area, there are a number of safeguards recommended by the Centers for Disease Control and Prevention if it is suspected that an anthrax letter has been received:

1. Do not shake or empty the contents of the suspicious letter.
2. Do not carry the suspected letter to others or allow others to examine it.
3. Place the envelope on a level surface.
4. Do not touch, smell, taste, or closely examine the suspected powder.
5. Warn those in the area and leave immediately.
6. Do not open windows and, if possible, shut off any ventilating systems.
7. Wash your hands with soap and water to prevent spreading the potentially infectious material to the face or other areas of the body.
8. Notify security or law enforcement.
9. If possible, complete a list of all people who were in the area or may have handled the suspected item. Provide the list to law enforcement and first responder emergency medical personnel.

Chemical and Biological Agents

In the past, when the term *chemical weapon* was used, it usually brought to mind the military application, such as occurred during World War I. During the war, phosgene, chlorine, cyanide, and mustard gases were all put into play. After World War I, the rules governing warfare all but outlawed the use of such WMD. In 1925, a Geneva Protocol governing the rules of war prohibited the further use of chemical and biological weapons. The United States signed the document, but it was never ratified by Congress. In 1997, a more modern chemical weapons ban was signed by 160 nations, but obviously not by any terrorist organization.

In other major wars of the twentieth century, including World War II, Korea, and Vietnam, deadly gas was not an option to be used on the battlefield. Although many nations stockpiled biological and chemical weapons, none were used until the war between Iraq and Iran during the 1980s, which saw the reintroduction of the deadly chemical agents. Iraq's leader Saddam Hussein used chemical weapons to quell dissent among the Kurdish people seeking autonomy for a homeland that they hoped would eventually unite Kurds in Iraq, Iran, and Turkey.

Today, chemical, biological, and nuclear weapons are linked with terrorists and rogue states, such as North Korea and Iran. There are literally thousands of combinations that can be deadly to humans, although for practical reasons, including cost and method of delivery, only a few must to be considered in counterterrorism efforts.

Transmission of Infectious Agents

Direct transmission is immediate, as the transfer of the infectious agent goes directly into the body. This is accomplished by personal contact, such as touching, kissing, or biting, as the agent enters through the mouth, openings in the skin, or other body cavities. Direct transmission via aerosol occurs when tiny droplets enter through the nose, mouth, or eyes during spitting, coughing, and the like.

Indirect transmission includes a variety of methods:

1. Vehicle-borne transmission is when the agent is introduced through food, drink, or sera ingested into the system.
2. Vector-borne introduction comes through contact with insect or parasite bites or other injection methods.
3. Airborne transmission involves aerosols that usually enter the victim through the respiratory tract. These aerosols could linger in the

air for days, with some retaining their ability to cause harm, while others lose potency when exposed to sunlight or other elements.

Chemical Agents

Chemical agents may come in the form of solids, gases, or liquids. The form in which the chemical is presented often depends upon temperature and pressure under which the agent is maintained. Most chemical agents come in some variety of liquid form, but there are exceptions, such as riot control agents that are solids, usually in the form of a very fine powder. Chemical agents can produce a variety of effects, depending upon their volatility and resistance to evaporation. Some effects can occur within seconds, while others may not appear until days after contact. The components of the chemical agent and the ambient factors such as temperature, wind velocity, and the texture of the surface upon which the agent comes to rest all affect the volatility and potency of the agent.

There are a number of specialized terms used in association with chemical weapons, including:

Aerosol: Fine liquid or solid particles suspended in a gas, including fog or smoke.

Atropine: First aid treatment for a nerve agent, such as sarin, tabun, or VX.

Blister agents: Substances that cause blistering of the skin; may occur by liquid or vapor contact with exposed tissues, such as eyes, skin, and lungs.

Blood agents: Injure by interfering with the exchange of oxygen and carbon dioxide between blood and tissue.

Casualty agents: Produce incapacitation, serious injury, or death; these agents are the choking, blister, nerve, and blood agents.

Central nervous system depressants: Compounds that have the effect of blocking the activity of the central nervous system and interfering with the ability to think; can reduce motivation.

Central nervous system stimulants: Compounds that have the effect of flooding the brain with too much information, resulting in a loss of concentration and causing indecisiveness and the inability to act in a purposeful manner.

Choking agents: Damage the lungs through inhalation; in extreme cases, membranes swell and lungs become filled with liquid, and death results from lack of oxygen.

Cutaneous: Pertaining to the skin.

G-series nerve agents: Chemical agents of moderate to high toxicity that were developed during the 1930s; examples include tabun (GAO), sarin (GBO), and soman (GD).

Incapacitating agents: Produce physical or psychological effects or both that may persist for hours or days after exposure, rendering victims incapable of performing normal physical and mental tasks; these agents are not likely to produce permanent injuries.

Industrial agents: Manufactured for use in industrial operations and processes or for use by government or other researchers; produced for the purpose of causing casualties; examples include hydrogen cyanide, cyanogens, chloride, phosgene, and many herbicides.

Lethality: Refers to whether an agent will cause fatalities or the degree of incapacitation.

Liquid agent: Usually appears as an oily film or droplets; color ranges from clear to brownish amber.

Nerve agent: Interferes with the central nervous system; exposure is primarily through the skin and by inhalation. Three major symptoms are pinpoint pupils, extreme headache, and severe tightness in the chest.

Nonpersistent agent: Agent that generally loses effectiveness after 10 or 15 minutes. It has a high evaporation rate and, since lighter than air, will disperse rapidly; although a short-term hazard, in unventilated areas it will be more persistent.

Percutaneous agent: Retains its casualty-producing effects for an extended period of time, anywhere from several minutes to several days. It has a low evaporation rate since its vapor is heavier than air and tends to hug the ground; considered a long-term hazard.

Toxicity: A measure of a quantity of an agent required to achieve a given effect.

Vapor agent: A gaseous form of a chemical agent. If heavier than air, the cloud will lie close to the ground, and if lighter, it will rise and disperse more rapidly.

V-series agents: Developed in the 1950s, with moderate to high toxicity; examples include VE, VG, VM, and VX.

Volatility: A measure of how readily a substance will vaporize.

Common Nerve Agents

Intended to disrupt the way in which the body's nervous system and organs interact, nerve agents can be extremely toxic and, in almost all cases, have a very rapid effect on the victim. Nerve agents can be in the form of gas, aerosol, or liquid and can enter the body through inhalation or through the skin and are usually clear and colorless. Heavier than air, when they are released, they settle along the ground and lower terrain features. Exposure to even a low dose of a nerve agent will cause the victim to display such symptoms as an increased production of saliva, a runny nose, and a feeling of pressure on the chest; eye pupils contract, impairing vision, especially at night; in addition, the capacity of the eye is also reduced so that short-range vision deteriorates and the victim feels pain when trying to focus on nearby objects. Effects also include headaches, tiredness, slurred speech, hallucinations, and nausea. At higher exposure levels, the victim suffers a much more severe reaction, including involuntary discharge of urine and feces as well as running eyes, sweating, muscular weakness, local tremors, and respiratory system effects, usually causing death by suffocation. The common nerve agents are:

Sarin (GB and GF). This item is classified as a nerve agent that disrupts the transmission of nerve impulses in the body. It is a colorless, odorless liquid that mixes readily in water and may be ingested, inhaled, or absorbed through the skin. Depending on the dose, onset of clinical manifestation can vary from within a few minutes to one hour, although most occur within minutes. Signs and symptoms include visual disturbance, runny nose, chest tightness, nausea, vomiting, convulsions, and death. Treatment includes atropine, pralidoxime chloride, and diazepam. Sarin can, depending on the environmental conditions, persist from a quarter of an hour to as long as two days.

Soman (GD). This is classified as a nerve agent, one that disrupts nerve impulses in the body. It is a colorless and tasteless liquid that mixes readily with water, and when released, soman evaporates rapidly, dissipates, and eventually breaks down in the environment. Clinical manifestations include visual disturbance, runny nose, chest tightness, nausea, vomiting, convulsions, and death. Treatment consists of decontamination, drugs such as atropine and pralidoxime chloride, and care. This agent may persist anywhere from 2½ days to six weeks.

Tabun (GA). Tabun is classified as a nerve agent that interrupts the transmission of nerve impulses in the body. It is a colorless to brownish liquid. Under average weather conditions, tabun can persist for one to two days. It is primarily released as an aerosol or a vapor. Clinical signs and symptoms include visual disturbance, runny nose, chest tightness, nausea, vomiting, convulsion, and death. Treatment includes atropine, pralidoxime chloride, and diazepam. The agent may be persistent from one day to two weeks.

V-series (VE, VG, V-gas, VM, and VX). These agents, originally produced by the British, disrupt the transmission of nerve impulses in the body. Amber-colored and oily liquids, they can enter the body through ingestion, inhalation, or through the eyes or skin. Health effects include constricted pupils, visual disturbance, runny nose, chest tightness, nausea, vomiting, convulsions, and death. Treatment includes atropine, pralidoxime chloride, and diazepam; ventilation to support respiratory function; and supportive care. V-agents are some of the most persistent agents and can last anywhere from 3 days to 16 weeks.

Blood Agents

Blood agents are absorbed into the body through the action of breathing, and once in the body and bloodstream, they can cause lethal damage by acting on an enzyme known as cytochrome oxidase. The overall cause of death with these agents is suffocation. The major blood agents are:

Hydrogen cyanide (AC)
Hydrogen chloride
Cyanogen chloride (CK)
Arsine (SA)

Blister (Mustard) Agents

Blister or mustard agents are named for the wounds they cause, primarily blisters or burns. Mustard gas was first used by the Germans in July 1917 during World War I. These agents also cause severe tissue damage to the eyes, respiratory system, and internal organs. Blister agents in their pure state are colorless and almost odorless, but when weaponized there is an odor of rotten onions or mustard. The agent is absorbed into the skin, eyes, or respiratory system within minutes of contact. On exposed skin, the symptoms are similar to a sunburn, with itching and small blisters that may develop within the reddened area. Eye lesions will develop before those on the skin. Blister agents include mustard gas (H and HD). At room temperature, mustard agents are liquids that are stable with a low volatility, but very persistent, with a life of from about two days up to eight weeks.

Nitrogen mustard (HN) agents are oily, colorless to pale yellow liquids, with some of these agents being odorless while others have a faint odor of fish.

Lewisite agents have the odor of geranium flowers and produce more severe skin lesions than the sulfur mustard-type agents. Pain begins almost immediately, with blisters forming in almost half the time that they take to develop with sulfur mustards. These agents are heavier than air and will settle on low areas.

Choking/Lung/Pulmonary Agents

These agents, which attack lung tissues and cause pulmonary edema, were used extensively during World War I. Prior to the use of mustard gas, these were the most casualty-producing agents in use. There are a number of these agents, but the most widely recognized are chlorine, cyanide, and phosgene.

Chlorine: Known to millions as an agent to sanitize water in swimming pools, chlorine was first used in a gaseous form during World War I as a choking agent. The extent of poisoning caused by chlorine is determined by the duration of exposure. Chlorine attacks the eyes, throat, and lungs with symptoms that include coughing, chest tightness, burning of the eyes, throat, and nose, blurred vision, nausea and vomiting, and fluid forming in the lungs within two to four hours. Because chlorine is heavier than air, it will sink to low-lying areas.

Cyanide: This rapidly acting and potentially deadly chemical is also used in the manufacture of paper and textiles. The military designations are AC (hydrogen cyanide) and CK (cyanogen chloride). AC was also known as Zyklon B and was used as a genocidal agent in World War II. Less dense than air, it will rise. The agent is absorbed through the skin and inhalation and deprives the cells of oxygen. Some of the symptoms include rapid breathing, restlessness, dizziness, convulsions, low blood pressure, loss of consciousness, and respiratory failure leading to death.

Phosgene: This chemical is colorless in liquid form and yellowish brown in solid form. It can be delivered as a gas, liquid, or a solid. Depending upon how the agent is delivered, symptoms include pain within a few seconds, with red rings appearing on the exposed skin area shortly afterward; pain and irritation in the eyes coupled with temporary blindness; irritation to the upper respiratory tract; and sinus pain. At this time there is no known antidote for the agent.

Riot Control

Tearing Agents

Many times these are commonly referred to as simply tear gas. Tearing agents are used mainly as crowd control agents by law enforcement and on occasion by private individuals, in the form of pepper spray, for self-protection. The most common of these are CS and CN, which can be released in either fine droplets or particle form. These agents are designed to cause irritation to areas of contact, i.e., eyes, skin, and nose. The effects are short lived, usually

15 to 30 minutes after the sources of contamination are removed. The effects may cause excessive tearing, blurred vision, runny nose, burning and swelling in the nasal passage, difficulty swallowing, shortness of breath, nausea, and vomiting. Long-term exposure or a heavy dose may cause blindness, or death due to severe chemical burns to the throat and lungs causing respiratory failure.

Vomiting Agents

More severe than tear gas, these agents in the riot control family are identified as DA, DM, and DC. Probably the most noted is Adamsite, or DM. When this odorless agent is used in an aerosol form it will irritate the eyes, but not necessarily the skin. When released in a solid state, it can range from yellow to green in color. The agent has effects similar to those of other riot control agents, as evidenced by the absence of skin irritations, but may be able to induce irritation of the mucus membranes, coughing, sneezing, severe headache, acute pain and tightness in the chest, nausea, and vomiting. The onset of the symptoms is very rapid and, depending upon the temperature, persists from one to four hours. If released indoors where ventilation is inadequate, it can cause serious injury or even death.

Biological Agents

Biological agents can appear in either liquid or dry form. In the hands of a well-organized, trained, and determined terrorist organization or individual, biological weapons can be among the most deadly and terrifying. It has been estimated that as little as one gram of anthrax or similar agent dispersed properly has the potential of killing a significant portion of the U.S. population over time. And although there are numerous benefits and beneficial uses of modern advanced biochemical manufacturing technologies, they also allow for the possibility of an almost endless progression of lethal pathogens to be produced.

The Centers for Disease Control and Prevention classifies biological agents on their potential risk to national security and ranks them as class A, B, or C:

- *Class A agents* can be easily disseminated or transmitted person to person and can cause a high mortality rate with the potential for major public health impact. This may cause public panic and social disruption and require special action for public health preparedness.
- *Class B agents* are moderately easy to disseminate and can cause moderate health issues with a low mortality rate.

- *Class C agents* include those that can be engineered for mass dissemination in the future due to availability, ease of production, and dissemination. They have a potential for a high mortality rate and having a major health impact.

Common Terms Associated with Biological Agents

Aerosol: A fine mist or spray that contains solid particles, typically in a fog or smoke.

Antibody: Proteins produced by an organism's immune system to recognize a foreign substance.

Antigen: Any substance that stimulates an immune response by the body. The immune system recognizes such substances as foreign and produces cellular antibodies to fight them. Antigen/antibody response is an important part of the person's immunity to disease.

Bacteria: Single-celled organism that multiplies by cell division and that can cause disease in humans, plants, and animals, although there are also many useful and helpful bacteria.

Biological warfare agents: Living organisms or materials derived from them that cause disease or harm to humans, animals, and plants. Biological agents may be used as liquid droplets, aerosols, and dry powders.

Biosafety level: Classifies the safety equipment required for a hazard threat in relation to exposure.

Level 1: Applies to agents that do not ordinarily cause human disease.

Level 2: Equipment appropriate to agents that cause human disease.

Level 3: Applies to agents that may be transmitted by the respiratory route and can cause serious infection.

Level 4: Used in dealing with exotic agents that pose a high risk of life-threatening diseases that may be transmitted by aerosol methods and for which there is no vaccine or treatment.

Contagious: Capable of being transmitted from one person to another.

Culture: A population of microorganisms grown in a medium.

Epidemic: The occurrence of cases of an illness in a region that is in excess of the number of cases normally expected for that disease in that region at the time.

Host: An animal or a plant that harbors or nourishes another organism.

Line-source delivery: A delivery system in which the biological agent is dispersed from a moving ground vehicle or from an aircraft moving in a line perpendicular to the direction of prevailing wind.

Mycotoxin: A toxin produced by fungi, plants characterized by the lack of chlorophyll, including mold and mushrooms.

Pathogen: Any organism (usually living) that is capable of producing serious death or disease.

Point-source delivery system: A delivery system in which the biological agent is dispersed from a stationary position. This method of delivery results in coverage over a smaller area than a line-source would accomplish.

Rate of exposure: The path by which a person comes into contact with an agent or organism, e.g., breathing, ingestion, or skin contact.

Reservoir: Any person, animal, or substance in which an infectious agent normally lives and multiplies. The infectious agent primarily depends on the reservoir for its survival.

Spore: A reproductive form some microorganisms take in becoming resistant to environmental conditions, such as extreme heat or cold while in a "resting stage."

Toxicity: A measure of harmful effects produced by a given amount of toxin on a living organism. It is expressed in milligrams of toxin required per kilogram of body weight to kill an experimental animal.

Toxins: Poisonous substances produced by living organisms.

Vector: An agent, such as an insect or rat, capable of transferring a pathogen from one organism to another.

Venom: A poison produced in the glands of some animals, such as snakes, scorpions, etc.

Virus: An infectious microorganism that exits as a particle rather than as a complete cell; these particles can be as small as one billionth of a meter. Viruses are not capable of reproducing outside of a host cell.

Zoonotic disease or infection: An infection or infectious disease that may be transmitted from vertebrate animals, such as rodents to humans.

Common Biological Agents: Class A

Anthrax (Baccillus anthracis), due to its high casualty rate, is the terrorist's preferred biological agent. The germ is fairly easy to produce in large quantities, inexpensive, easy to weaponize, and can be stored indefinitely in a dry powder form. Another feature is that there are only limited detection capabilities. Anthrax is a single-cell organism that is produced through a fermentation process—basically along the same lines in which beer is manufactured. Anthrax is most commonly found in agricultural regions and is natural in plant-eating animals. The bacterium that causes anthrax is *Bacillus anthracis*. The name is derived from the Greek word for coal, *anthracis*, because of its ability to cause black, coal-like lesions on the skin.

An individual can contract it in three different ways:

1. *Inhalation* is the deadliest form of the disease, with doses ranging from 2,500 to 55,000 inhaled spores that will prove fatal 50% of the time. The body's immune system will destroy some of the invading spores, but the larger spores will become trapped in the upper respiratory tract and the smallest in the tiny sacks of the lungs. The anthrax bacteria will begin to multiply quickly and infect the chest tissues, possibly as quickly as 24 hours. The incubation period, however, may take as long as six days. As the infection takes hold, a toxin is released into the blood stream, attacking the lungs and causing hemorrhaging and death. Treatment with very high doses of antibiotics can lower the death rate substantially.
2. *Cutaneous*, or skin form, is the most common type of the disease caused by direct contact with anthrax spores, and the bacteria may enter the body through any openings in the skin, such as cuts and scrapes. A painless blister, red around the edges, will form and after two days becomes a black open sore. After a couple of weeks, the sores dry and then often clear up on their own. Death rarely occurs with these cases.
3. *Gastrointestinal* is a very rare form that is contracted through ingesting contaminated meat. This form leads to acute inflammation of the intestinal tract. Symptoms include loss of appetite, vomiting, and fever, which is followed by abdominal pain, vomiting blood, and severe diarrhea. Untreated, this form can lead to death in 25 to 60% of cases.

Anthrax in its purest form is highly lethal, easy to store, and able to survive for decades, making it a prime weapon for the terrorist community. Under the right circumstances, it is possible to release a lethal cloud in a large area that would not be detected until people began to report symptoms.

Botulinun toxin is one of the most toxic substances known, and the amount of exposure determines how quickly the victim will die. It can be contracted in three ways, but the most common is through ingestion of food. The agent attacks the nerve cell synapses and causes palsy, spasms, and then paralysis. Although the military maintains a supply of vaccine for this agent, is not yet cleared for general use by the civilian population.

Merely mentioning the term *plague* in connection with a disease outbreak will send shivers up the spines of even the stoutest people. During medieval times, the plague killed an estimated 25 million people in Europe, more than a third of the region's population at the time. The *plague* is an infectious disease transmitted by bacteria commonly found in rodents (or other burrowing animals) and the fleas that they carry. A person usually becomes ill with bubonic plague two to six days after being infected. This killer disease is attractive to terrorists because of its potential for developing a huge body count, but a major drawback is the difficulty in effectively deploying it. Sustaining the virulence of the germ is hard, and as a result of this instability, it is difficult to turn the disease into a viable WMD. Pneumonic (bubonic or Black Death) plague occurs when bacteria attack the lungs. The first signs of the illness are high fever, headache, weakness, and a cough that produces blood. If the victim is left untreated, death may occur in several days or even as quickly as 24 hours. There is no known vaccine against the plague, but it may be treated in its early stages with streptomycin, tetracycline, and similar antibiotics.

Smallpox (*Variola major*), due to its high mortality rate and rapid method of transmission to others, represents one of the more serious bioterrorism threats to civilian populations. Over the centuries, naturally occurring smallpox, with its case fatality rate of 30% or more and its ability to spread in any climate and season, has been universally feared as the most devastating of all the infectious diseases. The variola virus that causes smallpox was once a worldwide scourge and had been all but eradicated throughout the world by the 1970s. This virus has an incubation period ranging from 7 to 17 days, but usually surfaces in 12, following exposure to the virus. It is highly contagious, especially during the first week of the illness, and can readily spread from person to person by infected saliva.

Initial symptoms include high fever and fatigue accompanied by head and back aches. After two to three days, a characteristics rash, most prominent on the face, arms, and legs, begins to develop. The rash usually starts as red lesions that gradually become pus filled and three to four weeks later scab and fall off. The disease was declared eliminated on a global basis by the 1970s, and in 1972 routine vaccinations against the disease were discontinued in the United States. Although there is no known treatment for smallpox, the United States maintains an emergency supply of smallpox vaccine.

Tularemia (*Francisella tularenis*) is considered a potentially dangerous biological weapon due to its extreme infective properties and the ease with which it can be disseminated. It has the capacity to cause illness and death. The disease is usually contracted via bites from an infected insect, handling an infected animal carcass, eating or drinking contaminated food or water, or breathing in the bacteria. Symptoms usually appear three to five days after exposure, but could be as long as 14 days. It is one of most infectious pathogenic bacteria known, and an extremely small amount can prove fatal. Symptoms of the disease include sudden fever, chills, headaches, diarrhea, muscle aches, joint pains, dry cough, and progressive weakness.

According to the Center for Civilian Biodefense Studies, tularemia was one of several biological weapons that were stockpiled by the U.S. military in the late 1960s, all supplies of which were destroyed by 1973. The Soviet Union continued weapons production of antibiotic- and vaccine-resistant strains into the early 1990s. The agent attacks the respiratory system. An aerosol application in all probability is the best weapon dispersal system.

Viral hemorrhagic fever (VHF) refers to a group of illnesses caused by several viruses, ranging from mild to extremely deadly. Most viruses that are associated with VHF usually reside in an animal reservoir, mainly rodents. Although initially transmitted to humans from animals, some viruses can be spread from one person to another. This can occur when one comes in contact with infected persons or their bodily fluids, or from infected syringes and needles. There are four distinct families of viruses that may cause the disease:

1. Arenaviruises
2. Filoviruses
3. Bunyaviruses
4. Flaviviruses

Symptoms of the disease vary, depending on the type of VHF that has been contracted. In almost all cases initial symptoms include fever, fatigue, dizziness, muscle aches, loss of strength, and exhaustion. In severe cases, VHF will produce bleeding under the skin, in the internal organs, and from body openings, such as the eyes, mouth, and ears, but death from loss of blood is rare. Death usually occurs due to complications with the central nervous system, shock, and sometimes kidney failure.

There are virtually no vaccines that can prevent these diseases, except for the Argentine variety of the fever. Once VHF is contracted, there is virtually no cure. There are certain strains that can be treated with particular antiviral drugs, but the mortality rate for VHF cases is extremely high.

Common Biological Agents: Class B

Q-fever, or *Coxiella burnetii*, is a zoonotic disease. The primary reservoirs are cattle, sheep, and goats. This disease is known throughout the world, but due to irregular reporting methods, it is not known how many cases occur each year. About 50% of the people infected with this disease show signs of clinical illness. The most acute cases are marked with high fever—ranging from 104°F to 105°F—accompanied by severe headaches, general malaise and confusion, sore throat, chills, sweats, coughing, nausea, vomiting, diarrhea, and abdominal and chest pains. Only 1% to 2% of the severe cases result in death. *C. burnetii* is a highly infectious agent that is rather resistant to heat and drying. It can become airborne and inhaled by humans. A single *C. burnetii* organism may cause disease in a susceptible person. This agent could be developed for use in biological warfare and is considered a potential terrorist threat.

Brucellosis is an infectious disease caused by the bacteria of brucella. This disease usually affects sheep, cattle, pigs, dogs, and some other animals, and can be transferred to humans through contact with the infected carrier. Humans are generally infected in one of three ways:

1. Eating or drinking contaminated foodstuffs
2. Inhalation of the brucellosis bacteria
3. Having the agent enter through an opening in the skin, such as an open wound or cut

This disease can cause a range of symptoms that are similar to the flu and may include fever, the sweats, headaches, back pain, and physical weakness. In severe cases the disease may affect the central nervous system or the lining of the heart. Although the disease can be treated with antibiotics, the recuperation period could be quite lengthy. A combination of antibiotic drugs must be used for at least six weeks to prevent recurrence. The mortality rate is low for the illness, and death is usually due to complications associated with brucellosis.

Ricin is derived from the castor bean. In very concentrated quantities, only a small amount is required to kill an adult. The agent can be delivered in a liquid or powder form that can be used as a poison to contaminate water or food sources. First symptoms include abdominal pain, vomiting, and bloody diarrhea, and within several days there is severe dehydration, decreased urine output, and elevated blood pressure. If death does not occur within three to five days, the patient usually recovers.

According to the Animal Science Department at Cornell University, ricin was used in the assassination of a Bulgarian journalist in 1978. The victim, who was living in London, was a critic of his government and was stabbed with the point of an umbrella while waiting at a bus stop. An autopsy found a metallic pellet embedded in his leg that presumably contained the ricin toxin.

Common Biological Agents: Class C

Yellow fever is a tropical disease that appears in two different varieties and is found only in South America and Africa. The first is the jungle variety and the other is the urban variety. The jungle variety is spread by mosquitoes biting an infected monkey and in turn biting a human. Urban yellow fever is spread by mosquitoes that have been infected by other people. The female *Aedes aegypti* is the variety of mosquito that usually carries the disease from human to human. The symptoms, starting from three to six days after being bitten, include high fever, chills, headaches, muscle aches, vomiting, and backache. After what seems like a recovery, the disease can lead to shock, bleeding, and kidney and liver failure. A severe case can be fatal.

Other Biological Agents

Cholera is caused by the bacteria *Vibria cholerae*, which infects the intestines. This will result in bouts of diarrhea, vomiting, and leg cramps. If untreated, cholera can prove fatal. The disease very often occurs after a severe disaster where the water and food supplies have become tainted. The treatment of cholera is relatively simple and effective when administered soon after the first symptoms are observed. A mixture of sugar, salt, and clean water in sufficient amounts to replenish lost fluids can effectively fight cholera.

Typhoid fever is caused by the virus known as *Salmonella typhi* and lives only in humans. This virus is carried by humans and spread by wastes that the carriers transfer to their hands from contaminated sewage or other sources. Typhoid is very common in developing countries. Symptoms include high fever, a weak feeling, stomachaches, and headaches, as well as a loss of appetite.

Nuclear Weapons

In the past several years, threat of a terrorist attack with nuclear weapons has been pushed to the front of the concerns of counterterrorism defense planning, especially in the United States. The threat deals with not only the possibility of an actual nuclear explosion or the detonation of a so-called dirty bomb, but also an attack on a nuclear power plant by a hijacked aircraft or some other means. The concern centers on well-organized terrorist groups either developing a weapon on their own or purchasing a tactical nuclear weapon, more commonly referred to as a suitcase bomb, from a rogue nation or foreign organized crime group.

Development of such weapons began during the mid-1950s, when both the United States and Soviet Union began to develop a new family of nuclear weapons that could be used in tactical combat situations that allowed for limited capabilities for a ground forces attack. By the early 1960s, the United States had developed and deployed a substantial number of fielded tactical nuclear weapons. The warheads on these weapons typically have yields of less than five kilotons.

The so-called dirty bomb, formally referred to as a radiological dispersal device (RDD), is a more realistic scenario than an actual attack carried out using a conventional nuclear weapon. A dirty bomb combines a conventional explosive, such as dynamite or trinitrotoluene (TNT), and a radioactive material. When exploded, the device will disperse the radioactive material in the immediate vicinity, and if the radioactive material is in the form of pellets or powder, it will be even more effective. The severity of the damage done will depend upon the grade of the radiological material used. The ability of terrorists to obtain nuclear material, particularly from sources outside the United States, poses major challenges. A worse possibility is that terrorists may obtain an intact tactical nuclear warhead from newly emerged former Soviet republics or a rogue nation such as North Korea or Iran. According to the Center of Defense Information, in 1996 Chechen insurgents placed a dirty bomb in a park in Moscow but did not explode the device. The act showed that the threat of using such a device was more reality than mere theory.

The extent of contamination resulting from detonation of a dirty bomb depends on a number of factors, such as the amount and type of the explosive used, the amount and quality of radioactive material used, and the prevailing weather conditions. The following are steps that may be taken in the event that a radiological explosion occurs:

1. Evacuation from the immediate area of the incident, if possible, for at least several hundred yards from the site of the explosion. Those evacuating should seek shelter indoors in order to reduce exposure to any radioactive airborne dust. This of course will be easier if the event occurs in an urban area.
2. If possible, tune to local television or radio for advisories from public safety officials.
3. Remove clothes and place them in a sealed plastic bag. Take a shower as quickly as possible to wash off dirt and dust.
4. If a radioactive material release has been confirmed, seek medical attention to monitor radiation exposure and perform other tests, as may be needed. Potassium iodide (KI) protects only the thyroid from radioactive iodine, offering the body no other protection.

Common Terms Associated with Nuclear Weapons

- *Acute radiation syndrome*: More commonly referred to as radiation syndrome and is caused when a person gets a high dose of radiation in a very short period of time. Symptoms include nausea, vomiting, diarrhea, loss of bone marrow that may lead to loss of weight, loss of appetite, flu-like symptoms, infection, and bleeding. If an individual survives, recovery can take two years.
- *Alpha particles*: Have a very short range in the air and a low ability to penetrate other material. Alpha particles are not an external radiation hazard, but present an inhalation or ingestion threat.

- *Beta particles*: High-energy electrons emitted from the nucleus of an atom during radioactive decay. The skin or other thin material may stop these particles.
- *Cesium-137*: A strong gamma ray source; can contaminate property, entailing extensive cleanup.
- *Decay*: The process by which an unstable element is changed to another isotope or another element by the spontaneous emission of radiation from its nucleus. This process can be measured with a Geiger counter.
- *Gamma rays*: High-energy photons emitted from a nucleus of atoms, similar to x-rays. These rays can penetrate deep into the body and are potentially lethal.
- *Half-life*: The amount of time needed for half of the atoms of radioactive material to decay.
- *Highly enriched uranium-235 (HEU)*: Uranium that is enriched to above 20% in uranium-235. Weapons-grade uranium HEU is enriched to above 90% in uranium-235.
- *Lethal dose (50/30)*: The dose of radiation expected to cause death within 30 days to 50% of those exposed without medical attention. It is generally accepted that 400 to 500 rem received in a short period will be fatal.
- *Plutonium-239 (Pu-239)*: A metallic element used for nuclear weapons. The half-life is 24,110 years.
- *Radiation*: High-energy alpha or beta particles or gamma rays that are emitted by an atom as the substance decays.
- *Radioactive waste*: Disposable radioactive materials resulting from nuclear operations. They are classified as either high-level or low-level waste.
- *Rem*: An acronym for roentgen equivalent in man, it is a unit of absorbed dose that will cause harm to human health.
- *Shielding*: Materials, such as lead and concrete, used to block or retard radiation for protection of people or materials.
- *Uranium-235 (U-235)*: Natural uranium found at 0.72% enrichment. U-235 is used as fuel for reactors and weapons. For weapons it is enriched to 90%.

Response to a WMD Incident

In light of the major attack on September 11, 2001, the war on terrorism took on a new meaning. Now it is even more important that an integrated response concept, especially dealing with WMD, be in place at all levels of government and with appropriate components of the private sector. Meaningful working relationships need to be formed prior to an attack to avoid not making the actual occurrence an on-the-job training experience. Since the attacks of 9/11, the federal government has greatly upgraded existing antiterrorist measures and implemented a number of initiatives, most notably the creation and organization of the Department of Homeland Security.

First Responders

A community that is the target of a terrorist attack provides the emergency first responders to the scene. As a result, local law enforcement agencies must become more proactive in deterring terrorist attacks. If an event includes a WMD, there are differences in gauging what has occurred. Where a massive IED is used, the first responder will quickly be cognizant of what has occurred. In other instances, the following applies:

Chemical incidents usually display a quick onset of symptoms and may have easily discerned characteristics, such as odor, color, victim reaction, and a concentrated affected area.

Biological incidents may or may not be apparent for several days. Many symptoms (rash, fever, etc.) may not appear until days or even weeks later. This, coupled with a dispersal of the victims after exposure, may cause it to take time for health officials to realize an attack occurred.

Radiological attacks utilizing a dirty bomb or any other release of this type of nuclear material will not typically manifest any characteristics since radiological materials are colorless or odorless.

Some of the actions or safeguards that a first responder may take when a WMD event has occurred are:

1. Approach the location from upwind of the incident site and also evacuate to upwind locations.
2. Don protective gear immediately to cover all skin, and protect the respiratory system with a self-contained breathing apparatus. Remember, think before rushing into a situation; there will be enough casualties, so don't add to the count.
3. If the incident is inside, evacuate to outdoors, minimizing traffic past the affected area, and keep all the windows and doors closed.
4. If inside and the incident is outside, have citizens stay put; instruct them to turn off the air conditioning and seal windows and doors with plastic tape if possible.

5. If radiological material is suspected, remember to minimize exposure by spending as little time in the area as possible.
6. Try to place shielding (building, land features) between yourself and the direct line of sight of where the incident occurred.
7. If available, deploy chemical-biological-radiological (CBR) detection equipment as soon as possible around the outlying areas to monitor the spread of radiation.
8. Once clear of the contaminated area, remove all external apparel, including shoes, hats, and gloves, and leave them at an isolated designated point. Proceed to a shower, within minutes if possible, and wash with soap and water. Simple flushing with water is not enough— rigorous scrubbing is required.

Federal Assistance

Although local public safety and emergency medical personnel will be the first on the scene in the event a nuclear incident occurs, they will be augmented by specially trained federal authorities.

The Joint Task Force Civil Support (JTF-CS) is headquartered in Fort Monroe, Virginia, to provide command and control over Department of Defense forces in support of a lead agency. This command is a subunit of the Joint Northern Command.

An integral part of the JTF-CS is the WMD Civil Support Team. The team was established to deploy rapidly to assist local officials in determining the extent of the attack. The WMD Civil Support Team members can provide expert technical advice and supply any follow-up federal and state military assets that may be required. Specifically, they can provide initial advice on what agents and substances may have been used and assist first responders in the detection-assessment process.

The joint units consist primarily of Army National Guard and Air National Guard personnel. These WMD support teams are not connected to the counterterrorism initiative, nor do they have any counterterrorism capability. In addition, the military has several rapid response units that can perform a civil support mission for consequences management. The U.S. Army has technical escort units and the Marine Corps has the Chemical and Biological Response Force. They will respond as part of a federal response effort initiated by the president in the event that state and local efforts prove incapable of handling the situation. These units will respond with a mobile analytical laboratory that can be used for analysis of biological or chemical agents.

Local Initiatives

Since the attack of 9/11 the threat of out-of-the-box terrorist attacks has presented a new challenge for law enforcement agencies. Many large and midsize cities have met that challenge by equipping the public safety officers with vehicle-portable and handheld chemical, biological, and radiological detectors. Detection technology is not new and has been used extensively in industrial contexts.

One example of enhanced training since 9/11 involves the New York City Police Department, which has trained hundreds of officers from its Emergency Services Division and the COBRA (Chemical, Ordnance, Biological, Radiological Awareness) program to respond to an attack using a WMD. The COBRA program is a two-day training course for front-line officers, as well as ranking personnel, that includes classroom instruction and practical exercises. The exercises include putting on level C protective equipment (see below), downwind hazard awareness, and decontamination and triage procedures.

There are a number of products on the market today that fill the needs of the law enforcement community. A list of companies that manufacture WMD detection devices was published with the article "WMD Detection Devices" by Scott Oldham, in the October 2006 *Law and Order Magazine*. This was also reprinted by Hendonpub.com. The following have been excerpted from that article:[2]

- AsistaTek: Produces a software package that will predict the dispersion of toxic or flammable vapor clouds. This software can be used on most laptops and most PC-based mobile data terminals. AsistaTek does not make any detection or protective equipment.
- BW Technologies: A division of Honeywell that manufactures gas monitors and detection equipment. The company offers a wide range of portable devices that are designed to operate under the most severe conditions.
- AutoClear: Offers a variety of products that are useful to the law enforcement community, and the article highlights the E3500 series of explosive detection equipment, calling it "one of the few products that is able to reliably detect trace amounts of explosives, including TATP and peroxide-based explosives in the vapor or particulate mode, as well as taggants that are chemically included in the manufacture of both military-grade and high-grade commercial explosives."
- Canberra: Has several items of value to law enforcement, with a number being in the radiological field, especially a handheld radiation monitor that displays dose and dose rate information on an LCD.

- Radiation Shield Technologies: Manufactures garments that protect against nuclear radiation and shield against gamma and x-ray emissions. Oldham notes, "While there are many companies that manufacture suits for chemical and biological warfare agents, there are few that are capable of handling the hazard of ionizing radiation."
- RAE Systems: Offers a variety of detection equipment for radiological and chemical incidents, including several usable by first responders. These include the GammaRAE II Responder, a radiation detector, and the ChemRAE, a chemical warfare (CW) agent detector.
- Smiths Detection: Manufacturers handheld detection devices among other items for both military and civilian applications, including the Smiths Sabre 4000 portable detection device for use in screening people for explosives in an unobtrusive manner. The detectors were tested on the New York City subway system for several months before being purchased. It was reported that the device is capable of detecting PETN, TNT, Semtex RDX, and ammonium nitrate, among other explosives, as well as such chemicals as tabun, sarin, VX, and nitrogen mustard 3.
- Thermo-Elecron Corp.: Has a full line of biochem detection equipment with the first responder in mind. The company also manufactures a line of covert detection equipment.

Protective Gear Requirements for WMD Response

The U.S. Environmental Protection Agency (EPA) standards should be used as a guideline for assembling protective gear for emergency personnel responsible for responding to WMD incidents. According to the EPA, there are four levels, A to D, with A representing the highest level of protection to be worn.

Level A: The highest level of protection is needed for the respiratory, skin, eye, and mucus membranes and requires:
  - National Institute for Occupational Safety and Health (NIOSH)-approved positive-pressure, self-contained breathing apparatus or positive-pressure supplied air respirator with an escape self-contained breathing apparatus
  - Fully enclosed chemical protective suit
  - Gloves—inner and outer, chemical resistant
  - Steel-toed and chemical-resistant boots
  - Optional two-way communication, hard hat, and coveralls or undersuit

Level B: A high level of protection is required for respiratory protection, but less is needed for eye and skin protection. The following should be the minimum level of protection worn upon an initial entry scenario:
- NIOSH-approved positive-pressure, self-contained breathing apparatus or positive-pressure supplied air respirator with an escape self-contained breathing apparatus
- Chemical-resistant clothing (overalls and long-sleeved jacket, coveralls, hooded two-piece chemical splash suit, disposable chemical-resistant coveralls)
- Chemical-resistant outer and inner gloves
- Chemical-resistant steel toe and shank boots
- Optional hard hat, two-way communication system, face shield, and disposable boot covers

Level C: The type of airborne threat has been established, the requirement for using air-purifying respirators is provided, and skin and eye exposure is unlikely.
- Full face or half-mask air-purifying respirator (NIOSH approved)
- Chemical-resistant clothing: one-piece coverall or two-piece hooded splash suit
- Steel-tipped and shank chemical-resistant work boots
- Optional chemical-resistant boot covers, two-way communication system, hard hat, and face shield

Level D: The lowest level of protection is required. Prior to equipping a team, one must conduct further research to ascertain the type of protection that may be required. (Refer to the Office of Emergency and Remedial Response, Environmental Response Division.)
- Coveralls and safety boots

Endnotes

1. Neal R. Chamberlain, History of Biological Weapons (5 pages). www.atsu.edu/faculty/chamberlain/bioterror/history.htm (accessed on April 1, 2011.
2. Scott Oldham,"WMD Detection Devices," *Law and Order*, October, 2006, n.p. (accessed online).

Domestic Terrorism 9

Leaderless Groups and Lone Wolves

Many, if not most, terrorist acts are perpetrated by groups organized—tightly or loosely—with a structure that may be paramilitary. They are focused on terrorist action, or they may include nonviolent political, social, or religious segments as well as extremist and activist arms. However, there are also groups that are leaderless (at least outwardly) but still supportive of direct, radical action. Terrorist acts committed in the name of such groups as the Earth Liberation Front (ELF) and Animal Liberation Front (ALF) may appear to be executed by lone wolf perpetrators, but in reality there are whole networks of supporting enablers for these operatives, including publicists, counselors, tacticians, and legal advisors who communicate via websites, publications, blogs, and other media to encourage and advise. Even structured groups, such as Yemen-based al Qaeda in the Arabian Peninsula, have so-called lone wolf adherents who commit small-scale or low-level terrorist acts in the United States.

Ecoterrorism

They call themselves "elfs," act in autonomous groups with little or no chain of command, and recruit loyalists though a website that had been maintained by a publicist in Portland, Oregon, who claimed not to know the names of any members of the group. Making it even more difficult for the police and the private security professionals to track their activities, members of the Earth Liberation Front (ELF; hence the term *elfs*) have claimed credit for activities that cross the jurisdiction of a number of law enforcement agencies, including the FBI; Bureau of Alcohol, Tobacco, Firearms, and Explosives; Bureau of Land Management; and U.S. Forest Service. In addition, because of the ill-defined organizational structure, members who may or may not be acting independently have committed crimes in many parts of the country and have targeted prime companies, universities, researchers, farmers, and real estate developers, resulting in a nightmare of cross-jurisdictional problems for any investigator trying to determine where the elfs might strike next. The movement is so loosely organized that trying to get a handle on it has been described as trying to grab a fistful of water. ELF opposes urban sprawl, deforestation, and more vaguely, any acts its members view as "harmful to the environment," which includes work with genetically modified food stocks, typically referred to as Frankenfood.

ELF traces its origins to a gathering of members of Earth First, an environmental group that was active in England in the early 1990s. Those who believed that Earth First was not radical enough or lacked the will to undertake guerrilla activities split from the group. ELF has been active in the United States since at least 1996, when it set fire to a fire service truck in Willamette National Forest in Oregon. The group has a tradition of leaving a signature message, such as "if you build it, we will burn it," or just its initials. By 2001, ELF claimed responsibility for more than 100 attacks that had caused more than $37 million in damage in at least eight states, including Oregon, Colorado, Arizona, Indiana, Wisconsin, Michigan, Pennsylvania, and New York. By 2003, reflecting the increased activism and higher profile of the group, damage estimates attributed to it had risen to more than $100 million.[1] Since then, the ELF "press office" has been intermittently inactive for periods of several years and has rarely issued any more damage estimates.

Although many continue to portray environmentalists as tree huggers whose idea of civil disobedience is to hug a tree rather than allow it to be cut down, radical ecoterrorists view arson as a viable tool to prevent what they see as the continued destruction of the planet. While there has been more questioning of what turns a religious fundamentalist into a suicide bomber since 9/11, those who monitor the domestic terrorist scene are as likely to ask what turns a tree hugger or animal lover into an arsonist and potential murderer.

The difficulty in recognizing the violent nature of some of their activities, as well as the elusive nature of many of the domestic terrorist groups, makes them particularly difficult to protect against. Members of the groups are often young, upper-middle class, and white, and their activities are often centered on areas close to where they live.

Few have had any involvement with the police other than possibly other ecoprotests, so they are difficult to trace, and only rarely are their fingerprints or descriptions already on file. In some cases the activists have been employed by or for their targets, making it even more difficult to prevent their access to a facility or their ability to learn the facility's vulnerability.

In August 2003, ELF claimed credit for a fire that destroyed about 20 Hummer H2 sport utility vehicles (SUVs) worth about $50,000 each, damaged another 20 vehicles, and burned a warehouse at an auto dealership in the Los Angeles suburb of West Covina. Three other dealerships, where additional vehicles were destroyed, were spray-painted with slogans that included "fat lazy Americans," "gross polluter," "ELF," and "you build it, we burn it"— the ELF slogan. SUVs were also damaged in Seattle; Eugene, Oregon, and Erie, Pennsylvania, indicating a concerted effort that was somewhat unusual for the loosely affiliated sympathizers upon whom ELF depends.

Other activities have included cutting fences that freed about 5,000 minks at a ranch in Mermansville, Michigan, and the destruction of offices on Christmas Day 1999 of the Boise Cascade Corporation in Monmouth, Oregon, because the paper manufacturer allegedly "ravaged" Pacific Northwest forests in the course of its business activities. Various websites devoted to "nighttime gardening," a euphemism or a code word for vandalism, suggest that activists target private companies and universities rather than small farmers because they are less sympathetic as victims.

Universities have been hard hit by ELF. In October 2001, ELF left firebombs next to two forestry buildings on the Houghton, Michigan, campus of Michigan Technical University. The university had previously received e-mail threats from ELF after it received funds for research that included the genetic manipulation of trees. On January 26, 2002, members of the group caused an estimated $250,000 in fire damage to a University of Minnesota construction site where a plant genetics center was under construction. On August 1, 2003, environmental groups claimed credit for a $50 million fire that destroyed a construction site for 1,500 apartments near the campus of the University of California at San Diego, and in May 2004, ALF, closely related to ELF, took responsibility for an arson attack and other acts of vandalism at Brigham Young University, threatening that the Provo, Utah, institution would face continuing attacks until it ceased participating in animal testing.

A fire on New Year's Eve 1999 at Michigan State University at Lansing resulted in the burning and trashing of Agricultural Hall, a genetic engineering research facility. Although no one was hurt, hundreds of thousands of dollars in damage was reported, and the fire cost an academic researcher her academic records, lecture notes, slide presentations, books, and passport. The program was targeted because it accepted funding from Monsanto, the St. Louis, Missouri-based company that is the world's largest producer of bioengineered products. It was not the first time MSU had been attacked. In 1995, Rodney Coronado, an animal rights activist, was convicted of setting fire to an animal research laboratory on the campus. Despite more than $70,000 in funds for his defense, donated by PETA, Coronado was found guilty and also pleaded guilty to similar crimes at Oregon State University and Washington State University. Another arson fire at the University of Washington in Seattle and a fire at a genetics lab at the University of Minnesota have also been attributed to ELF, as was an arson fire at the University of California at Davis that set a graduate student's research back at least six months after her three-acre corn field was ripped out.

The University of Washington arson gutted a research laboratory at the Center for Urban Horticulture on the same night in May 2001 that two buildings and several vehicles at a tree nursery in northwestern Oregon were also targeted. The center was conducting research on genetic modification to trees that would alter the number and size of branches, issues that could be of great importance to the logging and paper industries, and was supported by the Department of Energy and two large timber companies, Weyerhauser and Boise Cascade.

A Chevrolet dealership that had been firebombed in 2000 seemed to have been chosen in part due to its location at the end of the University of Oregon campus. This is one of the few cases that has resulted in arrests and convictions. In this case, the two arsonists, Craig Marshall and Jeffery Luers, had been under surveillance by the Eugene Police Department. Although the officers did not actually see the two set the fire, they were observed acting suspiciously around the dealership and were arrested. Marshall pleaded guilty to conspiracy to commit arson and unlawful possession of a destructive device, for which he received a 5½-year sentence. Luers was linked to an earlier arson and, after being found guilty in both cases, was sentenced to almost 23 years in an Oregon prison. The two had met while tree sitting during environmental protests.

Academic institutions being ecoterrorism targets has implications for first responders, since university security or police personnel may be less likely to be aware of ecoterrorism groups operating in their areas than local police or federal officials. University personnel particularly may be unlikely to have their suspicions aroused by young people dressed casually—or even sloppily—hanging around university office or research buildings. Further complicating protecting against such crimes, such facilities are often in remote areas where there is little chance of perpetrators getting caught. The elusive nature of the attackers makes it fairly easy for them to undertake detailed preraid surveillance of a facility without being detected.

The shadowy nature of ELF is exemplified by its self-proclaimed former spokesperson, Craig Rosenbraugh, of Portland, Oregon, who claimed in 2002 that he had resigned his position as spokesperson after invoking his Fifth Amendment right against self-incrimination before a U.S. House of Representatives subcommittee. Still speaking for the group at a time when three Long Island, New York, youths pled guilty to federal arson charges, he agreed with his attorney's view that the pleas would have little effect on the group because it "operates under an ideology, not a physical membership, so it really impossible to dissolve."[2] Yet James F. Jarboe, an FBI domestic terrorism expert, called the group one of the most dangerous domestic terrorist groups based on two factors: its increased activities and the amount of damage its supporters have caused. According to FBI estimates, ELF and its partner in crime ALF have committed more than 2,000 criminal acts and caused more than $110 million in economic losses and damages since their inceptions.

A Eugene, Oregon, detective attributed the group's danger to its impossibility to infiltrate. Since few of the members know one another and they hold no meetings or issue no instructions to one another, there is little or nothing to track. He contrasted it with the Mafia, where a potential undercover operative can sometimes gain access through recommendations from a made member of a particular family. But among ecoterrorists there is no family to infiltrate; there is only a very small group of people who get together to commit a crime and take credit for their act only through a press release or on a website.

In a self-published monograph, ELF boasted that very few of its actions have resulted in arrests, claiming that the group "has been extremely successful in evading law enforcement due to its anonymous cell structure."[3] ELF describes itself as an environmental group "that realizes the true cause of murder and destruction of life," and that it must work against "the capitalist state and its symbols of propaganda" through economic sabotage. In recruiting members, the group notes that if someone believes in the ELF ideology, follows its guidelines, and "conducts actions," he or she will become part of ELF.

The guidelines are:

- To cause as much economic damage as possible to a given entity that is profiting off the destruction of the natural environment and life for selfish greed and profit
- To educate the public on the atrocities committed against the environment and life
- To take all necessary precautions against harming life

Discovery Channel Hostages

Ecoterrorists, animal rights extremists, and similar groups traditionally favor property destruction tactics such as bomb attacks, arson, vandalism, and criminal trespass to terrorize their intended victims. That changed in September 2010 at the headquarters of Discovery Communications in Silver Spring, Maryland. Radical environmentalist James J. Lee was well known to the people at the building, home of the Discovery Channel and such sibling networks as Animal Planet and Green Planet, for the frequent protests he staged outside the building, exhorting the organization to live up to its "commitment to save the planet" and "stopping the human race from breeding any more disgusting babies." When Lee was not picketing or protesting in person, he would rant on his website, SaveThePlanetProtest.com, with such observations as "humans are the most destructive, filthy, pollutive creatures around and are wrecking what's left of the planet with their false morals and breeding culture."

On the first day of September, toward the end of lunch hour, Lee strode into the lobby of the Discovery building, approached the security checkpoint, fired a shot, and announced, "Nobody's going anywhere." Lee was armed with a pair of handguns, canisters hanging from his body attached to what looked like a propane tank, and he carried a flashing light in one hand. Thus began a four-hour standoff, with Lee holding three hostages, one of whom was a security guard. In the work areas behind the lobby, the initial gunshot had trigged emergency procedures that began with a public address system announcement advising the 1,900 employees and visitors to stay put. Within 10 minutes, however, they began to evacuate the building through rear entrances, staying out of Lee's sight.

The Montgomery County Police Department arrived at the scene; officers were able to follow events in the lobby via the video surveillance cameras trained on the area. Police tried to negotiate with Lee, but the incident came to a deadly conclusion after Lee pointed a pistol at one of the hostages and a police sharpshooter took him out, shooting and killing him. The guns Lee carried turned out to be starter's pistols, incapable of killing anyone, but the canisters contained enough explosives to cause harm and possibly kill someone. A search of Lee's home in nearby Wheaton turned up four more improvised bombs and much more evidence of his obsession with preserving animals and nature while ending human births. Subsequent investigation also produced indications that Lee may have been an unstable personality.

Other Ecoterror Groups

Among the groups claiming credit or suspected of being involved in terrorist acts, in addition to ELF, are the Cropatistas, the Strawberry Liberation Front, the Anarchist Golfing Association, and Reclaim the Seeds. Although the names may sound amusing, the groups' activities are not and are termed "serious violations of federal law" by FBI agents assigned to the cases. Mainstream environmental groups, such as the Sierra Club, have worked to separate themselves from ecoterrorists. Carl Pope, executive director of the Sierra Club, made the distinction in November 2003, stating that these groups contained members that were not environmentalists, but strictly arsonists.[4]

Targeting not only farms that raise animals, but also farms experimenting with genetically altered crops and facilities housing genetics researchers has a long history among ecoterrorism groups and is similar to tactics engaged in by animal "rights" groups dating to the nineteenth-century antivivisectionists. The concerns over genetically altered agricultural products began in Europe and, according to some political observers, gained strength in the United States in January 2000 at a trade meeting at Montreal, Canada, when the administration of then-President Bill Clinton agreed to a treaty that allowed countries to close their markets to genetically engineered crops—so-called Frankenfood. The group had gained strength earlier, in 1998, when Great Britain's Prince Charles declared that he would never knowingly serve or eat genetically modified food.

Relying on traditional physical security measures, one victimized company installed a chain-link fence with razor wire, motion sensors, and an alarm system on its 110-acre property in 2001. The precaution, though, had the effect of making the Pure-Seed Testing Company more visible than it had been previously. The firm, located in the small community of Canby, Oregon, and the area surrounding its greenhouses now look "like a prison."[5]

The firm was targeted by a group calling itself the Anarchist Golfing Association, which caused about $500,000 worth of damage to Pure-Seed primarily because it experiments with genetically modified grass that could be used for putting greens on golf courses.

Other types of companies have also been forced to enhance physical security. At least one of the many car dealerships that was vandalized because it sold SUVs increased fencing around its lot and hired security personnel to patrol the area, something it felt was not required prior to the attack. Others placed cameras on exterior fencing and added closed-circuit television and security personnel to monitor activity in remote areas of their property.

The courts have provided a number of victories for the ecogroups. Members of Earth First, from whose hit list Unabomber Ted Kaczynski selected two of his victims, and one of the groups the ELF styles itself after in 2002 won a $4.4 million award in a federal civil rights suit in California that contended the group's civil rights had been violated by local federal officials who arrested members for carrying a bomb 12 years earlier. The 1990 case stemmed from the arrest of two defendants—one of whom died in 1997—by a task force of FBI agents and Oakland, California, police officers. The defendants were arrested after a homemade pipe bomb exploded in their car while they were on the way to promote demonstrations against logging. The two were arrested but charges were dropped six weeks later for lack of evidence. Darryl Cherney, who has remained active in Earth First, and Judy Bari, who died from cancer in 1997, vowed to clear their names and sued for false arrest, illegal search, and a variety of other charges. After seven days of deliberations, the jury agreed with them and ruled that Cherney's and Bari's estates receive more than $2 million from the FBI and another $2 million from the Oakland Police.

The Forest Guardians, an antigrazing group, has found another way to make use of the courts to sustain its agenda of clearing every head of cattle from the 265 million acres of wildland that the U.S. government owns in 11 western states. Following a technique learned from Gila Watch, which in 1995 successfully sued the U.S. Forest Service to remove all cattle from the 125,000 acres of the Gila National Forest, the Forest Guardians used the Endangered Species Act to force ranchers to remove cattle from publicly owned lands.

The group is more centralized than many of the other ecogroups and more sophisticated in its methods. Formed in 1989, it had at least 2,000 members in 2002 and a budget of about $400,000. Its tactics are disarmingly simple. Rarely resorting to the physical violence with which the other ecoterrorists are associated, the Guardians use the Freedom of Information Act to learn the names of participants in what is known as the escrow-waiver loan program. The program permits ranchers to borrow money, using as collateral their government-issued permits to graze their cattle on government lands, which is substantially cheaper than relying on other pasture areas. About 25,000 ranchers have such permits, which are issued by the Forest Service.

The Guardians have won more than a dozen suits claiming that such grazing results in mismanagement of the land, in dangers to various protected flora or fauna, or in destruction of land that is home to protected species. As a ruling in the successful suits, the individual rancher must reduce the number of cattle grazing on the land, which affects the basis of his or her loan, decreasing the amount of grazing on the land but substantially increasing the rancher's operating costs. Despite the absence of any violence in its agenda, and because it so often targets smaller, more vulnerable ranchers who are at risk of losing their livelihood, the First Guardians is a group from which the Sierra Club has distanced itself. George Grossman, an official in the Sierra Club's office in Santa Fe, New Mexico, where the Guardians are also based, called them "a little extreme ... zero anything is not the way to go," particularly when people are losing their livelihoods.[6]

Animal Rights Groups

Although most people are familiar with PETA and its tactics of splashing paint on the fur coats of wealthy and prominent fur wearers—usually women but sometimes men—it is only one of a number of active animal rights groups, and its activities have ranged far beyond coat splashing. PETA has had considerable impact in changing techniques employed by the country's poultry growers, primarily by direct action against the largest companies that purchase from the growers. Campaigns against McDonald's, Burger King, Wendy's, and more recently KFC (once known as Kentucky Fried Chicken) have resulted in more humane treatment of the chickens, primarily providing more space in pens, cleaner coops, and alternate killing methods. PETA has benefited from its association with a number of popular cultural icons, including former Beatle Sir Paul McCartney, actress Alicia Silverstone, and former Baywatch beauty Pamela Anderson, all of whom have publicly supported the campaign against KFC, which purchases more than 700 million chickens annually from many of the nation's largest poultry farmers and processors.

Other groups less known than PETA have followed its lead by concentrating on protesting and, in a number of cases, abducting fowl raised for the dinner table from farms that raised them. Members of Compassion over Killing have been arrested for entering chicken sheds in Maryland and filming rows of hens crammed into cages the size of filing drawers. In addition to photographing conditions, members have, using their term, "freed" birds and taken them home, arguing that, in the words of the group's founder, Paul Shapiro, "Chickens have the right to be chickens; to walk on the ground, scratch the earth, spread their wings, roost, take dust baths."[7] Groups in other states, including Ohio's Mercy for Animals and Minnesota's Compassionate Action for Animals, have engaged in similar "rescues." A group calling itself Gourmet Cruelty has used the same tactic to highlight the condition under which ducks raised for foie gras are kept and force-fed. A number of restaurants in California that serve foie gras have been spray-painted and flooded by vandals trying to convince them to take the haute cuisine delicacy off their menus. In response, the state of California has adopted a ban on the production of foie gras that goes into effect in 2012.

Most of the groups were formed in the 1990s, often by college students who believed that following a vegetarian diet and refusing to eat meat or meat by-products was not a sufficient way of destroying factory farms that raise fowl, cattle, or pigs for food or laboratory research.

Animal Liberation Front

In addition to spawning groups with aims similar to it, PETA has also provided financial support to ELF and ALF. Both groups are more violent than PETA has been, and PETA's support may reflect the views of its longtime president, Ingrid Newkirk, who has been quoted frequently as stating that if she "had more guts," she would light a match to research laboratories doing work for food and cosmetic companies. By supporting ELF and ALF, PETA is able to provide the financial spark to those who have shown the guts to light the matches.

With ELF, ALF has claimed responsibility for a number of post-9/11 protests that failed to garner national headlines at a time when international terrorism was uppermost in the minds of law enforcement executives, the press, and the public. Included in these were a firebombing at a federal corral for wild horses near Susanville, California, that caused about $80,000 in damage; a fire at a primate research center in New Mexico; and two break-ins in Iowa, one at a fur farm that resulted in the release of more than 1,000 minks and another that freed pigeons that were being raised for use in research. These were not the first break-ins or animal releases in Iowa, although the earlier events had been attributed to ALF until a Canadian-based faction of the group claimed credit for the 2001 actions.

ALF is reputed to have been behind a number of arsons at labs of companies with ties to Huntingdon Life Sciences, a research lab that conducted animal testing for pharmaceutical, agrochemical, and biotechnology products. Among the targets in the summer of 2003 were Chiron Corp. in Emeryville,

California, and cosmetics manufacture Shaklee Corp. in Pleasanton, California. The animal rights group's concerns with Huntingdon were sufficiently strong that the company has become the sole target of a subgroup that calls itself Stop Huntingdon Animal Cruelty (SHAC).

Huntingdon was a British company that performed most of its research, all of which is required and approved by the Food and Drug Administration (FDA), on rats, dogs, and primates. The company's U.S. offices were located in East Millstone, near Princeton, New Jersey, and in May 2004 seven animal rights activists were charged by the U.S. Attorney's Office with committing a number of offenses between October 2001 and February 2004 that were aimed at recruiting sympathizers online to vandalize property not only at the company's offices, but also at the homes of a number of its employees.

SHAC, like its sister ecoterrorism and animal rights groups, has come to rely strongly on Internet communications. This has become a favored method of exchanging information among its mostly male, white, well-educated supporters under the age of 30. In the instances that resulted in federal charges, the group, according to then-U.S. Attorney for New Jersey Christopher J. Christie (currently New Jersey's governor), posted what it called the top 20 terror tactics to be used against corporate and individual targets. The tactics included invading offices, chaining shut office gates, writing graffiti on cars and houses, flooding suburban houses by using available garden hoses, smashing windows of homes and offices, and sending defected or infected e-mail messages as a way to disrupt a company's computer network.

Indicating the range of the group's activities and membership, FBI agents arrested suspects in New York, New Jersey, Seattle, and a San Francisco suburb. Six of the seven were male; all were under 30. All were accused of engaging in a conspiracy to commit terrorism against animal enterprises; additional charges against some of the accused included interstate stalking and using the Internet illegally to instill fear. The nature of the charges reinforces the difficulties for police in investigating these incidents solely on the local level.

The arrests have not halted SHAC's activities in targeting individuals rather than solely corporate entities. In late May 2004, members of SHAC and ALF were implicated in a brick-throwing incident in Monrovia, California, that injured an off-duty police officer who was guarding the home of an executive of a firm whose company is a subsidiary of a company that has had business dealings with Huntingdon. Despite this somewhat tangled relationship, the executive, his wife, and their two children were the target of demonstrators outside their home who wore masks and black robes and spray-painted "puppy killer" and "you can't hide" on their home. It was these activities that led to the off-duty police guard.

SHAC's violent orientation earned it a place on an FBI list of special interest extremist groups, referred to by Deputy Assistant Director of the Bureau John E. Lewis as the "most serious" of domestic terrorism threats. Law enforcement responded vigorously, and a number of SHAC operatives, in both Europe and the United States, have been arrested, tried, and are still serving time in prison. This includes the group's founders, Greg Avery, Heather Nicholson, and Natasha Dellemagne.

About the same time the SHAC violence was at its height, there were a series of attacks on researchers at the University of California Los Angeles (UCLA) who worked with animals. One neuropharmacologist's house was flooded, causing serious damage, after a garden hose was run through a broken window and turned on. Five months later, a Molotov cocktail was ignited at the woman's front door. Another UCLA researcher found a bomb placed under his BMW. Bomb squad technicians said the fuse on the IED had fizzled and failed to set the device off. In another incident, for which ALF claimed responsibility, a bomb was placed in front of a house owned by UCLA animal researcher Lynn Fairbanks. Fairbanks didn't live there, but her 70-year-old tenant did, and the FBI said the device was large enough to kill the occupant.

The UCLA chancellor appealed for assistance, and Congress took up the issue and passed the Animal Enterprise Terrorism Act (AETA), which was signed into law by President George W. Bush on November 27, 2006. The law increased the penalties for persons convicted of animal terrorism crimes and broadened the definition of "animal enterprise" to cover both academic and commercial organizations using or selling animals or animal products. AETA also extended protection to animal enterprise associates and employees and their homes by prohibiting "tertiary targeting."

Food Fights

Closely related to the animal rights groups are those groups that use terrorist tactics in opposing such things as research into and distribution of genetically modified (GM) food products; irradiated perishable items such as meat and produce; meat, dairy, and other products from cloned animals, and even traditional foods such as veal and foie gras, which they maintain are produced through inhumane methods. Many of these groups originated in European countries, but a number have established themselves in the United States. The most active, Greenpeace and Friends of the Earth, are now considered mainstream by many, particularly since there has been little radical activity in the United States specifically on the issue of GM foods in the past few years. A big reason for the diminished activity has been the success of the movement, particularly in European Union (EU) countries, where genetically altered food must be precisely labeled. With so many consumers believing the worst about GM foods, product growth has been hampered by fears of farmers that they will be unable to market their goods outside the United States, Argentina, and Canada, where genetically altered crops are grown and regularly consumed by shoppers.

The movement against GM crops and animals, and therefore the food-stuffs derived from them, may be refueled by the changes sanctioned by the EU in mid-2004 that began to open the 25-nation market to bioengi-neered foods. Under pressure, especially from Greenpeace, the EU has kept to a minimum the number of types of GM products that can be sold on the grocery shelves. But beginning May 1, 2004, new regulations permitted up to 0.9% GM products to be sold, although the labeling requirements are so detailed that the new ruling may have little impact. In England, Greenpeace regularly destroyed GM foods during televised protests and picketed super-markets that carried GM products.

A number of food retailers in Western Europe, particularly among coun-tries that made up the original EU, have signed pledges with Greenpeace to keep genetically modified brands out of their stores. Indicating the type of protests that could be anticipated, in January 2004 Greenpeace shadowed trucks through the streets of Copenhagen that were delivering a new Swedish beer that was the first European food product labeled with a GM advisory to reach the store shelves. No violence occurred, but what Greenpeace termed chase cars followed the delivery trucks, while its members handed out litera-ture at the stores, warning consumers about the product and asking them to refrain from purchasing it.

Supporters of biotechnical research and modified crops have argued that the crops are the primary hope of feeding hungry people around the world, primarily because more can be grown on smaller plots and because the crops are weather and pesticide resistant. Despite a report by the United Nation's Food and Agricultural Organization reinforcing that GM crops could help feed the more than 800 million people in the world who are chronically hungry,[8] opponents remain unconvinced and continue to support protest actions and, worse, to work against the introduction of the GM seeds into farming around the world and against individual products that contain GM ingredients.

ALF Lone Wolf

The existence of AETA in protecting animal enterprises has not deterred radicals from committing acts of terrorism, such as those in which Walter Bond was charged. Bond, who refers to himself as a lone wolf and has the word *vegan* tattooed across his throat, was arrested in July 2010 for arson at a Glendale, Colorado, business called the Sheepskin Factory, a retail establishment that carried a variety of products, including hats, mittens, seat covers, rugs, boots, and slippers. The merchandise was also sold through an e-commerce website. According to the affidavit with the charges against the 34-year-old Bond, he had at one time lived near the Sheepskin Factory and had been angered that the business profited from the deaths of animals. He also called the building housing the business a "box of matches," and indicated it was a prime candidate for a fire. By the time Bond was arrested, almost four months after the crime, the Sheepskin Factory had reopened for business with new inventory in another location. Bond vowed to "torch" the new store "in a couple of years."

After the Sheepskin Factory fire, which caused $500,000 in damages, but prior to Bond's arrest, someone using the tag "ALF Lone Wolf," who may or may not have been Bond, made an Internet post stating: "The arson at the Sheepskin Factory in Denver was done in defense and retaliation for all the innocent animals that have died cruelly at the hands of human oppressors. Be warned that making a living from the use and abuse of animals will not be tolerated. Also be warned that leather is every bit as evil as fur. As demonstrated in my recent arson against the Leather Factory in Salt Lake City. Go vegan!"

The fire at a Tandy Leather Factory store in Salt Lake City and at the Tiburon Restaurant in Sandy, Utah—which serves foie gras—have been attributed to Bond, but investigators say the actual perpetrator may be another animal rights activist who is using Bond's arrest to publicize other ALF-oriented activities.

Islamic Lone Wolves

The issues surrounding the difficulty in anticipating lone-wolf terrorist acts and in trying to discern a pattern in them are exemplified by a shooting that occurred on June 1, 2009, in front of an Army/Navy recruiting center located in a strip mall in west Little Rock, Arkansas. Abdulhakim Mujahid Muhammad, a 23-year-old African American who had been known as Carlos Leon Bledsoe before converting to Islam, shot two young soldiers as they took a smoke break outside the recruiting station to which they had been temporarily assigned. The suspect, originally from Memphis but living and working in Little Rock, made a number of incriminating statements to local police. According to the officer's report filed with Mujahid Muhammad's arrest report, he told police that after putting three weapons in his Ford Sport Trac, he drove around and saw the Army military recruiting station with two soldiers standing out front smoking, and that he "pulled onto the parking lot in front of the Recruiting Station, stopped his vehicle, and began shooting at the soldiers." He further stated that he fired several rounds at the soldiers with the intent of killing them before fleeing.[9]

The degree to which the local police were left to handle the case on their own is not unusual in these "lone wolf" terrorist actions. Both the arrest report and the 12-page request for a search warrant were filed by local police officers after stopping Mujahid Muhammad's vehicle based on eyewitness identifications. Despite these similarities to any local vehicle stop, in this instance the defendant was charged with a total of 16 counts of terrorist acts in addition to one count of capital murder. As information about the suspect became known, it became obvious that the case was more than a random shooting.

Little Rock Chief Stuart Thomas reported that Mujahid Muhammad had admitted that he was specifically targeting soldiers because he was angry at the Army because of attacks against Muslims overseas. Despite the fact that the suspect was determined not to be part of a larger group planning attacks, there were also reports that he had traveled to Yemen. Subsequent investigation revealed that he had gone to Yemen to teach English, had married a Yemeni woman, and had been arrested in Yemen for carrying a fraudulent Somali passport. He had been interviewed by the FBI while in a Yemeni prison and was deported by Yemen at the urging of the American Embassy. But despite the FBI having opened a preliminary investigation on him, no further action was taken when he was returned to the United States on January 29, 2009, barely 6 months before the shooting.

This illustrates one of the problems in keeping track of lone wolves and opens questions about whether law enforcement agencies are the best choice as counterterrorism tools. Although it may not release exact figures, the FBI undoubtedly receives thousands of bits of information on people like Mujahid Muhammad. Whether obtained from authorities in other countries, from its own agents, from other government agencies, or through tips that outsiders provide for any number of reasons, the number of leads make it impossible to do more than cursory follow-up on all but a few.

As with all police investigations, a case file is opened, the matter receives attention, and unless the inquiry turns up additional information that indicates an actual violation, the case is closed. Generally, in the course of normal policing, the case is unlikely to be referred to again unless something similar is reported about the same individual or if a group of similar cases are opened. In the latter instance, there is no guarantee the cases will be linked until after something occurs. This is similar to what happened after 9/11, when deeper postevent analysis turned up bits of information about Middle Eastern men who applied to a number of flight schools around the nation, but there was nothing to point to this information as particularly relevant.

The other danger of overlooking lone wolves is that, by definition, they work alone. This means it is difficult to catch them ahead of time; there are no groups, there is no buildup, there are no messages to intercept. With a cell, someone may make a mistake, someone may want to back out, someone may upset the plans, or even spill the beans, but with a lone wolf, the person may strike any time with little or no advance planning. Like regular crime, some lone wolf activities could be terrorism of opportunity, meaning that although the person intended to commit a terrorist act, the actual event was somewhat unplanned and occurred at that time and in the location because the opportunity presented itself.

For instance, if the two soldiers had not been outside, would Mujahid Muhammad have entered the career center and started shooting? Although his original statement to the Little Rock police tended to reinforce the random nature of the actual act, if not of his motivation, his later statements indicate a different story. In January 2010, in a letter to the local judge presiding over the case, Mujahid Muhammad changed his plea to guilty, claiming affiliation with al Qaeda in the Arabian Peninsula (AQAP), although this has not been confirmed. The suspect's father, Melvin Bledsoe, doubts it, though, believing rather that his son was trying to fulfill a sense of martyrdom. Most terrorist experts seem to agree.[10]

Abortion Clinic Violence

Despite their activities having receded in recent years, antiabortion activists frequently are involved in firebombings of abortion clinics around the country. Although they are often sole-issue activists, some have also been associated with violence against bars that cater to homosexual clients and churches that welcome homosexuals into worship services, or that do not take what is perceived to be a strong enough stand against abortion. Not only do they differ in their political orientation from the ecoterrorism, animal rights, and antiglobalist groups, but they also differ in their organizational structure. They are usually parts of small, very close-knit groups, and cracking these cases often depends on informants, although the FBI's Joint Terrorism Task Force has been heavily involved in investigating clinic bombing cases for many years.

Despite their different political and organizational orientation, the antiabortionists have also made considerable use of the Internet to publicize their cause and, in some cases, to recruit supporters and raise money. They have used a variety of websites to publicize the names of doctors who perform abortions, particularly since 2001, when the U.S. Court of Appeals for the Ninth Circuit, one of the most liberal in the nation, overturned a $109 million verdict against a group of antiabortionists, ruling that the website maintained by the group that featured wanted posters of doctors who performed abortions was protected by the First Amendment. The appeal overturned a

Portland, Oregon, jury verdict that had ordered the group to pay damages to Planned Parenthood and four doctors who had used the federal racketeering (RICO) law to claim that the site incited violence. The court ruled, in a decision that had obvious implications for cases involving web advocacy, that if the group did not threaten to commit violent acts, but "merely encouraged unrelated terrorists," its words were protected by the First Amendment.

Antiglobalism

Since 1999, when an array of groups brought havoc to the streets of downtown Seattle during anti-World Trade Organization (WTO) protests, the antiglobalism movement has been associated with activities against trade meetings held by the major industrialized nations in countries around the world. The groups that make up the movement, many of which claim to be anarchist and therefore lack identifiable leaders, may have played the same card too often, though. Despite their success in catching Seattle law enforcement authorities so unprepared for violence that they cost the police chief his job, similar events in 2003 in Miami to shut down meetings to set up a Free Trade Area of the Americas were met by a police department that virtually closed off the downtown area and severely curtailed protest activities.

The concept of antiglobalism is an amorphous one; it includes concerns ranging from fast foods to GM foods, from environmental to economic exploitation, and from profits to free trade. What the groups share is a Marxist-influenced distaste for big business, particularly multinational corporations. Among the individual companies that engender particular hatred are McDonald's and Nike—the first for bringing fast foods into the world and the second for exporting the manufacture of its goods to Third World countries, where it is accused of exploiting workers through low wages and inferior working conditions.

Prior to relying on mass demonstrations keyed to major economic summit meetings, the movement was best exemplified by a lone French farmer and by American students protesting Nike products at their college campus stores. The lone French farmer, José Bové, led a group that smashed the windows of his local McDonald's restaurant in southern France and then attacked a field of GM crops. In 2002, France's highest court denied his appeal of a 14-month prison sentence for his activities. The form that Bové's protests took were similar to those of U.S. ecoterrorists, striking at individual targets with small groups of activists; but ironically, since 1999, the antiglobalists have gone global themselves, eschewing small protests for massive protests at international trade meetings around the world.

While Bové attracted a disproportionate amount of worldwide press by painting himself as a poor, beleaguered French farmer facing up to the ever-present global colossus McDonald's Corp., that paled in comparison to the attention the antiglobalists achieved in Seattle. The irony was that Seattle's mayor had actually sought to deny the protestors a forum by providing minimal police presence at the WTO meeting in December 1999 that brought to the city negotiators from more than 130 countries. The WTO, formed in 1994, has become a major target of a wide collection of antiglobalism trade groups. Countries that join agree to abide by its rules to eliminate trade barriers, and critics complain about its ability to override national, state, and local laws on labor and environmental issues.

Seattle, which views itself as a city dependent on world trade and which sought to host the 1999 meeting, had been involved in what were considered cooperative meetings with at least some of the groups planning to protest. Brent Wingstrand, the Seattle police captain who was in charge of the unit that was designated to work with the protestors, was confident of the department's ability to handle the demonstrations, noting that the city had a long history of working with protest groups and with helping them protest without their actions becoming illegal, disruptive or violent. "We have to plan for something big and then adjust our deployment to what the reality turns out to be," Wingstrand said.[11] But when the anarchists of the many groups that had gathered in the city rampaged through downtown streets, breaking windows and battling 1,000 police in riot gear, Mayor Paul Schell was forced to declare a state of emergency that imposed a dusk-to-dawn curfew. Despite mobilization of the entire 1,300-person police department by Mayor Schell and the police chief, Norman Stamper, two units of National Guard troops were called in to assist the police. The publicity the protesters garnered brought them a level of attention that had previously not existed, and their ability to prevent the trade talks from getting off the ground infused the groups with enthusiasm of future protests.

The various antiglobalism protestors are difficult to describe or prepare against because they are so diverse and so loosely affiliated. Participants include mainstream organizations such as the AFL-CIO and individual member unions protesting the loss of jobs in the United States and other first world countries through outsourcing to countries around the globe where wages are lower and worker protection laws weaker. Other groups have shorter histories and less targeted agendas, and some are formed specifically for individual protests, such as Public Eye on Davos and Anti-WTO Coordination. A group of academics called themselves The Other Economic Summit (TOES), while other groups represent environmental or animal rights concerns. Antiwar groups opposing U.S. and its allied presence in Iraq were also been involved in the protests. Although the majority of these groups claim to eschew violence, anarchist groups have taken the opposite tactic, believing that goading the police into violent reactions to their activities aids their cause.

The antiglobalism demonstrators regrouped at subsequent economic meetings in Prague and Washington, D.C., in 2000 for International Monetary Fund–World Bank protests; in Davos, Switzerland, and Melbourne, Australia, for the Anti-World Economic Forum in 2002; in Quebec, Canada, Genoa, Italy, and Salzburg, Austria, in 2001 for World Economic Forums held in those cities; in New York City for the World Economic Forum in 2002; in Montreal and Cancun, Mexico, in 2003 to protest additional WTO meetings; in Miami at the end of 2003 to disrupt the meetings of countries hoping to set up a western hemisphere free trade area; and in 2004 in Sea Island, Georgia, to protest a G-8 Summit meeting.

Certainly after Seattle, police and other responders, particularly fire and emergency medical personnel, were on notice that ignoring the protestors was not a viable course of action. This was particularly apparent to police chiefs after Seattle's Chief Stamper announced his resignation within months of the protests amid criticism that the police had first been too soft, ignoring the possibility of violence, and then in response to the violence, too heavy-handed. Although Stamper claimed that he intended to resign and was only moving his timetable forward, the nearly $20 million lost in sales and property damage to downtown Seattle merchants and the repeated television videos and still photos of raging demonstrators and tear gas-tossing police did not aid his image locally or nationally.

Since Seattle, police have employed a variety of tactics at international trade meetings. In addition to the different cultures of policing worldwide, the physical layout of the meeting sites had played a role in strategic considerations. One way in which some countries and cities assisted the police was holding the meetings in areas that could easily be separated from the cities closest to where the delegates would meet, although New York City and Miami did just the opposite. In New York the meetings were held at the Waldorf-Astoria in midtown Manhattan, and in downtown Miami, in the business and government district.

In many locations, the police attempted to use undercover officers to infiltrate groups planning protest actions. In response to past abuses of this tactic, many federal agencies and a few local police prohibit officers from this sort of activity, but even departments that permit it have found it difficult to infiltrate groups that are as amorphous as some antiglobalists, who shun organizational structure, meetings, or designating certain members as leaders, and opt for what has become known as leaderless resistance. Information is often exchanged on the websites, via e-mail or other social media, and when meetings occur, they are often more likely to be free-form discussions that range from the possible to the highly fantastic.

When Pennsylvania state troopers attempted to infiltrate groups planning to protest at the Republican National Convention in Philadelphia in 2000, a few were identified and "outed" because they ate meat (in McDonald's no less), looked bigger and healthier than other potential protestors, and wore Nike sneakers among antisweatshop protestors. These are excellent examples to undercover officers of the importance of knowing the habits of those you are observing and not committing such obvious acts or omissions that you are easily identified as an outsider.

In Cancun and Sea Island, planners chose locations that the police could isolate from the demonstrators, a plan that proved to be fairly successful. The city of Cancun is separated from the narrow strip of land that comprises the hotel zone, where the meeting took place. The police were able to fence off the area from protestors, and although the fence was breeched, most successfully by a group representing a Korean farmers' union, the meetings took place with minimal damage. Similarly, the 2004 meeting hosted by President George W. Bush on Sea Island took place at an inaccessible resort in a state with strict local rules on public conduct and limits on the size of public gatherings. Further, the island contains only private homes, and only residents and those affiliated with the meetings had authorization to go beyond the security checkpoint on the only road leading to the resort.

The other U.S.-based meetings were in far different locations. Washington, D.C., Police Chief Charles Ramsey dealt with a variety of protests; New York City's Commissioner Ray Kelly kept disturbances to a minimum; and Miami's Police Chief John Timoney (a former police executive in New York and Philadelphia's chief during the 2000 GOP convention) flooded downtown Miami with so many cops that they outnumbered the demonstrators and a year later would still be accused of unnecessarily heavy-handed tactics. Although each of these police executives was criticized by human rights groups, none suffered the fate of Seattle's Stamper.

Timoney came under particular criticism for designing what has come to be called the Miami model, shorthand among civil liberty groups for quashing dissent and shorthand among police for curtailing anything resembling the "battle in Seattle." The mayor supported Timoney's tactic of saturating the downtown zone with police even though only $8.5 million of the almost $24 million in costs were reimbursed by the federal government, the rest to be paid from tax levy funds. Although about 10,000 protestors showed up in Miami, the numbers were fewer than expected and the demonstrations were tamer. At some events, police outnumbered demonstrators, but the city and state may have willingly foot the bill because they were competing with about a dozen other cities to become international headquarters for the Free Area of the Americas. All indications are that future world economic meetings will receive high-visibility police presence, similar to the Miami model, as long as protests are a featured side event of these gatherings of world leaders.

Contemporary Homegrown Islamic Terrorists

Since 9/11, the FBI and other government agencies have arrested more than 20 American-born or naturalized citizens on terrorism charges. The reasons for their arrests ranged from committing violent acts, to offering support to violence, to helping finance a terrorist operation, to recruiting new terrorist operatives. Here are a few examples:

Two Brooklyn, New York, men, Wesam el-Hanofi and Sabirhan el-Hasanoff, were arrested in Virginia, after returning from Yemen, where el-Hasanoff took an oath to al Qaeda. While in Yemen, he purchased software to secure communication and seven Casio watches that matched a model that had previously been used extensively in creating timing elements of IEDs. In addition, he received $50,000 from another conspirator to further terrorist actions.

"Jihad Jane," Colleen R. LaRose, a striking blue-eyed blonde born in Michigan around 1964, had never been in any serious legal trouble. By the age of 24, after two failed marriages, she had been living for the past five years in a suburb of Philadelphia with a man whose father she cared for while her companion worked. She spent a good deal of time online and posted a YouTube video saying that she desperately wanted to in some way help Muslims, although she was not specific on how or why. She somehow became involved with a group of violent coconspirators from around the world. On the day of the funeral of her companion's father, she disappeared with her computer hard drive (probably having been advised to do so) and flew to Europe. She was arrested in Ireland with two Libyans, a Palestinian, a Croatian, and two Algerians, one of whom she had married. Because she was a blue-eyed blonde, she and the members of her group believed that she would not attract attention moving to Sweden to assassinate a Swedish cartoonist who Muslims say blasphemed Mohammed. In 2011, she pleaded to providing material support to terrorists, conspiracy to kill in a foreign country, making false statements, and attempted identity theft.

George Tech student Syed Haris Ahmed, born in Pakistan in 1984, came to the United States with his family when he was 12 years old and became a naturalized citizen at 19. He and other Muslim youths who met in Canada talked themselves into becoming jihadists and were ready to take action. On his own, Ahmed visited Washington,

D.C., and videotaped a number of landmarks, a fuel depot in the area, and a Masonic Temple in Virginia. He then bought a one-way ticket to Pakistan and attempted to interest the Pakistan terrorist group Lashkar-e-Taiba in the tapes he had prepared. They spurned his offer due to their suspicions about the arrival of an unannounced Westerner. He returned to Atlanta where, because the authorities were aware of his actions, he was arrested and subsequently pleaded guilty to conspiracy to provide material support for terrorism in the United States and abroad.

Radical Islam for non-Arabic-speaking Muslims. Anwar al-Awlaki was born in New Mexico in 1971 to foreign parents. His father was a low-level Yemeni governmental employee. Anwar spent his later childhood back in Yemen, returning to the United States in 1991 for his education. Evidence indicates that three of the 9/11 attackers interacted with al-Awlaki and received spiritual advice from him prior to the attacks. When al-Awlaki returned to the United States, he attended Colorado State University and received a BA in engineering, and subsequently earned an MA in education at San Diego State University. He served as an imam at a mosque in San Diego. Some who knew him at the time of the 9/11 attack say that his lectures identified him as a moderate; however, this description has been disputed. Court records show that he was arrested twice in San Diego for soliciting prostitutes. He returned to Yemen and spent various stints in jails, where he voraciously read the works of radical Muslims. His writings and lectures, in English, have been directed at young American and British Muslims, where he had his greatest influence. One of his most read works is entitled "44 Ways to Support Jihad."

One of his disciples was U.S. Army Major Nidal Malik Hason. Born in the United States to Jordanian emigrants, after high school, Hasan joined the U.S. Army and received all of his higher education from the military. He completed his undergraduate work, medical school, and internship at Walter Reed Hospital as a psychiatrist at taxpayers' expense. Hasan's fitness reports were marginal, but no action was taken by the Army hierarchy. After consulting with al-Awlaki on whether the killing of his brother soldiers would be acceptable in the Islamic religion, Major Hason killed 13 soldiers at Fort Hood, Texas, before being shot by a responding local police officer. Nearly two years after the incident, Hason had yet to be tried for his actions.

Another devotee of al-Awlaki was the so-called Christmas Day bomber, Umar Farouk Abdulmutallab, a 23-year-old Nigerian national who boarded a plane in Amsterdam with an explosive device in his underwear and unsuccessfully tried to blow up the airliner over Detroit.

Yet another adherent of al-Awlaki's teachings was Faisal Shahzad, also a naturalized citizen, who became known as the Times Square car bomber. He told authorities he was moved to action by al-Awlaki's writings that called for holy war against Westerners. He considered himself a follower of al-Awlaki and had contacted the Internet-savvy imam via computer. Using his U.S. passport, Shahzad returned to Pakistan in an attempt to connect with an unnamed militant group for training. Although he has claimed that he received training for a number of weeks by the group, terrorist experts believe that he was probably viewed with suspicion and did not receive high-level instruction. As evidence, they point to the inept device he constructed. In May 2010 Shahzad constructed a VBIED in a Nissan Pathfinder and parked it on West 45th Street in the Times Square area. He set the fuse and left the area, but a T-shirt vendor saw smoke and alerted police. Had the device been properly prepared, it could have caused great damage and significant loss of life. Shahzad was captured two days later while trying to flee the country.

Al Qaeda's public relations man, Adam Pearlman, aka Adam Yahiye Gadahn, aka Azzam the American, was born in Oregon in 1978. His grandfather was Jewish and his grandmother Christian. He was raised Christian and at 17, while living in California with his grandparents and attending college, he converted to Islam. At 20, he moved to Pakistan where he married an Afghan refugee. Until he lost contact with his family in 2001, he had told them that he was a journalist. He would in fact become the public relations expert for al Qaeda and a senior advisor to Osama bin Laden, including preparing cultural transcripts, producing propaganda videos, and translating for al Qaeda. He has prepared or appeared on various recruiting videos criticizing the United States and has assisted in a number of attacks and the bombing of embassies. One of his messages was an invitation to Americans "to be lead out of darkness into the light" of al Qaeda. He has been involved or appeared in every video or communication released by al Qaeda "commemorating the 9/11 attack to the World Trade Center." These actions led to his being indicted by the United States for "treason, for providing material support to al Qaeda," and he has been placed on the FBI's Most Wanted Terrorist List.

Non-Islamic Homegrown Contemporary Terrorists

Antigovernment militias have existed for decades, but a more recently formed group has attracted considerable attention. Formed in 2008, the

Hutaree Militia, whose name the group say means Christian Soldiers, is based in Michigan with outreach to Ohio and Indiana. It is believed that this group has connections with other militia groups, but it is not a clandestine organization. The militia maintains a website and members have appeared on radio talk shows. While most other militia movements are paramilitary organizations, usually survivalist, antigovernment and antitaxes, and Second Amendment adherents, the Hutaree group states a more Christian aim and a belief that the apocalypse is near. In one indictment against the group, members are accused of plotting to entrap and kill police officers by placing a false 911 call and attacking responding officers. They also hoped to attack ceremonial funerals generally attended by a large number of law enforcement personnel. This is not unlike a tactic used in Ireland by the IRA.

Early Homegrown Terrorists

Although recent terrorist activity has focused on radical activity fostered by international concerns, the history of terrorism is replete with actions that were either purely domestic in nature or focused on international events quite different from today's. Among these were:

> *First VBIED in the United States.* Probably the first vehicle-borne improvised explosive device (VBIED) was a horse and wagon loaded with 100 pounds of dynamite that detonated mid-day on September 16, 1920, in New York City's Wall Street area, killing 38 people and injuring more than 400. Despite vast resources expended by local and federal law enforcement and by private security firms, the crime has never been solved.
>
> *World's Fair 1939–1940.* During the fair in Flushing Meadows Park, New York, a suspicious package was removed from the British Pavilion by two members of the NYPD Bomb Squad. While they were attempting "render safe procedures," the device exploded, killing the two detectives. Like the Wall Street area bombing, this case has never been solved, although in this case investigators believed the package had been placed by Nazi sympathizers.
>
> *The Mad Bomber.* Between 1940 and 1956 a disgruntled former employee of Consolidated Edison, the power company in New York City, George Metesky, placed 33 IEDs, 22 of which detonated. Most were placed in movie theaters, railroad stations, throughout the subway, and in other locations that attracted large crowds. Although many people were injured and there was considerable property damage, his activities did not result in any fatalities. Metesky used the nom de plume "FP," but the news media dubbed him the "Mad Bomber."

Upon capture, Metesky was judged legally insane and institutionalized. He was released after 13 years on the basis of judicial error. He
never engaged in any further violence and died in Connecticut, 20
years later, at the age of 90.

Anti-Vietnam war activists. On August 24, 1970, at the Mathematics
Research Center, a U.S. Army-funded facility located in Sterling
Hall on the University of Wisconsin campus in Madison, a Ford
Econoline van blew up in the early morning hours, killing one person (a scientist whose work was unrelated to the Math Research
Center), wounding many others, and causing tremendous damage
to many buildings in the area. The van was loaded with six 50-gallon
drums of ANFO (ammonium nitrate and fuel oil), with an explosive
booster. A book about the case by Michael Morris included a dia-
gram of the VBIED.[12] Since a Ford Econoline van packed with ANFO
was also the delivery system used in the 1993 World Trade Center
bombing, many believe the WTC bombers may have gotten some
of their ideas from the earlier bombing. The four perpetrators of the
Madison bombing were anti-Vietnam war protestors affiliated with
Students for a Democratic Society (SDS). Three were arrested and
convicted; the fourth fled to Canada and has never been captured.

Black Liberation Army. Starting in 1971 and continuing for almost 10
years, members of the Black Liberation Army, a radical offshoot
of the Black Panther Party, executed a number of assaults against
police officers and buildings across the country. Members of the BLA
set off a number of bombs across the nation, from San Francisco to
New York. Arrests were made of many of the group's leaders in a
case involving the murders of two police officers in New York,
which eventually led to the demise of the group. However, a few
members remained active, working with members of the Weather
Underground Organization and taking part in the 1981 Nanuet,
New York, armored car robbery that resulted in the deaths of two
police officers and a Brink's truck guard.

Weather Underground Organization. The Weathermen, another offshoot of SDS, formed in 1969, took its name from a Bob Dylan
song. The group declared its intention to overthrow the U.S. government; as women began to take more prominent roles in its activities, it changed its name to the less sexist Weather Underground
Organization. Between 1969 and the mid-1970s members engaged in
public demonstrations causing violence and riots and were especially
active during the Democratic presidential nominating convention in
Chicago in 1968. They continued to place bombs at various locations,
often targeting banks. Although they prided themselves on sending
warnings about the devices, many resulted in casualties. Among the

group's major bombings were those at a police memorial in Chicago, a federal judge's home, New York City's police headquarters in Lower Manhattan, and the Pentagon building near Washington, D.C., which involved Bill Ayres, who later befriended Barack Obama in Chicago.

While members of the Weather Underground were preparing IEDs in a townhouse in New York City's Greenwich Village neighborhood in March 1970, the building exploded and was leveled. Group members had been preparing nail bombs for placement at the Fort Dix Army base in New Jersey. Three died in the explosion, while two others, Cathy Wilkerson and Kathy Boudin, escaped virtually unharmed. After the end of the Vietnam War most of the violence ended and members tried to pursue a more purely Marxist-Leninist ideology, laying out their plans in a manifesto entitled *Prairie Fire: The Politics of Revolutionary Anti-Imperialism*. This was not unlike Carlos Marighella's publication *Minimanual of the Urban Guerrilla*. The organization eventually split into two units: the May 19th Communist Organization and the Prairie Fire Collective. Bill Ayers and Bernadine Dohrn were in the latter group. In 1973 the government dropped charges against most of the members of the group following a Supreme Court decision on permissible evidence, and the possible revelation of foreign intelligence information at a trial. Many members surfaced, like Dohrn and Ayers, who used assumed names underground until they turned themselves into authorities in the 1980s. It was reported that among other things, both Ayers and Dohrn helped organize the May 31, 2010, Free Gaza Movement's attempt to break the blockade instituted by Israel in 2007 to preclude weapons from being shipped to Gaza. After six ships left a Turkish port, the Israel Defense Forces (IDF) boarded the ships as they approached Gaza waters. On one ship there was a violent encounter; nine people were killed and a number injured. The Israelis indicated that seven soldiers were also injured, two seriously.

Other members of the WU organization continued with violent actions, culminating in the 1981 armed robbery of a Brinks armored car in Nanuet, New York. Susan Rosenberg, Kathy Boudin, and four other WU members, along with five members of the BLA, ambushed the armored vehicle, robbing it of $1.6 million. During the robbery and escape, group members killed two police officers and one of the Brinks guards. All the suspects were apprehended over a period of years.

The FALN. Fuerzas Armadas de Liberacion Nacional Puertorriquena was an organization fighting for complete independence for Puerto

Rico. The activists brought their fight to the mainland, primarily to New York City. In December 1974, one of their first devices, placed in a tenement in New York's Harlem neighborhood, injured a police officer who was responding to investigate a possible dead person. Their next bombing, in January 1975, was at the historic Fraunces Tavern restaurant in Lower Manhattan, where President George Washington had bid farewell to his troops after the Revolutionary War. The restaurant was a popular Wall Street lunchtime destination, and the explosion killed four people and injured more than 50 others. Later that same year, in April, members of FALN planted and exploded four IEDs at four locations in Midtown Manhattan, injuring about a half-dozen persons. In August 1977 they placed devices in additional Midtown locations, this time causing one death and several more injuries. They invariably left communiqués in telephone booths. One of their key bomb makers, William Morales, was arrested in his Elmhurst, New York, home after accidentally exploding a device he was working on. As firemen and police responded, he stuffed papers and files down the toilet even after having nine fingers severed. With only one finger, he would later escape from the hospital prison ward and make his way to Mexico. Who helped him was never completely ascertained. He claimed he did it alone.

On New Year's Eve 1982, two members of the NYPD Bomb Squad were severely injured and maimed while trying to render safe a FALN device that exploded prematurely. This group would be responsible for almost 110 bombings in New York and more in Chicago, Philadelphia, and San Francisco over a period of almost 10 years. A number of individuals were arrested for various bombings, attempted bombings, bank robberies, and other felonies. The FALN was one of the first terrorist organizations to use the double-bang tactic. This involved placing a second bomb in close proximity to the first, so that when responding officers and investigators arrived, while they were shaking hands and greeting each other, the second device would go off. After this, future first responders built defenses against this tactic into their response procedures. In 1999, to the astonishment of the entire law enforcement community as well as a large part of the general population and an overwhelming majority of the U.S. Congress, President Bill Clinton pardoned 16 members of FALN. His justification was that none of those pardoned had been convicted of actually harming anyone. They had been convicted of conspiracy to commit robbery, bomb making, and sedition. Though perhaps they were not the persons actually placing the bombs, they helped accomplish the deed. The government wanted those pardoned to denounce any further violence; not all did.

Using America as a Battleground

Omega 7

The anti-Castro organization got its start in the early 1960s in Miami, Florida, after the Bay of Pigs disaster, becoming active in the New York area in 1975. During an eight-year period it was responsible for between 30 and 50 bombings and 2 assassinations. Many of the incidents involved small incendiary devices in department stores and bodegas. Their main targets were the Cuban Mission to the United Nations and any businesses that were involved in trade with the Castro government. Though viewed as freedom fighters by many Americans, they were using U.S. soil as a battleground. The possibility of collateral casualties is always something that law enforcement must consider in bringing members of these types of organizations to justice. With many of the leaders having been convicted and incarcerated, the organization just seemed to disband.

ASALA

The Armenian Secret Army for the Liberation of Armenia was formed in 1975 to compel the Turkish government to acknowledge the 1915 genocide of Armenians in Turkey. Although most of their activities took place in Europe, ASALA members took part in assassinations and bombings in Los Angeles and New York. The targets were usually Turkish diplomats or Turkish businesses. Some operatives were trained in Palestine Liberation Organization (PLO) camps in Beirut, Lebanon. In the blasts that took place in New York City, the postblast examination of evidence noted that many of the components were bought at Radio Shack, resulting in the bomber being nicknamed the "Radio Shack Bomber." The bomb maker was later arrested; because he was elderly, the court tried to work out a lesser penalty, but he said he wanted to go to jail for Armenia. The organization was dissolved in late 1983 for a number of reasons. For one, Israel's invasion of Lebanon in 1982 cost the group much of its support from the PLO. In addition, the attack at the Esenboga Airport in Ankara, Turkey, where the ASALA operatives targeted nondiplomatic civilians, killing many and taking hostages in a crowded passenger waiting area, resulted in a loss of support for the group. Similarly, the killing of eight innocent passengers at Orly Airport near Paris, France, cost the group the financial support of the Armenian diaspora.

American Militia Movement

The Oklahoma City bombing on April 19, 1995, was a VBIED truck bomb containing almost 7,000 pounds of explosive material (ANFO) driven to, and parked in front of, the Alfred P. Murrah Federal Building. The driver was Timothy McVeigh, who was an antigovernment believer. He was assisted in putting together the device by Terry Nichols. The blast killed 168 (19 under six years old) and injured more than 680 people. The date was selected to coincide with the end of the Waco siege in Texas in 1993 and the Ruby Ridge siege in 1992. The blast destroyed or damaged more than 300 buildings and shattered windows in an even greater radius. McVeigh had a copy of the *Turner Diaries*, a fictional book outlining militia-type antigovernment operations. This event is similar to the book's portrayal of the bombing of FBI headquarters in Washington, D.C.

The LaGuardia Airport Bombing

At the TWA terminal at New York's LaGuardia Airport on December 29, 1975, shortly after 6:30 p.m., an IED that had been placed in a luggage locker (a common amenity at that time) detonated. The location was near large windows of the ticketing area, facing the driveway and walkways. It resulted in 11 deaths and 74 injuries. A taskforce of more than 700 NYPD detectives, FBI agents, ATF agents, and Port Authority of New York and New Jersey (PANYNJ) Police worked on this investigation, which spread across the entire country to no avail. In September 1976, a TWA flight left LaGuardia Airport en route to Chicago; shortly after takeoff a group of Croatian freedom fighters, led by Zvonko Busic, hijacked the plane. They claimed to have a bomb on board. To give credibility to their threat, they said they had planted a similar device in a locker at Grand Central Terminal in New York. The NYPD Bomb Squad responded and removed the device, a pressure cooker cooking pot. At the police firing range where such devices are rendered safe, the IED detonated prematurely, killing one bomb technician and seriously wounding four others. The hijacked plane continued to Canada, where it was refueled and continued on to Paris, France. Eventually, after the authorities shot out the tires on the aircraft, the hijackers surrendered. Busic was flown right back to New York and charged with the hijacking and death and injuries of the detectives. He was later convicted at trial and sentenced to life imprisonment. The MO, or modus operandi, i.e., the use of a locker, was similar to the LaGuardia bombing. Busic was questioned extensively, but denied involvement, though there were many inconsistencies in his responses. To this day, this case remains unsolved. Busic was paroled in July 2008, after 32 years, and deported to Croatia, which had gained independence from Yugoslavia in 1995. He was greeted at home as a hero patriot.

Endnotes

1. Nick Madigan, Crimes of Activism and Terrorism in S.U.V. Torching, *The New York Times*, August 31, 2002, p. 20.
2. Al Baker, Youths Held in Eco-Terror Are Reported Nearing Plea, *The New York Times*, February 14, 2001, p.B5, col 1.
3. North American ELF Press Office, *Frequently Asked Questions about the Earth Liberation Front*, Portland, Oregon: 2001.
4. Patricia Leigh Brown, Enabling, Disabling, Eco-Terrorists, *The New York Times*, November 16, 2003, security. 4, p. 14.
5. Sam Howe, S.U.V.s, Gold & Even Peas Join Growing List of Eco-Vandals, *The New York Times*, July 1, 2001.
6. Jim Carlton, Green Soup Tries to Drive Ranchers Off Federal Lands, *The Wall Street Journal*, September 11, 2002, p.1 and A9.
7. Elizabeth Becker, Advocates for Animals Turn Attention to Chickens, *The New York Times*, December 4, 2002, p. A20.
8. Andrew Pollacks, U.S. Unit Sees Giant Promise in Biotech Research on Crops, The New York Times, May 18, 2004, p. C8
9. Arkansas Arrest/Disposition Report, defendant Abdulhakim Mujahid Muhammad, filed June 2, 2009, available online from Investigative Project on Terrorism, www.investigativeproject.org/case/330 (accessed November 4, 2010).
10. James Dao, A Muslim Son, a Murder Trial and Many Questions, *The New York Times*, February 17, 2010.
11. David Postman, Resistance Takes Fast Track—Protesters Training Now for Sit-Ins, Blockades, *Seattle Times*, September 10, 1999, p1.
12. Michael Morris, The Madison Bombings: The Story of One of the Two Largest Vehicle Bombings. London: Research House, 1988.

Bomb Searches

10

Overview

The general concepts of building evacuations, bombers, and their motivations for using explosive devices were discussed earlier, as was the insight into bomb threats. Here we discuss the concepts and mechanics of conducting searches for bombs, as well as equipment that may assist in reducing the threat of an attack. Reducing the threat of an attack begins with good security based upon a real assessment of the threat faced.

General Concepts

Regardless of the advances terrorists make in constructing explosive devices, the methods of conducting a search remain fairly constant. With the number of bomb threats increasing and heightened security awareness so widespread, training among first responders is as important now as it ever was. Some of the material is basic, but if basics are overlooked, security will be compromised.

Typically, there are four types of searches that a security professional or law enforcement officer conducts:

1. The building search, where the premises may or may not be occupied at the time the search is conducted
2. The search of a suspicious vehicle
3. The VIP or preincident security bomb sweeps of locations or vehicles or both
4. A search using explosive detection canines

Unless extenuating circumstances exist, two general rules should always be followed when conducting a bomb search:

1. All searches should begin from the outside and gradually work toward the interior.
2. Once inside, start with the lowest level and work upward, unless the search is in the basement of a building, when the converse is true: begin at the entry level and search downward from there.

The operative philosophy, and a very important point, is to never let an explosive device get between the searchers and a point of egress.

Building Searches

Traditionally, building searches usually were conducted as a result of a bomb threat notification being received, but in the current climate of an elevated threat level many searches are now conducted as part of routine security procedures, particularly where sensitive personnel or locations are involved. Targeted buildings for the most part are multistoried structures or large sprawling buildings, including schools, transportation facilities, commercial office buildings, tourist attractions, and in some cases, private residences. Less frequently, searches may be conducted in safe houses used by fugitive radicals and terrorists, suspected bomb factories, or even major drug trafficking locations that may be booby-trapped, or where hazardous chemicals may be used in the manufacture of drugs. When a private industrial or corporate building is the subject of an anonymous bomb threat, a search will often be conducted by the company's security personnel or volunteer employee search teams (or both), assisted by law enforcement personnel.

Exterior Searches

The number of teams or individuals required to properly search the exterior portion of any location will depend on the size of the building, the area and nature of the grounds, i.e., the presence or absence of shrubbery, and the degree of experience of the searchers. A general rule for exterior search team assignments is that about 25% of the total personnel involved in the search operations be assigned the task of conducting the exterior search. Not only is a primary improvised explosive device (IED) a concern, but also the fact that a secondary IED may sometimes be planted. This task will be greatly reduced, not only in effort but also in time, if explosive detection dogs are available, but the key factor is still the nature of the exterior area.

The initial search should be concentrated on the area closest to the building and extending out from the building line for a distance of about 20 to 25 feet, depending upon the physical layout. Special attention should be given to shrubbery, window ledges, loading docks, waste containers, and entranceways. Searchers should also look for any indication of loose ducts, ventilation grills, freshly dug earth, or anything out of the ordinary. Search time can be reduced and safety enhanced by a regular program of maintenance that includes keeping the area free of unnecessary obstructions and keeping shrubbery well trimmed, removing accumulated trash, and generally reducing the chance of providing a hiding place for an explosive device.

If the building or facility maintains a parking lot for use by the building occupants, that presents a new set of potential problems. The threat may be designed to get people out of the building and into an area where an explosive device can cause the greatest number of casualties. In this case, we do not want an evacuation area to include the parking lot or around any large refuse containers, such as trash dumpsters.

Interior Searches

The interior of a building should be divided into two distinct segments for searching:

1. Areas to which the public or other such visitors as delivery people have general access
2. Areas within the building that have restricted access or to which access is limited in any way

Public access areas are the most vulnerable to the covert or even an overt placement of an explosive device, and therefore should be searched by the most experienced and best-trained members of the search team. Public access areas include lobbies, restrooms, unlocked maintenance and utility closets, hallways, fire stairs and unsecured stairwells, and reception and storage areas. Areas where outside deliveries or vendors have access should also be considered public access areas for search purposes.

Restricted access areas are places to which the public does not have regular access and that are usually under employee observation, supervision, or control. Even though these areas are supervised, they may still be vulnerable to bomb attack by determined terrorists willing to attempt penetration by posing as repair technicians, messengers, and the like. The U.S. Navy was reminded of this on October 12, 2000, when the USS Cole entered the port of Yemen. An explosive-laden skiff, which the seamen apparently thought was part of the harbor fleet helping to moor the ship on a refueling call, was able to approach the vessel to inflict considerable damage. The al Qaeda-sanctioned attack saw 17 sailors killed and more than 100 others injured.

The members of the search team assigned to restricted areas should be personnel who are most familiar with the areas to be searched since they would be aware of an item or object out of place or out of the ordinary. It is here, then, that nonsecurity personnel will be most helpful as members of the search teams.

A word of caution: When employees or volunteers are used in conducting a search for IEDs, it should be an "eyes only" search. Searchers must refrain from probing or physically disturbing any areas or objects of a suspicious nature or that otherwise may cause concern. Training must stress that the search team members are concerned with locating the obviously out-of-place item or package that is deemed suspicious. A suspicious package should not be touched or moved under any circumstances. Further examination should be conducted only by personnel trained for that task.

Search Teams

Search teams, if organized within private companies or organizations, such as businesses and schools, should be formed on a volunteer basis. Security personnel may be automatically included if the bomb search duties are specified as part of the job description when the individual is hired. The size and composition of the team will depend upon a number of factors, including the location and size of the facility to be protected, the type and number of employees, the professional capabilities of responding public safety agencies, and the company's vulnerability to terrorist activity.

The voluntary nature of the search team cannot be emphasized enough, because nonvolunteers are likely to conduct inadequate searches. In assembling a search team, the assistance of the personnel director or human resources manager is vital. This individual can be very helpful in screening potential candidates. It is also that first- and second-line supervisors and managers realize and understand the reason for using nonsecurity personnel in certain situations. These supervisors should also be made familiar with the eyes-only restrictions that are placed on search team members.

Setting Up a Program

It should be anticipated that nonsecurity supervisors and managers who do not want their personnel exposed to danger or taken away from their primary duties may show resistance. As a result, the security director may want to establish an orientation program for supervisors and managers to explain the training and utilization of search team members. The orientation should stress the benefits to the company of a search team and its importance in cutting down on lost time during a bomb threat. The traits to look for when screening for search team members are:

1. Level-headedness and the absence of gung-ho bravado that may lead to brash or foolish acts
2. Willingness to accept training and instructions along with a demonstrated ability to follow established guidelines
3. Familiarity with the sections of the building/facility/location that require searching
4. A reputation for thoroughness and completion of assigned tasks

In many companies, especially those located or headquartered in suburban areas, a pool of employees with backgrounds that include volunteer firefighting service, auxiliary or past experience, or military experience should be sought out, as should members of the existing fire brigade, if the company has one. In selecting personnel for search teams, employees with established track records with the company should be given preference over new or entry-level employees. Again, it must be stressed to each individual searcher that any search will involve an eyes-only, hands-off approach.

Surprisingly, supervisory and management personnel often do not make effective search team members. This is in part because they are used to giving orders rather than taking them. They also may not be broadly familiar with the day-to-day operations of the company, spending the majority of time in the area of their expertise. They may also be reluctant to search dirty, out-of-the-way areas. In addition, such personnel may be difficult to locate in an emergency as a result of the company's primary demand on their time or location.

Another important item to remember is that in the face of hard economic times, layoffs and early retirements may greatly impact the composition of any team that may be formed. As a result, it is imperative to frequently review team members and find replacements for employees who have left.

Alternative to Search Teams

If a volunteer search team program is not feasible, all employees should be used to search their own work areas to determine if anything is suspicious there. Although this may be the fastest of the search methods, it has a number of drawbacks. First, all employees have to undergo some kind of training in what to look for, how to search, and how to react to suspicious packages. All employees are also potentially exposed to danger should an explosive device actually be planted. Additionally, a search team still must be employed to look through public, exterior, or other areas where no employees are ordinarily assigned.

Mechanics of the Search

Whether a search is being conducted by police officers, security personnel, or employees at the location, the mechanics of the search are the same. The search team should be divided into subteams, or units, of two persons each, with members deciding between themselves how they will divide the labor, such as who will handle the reporting and what search pattern will be utilized. The search pattern can be a grid, a circular or ever-enclosing spiral pattern, a pie wedge, or other geometric design. No pattern is necessarily better than any other, although on occasion, the layout of a particular area may dictate a specific search pattern. Whatever pattern is employed, the most important thing to remember is that the search must be systematic, thorough, and include all confined spaces. A person familiar with the area may, with a quick eyeballing, be able to determine if anything is strange, out of place, or has been tampered with.

The next thing a team should do upon entering a room is initiate an audio check. To accomplish this, the team members simply remain silent and listen for any background noises. The idea is so that if a mechanical timer was used, the sound emitted by that timer may be heard. To enhance the searchers' concentration on listening, they should close their eyes and stand quietly in one spot. The searchers should try to identify each sound and source (e.g., air conditioning, fluorescent light buzzing, constant-run machinery, traffic, or other exterior noises that filter into the building). All equipment and machinery that can be shut off should be, in order to reduce the amount of ambient sound. This will make it easier to recognize the sound of a timing device ticking away, should an actual bomb have been planted.

Room Search

Under normal circumstances the starting point for a room search is the entranceway. The search team should follow whatever search pattern was selected, remembering that although speed is important, thoroughness is more so. Safety is the most important factor of all. Searchers must always remember not to disturb anything that appears unusual, and not to touch anything that is in the least suspicious. In searching a room, the searchers should mentally divide it into three horizontal layers or sections. Searchers should be moving their eyes and heads left to right, back and forth, and not up and down. The up-and-down movement is the easiest way to miss something of importance, because searchers will tend to be moving. The first horizontal zone of search is from the floor to the waist, following the general rule that searches are conducted from the outside in and from bottom to top.

The floor-to-waist zone is the area where IEDs are most likely to be placed. Once this zone is cleared, the searchers should concentrate their efforts on the layer comprising the waist to the top of the head. The third segment—which may require standing on desks, chairs, other office furniture, or a ladder—includes the area from the top of the head to the ceiling. Under certain tactical conditions, the areas may be consolidated into two. This might occur where the room has virtually no hiding place along the walls, such as in conference rooms or windowed dining rooms.

A fourth search zone is the plenum, or that area above the acoustical tiles or false ceiling. This step is not required if an observable ceiling is permanent; if this step is required, it is usually the most difficult and time-consuming to complete. To conduct a search of a ceiling, remove a ceiling tile in each corner of the room and, standing on ladders, have first one searcher, then another, sweep the area with a flashlight, outlining objects in the light's path. If the area is cluttered with wires, cables, or storage articles, if there are pillars blocking vision, or if the ceiling is particularly large, the plenum search will have to be accomplished in small sections. Throughout the search, eye and head movements should be from left to right, back and forth, and not up and down.

As the search progresses and sections of the building or individual rooms are completed, this information should be relayed to each search coordinator or command post so that the progress of each search can be monitored and recorded. It is most important to convey this information in order to track time, especially if a deadline has been specified by the threat maker. It is also important to keep track of the search time so that in the event a search is progressing more slowly than anticipated, additional searchers can be added when the plan is critiqued and updated on the basis of actual performance. The time factor is also important in determining whether or not to keep evacuated personnel in the area or to send them home for the remainder of the day.

Common Bomb Placement Locations

Over the years, terrorist operatives have penetrated security defenses to place explosive devices in a wide variety of target locations. In this age of suicide bombers, terrorists often have not been very subtle in their delivering explosive devices with bombs that have been placed outside the targeted building. In many cases, however, these exterior bombs were powerful enough to cause major structural damage to the target. On other occasions, IEDs have been placed inside a critical area of the targeted facility. More typically, however, domestic bombers for the most part have placed IEDs inside a building, secreted in places with relatively easy access. The most common placement locations include:

1. Restrooms, particularly women's restrooms, where devices have been placed in trash receptacles, behind toilet bowls, and in false ceilings or ceiling air vents.
2. Lobby areas, particularly reception areas where heavy traffic can mask a terrorist or bomber's moves. Favorite locations include behind and in planters, under couches or chairs, or just inside the main entrance doors.
3. Upper floors of multistoried buildings, particularly in hallways, fire exits, stairwells, restrooms, and adjacent to or in elevator shafts.
4. Fire stairwells, open by law, are easily accessible and lightly traveled.

Precaution

When conducting a search for an explosive device, the searchers must be constantly on the alert for booby-traps and other antidisturbance devices that may be affixed to the IED or incorporated in the device's firing system. These include trip wires and similar action-activated initiating switches. The importance of eyes only cannot be overemphasized as the primary caution in a search for explosive devices.

Vehicle Search

Motor vehicles are routinely becoming subjects of bomb searches. Such a search can be prompted by an anonymous bomb threat, as part of a VIP, executive protection, or preincident search, as a routine security search at entrances or restricted parking areas, or as the result of finding a suspicious vehicle on the premises. The same principles guiding a building search can be used in a vehicle search. The search starts on the outside and proceeds inside. Once inside the vehicle, the search is conducted from bottom to top, including the use of mirrors or optical-fiber scoping devices for the undercarriage. These can be the same type of long-handled mirrors or scopes used in interior searches for checking under and behind heavy furniture and equipment.

There are two primary methods in which passenger cars and other vehicles are used in bomb attacks. The first involves the placement of an explosive in a vehicle with the intent to kill, maim, or otherwise injure the target within. In other situations, the vehicle is used to conceal a large amount of explosives or an IED. The trunk areas are usually used for this purpose. The use of car bombs is a method of delivery particularly favored in Western Europe and the Middle East.

In almost all cases, the actual explosives will be out of sight, so any searches of a suspicious vehicle should be conducted by a qualified public safety official. The role of a private security professional should be limited to the identification of the suspicious vehicle. However, if the search is of vehicles in executive protection programs, professional security personnel are actually the ones to conduct the vehicle search.

Antipersonnel Car Bombs

An antipersonnel device is typically wired to the internal electrical system and is initiated by the actions of the driver or passenger or by remote means. Usually the explosives are placed under the driver's seat or in the engine compartment, often adjacent to the firewall. Typically, no more than two or three pounds of high explosives are required to do extensive damage to the automobile and most certainly kill the occupants of the car. Although an action switch is the most common type of detonating device in vehicle bombs, the use of remote control devices is becoming more frequent.

Because of the prevalence of action switches and command-detonated devices, vehicles searches should be conducted only by persons with extensive training in search operations. If a vehicle search must be done, steps to follow are:

1. If time permits, a background check on the vehicle should be made to determine whether the owner or regular driver(s) might be targets and why. The check should also determine who has regular access to the vehicle, and why the vehicle is suspected of having an explosive device within it or explosives hidden inside.
2. An external search must be completed prior to entering the vehicle. This involves searching not only the exterior of the vehicle itself, but also the area immediately surrounding it. Things to look for include obvious tampering with doors, hood, or trunk area; evidence of tape, wire, or other foreign matter on the outside of the vehicle; impressions in the ground of footprints or any sign that a jack may have used to raise the vehicle; and any signs that dirt or other material has been dislodged and knocked to the ground, as might occur if a device had been placed on the underside of the vehicle.
3. The search of the vehicle's exterior should precede very carefully, ensuring that nothing causes excessive movement, jarring, or shaking of the vehicle. The use of a hydraulic or other type of jack in conducting the search should not be considered. To reduce search time, a long-handle inspection mirror is ideally suited for checking

the underside or, if available, a scoping device utilizing optical fibers. It nothing suspicious is found, the interior search can begin.

4. Gaining entrance to the interior of the vehicle should be attempted remotely rather than manually, if possible. The opening of all compartment doors—hood, trunk, doors, glove compartment, etc.—should be done with remote devices, which should be part of any search team's basic equipment. The first interior area to inspect is the engine compartment. Because the battery under the hood is a source of power for a concealed explosive device, it is the logical place to start. Beginning the interior search in the engine compartment allows for clearing any connection that might be affixed to the vehicle's electrical system. Once the engine compartment has been cleared, other areas, such as the trunk and seating, may be addressed.

Vehicle-Borne Explosive Devices

In the past several years, the use of vehicle-borne IEDs has increased significantly. These bombing attacks have usually occurred in areas where security operates in a business-as-usual atmosphere. In this country, in 1993 the World Trade Center in New York City and later the Murrah Federal Building in Oklahoma City sustained extensive damage when large explosive devices were delivered in vehicles. Overseas, the 1983 attack on the U.S. Marines' barrack in Beirut, Lebanon, involved the largest IED ever used in a terrorist attack. It is estimated that the truck-borne device used approximately 15,000 pounds of high explosives and propane in the attack. There were 243 killed in the suicide bombing. The October 2000 bombing in which the U.S. Navy destroyer *USS Cole* was attacked within Aden Harbor in Yemen resulted in the deaths of 17 sailors. The attackers used a small Zodiac dinghy loaded with a large quantity of high explosives. Due to the lax observation of security procedures, the dinghy was allowed to approach the ship in broad daylight. Another example of operating in a high-risk area was the destruction caused to U.S. Air Force personnel housed in Khobar Towers in Saudi Arabia. The structure was adjacent to a public thoroughfare, and on March 22, 1997, a tanker truck filled with explosives detonated in front of the building, virtually destroying it. Nineteen were killed and 200 injured. One of the more recent VBIED incidents in the United States was the failed attempt by terrorist Faisal Shahzad to ignite a Pathfinder filled with explosives and tanks of propane gas in New York's Times Square on May 1, 2010.

Aircraft Searches

The extensive use of privately owned aircraft by businesses and wealthy individuals requires that these now be included in any executive protection program that includes bomb sweeps being conducted in the general course of business. Once again, the search of the aircraft should be conducted in the same manner as other types of searches, from outside to inside, and proceeding along the same lines as automobile and other vehicle searches. An additional security concern in the case of aircraft should be the search of baggage and other items, such as catered foods, that are loaded onboard. Food caterers and cleaning and maintenance services should be subjected to background checks. In protecting an aircraft against a potential bomb attack, there is very little margin for error because a small quantity of explosives can bring an aircraft down.

Preincident Executive Search

A preincident sweep is handled in much the same manner as a search following an anonymous bomb threat. Searchers who conduct the sweeps of meeting rooms, vehicles, public areas, or other locations in advance of an appearance by anyone who is a possible target of a terrorist attack should be particularly alert to the use of action switches or command-activated devices. Often, searchers will not have the luxury of much time between the start of the search and the arrival of the VIP. Also adding to the difficulty of this type of search is that searchers are combing unfamiliar locations, making it easy to overlook small changes. Areas of concern should be those where the executive is most vulnerable, namely, hotel rooms, dining rooms, or public pathways that take the subject from one point to another. Special emphasis should be placed on areas where trip wires, pressure switches, or similar devices can be hidden. In order to speed up searches, the use of explosive detection canines should be considered. In recent years, a number of private security companies have added dogs to their arsenal of search equipment. In the current environment of increased security concerns, financial institutions and other businesses with global interests, as well as companies and headquarters or other facilities in New York City, use privately owned canine patrols on a daily basis to sweep incoming packages and bulk deliveries.

Explosive Detection Canines

Although canines have been an important part of police work for years, especially in the patrol and detection functions, the use of dogs for specialized searches such as narcotics and explosives is on the increase. Due to the increased call for bomb detection dogs in the private sector, a number of security agencies now provide canines on a contract basis. It is important to note that any business or organization contracting for such services should thoroughly check the credentials of the contract agency, if only for the numerous liability issues surrounding the use of such programs. Using canines to detect explosives received a major boost in 1972, when the federal government awarded the University of Mississippi a grant to study dogs as bomb detectors. The first dogs the study produced were used in New York, Los Angeles, and Baltimore. Although the dogs are extremely reliable, it must be remembered that they are just another tool for the bomb technicians. Of course, canines cannot be expected to be foolproof either. Dogs are used to assist search operations and to detect the existence of explosives in suspicious packages.

Maintaining a bomb-detecting canine program can be an expensive and time-consuming project. There are training cycles, rest and work periods, and the physical care of the canine to consider. To maintain adequate coverage, more than one dog and handler will be needed, adding to the expense. If a dog fits into a department's or company's needs, there are numerous private firms available for training and related services. An organization contracting for such services must thoroughly check the credentials of the contract agency, for again, numerous liability issues surround the use of canine detectors, not to mention reliability or possible subversive intentions. According to many canine practitioners, the best dog is one that is trained for solely one task. This means that a dog is best used for only explosives, and not cross-trained for narcotics or other scent work. Today there are a number of security firms that are solely in the business of training and certifying bomb dogs that are sold to other security firms or government agencies.

Dogs used in bomb detection work are usually trained on the reward system. When a dog locates something, or to use the handler's phase, "makes an indication," the dog is rewarded with a biscuit, a short play period, or some other style of positive reinforcement for its efforts. Since search is a bit of a game for a dog, it must find something on every search to keep its attention on the search. To accomplish this, the handler carries a "plant" to be placed every so often to ensure that the dog finds something. Even with this approach, the dogs quickly lose interest in searches and begin to lose their effectiveness after about 20 or 25 minutes. After a short rest period, the search can resume if sufficient time exists.

What a dog actually reacts to when sensing certain explosives has been the subject of some debate in the field. Much of the debate relates to what makes up the sense of smell and how the sense actually functions. One theory holds that molecules of substance vibrate at different rates, with pungent substances having quite different rates from stable substances, and that it is to the vibration rates of the molecules that the dog actually reacts.

A somewhat different theory proposes that there are seven primary odors, just as there are three primary colors, and that each of the primary odor molecules has a different geometric shape. Receptors in the nose of the dogs (and humans, for that matter) have cells corresponding to the various shapes of the odor molecules, and elicit the appropriate or associated smell response.

Whatever the reason for their behavior, bomb detection canines are valuable tools for the bomb technician and security professionals and are especially useful when used in a preventive role.

Suspected Packages

Once a bomb threat has been received and a search begun, the first, last, and most important rule is *do not touch* any suspected package. As part of their training, searchers should be kept informed of current trends among terrorist bombers, such as how deliveries of IEDs have been masked. Over the years, terrorists have hidden devices in containers designed or specifically chosen to blend in with the surroundings of the targeted site. Containers used in the past include boxes of long-stemmed roses, lunch boxes, take-out and delivery containers from fast food chain restaurants, and similar everyday items. The backpack is a popular item used by terrorists since it is so common. In the Middle East, suicide bombers have taken to using a custom-fashioned "explosive vest" worn under loose outer garments. In incidents where antipersonnel devices are involved, the bomb makers have been especially ingenious. One such incident involved a Hamas terrorist, Yihya (The Engineer) Ayyash, who was assassinated in 1995 (reportedly by Israeli agents) when operatives were able to secret a small IED into his cellular telephone. Given such examples, search teams must be composed of individuals with a keen working knowledge of the assigned area so that they can ascertain very quickly what does and does not belong. Items become suspicious packages when there is no one who can account for a specific thing being in that particular area, especially when a threat has been received or if the facility previously has been the target of a threat.

When searchers discover something they feel is suspicious, the immediate area should be vacated quickly. When the searchers are out of the immediate area, the command post or search coordinator should be informed of the situation. The suspicious item should be considered, and thus treated as, an explosive device. Only after the item is positively identified as harmless or innocuous (such as an identifiable backpack or tote bag left behind), or the item has been examined and cleared by a qualified bomb technician, should the search be resumed. The searchers and others involved in a bomb incident operation should be aware that a secondary explosive device may also be present. Several terrorist groups have done this in the past, particularly the Irish Republican Army in Europe and the Puerto Rican group FALN when it was active in the United States. The primary purpose for planting a secondary device is to kill or maim any emergency personnel who have responded to the scene. These secondary devices are usually only a short distance from the initial explosive device.

A suspicious package should never be disturbed in any way, and this includes bomb suppression items such as bomb blankets over the device. A bomb blanket is strictly a tool for the bomb technician. If used improperly it may cause a premature detonation of the explosive device. If hasty damage control functions are to be performed, they should be limited to venting the area (opening doors and windows) and shutting down any utility feeds that may be in the immediate area.

Major terrorist groups such as al Qaeda are masters at manufacturing explosive devices. Those involved in any business that concerns itself with IEDs or may be the target of terrorist groups must stay on top of their game and treat every suspicious package as though it were the real thing.

Energetic Materials and Explosive Devices

11

Energetic Materials

In recent years, the term *energetic material* has been used to describe what were traditionally identified as explosives, powders, etc., in both civilian and military applications. Energetic materials can simply be defined substances capable of producing heat, chemical reaction, and releasing energy. This includes explosives, pyrotechnic compositions and materials, propellants (powders and rocket fuels), and regular fuels, such as gasoline, diesel, etc. The improvised explosive device (IED) remains, far above all others, the weapon of choice of the terrorist.

Explosives Defined

As defined by the *Military Explosives Technical Manual*, "an explosive produces an explosion by virtue of a very rapid, self-propagating transformation of the material into more stable substances, always with the liberation of heat and almost always with the formation of gas."[1] Explosives can be solid, such as trinitrotoluene (TNT); liquid, such as nitroglycerine; or gaseous, including elemental hydrogen or oxygen. The solid explosive is used most often in terrorist operations. Explosives are further categorized into two major classifications: high explosives and low explosives. Much like fire, an explosive requires three elements to achieve required results: oxygen, fuel, and the introduction of heat, to begin the action between the oxygen source and the fuel. The only difference between fire and an explosion is the speed in which the chemical action occurs.

The major differences center on three characteristics:

1. *Burning rate.* A low explosive generally has a burning rate of under 3,200 feet per second (fps), while a high explosive has a burning rate in excess of 3,200 fps. The faster the burning rate, the more powerful the explosive, creating a greater shattering effect.
2. *Container.* A necessity for using a low explosive in order to create an explosion. The container may be a galvanized pipe, cardboard cartons, or similar items that capture the expanding gases. Conversely,

a high explosive needs no container to achieve detonation, and thus can be removed from its wrapper.
3. *Firing techniques.* A low explosive requires only the introduction of heat, flame, or spark to achieve initiation. A high explosive needs the introduction of another high explosive, called the primary explosive, to produce sufficient shock for initiation.

Low explosives are generally classified as propellants and are used in a variety of products that include small arms muzzleloading weapons, small arms ammunition, fireworks, and propellants for amateur rocketeering. Among the more common low explosives are smokeless powder, black powder, and nitrocellulose powder. In order to achieve detonation, the powder must be enclosed in a vessel or container that will capture the expanding gases until a sufficient force is built up that overrides the strength of the container wall and an explosion is achieved. Such powders are common fillers in pipe bombs and similar IEDs. Low-explosive powder is generally manufactured through a mechanical blending where raw materials are reduced to a fine powder and mechanically mixed together. A bonding agent may be used to form a paste that is then dried, reduced to small pieces, and ground to the desired degree of fineness.

High explosives are designed to shatter or destroy the intended target. They are available in a wide range of detonating velocities (burning rates), from 3,300 fps for ammonium nitrate to 29,900 fps for HMX. The faster the burning rate, the greater the shattering effect. High explosives are generally considered compounds rather than mixtures, because the combustibles and oxidizers are molecularly blended. Some high explosives are more sensitive than others. These are used as initiating charges and are considered primary explosives, while less sensitive explosives are classified as secondary explosives.

Types of High Explosives

- Primary: Have an extreme sensitivity to heat, shock, and flame and are usually used as initiating agents.
- Secondary: Less than primary and require an initiator, such as a blasting cap, to function.
- Tertiary: The least sensitive of the explosives and need the introduction of a substantial shock to cause a detonation.

Common Primary Explosives

- *Mercury fulminate.* An explosive that appears in crystalline form and is white when pure, but usually has a brownish yellow or gray tint. It is extremely sensitive to shock, friction, or heat, and accidents during manufacture are not uncommon. This explosive is used in detonators, and it fires in the range of 13,400 to 17,000 fps.

- *Lead azide.* A crystalline, cream-colored compound with a high ignition temperature, and is less sensitive to shock, heat, and friction than mercury fulminate. It is used for major caliber-based detonating fuses and point detonation fuses, as well as a number of other detonators, and has a burning rate of 13,400 to 17,000 fps. This explosive should not come into contact with copper, zinc, and similar alloys due to the possibility that more sensitive azides will be formed.
- *Lead styphnate.* Even with its lead toxicity, this explosive is still one of the most widely used as an initiating agent. The explosive varies in color from yellow to brown and is extremely sensitive to fire and heat; when in a dry state, even a small charge of static electricity may cause a detonation. Firing at 17,000 fps, lead styphnate is use as a component in primer and detonating mixtures, mostly in small arms ammunition and blasting caps.
- *Tetracene.* A pale-yellow explosive that burns around 13,000 fps and is extremely sensitive to flame, producing a large volume of heavy black smoke. Due to its low detonating velocity, it is usually combined with other explosives.
- *Diazodinitrophenel* (DDNP). Yellowish brown powder that is less sensitive to impact than mercury fulminate and lead azide, but more powerful upon detonation. DDNP is usually mixed with other explosives and used as a priming mixture. It can be destroyed by a solution of cold sodium hydroxide and desensitized by emersion in water.
- *Triacetone triperoxide* (TATP). A white crystalline powder that is extremely sensitive to impact, temperature changes, and friction. It is one of the most sensitive explosives known, especially when impurities are present in it. In a pure state it is relatively stable. It was this explosive that was improvised by Islamic terrorists when they attacked the London Underground system in July 2005, and used in the compound carried by Richard Reid, the "Shoe Bomber."

Common Secondary and Tertiary Explosives

Common explosives are high-explosive mixtures and compositions that are designed to release vast amounts of force to accomplish a particular task. These explosives usually reach a burning or deflagration rate in excess of 3,300 fps.

- *Amotol.* Mixture of TNT and ammonium nitrate that was developed during World War I. It is crystalline and yellow or brownish in color.

It may be a substitute for TNT and is usually used as filler for large caliber artillery shells.

- *Ammonium nitrate–fuel oil.* Commonly referred to as ANFO, this mixture was developed for commercial use in the 1950s, employing "prilled" rather than crystallized ammonium nitrate. The explosive is prepared with 94% prills and 6% no. 2 fuel oil and detonates at a very low speed, which produces an excellent pushing and heaving effect. This explosive has largely replaced dynamites and gelatins used in legitimate blasting operations. ANFO, whether improvised or manufactured, is also the terrorist's explosive of choice for large vehicle-delivered explosive devices. According to Global Security. org, a usually reliable source for military-related information, in November 2009, Afghan police seized some 250 tons of ammonium nitrate fertilizer in the city of Kandahar. Ammonium nitrate fertilizer is used in 95% of the IEDs used in Afghanistan. ANFO is not cap sensitive and requires a heavy booster charge to cause a detonation. It is also important to note that the uniform mixing of oil and ammonium nitrate is necessary to ensure full explosive force is achieved. This is a tertiary explosive.

- *Composition B.* Made from 40% TNT, 59% RDX, and 1% wax, with the TNT reducing the sensitivity of the RDX. Composition B is used as filler in land mines, rockets, and other projectiles. It has a detonating velocity of 25,000 fps and may be used as a primer and booster for blasting agents. Comp B is no longer used in the newer projectiles, but may still be around as Comp B main charges. When first developed it was found to be somewhat sensitive to impact shock. This explosive was used in 500-pound bombs that were marked with two yellow bands and, according to an article appearing in the *Journal of the Company of Military Historians* (Summer 1993),[3] caused several incidents of low-order detonation when they accidentally fell from the bomb bay sling and onto the concrete runways.

- *Composition C-3.* Composed of 77% RDX, 3% tetryl, 4% TNT, and the remainder bonding agents, but was replaced by C-4 as the primary field explosive. C-3 is approximately 1.35 times as powerful as TNT and has a detonation velocity of approximately 26,000 fps.

- *Composition C-4.* One of the best known of all military explosives. It is made of 91% RDX and 9% plastic binders and motor oil. It is ideal for the military since it keeps its plastic form from –20°F and will not leak oil up to 170°F. Because of its high brisance and insensitivity to shock, C-4 is a basic combat demolition charge for the U.S. military. Given the military designation of M112, it comes in rectangular blocks that measure $2 \times 1.5 \times 11$ inches and weighs 1.25 pounds. Because of its flexibility, it is an ideal explosive in special operations scenarios and the explosive of choice among terrorists. With a little modification, a 1.25-pound block of C-4 can be made into a paste with the addition of a little mineral oil. This extremely pliable substance can be used with only slightly diminished results. C-4 has a detonating rate of 26,400 fps and can be detonated using military J-2 caps.

- *2,3-Dimethyl-2,3,-dinitrobutane* (DMDNB). A unique compound added to explosives as a taggant. Factories in what was once Czechoslovakia produced a version of this substance, called Symtex H, which is reddish to orange in color and used by terrorists in both Western Europe and the Middle East.
- *Cyclonite* (RDX, for royal demolition explosive). In the nitramine class of organic nitrate explosives,[2] it is rarely used alone except in the case of military detonators. It is an extremely fast-firing, white crystalline solid with a high degree of brisance, used in detonating cord, bursting charge in shells, blasting caps, and in the manufacture of C-4 with both military and civilian applications. RDX has a high degree of stability in storage and is considered one of the most powerful of the military explosives, and in fact forms the base for military explosives composition A, composition B, composition C (C-4), and HBX, among others. Except for C-4, the explosives mentioned are used as bursting charges in a number of shells and bombs. RDX is not produced commercially in the United States, but it is produced in Army munitions plants, such as Holston Ammunition Plant in Kingsport, Tennessee.
- *Flex-X* or Data Sheet. Another type of plastic explosive that is used as a cutting charge. This flexible explosive is waterproof and insensitive to shock, with a burning rate of 23,000 fps. Commercial items are usually reddish or orange in color, while the military version is green. It is used for precision cutting, especially steel beams in both civilian and military applications. In the military, this explosive is referred to as the M118 demolition charge; it consists of four half-pound sheets of the explosive packed in a plastic envelope. Each sheet measures 12 inches long, 3 inches wide, and 1/4 inch thick. Makers of this explosive use either RDX or PETN as the base.
- *High melting explosive* (HMX). One of the most powerful explosives made on a large scale in the United States today. This explosive can produce a high degree of shattering effect due to its extremely rapid detonating rate. RDX is a white-colored explosive with a firing rate of 29,900 fps. It is often mixed with TNT in the manufacturing process to reduce its sensitivity. Generally used in the manufacture of high-blast munitions.

- *Nitrostarch.* Closely related to nitrocellulose, and is less sensitive and less powerful than TNT. It was not until early in the twentieth century that is was possible to produce a stable form. Nitrostarch is similar to the straight and ammonia dynamites, except that nitrostarch is used in place of nitroglycerine. It is white in color, and burns about 16,000 to 20,000 fps. It has been used as a base charge in grenade and mortar ordnance. This explosive is highly flammable and can be ignited from a spark caused by friction.
- *Nitrocellulose* (NC). Also known as guncotton, it was discovered in the early 1830s and later refined in the 1840s by treating cotton wool with nitric and sulfuric acids to make an explosive.
- *PETN.* An odorless white crystalline with a detonating rate in excess of 25,000 fps. This extremely powerful explosive is used extensively in the manufacture of detonating cord (primer cord), blasting caps, and boosters for blasting agents. It is more sensitive to shock and friction than TNT, and in some cases it is used as an initiator. It is a component of Semtex-H, the Czechoslovakian version of C-4. It was the explosive of choice on at least two occasions. The first was Richard Reid (a.k.a. Abdul Raheem and Tarriq Raja), who became known as the "Shoe Bomber." Reid, in December 2001, tried to ignite his explosive-laden shoes during a commercial airline flight to New York, using PETN as a base charge and TATP as an initiator in attempting to turn his shoes into IEDs. In the second case, Umar Farouk Abdulmutallab, the Nigerian who became known as the Christmas Day "Underwear Bomber," attempted to ignite a PETN-based explosive device secreted in his underwear aboard a Northwest Airlines flight from Amsterdam to Detroit. It failed to function as designed, but severely burned the bomber in the process.
- *Picric acid* (trinitrophenol). Highly explosive in a crystalline state with a burning rate of approximately 19,000 to 23,000 fps. The Japanese used picric acid as a base explosive during World War II. It is available in a powder configuration that is used in various dye tests under laboratory conditions. When stored for a long period of time, picric acid can become extremely unstable and sensitive to shock and friction. When the chemical comes in contact with lead, it forms lead picrate, a sensitive and violent explosive. Bottles of unstable picric acid are routinely found in school chemistry labs, presenting another challenge to bomb technicians. It is lemon-yellow in color and soluble in alcohol, benzene, and other organic solvents.
- *Tetryl.* Clear to yellow crystalline material with a very high degree of shattering effect, or brisance. It has a burning rate of 25,800 fps, and is sometimes used as a booster and in blasting caps.

- *Tetrytol.* Light tallow to buff in color, and a high explosive that is 70% tetryl and 30% TNT and used primarily as filler in artillery shells and bursting mines. It is similar to TNT and tetryl. It fires at 24,000 fps. It is also used in demolition satchel charges.
- *Trinitrotoluene* (TNT). A solid-cast explosive that was first used in 1905. TNT is yellow crystalline substance with a high brisance, or shattering effect, and is well suited for cutting steel, breaking concrete, and similar demolition work. Primarily a military explosive, it is issued in ¼-, ½-, or 1-pound blocks for demolition work and as a filler in bombs and artillery ammunition. It is used by the military as a standard in comparing the strengths of other explosives to TNT. It is given an index of 1.00 and has a burning rate of 22,500 fps.
- *Torpex.* A mixture of RDX, TNT, aluminum, and wax desensitizer that was used as the explosive filler for torpedoes and naval mines during WWII. It was replaced with HBX later in the war.

Common Commercial Explosives

- *ANFO.* Commercially manufactured ammonium nitrate-based explosive that was first introduced in the 1950s to the replace the more sensitive nitroglycerin dynamite. The uniform mixing of fuel oil is essential in achieving maximum effect. This product has a wide range of detonating velocities that run from 10,000 to 16,000 fps. ANFO is a blasting agent and not blasting cap sensitive; therefore, it needs a secondary high explosive to achieve detonation. ANFO is an explosive easily improvised and is a favorite of terrorists in making large vehicle-delivered explosive devices.
- *Detonating cord.* Also known as detcord or primer cord. This explosive can be used in both civilian and military applications. Looking very much like a safety fuse, which has a black powder filler, detonating cord has a filler of either PETN or RDX and is usually manufactured in bright colors for easy visibility. The core is white in color. The military version is olive drab in color. It should be noted that the olive-drab military safety fuse has yellow bands every 3 feet and is designed to burn between 35 and 45 seconds per foot. The core of the time fuse is black in color, while detcord is white. Detonating cord is usually used as a cutting charge, but it may used as part of a firing train (see below) to initiate another explosive charge. Detcord has a burn rate of approximately 25,000 fps.
- *Dynamite.* Developed by Alfred E. Nobel in 1867 as a substitute for the highly volatile nitroglycerin, which was the primary blasting agent at the time. Originally, dynamite was made with a train of nitroglycerin running through an inert binding material and was

known as "straight dynamite." These dynamites were classified as 20, 30, 60%, etc., depending upon the amount of nitroglycerin present, and also came in a variety of sizes, ranging from 0.50- to 50-pound cartridges. Today, the nitroglycerin has been replaced largely by ammonium nitrate to make it more stable and easier to maintain in storage. Military dynamite, composed of RDX, TNT, nitrostarch, and motor oil, contains no nitroglycerin, nor does it absorb or retain moisture. It is much easier to use and store than the commercial variety and is generally used in noncombat construction projects and has a detonating rate of approximately 20,000 fps. In the commercial sector, there are so many formulas for commercial dynamite that there are no agreed-upon standards for coloring, firing speed, or size. Nitroglycerin-based dynamites become extremely dangerous if not properly cared for while in storage. Nitrate salt crystals form on the outside of the cartridges, or the nitroglycerin may leach through the wrapper, leaving dark or wet spots on the cartridge.

- *Water gels.* Also called slurry, these were introduced in the late 1950s, and are composed of ammonium nitrate, TNT, water, and a gelatinizing agent with a bombing agent. This explosive is used primarily for quarry blasting because of its concentrated strength.

Powders and Propellants

- *Black powder.* The exact date of origin is not known, but it is believed to have been invented in China sometime around the ninth century and has been used in various applications throughout its long history. Today, black powder consists of a mixture of carbon, powdered sulfur, and potassium nitrate (saltpeter). The product is usually formed in large cakes that were treated with water and alcohol to reduce the chance of accidental ignition and left to dry. Black powder is unique in that even though it is a low explosive, it can under certain conditions detonate with high-explosive force. Black powder comes in four classifications, from fg to ffffg, with fg being the largest and used in only the largest caliber firing weapons; ffg is a smaller grain and is commonly used in larger bore weapons, usually .45 caliber and up; fffg is yet a smaller grain and is obviously used for smaller caliber weapons; and lastly, the finest of the powder is ffffg, which is usually used in firing old flash pan flintlock muzzleloaders. When black powder is burned it leaves a thick heavy fouling residue. During the Civil War, the rapid firing of soldiers' weapons would cause them to become so fouled with residue it would be nearly impossible to ram new rounds into the piece. Black powder deteriorates with age, but when saturated with water and later dried out, it still retains is

Figure 11.1 Smokeless powder: relatively easy to obtain, smokeless powder is a common filler used in improvised explosive devices, particularly bombs.

potency. Civil War cannon balls removed from rivers where combat occurred, when dried out, were just as potent as the day they were manufactured. Due to its ready availability, black powder is a favorite explosive filler for pipe bombs built by not only amateur bombers or occasional experimenters, but terrorists as well.

- *Smokeless powder.* Smokeless power is generally produced by dissolving gun cotton with a mixture of ether and alcohol and blending into a paste (Figure 11.1). This paste is then formed into a rope-like shape of various thicknesses and cut into different lengths. Smokeless powder of this type is known as single base; if nitroglycerin is added it is known as double-base powder. These powders come in various forms and colors. It is generally considered the standard propellant for small arms ammunition and for certain types of cannons. Smokeless powder can be purchased in most sporting goods stores and is available in cans from 1 to 25 pounds in weight. This powder is sensitive to friction, flame, shock, and static electricity, but it is not as sensitive as black powder.

250 The Counterterrorism Handbook

Explosives Used in Making Improvised Devices

Virtually any type of explosive can be improvised by those with a background in chemistry or trained by someone with that type of expertise and access to the chemicals required. In addition, some explosives can still be purchased over the counter.

- *Powders.* The most common type of explosive used in making small improvised explosive devices. They are frequently found in pipe bombs fashioned by young experimenters, amateur and domestic terrorists, and radicals. Black powder and smokeless powder, both readily available in sporting and outdoor stores, are used most in the construction of pipe bombs. Potassium chlorate, mixed with a catalyst substance, such as sugar, is used in either making pipe bombs or incendiary devices.
- *Improvised plastic explosives.* Knowledgeable bomb makers and terrorists commonly manufacture their own explosives. A mixture of easily obtainable potassium chlorate, ground very fine, and petroleum jelly can be detonated with a blasting cap. In addition, when potassium chlorate is mixed with an enhancer, such as sugar, it can be a very potent incendiary mixture.
- *Fuel-oxidizer mixes.* There are an almost infinite variety of improvised fuel explosives that can be made by a determined bomber. Some of these mixtures are difficult and dangerous to manufacture; others are fairly simple (Figure 11.2). Raw materials for the devices are regularly found in areas where there are agricultural, mining, and quarrying activity. Improvised mixtures of ammonium nitrate and fuel were used in both the New York City World Trade Center and Oklahoma City federal building bombings. These explosives require booster explosives to achieve detonation.

Identifying Improvised Explosive Devices

A point made several times in this book is that an improvised explosive device is limited only by the ingenuity of the bomb maker. This holds true not only for the IED itself, but also in the method of delivery. You do not have to be a qualified bomb technician to recognize the types of IEDs, explosives, and firing devices that are commonly available. The great majority of IEDs used in terrorist attacks are of fairly simple construction,

Figure 11.2 A reconstruction of the vehicle-borne IED used in the Oklahoma City bombing. (Courtesy of F. Guerra.)

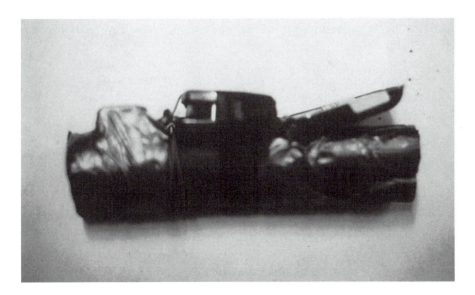

Figure 11.3 Pipe bomb pictured above is the type used in the bombing of Atlanta abortion clinics. (Courtesy of F. Guerra.)

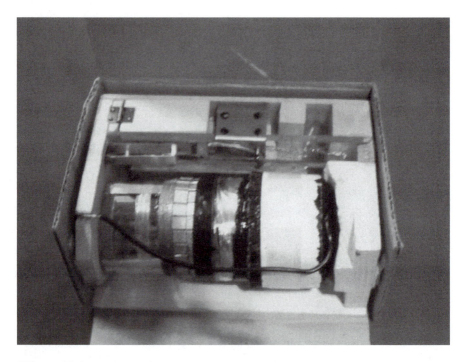

Figure 11.4 Mock-up of a pipe bomb that was used by the Unabomber in his long-running bomb campaign. (Courtesy of F. Guerra.)

utilizing electrical or mechanical firing systems. Generally, IEDs contain these components:

1. Explosives' main charge.
2. Firing or initiating system.
3. Delivery system (package, container, or vehicle in which the IED is placed). IEDs can also be delivered utilizing firing systems such as homemade mortar tubes and rocket launchers.

Firing Train

Basically the firing train is the number of steps that are required to achieve the desired end results. For instance, if a blasting agent or tertiary explosive is the main charge, it would be a five-step process: (1) the introduction of flame to (2) the time or safety fuse that in turn will (3) initiate the blasting cap or primary explosive that will (4) detonate the secondary or booster charge that will (5) in turn cause the blasting agent to detonate.

Figure 11.5 Trinitrotoluene: TNT manufactured for the military comes in a variety of shapes and sizes.

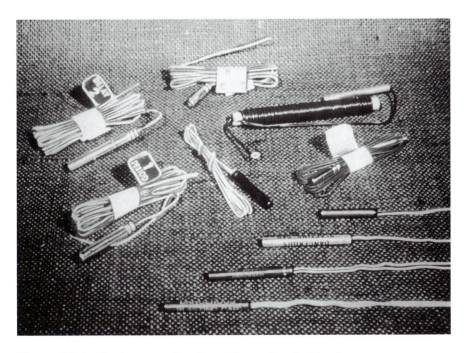

Figure 11.6 Blasting caps: by themselves, electric blasting caps are easy to obtain and may seem relatively harmless, but are powerful and must be handled with extreme care.

Initiation Systems

A low explosive (e.g., black or smokeless powder) needs only a spark, flame, or friction to be initiated, whereas a high explosive (such as TNT or C-4) requires the introduction of an explosive shock to achieve detonation. This shock is usually accomplished through the use of a detonator or blasting cap. Blasting caps come in two functioning varieties: electric or nonelectric. Blasting caps generally consist of a metallic sleeve containing a small amount of primary explosive and measuring approximately ¼ inch diameter by 2 to 5 inches in length, depending on design and intended use.

Electric blasting caps are detonators designed to function when an electric charge, from such sources as batteries or generating equipment, is transmitted into the cap. Electrical impulses are transmitted through leg wires of various lengths that initiate the base charge. The electric blasting cap will function with the application of a very small electrical charge and low amperage into the primary explosive. The electrical charge is usually introduced by using what is known as a blasting machine. There are two categories:

1. Generator type, which is usually activated by a rapid twist of a handle or a downward thrust of a plunger. The twisting handle type is usually held firmly in the hand and is known as a 10-cap machine. The other is box-like and has a t-handle that is vigorously pushed downward. This type is commonly referred to as a 50-cap blasting machine.
2. The generator types have for the most part been replaced by a capacitor discharge, which is much smaller than the generator type and utilizes dry cell batteries to charge the capacitor. The electric charge is then discharged into the cap. In addition, the caps are manufactured in a wide range of time delays, from the instantaneous to a delay of several seconds.

Nonelectric blasting caps are small metal cylinders, closed at one end and containing a small amount of primary explosive as a base charge. They are designed to function when a small spark or flame is introduced to the base charge, usually from a burning length of safety fuse. The fuse transmits a flame of uniform rate in order to provide a time delay prior to detonation. The fuse usually consists of a train of black powder encased in a waterproof covering, measuring approximately ¼ inch diameter, which provides a fairly constant burning rate of 35 to 45 seconds per foot. Burning rates may vary with manufacturers, climate, or other such factors. A sample length of fuse would be test-burned to establish a burning rate for the particular items prior to using on a charge. Fuse colors may vary from highly visible, colorful shades for commercial use to olive drab for military use. Although ordinary matches can be used to light the safety fuse, more efficient methods include fuse igniters manufactured for either military or civilian use. In addition, igniter cord, a flexible incendiary cord, may be used when initiating a number of different safety fuses.

With low explosives or propellants, only an introduction of a spit of flame, heat, or spark is required to initiate the mixtures. A favorite initiator in IEDs utilizing smokeless powder and an electric firing system is common photographic flashbulbs, which are no longer so easy to come by. Not only will they initiate propellant powders, but they also work very well with an assortment of incendiary materials.

There are other initiators used for, and found in, IED construction. Among them are:

1. Hot, or bridge, wire elements that consist of a wire bridged across the ends of two leg wires carrying the current. The bridge wire, being less resistant than the leg wires, will heat up and glow quickly when power is applied, thus initiating the charge.
2. Electronic squibs or "matches" that not only function much the same way as an electric blasting cap, but appear similar. The difference is that they lack the explosive main charge and are used primarily to initiate low explosives. There are basically two types: the vented, which allows the flame to vent through holes in the cylinder, and the nonvented, which bursts from the flame confined in the cylinder.
3. Any type of safety, firework, or other improved nonelectric fuse capable of transmitting a flame or spark.
4. Non-el, or "shock tube," is made from a very thin hollow-core plastic tube that is dusted with the powerful HMX and fine aluminum powder. When initiated by the introduction of a shock, it detonates at 6,500 fps.

There are three primary methods for firing systems utilized in the construction of IEDs, and each has its variations:

1. Time delay, provided by electronic or mechanical timers, a fuse, or the use of chemicals
2. Action, a mechanical system that can be fired by an individual pushing, pulling, or applying pressure
3. Command, which functions by electrical or radio signal

All three types of time-delay options have been used by terrorist operatives. The choice of system depends more on personal or group preference and availability of materials than on the performance advantage of any one option. Improvised versions of various time-delay options can be simplistic or sophisticated:

- Mechanical time-delay devices include everything from an altered alarm clock to a long-delay miniature electronic circuitry. Time delay is limited only by the power source the bomb maker can provide. Mechanical time delay is still used by bomb makers who employ such timepieces as alarm clocks, wristwatches, and kitchen timers in a wide variety of electrical circuitry hookups. The alarm function on cell phones is now in use for timing delays. Unless a very large action is planned, terrorists tend to use short time-delay devices, with many of the IEDs being placed at the target within an hour of detonation. When a timepiece is used in a mechanical firing system, it may be altered in several ways to provide time delay. Among the more common methods are:
  1. Using the hour hand to achieve a time delay of up to 12 hours, or the minute hand for a delay of up to 59 minutes
  2. A stem-wound watch where the mainspring is used as a contact, thus increasing the potential delay up to 36 hours or more
  3. Using a mechanical alarm clock winding stem as the contact point
     The rapid evolution of technology in electronic circuits and the miniaturization of programmable timing devices provide more options for today's bombers. Bomb attacks, which can result in detonations being set far in advance, days and even weeks ahead of time, can be carried out.
- Chemical delays are used effectively in both incendiary and explosive devices, including those employing high explosives. Chemical delays are not used as frequently as mechanical delays, because the measurement is neither as exact nor as accurate. As a result, chemical delay fuses are not used in everyday demolition operations. The delays may be either improvised or manufactured, the latter usually being prepared for the military. The most common of these is the delay fuse usually referred to as a time pencil. There are foreign-manufactured equivalents with a different nomenclature. The time pencil has an effective time delay from as little as 2 minutes to as much as 23 days, although the longer the delay, the less accurate the timing device will be. Terrorists have made extensive use of chemical delays, especially improvised chemical delays employing acid solutions. Hydrochloric and sulfuric acids are the most common because they are easy to obtain through legitimate sources. In addition, gasoline, lye, and other common caustic substances can be used as chem-

Figure 11.7 Improvised hand grenade: an empty soft drink can refilled with BBs and a high explosive became a deadly, easily throwable hand grenade.

ical initiators and delays. Chemical delay fusing systems were fairly popular among Latin American terrorist groups in past decades.

- Time-delay fuses are commonly encountered with nonelectrical systems, the most common of which are safety fuses (Figure 11.7). Although the safety fuse is designed for use with nonelectric blasting caps, it can be used in the initiation of low-explosive powder and propellants. This type of delay initiating system is commonly used in the construction of pipe bombs. Safety fuses are often employed in pipe bombs. Although there are a number of safety fuse manufacturers, the chief differences among the brands are the types of exterior waterproofing and color-coding systems employed for easy identification. Military issue is generally olive drab in color. Improvised burning-type fuses can be made from such readily available materials as cotton string that has been impregnated with black powder or drinking straws filled with a smokeless powder mixture. Easily found manufactured items that can be used as safety fuses are firework fuses and those used to initiate model rockets.

Action switches are set off by the action of an individual, either the person planting the bomb, the targeted individual, or a person tampering with the device. They are often referred to as booby traps or antitampering devices. There are different types of action switches:

1. Pull release, which is designed to function when tension on a wire is severely decreased by pulling or yanking. These switches come in a variety of configurations specifically manufactured for military use. The most common item in improvising the switch is an ordinary spring-type clothespin, which also can be used for a pressure-release or pressure-applied switch. The action switch is used primarily in antipersonnel devices, particularly in letter and parcel bombs, such as those crafted by the Unabomber.

2. Pressure application switches are designed to initiate a device through the release or application of pressure or tension. There are a wide variety of these switches available, particularly for military application in mine warfare. Pressure switches are also easily improvised. These types of switches are of particular concern for a searcher undertaking a VIP or preincident sweep.

3. Tilt switches are usually found on devices fired by an electric circuit. The switch functions when it is tipped, tilted, or jarred in any direction, or in a single, predetermined direction. The most common is the mercury switch, with numerous mechanical and electrical applications, and is available at virtually any electronic components store. These switches also are easily improvised using glass tubes, ball bearings, and other common items. These types of switches are of particular concern for a searcher undertaking an executive sweep or preincident search.

4. Command detonation is a method employed when a bomber wishes to activate a device at a precise but undetermined time, such when an individual walks or drives past it. Command detonation can be achieved by electrical ignition or radio transmission or other wireless devices. Such explosive devices are becoming more frequent in terrorist bombings, particularly in the Middle East. The drawback with firing a radio control device is that line of sight with the target is required, although modern electronics and cell phones have eased this limitation. The ETA, the Basque terrorists in Spain, make frequent use of radio-detonated IEDs. Electrical control of a command detonation is the more traditional method because it is routinely employed by demolition teams in legitimate work. It is accomplished simply by introducing an electrical charge into wires connected to the explosive charge, using either batteries or handheld generating equipment manufactured for that purpose.

IED Packaging

During the late 1960s and 1970s domestic terrorists used smaller IEDs than what is common among today's terrorists. Just as IEDs are limited only by the bomb maker's ingenuity, so are the methods that past terrorists used to penetrate security to get inside and deliver the device. Over the years, as security tightened and access to buildings became more difficult to achieve, more and more explosive devices were placed on the building's exterior. As perimeter security tightened, terrorists began to deliver vehicle-borne IEDs that can deliver a massive payload. Some delivery methods, the amount of explosives that each may contain, and the recommended stand-off distances follow:[4]

- Pipe bombs. The most common of these devices are constructed from galvanized pipe, usually 6 to 10 feet in length and 2 to 2½ inches in diameter, and which hold upward of 5 pounds of explosives. If high explosives, the minimum evacuation distance from a bomb in a building is 70 feet, and if left in the open, 850 feet.
- Briefcases/suitcases and backpacks. Depending upon the size, can hold as much as 50 pounds, with building evacuation of 150 feet, and if outside, as much as 1,850 feet.
- Automobiles. Once again, depending upon the type of vehicle, a full-size sedan to a compact car can be packed with between 500 and 1,000 pounds of explosives. Thus, the stand-off distance is as much as 1,750 feet.
- Passenger/cargo vans/small trucks. These vehicles can be loaded with between 4,000 and 10,000 pounds of explosives. The safe stand-off distance varies from 2,750 to 3,750 feet. If in an urban area, this stand-off distance can present a serious problem, especially from collateral damage, as occurred in the Oklahoma City bombing in April 1995.
- Large trucks/moving vans/semi-tractor trailers. Can be loaded with high explosive, between 30,000 and 60,000 pounds of explosives. We have witnessed these types of VBIED in the bombing of the Marine Corps barracks in Lebanon and the Kobar Towers bombing in 1996 in Saudi Arabia.

Packaging of IEDs to defeat a security system can come in almost any innocent-looking container, such as:

- Radios
- Toys

- Cell phones
- Computers
- Fruit baskets and gift-wrapped packages
- Through the mail or private delivery services such as Fed Ex, etc.
- Household items, such as lamps

Characteristics of Military Ordnance

Of the secondary explosives discussed, the majority are used in military applications. The same criteria that make certain explosives acceptable for military use also make them attractive to terrorist organizations. These include:

- Relative insensitivity to shock, heat, or friction, such as small arms bullet impact
- Good shattering effect
- Convenient shape and size for handling, storage, and placement under combat conditions
- Manufacturability from readily available raw materials
- Usable under water

Endnotes

1. U.S. Army TM-9-1300-214/11A-1-134, *Military Explosives Technical Manual*, November 1967, U.S. Department of Defense, Washington, DC.
2. Global Security.org, military/systems/munitions/introduction/Explosives.
3. Roy Rayle, Bombs Explode on Rough Handling, Journal of the Company of Military Historians, summer, 1993.
4. Technical Support Working Group of Combating Terrorism.

Hostage Incidents

12

What Is Involved

Dealing with hostage incidents means setting up communications with the hostage takers. Also, a command post must be established and a support system created for the one person actually dealing with the perpetrators: the hostage negotiator. Though only one person should be speaking directly with the perpetrator, he or she will be closely backed up by a secondary negotiator. The secondary negotiator will listen to both sides of the negotiations and will feed the primary negotiator appropriate intelligence as it is passed up to the point of negotiation. He or she also will act as insulation to permit the primary negotiator room for concentration. There also will be a person who acts as coach and who will monitor both the primary and secondary negotiators and feed intelligence through the backup to the primary. The coach will coordinate the efforts of those gathering information and intelligence. While all this is happening, more intelligence gathering should be ongoing in order to formulate a negotiating strategy and tactics.

Communicating with the Hostage Taker

We already have learned about the physical and mechanical parts of establishing communication, such as the use of bullhorns, telephones, etc. Equally important—possibly more important, really—is what kind of stance the negotiator is going to take in dealing with the hostage taker, or if it is a group, with the leader or spokesperson.

For law enforcement agents dealing with a hostage situation, a conservative approach is probably the safest. Police officers might not be of much help in making the situation any better, but most assuredly, no one wants to make the situation worse. Being conservative does not mean being inactive or taking no action whatsoever, but neither is there any reason to rush into action. Certainly, it takes time to gather as much intelligence as possible. Once that intelligence begins to filter in, it should be weighed so that a negotiating strategy can be formulated.

The first decision to be made is whether to take a hard-line or soft-line stance. Few would question that the State of Israel probably has the hardest line anywhere in dealing with terrorist hostage situations. Exaggerating only slightly, it is said that hostage takers confronted by the Israelis are given about 10 minutes to come out with their hands up or they will be brought out with their feet up. However, this policy certainly has not stopped acts of terrorism from being perpetrated against Israel.

On the other hand, the so-called soft-line approach to dealing with hostage takers has critics, too. The New York City Police Department (NYPD), for example, has been accused of dealing too softly with hostage takers. One judge reportedly said that in New York, if you were robbing a bank and things went bad, all you had to do was grab a few hostages. Then, the NYPD would help you pack the money and drive you to the airport. The exaggeration here is greater than it was in describing Israel's hard-line approach.

The differences between hard-line and soft-line approaches and the arguments over which is preferable are not as important as what will achieve the desired outcome in the hostage situation. Will the hostages be harmed? Will a martyr be created? Will the stakes be raised in a sequel or imitative incident?

The policy and approach of the NYPD, for example, does not encourage imitative or copycat actions. Generally, when hostage incidents end and the perpetrators surrender, they are taken away to a city hospital, where they are given a cursory physical and psychiatric examination by a mental health professional. The physical examination is made to preclude any allegation of beating or other police brutality, while the psychiatric examination determines whether there is a mental health problem. If there is, the subject can be treated. If no mental health problem is apparent, the subject can be returned to the criminal justice system and a defense plea of insanity is almost certainly precluded. This approach helps prevent imitative copycats, since people want to emulate heroes, not persons with mental problems.

The whole question of martyrdom is based upon putting tremendous value on the cause for which one gives his or her life. The fact that such martyrdom now is often associated with Islamic fundamentalist terrorists does not mean that others before have not been so motivated. As far back as the Crusades, Pope Leo told Christian crusaders that if they died in the service of the cross, they were assured a place in heaven.

The Making of a Hostage Incident

In order to know how to negotiate, what attitude to adopt, and what stance to take, it is necessary to understand what goes into the making of a hostage incident staged by terrorists. Dr. Brian Jenkins of the Rand Corporation, a research group located in California, coined the phrase "the theater of terror." The perpetrator is the star of the production, that is, the leading actor. The police are the supporting cast, the hostage is the costar, and the public, the rest of the world, if you will, is the audience. The vehicle used to make this presentation is the hostage taking. This is what attracts an audience and what draws media attention, which in turn creates an even larger audience. Whether the incident is local (with news coverage) or global (with worldwide satellite coverage), the incident reaffirms Shakespeare's observation that "all the world's a stage."

The publicity value of holding hostages can almost never be underestimated, as terrorists from the Middle East to North Africa and the Philippines have demonstrated in recent years. A person who is ignored by society, as terrorists claim they are, or by the bureaucracy of government, or by friends and neighbors, can become the center of attention, the number one attraction in town, simply by taking hostage an unsuspecting person, even a relative, and holding the police at bay with the mere threat of doing that person bodily harm.

A classic example, though it does not involve a terrorist incident, illustrates this very well. In the early 1970s, Anthony Koritsis in Indianapolis, Indiana, felt he had been cheated out of his life savings by a financial company. He did not demonstrate his anger by simply storming into the company offices and shooting the principals. Instead, he purchased a shotgun, cut down the stock, and sawed off the barrel. He affixed a wire noose to the end of the barrel. He then went to the financial company's offices and forced the manager to put the noose around his neck. Koritsis then proceeded to parade the man through the streets of Indianapolis. They eventually wended their way to Koritsis's previously booby-trapped apartment, where he held the manager hostage for many hours. After receiving a promise of immunity from the state attorney general, Koritsis held a press conference with the hostage still in a noose at the end of his shotgun. Koritsis was able to manipulate the media—all the major television networks provided coverage, as did local television stations, numerous print reporters, and photographers. Finally, after forcing the hostage to read a prepared statement, Koritsis did surrender. The grant of immunity, incidentally, was held to be null and void, but Koritsis was eventually found not guilty by reason of temporary insanity and was institutionalized.

A similar event happened more than 20 years later in Hawaii when a disgruntled former employee by the name of John Miranda returned to his former place of employment and shot and wounded a supervisor. He then forced another employee, who normally would not have been in the office, to place around his neck a wire that was attached to a shotgun. After a few hours of talking to the media and negotiating with police, Miranda forced the employee down an outside stairway. The two pirouetted in a macabre dance in the company parking lot, surrounded by police who could not fire at the perpetrator for fear of hitting the hostage. After setting a series of deadlines, Miranda told his captive to count down from 100 and then he would fire.

When the count reached 13, the hostage spun around and tried to grab the gun. It was now away from his head. Miranda fired but missed. The police fired and didn't miss. The hostage was saved. This illustrates the familiar axiom: "Everything old is new again." Researching and learning from previous incidents will always be helpful in responding to current situations.

Nearly every day we see the principle of theater being applied in international terrorist operations, whether perpetrated by dissident Chechens, Islamic Jihad, or any of the too numerous to mention national, political, and ethnic groups using terror as a political weapon.

In Chapter 5, we examined the expropriation of media attention during the 1972 Olympic Games by terrorists of the Black September organization. An even more effective example of media manipulation was effected by the Symbionese Liberation Army (SLA) operating in the United States during the 1970s, one of whose members was pardoned by outgoing President Bill Clinton in January 2001. The SLA was a group that probably never had more than 12 active members, but that managed to lead the media and general public into thinking that it was in fact a large, well-organized army. This organization staged the highly publicized abduction of Patricia Hearst, heir to the Hearst publishing fortune. The SLA demand that the Hearst family distribute food to the poor, and the subsequent distribution of this food caught the attention of the whole world. Journalists reported how some United Nations officials were calling for an investigation into the "plight" of the Symbionese people, because their liberation army had been pushed to such extremes for attention. The name *Symbionese*, of course, is related to *symbiosis*, a biological term describing the relationship of two dissimilar organisms living in an association that is beneficial to both (as opposed to parasitism).

The Announcement

If a person were holding one, two, or more persons hostage and no one was aware of the situation, there would be little value in continuing to hold the hostages. Because hostage situations are designed to influence authorities or obtain something of value, the perpetrators do not want anonymity. They want an audience. Not unlike the traditional circus parade through town to herald the arrival of the greatest show on earth, hostage-taking perpetrators may stage a robbery, crash a bus through a fence, or fire a couple of gunshots in order to bring attention to themselves. Only then can they move on to the next step, the position of power.

This is why, in planning negotiating strategies, it is so important to have all of the information and intelligence possible about the incident: who, what, when, where, how, and why? How was the announcement made? Was anyone hurt in the takeover? How many perpetrators are there? What weapons do they have? How many hostages? Where are they located? What are the demands, and how logical are they? It is important to note, however, that logic does not necessarily set the value or seriousness of the demands. Another question that should be answered quickly is whether any demands were granted by those individuals first responding to the announcement. All of this information will assist in securing the safest possible outcome.

Reaction of Law Enforcement Professionals

Hostage negotiation is based on the theory of cognitive dissonance, which, explained in everyday language, means that something is worth whatever someone is willing to pay for it. This is the principle involved in the pricing of objects sold at auction, whether art or antiques or racehorses. What was last paid for the object, or similar object, sets the basis for the new price. What is the highest price that can be paid for anything? A human life! So if someone is willing to give his or her life for a cause, others will evaluate that particular cause in a similar manner. Making a martyr out of a hostage taker will only encourage imitation. Negotiation offers the optimum chances of recovering the hostages alive, while at the same time providing the least opportunity for creating a hero or martyr of the hostage takers.

There are certain principles that have been gleaned from our work in hostage recovery. One of these is that it is in neither the hostage taker's nor law enforcement's best interest to have a situation become violent. The hostage taker knows that ultimately the police will win. Although there could be temporary setbacks for the police, if it comes to an all-out confrontation, the authorities have the equipment and manpower to eventually overcome any violence that the perpetrator can muster. This leads to the obvious conclusion: hostage situations are really not as delicate as many observers tend to think they are. If a hostage taker truly intended to kill his or her victim, the police would be there investigating a homicide rather than dealing with the dynamics of hostage negotiation. On the other hand, hostage takers must be regarded as potential killers. If pushed to a point where they must demonstrate power and control, they may resort to violence.

The Application of Time

The concern of many people on the periphery of hostage situations, be they civilians or ranking police officials, is that the negotiating is taking too long. The police should hurry up and "do something." The use of such statements as "We're running out of time," "You're wasting your time," "Time is running out," and "This is costing too much overtime" should not influence the negotiators in their efforts to bring about the release of the hostages. A job is over when it's over. In discussing deadlines, we learned that perpetrators will often set a deadline for whatever demand they are making. Most perpetrators are not likely to kill on a deadline, but obviously there are no guarantees.

Over the years, through empirical data, we have concluded that negotiators should seemingly ignore the deadlines. By that we mean do not call attention to "the clock" in communications with the perpetrators. Try to keep them talking through the set time. Most often when the perpetrators realize the time has past, they will establish a new deadline. This tactic can go on indefinitely, sprinkled with the granting of a few insignificant requests, such as food or cigarettes.

The importance of patience was demonstrated at a prison in Buckeye, Arizona. On January 18, 2004, two inmates of the Arizona State Prison Complex attempted to escape from that facility. Overpowering a correction officer and a kitchen worker, one of the prisoners, using the officer's uniform, gained entry to a security watchtower. At the tower, the inmate took captive two officers assigned to the tower, a male and a female. He was later joined by the other inmate, and thus began a 15-day odyssey for the officers and prison officials.

Negotiations began almost immediately with the assistance of the Phoenix Police Department. During the course of the negotiation, the hostages' safety was verified and various simple demands granted. Demands included "a helicopter and a pizza"; the pizza was delivered. The media, as well as some government officials, created pressure for a quick resolution of the incident, which eventually cost a reported $3.6 million. On the twelfth day, the male correction officer was released after an interview of the inmates by a local radio station. The next three days brought about great concern for the safety of the remaining hostage, the female officer. But on the fifteenth day she was released and the inmates surrendered. There were concerns about the possibility of sexual assault on the female, but it was more important to bring her out alive.

Upon her release she made the following statement: "Thank you for not forgetting me, and thank you for not rushing the tower; they would have killed me." It was also stated, "This was not a TV show or a movie." This was the longest prison hostage situation in Arizona's history, and one of the longest in the country, but it demonstrated the importance of the proper use of patience and negotiating skills.

Criminal Role

There are roles played by both the criminal and the police. Many times, the criminal role is to play the unbalanced person, the crazy person, if you will.

This is especially true if there are two perpetrators. One will speak with the authorities in a rational manner, usually warning that he doesn't know how long he can control the other, apparently more irrational culprit. The other will be just that, apparently and overtly irrational, unstable, and volatile. If the perpetrator is alone, he may do things such as seeming to play Russian roulette with himself or the hostage. Depending upon how extreme the response of the negotiator or authorities is, the more or less likely the hostage taker is to engage in these actions. However, total disregard of such actions could provoke a demonstration of power; therefore, some slight acknowledgment of power will placate the hostage taker's ego.

Police Role

The police also have a role to play. They have been called the good daddies of society, and the mere presence of a uniformed officer many times can calm the anxieties of the public in a crisis situation. It is not uncommon for two persons in a fender bender traffic accident to leave their vehicles in the middle of the roadway to await the arrival of a police officer. It is as though once the officer surveys the situation, everything will work out all right. Simply exchanging driver's license information and insurance company data is all that is required, and this is all the officer will do upon arriving at the scene (often delayed because the accident participants have left their vehicles in the middle of the roadway).

What officer, when donning a uniform on the first day on the job, has not looked in the mirror and believed that he or she could make a difference to the public waiting to be served? It is no surprise, then, that most police officers become action oriented. When they get to the scene of an incident, they are usually under the gaze of a crowd that has gathered, and many times feel the need to do something. Usually, this starts with moving back the crowd, an action not always appreciated by the curious onlookers. At a hostage or barricade situation, the first things the officers should limit themselves to are containing, evacuation, and intelligence.

Containment

Generally, containment is a physical exercise, although there is also a psychological component to the activity. First and foremost, however, is physical containment, keeping perpetrators within the smallest area practicable. A locked or wedged door creates a barrier that cannot be opened or moved by the perpetrator yelling or threatening. It is preferable that the police prohibit, or at least restrict, the movement of the hostage taker and the hostages, because a mobile situation is usually not in the best interest of law enforcement personnel or the hostages, although there may be times when going mobile produces a tactical advantage for the authorities.

Containment also has its psychological aspects, i.e., in the initial stages of the incident, not trying to converse with the perpetrator, and letting him or her get over panic and calm down in order to assess the situation. Often, this is all that is needed to bring an incident to a safe conclusion. On the other hand, it is possible that police actions could provoke a violent reaction, particularly if the perpetrator has power over the situation, or worse, intends to commit suicide. Frequently, such individuals do not have the wherewithal to pull the trigger on themselves and will kill or otherwise harm a hostage in order to draw police fire, which has been termed suicide by police.

Evacuation and Intelligence

The orderly evacuation of innocent persons is important to preclude injury or death or the possibility of the perpetrator taking additional hostages. The hows of evacuation were covered earlier. The gathering of information as quickly and accurately as possible will greatly affect the outcome of any hostage situation, be it terrorist or otherwise. When evacuating people from the hostage scene, it must be done in an orderly manner, trying to account for all of the inhabitants, customers, and the like. When there is a fire in a multiple-unit dwelling, firefighters try to account for all the residents. When they can't, they often send firefighters into the burning building to search for possible victims. In a hostage situation, if there are people unaccounted for, the assumption must be made that they are being held hostage. In this situation, the risk taking is to save the lives of innocent victims. If it is convincingly established that there are no hostages, then it becomes a barricaded situation. Never ask the perpetrator, who has nothing to lose by lying. However, intelligence, no matter how accurate, becomes valueless and useless unless communicated to the appropriate individuals.

Advances in Technology in Gathering Intelligence

In earlier days of handling hostage/barricade incidents, the means used to gather intelligence required innovation and imagination. Much of the equipment was jerry-rigged, and a good deal was hit and miss. Some officers assigned to observation positions used binoculars and portable radios to gather some basic intelligence. Often from those positions they could see into the building or apartment. They would then advise the command post on the actions of the perpetrator(s) and the condition of the hostages. At times these abilities were hampered by the physical location or structure of the building. Early on, in order to get a closer look into windows, we taped a lady's hand mirror to a mop handle and looked from the window above or next door. We also used children's toy periscopes, especially if there was a possibility of coming under gunfire from the perpetrator. Though new to law enforcement, this was not new to the battle between good and evil. Periscopes had been used in trench warfare in World War I. Many had also been seen at golf tournaments and parades. To see into a room or apartment, we again used lady's makeup mirrors. Placed under the doorframe halfway with the proper angle, we could see who was in the room and where they were located. Though quite primitive, these could be very effective. (Note: When viewing with a mirror, the images are reversed, whereas when using a periscope, the images are correct.)

In establishing communications with the person(s) involved in a hostage/barricade, one of the first things we would try to do was call him or her by the in-house telephone. We would try to capture control of the line either with the cooperation of the telephone company or by physically depriving the subject of service, thereby isolating the subject and requiring him or her to deal with the negotiator. Sometimes in the panic of the initial confrontation, subjects have been known to rip out the telephone. In order to maintain control of communication, we created a field phone—a simple telephone mounted on a small board that was placed outside a door for someone to pick up and take inside, or we would throw a rope with the phone attached to it and have the subject pull it into the room or apartment. The telephone was attached to a long length of wire and a telephone at the point of negotiation. A 6-volt battery supplied the power to the carbon speakers. Of course, over the years we have seen tremendous improvements of the "throw phone." Some phones can act as both video and audio "bugs" surreptitiously (in some jurisdictions this might require a court order). The console allows as many as four or five persons to monitor the conversations at the point of negotiations. It can also be bridged to the command post as well. When the hostage negotiation program was started, we did not have a protocol with the telephone company in order to deprive the subject of telephone service. During one ongoing incident, in attempting to get assistance from the telephone operator supervisor after normal business hours, we had to resort to chopping a 202 pair of telephone cables with a fire ax. After that incident, we received extremely good cooperation from the local telephone company. Now, there are many different companies supplying telephone service to subscribers, including VOIP (voice-over Internet protocol) and various cell phone service providers. Preincident liaison with these companies in your local area would be a good policy. Not only is this important for hostage and barricade incidents, but for kidnap investigations as well.

One of our earliest technical improvements was the introduction of hard-wired black-and-white video. The camera was about the size of a large book, but it seemed amazing at the time. We were limited by the length of the cable as to where we could watch it. Then came the 1980s and the introduction of cell technology (a by-product of the original NASA moon trip program, the silicon chip). First came the introduction of car phones with limited coverage. These were semimobile because the battery pack that you had to remove from the car was the size of a small suitcase. In a few short years personal cell phones became available and cell coverage kept getting better and better. Today just about everyone who leaves his or her home for work, school, or shopping carries at least one cell phone. It is reported that as many as 89% of adults have cell phones, PDAs (personal digital assistants), or so-called smartphones. The sophistication of these instruments has reached a fantastic plateau. The capabilities include connecting to the Internet, downloading music and information, and capturing and transmitting photos and video, to name just a few basic applications. These mobile phones are handheld computers that can do everything a desktop or laptop can, plus have communication capability.

From the outset, when responding to a hostage or barricaded situation, we are trying to gather intelligence: the who, what, when, where, how, and why. Conversely, we are trying to deprive the subject of the movements of the responding law enforcement personnel. Even when establishing the mobilization point, care must always be taken to keep that location out of the view of the subject so that he or she will not know the capabilities of the responders. However, currently there are thousands of video surveillance cameras in almost every community. The quality of the images has come a long way from the grainy, almost impossible head shots at bank ATMs. Besides the official cameras set up by various government entities as in London and New York City and other venues, businesses from large corporate structures to local bodegas and convenience stores have surveillance camera systems. The quality can vary greatly, but is constantly improving. Currently detectives and investigators, in addition to the standard canvas looking for witnesses, also search for possible images caught on tape or digitally. An example of the significance would be at the truck bombing of the Alfred P. Murrah Federal Building, Oklahoma City, Oklahoma, on April 19, 1995. The image of the explosive-laden Ryder truck that was rented by Timothy McVeigh was captured and preserved by a video camera in a building across the street from the Murrah Building. The camera was focused on the lobby of the building, but in addition, it actually saw out into the street.

One of the first cities to employ video cameras was Munich, Germany. In the early 1970s these cameras assisted in the city's vehicular traffic control. In the 1990s London was one of the first major cities to install surveillance cameras specifically for counterterrorism purposes as part of the Ring of Steel. This was an attempt to thwart the IRA's (Irish Republican Army) bomb campaign. The cameras were as much a public relations gambit as a crime prevention effort. As with any video system, if there is no one assigned to monitor the images, it loses effectiveness as a deterrent. However, as we see, it is a very good investigative tool even after the fact.

In 2005, 52 people were killed when terrorists detonated a bomb in London's Underground subway system. Within a few days, the terrorists decided to strike the transit system again, targeting the subway and three double-decker buses. The IEDs, which were carried in backpacks, did not completely explode, and postblast examination identified the backpacks. Review of the tapes showed that images of four suspects carrying the bags were captured by surveillance cameras. The images were broadcast on the local television channels, which led to the suspects being taken into custody. The thousands of cameras that make up the network lining intersections and neighborhoods again assisted investigators in 2007, when terrorists attempted to detonate two car bombs in London. They were able to unravel the plot and tracked the suspects to an airport parking area in Glasgow, Scotland, where several arrests were carried out.

New York City Police Department has installed a large number of video surveillance cameras starting in Lower Manhattan, the First Ring of Steel in New York. This covers the area of the two major terrorist events at the World Trade Center in 1993 and 2001. In addition, it also covers the financial district, considered a prime target. Also, there are electronic automatic license plate readers that can identify reported stolen vehicles that may be used to transport terrorists or explosives. Plans are in place to expand the video surveillance to Midtown Manhattan, between 34th Street and 59th Street from the East River to the Hudson River. It has been estimated that between the public and private systems, there are more than 40,000 surveillance cameras in New York City. The number is still growing and is exceeded only by London and one city in China. The number of cameras has not been lost on the American Civil Liberties Union and others concerned with personal privacy.

Surveillance cameras are not just the domain of government and businesses. Private citizens have been using them in and around their homes for many years. Their uses range from keeping an eye on the nursery—the so-called nanny cams—to overall internal and external residence observation. Many of these systems can be monitored via the Internet on laptops or handheld smartphones. In a recent double homicide (July 9, 2009) in Beulah, Florida, a well-to-do husband and wife, the natural parents of four children and adoptive parents of 12 children, some with special needs, were killed. Many of the children were in the home at the time. The probable motive was larceny because a small safe was removed from the home. The investigating officers were able to examine the in-house video security system, which covered inside and outside the home. The video showed the perpetrators arriving outside the building, some attired in ninja outfits, and the vehicle they used. The information gained from the tapes led to the location of the vehicle and the arrests of seven individuals believed responsible for the crimes.

This same type of security system, if taken advantage of by a barricaded subject, could very well expose the law enforcement personnel and their tactics to that subject. In visually searching for security cameras, especially inside buildings, be aware that surreptitious cameras can be disguised as various items, such as clocks, radios, smoke detectors, lamp bases, etc. When investigators review tapes for information and the time of occurrence is significant, be sure to ascertain that the built-in time stamp is correct for either daylight savings time or standard time. As previously stated, some of these systems can be accessed via the Internet, making the images available to many persons and organizations. Some viewers may be media and the images may be used, as in the Mumbai incident in November 2008. Images can be broadcast over television, where even the terrorist handlers can view them and use this information to remotely guide the terrorists.

Not everything is bleak for law enforcement. There has been much advancement since the periscope and hand mirrors. Thermoimaging can ascertain if there are live persons or animals inside a house or apartment, and where they are located. This information can be of assistance so we don't have to negotiate to an empty room or house. Also, if an entry is necessary, officers will be better aware of the possible dangers. Fiber optics, with controllable lenses, allow for surreptitious visual observations under doors or through small holes in walls. Military equipment has also been used to gain visual and audio intelligence. Smith and Wesson has produced a device the size of a softball. The device can be thrown through a window or over a wall. Once in place, the device will right itself and engage a video camera with audio capability. The camera can be controlled with 360° horizontal control and about a 35° elevation. The video and audio are transmitted to the control receiver nearby. However, not all agencies will have the budget to acquire some of this more exotic equipment. Mutual aid or preincident liaison with other agencies may make this equipment available.

In the end, basic innovation and resourcefulness may be necessary to make up for some lack of funding to accomplish the task of saving lives.

Why Police Do the Negotiating

A hostage negotiating situation and the employment of hostage recovery methods obviously involve the use of certain psychological principles and techniques. This leads to the question of why mental health professionals or others trained in psychology are not involved in the negotiating and why police officers are used instead. The answer revolves around the environment in which mental health professionals work. More often than not, a person using the services of a mental health professional is either a voluntary patient paying good money per session or an institutionalized individual in a hospital or prison who is required to see a therapist as part of a legal obligation or rehabilitation program.

The patient will usually see the therapist one or two sessions a week for anywhere from three to six months. During that time, the mental health professional will learn a great deal about the patient, such as likes, dislikes, emotional needs, and feelings about people and situations. The mental health professional may or may not have a lasting impact upon the subject. In an active hostage or barricade situation, there is no such expansive time luxury. The police officers at the scene must deal with an immediate crisis, albeit one of uncertain duration. Police officers are trained in, and experienced at, dealing with situational occurrences, such as an accident, burglary, assault, rape, murder, or similar on-the-spot situations. There are also some pragmatic reasons for using police officers rather than mental health professionals, or others, as hostage negotiators. There are, in sheer numbers, more police officers than mental health workers. Also, police work around the clock. In the end, it is easier to teach police some basic psychological principles than to teach mental health workers basic police techniques (Figure 12.1).

The early models for police hostage negotiators were detectives who, by virtue of their street experience in interviewing and interrogating, had empirically discovered many psychological principles. This practical experience was then reinforced with theoretical, academic, and clinical approaches provided by mental health professionals. Police hostage negotiators are not dealing in long-term therapy, but rather are applying a kind of psychological first aid. For those who are critical of not using mental health professionals, the analogy can be made with emergency medical situations during which a police officer applies first aid only to stabilize a situation until medical professionals can be utilized. Examples are treating severe bleeding, cardiopulmonary resuscitation, and artificial respiration.

This is not to say that nonpolice personnel cannot be successful negotiators. There are cases when a mother, other relatives, or clergy have been successful. An occasional success should not, however, be the criterion for use. Remember that often it is strained relationships with spouses, parents, or friends that precipitated or contributed to the incident. On numerous occasions, the appearance of a wife or mother at a hostage incident has resulted in the perpetrator becoming violent. This has led to both suicide and the killing of hostages. It is also best to have only one primary negotiator at a time, because multiple negotiators have at times created a competitive environment. The purpose of negotiating is to lead the hostage taker on a path toward a specific course of action or solution. Anything that distracts attention from that goal is counterproductive. If a second

HOSTAGE NEGOTIATOR CHECKLIST

The Purpose of this checklist is manifold:

1. To gather information about the incident and its participants thus aiding in the application of psychological tact. The Who, What, Where, When, How, and Why, briefly indicated, starts your Intelligence.

2. To ensure that the Intelligence is disseminated to and exchanged with all who require it. REMEMBER, COMMUNICATE.

3. To prepare this format permitting all actively engaged to evaluate what has occurred and how to proceed accordingly. REMEMBER, TIME IS ON YOUR SIDE.

4. To assist with covering the basis of the negotiations and to psychologically prepare you to enter and conduct purposeful negotiations with the subject(s).

5. Properly prepared, you will better cooperate with the Emergency Service Unit personnel in assisting the Area Commander. REMEMBER ...SLOW IT DOWN...

Figure 12.1aa Negotiator checklist.　　(continued)

person must speak to the perpetrator, for example, to combat fatigue of the primary negotiator, it would be best to have someone with a distinctly different voice so the hostage taker does not feel a trick is being played. If one negotiator is making no progress with the perpetrator, then it may be a police decision to use a different negotiator in order to change the pattern. If things are going well, however, the introduction of a second voice would only complicate matters.

Postincident Crisis Intervention Teams

In the past few years we have seen a proliferation of mental health professionals and social workers who are available to respond to victims of terrorist or hostage incidents, multiple homicides in public places, such as schools or office buildings, or other horrors. Examples of this include the survivors of the bombing of the federal building in Oklahoma City; students, parents, and teachers connected to the Columbine High School shootings in Littleton, Colorado; as well as individuals present at the aftermath of the 9/11 attacks at the World Trade Center in New York and the Pentagon in suburban

NEGOTIATOR CHECKLIST

What:

A. What occurred:
(emotional dispute)
(crime, i.e., robbery)
(political terrorism)

B. Time of occurrence: date _____ day _____ time _____

C. Who called Police Department:

D. Time notified: date _____ day _____ time _____

E. From where: scene _____ telephone _____

F. Injuries: Yes   No   Describe
   1. Hostage   ____ ____ _____
   2. P.D.   ____ ____ _____
   3. Perpetrator   ____ ____ _____
   4. Other   ____ ____ _____

G. Contact with suspect:
   1. When
   2. How
   3. By Whom
   4. Anything promised

H. Contained:
(P.D. deployed)

I. Weapons (what):
   1. Verified

J. Number of suspects _____

K. Number of hostages _____

Where (location):

A. Suspects
B. Hostages
C. Police
D. Floor plans (separate sheet)
E. Containment (separate sheet)
F. Observation posts (number on sheet)
G. Entrances, exits (indicate on sheet)
H. Telephones (indicate on sheet)

Communication (how) [radio (frequency), telephone, field phone]:

A. Police to Police (frequency) _____
B. Police to suspect   bullhorn _____ face to face _____
   telephone _____
C. Command post to operations unit _____
D. Other _____

Figure 12.1ab (continued) Negotiator checklist.

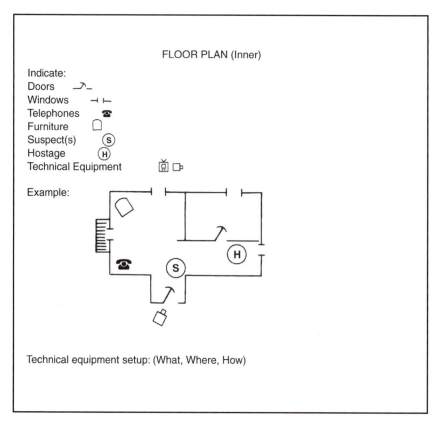

Figure 12.1b (continued) Initial floor plan.

Washington, D.C. The same principles of posttraumatic stress disorder that people may experience after surviving devastating floods, earthquakes, tornadoes, airplane crashes, and bus and car accidents also are experienced by those affected by urban terrorism. The counseling offered helps victims first to recognize the pattern and symptoms of the disorder, and then to overcome the fear, confusion, and stigma that once were attached to seeking or receiving treatment or help.

Controlling the Environment

Controlling the environment has two meanings, referring to both the physical environment (including characteristics such as light, temperature, noise, the view outside, access, and egress) and the atmosphere in which the negotiations are conducted (including things such as initiating communication, controlling the discussion, and regulating the pace of negotiation). Once control of the environment has been established, its manipulation becomes a

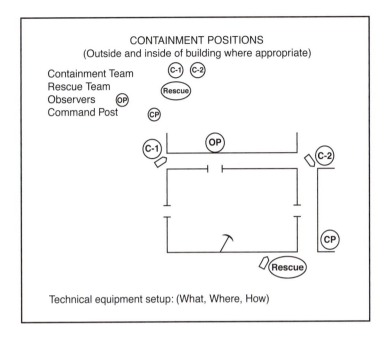

Figure 12.1c (continued) Initial containment position.

viable option in the negotiator's tool kit. Raising or lowering the temperature, controlling the amount of light, raising or lowering the amount of outside noise, even odors such as cooking smells or the scent of perfume can be used to influence the situation.

Manipulation of the environment should be done as unobtrusively as possible, in increments that are not readily noticeable. A sudden change could provoke a violent response, because a hostage taker might interpret the change as an attack. Conversely, a gradual raising of the temperature in the room might be discerned only after a period of time. The perpetrator's reaction, if there is any at all, would likely be in the form of a complaint to the negotiator, who then would be in a position to offer assistance to remedy or at least alleviate the situation in exchange, of course, for some concession by the hostage taker. Bargaining chips are hard won and must be used judiciously.

There are situations, however, in which manipulating the environment can have negative consequences. There has been concern, for example, that hostage takers might have police scanners or other equipment obviously requiring a power source. This could be a reason to deprive them of electricity. If this is the decision, however, it must be done in a manner that does not induce panic. There was a situation in 1986 when the deprivation of electricity by Pakistani authorities during the hijacking of Pan Am Flight 73 was accomplished in such a manner that it put the hostage takers in a panic situation, contributing to the loss of hostages' lives in the ensuing gun battle.

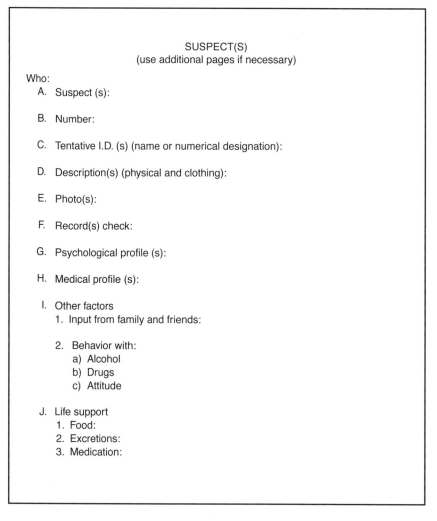

SUSPECT(S)
(use additional pages if necessary)

Who:
  A. Suspect (s):

  B. Number:

  C. Tentative I.D. (s) (name or numerical designation):

  D. Description(s) (physical and clothing):

  E. Photo(s):

  F. Record(s) check:

  G. Psychological profile (s):

  H. Medical profile (s):

  I. Other factors
    1. Input from family and friends:

    2. Behavior with:
      a) Alcohol
      b) Drugs
      c) Attitude

  J. Life support
    1. Food:
    2. Excretions:
    3. Medication:

Figure 12.1d (continued) Suspect profile.

One of the most effective instances of environment manipulation took place in West Chester, Pennsylvania, where the millionaire heir of the DuPont chemical fortune, John DuPont, shot and killed a former Olympic wrestler who served as a caretaker on his estate. When police responded to the estate, DuPont retreated to his mansion and barricaded himself there. It was known that DuPont had all kinds of exotic and powerful firearms, including an armored personnel carrier. Any attempt at an assault would be extremely dangerous to officers. The subject was contained and negotiations commenced. The talks went on for two days in rainy and cold weather. The police were even castigated by the media, some saying it was DuPont's money and influence that prolonged the negotiations and kept the police from going in after him. However, it was a correct decision on the part of the incident commander not to risk the lives of his officers against heavy weapons just for expediency and possible overtime pay considerations. After fruitless negotiations, it was ascertained that the heating boilers for the main house were located in an outbuilding. Members of the tactical team shut down the boiler and the cold weather soon permeated the house. When the subject, speaking with the negotiator, commented on the cold, the officers told the subject to go to the basement to check it out. The subject stated that the boiler wasn't in the basement but in an outbuilding, something the negotiator knew but kept to himself. The negotiator told DuPont that the only way to check was to leave the weapons in the house. He agreed, and when he went to the outbuilding unarmed, the tactical team was there to take him into custody without having to fire a shot.

Dynamics of Hostage Negotiation

Negotiations (or even simple two-way discussions) have been broken down into win-lose, lose-win, and various other configurations, depending upon the results of the talks. We always have viewed a hostage negotiating situation as a win-win dialogue, meaning that both parties get something they want out of the situation. This is preferable to a win-lose approach, where one party obtains satisfactory results and the other is unhappy, displeased, or possibly humiliated. Avoiding this latter outcome is as important in the area of international terrorism as it is in the field of international diplomacy.

Part of the dynamics of negotiations utilizes a frustration-aggression equation. Frustration is considered a negative factor in life, as in situations in which a specific goal or end cannot be achieved and frustration results. Not all aspects of frustration are negative, for it is an important part of the learning process and is the driving force behind ambition. If an infant had everything he or she could possibly want, there would be little reason for the child to learn how to grip, how to talk, or how to cope by manipulating the people and things in the larger world.

As that child grows and develops, he or she moves from learning how to cry in a certain way to be fed, to learning that something out of reach can be obtained by crawling or standing up. The desire-frustration-solution process continues throughout our lifetimes. However, as we know, at times there may be some things that appear to be attainable but remain just beyond reach. In the frustration-aggression equation, the presumption is that if a person is sufficiently frustrated, this will lead to aggressive behavior, whether it is a big kid taking a toy away from a smaller child or an adult pounding on a countertop looking for service in a store. Most people, however, do not move

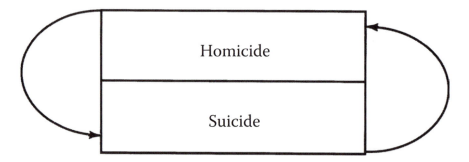

Figure 12.2 Internalized vs. externalized aggressive behavior. Suicide is internalized aggression. Homicide is externalized aggression. Aggression, like love and hate, is a two-sided coin, and it is difficult to predict which type of behavior a perpetrator will enact. Sometimes it is both—for if homicide does not satisfy, a suicide may ensue.

into aggressive behavior as long as they believe there may be a remedy for the source of their frustration.

In an effort to eliminate frustration from a hostage situation, the negotiator must eliminate the word *no* from his or her working vocabulary. Rather than saying no or using negatives, replace them with such phrases as "let me see what I can do," "I'll work on it," or "I don't know, let me check that out." Even when the request cannot possibly be granted, such as one for weapons, never use the word *no*. Were the response to a request no, this could close off the option of problem solving and force the subject into the aggressive behavior part of the equation. Aggression in these situations can be focused in either of two ways: internalized or externalized. Carried to logical extremes, internalized aggression could result in suicide, and externalized aggression to murder. The dynamics are interchangeable; suicide and homicide are two sides of the same coin (Figure 12.2).

Persons who could commit homicide could commit suicide and vice versa, as strange as that may sound. Many persons who have committed homicide, when incarcerated, hang themselves in their cells. Experienced homicide detectives, when faced with a list of three or four possible suspects of apparently equal culpability, will research whether any of the suspects has a history of suicide attempts or a series of self-destructive incidents, such as driving off the side of a road, driving into a wall, and similar one-car accidents.

Gathering Intelligence of the Hostage Taker

When we speak about the gathering of intelligence of the individual or individuals holding a hostage or hostage, some might think all that is required is his or her name, age, address, marital status, and place of employment. We might also try to ascertain what precipitated the situation. Though this is the basic information, there is so much more that we can use to safely and successfully conclude the incident.

The individual's likes and dislikes of various things can influence the outcome and be extremely important, especially in protracted incidents. The negotiator will often be able to effect and influence a "nonresponder." There is nothing that can be so frustrating as dealing with a subject who will not speak or respond to efforts to establish communication.

Let us look at one condition that we might have some control over in order to establish communication. The introduction of music. Music? Why and how would you play music at the scene of a life-and-death situation? Well, music has a great influence in just about everyone's life. We see almost every jogger and many casual walkers with "buds" plugged into their ears. Just watch an exciting movie in a theater or on television. Listen how moods are created, how a crescendo builds to enhance an important point in the story. Watch a chase sequence or a cowboy flick. Then press the mute button and observe that there is little excitement and the actions can at times seem silly. Military bands are used not only to establish a marching cadence, but also to boost the morale of the troops.

We will find that information about his or her likes and dislikes from family and friends. We will try to use that information to gain a psychological upper hand. We know that some music can speed up the heart rate of some, and other times soothing music can actually calm a person down. Of course, different individuals will be affected differently by the same music, so this is where the interviews with family and friends are important.

If after a long period of time, and each incident may be different, communication has not been established, this may be an effective way for us to elicit a response. From intelligence gathered, have the music that the subject does not particularly care for played softly for a period of time (no set time but long enough to gently annoy the subject). You do not want to drive him or her to violence. This should be done prior to the negotiator attempt to speak with the subject. A few minutes before the negotiator intends to speak, fade in the music that the subject is believed to enjoy. When contact is attempted, the voice of the negotiator will be equated to music that the subject enjoys, and he or she is more likely to establish communication at that time. We do not want to create discord or anger, but to establish a positive relationship between the perpetrator and the negotiator. This use of a psychological principle should not be confused with some principles of the *First Earth Battalion Operational Manual* by Lt. Col. Jim Channon, or some of the military psychological operations reported in the book by Jon Ronson, *Men Who Stare at Goats*, where even a passage pleasant for children, such as the "I Love You" song from *Barney the Friendly Dinosaur* children's TV program, when played over and over for many hours, was called torture by some. Some of the tactics used at the siege of the Branch Davidians in Waco, Texas, in 1993 by the federal authorities included the use of loud blaring music and sound effects in a very different manner than we suggest here.

Words and Phrases

The exact phrasing of statements by a negotiator to a hostage taker can be extremely important to avoid misunderstanding and misinterpretation. Nonjudgmental words and phrased are preferred. Be nonjudgmental, encourage talking, and deal with feeling:

1. First, I'd like to get to know you better.
2. Could you tell me about it?
3. I would like to hear your side.
4. Could you share that with me?
5. I guess that's pretty important to you.
6. Tell me about it.
7. That's interesting.
8. I see.
9. Is that so?
10. Oh.
11. Uh huh.

A Note on Weapons

When gathering information and intelligence, it is important to note that the use of a checklist is important. It permits an orderly gathering of information. It also helps to know who contributed what. For example, whenever a statement or allegation is made that the subject has a weapon or a device, even if it is not displayed, the assumption must be that this weapon or device does exist and appropriate tactics are used to counter it until contradictory information can be verified from the contributor or source, or can be discounted from other sources. It is best to operate on a worst-case scenario basis.

Saying No

When we say a negotiator should never say no, this does not mean there are not any no-nos in hostage negotiations. There most assuredly are, and here are four of them:

1. *No exchange of hostages.* No person—not the negotiator, the first responding officers who make the initial contact with the hostage taker, or any volunteer—should be exchanged for a hostage or otherwise sent into a hostage situation. Even if a hostage slips out undetected, that individual should not be allowed to reenter captivity, regardless of pleas or circumstances. There is no circumstance that would justify such action. First, there is no guarantee that any deal struck with the perpetrator will be honored. Second, any hostage, or all hostages, may be killed. No one has a right to send a person into such a situation. Even a police officer should not be sent in because cops remaining on the outside will lose their objectivity. Just as doctors do not perform operations on members of their own families, police officers can be emotional and may use different criteria and judgment when another officer is involved. Once a person is a hostage, he or she cannot be a negotiator. There will always be a time when the subject will say something like, "You want me to trust you, then you gotta trust me. Take off your gun and come in here like a man and sit down with me." Under no circumstance should a negotiator be permitted to go inside. This should be distinguished from what is called face-to-face negotiating, as we discuss later. A negotiator must always leave an avenue of escape. Though we are aware of a few instances where negotiators have violated this principle and have succeeded, the luck of those incidents may not carry over to all cases. Last, from a strictly pragmatic point of view, allowing a person to enter a hostage situation and become a hostage leaves the police open for vicarious liability court action should that person be killed.

2. *No weapons.* Do not give the hostage taker a weapon. The one he or she has may be bogus or may not work. Even if the weapon has been fired, it may have jammed or there may be no more ammunition. There was a case several years ago where a security guard surrendered his gun, figuring there was no harm since the hostage taker was already armed. The sad fact was the hostage taker had only a starter's pistol that fired blanks and was not really armed until he had the security guard's gun. Again, picture the scene in court with you, the police officer, on the witness stand admitting that it was your gun that was used to kill a hostage, that the lawyer's poor,

demented client had not even been in possession of an instrument of death when the situation started. Does the negotiator say no when a hostage taker demands a gun? Of course not, delaying language is used. "I don't know, I'll have to check on that," or "I'll work on it, let me talk to my boss," would be appropriate responses. Never say no and never give a perpetrator a gun.

3. *No prisoners released from jail or prison.* Once prison doors swing open, this will only encourage others to try the same tactic to free their comrades. Even in hostage-taking situations in prison disturbances, most prisoners know they cannot get out. There are no demands for escape, but rather for better conditions, tastier food, more recreation, longer family visits, etc. They want to save face after taking hostages, so they have to demand something. Have there ever been hostage situations where prisoners have been freed? Not in the United States, although it has happened elsewhere. The West Germans were ready to free domestic terrorists in their jails during the hostage incident at the 1972 Munich Olympics. Several years later, Salvadoran President José Napoleon Duarte released some prisoners when his daughter was kidnapped and held hostage by rebels. He ran two risks. First, he could have wound up with a dead daughter and some free anti-Duarte terrorists running around the country. Second, he encouraged others to attempt kidnapping members of his family, even after he moved them to Florida. It is difficult to be objective when your own family is involved; however, in this case Duarte had a greater responsibility to his people and his country.

   To demonstrate the significance of not releasing prisoners from jails, there are two incidents that occurred in Louisiana. On December 13, 1999, seven Cuban nationals and one Bahamian at the St. Martinville Prison were involved in the taking of six hostages. Four of those in the uprising were being held at the facility since the 1980 "boat lift" from the Cuban port of Mariel for the federal agency then known as Immigration and Naturalization Services. The disturbance continued for six days, when the mother of one of the inmates helped broker a deal to send the detainees to Cuba. By December 20, 1999, six of the hostage takers were on a federal plane bound for Cuba. This was done with very little press coverage. However, it did not go unnoticed by everyone. On December 28, six inmates tried to break out of the state prison at Angola, Louisiana. During the course of their failed attempt they beat a correction officer to death when he refused to give up his keys. They then took three other officers hostage, having been inspired by the success of the Cuban detainees.

During the course of a short conversation, the warden said, "We might as well do what they did in St. Martinville." In this case, however, the authorities refused the prisoners' demands and when two of them tried to escape, a shootout ensued. Two inmates were shot, one died, and the other was seriously wounded. The correction officers were rescued unharmed.

4. *No special nuclear materials should leave a facility.* Whether it is a weapons facility, a nuclear power plant, or some other source of fissionable material, special nuclear material should never be given to terrorists. The amount involved may not be enough to construct a nuclear weapon, but when combined with dynamite or another conventional explosive, it can make a very hazardous dirty bomb. From the standpoint of the federal government, police may use deadly physical force to protect nuclear material; that is how potentially disastrous the material is regarded to be.

Another "never" to remember for hostage negotiators is: never leave yourself without an avenue of escape. Do not position yourself in such a way that if the hostage taker decides to make a break for it, the hostage negotiator will be unable to head for cover. One other admonition, which is covered in more detail later in this chapter, is never take the weapon from the hand of a surrendering perpetrator; there may be a change of heart at the last instant. Have the individual leave the weapon inside or send it out. If it is a gun, have him unload it if he intends to give it to a hostage to bring out.

The Art of Negotiation

Negotiations are conducted in order to avoid confrontation, which almost invariably leads to violence. The question of confrontation in a hostage situation is a perplexing one for most law enforcement agencies. No one wants to be responsible for precipitating violence, yet police cannot sit back and watch as the bodies of hostages are thrown out of a building one by one. The determination must be made, however, whether these killings are happening during a panic reaction on the part of the perpetrator, on a deadline, or perhaps for some other reason. When people are killed on a deadline, this evinces the workings of a depraved mind and may indicate that an assault is the necessary alternative, if only to save the lives of the remaining hostages. If, however, a person has been killed during the initial takeover, it might be the product of a panic reaction. Though this death would not be excusable, it could be understandable and not rule out negotiation as an option. Therefore, though it may appear arbitrary, we will make an assumption that anyone killed prior to our establishing contact with the perpetrator is the product of a panic reaction. We could therefore negotiate.

Courses of Action

Before negotiations begin, or at any time during the negotiations when the talks may get bogged down or the perpetrator's actions indicate a depraved mind, three courses of action remain open to the incident commander:

1. Rescue
2. Sharpshooters
3. Chemical agents

Of the three courses, rescue presents the greatest challenge.

Rescue

The Rand Corporation conducted a study of hostage situations throughout the world. One of its findings was that of all the hostages killed in all situations studied, 78% were killed during the rescue effort. This indicates the danger involved in undertaking a rescue. However, the capability must be there in the event the perpetrators start killing hostages and rolling out the bodies. That 78% is a high rate and underscores the need for serious consideration before the decision is made to go in on a rescue. In considering a rescue, the CID triad (communications, intelligence, and discipline of firepower), as discussed earlier, comes into play. It must be determined beforehand how many perpetrators there are, what kind of weaponry they have, their exact locations inside the building, who they are, and what they look like (beyond description of their clothing), in addition to how many hostages there are (Figure 12.3). Useful, and absolutely essential, is information on whether or not there are any booby traps. Lacking such intelligence, the possibility of booby traps must always be considered.

Rescue attempts present special problems. In spite of lessons learned earlier, mistakes are made in assault attempts to recover hostages. In 1986 in Malta, Egyptian commandos stormed an Egyptian airliner that had been hijacked by Palestinian terrorists. In the rescue attempt, 58 hostages died during the assault and only 12 of them, it was later determined, had been killed by the terrorist hijackers from the Palestinian Liberation Organization. The classic hostage rescue case, although it does not involve terrorists, occurred at Attica State Prison in upstate New York in 1971. In that situation, 11 hostages died, one as a result of injuries sustained during the takeover by inmates. The

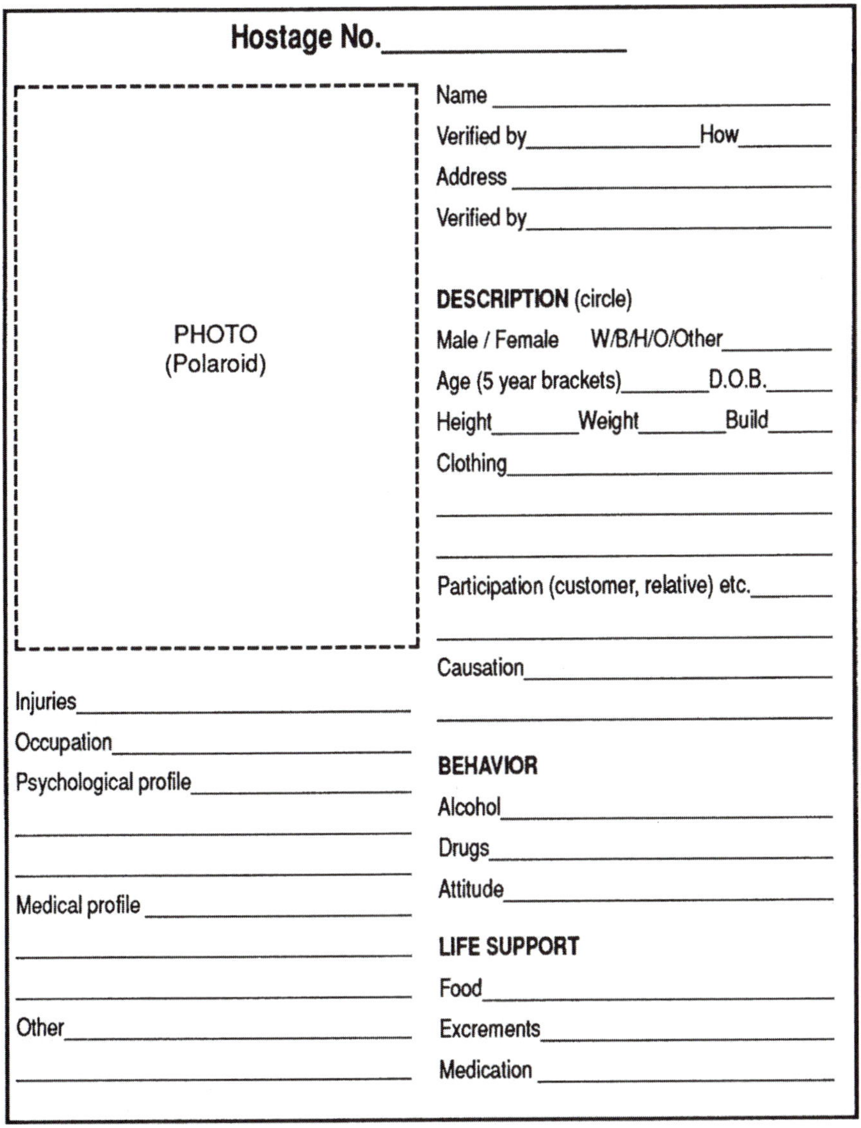

Hostage No._____

PHOTO
(Polaroid)

Name _____

Verified by_____How_____

Address _____

Verified by_____

DESCRIPTION (circle)

Male / Female   W/B/H/O/Other_____

Age (5 year brackets)_____D.O.B._____

Height_____Weight_____Build_____

Clothing_____

_____

_____

Participation (customer, relative) etc._____

_____

Causation_____

_____

Injuries_____

Occupation_____

Psychological profile_____

_____

_____

Medical profile _____

_____

_____

Other_____

_____

BEHAVIOR

Alcohol_____

Drugs_____

Attitude_____

LIFE SUPPORT

Food_____

Excrements_____

Medication _____

Figure 12.3a Biographical sketches: Forms should be created for recording intelligence about both hostages and their captors. It is important that two formats—one horizontal, one vertical—are used to help maintain distinction between suspects and victims.

other 10 died several days later during a direct assault by various law enforcement agencies—national guardsmen, state troopers, corrections officers, and police from local municipalities. The cause of death was gunshot wounds; however, it was later learned that the inmates who were holding the hostages had no firearms. A prudent person would have to assume that the would-be rescuers brought about the deaths of the hostages. The lengthy civil litigation

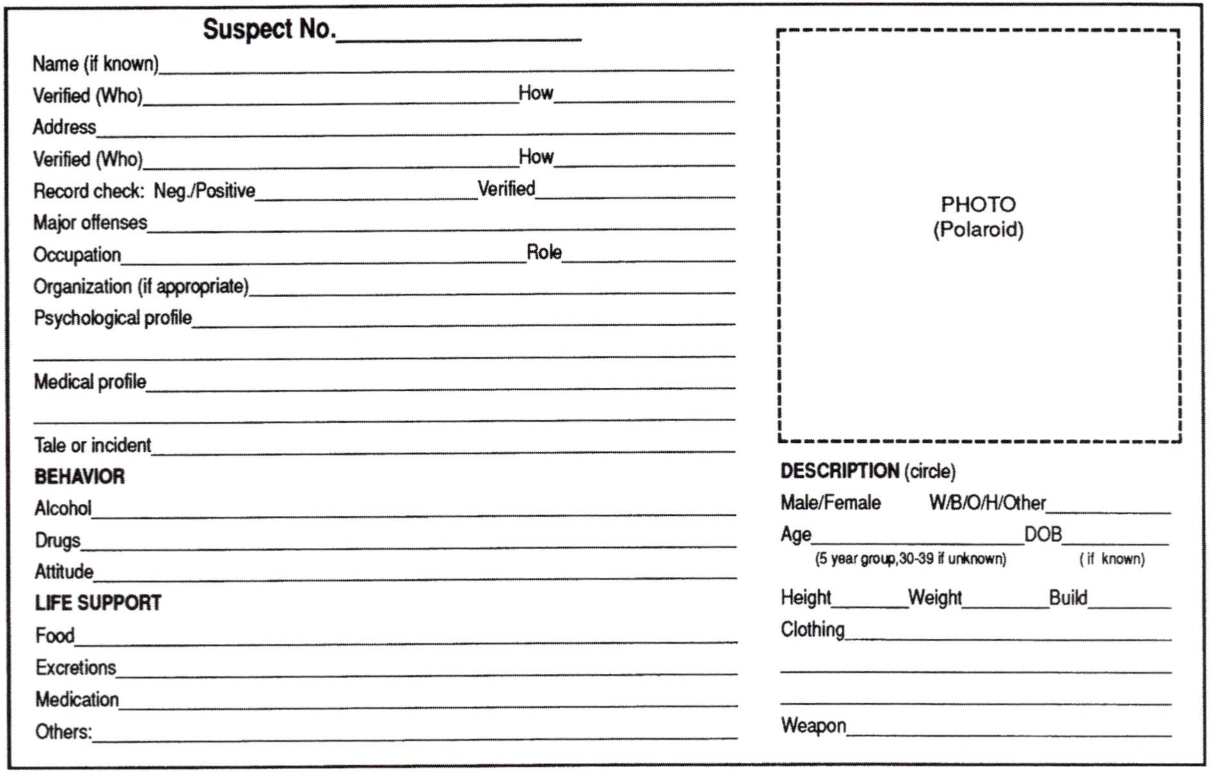

Suspect No. _____

Name (if known) _____

Verified (Who) _____ How _____

Address _____

Verified (Who) _____ How _____

Record check: Neg./Positive _____ Verified _____

Major offenses _____

Occupation _____ Role _____

Organization (if appropriate) _____

Psychological profile _____

_____

Medical profile _____

_____

Tale or incident _____

BEHAVIOR

Alcohol _____

Drugs _____

Attitude _____

LIFE SUPPORT

Food _____

Excretions _____

Medication _____

Others: _____

PHOTO
(Polaroid)

DESCRIPTION (circle)

Male/Female   W/B/O/H/Other

Age _____ DOB _____
(5 year group, 30-39 if unknown)   (if known)

Height _____ Weight _____ Build _____

Clothing _____

_____

_____

Weapon _____

Figure 12.3b Biographical sketches: Forms should be created for recording intelligence about both hostages and their captors. It is important that two formats—one horizontal, one vertical—are used to help maintain distinction between suspects and victims.

involving the Attica inmates was not completed until the summer of 2000. The corrections officers and their families had been urged to settle their lawsuit shortly after the incident, and it has been said by some critics that they were forced into settling for the good of the agency.

The Surrender and Suicide Ritual

For the perpetrator of a hostage situation, there are four perceived options:

1. Escape
2. Surrender
3. Suicide
4. Homicide

For two of these options, a subject will go through a ritual. The ritual preparations for both suicide and surrender are similar and may be difficult to differentiate. Many hostage takers feel they will be killed when they come out. No matter what crime or action may have created the hostage incident, most perpetrators perceive that if and when they come out, they will be killed, shot, or beaten. Violent police/action television shows and movies have helped create such an image in the minds of emotionally charged persons, who when they become hostage takers, feel they will be punished and fantasize about how this punishment will be administered.

Although many hostage takers expect punishment, and even death, they want to look good. They know family and friends will be there, and the media too. So as part of the ritual, they will primp and preen, or at least make themselves look presentable. The perpetrator is saying, "It's all over now; the end is near." The only question is whether the end will bring surrender or suicide. The police don't know. The negotiator can only guess. The perpetrator himself may be uncertain up to the last second.

The negotiator must be aware of his or her own body language. This helps determine how the individual will come out. The perpetrator has to know that the negotiator is in control, so it is incumbent upon the negotiator not to look nervous, confused, or disorganized.

In setting the stage for a surrender, the word *surrender* should not be used, but instead phrases such as "coming out" or "meeting halfway" are employed. The negotiator should soothe the subject, telling the subject to take his or her time, explaining what to expect ("there will be a few other officers with me," etc.), painting a verbal picture that conveys the sense that the negotiator will protect the perpetrator from any harm.

Even though the negotiator will meet the subject halfway, under no circumstances should the negotiator place himself or herself in the position of not having immediate cover available. Care should be given in coordinating the apprehension with the tactical team. By giving the subject direction, he or she can come out without adding any danger to the apprehension team. This will also obviate the need to apply force. We have seen where the subject came to the door, unloaded his gun, and surrendered his weapons. He expected to be interviewed by the media. Instead, the subject was thrown to the ground, and three or four officers piled on top and forcibly handcuffed him. If they had told him to turn around and place his hands out, the same control of the subject could have been accomplished. The importance of tactical discipline in the final apprehension was demonstrated when a man who had been holding his wife and child hostage decided to surrender to police. He said he had been influenced by the careful apprehension of his brother during another hostage situation four states away three weeks earlier.

Thought Interruption

Although suicide and surrender rituals may appear similar, one critical indication of a suicide is the disposing of worldly possessions. When this occurs, a person contemplating suicide can sometimes be dissuaded.

An incident illustrating the suicide ritual took place in the finished basement of a suburban home. The subject had stabbed a man in the chest and, at the approach of responding police, took hostage his common-law wife's 6-year-old son and the wounded man's 20-year-old girlfriend. Negotiators progressed to the point where the mechanics of surrender were being worked out. Upon hearing his mother's voice at the scene, the hostage taker requested that the negotiator (who was now negotiating face-to-face, blocked by furniture, since the weapon involved was not a firearm) pass along his money to his mother. This was followed by the perpetrator's jewelry and keys, as he explained he would have no need for them in jail. Before emerging, the subject washed his hands and face and put on a clean shirt. He then walked with the young boy toward the darkened rear of the basement. A few moments later, the child returned carrying a folded knife: the weapon with which he had been held captive. Responding to the beckoning police negotiator, the lad explained that the perpetrator was fixing a lamp. Within seconds, there was a large bright blue flash from the darkened rear of the basement. This was followed by another flash and the sound of a body crumpling to the floor. The negotiator and backup tactical team entered the area and found the subject grasping two hot wires of a dissembled lamp. The quick disengagement of the lamp's plug and application of CPR techniques revived the subject.

There was another case in which a man was holding his infant child hostage on the roof of a building. After a long and tiring confrontation

with the police, the man leaned over the edge of the roof and began emptying his pockets, indicating who should get his money, his keys, jewelry he
was wearing, etc. Disposing of his worldly goods was a catharsis of sorts.
Although it was the middle of summer, the negotiator asked if he thought
it was going to snow. The man stood upright and asked the negotiator,
"Snow? Are you crazy?" The officer quickly corrected himself and asked
about rain. The man's thought pattern had been broken. Suicide was no
longer foremost in his mind. Eventually he gave up the baby unharmed
and surrendered.

Never Take a Weapon from the Hand of a Surrendering Perpetrator

No matter how sincere or well intentioned a surrendering hostage taker may
seem, never take a weapon from his or her hand. It may all be a trick, or there
could be a last-minute change of heart. Even if the weapon is offered handle
side toward you, it could be swung around swiftly in one last violent act. It
may even be that the perpetrator wants to commit suicide, but cannot pull
the trigger. Death can usually be ensured by killing a police officer in full
view of all the tactical people with their guns drawn. The appropriate course
of action is to have the perpetrator throw the gun out, give it to a hostage
(unloaded to prevent any further confrontation), or leave the weapon inside.
Throwing the weapon out of a window would be the last resort because certain weapons can fire and may injure someone accidentally. Remember, even
if a weapon is recovered, use caution because there could be more weapons
available to the perpetrator.

Special Qualifications

Occasionally, there may be demands to match the race or sex of the negotiator and hostage taker. There is no reason to match black negotiators to a black
perpetrator or white to white. The police must control the situation and use
the best negotiator available. Language, training, and ability are the criteria.
Communication is the key. The ability to take criticism, even ridicule, is important, because hostage takers will often test a negotiator by hurling invectives.
A negotiator cannot be thin-skinned, for a perpetrator will do everything he
or she can to test the negotiator, just to see who is in control. The hostage takers are trying to determine if the negotiator really cares about them.

Women police officers have often been successful negotiators, especially in instances involving young girls. It has been observed, however, that the insults male perpetrators direct toward female negotiators often become explicitly sexual. An officer might say, "I'm here to help you." The perpetrator might respond by saying the only way she could help is to have sex with him.

There are a number of other factors to consider when designating a negotiator, such as the cultural background of the hostage taker. It may be unthinkable for him to surrender to a woman. On the other hand, a female negotiator might have an advantage because the perpetrator may think he is pleasing his mommy or doing the woman a favor, that he is being charming by surrendering.

There are no hard and fast rules on matching a negotiator with a particular situation. This is a commander's decision. The perpetrator will eventually have to talk to whomever is the negotiator, or he speaks to no one. As hard-nosed as that might sound, remember that the perpetrator initiated the hostage taking in order to get an audience and announce his message. Eventually, he will speak to whoever is available.

Certification of Hostage Negotiators

The climate in law enforcement today is to ensure that the agencies and their officers meet the requirements for accreditation. This is not only to qualify for grants and other funding, but also as a shield for possible liability litigation. The agency, as well as the units that comprise the department, is scrutinized to ensure that it meets the standards required for that recognized accreditation— that training in the use of deadly physical force, emergency vehicle operation, internal affairs and supervision, and proficiency with firearms meets acceptable standards that have been established. Currently there does not seem to be a standard for the selection, training, and deployment of hostage negotiators or, as they are now called in some agencies, crisis negotiators. When the program was established in 1972, by the New York City Police Department, the title of it was Guidelines for Hostage and Barricaded Incidents. That included a variety of crises, including criminal, terrorist, and emotionally disturbed person (EDP). Every hostage situation is a potential life-and-death event and a crisis. However, every crisis is not a life-or-death situation.

More often than not, the question of the qualification and training of the negotiator will come up in the courtroom—whether by the defense attorney in a criminal case or by plaintiff's counsel in the almost inevitable civil action following many incidents. It seems it doesn't matter if the incident was resolved successfully or not. If the results were less than the officers had wished for, someone will attempt to assign blame. Yet we have seen litigation even in successful cases: cause of action, "what took so long."

During the examination to determine if the negotiator and supervisor were qualified, the questions asked will always include education, training, and experience in hostage recovery. If the officers work in a larger jurisdiction, the number of incidents and occasions for experience will be greater. Those who do not have that opportunity will have to rely on education and training. Certainly attending one or two seminars on hostage negotiation and recovery by reputable, experienced trainers and getting a certificate of attendance will be helpful. But unless there is follow-up retraining, the knowledge gained will slowly fade in the memory. Even in a department with a large number of callouts, such as the NYPD, retraining is usually conducted twice a year to update and refresh the team members.

I have trained an officer from a six-person police department in Iowa, an agency with a limited budget, even before these difficult financial times. Two weeks after the three-day seminar he was called out to deal with a barricaded subject. Utilizing the principles we imparted, after about six hours the officer was able to get the subject to put down his weapon and come out peacefully. This might have been the only incident for the next year or two. However, this officer initiated mutual aid in training and support from adjacent agencies, both local and state, with role playing and tactical training. This procedure demonstrates the possibilities of getting experience even in a community with very few callouts.

Seeking out and joining the various state associations of hostage/crisis negotiators is another avenue to keep up-to-date in both intelligence and training. The California Association of Hostage Negotiators has been sponsoring annual training seminars, statewide, as well as local programs for more than 20 years. The International Association of Hostage Negotiators has also been around since 2000. The founder, director, and principle trainer is Dominic Misino, a retired NYPD detective. He first had tactical experience as a member of the NYPD Emergency Service Unit. He then became a member of the hostage negotiating team. In addition to responding to hostage incidents, he also became responsible for training new members and scheduling retraining for the almost 120 team members. He was in that position for six years. About three years ago, in conjunction with the Public Agency Training Council, Misino, along with Hugh McGowan, PhD, retired NYPD lieutenant, former CO, HNT (13 years), developed a certification procedure. This is especially significant for negotiators who work in agencies that have less frequent callouts and subsequently less on-the-job training.

The program consists of three phases of training over a period of 10 or 11 days. Phase I includes the history and principles of hostage negotiation. Phase II reviews phase I and includes hands-on negotiating role playing. Phases I and II can be presented as either two- and three-day seminars or combined into one five-day seminar. Phase III is presented only as a five-day seminar with multiple instructors with both hands-on testing and written testing. There are no numeric grades, only "meets standards," "needs improvement," or "does not meet standards." Those who need improvement or who do not meet standards are given the opportunity for retesting by different instructors and different role players.

The program has been subjected to the court process and has been accepted in a state court. It is suggested that negotiators interested seek out information about the aforementioned associations or groups in their own states, via the Internet.

Transportation Terrorism Countermeasures

13

DOROTHY MOSES SCHULZ

Overview

Transit agencies are well aware of the potential for crime and terrorist activities to occur on their facilities. They have instituted new policies or strengthened existing strategies to overcome some of the challenges presented by the openness of public transit facilities and their multiple uses. Strategies must be developed for apparent contradictions; some facilities are potential targets because of their iconic status or strategic locations in busy business districts; others are targets for the opposite reason: they are isolated and used infrequently, but on a regularly occurring pattern.

Many countermeasures developed to minimize the possibilities of becoming sites of terrorist activities are no different from general crime prevention strategies. In some cases, the knowledge that certain types of incidents, such as fires or explosions, may be met by a higher level of patron fear because of terrorism-related concerns has raised transit systems' awareness of the need for better planning and coordination of response to all emergencies.

Although many strategies are still evolving, protection of airports and passenger screening techniques are highly regulated by the federal government. Through the efforts of the Department of Homeland Security's (DHS) Transportation Security Administration (TSA), patrons have become familiar with the highly regulated airport environment. With rare exception and other than as tests, similar policies have not been implemented at mass transit facilities. Yet, while procedures may be less regulated and less obvious to outside observers, this is not an indication that nothing is being done.

This chapter describes many of the strategies currently employed by transit agencies to prevent attacks against their systems and to mitigate the consequences of serious incidents that may threaten the transit system and the surrounding areas. A number of these countermeasures rely on outside agencies and are designed specifically to involve nontransit first responders in planning and response activities.

Tabletop Exercises

Tabletop exercises and drills are the two methods most often used in emergency management to rehearse for actual events. They are specifically designed to practice response skills and to test the adequacy not only of decision making but also of implementing those decisions. All law enforcement/security professionals are aware of the problems that can occur when multiple agencies respond to a scene. Different procedures, radio transmission codes, and myriad other operating differences frequently bring additional confusion to what may already be a chaotic scene. To rehearse for what may be the real thing, more and more agencies are taking part in tabletop exercises and drills that involve not only multiple layers of law enforcement, but also all area emergency response agencies, including fire, emergency medical, and hospital personnel.

Many local police and fire personnel may not be aware of transit industry recommendations that all agencies conduct two tabletop exercises and one full-scale drill annually. Tabletop exercises take their name from the practice of having available a scale model of the exercise site and miniature pieces of equipment to move about the site. These types of activities are designed to test response readiness and provide warning of procedural and policy gaps, confirm duties and responsibilities, identify resources that must be obtained, and provide responders from different agencies with opportunities to practice working as a team.

Most emergency response managers are familiar with these exercises, which in recent years have become standard features of executive training programs. They are also regular features of emergency incident training for first responders to crisis situations, including fires, natural disasters, derailments, hostage situations, or terrorism-inspired emergencies.

Following guidelines established by the Federal Transit Administration (FTA), most tabletop exercises include all personnel who will respond to any emergencies. Many emergencies are not specifically law enforcement related, although they may require evacuation or crowd or traffic control. These types of situations include, for instance, power outages, trains stalled between stations, minor derailments, bus breakdowns, or weather-related delays of ferries, or similar operating issues. Tabletops are also used to practice law enforcement scenarios, such as hostage situations, shootings, or other crimes on railcars, buses, boats, or as in recent years, terrorism-inspired emergencies.

Most agencies include local police and fire personnel, even for non-law enforcement-specific exercises, since it is likely that nonagency first responders will be involved in assisting even when the emergency is not crime related. These exercises also provide local agencies with an opportunity to establish working relationships with a wider range of agency employees than those in law enforcement roles.

If you have not been invited to participate in these activities, it may be the result of a separation in the transportation industry of the safety and security/police functions. Safety is defined by the transportation industry as "freedom from harm resulting from unintentional acts or circumstances," while security is defined as "freedom from harm resulting from intentional acts or circumstances," generally what police refer to as crimes.[1] Safety department personnel, who are usually responsible for organizing tabletop exercises and drills, may overlook the importance of involving local emergency responders in their preparations.

This is particularly true in bus-only agencies. Because they are unlikely to have their own police or security staffs and may require outside assistance fairly infrequently, they may need to be reminded of the importance of regional participation in all emergency-related training activities.

As fears of terrorism-related events have increased, so has the formality of tabletop exercises. It is common today that there is a predetermined script outlining the specific incident for which response is being tested. Many exercises include a realistic scale model of the location that includes moveable pieces or a computer simulation representing the scene and actions occurring throughout the situation or a computer-based simulation. Frequently outside evaluators observe the "responders" and provide onsite commentary as well as a formal after-action report.

Transit or emergency management professionals, including sometimes local police or fire executives, may be invited to observe and make recommendations for improving an agency's response.

Drills

If a tabletop exercise can be compared to a rehearsal, a drill would be the final dress rehearsal. This is because a drill is where the participants "act out" a situation where it would occur. A drill is designed to incorporate a high degree of realism, extensive involvement of resources and personnel, and an increased level of stress due to its realism and on-scene activities.

Most agencies—and all large rail transit agencies—hold one full-scale drill annually. As with the tabletops, drills are likely to be coordinated by safety personnel, but because of their wider scope, will generally also involve members of the police and public affairs staffs. The Federal Transit Administration (FTA) recommends that drills simulate a critical rather than a minor incident, and that they be held in critical locations, such as a downtown subway station or at a bridge or tunnel that is vital to local transportation and business networks. The theory behind this recommendation is that while minor incidents are more likely to occur than major ones, it is the latter that will require full-scale mobilization of multiple agencies.

Not all drills are terrorism related, but in many situations, the same emergency response skills and coordination are required. In January 2005, the American Public Transportation Association (APTA) published on its website a transit application for a proposed national tabletop exercise based on FTA-defined priorities. In addition to terrorism, scenarios would focus on natural disasters or on activities such as a deranged gunman taking over a transit office or a hostage situation on a train, bus, or boat.

Depending on the event the drill simulates, many agencies will be invited to provide planning and logistical support and to participate in the actual drill. Each agency will also be asked to participate in the formal debriefing. It is also common for a written critique to be circulated to all participants, including outside agencies.

Some agencies involve local schools by asking students to portray victims; others involve their staffs by having them portray injured passengers, crew members, or curious onlookers. While the former helps generate publicity for the drills and makes the public more aware of emergencies that may occur, the latter helps transit agencies provide their nonemergency employees with an idea of what may occur during critical incidents. In addition to transit authority employees, union representatives, contractors, and labor groups representing contract employees may also attend and participate. In some areas, local elected officials also take part.

As members of the public have become more aware of the police role in terrorism prevention, drills have begun to receive considerable press coverage. Contrary to earlier years, when police tended to downplay these activities so as not to engender additional fear, the current strategy is to show the public that law enforcers are on alert and are there to protect them. For example, the *Washington Post* reported on antiterrorism drills by Washington, D.C.'s Metro Transit Police as part of its Blue TIDE (Terrorism Identification and Deterrence Effort) initiative launched in early 2010. Among the agencies that participated were local police, other transit agency police in adjacent jurisdictions, and two federal law enforcement agencies.

As part of the this new openness, the D.C.-area drill on June 29, 2010, was one of many that occurred on the East Coast, when a number of cities carried out antiterrorism exercises, including more than 100 officers in New York City's Penn Station and Grand Central Terminal and in the Herald Square area adjacent to Macy's department store. Earlier, in April, in an operation dubbed Multiagency Super Surge (MASS), members of the New York City Police Department Transit Bureau (which polices the subway system), Amtrak, Metropolitan Transportation Authority (MTA), and New Jersey Transit police, and the National Guard responded to "incidents" at Penn Station and Grand Central Terminal.

With only some exaggeration, 2010 may be labeled the summer of drills. Across the nation, many areas held similar multijurisdiction exercises. For instance, in May, Long Beach and San Francisco conducted waterfront drills in cooperation with the FBI; the exercise centered on a number of port-related problems, including cargo examination. Creating both a figurative and literal splash was the inclusion of "mine-detecting dolphins" in the program. In the same month in Los Angeles, the drill was based on the threat of an improvised nuclear device placed in the Los Angeles Memorial Coliseum, a landmark sports complex built in 1923. The drill, which involved local, state, and federal agencies, was scripted to include multiple detonations over a three-day period.

In addition, Amtrak, TSA, and a number of local railroads from Virginia to New Hampshire tested their combined responses to incidents in stations, on the tracks, and along the right-of-way. A major aim was to achieve a greater level of interaction, communication, and coordination.

In another drill, commuters in New Jersey observed a similar exercise. In this instance New Jersey State Police troopers were sent to station platforms, parking lots, and waiting rooms to familiarize themselves with these locales. According to the local area commander, the two-hour exercise was meant to be visible to commuters, who were given pamphlets with information about security measures. That same month, Boston's Massachusetts Bay Transportation Authority, known locally as the T, joined with DHS to review the effects of airborne chemical or biological attacks on its subways by introducing inert toxins and luminescent tags. This type of test is particularly important in Boston; many of the tunnels that carry trains were built in the early years of the twentieth century, and are poorly ventilated and poorly marked for emergency evacuation. More recently, and possibly in response to the drill's findings, the MBTA has received funding to upgrade tunnel lighting and evacuation protocols.

Some drills are international; in July 2010 Pakistan and China joined to hold a weeklong exercise that included searching mountain areas by helicopter and on foot to locate and destroy terrorist training bases. In August, the United States joined Canada and Russia in a drill dubbed Vigilant Eagle, which centered on a jet containing military officers from each nation being hijacked over the Pacific Ocean.

Public Information and Outreach

A major area of public information and outreach has involved transit agencies simply becoming more open with the public, whether in publicizing drills, security improvements, installation of video surveillance, or a greater level of participation in area task forces and joint exercises.

Many agencies have created programs and telephone numbers to encourage patrons to report suspicious activities. Many are in conjunction with local police, but even if the phone number provided for tips is unique to the transit agency, local police may receive these calls and should be aware of the existence of such programs. These programs tend to have catchy slogans, most based on some variation of "see something, say something."

In the New York metropolitan area, the MTA ran television commercials publicizing its antiterrorism tagline, "if you see something, say something," and the hotline to call. Ads in local newspapers also introduced the public to the agency's explosive detection dogs and their police officer partners. The agencies that now combine to make up the MTA's law enforcement component had patrol dogs long before 9/11, but none took out ads publicizing this. In fact, there was initial concern that the public would complain about, rather than be pleased, to see uniformed police officers patrolling with dogs.

Outside the largest cities, where agencies might not have millions of dollars to spend publicizing their antiterrorism efforts, they are more likely to rely on public service announcements, seat notices, and posters in stations and shelters, as well as on railcars, buses, and ferries, to convey the same message, often in both English and Spanish. These too are based on earlier crime prevention efforts, which previously reminded patrons to watch their packages or purses and not to leave them unattended, and how to evade pickpockets and various scammers who are known to frequent large depots.

Today these programs are more likely to encourage members of the public to report suspicious activity, particularly unattended packages or large groups congregating near nonpublic areas. The effectiveness of these efforts is difficult to gauge. Because a more aware public may also report miscellaneous activity that is neither crime nor terrorism related, few agencies have publicized the results of the calls they have received. The MTA, which heavily promotes its 1-888-NYC-SAFE hotline, reported that in 2007 it received close to 13,500 calls. In 2006, almost 9,000 calls were received, although some came from the city's emergency (911) and nonemergency (311) numbers. Many calls were deemed serious enough to be investigated, but only 18 over the two years resulted in arrests, none of which had a direct connection to terrorism.[2] Nonetheless, the MTA and the New York City Police Department consider the number a success.

A recently established national crime reporting program follows a similar model. The Nationwide Suspicious Activity Reporting (SAR) Initiative (NSI), established within the Department of Justice, is based on developing a data collection process to bring together in one place suspicious activity information to be shared with a variety of public safety entities, including state and regional fusion centers and Joint Terrorism Task Force (JTTF) members.

Employee Information, Outreach, and Training

A number of training programs have been developed within the transit industry to help individual agencies provide employee training, primarily to help them recognize and act on their roles in antiterrorism efforts. Many of these operate under the auspices of the National Transit Institute and have been packaged so that they can be taught during one-day or half-day in-service training programs at the individual transit agencies. NTI, which is located at Rutgers University in New Jersey, has packaged a number of workplace safety and security courses; many teach awareness and violence prevention, or instruction for civilian employees on how to respond to emergency conditions.

Emergency Responder Information, Outreach, and Training

The emergence of state offices of homeland security around the country has resulted in greater levels of cooperation among agencies and also in the development of public outreach to a wider range of agencies that might become involved in emergency response.

Typical, for instance, are the brochures published by the New York State Office of Homeland Security on a number of topics. A brochure aimed at the public and at transit system employees provides tips on helping to prevent terrorism, including specific activities to look for. Another, aimed at fire and emergency medical personnel, points out that terrorist groups have been known to target first responders and provides tips on how these employees can best protect themselves.

Operation Lifesaver, a private group that has for many years worked closely with railroads on safety campaigns, including a grade-crossing collision investigation course, has also increased its training for local agencies and has issued a number of safety brochures similar to those published by state homeland security departments. NTI, although primarily aimed at transit employees, also makes its courses available to other public agencies that would be expected to respond to a transit emergency.

Some police academies and individual departments have for many years included transit-related training as part of their curriculums, particularly for Special Weapons and Tactics (SWAT), Special Response Team (SRT), bomb squad, and hostage teams' training. These courses generally involve a drill-type course that includes unit members participating in a mock event on transit equipment. An unusual course developed in 2002 by the Miami-Dade Police Training Bureau involved a two-day bus takedown that simulated the unique problems a tactical unit could face storming a hijacked bus. The training was based on an actual hijacking in 1995 of a special education school bus in Miami by an emotionally disturbed individual who claimed to have been armed with bombs; all the children were successfully rescued.

Patrol by Uniformed and Plainclothes Police/Security Officers

One of the most obvious countermeasures for all law enforcement agencies is increased patrol presence. In many large cities uniformed presence has been augmented by members of the National Guard, particularly immediately after transportation-related events occur anywhere around the world. In addition to simply adding police or security officers to their locations, transit systems and local police have turned to a number of tactics designed to maximize the visibility of uniformed officers. Transit systems have met with limited success in barring photography in stations or of buses and trains. Taking photos of transit equipment has been controversial for many years. Well prior to 9/11, transit agencies, and particularly freight railroads, attempted to bar or at least limit photographers from their property, including hobbyists and train enthusiasts. Because an agency may have a policy of not allowing photography without a permit, even though the activity may not violate local laws, police officers responding to this type of complaint should exercise discretion before making an arrest.

Just as many shopping centers and retail establishments have encouraged local police to set up mini-substations, transit agencies have done the same, providing a small office or desk for report writing as a way to enhance uniformed presence.

Many bus-only systems are encouraging local police to ride in uniform as part of their patrols. Similar to park-and-ride strategies whereby uniformed officers would park their marked vehicles and walk around in a downtown area, these bus riding details involve prearranged patterns of officers riding bus routes and then resuming motor patrol in a marked vehicle that had been assigned with another officer to trail the bus. Another tactic has been for officers to board a bus at a particular stop, walk through while passengers are entering or exiting, and then also exit at the same location. Transit police who normally concentrated their efforts on rail patrol have also become more involved in patrols of buses and at bus depots and shelters.

Behavioral Recognition

Higher visibility patrol has often been combined with elements of so-called behavioral recognition programs. These programs may involve both uniformed and plainclothes officers. Going under a variety of acronyms, the programs are modeled after one used by Israel's El Al Airlines. Security personnel observe the behavior of individuals and then ask probing questions of those who appear suspicious. One program, the Behavioral Assessment Screening System (BASS), is modeled after one developed at Boston's Logan Airport, modified by the MBTA police and subsequently by other transit police departments. TSA has developed a variation known as SPOT (Screening of Passengers by Observation Technique).

Canine Teams

Also as part of their more visible and aggressive patrol tactics, a number of agencies have added canine programs. Although a small number of transit police employed canine well before their terrorist prevention efforts, today many more do so, including having added patrol dogs with explosive detection training. In many jurisdictions, local responders are well aware of transit canine capabilities because the teams are often available to other agencies.

The TSA has played a large role in the expansion of canine teams throughout the transit environment. Under its auspices, the National Explosives Detection Canine Team Program has graduated more than 500 teams in the last nine years. While most are assigned at airports, a number of ground transportation agencies have participated in the program, which trains an officer and canine partner in search techniques in parking lots, cargo and luggage areas, and general patrol. The program partially reimburses participating agencies for the costs associated with the teams, including salaries, overtime, and the canine's food and veterinary care, in return for cooperative agreements on use of the handler-canine teams by other agencies. Transit agencies in Atlanta and Baltimore are among those with TSA-trained dogs; other transit systems prefer to continue with programs in existence prior to TSA, in which the dogs may be trained only for regular patrol or for narcotics rather than explosive detection.

In addition to canine teams, a number of transit agencies include officers who have been trained in accident reconstruction and investigation of grade-crossing accidents. To foster cooperative relationships, these units, such as canine, accident reconstruction, and explosive specialists, are available to assist local departments either through formal memoranda of understanding

(MOUs) or through less formal arrangements whereby local agencies pool services when specialists are needed.

Passenger and Baggage Screening

Unlike air travel, full passenger screening of all mass transit passengers is not a realistic option. Transit terrorist expert Brian M. Jenkins and his colleague Bruce R. Butterworth, in a report published in 2007 by the Mineta Transportation Institute, observed that "the human resources required, added security costs, and delays" that would be required to institute 100% screening of mass transit passengers "would destroy urban mass transit."[3]

The assessment is based on the number of passengers that would need to be screened and the number of trains or buses departing within a small area. Particularly in the case of commuter trains, with multiple doors on each train car, the logistics of total screening are overwhelming.

Yet experimental random passenger screening has been undertaken at a number of transit systems, often at the urging of TSA or in cooperation with its Visible Intermodal Protection and Response (VIPR—pronounced *viper*) teams. As with use of canines, many agencies have participated with TSA or used its protocols in these screening activities, or have operated them independently. The VIPR teams were instituted in 2005 along with an expanded Air Marshal program under TSA auspices; despite being highly visible when deployed, they have generally received less public recognition. Initial plans to have them work independently of local or transit police at train, bus, and ferry stations have generally been scaled back to their assisting in periodic high-visibility patrols and in baggage screening activities at selected stations, generally during morning rush hours.

Whether working with VIPR or on their own, agencies undertaking random bag screening generally set up at a place near the entry point or points of a station and inspect all bags, including purses, backpacks, briefcases, shopping bags, etc., carried by all or by randomly selected patrons. Generally the checkpoints use a selection system similar to intoxicated driver checks; namely, a number is chosen randomly. Thus, if the number is, for instance, 15, every fifteenth person will be stopped for a baggage inspection before boarding the bus or entering the rail or ferry station. Under certain circumstances, those acting suspiciously or attempting to leave the area without being checked may be stopped for inspection.

Although they have been set up more frequently at rail stations than at bus depots or shelters, they can be used at either. Ferry systems, particularly on the West Coast, have also experimented with screening passengers prior to their entry onto boats. Since this access is generally more controlled than bus or rail access, the experiments have involved screening passengers and their bags in the general terminal area before permitting them to enter into an area that opens directly onto where the boat will dock. Challenges by local civil liberties groups as well as the American Civil Liberties Union (ACLU) have not been successful. Although systems retain the right to search bags in this way, the tactic is used selectively because it is labor-intensive, costly, and transit systems, particularly in cities where riding is discretionary, do not want to discourage people from using the system by compromising its accessibility.

A few systems have also experimented with selective screening, generally in conjunction with behavior recognition programs. In these situations, the staff members assigned to screening look for factors that tend to indicate a possible attacker. As with random screening, this is more difficult in public transit than it would be at an airport. For instance, purchasing an expensive, one-way ticket with cash, which may trigger further questioning at an airport, does not have the possible significance at a rail, bus, or ferry depot. Officers must rely on more common investigative clues, such as individuals wearing loose heavy garments in summer, congregating near nonpublic areas, or possibly creating a disturbance that seems to be a diversionary tactic. The concerns about such activity becoming little more than racial or ethnic profiling have made transit systems reluctant to rely on selective screening as a general deterrence tactic.

Surveillance Technology

One area that has undergone a quiet revolution in transit is the reliance on security cameras in stations and on rail vehicles.

The major source of funds for transit surveillance systems is the DHS Transit Security Grant Program (TSGP). In addition, DHS has awarded transit agencies grants for planning, training, equipment, and other security enhancements. Since receipt of funds requires the agency to have undertaken a risk assessment, this is a source of local responders learning more about an agency's needs and priorities.

A major impetus for the expansion of funds for surveillance was the existence of the somewhat blurry images of the four young London bombers that showed them with backpacks as they set out toward Kings Cross. Although the video was seen by many as reinforcing the value of closed-circuit television (CCTV) as a preventive tool, many others pointed out that it may serve more appropriately as a postinvestigative tool, and that it is not viable as a deterrence or prevention mechanism. This is particularly true when perpetrators are planning to die while carrying out the crime or have no fears of being identified. In some cases, knowledge that they will be identified may encourage those whose primary aim is to publicize their cause.

This debate among law enforcement and security professionals about the value of video as a preventive or even a postincident (forensic) investigatory tool was reinvigorated in May 1, 2010, when surveillance photos released of an attempted bombing in New York's Time Square proved highly inaccurate; although images were widely circulated, they turned out to be of someone who was not a suspect. Despite this, New York City's Mayor Michael Bloomberg used the media attention to renew calls for an expanded surveillance network in the city.

Regardless of these caveats, most transit agencies share video with local police and have recently begun to work with local media outlets for assistance in identifying individuals observed in the act of committing various crimes. Surveillance video may assist either transit operators or local police in a variety of ways. Among them are:

- Criminal investigation. Although it may not be true that a picture is worth a thousand words or that pictures never lie, surveillance video can be useful in investigating past crimes. Even if suspects cannot be identified or an individual crime cannot be solved, video may provide hints as to how future crimes could be prevented by, for instance, improving lighting or signage or physically locating equipment, entrances, etc. This is an important area of collaboration between transit agencies and local police and fire responders, since minimizing these events will save resources and may contribute to an increased feeling of safety in a community.
- Protection of members of the public. Whether in stations, at shelters, in parking lots, or on transit vehicles, patrons generally report feeling less secure than, for instance, at a local shopping mall. Anything that contributes to a higher sense of security benefits the public, the transit agency, and local law enforcement.
- Vandalism, graffiti, and scratchiti prevention. Ill-kept facilities send to patrons the message that the area is unsafe and that no one is in control. Posting signs highlighting the presence of surveillance equipment helps to minimize actual disorder and many of its visible symbols.

In addition to video technology, transit systems have invested in a variety of intrusion detection devices and are experimenting with explosive detection equipment, including systems claiming to detect bombs under clothing. One such experimental program used passive millimeter wave technology to detect hidden weapons and is somewhat similar to equipment used at airports. Another uses heat-sensing cameras to detect objects hidden under people's clothing. Most of these tests are operated and paid for by TSA; whether and when they might become prevalent is difficult to predict.

Redesigning and Minimizing Station Furniture

A large number of transit systems have redesigned or minimized station furniture to make unattended parcels more visible. Benches are now frequently designed for single seating to discourage loitering, and with benches high enough for packages to be readily visible to anyone walking by. Trash cans have been removed or their numbers minimized. The same has occurred with lockers, and both trash cans and lockers are now placed where they are visible on surveillance camera monitors. Similarly, because stations with multiple access points have installed bollards and other vehicle barriers to protect facilities, it is important that emergency responders are aware of available access points, and whether there is sufficient turnaround space, especially for ambulances and fire vehicles, which are larger than patrol cars.

Crime Prevention through Environmental Design (CPTED)

Transit agencies have adopted many of the basic precepts of CPTED, which relies on using the design of the physical environment to remove opportunities for crime. Whether applied to the perimeter of a facility, its exits or entrances, or its inside design elements, CPTED relies on lighting, landscaping, and lines of sight to enhance visibility to provide informal surveillance. Features such as strategically placed patron information kiosks, fixed security posts, and staff deployed in visible areas are intended to minimize opportunities for suspicious and criminal behavior. Few of these mitigation tactics are of value only in terrorism detection. As with all crime prevention techniques, each serves more than one purpose and can be beneficial to responders to a variety of emergencies. Each tactic can be modified, depending on the type of facility being protected and whether the transit vehicle is a railcar or road vehicle such as a bus or van. Protecting water-based vehicles presents different challenges.

Protecting America's Ports

Waterborne passenger vehicles make up only part of the maritime industry, which also encompasses all ports and shipping facilities. The agency with primary responsibility for port security in the United States is the U.S. Coast Guard (USCG). Under the Maritime Transportation Security Act (MTSA) adopted by Congress in 2002, all U.S. ports, facilities, and vessels must develop and submit security plans to the Coast Guard. Approved plans vary, but many contain elements similar to those for land-based facilities. These include:

- Improving background checks and mandating that proper identification be displayed by all crew members and visitors to a facility
- Increased passenger and baggage screening, including use of x-ray machines on all large cruise vessels
- Use of canine explosive detection teams
- Installation of surveillance equipment and perimeter fencing
- Restricting access to secure areas of the ports and vessels
- Training of port staff through programs similar to "see it, say it" or NTI-type courses

A major concern in port protection is cargo container security. Similar to concerns about air freight entering the country, much of the cargo has not been inspected for bombs or chemical weapons at its origination point. Many international ports lack the ability or the interest in ensuring either port or container integrity.

The differences between air traffic and mass transit highlight differences in protection of waterborne vessels also. Ports where cargo is received present different terrorism-related concerns than passenger terminals. Terminals that cater primarily to large cruise ships have been able to institute procedures similar to those at airports, namely checking passengers and their bags individually, including use of handheld wands and walk-through screening devices. Similar tactics are not appropriate for local commuter ferries for the same reasons they have been deemed inappropriate for bus and rail patrons.

Deterring Piracy

Deterring piracy has until now remained an international rather than a domestic security issue. One of the major deterrents to piracy and water-based crime is weather. This is especially the case during the monsoon season, when seas are extremely high. Although better organized than when they began operations, the Somali pirates described in Chapter 7 continue to rely on small fishing skiffs, and during heavy weather conditions it is too dangerous for them to venture too far from shore. However, a newer tactic that involves capturing larger fishing boats to use as mother ships has given the pirates greater range from the shore.

Various groups have been put together to deal with the piracy in the western Indian Ocean and the Gulf of Aden. Among these are the NATO Maritime Group, which specifically aimed to protect shipments of the World Food Program, and the European Union's antipiracy task force, established in the United Kingdom. In addition, individual countries have established their own task forces.

The International Maritime Organization (IMO), formerly Intergovernmental Maritime Consultative Organization, has also become involved in the fight against piracy. Established in 1948, the IMO is today a United Nations agency headquartered in London. The 169 member states and three associate members work to maintain maritime safety and security and shipping efficiency. Other concerns include the environment, legal matters, and technical cooperation.

One of the most effective efforts seems to be the Combined Maritime Taskforce 151. This group coordinates the efforts of the navies of the many nations. The system relies on a Mayday-type radio broadcast for assistance from victim ships. The messages are retransmitted, giving latitude and longitude to various naval task force ships that are patrolling in the area. Initially, when dealing with the Somali pirating, confrontations were carried out by task force ships intending to disarm the perpetrators and release them (catch and release) and possibly sink their skiffs.

This strategy was developed in part because no judicial format existed for more formal processing of the pirates. Subsequently, Kenya started accepting the prisoners and trying them in national courts. However, after a while the numbers overwhelmed the court system.

On various occasions when task force ships responded to incidents on ships that carry the flag of their own nation, the prisoners were taken to that country and tried there. This is being carried out with greater frequency now that there are more naval ships, from a larger number of countries, patrolling these waters. This presence has been underscored when, on a number of occasions, pirates unknowingly attempted to hijack vessels that turned out to be armed naval ships. A turning point may have occurred on April 8, 2009, when four pirates seized the American-flagged merchant ship *Maersk Alabama*, which was carrying relief supplies bound for Uganda, Somalia, and Kenya. Captain Richard Phillips was held hostage by three pirates aboard one of the ship's lifeboats, while one of the pirates who had been injured came aboard the U.S. naval ship that had responded for medical assistance. On April 12, when it was determined that the captain's life was in "immediate danger," a Navy Seal team of sharpshooters killed the three pirates. Since then, other rescues have been accomplished by Danish, Dutch, and Russian marines and other nationals as well.

Some of these vessel boardings and rescues have been recorded and are available on the Internet. Videos of the disastrous results for some of the pirates have lowered the number of crimes but not stopped them from occurring. A report issued in mid-2010 referred to 20 hijacked vessels with close to 300 crew members that were still being held in Somali waters, and indicated that ransoms were still being paid by some ship owners via money transfers, parachute drops, and ship transfers.

Endnotes

1. The Public Transportation System and Emergency Preparedness Planning Guide (Final Report), Washington, D.C.: U.S. Department of Transportation, January 2003, 137.
2. William Newman, In Response to M.T.A.'s 'Say Something' Ads, a Glimpse of Modern Fears, *New York Times*, January 7, 2008, p. B1.
3. Brian M. Jenkins and Bruce R. Butterworth, *Selective Screening of Rail Passengers*, MTI Report 06-07, San Jose, CA: Mineta Transportation Institute, 2007, p. 5.

Postblast Environment 14

Getting Back to Normal

The components of preincident planning relative to a bombing attack were discussed in earlier chapters. Here we expand the subject as it relates to the consequence phase of the bomb attack. The events that occurred on September 11, 2001, demonstrated the need for security planners to think outside of the box. Even the best-protected targets can successfully be attacked by a determined foe given money and time to study and plan. The manner of the attack, and its resulting severity, as well as how sufficiently the target is prepared to meet the challenge, will determine how quickly a building, worksite, or other location will be able to return to normal operations. In the public safety arena, the response will be only as good as the trained personnel responding to the incident and the degree of preincident liaison planning with the private sector to accommodate the different perspectives, since the civilian population wants to return to normal operations, while the law enforcement community wants to bring the investigation to a successful conclusion.

The Incident

Terrorism is a global threat and the U.S. mainland is no longer virgin territory for such threats and attacks. The 1993 World Trade Center bombing was the first indication of this, although this observation went unrealized for nearly a decade afterward. The 1995 attack on the Murrah Federal Building in Oklahoma City showed that domestic terrorists are as capable as Islamic fundamentalists of wreaking havoc and claiming lives. A bomb attack involving an improvised explosive device (IED) can occur at any time—day or night, weekday or weekend. The blast may happen outside or inside and in any type of weather. The damage caused by the device, even if only a small amount of explosive is used, can be devastating. Even if a location was not the intended target, collateral damage caused by the blast can be quite substantial, both physically and psychologically to those involved. In the Oklahoma City bombing, more than 100 businesses sustained damage in some shape or form, many quite extensive. In the case of the 9/11 terrorist attack against the World Trade Center, Lower Manhattan's infrastructure components were severely disrupted. The damage included telephone landlines, water, gas, and electrical services, which were interrupted or severely damaged to the point that the business interruption was catastrophic, even among the companies and buildings that received no physical damage. Travel for the public was so restricted within the affected area that employees could not get to their workplace.

Types of Explosions

There are basically three types of explosions that can occur and cause a varying amount of damage:

- Mechanical. This occurs when sufficient pressure builds up within a vessel and, with no other method of escape, ruptures the wall of the vessel and causes an explosion. A classical example is that of a boiler explosion when a safety valve becomes stuck and pressure is not allowed to escape. Similar is a BLEVE (boiling liquid expanding vapor explosion), when a container with pressurized liquid inside is ruptured due to a weakening of vessel walls.
- Chemical. Associated with explosions generated by an energetic material.
- Gas. Explosions caused by the leaking of natural, methane, or butane gas when reaching a point of a proper air-fuel mixture and ignited by an external source of spark or flame.

First Responders

Regardless of whether the incident is one of catastrophic proportions or a minor one that occurs regularly, first responders are the most important individuals in any emergency situation. In almost all cases it starts with a 911 call that will generate a response by local police, fire, and emergency medical responders. If the incident is serious enough, it may also require the local commander on the scene to initiate a call for a larger response. The success or failure of a large response to a disaster depends on prior planning and training of those involved. In the past, emergency response departments were extremely territorial as to their responsibilities and, in particular, who would be the lead agency. Unfortunately, this remains the case to some degree in many of the larger urban areas, but more and more this thought process is slowly diminishing. In almost all suburban areas, mutual support and emergency management task forces are becoming the norm.

Every incident, while perhaps not unique, does have unpredictable aspects that will require a first responder to make adjustments and judgments. But as the events in the immediate aftermath of the 9/11 attack demonstrated, dangers to first responders can have deadly consequences. Whether these first responders are private security personnel, concerned civilians, or trained emergency technicians, assisting the injured becomes the paramount concern. Although injuries may be extremely severe, victims must be removed from the immediate area of danger so they can receive proper medical care.

Search and Rescue Phase

In a major IED attack where extensive structural damage occurs, the operation may develop along the following lines:

- Size up the scene as to the extent of the damage and what may be required. The initial response will always be local, with the arrival of emergency personnel who will do a quick assessment as to what additional services are required, usually provided by the county or state. In the event of a major incident, the Federal Emergency Management Agency would dispatch a regional task force to the scene.
- The task force will have specialists in structural engineering who can make a determination as to the integrity of the target building or structure and what is required to continue the rescue effort with a degree of safety. This may involve the use of heavy lift equipment to remove large debris that may endanger rescue team members. Heavy rigging specialists should be directing these efforts to help ensure the safety of the searchers as well any trapped victims.
- The rescue effort can be initiated while the shoring of the damaged areas is carried out. In order to facilitate the locating of victims in large collapsed structures, electronic listening devices, small search cameras, and specialized search canines can be used. Those victims trapped in rubble may be easily retrieved or, in worst-case scenarios, if covered by thousands of pounds of rubble and debris, will have to be cut out as noted later in this chapter, the FEMA marking system should be used during the search and rescue phase.
- In addition to having normal first responder medical care, it may be necessary to augment that team with trauma physicians, nurses, and medical technicians with a mobile medical facility to facilitate such functions as triage and other evaluations. In addition, the mobile medical unit will serve in the event of rescuer injuries.
- The situation may also require that hazmat specialists be on the scene in order to evaluate the area for hazardous chemicals and facilitate the handling of toxic fluids from decaying bodies if a lengthy recovery operation is required.

- Again, if the operation is going to be extensive, logistic personnel may be required to move and account for large amounts of equipment required to complete the task.

The actual search should be conducted with a buddy system, that is, working in teams of two, with one team in and the other team out. Most commonly, trapped victims came be found in the "voids" of the structure. These voids can be formed in a variety of ways, i.e., walls that have diagonally collapsed against another to form a lean-to-type void or multiple floors collapsing on each other and forming a "pancake void."

Command Post Operations

To facilitate the search and rescue effort, it is necessary to quickly designate an area for a command post to be utilized in the rescue operation and in the field investigation. It is important to establish a line of investigative responsibility from the onset. Within the scope of the investigation, it is important to maintain a line of communication among the investigative agencies, although this vertical communication chain can at times be a trying affair, particularly when local agencies are dealing with federal enforcement agencies. Today, in almost all cases of an IED attack of major proportions, a federal agency such as the Federal Bureau of Investigation or the Bureau of Alcohol, Tobacco, and Firearms will be the lead investigating agency or will be assisting the local enforcement authority.

The operational command post should be located at a sufficient distance from the scene of the explosion to ensure a certain degree of safety, yet close enough to maintain operational control. In the 9/11 terrorist attack, virtually the entire New York City Fire Department senior command structure was lost after the command post, which had been established within the lobby area of one of the towers of the World Trade Center complex, was destroyed when the towers collapsed.

Recovery

The site of any bombing or suspected bomb attack should be handled as any other crime scene, with appropriate measures being followed. There are basic investigative steps to be taken in dealing with any crime scene from which physical evidence can be properly collected. It is extremely important that the crime scene be quickly defined and secured so that it may be safeguarded against all unauthorized entry. It is also important to remember that key evidence is likely to be small and fragmented, and in this state can be very easily mistaken for unimportant refuse to the untrained eye and may be discarded in a rush to clean up the site.

Remember, the crime scene may be a very large area, such as in the case of the World Trade Center after the 9/11 attack or the bombing in Oklahoma City, making the initial control effort very difficult. With 9/11, the rescue effort was measured in weeks and months. Even in Oklahoma City, the rescue effort lasted several days, making evidence recovery a complex task.

Since blast damage caused by explosive devices can vary in type and in the area of destruction affected, the threat of fire or a secondary explosion should be an immediate concern. This could be caused by exposed electrical wires, ruptured gas lines, and similar hazards that can precipitate further damage to the area and injuries to those in it. There have been occasions a secondary improvised device secreted a short distance from where the original bomb attack was carried out. A search for secondary explosive devices should be made as soon as the injured have been removed from the area. Where there are sufficient personnel on the scene, the search can be conducted simultaneously with victim recovery efforts. Secondary devices are generally placed and timed to explode only a short distance away, thus targeting the responding emergency personnel. Other hazards include the possibility of structural collapse, hazardous chemicals, toxic fumes, and blood-borne pathogens that could be communicated while assisting victims.

In major attacks, the rescue, victim recovery, and investigative searches will run concurrently. In smaller explosions, the task is simplified. The first step is to locate where the device actually detonated; this is called the seat of the explosion. It should be pinpointed exactly. From there, all fragments usually radiate in a 360° pattern, depending on the physical location of the device, e.g., if it is out in the open or in a concealed area. Thus, the placement of the device will dictate the fragmentation pattern, i.e., the path the majority of fragmentation follows. The crime scene proper should include the area where the farthest piece of physical evidence can be found. The area comprising half again that distance should be marked and designated as a restricted area for only those on official or legitimate business. Safeguarding the crime scene may be difficult, especially when crowds of people are drawn to the scene, whether gawkers or well-meaning volunteers. In high-profile cases, a heavy media presence can be expected and will add another dimension to an already chaotic scene.

Blast Damage

Damage and injuries caused by IEDs result primarily from the effect of blast pressure and the fragmentation developed from that effect. There is also the incendiary or thermal effect. Let's look at these a little closer:

- Effect of pressure. This is also known as a shock front. This is caused by the blast pushing the air outwardly, causing a bubble to surround the seat of the explosion. This is what is known as the primary or positive pressure phase. Once the atmospheric pressure overrides the ambient pressure, a reverse flow of air occurs. This is called the negative pressure and can last much longer than the positive phase, thus giving a one-two-punch effect. This action will cause debris thrown by the explosion to be pulled back in toward the point of the blast. The shock wave can also be generated through the ground and cause damage to foundations of surrounding buildings. Exposure to this overpressure can be fatal or cause severe injury. The ear is the most sensitive to overpressure, and damage to hearing is a common injury. The second most common is damage to the lungs, and is a major cause of death among bomb victims. The gastrointestinal (GI) tract is also vulnerable to internal hemorrhages and perforations.
- Fragmentation. The material that is developed from the explosive device itself and from items that are thrown by the effect of the blast. Thus, we have primary and secondary fragmentation. Fragmentation can be hurled at a very high velocity and great distances, depending upon the type and amount of explosives used. Fragmentation can be produced from any number of sources. The most common source is glass, and it can prove to be efficiently fatal. Flying glass produced by the blast can range from large shards of plate glass to sand-like fragments pelting the body. Another hazard arises from hanging panes of glass that may fall free during rescue operations. Explosive devices inside a structure can send glass flying into the streets, and conversely, blasts originating outside a building can send glass flying throughout a room. In an urban environment, the pressure wave can bounce off the concrete building surfaces and cause glass damage surprising distances from the blast site.
- Thermal effect. The blast itself generates a great amount of heat for a very short period of time. Unless there is a ready source of fuel, the blast will not cause a fire, especially when a high explosive is used. In the case of fire, structural damage may very well be caused when high heat causes steel beams and concrete support columns to lose considerable strength. In these cases, collapse of the structure can occur due to the abnormal load that is placed on the beams.

Types of Building Collapses

A catastrophic building collapse lends a whole new set of challenges to the first responders. Although FEMA has a number of search and rescue teams

Figure 14.1 The destructive force that was generated by the blast virtually destroyed the building. (Courtesy of F. Guerra.)

(SARs) available, in all probability they will require a considerable amount of time to assemble. First responders will be faced with several rescue situations and search problems in carrying out vertical and horizontal rescues. Many believe that the rescue of people can be better achieved with vertical removal, rather than removing debris horizontally (Figure 14.1). The following are the likely types of collapses that you may encounter:

- Pancake collapse. Occurs when load-bearing walls are destroyed, causing the floors to come down; in addition, the added weight on the lower floors will cause further collapse. In these situations voids are minimal.
- V-shape collapse. Where a lower floor or joists fail, usually due to a heavy load, but still remain affixed to the bearing walls, leaving a void below, closest to the lower wall.
- Lean-to collapse. Occurs when the floor collapses due to the failure of floor supports on one side, causing it to fall, creating a lean-to effect. This creates a void closest to the supporting wall.
- Cantilever collapse. Occurs when one or more walls have failed and the other end of floor remains attached to a bearing wall and is hinged downward. This creates an extremely dangerous rescue environment and voids are sporadic throughout the collapse area.

- Inward-outward wall collapse. Occurs when a wall actually breaks in two and the lower part falls outward and the top inward. This usually occurs in wood frame buildings.

SAR Marking Systems

Standardization among methods and search activities helps the coordination of efforts among various regional search and rescue teams. One aid is a uniform task force marking system that is used to identify specific information pertinent to each search area. The symbols can be conspicuously made with spray paint of international orange color and permanently identify and mark safe entranceways, note actions taken, or hazards that may be present. The following section outlines the basic markings used in search efforts according to the FEMA emergency guide.

Exterior Marking

- The basic mark is a 2- by 2-foot square box that is painted at a particular rescue entry point. All the normal entry points should be marked to ensure that other rescuers can identify that they have been evaluated. This plain square means that the structure is accessible and safe for search and rescue operations. Damage is minor with little danger of further collapse.

- A single diagonal slash across the interior of the box indicates that the structure is significantly damaged. Some areas are relatively safe, but other areas may need shoring, bracing, or removal of falling and collapsing hazards. The structure may be completely pancaked.

- An X drawn within the box will indicate the building is not safe for search and rescue operations and may be subject to sudden additional collapse. Remote search operations may proceed at significant risk. If rescue operations are undertaken, safe haven areas and rapid evacuation routes should be created.

- An arrow drawn next to a marking box indicates the direction to the safe entrance to the structure in case the marking box needs to be remote from the indicated entrance.

- An HM marking indicates that a hazardous material (hazmat) condition exists in or adjacent to the structure. Personnel may be in jeopardy. Considerations for operations should be made in conjunction with the hazmat specialist at the scene. The type of hazard should also be noted—body fluids, toxic chemical spill, etc.

HM

- In addition to the above information, time, date, and specialist ID should also be noted outside the box at the upper-right-hand side. This could be written with chalk or a heavy-duty pencil, or written with a grease pencil or magic maker on duct tape affixed to the exterior of the structure.

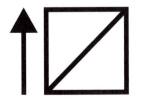

**7/15/91 1310 hrs.
HM - natural gas
OR-TF1**

There will most likely be a host of rescuers moving about the blast scene. To ensure that information is available to searchers within an affected building, an interior marking system should be utilized. For instance a single slash indicates that there is an active search operation within the area, and a cross or X indicates that personnel exited from the area.

Distinct markings could be made with each of the quadrants of the X. Thus, in the left quadrant will be the FEMA US&R task force identifier. The top part of quadrant will reflect the time and date task force personnel departed the search area. On the right should be denoted personal hazards that exist, such as rats present in the search area; and in the bottom quadrant, the number of living and dead within the area.

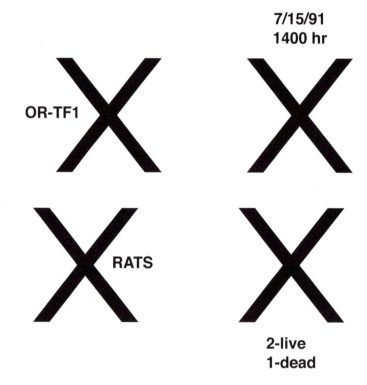

Investigative Phase

A bomb or not a bomb? That is the question. It is important to quickly establish whether the explosion was intentional or accidental. Thus, the investigation of the postblast or consequence phase of the incident should

Figure 14.2 Rescue and evidence recovery operations at the Murrah Federal Building in Oklahoma City. (Courtesy of F. Guerra.)

be conducted only by qualified investigators. When a large scene is being processed, searchers should be supervised by trained bomb investigators. In addition to bomb scene specialists, other technicians, such as evidence custodians, forensic specialists, still and video photographers, and representatives from the medical examiner or coroner's office may be required (Figure 14.2 and Figure 14.3). In blast sites involving more common crimes, i.e., burglary, robbery, and homicide, physical evidence is usually readily discernible and may be developed through traditional methods of investigation. Although postblast investigations make use of these techniques, much of the development of physical evidence requires a well-trained eye.

From the very beginning, the investigator should be taking written notes of his or her action at the crime scene. A new notepad should be initiated for a major incident, and this should be presented in as near chronological order as possible, while also being clear and concise. The notes should just record the facts that you see, not putting forth opinions or drawing premature conclusions.

Developing a premise for the exact nature of the explosion will be painstaking. Preliminary accounts gathered from eyewitnesses and victims may help to establish an initial starting point from which to launch the investigation. The seasoned bomb scene investigator will get a quick feeling as to whether it was an accident or intentional. It will take a tedious and many times consuming physical examination to come to a successful conclusion.

Figure 14.3 Closeup of the type of destruction of the Murrah Federal Building that challenged both the rescuer and the investigator. (Courtesy of F. Guerra.)

The process includes separating physical evidence into the known and the unknown. In other words, identify debris as either part of the design of the area or foreign to the area. It is important to keep in mind that the component parts of an improvised explosive device are not simply "atomized" by the energy generated by the blast, but are dramatically changed in shape or severely fragmented. Special attention must be given to fragmented components of the device itself, such as the bomb's container, timing mechanism, or wiring. If in doubt as to the origin of a particular fragment, always retain it for closer examination at a later date.

Once the crime scene is secured and defined, the search for physical evidence may begin. As in all crime scene investigations, the recording process is very important and must be accomplished by using photographs, including video, sketches, and diagrams, as well as written reports, both field notes and, at a later time, in formal agency format. An important fact to keep in mind is that all reporting is subject to open court review if judicial proceedings result. Once this has been accomplished, a preliminary search can begin.

Search Equipment

Be prepared is the byword of any police or crime scene operation, and this is no less true when handling a postblast scene. The evidence processing team or teams must be properly equipped to perform the assigned task. Although each scene is very different, agencies must be prepared to handle situations as they arise. The Department of Justice provided a fairly comprehensive list in a June 2000 research report titled *A Guide for Explosions and Bombing Scene Investigations*. It describes how required equipment can be broken down into several general categories:

1. Safety
2. General crime scene equipment
3. Documentation material
4. Evidence collection
5. Specialized items

Each category includes:

Safety

- First aid kits—both the personal type and those for treating victims
- Protective shoes and boots, preferably those with rubber soles
- Protective eye equipment and safety helmets
- Gloves—there should be a variety of hand protection available, both heavy work gloves and disposable latex
- Protective outerwear, kneepads, and portable protection against inclement weather, with appropriate identifying agency markings
- Respiratory—particle masks, breathing equipment including full-face respiratory types, as well as CPR pocket masks for protection when manually resuscitating patients
- Marked outerwear—to assist in identifying law enforcement personnel that have responded in civilian clothing

General Crime Scene Equipment

- High-visibility barrier tape or white engineer tape
- Various lengths and types of rope
- Communication equipment—multichannel portable radios with secure transmission capabilities, telephones (cell and temporary land line in the event wireless transmission is knocked out or overloaded, as occurred after the 9/11 attacks)
- Lighting—flashlights with extra batteries, auxiliary lighting fixtures, and mobile lighting equipment where available
- Hand tools—from heavy sledge hammers and pry bars to tweezers, forceps, utility knives, etc.
- Miscellaneous—flares, thermometers, binoculars, etc.

- Tents—open-sided tents may be required in the event of inclement weather or to shield workers from direct sun in warmer climates; sufficient tents provide privacy when dealing with casualties in light of the common use of rotary-type aircraft by the media

Documentation Material

- Official recording log books, writing pads, sketchpads, pens, pencils, permanent markers, and white boards and cork boards to hang charts, maps, etc.
- Photographic equipment—35mm, Polaroid and video cameras, tripods, etc.
- Laptop computers with accessible computer-aided design (CAD) programs
- Forensic mapping equipment, such as compasses, drafting tools, measuring equipment (tape measures, rulers, etc.), as well as portable tables
- Tape recorders and cassettes to assist in gathering field notes

Evidence Collection

- Evidence bags—plastic and nylon, boxes, cans, sealing tape, heat sealer, evidence tags
- Evidence flags and cones, placards, grid markers
- Vacuum, swabbing kits
- Sterile latex gloves

Specialized Equipment

- Field chemical testing equipment and vapor detectors
- Trace explosives detectors and canine detectors
- Specialized equipment—extrication/recovery
- Global positioning (GPS) equipment
- Aerial survey/photography—helicopter survey where appropriate

Establishing the Parameters of the Investigation

After the needs of the victims of the attack are properly addressed, the process of establishing a cause can be initiated. Prior to processing a scene, an overview of the scope of the incident must be examined. This can be accomplished by coordinating with first responders and senior public safety officials to establish the current situation and what actions have been taken. Actions and personnel required to properly handle the task will depend upon the magnitude of the incident.

The integrity of the scene must be assured. This can be accomplished via security perimeters and staging areas, evidence collection, and processing points all outside the actual designated crime scene. A walk-through examination should be conducted to establish the structural integrity, failed utilities, or hazardous materials in the target area.

During this period the following can be addressed:

1. Establishing entry and exit paths for authorized personnel. All persons should be made to sign in when entering and sign out when exiting. The sheet should indicate that all persons entering are subject to the possibility of having to appear before a grand jury to testify as to their actions within the crime scene. This caveat cuts down on the number of "ranking" sightseers to the site.
2. Advising crews of the possible hazards that may be encountered upon entering the site. In addition, all persons entering must be wearing the appropriate protective equipment.
3. Ensuring that victims and potential witness lists are developed, and that actions from that point forward are documented.

Preliminary Actions

A bombing will drastically change the appearance and characteristics of the targeted area. For this reason, it is important to gather as much information as possible about the preblast configuration of the location.

This information can be collected from a number of sources, including:

1. Floor plans and technical drawings from the building owners, management companies, or similar sources.
2. Public records—building or coding files from county or city agencies. It should be noted, though, that these records may not always be up-to-date or filed properly.
3. Architects who designed the buildings or office spaces within (including any remodeling or reconfigurations) are good sources of photographic information, especially if a commercial or corporate entity was targeted.
4. The building operating engineer and maintenance personnel should be able to provide up-to date documentation. In addition, the facility engineering staff should be retained at the scene in order to utilize their expertise regarding construction matters, as well as assisting in identifying items that are common to the area.

As indicated above, once the seat of the explosion has been located and a search area established—or, in the case of multiple bombings, several search areas established—the processing teams can be formed and the hunt for the cause of the explosion begun.

Remember that the search should be conducted only by trained bomb technicians or under their direct supervision. In the case of major bombings, dozens of teams may be composed of law enforcement officers working under direct supervision of bomb technicians. There should be no more than a four-to-one ratio in conducting an operation of this type.

During this time, photographs of the overall crime scene should be made in a number of media, including still and video. Still photographs should be taken in color and black and white. If possible, aerial photographs should be made, especially if a large explosion occurred and caused considerable collateral damage.

Seat of the Explosion

The seat of the explosion is the precise spot that the explosive device was placed and detonated (Figure 14.4). In theory, all damage and debris will radiate from that point outward in all directions, including up and down. In reality, because explosive force is directive, it radiates at a 90° angle from the surface of the explosive. There are certain physical manifestations that cause the explosive to follow the path of least resistance, which may dictate the pattern of fragmentation after an explosion.

The seat may or may not be located easily, and the location will be dictated by a number of factors:

1. The size and type of explosive used in the device will determine the amount of destruction to the target.
2. If the target is a vehicle, aircraft, or ship and it is totally destroyed, it must be reassembled. This is especially difficult when dealing with aircraft bombings such as Pam Am Flight 103, popularly referred to as the Lockerbie Bombing, where fragments were scattered over more than 50 square miles. The July 17, 1996, explosion of TWA Flight 800 from New York's JFK Airport to Paris was even more difficult since the aircraft explosion occurred over water.
3. If the explosive device detonated inside a building or similar structure, a fair amount of material must be removed in order to locate the seat.

In most cases, the experienced bomb scene investigator can get a feel of what occurred within a short time at the scene. The general area of where the

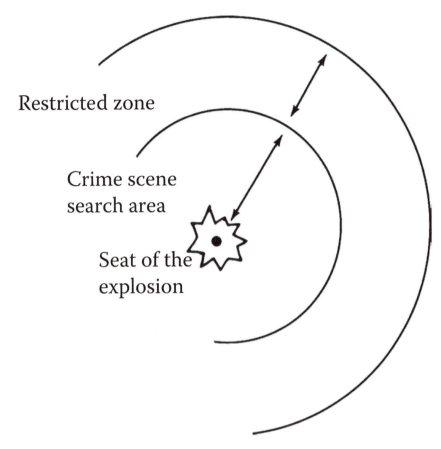

Figure 14.4 Crime scene: in a postblast investigation, the entire area needed to be searched for bomb fragments as part of the crime scene and should be protected by a buffer zone around the perimeter to which access is tightly controlled.

device detonated is first located, and will then become the focal and initiating point of the investigation. The lack of any defined seat may well point to a cause of the explosion other than a bomb. This supports a basic tenet of crime scene investigation: physical evidence will prove a theory of a crime. The corollary is that lack of physical evidence will indicate no crime was committed. A boiler explosion or natural gas explosion will generate force that leaves the impression of a bombing and will initially be treated as such, but once physical evidence is lacking, the bomb theory may be discarded (Figure 14.5 and Figure 14.6).

Gathering Physical Evidence

All the evidence gathered at the scene may well be categorized into primary evidence, that is, pieces that actually made up the IED, and other evidence,

Figure 14.5 The water-filled bomb crater in front of the troop barracks, Khobare Towers. The building was virtually destroyed by a large vehicle-borne IED. (Courtesy of F. Guerra.)

meaning objects and items in the immediate vicinity of the bomb. The IED remains typically are the smallest and most fragmented and distorted of the debris located at the scene. These may number in the hundreds, depending on the size and configuration of the device.

When examining the scene of a bombing, one can expect to gather a huge amount of physical evidence for examination. Much of the evidence will fall into the category of general debris, while other material will have to be retained. Bigger items, such as masonry wall debris, support beams, ceiling tiles, wall board, and lighting fixtures, may have to be cleared first to get at the scene of the explosion. All evidence that is recovered at the scene should be classified as either known items or unknown items, those that can be readily identified as belonging to the area and those that cannot be positively accounted for. One of the more challenging aspects of the bomb scene investigation is that no fragment or piece of evidence can be discarded automatically. There are several reasons for this: components of an improvised explosive device are limited only by the imagination of the bomb maker, and what at first may seem inconsequential may in fact be an integral part of the IED. In addition, items that may appear innocuous at the time of recovery may in fact be important evidence once all the pieces are put into place and fitted together. Very often it is not easy to identify items or their uses because they may be greatly distorted or deformed due to the force of the explosion.

Figure 14.6 Seat of an explosion: the cratering effect created by a blast is called the seat of the explosion. In this instance, this seat was created by a high-order detonation placed against a building foundation.

Examining Fragments

The seat of the explosion and the immediate area surrounding it, once again depending upon the amount and type of explosives used, will usually yield the most productive evidence (Figure 14.7). Evidence recovered from this area is critical because chemical testing for explosive residue is best accomplished from fresh, uncontaminated pieces. Trace residue is found not only on recovered bomb components, but also from soil and masonry fragments. Such evidence should be placed in proper evidence containers and submitted to a certified crime laboratory. In the majority of cases, this type of residue is processed at facilities of the Federal Bureau of Investigation (FBI) or the Bureau of Alcohol, Tobacco, Firearms, and Explosives (BATFE).

The search and investigation of a bomb scene are similar to an archaeological dig in that an attempt is being made to reconstruct a scene that has been greatly altered. For archaeologists, the alteration comes from time, natural forces, and perhaps disturbances by animals and humans. For the bomb scene investigator, an explosive force of an undetermined magnitude altered the evidence. In both instances, the only solution is slow, methodical examination of every scrap of evidence, distinguishing the known from the

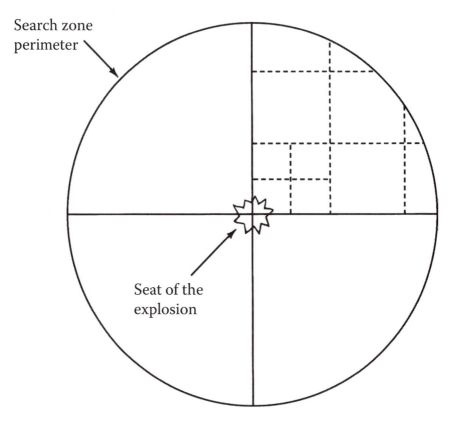

Search zone perimeter

Seat of the explosion

Figure 14.7 Postblast search: the area needed to be searched following an explosion should first be defined by a perimeter, and then divided into small segments that can be labeled in order to record the exact location were fragments are found.

unknown, the recognizable from the indeterminate, and segregating what could have been part of an explosive device from what is probably not.

Many fragments will initially be difficult to identify, and many more will be suspect. Gears, wire, electrical tape, and similar fragments could easily come from technical and mechanical equipment generic to the area or be part of the explosive device. Eliminating this type of fragment as part of the explosive device could be accomplished by utilizing site engineers or other specialists familiar with the area's equipment, or through forensic testing. This also applies to fragments of paper boxes, canvas tote bags, backpacks, and other items able to hide an explosive device. In most cases, elimination or identification of fragmented wire, switches, etc., can be best accomplished with the manufacturer's assistance (Figue 14.8a, Figure 14.8b).

The investigation of vehicle bombs proceeds very much in the same fashion, identifying bomb components vs. parts of the vehicle itself. Vehicle identification and type are extremely important because the recovery of vehicle

Figure 14.8a Bomb fragments: typical fragments from an IED that produced a low-order blast, in this case injuring one of the authors. (continued)

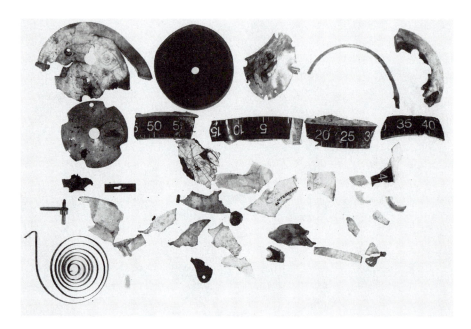

Figure 14.8b (continued)

identification numbers on key parts, ornaments that identify auto make, and other items will assist in the identification of a suspect. This was the case in the 1993 World Trade Center bombing when NYPD Bomb Squad detectives recovered a section of the vehicle's axle with a key identification number affixed to it. This key recovery subsequently led to the identification of those involved in the attack.

Evidence Recovery

Again, the recovery of evidence is a slow and demanding activity and should not be conducted haphazardly. To be successful, it takes a professional eye and a lot of luck. Once the large and obviously identifiable debris has been removed, the smaller debris around the seat can be carefully removed and examined. The best tried-and-true method is to sift the remaining debris through a variety of different-sized screens until only a granular substance remains.

Screens can be readily and cheaply made with 2- by 4-inch lumber constructed into rectangular boxes approximately 2 by 4 feet, with wire mesh screening affixed to one side. Ideally, the sifting should begin with 1-inch grids, then move down to ½-inch grids, and subsequently to ¼ inch or finer, depending on the situation. As a load of debris is worked through the sifting screen, the smaller pieces will fall through into a holding container. After examining the items that remain in the sifting screen and removing any suspected fragmentation, investigators should place the remaining debris in containers and store them in a secure location. The debris that fell through the screen will then be processed through the small grid screens and the process repeated (Figure 14.9 and Figure 14.10).

As the sifting proceeds, fragments that may be of investigative value should be closely examined, tentatively identified, catalogued, and properly packaged. Items that do not appear to be part of the explosive device should be retained in a separate and secure location in the event that future examination is required. Remember, none of the debris should be discarded until the physical examination is concluded without reservation. In addition, nothing should be discarded without proper appropriate prosecutorial permission.

It may take several rounds of sifting to ensure that all meaningful pieces of the evidence have been recovered. In many cases, the investigators will be under pressure to complete an on-site investigation so that restoration of the target area can begin. In these cases, it may be required to move the recovered debris to another area, where what may be a lengthy investigation can continue without disruption. However, the operation should not be moved until a through preliminary examination of the scene is completed and recorded.

There are certain advantages that a change of location may give to the investigator:

1. It allows the debris search to be completed without pressure to release the crime scene to the owners or operators.
2. It can provide sufficient space for the investigators to spread out the physical evidence for a more detailed examination.
3. It can protect debris from the elements and provide a secure location for the temporary storage of possible evidence.
4. It will allow the scene to be processed without external disruption from public or media scrutiny.

In almost all cases where prolonged sifting and search operations are going on, there is always a danger that the investigators will tire or become bored and possibly overlook important pieces of evidence. It is for this reason that searchers should be rotated in and out of the area if sufficient personnel are available.

Physical Evidence

The amount of evidence and its relative importance is predicated upon the severity of the explosion and the secondary thermal effect (Figure 14.11). As a general rule, the larger the device, the smaller the fragments and the

Figure 14.9 Typical sifting operation at the postblast scene. Debris is being worked through a fine sifting screen into a receptacle below. (Courtesy of F. Guerra.)

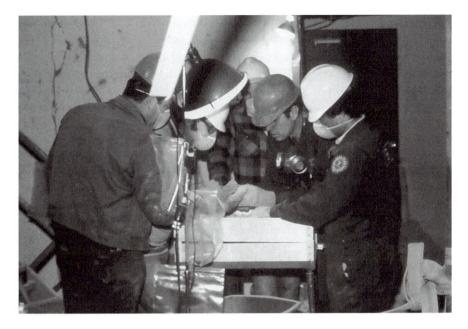

Figure 14.10 Closer view of the sifting operations.

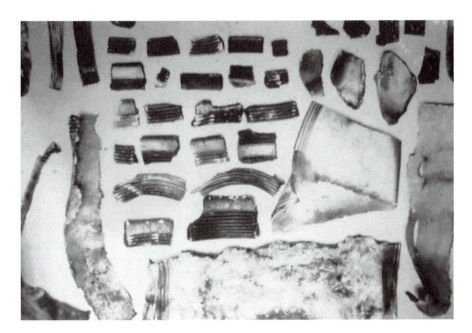

Figure 14.11 Typical evidence recovered from a pipe bomb that was exploded with a low-explosive filter. (Courtesy of Ken Dudonis.)

greater the area in which trace evidence will be distributed. When an explosion results in a fire, much of the nonmetallic evidence may be destroyed, and the metallic evidence even more distorted. When searching for physical evidence, it should be remembered that the device's degree of complexity is limited only by the ingenuity of the bomb maker, but the fact is that most bombs are constructed in a fairly simple manner. Physical or trace evidence recovered from the scene of a bombing can be grouped into two general categories, discussed below.

Container

The container is the package in which the explosive device has been placed and concealed and may be virtually any item.

Smaller devices can be secreted in common containers such as attaché cases, small pieces of luggage, shopping bags, and travel bags. Latches, catches, and inner and outer case coverings from these containers, although severely fragmented and distorted, may readily be found by the trained investigator. In cases where pipe bombs are used, the size of the fragments will depend upon what explosives were used in making the bomb. The more powerful the explosive, the smaller the fragmentation will be. The body of the bomb can be plastic, copper tubing, or galvanized pipe (Figure 14.12).

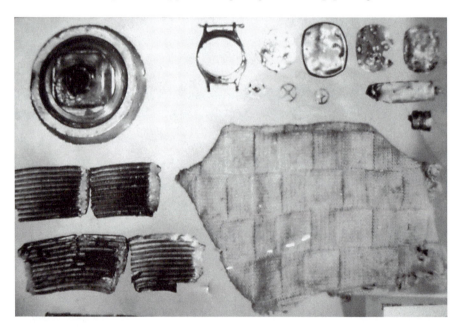

Figure 14.12 Pipe bomb evidence showing end caps, cloth used to tamp powder into pipe. Lower portion of photo shows fragments of wristwatch used as a time delay. (Courtesy of Ken Dudonis.)

A vehicle can also be considered a container in cases of large-delivered devices. Important items include ornaments, manufacturer's logo, and most significantly, the vehicle identification number (VIN). In addition to the main VIN located on the dashboard, a number of major component parts are also stamped with identifying numbers that will assist in tracing vehicle ownership.

Firing System

Physical evidence of the firing system will generally include fragmented mechanical or electronic timer-power units (TPUs). Common items recovered in sifting operations include the following:

1. The cell phone is becoming more common as part of the TPU, particularly among the major Islamic terrorist groups. It is used in command detonation or a timed event.
2. Even in this electronic age, the most common timers used in bombings are small clocks, pocket watches, or kitchen timers. These mechanical timers will produce gears and, in older pieces, mainsprings. Many times the mainsprings in mechanical timepieces are found easily due to their flexibility and resiliency. Even in cheaply made timepieces, recovered gears and other components may be stamped with date/shift codes that are valuable in tracing the origin of the item (Figure 14.13).
3. In addition to mechanical timers, an electrical power source is usually incorporated into the IED. A storage battery is the most common source of power. These batteries can range from the bulky type used in motorcycles to those small enough for use in hearing aids or musical greeting cards. Fragments commonly recovered are the outer casings, carbon interior, and connector studs and plugs. A smaller device, or one utilizing low-explosive main charges, may leave substantial portions of the battery. In many cases, fragmented outer casings will be located in sufficient quantity to establish identity. Commonly used batteries are 9-volt transistor, A series, C or D cell, lantern, or similar items.
4. Time delay can also be accomplished in a nonmechanical manner, through the use of commercial safety fuse, fast-burning common firework fuse, or an improvised burning fuse. Nonmechanical time delays have been used in several recent major terrorist bombings. The fuse must be of sufficient length to allow the bomber to escape unhurt, and it is not uncommon to have a sufficient portion thrown free of the blast site. In addition to the physical remnants of the fuse, there may be scorch and burn marks located in and around the seat. A fuse may also be used to ignite low-explosive filler. In

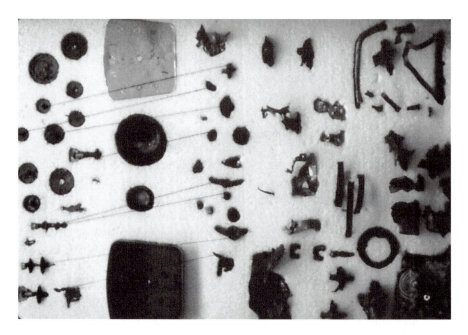

Figure 14.13 Fragments from a windup alarm clock used as a time delay in an improvised explosive device. (Courtesy of Ken Dudonis.)

small explosions, firework fuses may have been used with traces of ash found around the scene.

5. The lack of any mechanical or burning fuse residue may indicate the use of a chemical delay element. This may result in the deposition of chemical trace material at the seat of the explosion, particularly when an incendiary-type device is used. There are instances when military-type chemical delay fuses may be encountered. In such cases, metal tube fragments may be recovered. In most cases, however, the recovery of the chemical delay fusing system is difficult.

6. One of the more difficult portions of the explosive device to find is the actual detonator, particularly if a large quantity of high explosives was used. Fragments recovered from the scene may be from the outer shell, and if an electrical cap were used, may include the rubber waterproof grommet and pieces of the cap's leg wires. Locating and identifying portions of the leg wire can be vital, since manufacturers utilize color-coded systems for identification. In addition, crimps used to hold the waterproofing grommet and wires in place are identified by the manufacturer's different designs. In nonelectrical systems, the blasting cap fragments are almost impossible to recover unless the explosive functions in a low-order manner. As indicated, fusing fragments in nonelectrical firings may be recovered easily, more so than electrical leg wires. Blasting caps are not the only type

of initiators that may be used in an IED, especially if a low-explosive main charge is used. Common initiators employed in these systems are electrical bridge wires, old-fashioned photo flash bulbs, or just the spit of flame from a length of fuse.

7. The recovery of evidence at the scene of a bombing may indicate that booster charges were used to enhance the power of the main charge. These boosters may include volatile materials such as propane (added by attaching tanks to the device), like the device assembled by the Times Square vehicle bomber, Faisel Shahzad, in May 2010.

Postblast Investigative Process

The investigation will lie initially at the feet of the first responding law enforcement agency. The first step is to determine whether or not the explosion was caused by a bomb or by accidental causes. Once it is decided that an explosive device caused the explosion, the investigation can remain at the local level or fall to federal jurisdiction. If it is deemed criminal activity and in a relatively minor case, such as IEDs used in vandalism or extortion cases, local jurisdiction will most likely prevail. In major attacks, such federal agencies as the FBI, BATFE, or the Postal Inspection Service could be involved.

If it is a suspected terrorist attack, the FBI will assume the agency role. The bureau's explosives unit provides on-site explosives-related technical support in crisis situations to federal, state, local, and international law enforcement agencies. This unit responded to and directed the processing of the crime scene and the examination of the forensic evidence in the Oklahoma City bombing, the Unabomber bombings, the 1993 World Trade Center bombing, and a number of other high-profile terrorist attacks, including that on the *USS Cole* in Yemen in October 2000. In a nonterrorist situation, the BATFE will head up the investigation. If mail is involved in the delivery of any explosive device, postal inspectors will assist in the investigation. It should be noted that most bombings in the United States are non-terrorist related.

Mini Case Studies

The following are some examples of major bombings that have occurred in the past several years, and brief descriptions of the difficulties with which bomb investigators had to contend.

Pan Am Flight 103, Lockerbie Bombing—December 21, 1988

The bombing of Pan Am Flight 103 over Lockerbie, Scotland, was a crime scene of the most challenging proportions. The plane, a Pan Am 747-121, named *Clipper Maid of the Seas*, took off from Heathrow Airport after boarding a number of passengers from a transfer flight originating in Frankfurt, Germany. As the plane reached an altitude of 31,000 feet a bomb exploded, strewing debris over 50 square miles and killing 259 passengers and crew members on the plane and 11 people on the ground. The main wreckage plowed a 155-foot-long furrow in the ground, with the nose of the aircraft landing almost 4 miles from Lockerbie.

Because the aircraft was an American carrier and 189 people onboard were Americans, the United States offered any assistance that might be required to solve the bombing. In the end, personnel from the United Kingdom, the United States, France, and Canada participated in the investigation.

Almost from the beginning, an explosive device was suspected as the cause of the disaster. The preliminary investigation uncovered the cockpit voice recorder and disclosed a loud sound only milliseconds before the breakup. Another interesting point was that the number 2 engine showed heavy damage, as objects were sucked into the engine that was still functioning. Close examination indicated that the engine was subject to a strong blast while still operating, causing it to "eat" a number of items, including seatbelts, cable from the cargo area, and several passengers.

The scope of the case was enormous: more than 15,000 people were interviewed and approximately 180,000 pieces of evidence were examined. A break in the case occurred when a man discovered a T-shirt that had a piece of timer attached to it. Along with other evidence recovered, there were burn marks on a piece of luggage that were consistent with blast dynamics. The forensic investigation concluded that a bomb using Semtex explosives was detonated by means of a timer. The device caused a 20-inch-wide hole to be punched in the wall of the aircraft and was followed by a very rapid disintegration of the aircraft. The IED was secreted in a Toshiba radiocassette player inside a brown Samsonite suitcase. This conclusion was drawn by the fact that traces of high explosives RDX and PETN were found on the items that were in close proximity to the explosion. It is also believed that the device consisted of between 10 and 14 ounces of explosives with a timer or barometric pressure switch used as a delay.

The bombing of Pan Am Flight 103 was ultimately linked to Libya, and two suspects were arrested and tried in the International Court in the Hague. The trial ended with one of the individuals, Abdel-besset Megrahi, a Libyan intelligence officer and security chief for Libyan Arab Airlines (LAA), being found guilty and the other, Lameen Fhuima, the LAA station manager at

Luga Airport, Malta, being acquitted. Megrahi was sentenced to 27 years in prison, but was released after 8½ years on "compassionate" grounds after he was said to be suffering with terminal cancer.

The investigation of Pan Am 103 was extremely complicated in that it was multinational in scope, covered an area measured in square miles, and involved thousands of pieces of information to be processed. Yet the case was prosecuted to a successful conclusion. Libya eventually took responsibility and paid claims to the families of the victims.

World Trade Center Bombing—February 26, 1993

Early on a cold Friday morning, an explosion ripped through the parking garage of the landmark World Trade Center, killing 6 people and injuring as many as 700, setting off a national terrorist alert. The 1,500-pound vehicle-borne explosive device detonated in the underground garage area, ripping through three levels of the parking garage and starting a fire that sent smoke spiraling through the twin 110-story towers of the complex (Figure 14.14, Figure 14.15, Figure 14.16).

Within a short period of time investigators recovered a vehicle part with an identification number stamped on it, allowing a trace of the vehicle's history, which in the end turned out to have been rented in New Jersey. The vehicle was a yellow Ryder rental truck that was leased by Mohammad Salameh. He was

Figure 14.14 Overall damage to the basement area of the World Trade Center caused by the 1993 vehicle bomb explosion. (Courtesy of Ken Dudonis.)

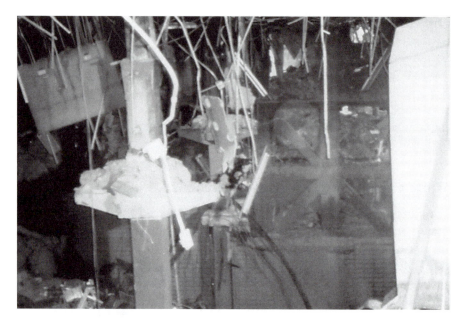

Figure 14.15 World Trade Center damage (1993) on a closer scale. (Courtesy of F. Guerra.)

Figure 14.16 World Trade Center damage (1993) on a ramp to the lower garage area. (Courtesy of F. Guerra.)

arrested after returning to the rental agency to collect the deposit on the truck, which he earlier reported stolen. His arrest led to 10 other Islamic terrorists, including the blind Egyptian cleric Sheik Omar Abdel al-Rahman. Osama bin Laden and his al Qaeda organization were also suspected of being involved.

As in the investigation of Pan Am Flight 103, hundreds of investigators from several jurisdictions examined thousands of pieces of evidence. Although the explosion was massive, it was contained within the confines of the World Trade Center basement. Despite this, the collapsed floors precipitated a search over a large area and tons of rubble that required the use of heavy equipment. Even though a major terrorist group plotted the action, the explosive device was really very simplistic. The base charge was 1,500 pounds of an improvised urea nitrate using nitroglycerine and ammonium nitrate dynamite as the booster charge. Three tanks of hydrogen were also added to enhance the explosive effects. The IED was initiated by a simple time fuse.

Another participant in the bombing, Ramzi Yousef, was later arrested in Pakistan. He was involved not only in the World Trade Center bombing, but also in a plot to blow up 12 airlines en route from Southeast Asia to the United States. The plot was part of al Qaeda's war on terror against the United States.

Oklahoma City—April 19, 1995

At 9:02 a.m. a massive truck-borne improvised explosive device detonated in front of the Alfred P. Murrah Federal Building in Oklahoma City. The bomb attack, which was the worst act of terrorism in U.S. history up to that time, was made against a target in a location that had no reason to suspect an attack of that kind. The massive explosion caused a collapse of a majority of the building and killed 168 people, including 19 children. The detonation of the Ryder truck used to transport the estimated 4,800-pound explosive device blew out the support columns of the nine-story building, resulting in the collapse of almost half the building. The crater in the street measured 30 feet long, 8 feet wide, and 3 feet deep. Local law enforcement and public safety officials were totally unprepared to handle such a devastating bombing. In reality, not many communities would be able to deal with the massive destruction wrought by the event. The problem faced by the local government was tremendous.

Initial Response

1. Even though there was a massive explosion, there was no fire at the primary target, but surrounding autos in parking lots were ignited. These fires emitted heavy smoke and made the initial medical response difficult.
2. Another difficulty was bringing emergency vehicles close to the scene. The streets were clogged with not only responding emergency

vehicles, but also private cars of responding emergency personnel, which quickly overwhelmed the area. Among other problems, this retarded the evacuation of those severely wounded in the blast.

3. Although there were massive casualties, a public call for medical personnel brought such a response that there was almost one doctor for each victim.

4. The massive influx of emergency and specialized investigators from throughout the United States created a massive logistical nightmare. These individuals had to be fed, housed, and equipped for a prolonged investigation. In the days following the attack, search and rescue and investigation teams came from well over a dozen cities. During the investigation, the Red Cross and Salvation Army provided 24-hour service to support the operation.

The Investigation

1. The size of the crime scene was so vast that it required hundreds of police officers just to secure it. Eventually, the perimeter was expanded to include a 20-square-block area.

2. The FBI was charged with the criminal investigation, but the Oklahoma City Fire Department retained responsibility for the search and rescue effort. The recovery of physical evidence was a massive and complicated undertaking. Collateral damage caused by the explosion was extreme. Many buildings within 12 square blocks were severely damaged and in some places collapsed.

3. Prior to processing physical evidence, digging and shoring up of large portions of the building was required. There was also concern that asbestos and other hazardous materials, in addition to the biohazards resulting from body fluids of the casualties, were a threat to the responders. To deal with this particular problem, a team from the Centers for Disease Control and Prevention was dispatched from Atlanta.

4. The search for physical evidence continued until the summer. In the end, 168 people were killed and 500 injured.

5. Timothy McVeigh, 27, was arrested 90 minutes after the Oklahoma City explosion because he had been driving without license plates. He was charged in the bombing, tried, and convicted. He was executed at 7:14 a.m. CDT on June 11, 2001. Brothers Terry and James McNichols were also taken into federal custody in connection with the bombing, and later stood trial.

TWA Flight 800—July 17, 1996

The destruction of TWA Flight 800 presented a unique challenge to crime scene investigators. The plane, a Boeing 747-431, exploded off the shores of Long Island, near East Moriches, about 12 minutes after taking off. The violent and immediate destruction of the aircraft had all the earmarks of a bomb attack. As any trained investigator knows, you don't build a crime scene around a theory, but you build your theory around the results of examining physical evidence. The media and public thought it was a foregone conclusion that a terrorist caused the tragedy and lit a fire under the conspiracy community.

The problems of evidence recovery proved to be a great challenge to the investigative team. The debris field was spread over a wide area of the ocean floor, and a fair amount of debris was being washed up on shore. In order to locate and plot the field, the National Oceanic and Atmospheric Administration (NOAA) hydrographic survey ship RUDE scanned the ocean floor and found the primary wreckage fields of the aircraft. This enabled Navy divers to recover the bodies of crash victims as well as the all-important flight recorder in a timely fashion.

Once the debris was recovered, it took months of painstaking effort to recreate the aircraft as much as possible. Still, it took quite a bit of time before investigators were able to determine that an accidental center fuel tank explosion brought the aircraft down.

As with all major explosions/accidents of this nature, conspiracy theories were rife and the disaster of Flight 800 was no exception. Topping the list was that a missile fired from a boat was used to bring down the jet as it flew overhead. Although a trace amount of "explosive" residue was found on several pieces of debris, it should be remembered that many chemicals used in the manufacture of certain explosives are also used in many peaceful manufacturing applications.

Centennial Olympic Park Bombing, Atlanta, Georgia—July 27, 1996

Some time after midnight on July 27, 1996, a powerful explosion ripped through a viewing area at the Centennial Olympic Park while a music concert contest was in progress. One woman was killed as she was struck by a nail from the bomb, and a Turkish TV cameraman died of a heart attack. A forensic examination of the scene indicated that the improvised explosive device consisted of three pipe bombs filled with low-explosive powder and wrapped with nails. This package was placed in an Alice-style military backpack. A steel plate was inserted inside the pack so the force of the explosion would be directed outward. The device was discovered by an alert security guard, Richard Jewell, and he began to evacuate the area. A few minutes later, a warning call was received by a 911 operator that a bomb was placed within the park, and at about 1:20 a.m. the device exploded. Richard Jewell was initially hailed a hero, but with great fanfare he quickly became a suspect. Then he became a major embarrassment to the FBI. Cleared of all suspicion, Jewell would later go into policing and won several lawsuits against a number of media outlets.

Eventually, a man named Eric Rudolf would become the prime suspect. On January 16, 1997, a bomb exploded outside the Northside Family Planning Services in a suburb of Atlanta, and that was followed by a secondary device exploding in a dumpster located in the parking lot a short while after the first blast. There were some major design differences with each bomb. The first was initiated with a burning fuse and contained no added fragmentation. The second was initiated with a mechanical timer and was wrapped with nails, designed with the clear intent of causing harm to first responders.

About a year later, a bomb exploded at the New Woman, All Women Health Clinic in Birmingham, Alabama, killing an off-duty police officer working a security detail and severely injuring a nurse who worked at the clinic. A witness saw a man take off a blond wig and leave very quickly in a 1989 Nissan truck—the license plate was traced to Eric Robert Rudolph.

On February 21, 1997, at 9:50 p.m. a bomb exploded in the Outside Lounge, a bar catering to the lesbian crowd of Atlanta, Georgia. The explosion injured five, and a second device was found unexploded outside. The Southeast Task Force, comprised of local, state, and federal law enforcement officers, found that the two abortion clinic bombings, as well as the Olympic Park bombing and the Outside Lounge incident, were of a similar nature, and Eric Rudolph, a white supremacist, among other things, was now the prime suspect. Rudolph would remain on the run for some five years before being captured in Murphy, North Carolina, hiding behind a trash dumpster. In order to escape the death penalty, Rudolph pleaded guilty to all the federal charges that were brought against him. He is currently serving a life sentence without the possibility of parole.

U.S. Embassy Bombings, East Africa—August 7, 1998

The twin bombings of the U.S. Embassies in Kenya and Tanzania in East Africa presented yet another challenge to U.S. investigators, complicated by the fact they were working in two separate foreign locations simultaneously. In Nairobi, the bomb killed approximately 200 people and injured thousands more. The explosive device consisted of approximately 2,000 pounds of TNT packed in various containers carried in a Toyota Dyna truck, which allowed closer access to the target. The vehicle was detonated just outside the embassy building. The powerful blast leveled an adjacent three-story building that housed a secretarial school and destroyed a number of passing commuter buses. Almost simultaneously, a large vehicle-borne IED exploded in front of the U.S. Embassy in Dar es Salaam, Tanzania, killing at least 11 people and injuring more than 70. The targets were chosen because the buildings were easily accessed, ironically because they were not considered to be located in high-risk areas.

Within a short period of time it was evident that the bombings were the work of Osama bin Laden's terrorist group al Qaeda. Federal officials dispatched a team of FBI investigators to process the crime scene. Although the attacks occurred almost halfway around the world, U.S. law enforcement agencies were able to respond quickly and to successfully process the crime scene and identify those individuals responsible for the deed. By May 2001, four Islamic radicals who were members of al Qaeda were convicted in connection with the attack, while a number of others were identified and placed on the FBI's Most Wanted List.

Bombing of the *USS Cole*—October 12, 2000

A suicide bomb attack against the guided-missile destroyer *USS Cole* saw 17 sailors killed and 39 others injured as the ship was refueling in the port of Aden, Yemen. The attack occurred when a small Zodiac dinghy came alongside and detonated the bomb. The boat was allowed to get so close to the ship because the crew assumed that it was part of the refueling operation. It was later estimated that approximately 700 to 1,000 pounds of high explosives (investigation determined that C-4 explosives were most likely used) were formed in such a manner as to act like a huge-shaped charge. The blast tore a 40- by 60-foot hole in the ship's side near the galley area.

First to respond to the attack area was the British Frigate *HMS Marlborough* with a full medical and damage control team. Within a short period a U.S. Marine response team arrived from its base in Bahrain to provide additional security.

Again, the attack was launched against a target by a cell of the al Qaeda network after carefully studying the target. The U.S. investigative team was able to determine composition of the explosive device and subsequently, in connection with Yemeni authorities, arrested a number of individuals in conjunction with the attack. The ship received emergency repairs in the harbor and then was brought back to the United States on the *MV Blue Marlin*, a semisubmersible heavy-lift ship from the Netherlands. The *USS Cole* was fully repaired and subsequently returned to active fleet service on April 19, 2002.

Madrid Train Bomb Attacks—March 11, 2004

On March 11, 2004, at least 10 bombs were detonated aboard four trains that were packed with rush-hour commuters. The near simultaneous attacks, with bombs detonating within a 10-minute period, killed 191 people and injured over 1,800. The domestic terror group ETA became an early suspect in the bombing case since there was a December 2003 bomb attempt on a train by that group. In short order, however, Islamic radicals belonging to a terrorist group that has ties to al Qaeda became the focus of the investigation. This was ascertained after the recovery of a stolen van from a parking lot near a hub train station. In that van were a number of detonators, explosives, and an Arabic language tape (Figure 14.17 and Figure 14.18).

Three unexploded devices were recovered and provided a wealth of information to forensic technicians. One of the devices was recovered at the El Pozo Station and was subsequently removed to the Vallecas police station, where it was mistaken for property of a victim of the attack. Once discovered, the device was rendered safe.

Inside the bag was a plastic rubbish bag that encased the explosive device. The IED consisted of:

1. Ten kilograms of a nitroglycerin-based explosive that was identified as Goma-Eco dynamite—a special mining explosive. From the dynamite recovered in the van it was indicated that the explosives were manufactured only a month prior to the attacks.
2. A No. 5 Union Espanola de Explosives electric blasting cap.
3. An altered Telefonica "Moviestar" model cell phone. Two wires were protruding from the phone as part of the TPU. The phone was switched off. Further examination showed that the IED was not designed to function with an incoming phone call, but by utilizing the alarm function on the phone. The device was mistakenly set for 1940 hours instead of 0740 as designed.
4. The van that was utilized to transport the explosives had been stolen in Madrid at the end of February 2004, and the license plates had been altered or changed.

The investigation indicated that the Moroccan Islamic Combatant Group, with close ideological ties to al Qaeda, was responsible for the attack. This attack was probably the most sophisticated one that Islamic terrorists carried out since 9/11. As with the 1993 World Trade Center bombing, early forensic discovery handed the Spanish authorities the evidence required to bring the attackers to justice swiftly.

London Underground Suicide Bombings—July 7, 2005

Early in the morning of July 7, 2005, three bombs exploded on different trains in the London Underground system, all within a minute of each other. An hour later, a suicide bomber detonated an IED on a double-decker bus at Tavistock Square. These attacks were carried out by four homegrown Islamic

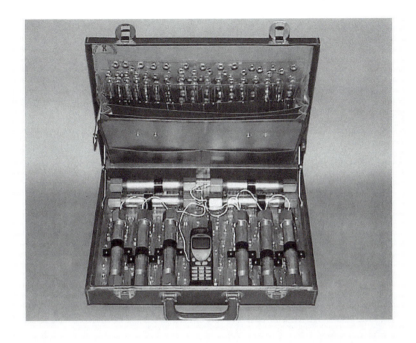

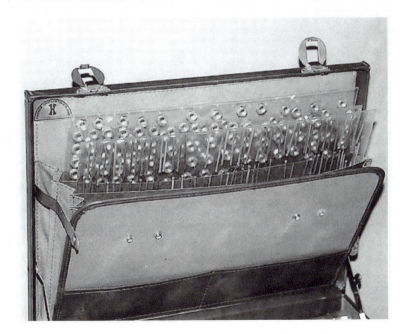

Figure 14.17 Briefcase bomb: terrorists may have used a briefcase bomb similar to this training mock-up device in the March 11, 2004, attacks on commuter trains in Madrid, Spain. (Courtesy of USAF/OSI.)

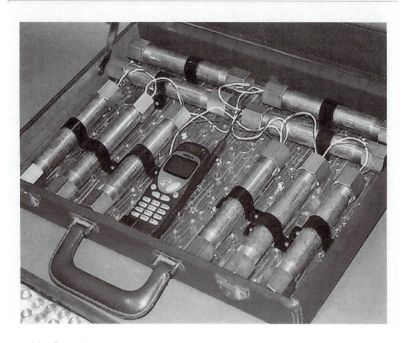

Figure 14.18 Additional views of the briefcase bomb. (Courtesy of USAF/OSI.)

radicals; three were of Pakistani descent and the other a Jamaican. In these attacks 52 people were killed and some 700 others injured, with all four bombers dying.

The first bomb exploded at 8:50 a.m. on the Circle Line train no. 204, traveling eastbound between Liverpool Street and Aldgate. The device, secreted in a backpack, detonated in the third car of the train just after it left the Liverpool Street Station. The explosion, which killed 26 and wounded 340, was powerful enough to damage the adjacent Hammersmith and City Line. This attack was carried out by Germaine Lindsay, age 19. The second bomb was detonated on a westbound Circle Line train just after it left the Edgware Road Station. The suicide bomber, Shehzad Tanweer, 24 years old, detonated his device soon after the train pulled out from the station. It was powerful enough to damage another train passing in the opposite direction. The bomb killed 7 and injured 171, 10 of them seriously.

The third attack occurred on southbound Picadilly Line train No. 311, which had left Kings Cross Street. The bomber, identified as Mohammad Sidique Khan, 30, waited until the train was about 500 yards into the tunnel before detonating his device. An hour passed before a fourth bomb was detonated aboard a double-decker bus in Travistock Square, a short distance from Kings Cross. The powerful explosion ripped off the top deck of the bus, sending fragments in all directions. The attack was carried out by 18-year-old Hasib Hussain and killed 13 people, mostly those in the upper and lower rear portion of the bus, and injured 110 people.

Multiple attacks such as these place a heavy strain on law enforcement resources, especially when it comes to specialized personnel who are qualified to conduct forensic examinations of bomb scenes. Another problem presented was the fact that three of the explosions occurred underground, where working conditions were most difficult: high heat and humidity became a drain on not only crime scene technicians but also first responders, forcing teams to work in shifts. High temperatures and quickly decomposing bodies quickly became a biological hazard, and vermin living underground made for an extremely difficult crime to process.

Shortly after the bombings police raided a number of apartments, including one in the Hyde Park section of Leeds, and uncovered what can best be described as a bomb factory. Further investigation ascertained that the apartment was rented by an Egyptian chemist, El Nasham. The police recovered a number of unexploded devices and bomb-making materials, including some studded with nails. The primary explosive that was used by the bombers was identified as TATP, an extremely powerful explosive. It was estimated that bombs weighed approximately 6 to 10 pounds each.

London Transit System Follow-Up Attack—July 21, 2005

In a follow-up attack on the London transit system, three small explosions occurred in the Underground. The attacks were made at the Shepherds Bush Station on the Hammersmith and City Line, Warren Street Station on the Victoria Line, and Oval Station on the Northern Line. A fourth bomb exploded on the no. 26 bus traveling from Waterloo to Hackney. In all the explosions, the IEDs failed to function as designed and no injuries were reported. Several days later an unexploded device discarded by a fifth bomber was found, and upon closer examination, the IED was found to be of similar construction to those used in the recent wave of attacks on the transit system. The reason for the failed attack was that the explosive, identified as TATP, had lost its potency, probably because of improper storage. Four Islamic terrorist were arrested in connection with this incident.

Glasgow (Scotland) International Airport Attack—June 2007

On June 29, 2007, a red Cherokee Jeep loaded with propane gas tanks drove into the main terminal at Glasgow International Airport. The barriers in front of the terminal kept the vehicle from completely entering the terminal, but it burst into flames directly outside. The two Islamic terrorists, a British-born doctor, Bilal Abdullah, and the driver, Kafeel Ahmed, both survived the inferno, but were badly burned.

"Underwear Bomber"—Christmas Day, December 25, 2009

On this day, Umar Farouk Abdulmutallab (aka-Omar Farooq al-Nigeri), a Nigerian Islamic radical affiliated with al Qaeda on the Arabian Peninsula, attempted to bomb Northwest Airlines Flight 253 inbound from Amsterdam to Detroit. Umar, who threw a blanket over his head, attempted to ignite an explosive device that was sewn into his underwear; with smoke wafting from under the blanket, a number of passengers jumped on and subdued the terrorist. Abdulmutallab was badly burned around the crotch area. The device consisted of 80 grams of PETN high explosives concealed in a plastic pouch inside his underwear, with a short length of fuse to be used as an initiating device. This device was similar to the one that was used in the attempted assassination of the deputy interior minister of Saudi Arabia in August 2009. That device was made with 100 grams of PETN and also failed to function as intended. By determination of the Obama administration, Abdulmutallab would be processed through the civilian federal court system.

Hostage/Kidnapping Aftermath

15

The Dangers Involved

Kidnapping victims, as we have seen, are in grave danger primarily because their physical whereabouts and their captors are unknown, and the victims are usually the only ones who can identify their abductors. In addition to the physical danger, there is also a mental health threat. To this extent, there is a common threat to the victims of both kidnapping and a prolonged hostage incident. A kidnapping can evolve into a hostage situation should the police track down and confront the kidnappers, as happened in the Tiede Herrema case in Ireland.

On October 3, 1975, Dutch industrialist Tiede Herrema was kidnapped near the Forenka Steel Cord Factory in County Limerick. He was seized by former members of the Provisional wing of the Irish Republican Army (IRA), Edward Gallagher and Marian Coyle. The kidnappers demanded that the Forenka plant be closed and that the Irish government release three imprisoned IRA members. The steel cord factory was closed by its Dutch parent corporation, but the Irish government did not release any prisoners and refused to negotiate with the kidnappers.

Investigators eventually located the hideout where Gallagher and Coyle were holding Herrema, and on October 21, armed troops smashed in the front door. The kidnappers, however, had taken their quarry and retreated to the upper floor of the house, where they were able to barricade themselves. A standoff ensued and the kidnapping became a hostage situation. Negotiations were conducted by a ranking police officer. During the course of the incident, food and changes of clothing were provided as part of the successful negotiations. Herrema was released on November 7. Although the Herrema kidnapping ended satisfactorily, sometimes the psychological states of both perpetrators and captives can frustrate police attempts to peacefully resolve such confrontations. Knowledge of what goes through people's minds in these instances can prepare authorities for the appropriate course of action.

The Immediate Reaction of Victims

The first reaction of most people when a kidnapping, hijacking, or hostage taking occurs is one of disbelief; what is happening before their eyes is not really taking place. Soon enough, the realization begins to sink in and the body reacts. In some cases, blood may drain from a person's head and rush to the stomach, causing dizziness to the point where the person will pass out. An even more common reaction will be involuntary responses of the nervous system: pumping adrenalin into the bloodstream, rapid heartbeat and heightened pulse rate, tensing of muscles, perhaps heavy and rapid breathing, perspiration oozing out of pores, or even hairs on the back of the neck standing out.

The next response is one of acceptance. As the situation continues to unfold and events take on a pattern, there are several different reactions: the body may begin to tremble uncontrollably; sobbing may start; there may be a loss of control over bodily functions, with the bladder or bowel emptying itself; or there may be a retreat into a catatonic state, perhaps even nodding off into sleep in order to escape from the reality of the situation. For those who remain conscious, there is usually some soul searching or a guilt reaction for somehow placing themselves in the situation. As the captivity progresses, a number of different psychological states or emotional responses can be adopted, often with the victim alternating between two or more. One reaction is to adopt a festive mood, as in trying to make the best of a bad situation. Thoughts of escape or overpowering the perpetrators are bound to arise. Eventually, however, most people accept their roles as captives, realizing that they have no control over the situation. Once this sense of reason returns, they can begin to protect themselves from possible harm.

Long-Term Reactions

Once the "why me" reaction fades and the body returns to close-to-normal functioning, the victim is able to assess the situation in fairly rational terms, and the whole incident takes on a different turn. Long-term incidents are usually kidnappings, since even the best-planned hostage takings are not designed to last more than a few days at most. With long-term incarceration, the group holding the victim or victims may be well organized, but this does not mean that they are professional. Any individual guard or member of the group may be high strung, tense, or easily shaken—or all three. The captors may have, and often flamboyantly display, weapons that they do not know how to use properly. Even if the organization behind the abduction is a professional terrorist group, the individuals employed on the operation may be recent recruits specifically brought on to handle this particular incident. A typical tactic of such hired help is to intimidate the victim with threats, verbal abuse, and all too often, physical beatings and death threats.

The common factor in such incidents is isolated confinement, often with deliberate attempts to disorient the victim by shutting out ambient sounds, obliterating light changes from day to night and back to day, and the removal of wristwatches and marking devices for keeping a calendar of captivity time. For a person in such circumstances, the obvious strategy is to counter these efforts by marking time with sleep habits or by noting the routines of abductors, such as when there is a changing of the guard. The important thing to remember in such circumstances is not to intensify apprehensions and fears, but rather to wait, observe, and note. One of the most comforting thoughts— even though a twisted observation—is that if the captors wanted you dead, they would have killed you. The fact that you are still alive means you are worth more alive than dead.

The Family

In any long-term abduction, the family suffers as much as the actual victim. Whatever contingency plans that were prearranged should be implemented. If the abduction occurs overseas and the preincident agreement is for the family to return home, arrangements should be made accordingly.

There is a possibility the family will be subjected to abuse. The media, of course, will be intrusive and at times appear insensitive in the pursuit of information or a new angle to a story. More threateningly, terrorist kidnappers may try to use the family for propaganda purposes, getting them to make statements they might not do otherwise in the belief or hope that this will win release of their loved one. Terrorists will, as has been demonstrated, pit the families of the hostage or kidnap victims against their own government, which is most often the real target of the terrorist action.

After the initial period of emotional adjustment, the family should try to resume its normal lifestyle. The victim wants the family to function. The family should celebrate holidays, birthdays, graduations, weddings, births, etc., and record them on film, tape, or photographs so that when the victim returns, he or she can share these milestones. Not only are such celebrations therapeutic for the family, but they will also help the victim in readjusting to freedom.

Unfortunately, there can be situations that are irretrievable, such as the death of a loved one. During U.S. journalist Terry Anderson's captivity in Lebanon beginning on March 16, 1985, his father died. Pleas to the kidnappers to release Anderson so he could attend the funeral fell on deaf ears. (Recently, Terry Anderson and some other international victims received court awards of monies from the governments that have supported international terrorism.)

Police Handling of the Incident

Upon verification of an abduction, standard operating procedure guidelines for a kidnapping should be implemented. Those assigned to investigate the case should be mindful that the victim's residence or place of business may be under surveillance by accomplices of the kidnappers. Plainclothes officers in unmarked vehicles should respond. Radio communications may also be monitored, so appropriate precautions should be taken and alternative means of communications employed whenever possible. A command post should be established and staffed, with appropriate procedures implemented and notifications made, as described in Chapter 18. The use of a time bar chart is helpful for rapidly orienting new or relief personnel. Half of the chart indicates the actions of the perpetrator, while the other half records the major activities of the police. The chart can be drawn on either a horizontal or a vertical axis, but the format should be consistent, at least through any one incident. Though originally used in kidnapping investigations, such a chart's usefulness in hostage situations became evident very quickly. A version of this chart is used on television's *Without a Trace* show dealing with the FBI's handling of missing persons and kidnappings (Figure 15.1).

The Stockholm Syndrome

In hostage situations and kidnappings, an almost perverse association between captives and perpetrators sometimes develops. This is called the Stockholm syndrome, a term coined by Harvey Schlossberg, a police officer psychologist, and colleague of the author, who was with the New York Police Department. The Stockholm syndrome derives its name from the reaction of the victims during a six-day siege in a bank vault in Stockholm, Sweden. Two gunmen, trapped during a robbery attempt, herded a man and three women into the vault and then demanded and received the release of a former associate who had been imprisoned.

For almost a week, under the most intolerable conditions imaginable, the two men held off police. Without plumbing facilities, all hostages were required to relieve themselves into wastebaskets. One of the women went through her menstrual cycle without sanitary napkins or tampons. Hostages were paraded to the vault door with a loaded gun held under their chins. They were tied to safe deposit boxes with metal wire around their necks, so if authorities bombarded the vault with tear gas, the hostages would faint

Time Bar Chart

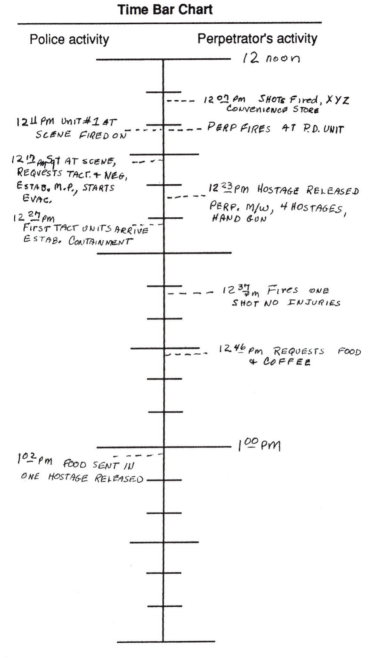

Police activity	Perpetrator's activity

12 noon

12 09 pm SHOTS Fired, XYZ CONVENIENCE STORE

12 11 PM UNIT #1 AT SCENE FIRED ON

PERP FIRES AT P.D. UNIT

12 19 am Sgt AT SCENE, REQUESTS TACT. + NEG, ESTAB. M.P., STARTS EVAC.

12 23 pm HOSTAGE RELEASED

PERP. M/W, 4 HOSTAGES, HAND GUN

12 27 pm FIRST TACT UNITS ARRIVE ESTAB. CONTAINMENT

12 37 pm Fires ONE SHOT NO INJURIES

12 46 pm REQUESTS FOOD & COFFEE

1 00 pm

1 02 pm FOOD SENT IN ONE HOSTAGE RELEASED

Figure 15.1 Time bar chart: A visual chronological record of events as an incident unfolds assists in updating backup and supervisors quickly. The left-hand side of the chart refers to actions of the police (i.e., activity outside of the hostage scene); the right-hand side refers to actions of the hostages or perpetrators on the inside. The axis line is broken into a timescale that will vary depending on the length of the incident and the amount of activity.

and collapse against the wire, choking to death. Eventually, police drilled through the vault, shot tear gas into it, and forced everyone out. As they fled, however, the four hostages encircled their captors because, they said, they wanted to protect them from possible harm by the police. Later, one of the women said she was in love with the bank robber and would wait for his release from prison to marry him.

Why? Because, psychologically, the captor has had life-and-death control over the victim and has allowed the victim to survive, earning a sort of everlasting gratitude. This is the ultimate in transference. Cruelty, it appears, only served to heighten emotional value for those susceptible to it. The pattern has also been called survival identification. The Dutch call it aggressor identification and note that it is hardly a new phenomenon. It occurred extensively amid the horrors of Nazi concentration camps, where some victims earned places of honor with the captors by emulating them and often outdoing the Nazis themselves in cruel treatment of fellow prisoners.

Transference

While the Stockholm syndrome is an extreme form of transference, there are other more common and less devastating types. Transference is a term used by psychiatrists and psychologists to denote the identification by one person with another. This is the key to what develops between a patient and a psychotherapist, for example. In a hostage or kidnapping situation, the cause of the perpetrator may well become the cause of one or more of the hostages. As a result of such transference, it is unwise to accept uncorroborated intelligence from hostages. They may tell you something is happening or not happening because they think this is what the perpetrator wants to hear. Even released hostages may not provide reliable information because of transference. By the same token, police plans should not be divulged to hostages because there is the possibility they, in turn, will relay the information to the perpetrators.

Transference can develop between the hostage taker or kidnapper and his victims, too, as well as between the negotiator and perpetrator (Figure 15.2). The only relationship in which transference is unlikely to develop is between negotiator and hostages, because there is so little interaction between them. In addition, the hostage perceives the negotiator as one of those prolonging the situation by not giving the perpetrator what he wants.

Transference is a coping mechanism, one that could well keep a hostage alive. The police—the negotiator, specifically—should do everything possible to encourage interaction between perpetrators and hostages. It is less likely that a perpetrator will kill a hostage when some degree of transference has developed. Some terrorist groups who have taken hostages have isolated a

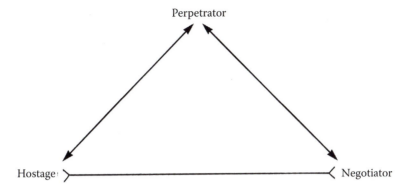

Figure 15.2 Transference: Transference is the relationship that can develop between the perpetrator and the hostages, or between the negotiator and the perpetrator. Transference rarely develops between hostages and negotiators.

designated triggerman from the hostages just to prevent any transference from developing in the event one of them is to be killed. Another tactic used with only limited success by terrorists is to cover the hostages' heads with hoods in an effort to frustrate the development of transference between the hostage takers and their victims.

Even when transference develops between the perpetrator and the negotiator, it is not necessarily a negative occurrence. The important thing is to control it so it doesn't get out of hand. The secondary or backup negotiator should monitor the primary negotiator so that he or she doesn't go off the deep end and almost fall in league with the perpetrator. Experienced negotiators may be aware of transference, but they cannot prevent it from developing. When people are in a crisis, they have to share that crisis with another human being, any human being. In a hostage negotiation situation, both the negotiator and the perpetrator are in a crisis. In fact, it may even be said that transference is the magic that allows negotiations to progress.

Because of transference, it is best that the negotiator not be the officer making the arrest complaint, in the event an arrest is made. The negotiator may be reluctant to fully prosecute the case or may otherwise try to give a break to the perpetrator. A second reason for not having the negotiator be the complaining officer is that it might be perceived as stealing an arrest from the first responding officer. Ideally, the cop in the street should get the arrest, if for no other reason than he or she might not be so quick to call for help in similar incidents in the future. Instead, the officer may want to handle it alone, without proper equipment, intelligence, or backup. This could lead to injury or even death. It is also probably better not to have negotiators testify in court, if at all possible, in order to maintain credibility with future hostage takers and to maintain the overall good guy image of negotiators.

When an Incident May End in the Use of Deadly Physical Force

There are two schools of thought about whether a negotiator should be told when the use of deadly physical force to neutralize a perpetrator may be necessary to recover hostages or when a sharpshooter will be used. The argument against telling the negotiator is based on the likelihood of transference. Because the death of the perpetrator is a very real possibility, the negotiator may give some indication of the impending assault or provide some warning to the hostage taker.

The opposite tack, telling the negotiator that deadly force is going to be used, is designed to protect the negotiator's mental health. Imagine talking with a person and not being aware of the commanding officer's decision to use deadly physical force. Suddenly, after what may have been several hours of sharing the same space, the other person's head explodes like a watermelon from a sharpshooter's round. This would, in all probability, have a devastating effect on the negotiator. Knowing ahead of time what is about to happen makes the action easier to accept, particularly if it does, indeed, result in the perpetrator's death.

It is preferable to take the negotiator aside and advise him of the impending assault. If he feels he cannot handle the situation, then have him introduce a new negotiator to the perpetrator. Because transference has not yet had a chance to develop, the new negotiator should be able to handle the assault situation better.

Ransom: To Pay or Not to Pay?

Before any ransom payment is made, verification must be made to determine if the people making the demand are, in fact, holding the victim. The request—really, it should be a demand—to verify that the victim is alive and well will not be perceived as unreasonable by any kidnappers. This has been called proof of life. Hoaxers, on the other hand, may object, saying they are not being trusted and, as a result, the life of the victim may be in danger. In many instances, a code word can be exchanged with the verified kidnapper when future communications are initiated to ensure that someone with cursory knowledge of the incident is not exploiting the circumstances for personal gain. On the first anniversary of the disappearance of a young boy named Etan Patz, a call came to the home of the parents indicating that the caller had information he would give the family for $10,000. Police were able to apprehend the callers. The ensuing investigation revealed the hoaxers knew nothing more than the anniversary date of the boy's disappearance.

Since the disappearance of six-year-old Etan Patz on May 25, 1979, investigation has continued. In 1990, a pedophile by the name of Jose R. Ramos, who had been a suspect in the investigation, pled guilty in another child molestation case in Pennsylvania. Two inmates who had served time with Ramos indicated that on separate occasions he had told them details of the Patz case. The Patz family, in 2000, with great difficulty, had Etan declared officially dead in an effort to force information from Ramos. The Patzes filed a wrongful death suit against Ramos. In the New York State Supreme Court, Justice Barbara Kapnick ordered Ramos to answer deposition questions of the Patzes' lawyers or risk being declared responsible for Etan's death. He refused and was so declared responsible, for failing to answer under oath.

While law enforcement agencies and police officers cannot advise one way or the other whether to pay the ransom, there are professional negotiators who can be engaged to handle the transaction. Such negotiators are usually engaged by businesses that have had an overseas executive kidnapped. Companies foreseeing kidnapping should establish preincident liaison. This means that security people within the organization should have, or have access to, people familiar with the geography, language, laws, customs, and different ethnic or religious groups from areas where such problems occur.

In some instances, negotiations by professional negotiators can decrease the amount of ransom payments. Obviously, the decision to pay or to yield or to make counteroffers will either fall within the preestablished guidelines or require approval of a company's crisis management team. If the ransom amount is very large or the money must be transported a great distance, there is insurance available to protect those funds. If the ransom is lost or stolen in transit, the payee could go bankrupt coming up with additional funds to meet the kidnappers' demands.

Making the Payoff

Once the decision has been made to pay the ransom, the next consideration is getting the money together. In a corporate context, arrangements must be made through the chief financial officer, who must authorize the outlay through the company's bank or banks. In most large cities, law enforcement agencies have arrangements with financial institutions to have available large amounts of cash in small bills, the serial numbers of which have been recorded or photographed. Corporate financial officers can usually arrange for a wire transfer of funds to cover the ransom monies.

In kidnappings involving individuals, the family or parties paying a ransom often will have difficulty in making their assets liquid in order to meet the demands. Once the decision has been made to pay the ransom, however, the police and law enforcement agencies will do what they can to assist. The specifics of how and where a ransom will be delivered are usually within the domain of the abductors, although counterspecifics can and should be made in an effort to ensure the safe recovery of the victim.

The perpetrators usually will have done a good deal of homework and reconnaissance on the victim and family or company. It is not unusual for a particular individual to be specified as the courier for the ransom funds. Often, domestic law enforcement agencies will want to plant a small radio transmitter on the courier. This is more for the individual's protection than it is for the safety of the funds, particularly if the courier is redirected to another drop location after receiving telephone instructions. Now there are all forms of electronic gear that can be of assistance to keep track of the ransom courier, everything from infrared fireflies (thermopackaging of the ransom) to global positioning systems. Tailing can be accomplished by all sorts of vehicles, even aircraft. However, tailing a walking courier, or one who might be directed to public transportation such as a bus or subway, requires investigators who have had training in this type of surveillance.

The surveillance teams following the courier should keep him or her in view, know what the person is wearing, and what he or she looks like, especially from behind. There may even be a hand signal or other sign so the courier can communicate with the surveillance team. Caution should be taken, however, to keep the tailing officer's identity and person out of the courier's view. There was one dramatic instance in which a father, acting as a courier, inadvertently revealed the identity of the tail team to one of the kidnappers making the pickup. There were no fatalities in the incident, but there was a great deal of anxiety and a felon fleeing with the ransom while the officers tried to regain their composure.

In some instances, law enforcement officers have been used to deliver the ransom. Their objectivity and training are usually very effective in assisting the investigation and eventual prosecution.

Proper packaging of the ransom can be used to assist in gathering physical evidence for eventual prosecution. The use of new, untouched paper or even new kraft paper bags is very helpful because they both hold fingerprints very well. Wrapping and taping the package so that the perpetrators must place their hands inside on the underside of a flap in order to open the package also will help in obtaining good fingerprints. In some cases, kidnappers will specify a certain type of receptacle, such as a briefcase or suitcase. In these circumstances, the container should be marked unobtrusively, with the mark being recorded on film or videotape. Another possibility is implanting an electronic device in the container, although if this is discovered by the perpetrators, it could result in harm to the victim.

When possible, the drop location of the ransom should be observed from concealed positions. If anyone retrieves the subject package or bag, that person should be followed, although not necessarily confronted, since the victim is still in danger. Several considerations need to be taken into account regarding confrontations, including the possibility of losing track of the pickup person or the inability to maintain a tail secretly. In both of these instances, it may very well be preferable to apprehend the person picking up the ransom package.

The Recovery

A kidnap victim may be returned alive in any number of ways. The easiest, and probably least traumatic, is for the victim to be released blindfolded on a deserted road or in an open field. The victim may be told to count up to 500 or more before removing the blindfold. During the countdown, there may be some trepidation, waiting for a bullet or some other life-threatening action. Another manner of return might be escape, or what appears to be an escape when abductors will sometimes offer no resistance or aid an "escaping" hostage. The best time to escape is at the beginning of an incident. The best time to get killed is also at the beginning of an incident, when everyone is in a state of panic. In one instance, the confusion may cover the escape. In the other, the perpetrators may perceive the escape action as a personal threat and strike out at the victim. However, after things calm down, and with the correct circumstances, escape may be possible. If the victim is in a hostile environment, such as an uncharted jungle or an unfriendly neighborhood, however, escape may be more dangerous than waiting out release or rescue.

One notably successful escape was accomplished during the recent turmoil in Iraq. Tommy Hamill of Macon, Mississippi, was a truck driver for a subsidiary of the Halliburton Corp. during the rebuilding phase of Operation Iraqi Freedom. He was captured with two other civilians and a soldier during an ambush of his convoy on April 9, 2004. He was held in an old house, and on May 2, 2004, when he heard the familiar sound of diesel truck engines, he pried open the door and ran about a half mile to a U.S. Army patrol where he was rescued. He then directed the soldiers to where he had been held and the abductors were taken into custody.

A different ending to a kidnapping incident could result from a successful cooperative investigation, as we noted earlier in the Tiede Herrema incident in Ireland that developed into a hostage standoff that was eventually resolved successfully through negotiations. Care must be taken that once the location of the victim is ascertained, appropriate action occurs. Ideally, quick, aggressive, and decisive action can bring about the safe rescue of the victim.

If there is a question of whether the abductors are aware of the police presence and possible assault or rescue attempt, then it is probably better to deploy a containment force and treat the incident as a hostage situation.

Victimology

Victims of terrorist action include more than just those who were killed or injured in a bomb blast, or who were taken captive in a kidnapping or hostage incident. The families of those involved are victimized, as are the police officers who work the incident, particularly in hostage situations. Even the public at large can be considered victims because there is more to be afraid of, and new regulations or procedures may be instituted, making everyday living just a bit more difficult. Traditionally, in the aftermath of such criminal acts as bombings, kidnappings, or hostage takings perpetrated by terrorists, psychological examinations, psychiatric treatment, and social counseling have concentrated almost solely on the criminals, with little thought given to the mental health of victims or their families (Figure 15.3).

Historical Background

The guiding light, if not founding father of victimology, is Dr. Richard Molders, a Dutch psychiatrist who participated in the negotiations involving the South Moluccans who took hostages in the Netherlands in the 1970s. Molders's principal American disciple is Dr. Frank Ochsberg, formerly of the National Institute of Mental Health. One of the first discoveries these victimologists made was that a victim's tribulations do not necessarily end with the termination of the criminal activity and the apprehension of the criminals.

Posttraumatic Stress Disorder

A short time ago, doctors at Harvard Medical School took part in a preliminary test of persons who had suffered traumatic experiences and the use of the pharmaceutical substance propranolol as treatment of posttraumatic stress disorder (PTSD). The study was conducted by Dr. Roger K. Pitman, professor of psychiatry at the school. The study involved a small group of persons who had suffered sufficient trauma, both physical and emotional, to require treatment at the emergency room of Massachusetts General Hospital. Forty-one persons were given four pills a day for 10 days. After three months an evaluation was conducted. Of 22 people who took part in the evaluation, 14 had taken placebos. All listened to audiotapes on which they had described

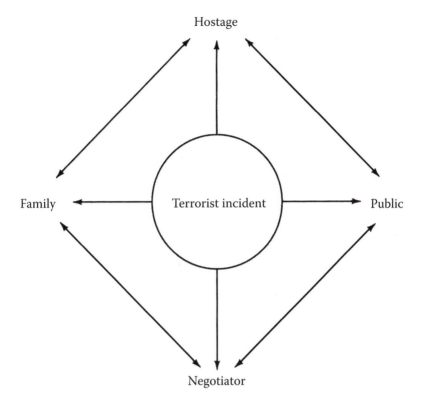

Figure 15.3 Victimology: All of the victims of a terrorist incident are not always immediately recognizable. The chart shows the lines and flow of relationships that develop in the aftermath of an incident.

the situations that they had experienced when they originally came to the emergency room. None of the patients who had taken the real drug, propranolol, demonstrated any negative response to the tapes. However, 8 of the 14 who had taken the placebo demonstrated significant physical signs of PTSD, including higher pulse rates, twitching muscles, and sweaty palms.

Dr. Pitman stated afterward, "The object of these drugs is not to make people forget their traumatic experiences, but to reduce the intensity of the memories to a more normal level, a level that a person can easily live with." He also indicated that more extensive testing needs to be done, but perhaps this is a step in the right direction for both victims and rescuers.

Courses of Action

Some former captives will be eager to talk about their experiences; others may grow reticent and prefer not to talk, or even think, about it. Both types of individuals, however, need counseling and guidance. Postincident counseling should be a total program involving a whole team, with initial debriefing interviews conducted by a law enforcement aide and a psychologist or psychiatrist. The victim should have a 24-hour phone number to call should problems arise at any time of the day or night. At least one other formal interview should occur, this one with the district attorney or prosecutor preparing the case against the perpetrators, at which the presence of a psychiatrist or psychologist may be helpful. One of the reasons for proffering official help is that former hostages or kidnap victims need to know that someone cares, and that someone in the system understands and is trying to help them readjust. This obligation is felt so strongly that the Dutch, for example, mandate such treatment for former captives. Talking about the incident and sharing the experience with others are generally good ideas. Many former hostages have indicated that they felt better after sitting down and writing about what had happened to them. This ventilating seemed to aid in getting their lives back on track. Media interviews, press conferences, and radio and television appearances pose another question. Certainly they can be part of the process, having a cathartic effect in relieving anxiety and other strong emotions. However, the danger exists that the victims or family members will grow comfortable with their newfound celebrity status, yet be unprepared for the inevitable letdown when the media's interest in the incident fades.

Immediate Postincident Reaction

Other than an overwhelming sense of relief, there is no universal reaction displayed by kidnap or hostage victims upon release. Some laugh, some cry, some do both. The closest thing to a typical postincident reaction comes when someone has been killed during captivity. There is almost always a sense of guilt among surviving captives, who wonder why they were spared and whether or not they could have done something to save the life of their dead comrade. Interestingly, at the time of the killing, when self-preservation instincts are running high, most captives are relieved that they were not the one killed, even while combating a new sensation of fear and apprehension at the perpetrators' escalation in violence. Only later does this sense of relief become a feeling of guilt and burden.

Longer-Term Reaction

Both the actual victim and his or her immediate family should be prepared to experience psychological trauma. There may be physical trauma as well. Fear, anxiety, sleep disorder, depression, aggression, digestive disorders, or sexual dysfunction may occur. Somatic reactions such as skin rashes, blotchy skin, loss of hair, or any one of a number of other maladies may develop. There also seems to be some distinction between hostages of opportunity and hostages of designation. In many cases, captivity of hostages of opportunity is of relatively short duration, typically less than 24 hours. An example of how one family was affected by a kidnapping involved a bank vice president who was taken from his home by three masked gunmen. The banker and his family were watching television when there was a knock on the door. His 17-year-old son opened the door without bothering to check who was on the other side. Three masked gunmen barged into the house. They tied up the mother, daughter, and son. One gunman stayed and guarded the hostages while the other two drove the executive to the bank. True, the gunmen could have forced their way in, but the ruckus and commotion might have alerted neighbors or allowed a family member to escape and call police. The planned bank robbery was unsuccessful because of vault timing devices, and the banker was eventually released unharmed. Afterward, his son required extensive psychiatric care to help him cope with the guilt he felt for putting his family in danger just by opening the door. For a long time afterward, the boy's mother experienced uncontrollable fits of crying. The man himself abandoned his banking career and found a job in another field.

Returning to Normal

However postincident reactions manifest themselves, there are two important points to remember: these reactions are completely normal, and they will usually fade with time. For most people who have been held captive, this means that returning to the preincident lifestyle as quickly as possible is the best course of action. Getting back to the routine of a job, or resuming normal school or household duties, has the reassuring comfort of normalcy to it. Various studies of former captives indicate those who are not kept busy have the most difficulty. For example, of the 52 people held hostage for 444 days in the U.S. Embassy in Teheran, Iran, in 1979–1980, the ones who had the most difficult period of adjustment were the Marines who left the service because their enlistments were up. The civilians who returned to work had an easier time readjusting.

Postincident Effects on Rescue Officers

The need for possible psychological assistance for officers involved in the rescue of victims of hostage situations or kidnappings cannot be underestimated. We have personally observed and experienced the immediate effects.

If right after the end of an incident the officers went directly home, many experienced severe bouts of insomnia, inability to eat or keep down food, and even sexual dysfunction. Two officers suffered heart attacks. Almost by accident, we found out that retiring to a bar or restaurant after an incident and spending an hour or two talking about the situation stopped the previously outlined symptoms from manifesting themselves. When relating this to our colleague, Dr. Harvey Schlossberg, he indicated that in actuality what we were doing was conducting a group therapy session, thereby providing a catharsis for any pent-up emotions. Perhaps this has worked well, because we have not gotten any further reports of those symptoms or any more dire effects of PTSD.

In other parts of the country and for other incidents, we have seen that when we speak of victims, we have to include many officers and rescue personnel. In 1987, an 18-month-old baby named Jessica McClure was rescued from an old well into which she had fallen some 20 feet. The entire country was riveted by televised reports during the 58 hours rescuers took to dig a parallel shaft before a slim fireman by the name of Robert O'Donnell wiggled down and freed the child. She was brought to the surface, cold, tired, but very much alive. O'Donnell was hailed a hero and was inundated by media coverage. After the media moved on, however, the hero had a downward spiral. In 1995, as he watched the rescuers and search crews looking for survivors in the Alfred P. Murrah Building in Oklahoma City, he told his mother that those rescue people were going to need lots of help, and that he didn't mean just for a couple of days or weeks, but for years. A few days later, April 23, 1995, O'Donnell took his own life.

One of the rescuers involved in the aftermath of the Oklahoma City bombing was Oklahoma City Police Sergeant Terrance Yeakey. He assisted in rescuing four people before part of a floor collapsed and he fell two stories, injuring his back. A little more than a year later, and three days before he was to receive his department's medal for valor, Yeakey shot himself to death. Similarly, a police lieutenant in New Jersey, shortly after completing a 36-hour tour of duty in the command center directing the rescue of hundreds of people from floodwaters caused by the remnants of a tropical hurricane, apparently took his own life. His stressors appeared to manifest themselves more quickly than those of the other officers.

Surviving Hostage-Taking Situations

Hostage-taking situations can happen almost anywhere and anytime. It is something that all should be aware of and should be prepared for. The following guidelines are meant as a basic introduction.

1. Don't be a hero; accept your situation and be prepared to wait.
2. The first 15 to 45 minutes are the most dangerous. Follow instructions.
3. Don't speak unless spoken to, and then only when necessary.
4. Try to rest.
5. Don't make suggestions.
6 Escape? Should you or shouldn't you? Think twice!
7. Advise on and request medication or aid if needed.
8. Be observant. You may be released and can help the authorities.
9. Be prepared to talk to the police on the telephone.
10. Don't be argumentative.
11. Treat the captor like royalty.
12. Be patient.
13. A black or red passport (diplomatic and official, respectively) may not bring you the best of privileges.
14. Get rid of items that could single you out as a person your captors may be fearful of.
15. If rescue comes, be prepared to hit the deck.

Follow Instructions

The first 15 to 45 minutes are the most dangerous. When the initial incident takes place, the hostages are in the gravest of danger. This is because the perpetrators are going through panic reaction, a high-anxiety situation that is manifested by the fight-or-flight mechanism. If the hostages hesitate or offer any overt resistance, the perpetrators will try to demonstrate that they have the power. In order for a small number of terrorists to control a large number of people, the captors often engage in a quick, violent act. They may beat someone, make a lot of noise, or even kill someone indiscriminately. If there is no resistance, just a lot of noise may be sufficient.

These first few minutes are the most dangerous for all concerned. This includes the hostages, the responding or confronting authorities, and even the perpetrator. In one instance, at Lod Airport in Israel, in the frenzy of the takeover, one of the terrorists accidentally shot one of his cohorts. Do not make suggestions to the perpetrator; if they go wrong, he may perceive this as a trick on your part.

Once the perpetrator feels comparatively safe in his cocoon, he will start to relax. This sense of calm settling in will become apparent in the voices of the captors. Then, as we discussed, the stage is set for the Stockholm syndrome to develop—a situation where both the perpetrator and the victim develop an unusual concern for each other's safety.

Try to Rest

As absurd as this may sound to anyone "under the gun," it is a very important and useful guideline. The effects of panic after the initial seizure will wear both victims and captors down, psychologically and physiologically. With the constant raising and lowering of anxieties, all concerned can become exhausted. This may not pertain to the captors if they are "chemically supported," using drugs or other stimulants.

It is not surprising or uncommon for everyone to fall asleep, hostage and hostage taker alike. This is especially possible in cases of a lone perpetrator, who must handle all stress and details himself. On many occasions, through the use of electronic listening and viewing devices, we were able to ascertain that everyone had in fact fallen asleep. Subsequent rescue and capture was then very easy.

Escape? Should You or Shouldn't You?

This is a very complex question. Most assuredly, everyone has the right to try for personal survival. Self-preservation is a very powerful and primary driver. In certain instances, where an aircraft remains on the ground, or the hostage incident occurs in a building, people have successfully escaped their captors. In a bank incident in Queens, New York, where police had infiltrated the basement, every time a hostage was permitted to visit the toilet located in the basement, they were spirited out of the building to freedom. This was accomplished without the perpetrators' awareness. During a hijacking of an airplane in the Middle East, a few hostages were able to escape by the tail cone door and fell into the darkness and safety. On another hijacked airplane in the United States on the ground, while one hijacker was on the flight deck, his female cohort fell asleep and the flight attendants used an elevator to evacuate all the passengers.

It is, of course, a very subjective topic and one that requires careful consideration. In other escape attempts individuals were caught by the hostage takers and severely beaten. In the hijacking instance of a Lufthansa aircraft that ended in Mogadishu, the perpetrators thought that the captain had tried to escape. This was not true, but nonetheless, when he returned to the aircraft the hijackers shot and killed him. If the escape attempt is done with great bravado, the hostage takers may feel that they must demonstrate even greater control over their remaining victims. They may harm or kill them to make public their seriousness to retain control. Some of these people may be strangers to you, but on the other hand, you may have friends or family left behind in captivity. While there are still hostages, play it low key and keep any plans for escape quite. And if you are successful, don't brag about your accomplishment until the incident is over for the remaining hostages. Attempting an escape is like attempting to broad jump a chasm. If you can jump 8 feet, but the distance is 8 feet 6 inches, you come close but you don't make it. Think about your opportunities and then rethink them again.

Be Observant

Mentally take note of everything you see and hear. After the initial panic subsides, this mental exercise will assist you in coping. Try to memorize things such as (1) the number of perpetrators, their appearance and conversations; (2) the kinds and numbers of weapons carried; (3) the number of hostages and their identities or descriptions; (4) where you are being held, and if any routine has settled in; and (5) the chain of command, and who is in charge.

On a train hijacking in Bellen, Holland, by South Moluccan terrorists, a hostage, who was a journalist, successfully kept a written journal. This is not a suggested procedure, since it may make you "stand out." In a more recent hijacking, one of the victims had a hidden camera and took photographs. Great care and thought should go into this kind of action. If you are released before the other hostages, your information will be invaluable to the other authorities in their tactical planning should a later rescue be necessary.

Don't Be Argumentative

This pertains to your actions toward the captors, and even to other hostages. Our studies have shown that those individuals who stand out or are perceived as a threat are often singled out by the captors. They may be treated violently, or even killed. Cooperate with your captors. Do everything that you are directed to do, short of harming another person, without an argument. Treating the perpetrator like royalty means to face him, make eye contact but do not stare, and when leaving his presence to go to another part of the room or location, sort of back away. This maintains your position as a person.

Be Patient

Be patient even though it may seem the authorities are doing nothing on your behalf. Most departments will be engaged in a complete program designed to bring you out of this crisis as safely and as quickly as possible. Remember that time is on your side. Everyone will get hungry and tired, and the hostage taker's resolve to continue will diminish. The biological functions of all concerned will work in your favor. In many instances, hostages have been traded for food, drink, or toilet facilities. There have been some cases in which the captors have surrendered rather than face the indignity of going to the toilet in the presence of others. This would be less likely to happen in a prison environment, where there is generally less privacy, and the perpetrators would be accustomed to these conditions.

Sleep has brought many hostage incidents to a safe conclusion. Physiologically, the stress and anxiety of the situation bears heavily on captors and victims alike. It has not been uncommon for authorities to have to wake everyone up after gaining control of the situation. Some perpetrators have been quite surprised to be awakened and placed in handcuffs, and several victims have been awakened to the news that "it's OK, it's all over." Sleep, from a psychological standpoint, is an acceptable way for the perpetrator to "surrender" without losing face. Everyone can identify with being unable to stay awake, and the perpetrator's excuse goes like this: "After all, if I only could have stayed awake, they never would have captured me. I never surrendered."

Get Rid of Items That Single You Out

Persons with diplomatic passports or law enforcement officers, federal or local, active or retired, should quickly get rid of their badges and credentials as surreptitiously as possible, even between the seats or in some other location. Many federal agents and police now place their credentials in their checked luggage. The carrying of other emblems, both military and religious, can also create problems. In the Middle East, the Marine Corps' eagle, globe, and anchor insignia is considered by many as a symbol of U.S. aggression against them, and those carrying that emblem or anything like it may be treated with greater harshness. Again in the Middle East, the wearing of a Star of David might also single the person out for specific treatment by certain terrorist organizations. In a free and open society, these privileges are taken for granted, but for safety's sake, discretion may be the better part of valor.

If Rescue Comes, Be Prepared to Hit Deck

The rescue might be loud with flash grenades. Stay down, cover your head, and keep your hands in sight. Expect to possibly be handled roughly until the rescuers can differentiate the hostages from the perpetrators.

Interviewing Victims

16

FRANK OCHBERG*

Whenever an investigator meets a survivor of traumatic events there is a chance that the interviewer will witness—and may even precipitate—post-traumatic stress disorder (PTSD). Therefore, it is important that professional investigators (including grizzled veterans) anticipate PTSD, recognize it, and report it, while earning the respect of those interviewed. The recognition of PTSD and related conditions enhances not only an investigator's professionalism, but also the interviewer's humanitarianism.

PTSD is three reactions at one time, all caused by an event that terrifies, horrifies, or renders one helpless. The train of disabling responses is:

1. Recurring intrusive recollections
2. Emotional numbing and constriction of life activity
3. A physiological shift in the fear threshold affecting sleep, concentration, and sense of security

This syndrome must last at least a month before PTSD can be diagnosed. Furthermore, a severe trauma must be evident and causally related to the cluster of symptoms. There are people who are fearful, withdrawn, and plagued by episodes of vague, troubling sensations, but they cannot identify a specific traumatic precipitant. PTSD should be diagnosed only when an event of major dimension—a searing, stunning, haunting event—has clearly occurred and is relived, despite strenuous attempts to avoid the memory.

---

* Frank Ochberg, MD, is a founding board member of the International Society for Traumatic Stress Studies and recipient of its Lifetime Achievement Award. He edited the first text on treatment of posttraumatic stress disorder, and served on the committee that defined PTSD. He was associate director of the National Institute of Mental Health and director of the Michigan Mental Health Department. At Michigan State University, he is clinical professor of psychiatry, formerly adjunct professor of criminal justice, and adjunct professor of journalism. Ochberg developed, with colleagues, the Academy for Critical Incident Analysis at John Jay College of Criminal Justice, Gift from Within (a charity for persons with PTSD), and the Committee for Community Awareness and Protection (responding to serial killer threats). Ochberg founded the Dart Center for Journalism and Trauma, served as its first chairman, and now helps journalists understand traumatic stress and traumatic stress experts understand journalists. As a Red Cross volunteer, Ochberg assisted families at sites of earthquakes, floods, fires, and aircraft disasters. He represents the Dart Foundation and directs its support of victimization programs around the world.

Intrusive Recollections

The core feature of PTSD, distinguishing the condition from anxiety or depression, is the unavoidable echo of the event, often vivid, occasionally so real that it is called a flashback or hallucination. The survivor of a plane crash feels a falling sensation, revisualizes the moment of impact, then fears going crazy because his or her mind and body return uncontrollably to that harrowing scene. A victim of the "cooler bandit," whose modus operandi was to rob urban convenience stores at gunpoint and force clerks into refrigerated storage rooms, had nightmares for more than a year.

There are important distinctions among traumatic memories. Some are clearly memories. The beholder knows this is a recollection, painful but not terrifying. Through time and (often) through telling and retelling of the trauma story, the memory is muted, modulated, and mastered. It no longer has a powerful, disruptive presence. It is a piece of personal history. On the other hand, that personal history may burst forth into awareness, and a trauma survivor may feel and act as though bombs are falling, a rapist is ready to strike, or the death of a loved one is witnessed again. (The loss of a loved one and the consequent bereavement are not, by definition, a source of PTSD, unless the death evoked imagery that is not usually part of natural death.)

Some repetitive recollections include regrettable acts by a person with PTSD. A patient of mine killed a boy in Vietnam. It was self-defense, in combat, but indelible in my patient's overactive conscience. Guilt, crushing guilt, was a major component of his intrusive recollection. An assistant principal at Columbine High School in Littleton, Colorado, ducked for cover as bullets flew during the massacre on April 20, 1999, then blamed herself for failing to rescue students. There was nothing she could or should have done.

Emotional Anesthesia: Constricting Life Activity

Numbing may protect a person from overwhelming distress between memories, but it also robs a person of joy and love and hope. While participating in a national PTSD research effort, I interviewed dozens of soldiers decades after their service in Vietnam. To these veterans, *survivor* meant being no more than a survivor and considerably less than a fully functioning human being. Painful memories might have subsided. Anxiety attacks were tolerable. But the capacity for feeling pleasure was gone.

These victims were not necessarily sad or morose, just incapable of delight. Why bowl or ride horses or climb mountains when the feeling of fun is gone? Some marriages survived, dutiful contracts of cohabitation, but devoid of intimacy and without the shared pride of watching children flourish—even when the children were flourishing. I saw this again as our soldiers and Marines returned from Iraq and Afghanistan.

Numbing and avoidance are less prominent, less visible, and less frequent than the more dramatic memories and anxieties. Early on, most survivors of trauma will consciously avoid reminders and change familiar patterns to prevent an unwanted recollection. For example, some ex-hostages from a notorious train hijacking in the north of Holland avoided all trains for weeks. Some avoided only the particular train on which the hostage incident had occurred. Others took that train, but changed to a bus for the few miles near the site of the trauma.

Numbing and avoidance are adaptive to a point, and then become a serious impediment to recovery. They can also mislead an interviewer of a survivor into seriously underestimating the severity of a traumatic event. There is a popular belief that victims of rape, kidnapping, and other violent crimes should be full of feeling, tearful shuddering, even hysterical, after the assailant leaves. When feelings are muted, frozen, or numb, the survivor may not be believed. When testimony in court is mechanical and unembroidered, jurors may assume that damages were minimal or never inflicted. I have testified as an expert for the prosecution (and for the plaintiff in a civil suit) on several occasions to explain this phenomenon.

Victims may be numb or withdrawn or both, and therefore do not come forward immediately. When they do, they appear to untrained observers to be indifferent, unconcerned, and unharmed, when in fact they are in a state of profound posttraumatic stress. This dimension of PTSD includes psychogenic amnesia. Along with loss of emotional tone and limited life pursuits are holes in the fiber of recollection. For example, an opera singer, battered by her husband, could not recall the most serious beatings. She was ready finally to divorce him, and she needed to testify in court at a settlement hearing. After several supportive sessions, including hypnosis, she remember his choking, almost strangling her. Eventually, all of the memories returned and she could joke, "He not only threatened my life but my livelihood! No wonder I put that out of my mind."

Lowered Threshold for Anxiety and Arousal

This is physiological. Unexpected noises cause the person to shudder or jump. The response is automatic and not necessarily related to stimuli associated with the original trauma. A patient of mine, a bank teller who was robbed, held hostage, then kidnapped, was not exposed to gunfire or loud sounds during her ordeal. But six month later, she was visibly startled and upset by the rumble of a train near my office.

It is as though the alarm mechanism that warns us of danger is on a hair trigger, easily and erroneously set off. A person lives with so many false alarms that he or she cannot concentrate, cannot sleep restfully, and becomes irritable or reclusive. A normal sex life is difficult with such apprehension. PTSD therefore impairs the enjoyment of intimacy, and this in turn isolates the sufferer from loved ones—the ideal human source of reassurance and respect.

Often, the anxiety takes familiar shapes: panic and agoraphobia. Panic is a sudden, intense state of fear, frequently with no obvious trigger, in which the heart beats rapidly, respirations are quick and shallow, and fingertips tingle. There is lightheadedness. There may be sensations of choking or smothering, and the person feels he or she is dying or going crazy, or both. After a few panic attacks, a person will often suffer agoraphobia, avoiding places such as shopping malls and supermarkets, where an attack would be particularly embarrassing.

Long after he covered the calamity on September 11, 2001, a nationally prominent press photographer had panic attacks whenever he heard an airplane, but only when he was inside a building. He was fine hearing jets overhead outdoors. He had no problem in an enclosed space without the aircraft sound. A particular combination of noise and confinement triggered his PTSD.

PTSD Is Not Always the Same

Thus, PTSD has not only a variety of dimensions and components, but vastly different effects and implications. Some trauma survivors are continually reminded of their victimization and experience relief when they tell details to others. Some survivors are humiliated by their dehumanization or laden with guilt for harming another person. They refuse to discuss details. Some are dazed, moving in and out of trancelike states. Some are full of fear, hypervigilant, easily startled, unable to concentrate, wary of strangers. The syndrome may be evident soon after the trauma or may emerge years later.

Who Gets PTSD?

Most current research shows that the intensity of traumatic events correlates positively with the occurrence of PTSD, but individuals exposed to the same extreme stress will vary in their responses. Heredity may play an important role. Just as some children are born shy and others exhibit a bolder temperament, some of us are born with a brain pattern that keeps horror alive, while others quickly recover. As a varied, interdependent human species, we benefit from our differences. Those with daring fight the tigers. Those with PTSD preserve the impact of cruelty for the rest of us.

I tell patients that there is nothing abnormal about those who suffer. It is, in a statistical sense, a normal reaction to abnormal events. Anyone could develop PTSD given enough trauma. But it also helps to consider PTSD an injury to the functioning of the brain. No one should be denied just compensation for PTSD. It is not merely excessive emotion. It is a significant change in the way the brain manages memory and modulates arousal as a result of extreme experience. People with no prior history of neurological or psychiatric conditions may develop PTSD.

Other Difficulties

Victims of human cruelty (as opposed to victims of natural disasters) experience additional emotional difficulties that are not listed in the official diagnostic manual and are not part of PTSD. Foremost among them is shame. Although violent criminals should feel ashamed, they seldom do. Instead, the victim who has been beaten, robbed, or raped is humiliated. This person has been abruptly dominated, subjugated, stripped of dignity, invaded, and made, in his or her own mind, into a lower form of life.

Who cannot recall being bullied as a child, forced to admit weakness, mortified by the process? As an adult, this shame quickly becomes self-blame: Why was I there? What could I have done differently? Why did I let it happen?

Self-blame may actually be a good sign, correlating with self-reliance and self-regard. But it may also be hostility turned inward, a relentless self-criticism and downward spiral into profound depression.

Hatred is another human emotional response to trauma with no reference in the diagnostic manual. On the path to recovery and possible forgiveness, victims of cruelty are entitled to hate their abusers. But survivors often do less hating than one might expect. Sometimes they are simply grateful to be alive. They may, ironically and paradoxically, love the kidnapper who could have killed them, but instead gave them life. This is called the Stockholm syndrome, named for the bizarre outcome of a crime in Sweden in 1973, when a hostage taker and a bank teller fell in love and had sex in the vault during a siege. Like Patty Hearst and countless others, the teller denied that her assailant was a villain, but responded passionately to his power to spare her life.

It is the Mothers against Drunk Drivers who are "mad." The covictims, the next of kin of the injured and dead, are more often the ones moved to rage and vengeance, if not hatred. Obsessive hatred is a corrosive condition, seldom the focus of psychiatric treatment, but of major concern to historians and journalists.

A Guide to Interviewing

A knowledge of posttraumatic stress disorder is vital to investigators in their understanding of the way victims experience emotional wounds, particularly wounds that are deliberately and cruelly inflicted. A rapidly developing area of clinical science, traumatic stress studies, teaches us that victims of violence have several distinguishable patterns of emotional response. These patterns are easily recognized once their outlines are understood. Seeing the logic in a set of psychological consequences rehumanizes and dignifies a person who may feel dehumanized and robbed of dignity. A sensitive explanation of the traumatic stress response aids recovery. When we as a society pay attention to the victim as he or she heals, we are less likely to be consumed by hate and focused on perpetrators, thereby contributing a contagion of cruelty.

Investigators can interview victims, understand them as multidimensional human beings, and possibly reduce some victims' impulses toward vengeance in the process.

Timing

When interviewers seek a trauma survivor's comments soon after the event, they are very likely to encounter one or more of the emotional states mentioned above. As time passes, emotional composure will increase. But a distorted recollection is also possible, i.e., selective memory and competition from many other interviewers, each with a different agenda, each raising new questions in the mind of the person interviewed. Therefore, even from a psychiatric point of view, no formula for setting the ideal time for a posttraumatic interview exists.

Assume you have access to a clerk who was robbed at gunpoint an hour ago. She appears uninjured. You might begin, "Have you had a chance to discuss this with anyone else?" This tells you where this interview is in the predictable sequence of police investigations, insurance and management inquiries, and conversations with family, friends, and others, including reporters. It also allows you to follow up with questions about those discussions, if they occurred. An interviewee reveals a lot about conversational preferences, when given the chance. For example, he or she might indicate a desire to talk at length, to be brief and to the point, to learn about the incident from you, or to get away from the scene—all in response to an open-ended question such as, "How was the previous discussion for you?"

Then you can set the stage for your interview, having assessed your subject's attitude and emotional state before he or she regards you as responsible for his or her feelings. Have subjects focus on how someone else made them feel.

Consider a very different interview. It is the one-year anniversary of a major catastrophe, such as the Virginia Tech massacre, and you are assigned to interview a survivor who now lives outside of Virginia in your small town. You telephone to arrange a meeting. This story, a year rather than an hour later, will deal with emotions throughout that year and on this anniversary date. The incident is less important than the impact of the incident on one individual through time. The interview may (probably will) cause vivid recollections. Do you mention this over the phone? Or do you assume that agreeing to be interviewed signifies a willingness to revisit painful memories?

The fact that this is an inquiry long after the event gives you more flexibility in arranging the time and place, meeting once or on several occasions. But you, the investigator, may be the cause of emotional injury, since this person was exposed to major traumatic stress and has reached some new adjustment state that you will disrupt. In a way, this is a more delicate, difficult situation.

Setting the Stage

Setting the stage is important regardless of the timing of an interview. A trauma survivor should be approached with respect, neither gingerly nor casually. This is a person who has witnessed and lived through a major event outside normal experience, someone who has something significant to share and who undertakes some reexposure to traumatic memories by talking with you. If you convey respect for this situation, then you are off to a good start.

Consider the possibility that a survivor might be more comfortable at home or might want to be out of the family circle. Some might feel more secure with a friend or relative present. The clerk robbed at gunpoint would probably be encountered first at the convenience store. But if she had the authority to leave or be joined by a friend, you might get more details, more spontaneity, than if you stayed at the scene of the crime. Of course, other professional deadlines might preclude taking an extra hour to learn about the emotional impact of the robbery on your witness/victim. Obviously, if you can remove someone to a comfortable, secluded place, the chance of interruption is reduced and concentration is enhanced.

Interviewing people as a Red Cross volunteer at disaster sites resembles the field conditions investigators encounter. When serving in that capacity, I set the stage as best I can, trying to assess quickly whether a person wants privacy or the proximity of others, and whether the comfort level is greater with the door open or closed. One woman preferred to sit on the floor, surrounded by her soggy belongings, as she sought help at a shelter after the 1994 Northern California floods. This woman was agoraphobic (fearful of crowded public places) before the floods, more so afterward, and I earned her trust by bringing social workers and small business loan specialists to her, rather than having her join the crowd in the busy service center.

To set the stage for an interview, remember that the person may be in a daze, may be numb, may be easily startled, may be hypervigilant, may be confused. But the victim can tell you which setting will suit him or her best. This may require a companion, an open door, and several breaks for self-composure.

Eliciting Emotion

As an interviewer, you can either elicit or avoid emotion. Do you want to see and hear a person's emotional state? Or do you want the individual to describe his or her feelings without displaying them? A person can tell you, "I was very upset, crying all the time, unable to work," or she can sob as she speaks.

Most interviewers would prefer to have their interviewees describe rather than display strong emotions (TV talk show hosts excepted). So would I in initial interviews with trauma survivors. My ultimate objective is to help them master their uncontrolled feelings. Therefore, I usually say that we can, if possible, defer dealing with the full impact of the event until we know each other better, until some progress has been made. I explain how, several weeks hence, we will get to the central part of the traumatic experience. But that is done when I am treating PTSD, by definition a persistent problem of at least a month's duration, with intrusive emotional recollections. At other times, for example, when debriefing Red Cross volunteers, I want to see strong feelings, if they are present, to get them talked out before the volunteer goes home (and to show respect for the person and for his or her emotions). That is the point of the debriefing.

But police investigators are not PTSD therapists or after-incident crisis debriefers. You are interviewing a witness who is a subject of an investigative inquiry. It is not uncommon for tears to flow during the telling of an emotional event. Therapists offer tissues. I usually say, "I'm accustomed to hearing people while they are crying, so don't worry about me." I neither urge nor discourage someone from continuing to talk, but I do try to normalize the situation. Investigators should bring tissues if a tearful interview is anticipated.

When survivors cry during interviews, they are not necessarily reluctant to continue. They may have difficulty communicating, but they often want to tell their stories. Interrupting them may be experienced as patronizing and as being denied an opportunity to testify. Remember, if you terminate an interview unilaterally, because you find it upsetting, or you incorrectly assume that your subject wants to stop, you may be revictimizing the person.

Some people who have suffered greatly, for example, torture victims in Chile, have benefited psychologically from the opportunity to provide testimonials, and the benefits have been substantiated by research.

Members of the Michigan Victim Alliance, who serve as interviewees for the medical and law students at Michigan State University, report some PTSD symptoms afterward (anxiety and intrusive recollections for one or two days), and an overall increase in self-esteem, because their stories have been heard.

Often, the facts are told with considerable depth of feeling. So the issue is not really should you, the interviewer, attempt to control your subjects' emotions, but rather, how you can best facilitate a factual report, a full report, and give your interviewee a sense of respect throughout.

Informed Consent

Should investigators offer the equivalent of a Miranda warning? "You are not a suspect, but your testimony may be needed in court and you may be exposed to publicity and risk." I do not recommend that. But the medical model of informed consent could be adapted for interviews with trauma victims. You might explain: "This procedure—interview and subsequent proceedings—has benefits for the community and may benefit you. Remembering, however, may be painful for you. And your name will be used. You might have some unwanted recollections after we talk and after your story appears in public. In the long run, telling your story to me should be a positive thing. Any questions before we begin?"

Stages of Response

The first set of responses after a shocking event involves the pathways of the autonomic nervous system, connecting the brain, the pituitary gland, the adrenal gland, and various organs of the body. Blood is shunted from the gut to the large muscles. The pupils dilate. The pulse accelerates and the stroke volume of the heart increases.

These physiological changes, shared by all mammals, prepare for fight or flight. We are in a state of readiness for dealing with the threats our ancestors faced on the great plains of Africa: wild beasts, sudden storms, deadly enemies. We are not adapted for fine motor movements or for deep conscious thought. The surge of adrenaline and pounding heart we experience when the car skids on an icy highway do not help us maneuver that piece of machinery. Our danger biochemistry is atavistic. We have to fight these bodily changes as we respond to modern mechanical dangers, such as a high-speed skid.

There are perceptual changes as well. Our focus on a source of danger, be it a wild beast or a pistol pointed at us, is intensified. Objects in our peripheral vision begin to blur, not only a function of the organs of perception, but also the result of how impulses are received, recorded, and analyzed by the brain.

Detectives, doctors, and journalists all know the implications of this phenomenon: details are notoriously distorted except for a few central features, when eyewitnesses report incidents of threat and sudden danger. Sometimes, a powerful threat is prolonged, as in a hostage incident, a kidnapping, some assaults, and rapes. Many natural disasters, a flash flood or hurricane, may place one in mortal danger for hours rather than seconds or minutes. Short, deadly traumas include gunshots, explosions, earthquakes, and fires.

When extreme stress is prolonged (days or weeks), adaptive mechanisms collapse. This is rare. But in animal experiments, mammals suffer hemorrhagic necrosis of the adrenal gland, literally a bloody death of that organ and, soon after, death of the organism itself.

Far more frequently, humans in states of prolonged catastrophic stress enter a second stage of adaptation. Hans Selye, the physiologist whose stress studies guide the modern era, called this a stage of resistance following a stage of shock. Now the organism is in high gear, accustomed to the increased flow of adrenaline, consciously appraising what previously had been grasped automatically.

At this point, a crime victim knows that he or she is a victim, although the person may be thinking, "This can't be happening to me." At this point, details do become evident, particularly to the trained observer. And, in group hostage situations, there is often a ritual calm, when confusion and feelings of threat diminish. This is the time when negotiations may be successful.

Disaster workers recognize a heroic phase, a second stage after the initial bedlam, when all is shock and confusion. In the second stage, people help one another, lives are saved, lost children are found. Hope and exhilaration coexist with fear and grief.

Eventually, there is a return to some equilibrium in the body, the mind, and the community. This may be a time of depression and demoralization: the high-energy condition is gone. There is debris. There is loss. There is pain. Reality sinks in. This is also the time when the press leaves. A survivor who might have been annoyed by too much attention could feel abandoned and forgotten.

Several authors describe stages of impact and recovery after shocking events or disturbing news. Elisabeth Kubler-Ross defined the denial, fear, anger, and eventual acceptance after learning one has a fatal illness. An investigator may want to consider the particular sequence of stages or phases that an interviewee has experienced, where that person is now, and how each stage affects the perception of events.

A discussion of stages may help the interview process, without actually leading the witness. Consider saying, "Sometimes people go through a stage when they act without thinking, when they don't even know what is happening," and you may elicit an interesting narrative. Some people need to be reminded that they acted instinctively. Then they can recall what occurred just before that phase and right afterward.

My patient who was thrown to the floor by the cooler bandit recalled months later that she hid her wedding ring under a shelf, as she lay in the fetal position expecting to be shot. She forgot that particular event during the time that she was experiencing fear and shame and all of the diagnostic PTSD symptoms.

For me, of special note was her instinctive protection of a valuable symbol, her refusal to yield that icon to her assailant. This woman was full of self-blame for not sounding the secret alarm, for behaving like a coward.

Therapy required a diligent search for evidence to the contrary, proof that would convince her. (I was already certain that she had done what any reasonable person would have done to survive an armed robbery.) She recalled hiding her ring as we talked about the instinctive, automatic things that some people do. And she finally agreed that her instincts were correct.

The Humanitarian Role of the Investigator

Investigators and therapists face similar challenges when they realize their subjects are at risk of further injury. Techniques may differ, but objectives are the same: to improve societal health. A therapist is not a lawyer or a security consultant, but a battered woman and an abused child need to know that shelters, restraining orders, and a network of advocates are available. Therapy includes such referrals.

The investigator is not responsible for individual referrals, but could give information about community resources when interviewing individuals who would benefit from them.

Secondary Traumatic Stress Disorder

Investigators are candidates for secondary traumatic stress disorder, an empathic response that affects us, therapists included, when our professional detachment is overwhelmed by certain life events. Images of dead children leave an indelible mark. Firefighters, who would rather not admit they have tender feelings, find themselves vulnerable to the haunting memory of a burnt child or the sight of a tiny form in a body bag.

The sheer numbers of unexpected dead in one place will penetrate the defenses of hardened rescue workers. Plane crashes rank among the most difficult assignments for American Red Cross workers, who normally handle floods, earthquakes, and fires. At an air disaster, there is a concentration of death images that few doctors, nurses, or ambulance drivers have ever seen.

Writing about journalists covering Rwanda, Roger Rosenblatt mused in *The New Republic*:

> Most journalists react in three stages. In the first stage, when they are young, they respond to atrocities with shock and revulsion and perhaps a twinge of guilty excitement that they are seeing something others will never see: life at its dreadful extremes. In the second stage, the atrocities become familiar and repetitive, and journalists begin to sound like Spiro Agnew: if you have seen one loss of dignity and spirit, you've seen them all. Too many journalists get stuck in this stage. They get bogged down in the routineness of the suffering. Embittered, spiteful and inadequate to their work, they curse their bosses back home for not according them respect; they hate the people on whom they report. Worst of all, they don't allow themselves to enter the third stage in which everything gets sadder and wiser; worse and strangely better.[1]

PTSD is now universally accepted as a medical condition, but is not fully comprehended and remains a source of stigma and shame. To be dazed at first, then haunted by horrible memories and made anxious and avoidant is to be part of the human family. When deliberate criminal cruelty is the cause of PTSD, we often neglect the victim and become captives of collective outrage, focusing attention on crime and criminality and those who are to blame. By understanding PTSD, we disarm PTSD. We do not prevent it, but we minimize its degrading, diminishing effects. We help victims become survivors. We help survivors regain dignity and respect.

Endnotes

1. Battle-Scarred Journalists: Rwanda Therapy, Roger Rosenblatt, *The New Republic*, June 6, 1994, p. 16.

Role of the Commander 17

Who's in Charge?

It has been reported historically in many jurisdictions what may be described as the "Battle of the Badges." A competitive spirit often exists between members of the police and fire departments at disaster sites. There have been occasions in New York City that individual officers have engaged in physical combat, at times resulting in arrests. Prior to 9/11, then New York Mayor Rudy Giuliani tried to alleviate that competition by strengthening the Office of Emergency Management (OEM). This was a successor to the mayor's Emergency Control Board that was established to manage major disasters such as explosions, air crashes, blackouts, natural disasters, and building collapses. Giuliani tried to ensure—through communication and information from daily reports required by every city agency that were forwarded to the OEM at the beginning of each day—OEM would be able to coordinate all of the city's resources. Armed with that information, OEM became a formidable player in managing these incidents. It was perceived that this would dampen the friction between the police and fire services. Thereafter, the ranking member of the NYPD was in charge of any emergency or disaster, except a fire. The new OEM, equipped with state-of-the-art facilities, equipment, and communications, was located at 7 World Trade Center (WTC), on an upper floor. It became known via the media as Rudy's bunker.

On September 11, 2001, not only did the two World Trade Center towers fall, but number 7 WTC, housing the offices of OEM, was also totally destroyed. However, in the immediate aftermath of the tragedy, personnel from OEM relocated first to the police academy and later to one of the cruise ship piers on the Hudson River. They were very effective in assisting survivors and their families and assisting staff of the medical examiner in the identification of the missing and recovered remains. They coordinated the collection of material for DNA samples. They have since moved to a semipermanent location in Brooklyn, awaiting the possible construction of a new building nearby.

However, with changes in the city's administration, the effectiveness of OEM as the lead agency of any major terrorist incident has diminished to where its role is primarily to assist and support the police and fire commissioners. Attempts are still being made to delineate which will be the lead agency in any biological, chemical, or nuclear terror incident. Both departments have hazmat-trained people. Traditionally, the fire department has been involved exclusively in fighting fires and rescuing victims. The police department, however, must be concerned not only with the rescues, but also with preserving the crime scene and gathering evidence.

An incident commander may be the designated leader of a special unit charged with specific counterterrorism responsibilities. A commander may also be a ranking officer who finds himself or herself in charge of a situation involving terrorists, even for a short period of time, until the arrival of federal authorities. While specific responsibilities and a course of action vary department to department and agency to agency, the topics of discussion and guidelines for action offered here cover the major options open to both types of command situations. For the leader of a special unit, the responsibilities can be divided into three general areas, determined largely by time sequence:

1. Preincident
2. During the incident
3. Postincident

For the commander who might be thrust into a terrorist situation by virtue of being the duty officer at that moment or because of a particular assignment, the incident or postincident sections of this chapter will be most relevant.

Preincident: Developing Guidelines

Preparing for a confrontation with terrorists or domestic incidents begins with the development of guidelines, including such things as who will take what role and who will perform what functions. These guidelines are the exposition of the department's policy and should be based upon the belief that the preservation of human life is the most important aspect of any situation. This is not a radical statement. Perpetrators can be captured, money, property, or goods can always be recovered, but human life, once taken, can never be retrieved.

To start at the top, the incident commander should be of high enough rank to get things done vis-à-vis other units, yet low enough to still have knowledge of and familiarity with the community being served. In hostage situations, for example, some departments will have the tactical commander in charge of overseeing the hostage negotiations on one hand, as well as supervising the tactical people on the other.

In other departments, and this is our preference, the commander in such situations is the patrol commander. The rationale behind this is that patrol units are closer to the community. Special units (such as SWAT, tactical

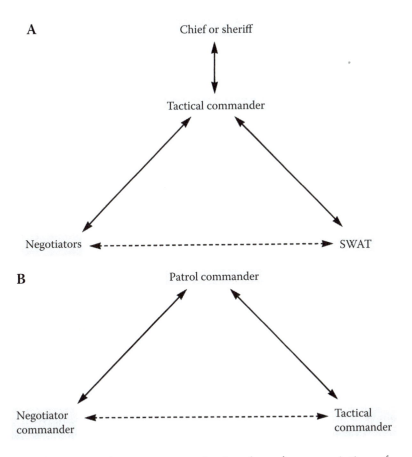

Figure 17.1 Command structure: organization charts for two variations of command structure, depending upon the makeup of the department. The shape of the structure is not as important as the fact that a structure exists, that it is documented, and that it is understood.

units, and hostage negotiating) come in, do their jobs, and leave. The focus is narrowly on the assignment at hand; it is possible to do the job they are assigned, but still leave the patrol people with special problems after they pull out. A patrol commander can make decisions designed to assist the special units, but that reflect sensitivity to the impact on the community. More importantly, however, is that the incident commander is clearly in charge, and even other unit leaders who may have higher rank are subordinate to that person in terms of the situation at hand. Thus (using the New York City Police Department rank structure as an example), a captain who is the incident commander may be outranked by a deputy inspector commanding the tactical unit, but the deputy inspector is "staff" to the incident commander for the duration of the incident. Whatever formula is used must be documented, thereby fixing authority as well as responsibility.

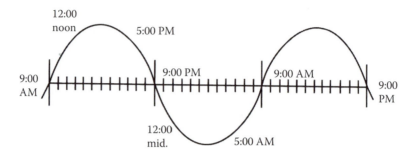

Figure 17.2 Daily biorhythm: the "ups and downs" of daily life are no old wives tale. Most people have performance peaks and valleys on a 12-hour cycle, with a psychological low usually coming in the early hours of the morning, between 4 and 6 A.M.

Makeup of the Team

How a special function unit is structured is not as important as the fact that there is some kind of structure. It is imperative that everyone know who is in charge, and somewhere it is delineated exactly who has what authority and what responsibilities. The operational guidelines should be just that, guidelines, and not a step-by-step formula or lockstep prescription for action. It is also important to develop mutual aid agreements with other agencies in the region that provide various services, because many departments are too small or under budgetary restrictions that prevent any one of them from having all emergency capabilities. Some police departments have disbanded their SWAT teams. This has been done for various reasons, some for budgetary problems and others because of liability losses in lawsuits. The city of Pittsburgh, for instance, disbanded its SWAT team after a person was kidnapped from a church and later killed by the kidnapper before backup teams could respond.

Some jurisdictions have established regional hostage recovery programs with two or three persons who are drawn from the various departments in the region and are assigned to the combined agency task force. They have regular training programs in which they become familiar with the guidelines, program, and equally important, each other. Teamwork and familiarity, particularly in life-and-death situations, build the confidence and trust necessary to accomplish the basic mission. A major recognition is that although several different departments in a county or a region may be involved in an incident, the jurisdiction in which the incident occurs is the one whose commander takes charge; all units, regardless of jurisdiction, follow his or her orders.

Maintenance of Manpower and Equipment

It is the responsibility of the commander to constantly monitor and maintain the strength of the special unit and the support equipment it needs. In smaller departments, this may mean a continuous updating of mutual aid agreements with agencies in contiguous jurisdictions. Equipment concerns should include availability of bullet-resistant garments and helmets (above and beyond the type utilized on normal patrol activities), the proper weapons and ammunition, and radio communications equipment with hands-free mouth- and earpiece capability that affords some amount of privacy so perpetrators at the scene of an incident are not privy to police communication.

Not all the equipment needs to be sophisticated and expensive. Night-viewing equipment would be welcome, but so are flashlights, periscopes, mirrors, and even mundane objects such as wedges and ropes to secure or maintain control of doors. Much of this equipment, if budget justifications are a concern, can be used in other police functions, but the problem here is that they must be available when an emergency situation occurs and not in the back of a car belonging to someone who has gone fishing for two weeks.

Maintenance of equipment is extremely important, from a functional and safety standpoint for your officers, but also from a vicarious liability standpoint because lawyers will pounce on the fact that a single piece of equipment may not have been in working order. Replacing batteries in equipment immediately after using it ensures its readiness when the next incident comes up unexpectedly.

Keeping Up-to-Date on New Developments and Strategies

In terms of training the operatives, if there are enough incidents for the department to deal with, then only refresher training after the initial immersion period would be needed, in addition to some periodic critiquing and evaluation. However, in departments where these special units may not be greatly utilized, say only once or twice a year, training should be required on a regular basis, at least quarterly, and preferably once a month.

Retraining, updating, in-service training—however it is referred to—is never wasted. Weapons training for such situations results in greater control of firepower in everyday situations. Drills in hostage negotiations also can serve as aids in routine interrogation procedures. There is a spillover of specialized training into everyday assignments. We need to remember that we live in a litigious society where people bring lawsuits for the least slight or injury, especially when it comes to suing a municipality with supposedly deep pockets. So in addition to whatever training is given to keep officers current, that same training may also help defend against potential exposure to vicarious liability lawsuits.

How much training should be offered? Although this begs the question, the only real answer is as much as is necessary. All too often, hostage situations and kidnappings are covered in the initial training, but nothing is offered in the way of refresher or updated courses. Such training is needed, particularly when the specialized unit does not get to handle many incidents during the course of the year. The training is important not only for the individual officers involved, but also for the coordination of the tactical, communications, and other units involved. The training does not have to be in the form of classroom lectures. The use of tactical people, for example, can be based on simulated reenactments of recent kidnap or hostage incidents elsewhere. Negotiators can keep their communications and sensitivity receptors fine-tuned by working suicide or other crisis telephone hotlines. In addition, there are numerous seminars and training courses available through the federal government as well as private institutions and consulting groups. Attending these sessions is also an excellent way to network and garner intelligence in an informal manner.

An important note to remember is that training sessions must be documented as to who did the training, what kind of training it was, how long it lasted, etc. This documentation is needed primarily in the event of lawsuits, where trial lawyers on discovery proceedings will rip into training methods, procedures, and quality of training for police officers involved in a particular incident. More importantly, if follow-up training is not provided, then the hostage recovery team will be a special unit in name only.

Evaluate and Update

In evaluating members of the team, remember that some people may look good on paper and may even train well, but may not operate at the anticipated level of performance. Likewise, some individuals may experience burnout in a relatively short period of time, while others may function well for years, growing in the job as they gain experience. It is the responsibility of the commander to make personnel changes whenever necessary. Some departments have specified time limits for tours of duty in special units, usually two or three years, with officers transferred out automatically. The problem with this approach is that no one on the job has more than two or three years' experience, and conversely, there are a lot of well-trained, experienced people out there doing other police jobs.

A unit such as a hostage negotiating team or bomb squad is a voluntary assignment. Whenever an individual leaves, whether by choice or by commander's decision, the transfer should be made without prejudice. As volunteers, all team members should know they can leave, or be asked to leave, at any time without a negative evaluation landing in their personnel folders.

Liaisons with Other Agencies

The commander of a special unit should establish and maintain telephone contact, written communication, e-mail, social media, or face-to-face dialogue with various agencies, including, but not limited to, the Federal Bureau of Investigation, state police, and other police departments in cities the same size or larger in order to establish a line of communication prior to an incident. Depending upon the nature of the special unit and the constituent profile of the department's jurisdiction, it also may be necessary to develop dialogue with appropriate personnel in various state agencies, i.e., corrections department, university systems, the Department of Homeland Security and its various agencies, the Federal Aviation Administration, the Army Corps of Engineers, the Department of Energy's nuclear energy bureaus, the Department of State, various military police, etc.

The reason for developing these contacts is to gain intelligence and information regarding jurisdictional line of authority before a situation develops that then must be implemented during an emergency situation. The commander would know then that in an airport incident, the agency operating the terminal is in control if the incident is in a public area of the terminal. If the incident occurs in the airport operations area (i.e., in a location between security screening and the aircraft), the FBI has jurisdiction. If the incident is on an aircraft itself and the doors of the plane have not been closed, the FBI is still in charge. Once the aircraft doors have been shut, however, it becomes the Transportation Security Agency's (TSA) responsibility. In practical terms, the TSA does not have much of a law enforcement arm and will usually defer to the FBI, so the FBI remains functioning and active, but coordinates its actions with the TSA. Even then, although the FBI is running things, many times the local police department will be the first called to take up containment positions.

The scope of maintaining liaisons should be expanded to include other police departments, law enforcement agencies, enforcement arms of civilian agencies, and non-law enforcement government agencies, such as the fire, building, sanitation, and traffic and highway departments. Contacts in private industry are also important and should include security people at the electric, gas, and telephone companies, as well as the operators (private, municipal, or quasi-governmental) of airports, docks, and harbors, and even bus and train depots, since these are favored terrorist targets. Private security also affords another aid to the investigation process through the use of video surveillance or closed-circuit television (CCTV). There has been a great increase in the use of video surveillance by private concerns to monitor security on their premises. One such example involving a counterterrorist investigation was in the bombing of the Alfred P. Murrah Federal Building in Oklahoma City on April 19, 1995. A surveillance camera from a building across the street actually videotaped the truck used to carry the bomb as it drove up to the scene. Though the image was grainy, it was helpful in the investigation. Since the time of those grainy black-and-white pictures, much advancement has been made in the quality of video images. Many of these improvements were in direct response to the needs of private sector businesses such as banks and the gaming industry in Las Vegas and Atlantic City and elsewhere around the country. Optical devices and capabilities developed for military use have also contributed to enhancing video surveillance capabilities.

In investigating an incident, or even in developing a security plan for a site or facility, a survey of locations where surveillance systems and individual cameras are located can be very worthwhile. The information gathered should include the names and home telephone numbers of whom to contact on a 24-hour basis. The list of potential emergency situations is virtually endless. So it is important to include everything from how to cut off power into a building (or needing to know where underground pipelines are), to how to obtain building plans for a location, to how to have airport nightlights turned on or off with short notice. For instance, a simple thing like a telephone in a room with a hostage taker and his victims could play havoc with police efforts. The news media may be able to contact the hostage taker, or worse yet, he could initiate calls to the media, broadcasting his demands live. Knowing whom to contact in order to have that phone line disconnected in a timely manner forces the hostage taker to communicate with the police or negotiator. In these days of wireless communications, knowing who can do what is a bigger challenge, but no less important.

During the Incident: Intelligence Gathering

Another of the primary functions of the commander during an incident is to make sure that intelligence is being gathered. This information must be shared with the negotiator as well as the tactical and patrol people on a need-to-know basis. Communication is essential; information gathered but not communicated to the people who need it is worthless information. Initial intelligence gathering should seek to uncover the number of perpetrators, number and types of weapons, number of hostages, and location of the perpetrators and hostages. Then you want to know what precipitated the incident.

Personal information on the perpetrators and victims should include physical descriptions, medical history, and psychological backgrounds. Finally, as much information as possible should be gleaned on the physical location where the hostages are being held: floor plans; location and type of windows; door and emergency exits; height of ceiling; the heating, ventilation, and air conditioning (HVAC) system; what is above and below the location; etc.

A note of caution: Be wary of descriptions that involve only clothing. First, people can change or be forced to change clothing. Second, color perceptions vary widely from one person to another. One person's turquoise is another person's blue and a third person's green. Clothing descriptions alone should be avoided, particularly in target selection for sharpshooters.

At a major incident in which many innocent victims may be involved, it is inevitable that relatives and family members will begin arriving at the scene. Rather than having them mill around or wander off to restaurants or who knows where, it is wiser to set aside a building (or part of a building, or obtain a van or bus) and direct the relatives inside, providing them with coffee, and have detectives begin the systematic gathering of information. The last thing you want is some distraught relative being interviewed by a television or radio journalist whose broadcast could be monitored by the hostage taker. Having them all in a bus would ease transporting them to a police facility for reunions with their relatives once the hostages are released.

Evaluate Alternatives

Before deciding upon a course of action, it is imperative that the commander has as much intelligence as possible. The choice, then, can be reduced to four alternatives:

1. Rescue/dynamic entry
2. Sharpshooters
3. Chemical agents
4. Contain and negotiate

Originally, when we established the courses of action, we used the term *assault*. However, the term, especially used by plaintiff's attorneys in civil litigation, was also characterized as a crime. Law enforcement people should never be perceived as committing crimes. Though it may seem to be just a matter of semantics, it can be significant in court testimony. If there is a hostage, we can use the term *rescue*. If there are no hostages, just a barricade, then we call the action a *dynamic* entry.

One of the most dramatic rescues in recent memory took place in Lima, Peru. The incident started in late December 1996 at a diplomatic Christmas

Party at the Japanese Embassy. Shortly after the function started, members of MRTA, known as the Shining Path, disguised as wait staff, produced automatic weapons and explosives. They took almost 500 guests at the party hostage. Local law enforcement officers were the first to respond to the report of gunfire and the first to become aware of what had taken place. Within the first hour, the local police and MRTA arranged for the release of almost 400 hostages, persons whom the captors deemed unimportant. The demand of the terrorists was for a release of a number of their colleagues from Peruvian prisons. Negotiations continued for over four months, with everyone from the Red Cross to representatives of the media to church officials to family representatives of wealthy hostages getting involved. Peru's president, Alberto Fujimori, maintained a hard line, refusing to negotiate with the hostage takers. During the period of the ordeal, a tremendous amount of intelligence was garnered. Many listening devices were introduced into the compound in various manners. The number and description of the perpetrators and their routines were ascertained from some of the released hostages. During the protracted negotiations, the Peruvian government crafted an elaborate plan to carry out a rescue. One of the more novel aspects included digging an earthen tunnel to an inside garden area of the compound. Amazingly, the security of this information was maintained without any leaks to the media. One afternoon, while the perpetrators were playing their usual post-midday-meal soccer game in the embassy ballroom, the rescue was mounted by the Peruvian army. Amid the explosion of the flash bangs and the gunfire, the rescue of the hostages was effected, but not without casualties. In addition to the 14 perpetrators who were killed, 1 hostage and 2 soldiers also died in the rescue. In this instance it was a military operation, and in military operations, there are acceptable casualty rates. Thus, the operation was considered a success. In police operations, however, there is no acceptable casualty rate other than zero.

Overall, the rescue/dynamic entry option is an extremely risky one. The Rand Corporation has determined that between 75% and 80% of hostages killed in hostage incidents are killed during a rescue attempt, some of which have been disastrous. On January 31, 1980, at the Spanish Embassy in Guatemala City, Guatemala, 33 terrorists disguised as peasants took over the embassy, holding 8 individuals hostage, including the Spanish ambassador. Although the Spanish government pleaded with the Guatemalan authorities not to assault, an assault was mounted. A Molotov cocktail exploded, and in the ensuing fire and police assault, 32 of the 33 terrorists and 7 of the 8 hostages died. Only one terrorist and the Spanish ambassador survived. (The terrorist was subsequently abducted from the hospital and hanged in the public square.)

There is another potential problem area involving rescue attempts. Should the perpetrators sense that an assault is near, or if capitulation is possible, there may be a last-ditch effort to escape. Commotion and confusion could be created by "stampeding" the hostages, with the hostage takers trying to escape by blending in with the crowd. One response to this tactic that has been successfully employed is for the police to herd everybody into a large bus and transport the group to a secure area, such as a police facility, where the victims can be separated from their captors. Care must be taken because the terrorists may have already been singled out by their former victims, and may require police protection to save them from beatings and physical assault at the hands of the erstwhile captives.

There is one other consideration that should be made prior to going in on a rescue attempt. Make absolutely sure that there is a hostage inside. If not, it may be a simple barricade situation, which is a major difference. If hostages are involved, the police are expected to take greater risks to protect the lives of those innocent third parties. If there are no hostages and only a perpetrator who may be heavily armed, the best option is to wait him out. There is no reason to risk the safety and well-being of police officers unless the possibility of a suicide attempt exists. Police cannot just stand by if the perpetrator is bleeding to death.

One option that can be exercised in barricaded situations is to have less experienced negotiators use the incident for practice. If the negotiator makes a mistake in psychological procedure, no innocent person will get hurt. It would be best, however, not to call the effort practice, particularly in the presence of media representatives, who can be extremely hostile and make the police appear insensitive in their dealings with the barricaded perpetrators.

Sharpshooters

The decision to employ a sharpshooter requires highly reliable intelligence. Realistically, this is sniper fire; we refrain from using that terminology since the word *sniper* has a pejorative connotation in the public's perception. Sharpshooters should never be used to just kill the perpetrators, but rather to stop them, the fact that a perpetrator may die notwithstanding. Sharpshooters shoot to stop, not to kill. The intent is to stop the bad guys from doing whatever they are doing that is life threatening to the officers or innocents.

Prior to giving orders to shoot, it is important to remember the rules for target identification. More than one instance has occurred in which sharpshooters selected hostages mistaken for perpetrators. Even if everything goes right, the sharpshooter could miss, or there could be a miscalculation in the number of perpetrators. If the sharpshooters have taken good cover, there should be no need to return fire and further endanger the hostages should the hostage takers begin to exchange fire.

There are times when sharpshooters should definitely hold their fire. For example, if a person says he has a bomb, treat him as though he has a bomb. There was a case involving a bank robber in Kenora, Canada, in which the perpetrator passed a note to the teller saying he was carrying a bomb, in addition to being armed with a pistol and long gun. The bank robber wired himself with a pressure release switch in the form of a spring-action clothes-pin that he held open with his mouth in order to keep the contact points from closing. The note the robber passed explained that if he were shot, the clothespin would close, making contact and detonate the bomb. When the robber exited the bank using an unarmed constable to carry the money, a sharpshooter who did not believe it was an actual improvised explosive device fired and hit the bank robber. Unfortunately, the bomb was real and exploded, blowing thousands of dollars all over the area. Fortunately, the constable was only injured and not killed in the explosion, sustaining leg injuries and a loss of hearing.

Another bank robber, this one in Helsinki, Finland, claiming to be armed with a bomb, went mobile with three hostages. After a wild chase that ensued for nearly 100 miles, the perpetrator's car was stopped. Two hostages managed to escape, and the police opened fire on the vehicle. Seconds later, the car exploded with the perpetrator and one hostage inside. Most of the time, when a perpetrator says he has a bomb, it turns out to be hoax or a fake explosive device. However, that one time when there is a bomb, people can and have gotten hurt or been killed.

Many departments or police officers are afraid of being embarrassed by letting a perpetrator brandishing an infernal device tie up a community and a good portion of the police force for hours, only to have the criminal laugh as he tosses his practice grenade or harmless mock-up aside. Remember, it is easier for the police to live with embarrassment, since embarrassment doesn't kill. An IED can.

Assessments of improvised explosive devices should be made only by bomb squad personnel. With apologies to Gertrude Stein, a bomb is a bomb, until proven otherwise.

Chemical Agents

Intelligence is also important before a decision can be made to employ chemical agents, such as tear gas. Medical background on the hostages, for example, would determine whether any of them have allergies or breathing problems. Intelligence would also indicate if infants or small children are being held. Because of children's lung capacity, the mean lethal dose of a chemical agent (i.e., the amount of agent that would preclude oxygen from the system to sustain life) is much less than that for adults. Even in situations where participants are barricaded and have a variety of equipment, including gas masks, as in Waco Texas, with the Branch Davidians, it is not likely that there would be masks for children. A survey of chemical agent mask manufacturers in the United States revealed that none of them produced masks for children. The author's only experience is seeing children's masks was in Israel during the Persian Gulf War in 1991 and, reportedly, in England during World War II.

Information on the location could reveal there is volatile material or a volatile atmosphere inside that could be ignited by hot chemicals, or the agent could be rapidly dispersed by the building's ventilation system into other critical areas. There is also the possibility (more likely when it is a well-planned terrorist operation) that the perpetrators may have gas masks.

Use of a chemical agent, though intended to be nonlethal, can very nearly be the equivalent of using deadly physical force. Chemical agents come in various compounds, e.g., CS, CN, and Mace. Each has specific characteristics. For example, CS may be more nauseating and disorienting than CN; however, it is more difficult to decontaminate an area where CS has been used. Compounds such as CS and CN can be delivered in a variety of ways, including projectiles of various calibers, grenades, and large-area canisters to broadcast the agent more widely. The decision as to which delivery system to use will depend upon the location, distance, and type of structure, and possibly other physical characteristics. The form of agents delivered can also vary. Mace, for example, is usually in a liquid form, consisting of 1% CN and other components that could be squirted or streamed at the subject. It should be noted that the 9/11 hijackers on American Flight 11 used Mace to incapacitate crew members and passengers in the takeover of that airliner. CS and CN can be delivered as a vapor ignited by a burning pyrotechnic. These substances can also be micro-pulverized and released as a fine dust or powder. If a hot gas is involved, the fire department should be on alert and on the scene, because chemical agent projectiles can and have started fires. Another chemical agent option is oleo capstan, or pepper spray, which can be carried on the belt of responding officers and used in less than the lethal range of the force compendium. However, make sure that the suspension medium is not alcohol based. One agency, after spraying an emotionally disturbed person with capstan, which at the time had an alcohol base, then used a Taser gun to stun the subject. A resulting spark ignited the alcohol and immolated the person, killing him. Ambulances should also be readily available for those affected by the chemicals.

Delivery of chemical agents should be done with care since this aspect of the operation can cause special problems. Being struck with a projectile can kill or seriously injure a hostage. There are times when a subject may be under the influence of drugs, alcohol, or just adrenalin. When the chemical agent is introduced, the subject may be able to physically withstand more agent than his body can handle medically. Too much agent can coat the alveoli of the lungs, inhibiting the exchange of carbon dioxide and oxygen in the bloodstream, precipitating moisture, and possibly inducing chemical pneumonia.

Food

When sending in food, don't send in ready-made meals. Rather than sending in a dozen sandwiches, for example, send in a couple of pounds of lunch meat; two loaves of bread; jars of mustard, mayonnaise, and ketchup; pickles and all the trimmings; along with some plastic utensils. The idea is create a party atmosphere, with the people inside interacting with one another. It is less likely that a hostage taker will harm a hostage after interactive circumstances such as these.

Another thing to keep in mind when sending in food is that a great ritual should be made of getting food to the location. The negotiator should never deliver it personally, nor should anyone else since there is always the possibility of becoming another hostage. Rather, the negotiator should be viewed by the hostage taker as going to great pains and effort to get the food to the location. *Never* place the food on the floor, since the hostage taker could react extremely negatively seeing food placed before him as it would be placed before a dog.

The question of sending in food laced with sedatives or some other type of drug is a more serious one. The obvious reason this should be avoided is that it might kill somebody: an innocent hostage might eat the doped food. As long as everyone's medical history is not known and drug dosages are unpredictable in their effects on people, it would be best to not tempt fate. Even anesthesiologists working one-on-one in hospitals sometimes lose patients, and there are side effects to drugs. In one incident that involved a 55-year-old man who was holding a 5-year-old child hostage for more than 24 hours, a ranking officer, noticing that the perpetrator had requested and received some beer, but had not given any to the child, went to a nearby hospital with a six-pack of beer. He explained the situation to a doctor, who told the chief to empty about an ounce and a half of beer from each bottle. The doctor replaced it with a mixture that he assured the chief "would knock out an elephant for 20 hours" without any serious side effects. The chief returned to the scene of the incident with the six-pack, which he placed in a refrigerator for future use. The refrigerator was in a residential apartment adjacent to the command post for the incident. The chief directed an officer to watch the beer, but failed to communicate what was taking place. Half an hour later, when the chief went to retrieve the beer, three bottles were missing, apparently purloined by two tactical officers and a negotiator when the officer watching the beer went to relieve himself. When the chief indicated the beer was spiked, the three officers good-naturedly admitted they took the beer. The chief ordered all three of them to be driven home, lest the doctored beer take effect while driving themselves home. The result of the incident was (1) the beer was not served to the perpetrator, (2) none of the officers were knocked out, and (3) two of the officers reported back on the aphrodisiac power of the adulterated beer.

When South Moluccan terrorists took over a school in the Netherlands, they held a small group of teachers and 150 children hostage. On the second or third day of the incident, all the children got diarrhea. The Dutch authorities said overcrowding had caused the condition. One could speculate, however, that mild laxatives that affected only the children might have been introduced into food that was sent in for the group. In any event, the terrorists released the children rather than deal with that smelly situation directly.

Alcohol and Drugs

The question of whether beer, wine, or spirits should be sent in depends upon the circumstances. Intelligence here is very critical. If it is learned from family or friends that when the perpetrator drinks, he becomes belligerent or nasty, under no circumstances should alcohol be provided. If, however, intelligence indicates the subject gets mellow or sleepy when drinking, the negotiator has the option of bargaining for hostages in exchange for the drink. There is also a chance that the perpetrator will be partying while the hostage abstains.

Should negotiators drink? Probably not, but there may be circumstances when sharing a drink or a bottle can give the negotiator an advantage or some control over the situation. When in doubt, leave it out.

If a hostage taker asks for controlled substances such as heroin or cocaine, it is easy to turn down the request on the grounds that the police department does not deal in drugs. However, the refusal has to be stated in a way that does not say no to a request. As far as pharmaceuticals are concerned, such as methadone for an addict in a rehabilitation program, this would be acceptable, but only with approval of the perpetrator's drug counselor or the physician at the scene.

Contain and Negotiate

The alternative courses of action discussed above are all violent and irreversible. Once started, they cannot be stopped. An alternate is to contain the incident, using barriers and tactical people to confine the perpetrator(s) in the smallest practical area, and then negotiate in an effort to bring about a resolution without harm to anyone. One of the prime advantages of this strategy is that it provides time. Time can be used to gather intelligence, deploy forces, and weigh options. Any of the first three alternatives is still open to the commander even after the perpetrators have been contained and negotiations have begun. Time also works on the police side in that biological functions are constantly at work. People—even well-prepared terrorists—get thirsty, become hungry, and grow tired. Toilet functions impose themselves. All these factors work in the favor of police.

Impact of the Events on the Public

The commander should be aware of the potential effect a particular incident could have on both the community at large and the police department itself. One dramatic example of this occurred in a 1985 Philadelphia incident involving the radical group known as MOVE. Members of this group barricaded themselves inside a house, and after several months of confrontation, the decision to evict was made by authorities. After a long day of siege in which various attempts were made to remove them, including the use of fire department water towers, the decision was made to use chemical agents. In order to effectively place the chemical agent within the compound, the procedural plan called for breaching the roof using an explosive charge. The explosive charge that was dropped from a helicopter was blown onto a low wall dividing the buildings by the aircraft's propeller wash. Thus, the explosive force did breach the roof, but it also ignited a container of gasoline that had been stored on the roof, touching off a roaring fire. Another decision was made to let the fire burn and ensure that the hole in the roof would be large enough to allow the entry of the chemical agent. Unfortunately, the fire burned out of control, eventually destroying the building and approximately 60 other houses in a two-block area.

All the personal possessions, keepsakes, mementos, and other irreplaceable items of the families in the neighborhood were destroyed. The wrath of the affected public shifted away from the MOVE radicals and was redirected toward the police and city government. Although this incident was precipitated by the failure of other city departments, particularly social welfare agencies, the situation was finally thrust into the laps of the police. The outcome had a devastating effect on both the department and the community at large. The police department lost its credibility, and the police commissioner resigned in the wake of the incident.

Subsequently, it was learned that an inquiry had been made of a demolition company about whether or not its crane and iron ball would be effective in opening a hole in the roof of the building in question. The answer was yes, it would be effective, but the cost of the effort would have been $7,500 to cover labor and insurance costs to the contractor. Philadelphia city officials decided not to spend that much money, and the rest is history, with the result that millions of dollars had to be spent for physical rehabilitation of the area. No price has been set on the personal and psychological damage resulting from the incident.

In New York City, as a result of a liaison between the city police department and the local gas and electric utility, Consolidated Edison, at any explosion, building collapse, or other disaster, a Con Ed crane or other heavy equipment will be moved to the scene, usually within the hour, to provide whatever assistance is required. The utility stipulated that the tools can be used only in a rescue effort, not for law enforcement purposes.

Postincident Debriefing

Once an incident ends and the paperwork is finished, the commander should debrief as quickly as possible. Prior to the formal debriefing, however, an informal session should be held. This is simply a couple of hours with negotiators and key tactical people sitting around a restaurant or table or other informal setting, talking about the events that just transpired. At the very least, such a session helps relieve the stress created by the incident, and at best, the conversation will have a cathartic effect on the individuals involved. In the early days of the NYPD negotiating team, it was noted that if a hostage incident ended very late and each member of the team went directly home or back to regular duty, certain physical effects became apparent. Some experienced nausea, insomnia, loss of appetite, or sexual dysfunction. It was also reported that two officers sustained heart attacks—one while negotiating, the other shortly after returning to his home. It was further noted that under similar circumstances, members of the hostage negotiating team would call in with related aliments.

Quite by accident, it was discovered that if all the individuals concerned with any one incident retired to a bar or restaurant, these symptoms failed to appear or were very mild. Alcohol was not a major factor, since some of the officers eschewed beer or drink in favor of coffee or a soft drink. This could be viewed as a group therapy session, and participants should understand that it is primarily stress management. Even if overtime pay is a concern for the officers involved, the cost to the department will still be less than having some of the officers call in sick for a day or two.

After a major incident, the negotiator will be on a high, perceiving celebrity status as a result of news interviews and television appearances. Following this high, however, there will almost inevitably be a period of mild depression as the boredom of everyday routine and reality reimposes itself.

The negotiator, in fact, may be waiting for the next opportunity to star, while fellow officers may begin to exhibit resentment and jealousy. This reaction is something that negotiating team members must be told about, so they can anticipate and deal with it when it occurs. This is where a mental health professional with the operation can be most helpful in easing the pressures on everyone involved, reassuring them that these feelings are normal and represent just another challenge to be dealt with.

Formal Debriefing

Within 48 hours of the end of the incident, the commander should oversee a more formal debriefing, which should include all police officers who participated in the incident. Problems could arise, however, if too many persons of different ranks are involved. For example, a police officer may be reluctant to say that a ranking officer, contrary to regulations, was in the inner perimeter without a bulletproof vest. This could present particular problems if the ranking officer were in the room at the same time. It is probably wiser to have officers of two ranks, police officers and sergeants, lieutenants and captains, etc., participating in the same debriefing session. Later, representatives from each group can prepare the debriefing report.

During the debriefing, deficiencies should be noted, whether they are deficiencies in tactics, intelligence, equipment, or manpower. This is the essence of the debriefing: to provide information that will enable the unit to perform more efficiently during the next incident. This is the way the session should be conducted, as quickly as possible afterwards. In addition, everyone involved should be aware that the debriefing will take place so that they have some time to give the matter some thought and make notes, if necessary. A concern not to be taken lightly is the question of whether or not a debriefing should be recorded. Obviously there will be an official report, but whether or not the remarks and observations of the participants are recorded verbatim is really a policy decision for the commander of the negotiator, whether the chief or commissioner. On the one hand, the raw material will always be available for reference and reinterpretation. On the other hand, the existence of a written transcript could encourage trial lawyers to subpoena the material in lawsuits that may grow out of the incident. Once officers become aware of the possibility of court appearances and legal ramifications, they may be reluctant to provide a free and open discussion during the debriefing session.

Evaluate New Developments and Outcomes

There is something of an amorphous responsibility that basically involves the commander's responsibility to rate new products and techniques that may have been used during an incident. If a new containment configuration was employed, or a different negotiating tactic tried, it is the commander's job to gauge its success and effectiveness, as well as any deficiencies, either potential or real, of the method vis-à-vis prior procedures. It is also important to keep on top of new developmental procedures being used by other departments, and whether or not they may be appropriate for incorporation into the local department's guidelines.

Case History: Russian Theater Takeover

On the evening of Wednesday, October 23, 2002, a performance of *Nord-Ost,* a children's play inspired by a popular book about Arctic explorers, was taking place at the auditorium of the Moscow Cultural Center. It was a cold and drizzly night when the play was disrupted during the second act by a group of armed Chechen nationals carrying out a takeover of the theater and its almost 800 attendees and actors. Not only were the terrorists armed with firearms, but many also had improvised explosive devices strapped about their bodies. The perpetrators have been referred to in various newspapers and television reports as "terrorists," "armed dissidents," "criminals," and "freedom fighters," depending upon the political views of the reporters. Whichever designation was used by the media, there is no doubt that these Chechens were engaging in a truly terrorist action, the taking of men, women, and as might be expected at this performance, a large number of children with the threat of injury and death to further their cause.

The captors gathered their quarry from the stage and from some of the other halls of the cultural center and had all of them sit in the theater audience seats. The Chechens numbered approximately 50; 18 of them were said to have been women. We use the term *approximately* because it was initially reported that there were 54 militants involved. Later reports indicated that 50 of the hostage takers had been killed during the rescue efforts on the third day of the standoff. The Russian media said that the local police had reported two terrorists had been captured, and two had made an escape during the confusion. No further reports of prisoners or escapees were forthcoming from the media or Federal Security Service (FSB), the domestic successor to the KGB. The FSB was also the government agency responsible for the recovery operation to free the hostages. There were no confirmations of any living prisoners or escapees.

The Associated Press reported on January 25, 2003, that Russian police had detained three Chechens in the city of Penza on suspicion of being involved with the theater takeover. Penza is located about 300 miles southeast of Moscow. The Interfax news agency had reported that a local police official said that the three Chechens had been under surveillance since their arrival shortly after the takeover. Their actual participation or their presence at the theater has never been confirmed.

It was reported in November 2003 that a Moscow policeman was taken into custody on charges of supplying "official registration" in Moscow for one of the Chechens involved in the *Nord-Ost* theater takeover. The officer was charged with bribe taking and "abuse of office." The investigation of the takeover was ongoing well into 2004.

Panic Reaction

One young woman hostage was reported killed during the first few hours of the takeover. Barring any information to the contrary, it would appear that this killing took place during the panic phase, the beginning of the hostage taking. (The panic reaction is discussed in greater detail in Chapter 5.) After that incident, no other person would be harmed for two days. On two different occasions, "intruders" (those who had entered the theater) had passed police lines. Each of the intruders would be killed by the hostage takers. Later, a few hours before the deadline that had been established by the terrorists, one of the hostages, a man who was a heavy smoker with a nervous nature, apparently succumbed to the tension and stress and seemed to have a breakdown. Some of the hostages who survived the ordeal reported that he jumped up and started shouting and scrambling over people and seatbacks. As he was making for an exit, the Chechen gunman shouted at him to stop. One raised a weapon and fired. The distraught man was shot in the eye. The bullet continued on, wounding a female hostage and just missing one of the Chechen women dissidents whose body was fitted with explosives. The Chechens arranged for the wounded woman's release after requesting an ambulance. They released her so that she would be able to indicate that her being shot was an accident, and they were not executing the hostages. This killing would not seem to have indicated a depraved attitude of the hostage takers at that time. The killing was not part of the deadline that they had established along with their threats to kill hostages. Remember, once a hostage is killed on a deadline, all meaningful negotiation is over and a move to the more parochial tactical phase has to be implemented. Usually if a hostage is killed purposefully, the hostage takers will display the body to underscore their resolve. Sending it out of the building in a dramatic fashion to shock the authorities and the public at large is a frequent tactic.

Who

The perpetrators were Chechens, who have been in open conflict with the Russians since 1994. Reportedly as a result of the breakup of the old Soviet Union, the Chechens wanted an independent state. The war had been carried out in two phases. From 1994 until 1999, about 10,000 Russian soldiers were killed, as were approximately 80,000 Chechens. Thousands and thousands of civilians were forced from their homes and took refuge in neighboring Georgia. Much of the country was decimated during the almost decade of war. The war had ground down to a few terrorist encounters and kidnappings from time to time. When Vladimir Putin became acting president after Boris Yeltsin's resignation, in 1999, Putin launched an all-out war. Part of Putin's campaign for election included that he would put an end to the Chechen terrorism.

Negotiations at the Theater

Russia, in dealing with the perpetrators it considered a threat to national security, said it would not negotiate with them. This is a stance that most governments assume when faced with an international terrorism crisis. However, in the area of international diplomacy, "talking" might not be considered negotiating. National governments cannot appear to be weak or look foolish when dealing with a national crisis like this, or in addressing the demands of perpetrators. Local police agencies or police negotiators many times will take verbal abuse from perpetrators as a means of demonstrating the negotiator's concern for the well-being of the perpetrator as well as the hostage. In the two days of desperate negotiations or talking, the hostage takers had but one demand. The demand was for Russia to end the war and to pull its troops out of Chechnya. The Russians officials made only one offer. The offer was that they would let the hostage takers live if the hostages were released. Briefs filed in subsequent lawsuits indicate that two senior government officials had entered the building in attempts to obtain the release of the hostages. Early on, some of the younger children were released by the hostage takers.

Some additional negotiations that were very tense were carried out by journalists. They were able to communicate with the perpetrators and hostages over the many cell phones that the hostages had with them in the theater. Many hostages also communicated with their families, until the cell phone batteries started to fail. One journalist-negotiator, Anna Politkovskaya, felt that even though the perpetrators had set a deadline, there was a chance to reach an agreement. She told a radio station in an interview the day after the rescue effort, "It seemed to me that all options to release the hostages had not yet been exhausted that night."

Tactical Preparations

After the initial takeover, the FSB contained the area and evacuated the other parts of the complex. It has been reported by some of the hostages who had escaped or been released that the perpetrators had explosives. Some of the female hostage takers had explosives about their bodies, and other explosives had been placed around the building. The distance designated, when establishing the perimeters, must always take into consideration the type of weaponry the perpetrators have. In this case, Kalashnikov rifles and explosives would require some distance. The geography of the location will also affect the distances of the evacuation areas and the perimeters.

If negotiations are not successful or if a hostage or hostages are killed on deadline, the following options are available:

1. Use of a sharpshooter
2. Use of a chemical agent
3. Implementation of a direct rescue
4. A combination of two or three or all options

Sharpshooter

Obviously, with the large number of perpetrators involved, it would be almost impossible to neutralize all of them simultaneously. Additionally, since some of the perpetrators were armed with explosives that they would probably detonate if some of their associates were shot, this option would not be the best selection.

Chemical Agents

The chemical agents most law enforcement personnel are familiar with are CS, CN, and oleo capstan. These are used as less than lethal alternatives that can be easily decontaminated and broken up, often by merely flushing with water. The delivery systems of these chemicals can either be hot (incendiary) or cold (blast dispersion or liquid). However, at times these agents can be lethal. This can happen if the amount of chemical agent introduced into a confined area exceeds what is termed the mean lethal dose. This is reached when the amount of chemical agent placed into a specific area exceeds the oxygen in the area, blocking the person from getting sufficient oxygen to sustain life. This changes a nonlethal weapon into a lethal weapon. The efficacy of these agents, when used correctly, is not enough to incapacitate all of the subjects at the same time. It depends on the individual metabolism of each person involved.

For many years, both law enforcement and the military have been searching for an effective means of safely and totally incapacitating all the individuals in rescue attempts. (This includes both those who are threatening harm to innocent hostages and the rescuers themselves.) Researchers and developers of vendors to military and government agencies have been trying since the tragedy at the 1972 Munich Olympic Games to produce such an agent.

In April 1980, during an operation called Desert One in the Iranian desert, there was an attempt by the U.S. Army's Delta Force, under the command of Col. Charles Beckworth, to rescue American hostages. The hostages were being held by Iranian students at the U.S. Embassy in Teheran. After a series of misfortunes en route, the number of troops available to Beckworth was cut back considerably. Though no statements were ever made, it would appear that some type of incapacitating chemical agent was planned to knock out everyone at the embassy, hostages and captors alike. It would appear that the manpower needed for the operation was at least two troops for each hostage in the event it became necessary to physically carry them out. Again, though it was never stated, this might well indicate that that was the plan of action.

Finally, in the theater incident on the third day, when the FSB did make a rescue entry into the theater, it did so following the introduction of what it hoped was a nonlethal chemical agent. The "secret" gas used was believed to be based on an anesthetic-type agent, fentanyl. Others said that it may have been a derivative of a nerve gas. The results were that many of the hostages who were removed from the theater were so incapacitated that they were unable to breathe. There were reports of insufficient ambulances, and that the doctors in the hospitals were not informed of the agent or a possible antidote. This, according to the ensuing investigation and subsequent lawsuits, contributed to the loss of more than 117 hostages.

Rescue/Dynamic Entry

From the outset, the Russian tactical teams correctly prepared for the probability of the need to effect a rescue. The tactical teams cannot sit back and wait to see if negotiations are successful. Planning and practice must take place as soon as possible based on the information and intelligence gathered and available. If necessary, the plans can be altered as new information and intelligence become available. The rescue must always be an option for the incident commander. In this instance, the teams were fortunate enough to have a similar building complex somewhat removed from the affected location to carry out training and practice entries. This location was distant enough to afford privacy and security, especially from the media or unknown collaborators of the perpetrators who might have been in the area.

Russian Hostage Litigation

At least 44 of the former hostages sued authorities in Moscow for compensation. Lawyer Igor Trunov said the families of those who died in the rescue attempt had been awarded the equivalent of $3,100.

Theater Reopens

The Associated Press reported that on January 25, 2003, almost three months after the takeover by the Chechen militants, the Moscow Cultural Center had been reopened. It had taken that long to repair the damage and renovate the theater. This included revamping the security system, the audio system, and the orchestra pit. The cost, a reported $2.5 million, was incurred by the Moscow city government.

Continued Terrorism

In November and December 2003, suicide bombings took place in Russia. A commuter train in southern Russian was targeted, and many people en route to their work places were killed. In Moscow, six people were killed and many injured outside the National Hotel. A prosecutor reported that the type of explosive and the nature of the destruction were similar to an earlier suicide bombing at a rock concert in Moscow that had occurred in the summer of 2003. In each case the suicide bombers were women and were reported to be wearing the same type of improvised explosive device belts worn by the women who took part in the Moscow theater siege in October 2002. In August 2004, two commercial airliners were blown up minutes apart, shortly after taking off from the Moscow airport. Suspicion was placed on female passengers with Chechen names aboard each plane. The Russian press has labeled these terrorists the Black Widows because purportedly they were willing to engage in suicide missions because their husbands had been killed by Russian troops in earlier fighting.

No doubt there will be more actions on the part of the Chechens. These may take on the other types of engagements used by descendants of Chechens killed to make their point. They include assaults, assassinations, and kidnappings. As the media becomes less impressed by the repeated use of one type of action and gives it less coverage, the terrorists will move to a different form of enterprise.

The Command Post ⟨18⟩

The Nerve Center

Equally important as the role and responsibility of the commander are the location and administration of the command post. This is the nerve center and heart of an emergency operation. How it is set up and run could well make the difference between the successful resolution of a terrorist criminal incident and a botched assignment. It should be noted that there are regional differences in terminology in referring to command posts. They have been variously referred to as mobilization points, forward posts, and temporary headquarters, with those terms being used more or less interchangeably in some areas and having separate and distinct meanings in other jurisdictions.

The preferred definitions are:

1. *Forward command post.* The same as temporary headquarters; specifically, a formal location from which the operational administration of the incident is directed.
2. *Mobilization point.* Location near the site of the incident to which specialized manpower and equipment first report.
3. *Point of negotiation.* Used during a hostage incident and is the physical location of the negotiator when in communication or direct contact with the perpetrator. In a bombing incident, this may be known as the evidence collection point or some similar terminology.

Forward Command Post

The positioning of a forward command post is often dictated by the tactical situation of the incident. In some cases, however, preincident selection may be appropriate when incidents can be anticipated, such as mass demonstrations like those generated by World Trade Organization meetings and similar summit and economic conferences. In these cases, prepositioning in such locations as airports, recreation areas, shopping centers, or other likely target locations may be appropriate. In most instances, however, the site of the forward command post or temporary headquarters must be made under emergency conditions and may be a private home, an office, a store, or any protected location near the incident. Among some of the considerations in choosing a forward command post are the presence of communications capability, adequate lighting, floor area and workspace, heat (or lack of it, depending upon the weather), toilet facilities, convenience, and security.

In recent years the widespread availability of cellular telephones and other wireless communications devices has enhanced flexibility in the selection of forward command posts or temporary headquarters. In today's world of increased funding to combat terrorism, many jurisdictions have access to a mobile command vehicle. In fact, there may be a variety of vehicles that can serve as crime scene processing units, including bomb squad response vehicles, among others. These vehicles, which can be mobile or trailer, can be equipped with a host of telecommunication equipment, including wireless laptop computers, fax, video surveillance capabilities, as well as broadcast and television reception. In nonurban locations, if a mobile unit is not available, a recreational vehicle, trailer, or even a patrol car, if appropriately equipped, could fulfill the basic needs. Vehicles seized in other actions, such as vans used in drug operations, can be outfitted more elaborately. Remember that when placing these vehicles at the scene of an incident, safety and security are of paramount importance. A few key points to remember when selecting a location:

- Keep it out of a perpetrator's line of sight as well as out of the line of fire. In the case of an explosive device, remember: if you can see the bomb, it can see you.
- The command post must be accessible to responding officers and backup support teams, as well as to the negotiators and supervisors at the front line.
- Ensure a secure radio frequency is selected and communicated to the mobilization point so the newly arriving personnel can be informed.
- The physical placement of the command post should be carefully screened. More than once, a post has been established in a basement or next door to an incident, only to be hastily relocated when the perpetrator began firing random gunshots at the wall, ceiling, or floor.

One of the requirements to be met, at least under ideal circumstances, is that the command post be large enough to be physically separated into distinct function areas, such as for technicians (bomb squad, negotiating teams, etc.) and administration functions, with a third area for VIP or press briefings.

Mobilization Point

The primary location to which personnel and equipment report after the initial responding officers have arrived is the mobilization point. This location is usually selected by the first supervisor to arrive at the scene, and its location is communicated via the radio dispatcher. In the event that the incident includes a report of an armed person or persons, the safest route to the mobilization point should be indicated, as should any danger areas that may be in the line of fire. If the event is large enough to gain immediate media coverage, the possibility is very real that off-duty personnel may be rallying to the scene. Control must be maintained over well-meaning officers responding to the scene and jumping into the middle of situation, lest they become a casualty of friendly fire. The mobilization point should be selected based on convenience, accessibility, and capacity to accommodate responding personnel. Care must be taken to ensure that the location is out of the perpetrators' lines of sight, so they will not be able to assess the assembled resources. The idea is to increase police intelligence and information, while depriving the perpetrators of as much of the same as possible.

Point of Negotiation

In a hostage incident or a barricade situation, the point of negotiation may be closer to the location of the perpetrator than is the command post. There is no reason, though, why the point of negotiation could not be located in the area of the forward command post or temporary headquarters. However, the negotiators should have as much privacy as possible to allow them to establish rapport with the hostage taker and ensure that the he or she will not overhear planning, radio transmissions, or other statements made by nonnegotiating officers. If the negotiating team moves up to face-to-face negotiations, the location, of course, will change. Wherever it is physically situated, however, the incident command post should be able to communicate with personnel and perhaps even monitor the actual negotiations. This can be accomplished by placing a body transmitter on the negotiator's telephone and equipping the incident commander and tactical commander with body receivers.

Staffing the Command Post

Standard operating procedure, a department's policies and procedures manual, should specify who should be the overall commander and decision maker at an incident command post, tactical or otherwise. So too, the staffing of the command post should be spelled out in advance. While incidents may vary in nature and duration, there is always a need for a spelled-out chain of command. Besides the officer in charge (OIC), other positions likely to be needed are those of an operations officer, a logistics officer, a communications officer, and an intelligence officer. It should be noted that the communications officer should be versed in maintaining wireless as well as hardwired systems. There should also be clerical personnel responsible for the maintenance of a command post log and the situation map. Depending upon the incident-specific circumstances and size of the department, some of these responsibilities could be combined and handled by one individual.

In hostage situations, there is also a need for a support staff. The negotiator needs a coach, ideally, another trained negotiator who can provide advice and support, but who doesn't speak directly with the hostage taker. In smaller departments, the coach position could be filled by an officer who is familiar with tactical situations and the information the negotiator may need. Whenever possible, a mental health professional should be on hand to monitor the negotiator and, to whatever extent possible, observe the hostage taker and his or her actions. Unless the mental health professional is actually part of the department, there should be some preincident affiliation or interaction to be sure everyone's effort is integrated and coordinated.

There is also a question of how long any one person can negotiate. Perhaps 10, 12, or 18 hours is possible, although almost any negotiator will feel he or she can go as long as the perpetrator can. The idea is, however, to wear out the perpetrator, not the negotiator. The decision to change negotiators, or at least give one a rest, must be made by someone else, preferably the overall incident commander, upon consultation with the coach and the mental health professional. However, like a baseball manager changing pitchers, the decision is up to the on-site senior commander.

Bomb Incident Command Post

The aftermath of a major terrorist attack utilizing a large improvised explosive device may necessitate the initial use of an outside command post. In establishing a bomb command post, a number of things must be addressed. The first is to assess the extent of the attack, determine the size of the crime scene, and establish a secure perimeter. In the event that there are significant casualties, a triage area must be quickly established while simultaneously selecting a site where command posts can be established for rescue and control operations and another for technical and investigative teams. The crime scene tasks will thus be divided into three phases: concern for any persons who may have been injured; then the search for bodies, particularly in the event of collapse; and finally, the search for physical evidence.

Remember, the command post should not be located within the boundaries of the crime scene, lest evidence be contaminated or destroyed. If possible, the command post should be separated into two distinct areas: one for teams conducting the physical search, and the other for investigators and perimeter supervisory personnel. This division allows for greater safekeeping of evidence.

Record keeping is an important function at the command post. It is essential that once control of the bomb scene is achieved and the search for physical evidence is initiated, in order to maintain a "chain of custody," a record of the names of each and every person entering the crime scene area should be kept, regardless of rank or affiliation and what actions each has carried out. Such a record may also be required for subpoena purposes. In addition to an operations log to control movement, there should be a chronological log maintained to record the sequence of events, such as when certain pieces of evidence were recovered, when visitors arrived, when a wall collapsed, etc. These logs should be maintained by one person with sufficient authority to have all people make proper entries. The individual in charge of the log should be able to identify ranking officers by name and command.

When major explosions occur, a command post may have to be utilized for days, even weeks, until the thorough sifting of debris is concluded. The location where the on-site sifting for physical evidence is conducted should be protected from the elements. To accomplish this, there are a variety of low-cost pop-up tents readily available on the commercial market that are ideal for this purpose.

There will come a point in time when pressure will be brought to bear to complete the job quickly in order to clear up congestion of both pedestrian and vehicular traffic and otherwise get the location back to normal working order. In such instances, it may be necessary to physically remove all debris from the scene to a more remote location, where the material can be continued to be picked over, sorted, and classified.

Log and Situation Map

The command post log is a record of events and activities surrounding the particular incident. Once the basic data are recorded—when the command post was activated, its location, and the nature of the incident—information that should be recorded includes the exact location of the incident, a brief background of the incident up to the time the log was created, and the names, ranks, and affiliations of personnel assigned to the incident. Other relevant information includes the locations, names, and number of personnel deployed at the scene; which assignments are temporary and which are fixed for the duration of the incident; the number and types of vehicles and specialized equipment being employed; unit and personnel on standby or backup status; any intelligence received; any physical evidence recovered; names and arrival and departure times of any visitors to the command post or the scene of the incident; and names, time of arrest, and backgrounds of anyone arrested at the scene. The name of the authorizer should be noted.

The situation map may be a series of maps showing the location of the incident vis-à-vis major streets, highways, and transportation routes; its location within the neighborhood; and blueprints, floor plans, and other technical drawings showing the exact location of the incident within the building. Ready-made maps, whether in print form or downloaded from Internet sites, may be helpful in creating the incident-specific maps. There should also be a hand-drawn sketch of the scene showing locations of the individuals involved, whether police, perpetrators, hostages, or civilians who were trapped by the circumstances. Other features on the hand-drawn map should include pieces of furniture, light switches, windows, and anything else that may be relevant.

Equipment and Supplies

Regardless of whether or not a mobile command post is available, there are certain basic items that are required during an emergency incident that will assist in the smooth running of the operation. Many of these items are common to everyday operations, but easily forgotten in a shuffle of operational logistics.

The list of equipment required at a command post includes flip charts, markers, a blackboard (magnetic, if possible), masking tape, a large clock, a tape recorder with telephone attachment, walkie-talkies, flashlights, an instant camera for photos, a one-to-one adapter, bullhorns, a scanner, a laptop computer with fax capability, a printer and connecting cable or wireless connection, floor plans of the building and adjacent buildings, a map of the immediate vicinity, tools and equipment for gathering physical evidence, tape measures, an AM-FM radio, a police scanner, a television monitor equipped for both over-the-air broadcasts and cable, a first aid kit, paper or plastic cups, rope, wedges, and lastly, departmental forms and log books for chronological recording of events and for administrative purposes, such as recording overtime, etc.

Equipment at the scene should include a field phone or hostage phone in order to facilitate communication. While in the act of taking hostages, a perpetrator will often rip out a telephone to prevent anyone from notifying police, or the telephone may be torn out at some subsequent point. The field telephone or other limited communication device will allow for easier communication than shouting back and forth or using bullhorns. A cellular phone, on the other hand may provide the perpetrator with greater communication. One of the disadvantages of using a telephone for negotiations, however, is that the perpetrator may not get on the phone himself, but rather use one of the hostages to carry on the communication.

As departments get more sophisticated, they may be able to assign electronic technicians as part of the negotiation or hostage recovery team. The specialized personnel can assist in communication, intelligence, surveillance, and related areas. The equipment employed could include lock picks, mini television or video cameras, special optics, night-viewing equipment, and sophisticated listening devices. While some jurisdictions are absolutely prohibited from employing "bugs" to gather evidence, it may be possible to use electronic eavesdropping equipment purely as a means of gathering life-saving intelligence. If there is any doubt, the local prosecutor should be consulted.

Immediately after the incident, any equipment that needs cleaning or maintenance should be attended to the same day: batteries replaced, supplies replenished, whatever. It may be days, even weeks, before the equipment is needed again, but it may also be a matter of hours. On July 4, 1977, New York City had one major hostage incident followed by another in less than four hours. The likelihood of copycat hostage situations is great enough to make agencies want to be as fully prepared as possible.

Personnel who respond to the scene should be equipped with bullet-resistant garments and headgear and arm themselves with weapons appropriate to their assignments. This equipment may be standard to all officers, but any responding from other assignments or off duty may not be so equipped. Those in long-distance positions should have binoculars and scoped rifles; those closer in, shotguns and automatic weapons, or both. Upon arrival at the mobilization point, personnel should be given a quick briefing with as much intelligence as possible, told of the radio frequency in use at the scene, and then deployed as quickly as possible. Their first assignment should be to replace any underequipped or inadequately equipped first response officers occupying containment positions. Thought must be given to the availability of drinking water and other forms of nutrition. A heating coil or similar device and heatproof cups or containers could be useful for making instant coffee, soup, etc., particularly in rural locations.

Communications

There are any number of aspects to a terrorist incident that can be labeled important, with one key to the peaceful resolution of such incidents. However, lack of communication can do more than anything else to ensure

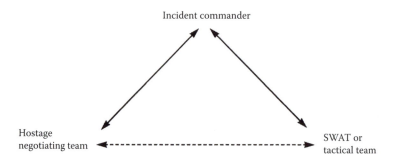

Figure 18.1 Lines of communication: in any terrorist incident, there must be two-way lines of communication between the incident commander and the hostage-negotiating team, and between the commander and the SWAT or critical team. Care must be taken that the communication between the negotiator and the SWAT team do not override the commander.

some degree of failure, if not total failure, in the handling of the situation. The communication network should obviously center on the commander at the scene, who in turn should be in direct communication with the SWAT or tactical commander and the leader of the negotiating team (Figure 18.1). The tactical and negotiating commanders also should be in direct contact, so each knows what the other is doing. In some jurisdictions, depending on the structure of the department, the incident commander may have to be in direct communication with the chief, the sheriff, or the police commissioner.

In addition to communicating orders and relaying intelligence, efficient communications are necessary to prevent tragedies, such as tactical forces taking up crossfire positions or having negotiators placed in the potential line of friendly fire. In Waco, Texas, for instance, the tactical team's command post was a considerable distance away from the point of negotiation and the official command post. Though all locations were linked by computer and there was communication, the nuances of that communication seemed to have been lost on some occasions because of distance.

As mentioned above, one of the first tasks upon arriving at the scene is to establish a tactical frequency on which communications will be carried. In jurisdictions with a large number of frequencies, a frequency predesignated for use in emergency or tactical situations may exist. In areas where there is a significant amount of interaction among different agencies, a netting frequency may be employed. There is usually at least one network, generally statewide, that employs a repeater system to permit any police agency in the state access, should it have to interact with any other police department during or in reference to an incident. If these alternatives are not available and multiple jurisdictions with differing radio frequencies are trying to work together, then a temporary communications center should be established and staffed by a member of each agency whose function is to rebroadcast any information transmitted over the other frequencies.

Concealment vs. Cover

In the deployment of containment and tactical teams, an important distinction should be made between cover and concealment. Concealment will block a police officer from the view of a perpetrator, but will not stop any projectiles. Concealment blocks only the perpetrator's ability to see the target. Cover, on the other hand, will protect the officer from projectiles, the amount of protection determined by the type of weapon involved. A high-powered weapon requires better cover than does a low caliber firearm. When adequate cover is taken, there is no need to return fire even if the perpetrator begins shooting. Police officers should not have to return fire until two things happen:

1. There is a clear necessity to shoot in order to save their own lives or someone else's life.
2. There is positive target identification and it has been determined by higher authority that deadly physical force is needed to stop or neutralize the perpetrator.

The importance of cover, or even concealment, in hostage situations is that instinctively most people will not shoot through things. They will usually wait for a good target view. Only specially trained officers, sharpshooters, and violent terrorists will shoot through objects. Randomly spraying with automatic weapons is a favorite tactic of terrorists. In such instances, mere concealment will afford little protection.

Good cover provides the police with time—time that can be used to gather as much intelligence as possible, time to identify targets, and time to get a clear target in the event the decision is made to use deadly physical force.

In cases where the operation involves a suspicious object or confirmed improvised explosive device, special care should include a safe stand-off distance, staying away from glass windows and avoiding anything an explosion may bring down.

Handling the Media

Newspaper reporters, photographers, broadcast journalists, and sound and camera technicians should be allowed inside the outer perimeter, but kept outside the inner perimeter. It is preferable to designate a special section for media representatives, so that they can be kept away from the immediate crime scene area where, in case of an explosion, they may destroy or disturb evidence, or in the case of a hostage situation, may incite the perpetrators to do something for the camera.

One of the most dramatic incidents of media interference occurred in Jasper, Arkansas, where members of a group called Father of Us had taken hostages to bring attention to their message. After members of the group were interviewed by a news crew from a local television station who said it would air the tape at 6 p.m., leaders of the group said that before the night was out they were going to provoke the police into shooting them. The television crew said that anything they did later might be too late to get on the evening news, so the hostage takers moved up their agenda. And they go out and get themselves shot and killed. There is no question that the media made the group members hurry to their conclusion. If the television reporters had not pushed them along, the individuals may have lost their resolve to die for the cause.

There are numerous other incidents, particularly hostage situations, where reporters or media personalities have tied up phone lines or otherwise occupied the perpetrators for on-the-air exclusives. At best, all this does is prolong a situation. At worst, it could result in the death of innocent persons.

The use of helicopters by various news agencies can also have a great effect on incidents. Sometimes it seems there are so many news choppers in the air hovering above a scene that they need their own air traffic controllers. At the 1998 Columbine High School tragedy in Colorado, the responding police and tactical teams and the scenes of escaping students were televised for all to see. Fortunately, the perpetrators did not see what was going on. Not so in Salem, Massachusetts, a year or so later. There, a bank robber led police on a multijurisdictional chase for many miles. After crashing the car, the robber continued fleeing on foot. He broke into the home of a sheriff's department officer, who was at home caring for his twin toddlers. The officer was able to negotiate with the intruder to permit the young boys to leave, although they were reluctant to go with their father still in the home. After the young boys were evacuated, the perpetrator changed the television channel from the one the boys had been watching. On the screen he found coverage of his situation, including an aerial view of the house and deployment of police around it. He also learned from one commentator that the father was a sheriff's deputy, something the perpetrator had not previously known. This led to a demand by the perpetrator for any weapons in the house. The incident ended successfully when the deputy wrestled with the perpetrator until the tactical team was able to immobilize him.

Media representatives have a job to do. In today's high-technology "eye in the sky" television coverage, a helicopter can be quite a distance removed from the scene and yet have the capacity for close-in shots. Keeping that in mind, always plan on the operation being under observation and act accordingly. News organizations serve a purpose in a constitutional democracy to keep the public informed. By providing them with enough accurate, up-to-date information that will not interfere with the incident or investigation, and that will limit or reduce speculation in the reporting process, police or corporate security personnel may be able to forestall or avert sensationalist tactics that a news blackout might precipitate.

Counterterrorism Command Center

In addition to incident command posts, which by definition are temporary in nature, there can be specialized command centers, discrete and physically separated from administrative headquarters. One such facility was established in June 1998 by New York City to direct operations in the event of a major disaster. The facility, which was located on the twenty-third floor of 7 World Trade Center, was selected due its close proximity to city hall and other major department headquarters. At the time it was a state-of-the-art facility and was in operation on September 11, 2001, when the hijacked planes hit the WTC's twin towers. When the towers collapsed, 7 WTC, in turn, was weakened enough to cause its collapse, taking the command center with it. Since then a new center has been constructed at an off-site location as well as another emergency situation room in the lower level of New York City Hall.

Following the horrendous event that took place at the World Trade Center—the 9/11 airplane attacks and keeping in mind the 1993 vehicle bombing of the WTC—the New York Police Department created a new facility through the financial assistance provided by government sources as well as the private sector, particularly the New York City Police Foundation, which funnels donations from the private sector to the NYPD.

This new counterterrorism center features a global intelligence room in which a dozen large, flat-screen, wall-mounted television receivers display satellite and cable news programming from around the world, including broadcasts from Al Jazeera, the Arabic language network based in the Persian Gulf. The newscasts are monitored, and sometimes recorded, and the personnel is fluent in such languages as Arabic, Urdu, Pashto, and Fijianese, among others. The center includes a computer network staffed by city, state, and federal investigators who maintain communications with other municipal agencies, as well as state and federal offices and selected private companies, such as utilities.

The counterterrorism command center is at the heart of an antiterrorism effort that includes such initiatives as in-service training in biodefense procedures for nearly a third of the entire force, equipping emergency service units with radiation detectors, and training and equipping tactical units (named Hercules teams and Atlas teams) to establish a high-visibility presence at major events, landmark sites, transportation centers, and other public facilities. The city has also established a terrorism tip hotline, which, among other things, provides information for the center's database.

The command center is staffed around the clock, and its design includes a sallyport at the entrance with bulletproof glass as well as ballistic sheetrock. An auxiliary generator provides for an uninterrupted power supply. During a power blackout in August 2003, some officers working in the windowless center were unaware of the loss of power until it became the subject of news reports. The transition to the backup generator was so smooth that it didn't even disrupt the computers they were using.

Though counterterrorism is the primary function of the command center, it could also function as a command center for natural disasters and other emergencies, whether dealing with evacuations due to flooding or hurricanes or the aftermath of such occurrences.

Appendix A: Government-Sponsored Terrorism

Legal Criteria for Designation as a Foreign Terrorist Organization

The legal criteria for designation as a foreign terrorist organization was set forth under Section 219 of the Immigration and Nationalization Act (INA), as amended.

The following apply:

- It must be a foreign organization.
- The organization must engage in terrorist activity, as defined in Section 212(a)(3)(B) of the INA, or terrorism, as defined in Section 140(d)(2) of the Foreign Relations Authorization Act, fiscal years 1988 and 1989, or retain the capability and intent to engage in terrorist activity or terrorism.
- The organization's terrorist activity or terrorism must threaten the security of U.S. nationals or the national security (national defense, foreign relations, or economic interests) of the United States.

How Terrorists Groups Are Designated

The Office of the Coordinator for Counterterrorism in the State Department continually monitors the activities of terrorist groups active around the world to identify potential new additions to the list. In this review the State Department looks at not only the attacks that have been carried out, but also if the group has engaged in planning and preparations for possible future acts of terrorism and retains the capability and intent to carry out such acts.

Once a group is identified, a detailed administrative record is kept; this record is a compilation of information, including both open-source and classified information, which demonstrates that the statutory criteria for designation have been satisfied. If the secretary of state, in consultation with the attorney general and the secretary of the treasury, decides to make the designation, Congress is notified of the secretary's intent to designate the organization and given seven days to review the designation. Upon the expiration of the seven-day waiting period, and if no congressional action is taken to block the designation, notice of the designation will be published in the *Federal Register*, at which point the designation takes effect. By law, an organization designated as an FTO may seek judicial review of the designation in the U.S. Court of Appeals for the District of Columbia Circuit no later than 30 days after the designation is published in the *Federal Register*.

In the past, the FTOs had to be redesignated every two years, or the designation would lapse. Under the Intelligence Reform and Terrorism Prevention Act of 2004 (IRTPA), however, the redesignation requirement was replaced by certain review and revocation procedures. This law provides that an FTO may file a petition for revocation two years after its designation date (or in the case of a redesignated FTO, its most recent designation date) or two years after the determination date on its most recent petition for revocation. In order to provide a basis for revocation, the petitioning FTO must provide evidence that the circumstances forming the basis for the designation are sufficiently different to warrant revocation. If no such review has been conducted during a five-year period with respect to a designation, then the secretary of state is required to review the designation to determine whether revocation would be appropriate. In addition, the secretary of state may at any time revoke a designation upon a finding that the circumstances forming the basis for the designation have changed in such a manner as to warrant revocation, or that the national security of the United States warrants a revocation. The same procedural requirements apply to revocations made by the secretary of state as apply to designations. A designation may be revoked by an act of Congress, or set aside by a court order.

Legal Ramifications of Designation

1. It is unlawful for a person in the United States or subject to the jurisdiction of the United States to knowingly provide "material support or resources" to a designated FTO. The term *material support or resources* is defined in 18 USC 2339a(b)(1) as "any property, tangible or intangible, or service, including currency or monetary instruments or financial securities, financial services, lodging, training, expert advice or assistance, safe houses, false documentation or identification, communication equipment, facilities, weapons, lethal substances, explosives, personnel (one or more individuals who may be or include oneself), and transportation, except medicine or religious materials." 18 USC 2339a(b)(2) provides for these purposes: "The term 'training' means instructing or teaching designated to impart a specific skill, as opposed to

general knowledge." 18 USC 2339a(b)(1) further provides that for these purposes, the term *expert advice or assistance* means advice or assistance derived from scientific, technical, or other specialized knowledge.

2. Representatives and members of a designated FTO, if they are aliens, are inadmissible to and, in certain circumstances, removable from the United States.

3. Any financial institution that becomes aware that it has possession of or control over funds in which a designated FTO or its agent has an interest must retain possession of or control over the funds and report the funds to the Office of Foreign Assets Control of the U.S. Department of the Treasury.

Additional Effects of Designation

1. Supports the efforts of the United States to curb terrorism financing and to encourage other nations to do the same.
2. Stigmatizes and isolates designated terrorist organizations internationally.
3. Deters donations or contributions to and economic transactions with named organizations.
4. Heightens public awareness and knowledge of terrorist organizations.
5. Signals to other governments U.S. concern about named organizations.

Appendix B: Foreign Terrorist Organizations

(As designated by the U.S. Department of State)

1. Abu Nidal Organization (ANO)
2. Abu Sayyaf Group (ASG)
3. Al-Aqsa Martyrs Brigade
4. al-Shabaab
5. Ansar al-Islam
6. Armed Islamic Group
7. Asbat al-ansar
8. Aum Shinrikyo
9. Basque Fatherland and Liberty (ETA)
10. Communist Party of the Philippines/New People's Army (CPP/NPA)
11. Continuity, Irish Republican Army (CIRA)
12. Gama'a al-Islamiyya (Islamic Group)
13. Hamas
14. Harakat ul-Jihad-i-Islami/Bangladesh (HUJI-B)
15. Harakat ul-Mujahidin (HUM)
16. Hizballah
17. Islamic Jihad Group (IJG)
18. Islamic Movement of Uzbkistan (IMU)
19. Jaish-e-Mohammad (JEM)
20. Jemaah-Islamiya (JI)
21. al-Jihad
22. Kahane Chai
23. Kata'ib Hizballah
24. Kongra-Gel
25. Lashkar-e-Tayyiba (LT) (Army of Righteous)
26. Lashkar I-Jhangni
27. Liberation Tigers of Tamil Eelam (LTTE)
28. Libyan Islamic Fighting Group (LIFG)
29. Moroccan Islamic Combatant Group (GICM)
30. Mujahedin-e-Khalq Organization (MEK)
31. National Liberation Army (ELN)
32. Palestine Liberation Front (PLF)

33. Palestinian Islamic Jihad (PIJ)
34. Popular Front for the Liberation of Palestine (PFLP)
35. PFLP—General Command (PFLP-GC)
36. al Qaeda in Iraq (AQI)
37. al Qaeda (AQ)
38. al Qaeda in the Arabian Peninsula (AQAP)
39. al Qaeda in the Islamic Maghreb (formerly GSPC)
40. Real IRA (RIRA)
41. Revolutionary Armed Forces of Columbia (FARC)
42. Revolutionary Organization 17 November
43. Revolutionary People's Liberation Party/Front (DHKP/C)
44. Revolutionary Struggle (RS)
45. Shining Path (SL)
46. United Self-Defense Forces of Colombia (AUC)

1. Abu Nidal Organization (ANO)

A.k.a.:

- Fatah Revolutionary Council, Arab Revolutionary Brigades, Black September, Revolutionary Organization of Socialist Muslims, Black June.
- It is also believed that ANO has used the names of Palestinian National Liberation Movement, the Egyptian Revolution, Revolutionary Egypt, Al-Asifa (the Storm), and the Arab Nationalist Youth Organization.

Organization:

- The founder, Sabri al-Banna, was born in Jaffa (now in the state of Israel) in May 1937. He later assumed the name of Abu Nidal, meaning "Father of the Struggle." He was at one time a member of the nationalist Baath Party and became involved with the PLO in 1967, forming the deadly Al-Fatah faction.
- The group was expelled from the PLO in 1974.

Area of operations:

- When the ANO was in its prime, it primarily operated in the Middle East and Europe. The remnants of the ANO are now believed to operate out of Iraq, and although expelled from Lebanon, they still maintain several cells within the Palestinian refugee camps in the Bekka Valley.
- In 1999 their offices were closed in both Egypt and Libya.

Aims/goals:

- The development of an independent Palestinian state and the elimination of Israel.

Strengths:

- Number of active fighters is unknown, but is suspected to be considerably lower from the peak years of the 1970s and 1980s. In addition, the group was weakened upon the death of Nidal on August 16, 2002, in Iraq.
- Once the most feared terrorist group operating out of the Middle East, its numbers and leadership have declined significantly since its height of power during the 1970s and 80s.
- In the past the group had received extensive support in the form of safe haven, training, logistics, and financing from Iraq, Libya, and Syria. It is believed that the group still receives some support from Iran.

Weapons/tactics/capabilities:

- With their leader dead and reduced in size, they have been inactive for the last several years.
- ANO used armed attacks and assassinations on high-profile targets utilizing both explosives and small arms weapons.

Major actions:

- ANO has targeted the United States, the United Kingdom, France, Israel, moderate Palestinians, the PLO, and various moderate Arab countries. Overall the group has launched attacks on some 20 countries and killed nearly 900 people.
- The group's deadly attacks included the 1972 attack on the Israeli Olympic team in Munich, Germany; attempted car bomb attacks against Israeli targets in New York City in 1973; the December 1985 attack on U.S. and Israeli ticket counters in the Rome and Vienna airports.
- An attempted hijacking of a Pan American flight in Karachi, Pakistan, in which 22 people died.

2. Abu Sayyaf Group (ASG)

A.k.a.:

- Mujahideen Commando Freedom Fighters, Al-Harakat Al-Islamiyya, Islamic Movement.

Organization:

- ASG was formed in the early 1990s, when under the leadership of Abdurajak Abubakar Janjalani, it split from the larger Moro National Liberation Front. In 1998, Abdurajak was killed in a clash with Filipino police and his younger brother Khadaffy assumed control of the group.

- Khadaffy was subsequently also killed by police, and the leadership void was filled by Radullah Sahiron.

Area of operations:

- Operates in the southern Philippine Islands, in particular the Sulu Archipelago, namely, in Basilan, Sulu, and Tawai-Tawi. The ASG has also ranged into the Zamboanga Peninsula and Jolo Island.
- A heavy force is also believed to be operating on Jolo Island.
- It has carried out attacks in the capital of Manila.
- The group expanded its operational reach to Malaysia in 2000 with the abduction of a number of foreign tourists from a vacation resort.

Aims/goals:

- The goal of the ASG is to bring about an independent Islamic state in the heavily Muslim-populated western Mindanao and the Sulu Archipelago.

Strengths:

- The number of fighters has dwindled over the years due to robust antiterrorist operations by the Philippine military assisted by U.S. special operation assets.
- Its forces on Basilan and Zamoanaga are reported to be under 100. A heavier force of ASG fighters is said to be operating on Jolo Island.
- It is believed that ASG has the strength of approximately 200 to 500 members. Some members have reportedly gained experience in fighting the Russians during their war in Afghanistan.

Weapons/tactics/capabilities:

- The ASG attack methods have included bombings, kidnappings, and assassinations. Extortion and ransoms from kidnappings are a primary source of income.
- The group is mostly armed with light weapons, including assault weapons and hand grenades procured from other Islamic groups. They also make liberal use of improvised explosive devices.

Major actions:

- April 2000: The group kidnapped 21 persons, including 10 Westerners from a resort in Malaysia.
- May 2001: Kidnapped 3 U.S. citizens and 17 others from a resort in Palawan, Philippines; several hostages, including a U.S. citizen, were later murdered.
- In November 2007, suspected in placing a motorcycle bomb that exploded outside the Philippines Congress, killing a congressman and three staff members.

3. Al-Aqsa Martyrs Brigade

A.k.a.:
- Palestinian National Liberation Movement, Al Aqsa Martyrs Brigades, Al Aqsa Brigades, Al Mujahedun Al Aqsa.
- The brigade has also claimed joint responsibility for attacks with groups like the Popular Front for the Liberation of Palestine and Palestinian Islamic Jihad.

Organization:
- The al-Aqsa Martyrs Brigade is a fundamentalist Islamic organization and began operations shortly after the outbreak of the Second Intifada, or uprising among the Palestinians in the West Bank. Named to honor the al-Aqsa mosque located on the Temple Mount.
- The brigade is made up of a loose network of localized, independent cells that have a loose alliance with Fatah, but act independently of each other. Due to its cellular structure, the identities of key leaders are difficult to ascertain.
- The brigade is considered the military arm of al Fatah (Palestine Liberation Authority).

Aims/goals:
- Driving Israeli settlers from the West Bank and Gaza and establishing an independent Palestinian state.

Area of operations:
- Al-Aqsa operates mainly in the West Bank but has conducted attacks inside Israel and the Gaza Strip.
- The group has members in refugee camps in southern Lebanon and overseas, although it has not demonstrated transnational capability.

Strengths:
- Unknown—believed to be several hundred.

Weapons/tactics/capabilities:
- Utilizes suicide bombers and mortar and rocket attacks against Israeli targets.

Major actions:
- January 27, 2002: Al-Aqsa sent the first female suicide bomber, who detonated a 20-pound bomb in central Jerusalem. The attack killed 1 person and injured over 100.
- January 5, 2003: Carried out a twin suicide bombing in downtown Tel Aviv that killed 23 people and wounded approximately 100.
- January 2004: Attacked a passenger bus in Jerusalem that killed 11 people.

- January 2008: Began a campaign with Hamas and the Palestinian Islamic Jihad to fire rockets into Israel.

4. Al-Shabaab

A.k.a.:
- Harakat Shabaab al-Mujahidin, Shabaab, the Youth, Mujahidin Youth Movement.

Organization:
- Al-Shabaab is a radical Islamic group, and although several senior leaders have received training at al Qaeda training camps, the group is linked more by ideology than operationally.
- The group is divided into three geographical units that act more or less independently: Bay and Bokoul Region, South Central Somalia and Mogadishu, and Puntland and Somaliland. It is reported that there is a substantial amount of friction among the groups that center on clan, operational, and ideological issues.

Aims/goals:
- Nationalistic in nature.

Area of operations:
- Southern Somalia and Uganda, and have clashed with Kenyan security along the border with Somalia.

Strengths:
- Comprised of several thousand fighters who control much of southern Somalia.

Weapons/tactics/capabilities:
- The group has used intimidation and violence (car and suicide bombs as well as armed attacks) to undermine whatever central government organization remains in Somalia.
- A part of the funding for the group's activity may come through the ransoms collected by pirate crews operating out of Somalia.
- There is some concern among counterterrorism experts that although this group is perceived by some as being strictly a regional threat, it has the capability to go global.

Major actions:
- July 2010: In its first activity outside of Somalia, al-Shabaab claimed responsibility for bomb attacks in Kampala, Uganda, that killed more than 70 people, most of whom were watching a public screening of a World Cup soccer match.
- May 2009: Coordinating an attack with Hizbul Islam, al-Shabaab launched an attack in the city of Mogadishou. In the ensuing

fighting several thousand people were either killed or wounded, and the greater part of the city fell under their control.
- February 2009: The group carried out a suicide car bombing that targeted the African Union military base that killed six peacekeepers.
- January 2007: The group produced a movie that warned the African Union peacekeepers that it was best for their welfare to leave Somalia.

5. Ansar al-Islam

A.k.a.:
- Supporters of Islam, Partisans of Islam.

Organization:
- Ansar al-Islam was founded in December 2001 with the assistance of Osama bin Laden providing seed money.
- The group's followers came from a merger of Jund al-Islam (Soldiers of Islam) and a splinter group from the Islamic Movement of Kurdistan. Initially the group's energies focused on combating the anti-Saddam Hussein group, the secular Patriotic Union of Kurdistan.

Aims/goals:
- The group follows the Salafi movement of the Wahhabi school of Sunni Islam and has a total disregard for human life in forcing these beliefs on others.

Area of operations:
- Operates in northern and central Iraq and maintains a large support operation of Muslims throughout Europe.

Strengths:
- The exact size of the group is really unknown, but it has been estimated to be between 500 and 1,000 active members.

Weapons/tactics/capabilities:
- Ansar al-Islam raises funds and recruits new members from among the radical Sunnis living in Europe. Additional funds are raised through dealing in the heroin and opium trades throughout Europe.
- Since the fall of Saddam Hussein it has expanded its operations to include actions against U.S. forces operating in Iraq.
- The group is suspected of giving refuge to al Qaeda fighters fleeing from coalition forces in Afghanistan.

Major actions:
- The group has been known to carry out coordinated suicide bombings using trucks and cars bombs against populated

areas or targets of prominent significance. It also includes the assassination of public key officials high on the list of actionable targets.

- In January 2009, Ansar al-Islam called for cooperation between the group and the resistance movement in the Gaza Strip and in Jerusalem.
- January 2008: It claimed credit for an ambush that killed five U.S. soldiers in Mosul. The attack was a coordinated effort using a roadside IED and small arms fire.
- January 2005: Claimed credit for the assassination of Sheik Mahmoud Finjan, an assistant to the senior Shiite cleric, Grand Ayatollah Ali al-Sistani, in the Salmon Park area of Baghdad.

6. Armed Islamic Group (GIA)

A.k.a.:
- Al-Jama'ah al-Islamiyah al-Musallah, Groupe Islamique Arme (hence the GIA from the French).

Organization:
- Founded in 1992 and a result of the government nullifying a 1991 legislative election in which Islamic Salvation Front was posed to win.
- The organization is suspected as being smaller than at its height of power—it was then organized in "companies" of 30 to 80 men. These were further divided into regional factions, with regional commanders who act independently of any central command. The exact number is somewhat vague, placing it between several hundred and several thousand.

Aims/goals:
- The aim of the GIA was the overthrow of Algeria's secular government, replacing it with an Islamic state.

Area of operations:
- GIA operates throughout Algeria, but mostly in the rural areas.

Strengths:
- Unknown, but key members of the group were Islamic radicals that were repatriated veterans returning from the 1978–1992 Afghan War.

Weapons/tactics/capabilities:
- The GIA targets those who it perceives as acting against its aims or goals. This is especially true with the media.

- The group has often been referred to as the Green Khmer, due to the fact it seems to mimic the violent action of the Khmer Rouge of Cambodia.
- In 1993 the group ordered all foreigners to leave the country and within a year had killed over 100, targeting mostly former French colonial bureaucrats.
- The GIA is suspected of receiving external assistance from the Sudan and Iran, as well as getting financial assistance from so-called charitable organizations in the United States and Western Europe.

Major actions:

- August 29, 1997: Rais Massacre—in one of Algeria's bloodiest attacks, hooded members of the GIA arrived by truck and assaulted the town residents with explosives, shotguns, axes, and knives. The official toll was put at 98 wounded and 120 wounded. A later BBC report placed the number of casualties at 800.
- September 22–23, 1997: Bentalha Massacre. In a follow-up attack, the GIA launched another mass attack against a population center. A neighborhood in the city of Bentalha witnessed an attack with explosives, automatic weapons, small arms, and machetes. Estimates of the total number of casualties vary from 85 to 400.

7. Asbat al-Ansar

A.k.a.:

- League of Partisans, League of Followers.

Organization:

- Organized in Lebanon during the early 1990s, Asbat al-Ansar aligned itself with Osama bin Laden's organization in order to obtain funding and support.
- The Lebanese government outlawed Asbat al-Ansar in 2002.

Aims/goals:

- Asbat al-Ansar is comprised of Sunni extremists of the Salafis school of Islam that want to return to an ancient caliphate form of government.
- It opposes any reconciliation with Israel and hopes to derail the Middle East peace process, as well as causing unrest in Lebanon.
- It is focused on supporting the jihad against U.S. forces operating in Iraq.

Area of operations:

- Lebanon.

- Operates from the Ayn al-Hilwah Palestinian refugee camp located near the seaside city of Sidon in southern Lebanon.

Strengths:

- Approximately 300–400 members, with some reports going higher.

Weapons/tactics/capabilities:

- Asbat al-Ansar carried out low-level attacks against anti-Islamic targets such as churches, bars, and foreign tourist locations.
- Small arms, mortars, rockets, and improvised explosive devices.

Major actions:

- 2000: The group claimed credit for firing rifled propelled grenades at the Russian Embassy to show solidarity with Chechen rebels.
- 2004: Operatives of the group are suspected of planning terrorist attacks against a number or targets, which include the Italian and Ukrainian diplomatic offices and Lebanese government offices.

8. Aum Shinrikyo

A.k.a.:

- Supreme Truth—the name is derived from *Aum* (a sacred Hindu symbol) and *shinri kyo* (supreme truth).

Organization:

- Chizuo Matsumoto, a partially blind son of a straw mat maker, who later changed his name to Shoko Asahara, founded the Aum in 1987. Asahara is currently on death row awaiting execution for his role in the 1995 Tokyo subway attack. His death by hanging sentence was reaffirmed by Japan's supreme court on September 15, 2006, and two subsequent retrial appeals were declined.
- In 2007 it split into two groups, one in Russia and one in Japan, with the focus on repairing its image in the eyes of the world. Fumihiro Joyu, a former engineer and leader of the Russian sect, has assumed the leadership.

Aims/goals:

- Aum started as a group of people interested in yogic meditation, but later gravitated into a terrorist group.

Area of operations:

- Japan and Russia.

Strengths:

- Due to the crackdown after the 1996 subway attack, the Aum Shinrikyo currently number approximately 1,500, divided between Japan and Russia.

- In 1995, at the peak of the strength, the group numbered some 40,000 members worldwide.

Weapons/tactics/capabilities:
- Aum Shinrikyo is presently more a cult than a terrorist group. Still listed as a terrorist organization by the U.S. State Department due to its past activity of using chemical weapons in terrorist attacks.

Major actions:
- July 27, 1994: Sarin gas was released using a truck-mounted dispersal system located outside a Matsumoto apartment complex. The gas traveled into the open windows of the building and before long there were 7 dead and 600 others sickened. This attack was launched with the intent of assassinating several judges who were about to hand down a ruling in a land dispute that the cult felt would be injurious to its members.
- March 20, 1995: Made an attack against the Tokyo subway system at the height of rush hour. The well-planned attack using high-grade sarin gas was carried out at the Kasumigaseki Station in Tokyo, where five train lines merge, close to the Tokyo police headquarters. The attackers hoped that releasing the gas on these trains would kill those who worked in police headquarters and other government buildings located in the area. The sarin was packaged in plastic bags and activated by a cult member who punctured the bags with an umbrella. Although sarin is an extremely deadly gas and caused close to 6,000 injuries of various degrees, only 12 people died. This was attributed to the fact that the chemical was only 35% pure, as well as to the efficiency of the air filtering systems in the subway.

9. Basque Fatherland and Liberty (ETA)

A.k.a.:
- Spain Separatists, ETA, Euskadi ta Askatasuna, Basque Homeland and Freedom.

Organization:
- The group was formed in 1959 as a response to the Spanish head of state Francisco Franco's attempt to suppress the Basque language and culture.
- Early in the group's history it was suspected of receiving terrorist training in Lebanon, Libya, and Nicaragua terrorists. In addition, fugitive members are suspected of being given safe harbor in Cuba and several South American countries.

- Financing for groups operations is gained primarily through extortion and kidnappings for ransom, with monies for the group claimed as "revolutionary taxes."
- The political wing, Batsuna, was declared illegal in 2003. A Spanish court found that the party was channeling public funds for use in terrorist activities. Between 1998 and 2001 it was known as Euskal Herritarrok, or "We Basque Citizens."

Aims/goals:

- The ETA wants to establish an independent Basque homeland, and during the mid-1960s the group adopted a Marxist-Leninist philosophy, but has altered philosophies over time.
- It usually maintains a socialistic orientation.

Area of operations:

- The ETA operates in the northern provinces of Vizcaya, Guipuzcoa, Alava, and Navarra. French departments of Labourd, Basse-Navarra, and Soule. They are suspected of operating outside their primary regions in attacking selected French and Spanish targets.

Strengths:

- Exact number of the group's members is unknown, but it is still believed to be significant.

Weapons/tactics/capabilities:

- Small arms, assault rifles, mortars, improvised explosive devices, both hand carried and vehicular borne.
- Targets selected included military and police installations, as well as Civil Guard barracks, judges, prosecutors, and journalists.
- Over the years the ETA has been responsible for some 825 deaths and 1,800 injuries in launching some 1,600 terrorist attacks. In the past, tactics have included mortar attacks, car bombings, assassinations using high explosives, extortion, and robbery to finance operations.
- Currently one of the last secular nationalistic terrorist groups operating in Western Europe, and although a number of key members have been arrested in both Spain and southern France, the ETA has proven to be a resilient terrorist group and will probably continue operations into the near future.

Major actions:

- June 2009: Exploded a powerful car bomb in the city of Bilbao. The attack killed one police officer.
- December 12, 2007: Killed two Spanish Civil Guards on counterterrorism duties in France. This attack ended the so-called permanent cease-fire and marked the first time since 1976 that a Spanish police agent was killed on French soil.

- December 30, 2006: Placed a bomb in a garage at the Madrid airport that injured 19 people.
- 1973: Assassinated Admiral Luis Carrera Blanco, the apparent successor to Francesco Franco, by planting a bomb underground where he usually parked his car.

10. Communist Party of the Philippines/ New People's Army (CPP/NPA)

A.k.a.:
- New People's Army (NPA).

Organization:
- NPA is a Maoist-oriented group formed in the spring of 1969 and is the military wing of the Communist Party in the Philippines. Very small from the onset, the declaration of marshal law in September 1972 drew thousands of students to its ranks.
- The group was designated as a foreign terrorist organization by the U.S. State Department in August 2002.

Aims/goals:
- Overthrow of the Philippine government.

Area of operations:
- The NPA primarily operates in rural Luzon, Visayas, and parts of Mindanao. It also has several cells that operate in Manila.

Strengths:
- The group reached its peak strength of some 25,000 members during the 1980s, but subsequently reduced to approximately 8,000 active cadre.

Weapons/tactics/capabilities:
- The NPA targets Philippine security forces, central government officials, and the local government. Also includes private businesses that refuse extortion demands or, as they are referred to, "revolutionary taxes."

Major actions:
- Prior to the U.S. base closures in 1992, the group targeted and killed several U.S. military personnel.
- The NPA primarily wages a guerrilla-type war against Philippine military and security forces.

11. Continuity, Irish Republican Army (CIRA)

A.k.a.:

- CIRA, Volunteers of Ireland, Continuity Army Council, IRA, Republican Sein Fein.

Organization:

- Organized as a paramilitary group in September 1986 after a split from the Provisional IRA.
- The CIRA has announced its intention to continue the struggle and not abide by the Belfast Agreement or participate in the decommissioning of weapons.
- The group has in all probability received financial assistance from sympathizers in the United States and arms from the Balkans with the assistance of other IRA factions. In addition, the CIRA may have links with the ETA in Spain.

Aims/goals:

- The CIRA is a radical, nationalistic terrorist group dedicated to the overthrow of British rule in Northern Ireland.

Area of operations:

- Active around the Belfast area and along the borders of Northern Ireland.
- The leadership of the CIRA is believed to operate from Ulster and Munster Counties.

Strengths:

- Approximately 50 hard-core members.
- Although reduced somewhat in strength over the last several years, it has been able to maintain membership through a selective recruitment program.

Weapons/tactics/capabilities:

- The group's actions include bombings, assassinations, kidnappings, extortion, robberies, and hijacking. The CIRA uses small arms weapons, improvised explosives, and improvised mortars in its attacks, as well as vehicle-borne IEDs and hoax devices.
- On July 13, 2004, the U.S. Department of State declared CIRA a foreign terrorist organization.

Major actions:

- 2001: The CIRA is suspected of carrying out bombings in Banbridge, Markethill, Moria, and Portadown, Northern Ireland.
- 2000: The group may have been complicit in the bombing of the BBC TV station in London, as well as the bomb attack at Hammersmith Bridge that June.

- November 1987: The group is suspected of detonating a 1,200-pound IED outside a hotel in Enniskillen, Northern Ireland. The explosion killed 11 and injured 63.

12. Gama'a al-Islamiyya (Islamic Group)

A.k.a.:
- The Islamic Group (GIA).

Organization:
- The GIA was formally organized in 1973 as an offshoot to the Egyptian Brotherhood after that group renounced the use of violence.
- The group was initially comprised primarily of militant students from the Asyut University located on the upper Nile. Almost from the beginning the GIA received spiritual guidance from Sheik Omar al-Rahman (who would later direct the 1993 attack on the World Trade Center in New York City) and soon began issuing a number of fatwas that justified the group's attacks on Christian targets in Egypt.
- In 2003 the group renounced bloodshed and in return the Egyptian government released over 2,000 suspected members from jail.

Aims/goals:
- Convert Egypt to a total Islamic state.

Area of operations:
- Operated throughout Egypt, particularly in the al-Minya, Asyut, Qina, and Sohja regions, as well in Cairo, Alexandria, and several other urban locations.

Strengths:
- At one time it was largest, most powerful, and deadliest terrorist group operating in Egypt, especially during the 1990s. Its numbers have been reduced through the concerted effort of Egyptian security forces after the 1997 infamous Luxor terrorist attack.

Weapons/tactics/capabilities:
- Many of the members fled to Afghanistan when the Egyptian government began an earnest crackdown on the GIA after the 1997 Luxor attacks. It was here that the group members forged strong ties with other Islamic radicals as well as Osama bin Laden.
- The Islamic Group primarily attacks secular targets such as bookstores, movie houses, banks, and tourist attractions.

- Since 2003, when the group renounced violence, it has been reported that a few members are slipping back into their old ways.
- In the past, the GIA has used small arms, automatic weapons, and explosives in its attacks.

Major actions:

- November 17, 1997: The group attacked a popular location for foreign tourists at the Luxor archaeological site located along the Nile River. The Islamic groups along with members of the Holy War of the Vanguard of the Conquest (Jihad Talaat al-Fatah) attacked with automatic weapons and knives, killing 63 people; 59 of the victims were foreigners.

13. Hamas

A.k.a.:

- Islamic Resistance Movement, Harakat al-Muqawamat al-Islamiyyah.
- Hamas operational cells: Students of Ayyash, Students of the Engineer, Yahay Ayyash Units (Ayyash was a Hamas bomb maker killed in 1996).

Organization:

- Hamas was created in 1987 by members of the Muslim Brotherhood's Palestinian faction, by Sheik Ahmed Ahmed Yassin, along with Abdel al-Rantissi and Mohammed Taha. The founding was coincidental to the first Palestinian uprising against Israeli rule, with the name *Hamas* first appearing on leaflets distributed to Palestinian youth.
- Currently a semilegitimized sociopolitical group that maintains a military force known as the Izzad ad-Din al-Qssam Brigades.
- In January 2006, Hamas was successful in carrying 76 of the 132 seats in the Palestinian parliamentary elections. The group succeeded in ousting former ruling party, Fatah, but in 2007 the two parties reached an agreement on unity of government. Shortly after this agreement was reached, it fell apart and factional violence broke out.
- The annual budget for Hamas operations has been placed between $50 million and $70 million. The funds were raised through so-called charitable contributions and direct funding from various Arab states, primarily Saudi Arabia.
- Besides being listed as a foreign terrorist organization by the United States, Hamas is also listed as a terrorist organization by Canada, the European Union, Japan, Israel, the UK, and Australia.

Area of operations:

- West Bank, Gaza, and within the borders of Israel.

Aims/goals:

- The aim of Hamas is to create an Islamic state in the West Bank and Gaza, and the breakup of the state of Israel.

Strengths:

- The military wing of Hamas is thought to have between several hundred to more than a thousand hard-core members, with several thousand more in support roles and as followers.

Weapons/tactics/capabilities:

- Hamas was the first terrorist group to use suicide bombers as a major weapon of choice.
- The group utilizes Qassam rockets to fire into Israeli territory. These are improvised, free-flying rockets with an explosive payload ranging from 1 to 22 pounds.
- Suspected of receiving funding, training, and weapons from Iran, with additional funding through donations from sympathizers and supporters in Western Europe and North America, as well as Palestinian expatriates.

Major actions:

- March 27, 2002: Passover suicide bombing. A 24-year-old suicide bomber breached the security of the Park Hotel in Netanya, Israel, and detonated a bomb in the dining room during a Passover celebration. There were 28 people killed immediately, with 2 dying later; in addition, 140 were injured.
- April 1993: Hamas uses suicide bombers for the first time, and by 1994 began a campaign of suicide attacks across Israel and Palestinian-occupied territories.
- 1994: Hamas launches its suicide bomb campaign within Israel and the Gaza Strip.
- October 19, 1994: Suicide bomber attacked a Dizengoff Street bus, killing 22 people. It was the deadliest suicide attack in Israel's history to date.

14. Harakat ul-Jihad-i-Islami/Bangladesh (HUJI-B)

A.k.a.:

- Movement of Islamic Holy War.

Organization:

- The HUJI-B was formed in 1992 with the aim of establishing an Islamic state within Bangladesh. Led by Shaugat Osman, it was formed with the assistance of Osama bin Laden's International Islamic Front.

- The group has established ties with Harakat ul-jihad-i-Islami and Harakat ul-Majahidin, which has suspected ties with the Pakistani intelligence services.

Area of operations:

- The HUJI-B operates from six camps that are primarily located along the coastal area of Bangladesh, from the port city of Chittagong south to the Myanmarese border.

Aims/goals:

- A Sunni-Islamic fundamentalist nationalistic-oriented terrorist group looking to establish an Islamic rule in Bangladesh.

Strengths:

- Believed to have a membership of 1,000 hard-core members, but that number is suspect.

Weapons/tactics/capabilities:

- From its coastal enclaves, the group's activities include gun running, smuggling, and piracy.

Major actions:

- Engaging in low-intensity warfare within Bangladesh, the group targets progressive intellectuals for assassination.
- Suspected in the attack of a veteran journalist who was making a documentary on the plight of Hindus within Bangladesh.
- HUJI-B members were named as responsible for the assassination attempt on Bangladesh Prime Minister Sheik Husina in 2000.

15. Harakat ul-Mujahidin (HUM)

A.k.a.:

- Movement of the Holy Warrior, Harakat ul-Ansar al-Hadid, Al-Hadith, Al-Faran.

Organization:

- HUM is a Pakistani Islamic militant group formed in 1985.
- Politically aligned with the radical Jamiat Ulema-I-Islam Fuzlar Rehman Faction (JUI-F) party. In 2000, many members of HUM defected to JEM.
- In 2003, HUM began operating under the banner of Jamiat ul-Ansar.
- HUM gets operating funds through donations from wealthy donors in Pakistan, Kashmir, Saudi Arabia, and other Gulf and Islamic states. The amount of funds raised is unknown.

Area of operations:
- Base operations in Pakistan, primarily in the disputed Kashmir region in the areas of Muzzaffarabad, Rawalpindur, and several other Pakistani towns in the Kashmir region.

Aims/goals:
- Originally formed to fight the Soviet incursion into Afghanistan, but later turned its efforts to the fight for an independent state of Kashmir.

Strengths:
- Comprised of several hundred fighters.
- The fighters are mostly of Pakistani and Kashmiri origin, but also include a number of Afghan and Arab veterans of the Afghan war.

Weapons/tactics/capabilities:
- HUM is mostly armed with light and heavy machine guns, assault rifles, mortars, and explosives.
- In January 2005, under suspected pressure by the Pakistani government, the long-time leader Fazlur Rehman Khalil was forced aside and replaced by Dr. Badr Munir. This change of leadership was due to Khalil's close ties to Osama bin Laden—Khalil's signature was found on a 1998 fatwa calling for attacks on U.S. and Western interests.

Major actions:
- Continuous operations against Indian troops and civilian targets in the disputed Kashmir region, as well as launching operations into Afghanistan.
- July 1995: Kidnapped five Western tourists in Kashmir; the group killed one in July and the remainder in December of the same year.
- December 1999: Hijacked an Indian airliner and demanded the release of a former Harakat ul-Ansar leader, Masood Azhar.

16. Hizballah

A.k.a.:
- Party of God, Islamic Jihad, Islamic Jihad Organization, Revolutionary Justice Organization, Organization of the Oppressed on Earth, Islamic Jihad for the Liberation of Palestine, Organization of Right against Wrong, Ansar Alla, Followers of the Prophet Mohammed.

Organization:
- It is a radical Shia Islamic organization that formed in 1982 in response to Israel's invasion of Lebanon. The group followed the

teachings of the late Ayatollah Khomeini and now follows the teachings of his successor.

- During the 1990s Hizballah transformed itself into a legitimate political force in Lebanon by winning and holding a number of elected seats in the 128-seat Lebanese National Assembly.
- Hizballah maintains close ties with Iran and often acts under its direction. In addition, the group has assisted Syria in advancing its political agenda in the region.
- The Hizballah organization receives training and logistical support (weapons and explosives) from Iran. Political, organizational aid is given by both Syria and Iran. Funding is gotten from private donations and both legal and illegal business enterprises.
- Hizballah has recently decreased its presence in southern Lebanon in accordance with the August 11, 2006, United Nations Council Resolution 1701 calling for a cease-fire in the Israeli-Lebanon conflict. Yet, it is believed that Hizballah has secreted large arms caches for future use.

Area of operations:
- This terrorist group operates primarily in the southern suburbs of Beirut, the Bekaa Valley, and southern Lebanon.
- Hizballah has also established support cells in Europe, Africa, South and North America, and Asia.

Aims/goals:
- The destruction of the state of Israel and replacing it with a Palestinian state.

Strengths:
- Estimates of the number of active members are all over the map, ranging from several hundred hard-core members to several thousand, with tens of thousands of supporters.

Weapons/tactics/capabilities:
- The group provides support to several Palestinian terrorist groups with weapons, explosives, training, and funding, as well as political support.
- The group claims to have some 33,000 various types of rockets in its weapons inventory, of which it regularly fires into Israeli territory.

Actions:
- July 2006: Fired more than 2,200 rockets into Israel, most coming from the area of the Sheeba farms; these attacks killed 17 civilians. In other attacks, more than 20 Israeli soldiers were killed.
- 1994: Jewish Cultural Center bombing in Argentina.
- 1992: Attack on the Israeli Embassy in Buenos Aires.

- Between 1982 and 1986, Hizballah claimed some 36 suicide attacks against U.S., French, and Israeli targets in Lebanon. These attacks include the 1983 Embassy and Marine barracks bombing.

17. Islamic Jihad Group (IJG)

A.k.a.:
- Al-Djihad al-Islami, Dzhamaat Modzhakhedov, Islamic Jihad Group of Uzbekistan, Jama'at al-Jihad, Jamiat al-Jihad al Islami, Jamiyat, the Jamaat Mojahadin, the Kazakh Jama'at, the Libyan Society, Islamic Jihad Union.

Organization:
- IJG was formed in 2002 as an extremist Islamic terrorist organization that splintered from the Islamic Movement of Uzbekistan.
- Unknown how the group is funded, but most certainly al Qaeda is a prime candidate.

Area of operations:
- The group operates throughout South and Central Asia.

Aims/goals:
- It is vehemently anti-Western and against secular rule in Uzbekistan and wants the government replaced with an Islamic governing body.

Strengths:
- The strength of the group is unknown.

Weapons/tactics/capabilities:
- The IJG makes extensive use of suicide bombers, as well as an assortment of small arms, including assault rifles and light machine guns.

Major actions:
- 2008: Three members of the IJG were arrested in Germany plotting to bomb U.S. military bases as well as Rhine Main Airport. The group acquired a large amount of hydrogen peroxide, which is an explosive precursor. All three suspects who were arrested had been trained at al Qaeda training camps in Pakistan.
- May 2005: Issued a statement supporting the attacks made against Uzbek police and military targets, while calling for the overthrow of the government.
- July 2004: Claimed credit for suicide bomb attacks against the U.S. and Israeli Embassies in Tashkent.
- March–April 2004: The IJG launched a series of attacks within the country that included female suicide bombers targeting police roadblocks and a popular bazaar. The attacks killed 47

people, including 33 terrorists, 10 police officers, and 4 civilians. Credit for the attacks was claimed on several Islamic websites. It also marked the first time that suicide bombers were used in Central Asia.

18. Islamic Movement of Uzbekistan (IMU)

A.k.a.:
- IMU.

Organization:
- In 1998, the IMU radical Islamic terrorist organization was formed in Uzbekistan under the leadership of Tohir Toldashev.
- The IMU embraces the anti-Western ideology prescribed by Osama bin Ladin and the al Qaeda group.
- The terrorist group receives both financial and material support from other Islamic groups and patrons in the Middle East, Central and South Asia.

Area of operations:
- Members of the IMU are spread out in Iran and South and Central Asia. They are active mostly in Afghanistan, Iran, Kyrgyzstan, Pakistan, Tajikistan, Kazakhstan, and Uzbekistan.

Aims/goals:
- Its prime mission is to overthrow the secular government in Uzbekistan and form a radical Islamic state in its place.

Strengths:
- Comprised of approximately 500 hard-core members.

Weapons/tactics/capabilities:
- The IMU has been predominantly occupied with attacks against the United States and other NATO troops operating in Afghanistan. It is also active in a number of Central Asian countries, with several members being arrested in Tajikistan in 2005.
- The IMU weapons of choice are the car bomb and the kidnapping of foreign nationals.
- Although relatively quiet since 2001, the group is still considered a viable threat in the area.

Major actions:
- November 2004: A suicide bomber exploded a bomb in the southern Kyrgyz city of Osh that killed a police officer.
- May 2003: Security forces in Kyrgyzstan arrested an IMU cell that was planning to attack the U.S. Embassy and a nearby hotel

in Bishkek. The group also claimed credit for a bombing in Osh that killed eight people.
- The IMU has claimed credit for several bombings in the city of Tashkent.
- August 2000: Took four U.S. mountain climbers hostage.
- August 1999: Took four Japanese geologists hostage.

19. Jaish-e-Mohammed (JEM)

A.k.a.:
- JEM, Army of Mohammed, Jaish-i-Mohammed, Khudamul Islam, Kuddam e Islami, Mohammed's Army, Tehrik ul-Furqaan.

Organization:
- JEM is an Islamic extremist group founded in early 2000 by Massod Azhar, a former member of the terrorist group Harakat ul-Ansar.
- Outlawed by Pakistan in 2002 and has since aligned itself with the radical political party Jamiat-i-Islam's Fazlur Rehman Faction. In 2003 the JEM splintered into Khuddam ul-Islam (KUI), headed by Azhur, and Jamaat ul-Furqan.
- Funding for the group is provided through other Islamic radical organizations as well as legitimate front business enterprises. Money is also gained from sympathetic supporters and fund-raisers.

Area of operations:
- Pakistan and Kashmir, with several training areas reported in Afghanistan.

Aims/goals:
- The aims of JEM are the overthrow of Indian rule in Kashmir and uniting it with Pakistan.
- The group openly declared war on the United States.

Strengths:
- JEM is reported to have several hundred hard-core fighters and a following of thousands throughout India's southern Kashmir and Doda regions.

Weapons/tactics/capabilities:
- JEM has launched a number of fatal attacks on soft targets within Pakistan and Kashmir, including a number of suicide car bombings in Kashmir.
- The group is armed with a variety of automatic weapons, assault rifles, mortars, improvised explosive devices, and rocket-propelled grenades.

Major actions:

- 2009: Indian security authorities detained several JEM members in connection with an attack on the Sri Lanka cricket team in Lahore.
- 2007: Participated in the Red Mosque uprising.
- July 2004: A JEM member was arrested in connection with the abduction and murder of U.S. journalist Daniel Pearl.
- December 2001: The group launched an attack on the Indian Parliament that killed 9 and injured 18.

20. Jemaah-Islamiya (JI)

A.k.a.:

- JI.

Organization:

- Abu Bakar Basir and Addullah Sunkar founded the group in 1969, incorporating several smaller terrorist organizations. Abu Baker Basir was implicated in the 2002 Bali bombings, sentenced to several years in prison and released in 2006. In a massive crackdown by Indonesian authorities following terrorism violence, more than 300 members of JI have been apprehended and jailed.

Area of operations:

- Although the group is based in Indonesia, it operates throughout Southeast Asia, notably in Malaysia and the Philippines.

Aims/goals:

- The Jemaah Islamiya is a terrorist group that wants to establish an Islamic caliphate, or ruling body, that encompasses the southern Philippines, Indonesia, Malaysia, southern Thailand, Singapore, and Brunei.

Strengths:

- It is difficult to determine just how large JI may be, although intelligence sources believe that the number could run into the thousands, but certainly there are at least several hundred hard-core fighters.

Weapons/tactics/capabilities:

- Operational funding and logistical support for the group are received from several sources in the Middle East and nongovernment organizations that are ideologically like-minded. The group is also capable of raising funds through various criminal activities.
- Uses small arms, automatic weapons, and explosives in attacks.

Major actions:

- May 2007: A bomb exploded in Sultan Kudarat in the Philippines in an attack that killed five people and injured scores more. It was the second bomb attack in Tacurong City within a six-month period.

- October 1, 2005: A suicide bomb attack in Bali left 26 people dead. One bomb was detonated in a restaurant in the Kuta Square shopping mall, and two others at a food court near the Four Seasons Hotel. A fourth bomb was later recovered unexploded.
- September 2004: Detonated a bomb outside the Austrailian Embassy in Jakarta.
- October 12, 2002: Island of Bali. The JI carried out the deadliest terrorist attack in Indonesian history. The attack killed 202 people and injured 240 others when JI terrorists attacked popular tourist locations on the island. The attack was carried out by three suicide bombers and a large vehicle-borne explosive device. An additional attack was made upon the U.S. Consulate in Denpasar. A number of JI members were arrested in connection with these attacks, and three members were sentenced to death.

21. Al-Jihad

A.k.a.:
- Egyptian Islamic Jihad, Egyptian al-Jihad, New Jihad Group, Jihad Group, Vanguards of Conquest, Talaa' al-Fatah.

Organization:
- The group emerged in 1979 as an extremely radical offshoot of the Muslim Brotherhood based in the Cairo districts of Boulaq, Nahia, and Kerdasa. Until about 1981, it grew by absorbing members of lesser underground radical groups.
- The early leader of the group, Ayman al-Zawahiri, connected with Osama bin Laden during the Soviet invasion of Afghanistan. During this time they combined their resources and tactical expertise to form a strong terrorist organization. From his number two position in the new organization, Zawahiri launched his war against the Egyptian government.
- Al Qaeda officially absorbed EIJ, and bin Laden and Zawahiri issued a joint fatwa—"World Islamic Front against Jews and Crusaders"—which denounced Israel and Western culture and urged the killing of Americans and their allies.

Area of operations:
- For the past several years, al-Jihad operated outside Egypt under the direction of al Qaeda leadership.

- Primary areas of operations are conducted in Afghanistan, Pakistan, Lebanon, the United Kingdom, and Yemen. It is also suspected that it has a presence in the Sudan.

Aims/goals:

- Initially founded with the aim of overthrowing the Egyptian government and establishing an Islamic state.

Strengths:

- The group is believed to have several hundred hard-core members, but a protracted campaign against the group by Egyptian authorities has greatly reduced its effectiveness in operating in Egypt.

Weapons/tactics/capabilities:

- External aid for the organization in obtaining weapons is not exactly known, but it is believed that the usual suspects are involved—Iran and the bin Laden organization. The group has the usual laundry list of small arms and explosives and makes extensive use of suicide bombers.
- Funding is achieved through donations from nongovernmental organizations, front business operations, and criminal enterprises.

Major actions:

- June 1995: The group failed in an attempt to assassinate Egyptian president Hosni Mubarak. In this attempt the Jihad group partnered with the Egyptian group al-Gama'a al-Islamyya and with the support of Sudanese intelligence services.
- October 1981: Assassination of Anwar Sadat. For this action Zawahiri was imprisoned for three years, and upon his release he moved to Pakistan.
- Since the 1998 issuing of the fatwa, attacks have been carried out against the U.S. Embassies in Kenya and Tanzania, the attack on the *USS Cole*, and of course the attack on the WTC on September 11, 2001.

22. Kahane Chai

A.k.a.:

- Kach, American Friends of the United Yeshiva, Committee for the Safety of the Roads, DOV, Forefront of the Idea, Jewish Legion, Judea Police, Kahane, Kahane Lives, Kfar Tapuah Fund, Koach, Meir's Youth, New Kach Movement, Repression of Traitors, Sword of David, Committee against Racism and Discrimination (CARD), International Kahane Movement, the Judean Legion, the Judean Voice, the Voice of Judea, the Way of the Torah, the Yeshiva of the Jewish Idea, Yeshivat Harav, among others.

Organization:

- It is an extreme right-wing political party founded in the early 1990s by the son of the late Rabbi Meir Kahane and based in Israel.
- The group traces its roots to Meir Kahane's Jewish Defense League, a U.S. domestic terrorist group that carried out a series of bomb attacks in the New York City area in the late 1960s and early 1970s.

Area of operations:

- The groups centers its activities in Israel and West Bank settlements, particularly Qiryat Arba' in Hebron.

Aims/goals:

- To restore the biblical state of Israel. The group was founded by Meir Kahane's son Binyamin after his father's assassination in 1990.

Strengths:

- Membership is unknown, but it has been reported that it disbanded in 2005.

Weapons/tactics/capabilities:

- The group received financial support from sympathizers in the United States and Europe.
- Smalls arms and explosive devices.

Major actions:

- Suspected in a number of low-level attacks against Palestinian targets since the al-Aqsa Intifada in 2000. It has also vowed revenge for the death of Binyamin Kahane and his wife, killed by Force 17 in December 2000.
- The Kahani Chai have harassed and threatened Arab, Palestinian, and moderate Israeli government officials alike.

23. Kata'ib Hizballah

A.k.a.:

- Hezbollah in Iraq, Hezbollah Brigades, Hizballah Brigades, Hizballah Brigades in Iraq, Hizballah Brigades-Iraq, Hizballah Brigades-Iraq of the Islamic Resistance in Iraq, Islamic Resistance in Iraq, Katibat Abu Fathel Al A'abas, Katibut Karbalah, Katibat Zayd Ebin Ali.

Organization:

- This terrorist group was organized in 2007 in the wake of the disbanding of the Sha'i Mahdi Army, but did not have any connection to that group.
- The U.S. Department of the Treasury designated Kata'ib Hezbollah and al-Muhandis foreign terrorist entities in July 2009, and the U.S. Department of State followed suit.

Area of operations:

- Operates within the Green Zone in Baghdad, Sadr City, as well as the traditional Shi'ite areas, especially around the al-Quds Mosque.

Aims/goals:

- To drive U.S. forces from Iraq.

Strengths:

- May have as many as 2,000 fighters, but it may be far fewer.

Weapons/tactics/capabilities:

- The group makes extensive use of roadside IEDs in attacking U.S. forces as well as other allied forces.
- Makes use of classic guerrilla tactics, i.e., using quick hit-and-run attacks and psychological warfare to get people to come to its side.
- Makes extensive use of snipers, especially in populated urban areas.

Major actions:

- February 2008: Rocket attack in Rustamiya area of Baghdad results in one U.S. civilian death and other injuries to U.S. civilians and Coalition Forces personnel.
- December 2009: Believed to have grabbed encrypted code information from a Predator drone.

24. Kongra-Gel

A.k.a.:

- Kurdistan Workers Party (PKK), Freedom and Democracy Congress (KADEK), Hulu Mesru Savunma Kuvveti (HSK), Kurdistan Freedom and Democracy Congress, Partiya Karkeran Kurdistan, People's Congress of Kurdistan, the People's Defense Force.
- Note: The organization is commonly referred to as the KGK/PKK, and thus will be referred to as such in this section.

Organization:

- The KGK/PKK is a Marxist-Leninist separatist organization consisting mainly of Kurds formed in 1978 by Abdullah Ocalan.

The People's Defense Force is reportedly the military wing of the KGK/PKK movement.

- Ocalan was arrested in 1999 and sentenced to death. He later announced a "peace initiative" ordering a retreat from violence, thus earning a commutation of his sentence to life in prison, where he still remains the symbolic head of the movement.
- In June 2004, a group of hard-liners took control of the movement and renounced the cease-fire.
- In the past, financial and material aid has been received in modest amounts from Iraq, Iran, and Syria, but recently Syria and Iran have cooperated with Turkey in efforts to combat the group.

Area of operations:
- The PKK operates primarily in Turkey, Iraq, Europe, and the Middle East.

Aims/goals:
- KGK/PKK wishes to establish an independent Kurdish state.
- In recent years the KGK/PKK has scaled back demands and turned toward gaining autonomy within Turkey that would include guaranteeing cultural and language rights.

Strengths:
- There are approximately 4,000 to 5,000 members, with approximately 3,500 located in the Kurdish area of northern Iraq.

Weapons/tactics/capabilities:
- The KGK/PKK launches raids from its bases in northern Iraq into eastern and western Turkey. Targets include Turkish security forces, local Turkish officials, and those who oppose the organization.
- KGK/PKK still maintains a robust extortion, fund-raising, and propaganda network throughout Europe.

Major actions:
- In 1984, the KGK/PKK began to launch a series of violent acts that included a number of urban assaults and bombings.
- Conducted attacks against Turkish diplomatic and commercial entities in Western Europe between 1993 and 1995.
- In 2000, the KGK/PKK carried out 5 attacks and after that steadily increased its acts of violence to more than 70 in 2007.
- October 2007: The Turkish army crossed the northern Iraq border in heavy force to operate against the KGK/PKK fighters in that area. The Turks drove some 30 miles into Iraqi territory, but pulled back after a short period of time.
- 2008 was the most violent year, with more than 140 deaths attributed to KGK/PKK attacks in eastern Turkey.

25. Lashkar-e-Tayyiba (LT)

A.k.a.:
- LT, Al Mansooren, Al Monsoorian, Army of the Pure and Righteous, Army of the Righteous, Lashkar e-Taiba, Paasban-e-Ahle-Hadis, Paasban-e-Kashmir, Paasban-I-Ahle-Hadith, Pasban-e-Kashmir, among others.

Organization:
- The group was formed in the late 1980s as the military wing of the Islamic extremist group Markaz Dawa il-Irshad, a Pakistani group opposing the Russian occupation of Afghanistan prior to its withdrawal in 1989. LT is led by Hafiz Muhammad Saeed.
- The majority of LT members are Pakistanis from Madrassas (Islamic schools) across Pakistan or Afghanistan or veterans of the Afghan War.
- Funds for operating the group are raised through donations throughout the Middle East, the United Kingdom, Islamic nongovernmental organizations, as well as Pakistani and Kashmiri business people. The exact amount of funds raised is not known.

Area of operations:
- The LT operates in the Muridke and Muzaffarabad regions of Pakistan, where it maintains several training camps, schools, and medical clinics. The group is active in southern Jammu and Kashmir, the Kashmir Valley, as well as the Doda region.

Aims/goals:
- Introduction of Islam throughout South Asia and the freedom of the Islamic people in Kashmir.

Strengths:
- Size of the group is unknown, but it is believed to be the largest and most proficient of the separatist groups operating in Pakistan.

Weapons/tactics/capabilities:
- The LT arsenal includes assault rifles, light and heavy machine guns, mortars, explosives, and rocket-propelled grenades.

Major actions:
- Since 1993, the LT has conducted a number of operations that target Indian military and civilians in Jammu and Kashmir, as well as carrying out a number of attacks against high-profile targets in India proper.
- November 2008: LT is the primary suspect in the five terrorist attacks in Mumbai (formally Bombay), India. There were 173 people killed in these attacks and 308 wounded.

- September 2006: Issued a fatwa against Pope Benedict XVI demanding that Muslims assassinate him for his statements about Mohammad the group deemed unacceptable.
- July 2006: LT suspected in the attack on the Suburban Railway system in Mumbai, India. Seven bombs were detonated within a short period of time, killing 209 and injuring 700.

26. Lashkar I Jhangvi (LJ)

A.k.a.:
- LJ.

Organization:
- Formed in 1996, LJ is an extremist group that is an offshoot of the Sunni Deobandi group Sipah-I-Sahaba Pakistan and was declared a terrorist group by Pakistan in 2001.
- Declared a terrorist group by the United States in 2003.
- Other than receiving assistance from the Taliban, other sources of external assistance are not known. The LJ has additional ties to al Qaeda and the Islamic Movement of Uzbekistan.

Area of operations:
- Active in the Punjab and Karachi areas, with members traveling between Pakistan and Afghanistan.

Aims/goals:
- To end the secular rule of Pakistan and convert it into an Islamic state.

Strengths:
- There are probably fewer than 100 hard-core members of LJ.

Weapons/tactics/capabilities:
- The group specializes in armed attacks and bombings against Shia targets. When the Taliban collapsed in 2002–2003, LJ members provided fleeing terrorists with safe houses and false identities in the Pakistani cities of Karachi, Peshawar, and Rawalpindi. With the resurgence of the Taliban in Afghanistan, LJ members have received sanctuary for their activities in Pakistan.

Major actions:
- December 27, 2007: LJ was implicated in the suicide bomb attack that killed Benazir Bhutto and 20 other people.
- March 2002: Claimed responsibility in an attack on a bus using an IED that killed 15 people, including 11 French technicians.
- January 2002: Linked to the kidnapping and murder of U.S. journalist Daniel Pearl.

- 1999: Attempted to assassinate Pakistani Prime Minister Nawaz Sharif.
- 1997: Killed four U.S. oil workers in Karachi.

27. Liberation Tigers of Tamil Eelam (LTTE)

A.k.a.:
- Ellalan Force, Tamil Tigers, Ellan Force, World Tamil Movement, World Tamil Association (WTA), Federation of Associations of Canadian Tamils (FACT).

Organization:
- Separatist group operating in Sri Lanka—formerly known as Ceylon.
- The LTTE had at one time controlled a substantial portion of northern Sir Lanka.

Area of operations:
- Throughout Sri Lanka.

Aims/goals:
- To create an independent state of Tamil in north and east areas of the island nation of Sri Lanka, known at one time as Ceylon.

Strengths:
- Unknown—the leadership and main body were defeated in a conventional military operation in the spring of 2009.
- At its height of power, the LTTE was believed to have a main body of some 10,000 part-time fighters and a cadre of around 5,000.

Weapons/tactics/capabilities:
- Evolved from carrying out small terrorist actions to a full-fledged military organization that specialized in unconventional warfare.
- Engaged in an ethnic cleansing of the Muslim population in areas under the LTTE control. An example, in 1991 the LTTE expelled the entire Muslim population of Jaffina.

Major actions:
- 2001: An attack on Colombo's international airport by suicide bombers killed 16 and damaged a number of commercial and military aircraft.
- 1995/1997: Involved in a number of ship hijackings.

28. Libyan Islamic Fighting Group (LIFG)

A.k.a.:
- Al-Jama'a al-Islamiyyah al-Mugatilah bi-Libya.

Organization:

- The Libyan Islamic Fighting Group emerged in the early 1990s comprised of Libyan veterans of the Afghan war with the Soviet Union. On November 3, 2007, a senior leader of the group announced that it has officially joined with al Qaeda.
- Designated an FTO by the United States in 2004.
- Method of funding unknown, but probably from other Islamic radical groups and contributions from sympathizers.

Area of operations:

- Since the 1990s many members have moved to various Asian, Arabian Gulf, African, and European countries.

Aims/goals:

- The overthrow of Libyan strongman Muamar Khaddafy because they deem him as un-Islamic.

Strengths:

- Several hundred active and support members.

Weapons/tactics/capabilities:

- LIFG has been known to use suicide bombers in attacking targets and has engaged Libyan security forces on a number of occasions.
- This group should be considered a serious threat for Americans traveling in the region.

Major actions:

- 2003: One of the groups that planned and participated in the Casablanca suicide bombings. Twelve suicide bombers attacked a number of Jewish-connected targets and well as the five-star Hotel Farah. The attacks killed 33 civilians, as well as the 12 bombers.

29. Moroccan Islamic Combatant Group (GICM)

A.k.a.:

- Groupe Islamique Combatant Group.

Organization:

- Organization first surfaced in 1990s, comprised of Moroccan recruits who were training in Afghanistan.
- The group has used drug trafficking in North Africa and Europe to finance terrorist operations, in particular the 2003 Casablanca attack.

Area of operations:

- Morocco, Western Europe, Canada.

Aims/goals:
- Establish an Islamic state in Morocco and assist al Qaeda in its global terrorist campaign.

Strengths:
- Many of the leaders and members have been either jailed or killed in the past few years, leaving only a handful of radicals to pose a threat.
- Many of the surviving members have taken up residence in the United Kingdom.

Weapons/tactics/capabilities:
- The GICM has all but disintegrated as an organization and probably does not operate as a group.
- It is reported that GICM served as a recruitment tool for extremists to be used in bombing missions in Iraq, and that at least one member did carry out a suicide attack against the coalition forces.

Major actions:
- 2004: GICM members were among those involved in the 2004 Madrid train bombings. In this attack, 13 bombs were detonated on a number of commuter trains, with 191 people killed in the attack.
- 2003: Carried out a number of suicide bombings in Casablanca.

30. Mujahedin-e-Khalq Organization (MEK)

A.k.a.:
- MKO, Mujahadin-e-Khalq (Iran's name for the group), Muslim Iranian Students Society, National Council of Resistance (NCR), Organization of the People's Holy Warrior of Iran, the National Liberation Army of Iran (NLA), the People's Mujahadin Organization of Iran (PMOI), National Council of Resistance of Iran (NCRI), Sazeman-e-Mujahadin-e-Khalq-e Iran.

Organization:
- MEK first emerged in the early 1960s in Iran as a violent political movement that opposed the rule of the Shah of Iran and his close ties to the United States.
- The armed wing of MEK is known as the National Liberation Army of Iran (NLA).
- In 2006, the European Court of Justice ruled that MEK was not a terrorist organization, but the decision was not upheld by the Council of the European Union.

Area of operations:
- MEK is a global organization, with its primary focus on Iran and Middle Eastern countries.

- The group maintains several bases of operation in various European countries, with its main office located in Paris.

Aims/goals:

- MEK aims for the violent overthrow of the Iranian government, with the group's ideology swinging all over the map.

Strengths:

- Estimated total membership of between 5,000 and 10,000.
- There are an estimated 3,400 members in a camp north of Baghdad that is "protected" by coalition troops under the rules of the Fourth Geneva Convention. Those members outside the coalition camp are not included, nor are those operating as a terrorist organization. As a result of the 2003 agreement, MEK surrendered all of its heavy weapons, including tanks and heavy artillery that had been primarily used in Iraq's war with Iran.

Weapons/tactics/capabilities:

- During the 1980s, MEK launched a terrorist campaign against the Islamic government of Iran.
- After being expelled from France, MEK received much of its support from the Saddam Hussein regime in Iraq prior to his overthrow. Now much of the funding and support is obtained through front organizations, but the amount is unknown.
- MEK primarily uses acts of terrorism and global propaganda against the Iranian government.

Major actions:

- Attempted assassination of the commander of the Nasr organization that was responsible for coordinating activities in Iraq.
- During the 1970s, MEK killed several U.S. military personnel and civilians, as well as supporting the takeover of the U.S. Embassy in Teheran.

31. National Liberation Army (ELN)

A.k.a.:

- Ejercito de Liberacion Nacional (ELN).

Organization:

- The ELN was formed in 1964 by a group of urban intellectuals who took their inspiration from Fidel Castro and Che Guevara. Cuba still provides some assistance in the form of medical and advisors.
- In 2005, the Colombian government opened peace talks with the group and as of yet, no arrangement has been agreed on.

Area of operations:

- The mountains of north and northeastern Colombia. It is also active in the southwestern portion of the country and along the border with Venezuela.
- The ELN also maintains several urban units in the larger cities.

Aims/goals:

- The destabilization of the Colombian government.

Strengths:

- Reported to have between 1,500 and 3,000 fighters along with a number of active supporters.

Weapons/tactics/capabilities:

- The ELN engages in kidnappings, extortion, and drug dealing as major sources of income.

Major actions:

- 2004: Kidnapped the Catholic bishop of the Yopal district.
- Ongoing campaign of bombings and other terrorist activities.

32. Palestine Liberation Front (PLF)

A.k.a.:

- PFL-Abu Abbas, Palestine Liberation Front-Abu Abbas Faction.

Organization:

- Formed in the late 1970s as a splinter group of the Palestine Liberation Front-General Command (PFLP-GC). The PLF later split into two factions, one pro-Syrian and one pro-Palestinian.
- In 1993, the PFL publicly denounced terrorism and agreed to abide by the Oslo Accords, but is suspected of supporting other Palestinian terrorist groups through the 1990s.
- Abu Abbas, the PLF leader, died in Iraq, allegedly of natural causes, in 2004.

Area of operations:

- The group currently operates out of Lebanon and Syria.

Aims/goals:

- The fall of the state of Israel and replacing it with an independent Palestinian homeland.

Strengths:

- Estimated to be between 50 and 500.

Weapons/tactics/capabilities:

- Bombings, assassinations, and hijackings.
- Small arms, automatic weapons, mortars, and explosives.

Major actions:
- 1985: Attack and hijacking of the Italian cruise ship *Achille Lauro* and the murder of U.S. citizen Leon Klinghoffer.

33. Palestinian Islamic Jihad (PIJ)

A.k.a.:
- Palestine Islamic Jihad-Shaqaqi Faction, PIJ-Shaqaqi Faction, PIJ-Shallah Faction, Islamic Jihad of Palestine, Islamic Jihad in Palestine, Abu Ghunaym Squad of the Hiballah Bayt al-Maqdis, al-Quds Squads, al-Quds Brigades, Saraya al-Quds, Al-Awdah Brigades.

Organization:
- Formed by militant Palestinians in Gaza during the 1970s, with the senior leadership maintaining headquarters in Syria.
- Declared a terrorist organization by the United States, Canada, Australia, United Kingdom, Japan, and Israel.
- Receives financial assistance and safe haven from Syria.

Area of operations:
- Israel, Gaza, and the West Bank.

Aims/goals:
- Destruction of Israel and the formation of an Islamic Palestinian state.

Strengths:
- Unknown, but believed significant in numbers.

Weapons/tactics/capabilities:
- Extensive use of suicide bombers, small arms, rockets, and mortars.
- Although inactive for several years, it remains a viable terrorist group to be reckoned with.

Major actions:
- June 2007: Attempted kidnapping of several Israeli Defense Force soldiers at a Gaza checkpoint.
- April 2006: Suicide bomb attack in Tel Aviv that killed 11.
- October 2003: Suicide bomber attacked a Haifa restaurant that killed 22 people and injured numerous others.

34. Popular Front for the Liberation of Palestine (PFLP)

A.k.a.:
- Halhul Gang, Halhud Squad, Palestine Popular Resistance Forces (PPRF), Red Eagle Gang, Red Eagle Group, Red Eagles.

Organization:
- George Habash founded this Marxist-Leninist breakaway group of the Arab Nationalist Movement group in 1967. It is not religiously oriented, but rather a force against Western influence in the region.

Area of operations:
- Syria, Lebanon, Israel, the West Bank, and Gaza.

Aims/goals:
- The formation of an independent Palestinian state and the elimination of Israel.

Strengths:
- Unknown, but still a substantial threat.

Weapons/tactics/capabilities:
- Waged a campaign of spectacular terrorist attacks during the 1960s and 1970s that saw at least 20 Americans killed. Stepped up activity during the al-Aqsa Intifada.
- Explosives, rockets, mortars, assault weapons, and small arms.
- Receives some external support and safe haven from Syria.

Major actions:
- 2007: Suspected of a number of rocket attacks into Israel from the West Bank and Gaza.
- November 2004: Conducted a suicide attack on a public market in Tel Aviv in which three civilians were killed.
- 2001: Assassination of Israeli tourism minister Rehavam Ze'evi.
- May 1972: Launched a major terrorist attack that became known as the Lod Airport massacre; 28 people were killed in the Ben Gurion International airport by members of Japanese Red Army Factions acting in concert with the PFLP.
- February 1970: Terrorists open fire on El Al passengers on a bus at the Munich Airport, killing 1 and wounding 11.
- December 1968: PFLP opens fire on an El Al airplane in Athens, Greece, killing an Israeli mechanic.

35. Popular Front for the Liberation of Palestine— General Command (PFLP-GC)

A.k.a.:
- PFLP-GC.

Organization:
- PFLP-GC split from the parent PFPL in 1968 to become more militant and violent in order to distance itself from the political process.

Area of operations:
- Maintains a headquarters in Damascus, Syria, and bases in southern Lebanon.
- The PFLP-GC also has a presence in the Palestinian camps in Lebanon and Syria.

Aims/goals:
- A Marxist-Leninist philosophy that opposed the PLO political orientation.

Strengths:
- Several hundred, but it may be as high as several thousand.

Weapons/tactics/capabilities:
- Carried out numerous cross-border raids into Israel and dozens of terrorist acts in Europe during the 1970s and 1980s.
- The PFLP-GC is known for its unusual means of attacking a target, such as using hot air balloons or hang gliders.

Major actions:
- February 1970: The PFLP-GC detonated two IEDs on airborne aircraft using barometric pressure switches. The two aircraft were headed for Tel Aviv, one a Swiss Air plane and the other an Austrian Airline craft; both went down with all aboard.

36. Al Qaeda in Iraq (AQI)

A.k.a.:
- Al Qaeda Group of Jihad in Iraq, al Qaeda Group of Jihad in the Land of the Two Rivers, al Qaeda in Mesopotamia, al Qaeda in the Land of the Two Rivers, al Qaeda of Jihad in Iraq, al Qaeda of Jihad Organization in the Land of the Two Rivers, al Qaeda of the Jihad in the land of the Two Rivers, al Tawhid, Jam'at al Tawhid Wa'al Jihad, Tanzeem Qa'idat al Jihad/Bilad al Raafidaini, Monotheism and Jihad Group, Organization Base of Jihad/Country of the Two Rivers, Organization Base of Jihad/Mesopotamia, Organization of al Jihad's Base in Iraq, Organization of al-Jihad's Base of Operations in Iraq, Organization of Jihad's Base in the Country of the Two Rivers, al-Zarqawi Network.

Organization:
- Began to emerge shortly after the insurgency in Iraq from the growing number of foreign fighters and former members of Ansar al-Islam.
- Formally created in January 2006 in an attempt to pull together Sunni extremists operating in Iraq; al Qaeda in Iraq created an umbrella group, the Mujahidin Shura Council. In order to give

AQI more legitimacy in its aims, it formed an umbrella group under which to operate, Abu Omar al-Baghdadi.

- The founder of the group was a Jordanian jihadist, Abu Mus'ab al-Zarqawi, who was killed in an air strike in June 2007. He was replaced by Abu Ayyub al-Masri, who announced the Islamic state of Iraq.
- Receives funding from several sources in Europe and the Middle East as well as supporters in Iraq.

Area of operations:

- AQI carried out attacks mostly in Iraq, but has ventured into Jordanian territory to launch attacks of opportunity.

Aims/goals:

- Establish a caliphate in the region by declaring the Islamic state of Iraq, in which attacks are now carried out.

Strengths:

- It has been estimated that AQI may have upwards of 10,000 fighters, making it the largest Sunni terrorist group in the Middle East. Although the vast majority of the fighters are Iraqi, much of the leadership is not.

Weapons/tactics/capabilities:

- The main weapon of this group is the improvised explosive device, whether it is vehicle-borne, a suicide bomber, or hand placed.
- This group carries out most of the suicide bombings that produce mass casualties, particularly of civilian targets in the Baghdad area, which are intended to produce widespread media coverage.
- In the past, AQI has claimed credit for attacks along with Ansar al-Sunnah and the Islamic Army in Iraq, but ideological differences have kept these groups from merging.

Major actions:

- 2007: Attacks included suicide car bombings of a mosque in Al Habbaniyah and several suicide attacks against Shia pilgrims in Al Hillas.
- August 2003: Bombed the Jordanian Embassy in Baghdad and followed up that attack by bombing the UN Headquarters, where 23 employees were killed.

37. Al Qaeda (AQ)

A.k.a.:

- International Front for Fighting Jews and Crusaders, Islamic Army, Islamic Army for the Liberation of Holy Sites, Islamic

Salvation Front, the Base, the Group for the Preservation of the Holy Sites, the Islamic Army for the Liberation of the Holy Places, the World Islamic Front for Jihad against Jews and Crusaders, Usama bin Ladin Network, Usama bin Ladin Organization, al Jihad, the Jihad Group, Egyptian al Jihad, Egyptian Islamic Jihad, New Jihad.

Organization:

- Formed in 1988 by Osama bin Laden, who staffed the organization with Arabs who fought against the Russian forces in Afghanistan.
- Some of the terrorist groups with direct links to al Qaeda are the Gama'at al-Islamiyya, the Islamic Movement of Uzbekistan, the Islamic Jihad, Lashkar-i-Jhangvi, Harakat ul-Mujahadin, Ansar al-Sunnah, the Taliban, and Jemaah Islamiya.
- Since the post-9/11 setbacks, al Qaeda has reconstituted itself while given safe haven in the Federally Administered Tribal Areas of Pakistan. During this time, Ayman al-Zawahiri emerged as al Qaeda's strategic and operational planner.
- Financial support is garnered from donations provided to front charity organizations for humanitarian purposes and some Islamic charities. Monies are also gained from drug trafficking, credit card fraud, and hostage taking. U.S. and international initiatives to combat these efforts have somewhat diminished the group's ability to raise funds.

Area of operations:

- Global, in that it interacts with other Sunni extremist groups and is capable of having attacks launched against Western interests throughout the world.

Aims/goals:

- The aim of al Qaeda is to unite Muslims to fight the United States and its allies and to overthrow governments that it feels are un-Islamic and expel Westerners and non-Muslims from that area.
- The group's ultimate goal is to establish a pan-Islamic caliphate throughout the world.
- In February 1998, under the banner of the World Islamic Front for Jihad against Jews and Crusaders, a fatwa was issued calling for all Muslims to kill U.S. citizens, both civilian and military, and their allies anywhere they are found.

Strengths:

- It is very difficult to assess the actual number of al Qaeda fighters, but it is believed that there are several thousand members with affiliated terror groups under al Qaeda control or who follow their philosophy.

- Affiliated groups have memberships that number in the thousands.

Weapons/tactics/capabilities:

- Considered the number one threat against the United States and continues to plot major terrorist actions against U.S. targets in conjunction with allied organizations.
- The major weapons routinely utilized are suicide bombers on foot as well as "suiciders" in vehicle-borne IEDs. Attacks utilizing these weapons have been made in Africa, Europe, the Middle East, Afghanistan, Pakistan, and Iraq.
- The group remains committed to planning attacks that would produce mass casualties, dramatic destruction, and have a major financial consequence.

Major actions:

- July 2005: Attack against the London transit system; although there is no link to a direct involvement, it was al Qaeda inspired. This holds true for the remainder of the attacks mentioned below.
- March 2004: Attack against the Madrid transit system. Killed 190 and wounded 1,400 others.
- November 2002: Suicide bombing of a hotel in Mombasa that killed 15.
- September 11, 2001: Attacks on the World Trade Center in New York City and the Pentagon in Washington.
- October 12, 2000: Directed an attack, in all probability in conjunction with Sudanese intelligence agencies, against the *USS Cole* in Yemen harbor. The attack killed 17 sailors and wounded 39 others.
- Is suspected, along with the Taliban, for the suicide bombing attempt against former Pakistan Prime Minister Benazir Bhutto in Karachi. There were 144 people killed in the attack. A few months later, a senior Taliban commander with ties to al Qaeda assassinated Bhutto.

38. Al Qaeda in the Arabian Peninsula (AQAP)

A.k.a.

- AQAP.

Organization:

- The group emerged in January 2009 to incorporate small groups of Yemeni and Saudi Arabian radicals under one umbrella.
- Initial leadership fell to Amir Masir al-Wahish and the military commander, Qasim al-Rimi, both veteran commanders.

- Al Qaeda and AQAP began to publish an English language magazine called *Inspire*, with the first edition released in July 2010. Articles encourage those who want to act on their own, outside the al Qaeda umbrella, to do so. The publication also provides how-to information on constructing IEDs and assists in making contact with similar-minded individuals.
- The group was listed as a terrorist organization by the U.S. State Department on December 14, 2009.

Area of operations:
- Yemen and Saudi Arabia.
- Due to the security crackdown within Saudi Arabia, many of the fighters have been forced to flee to bases in Yemen.

Aims/goals:
- To support the activities of al Qaeda and establish strict Islamic law throughout the world.

Strengths:
- It is of unknown strength but considered to have numerous operatives.

Weapons/tactics/capabilities:
- The CIA describes the AQAP as a major threat to U.S. security.
- Explosives, assault weapons, as well as an assortment of small arms weapons.

Major actions:
- December 25, 2009: The group claimed credit for the attempted bombing of Northwest Flight 253 as the craft approached Detroit, in the Christmas Day "Underwear Bomber" incident.
- February 2006: Staged a raid on a political security prison and freed 23 al Qaeda members.

39. Al Qaeda in the Islamic Maghreb (formally GSPC)

A.k.a.:
- Tanzim al-Qa'ida fi Bilad al-Islamiya, Le Groupe Salafite pour la Predication et le Combat, Salafist Group for Preaching and Combat, Salafist Group for Call and Combat.

Organization:
- The Salafist Group for Preaching and Combat merged with al Qaeda in September 2006 and changed its name to al-Qa'eda in the Islamic Maghreb.
- Funding for the group is received from Algerians and AQIM members residing in Western Europe. The group also makes use of extensive criminal enterprises to raise funds.

Area of operations:

- Algeria and the Sahel (a strip of land that transects the width of North Africa that covers parts of Senegal, Mauritania, Mali, Burkina Faso, Niger, Nigeria, Chad, Sudan, Somalia, Ethiopia, and Eritrea).

Aims/goals:

- The formation of an Islamic state in Algeria.

Strengths:

- Claims to have several hundred fighters across its area of operation.

Weapons/tactics/capabilities:

- Suicide bombers, small arms, and automatic weapons.
- Although the group has pledged not to attack civilians inside Algeria, its attacks in the past have caused a number of civilian casualties.

Major actions:

- April 1, 2007: The AQIM used suicide bombers for the first time in a series of attacks that included the Algerian prime minister's office, where more than 30 people were killed.
- December 11, 2007: Carried out two vehicle suicide bombings against UN offices and the Constitutional Council that killed 41 people and injured 170 others.
- AQIM has also been responsible for attacks against Mauritanian military targets that killed 15.

40. Real IRA (RIRA)

A.k.a.:

- 32 County Sovereignty Committee, 32 County Sovereignty Movement, Irish Republican Prisoners Welfare Association, Real Irish Republican Army, Real Oglaigh Na Heireann.

Organization:

- Formed in 1997 as the clandestine military wing of the 32 County Sovereignty Movement and identified as a political pressure group. It opposed Sinn Fein's adopting the principles of democracy and nonviolence.
- Did not participate in the 2005 weapons decommissioning program.

Area of operations:

- Northern Ireland, Great Britain, and the Irish Republic.

Aims/goals:

- The removal of all British forces from Northern Ireland and the unification of Ireland.

- The RIRA also strives to disrupt the Northern Ireland peace process.

Strengths:

- The group consists of approximately 100 active members and 40 members who are currently imprisoned.
- In addition, the group has a small number of hard-line supporters, in both Ireland and the United States, who provide financial aid.

Weapons/tactics/capabilities:

- Small arms and explosives.
- The former members of the IRA who came over to the RIRA have a wealth of knowledge on the construction and uses of IEDs and other terrorist tactics.
- Although the RIRA carries on low-level attacks in Northern Ireland, it still remains a threat to create higher levels of violence in areas in which it operates.
- Reported to have purchased weapons in the Balkans.

Major actions:

- August 2002: Attack of a London army base that saw a construction worker killed.
- Suspected in the August 1998 Omagh bombing.

41. Revolutionary Armed Forces of Colombia (FARC)

A.k.a.:

- Fuerzas Armadas Revolucionaries de Colombia, Revolutionary Armed Forces of Colombia—People's Army (FARC-PE).

Organization:

- FARC began operations in 1964 as a splinter outgrowth of a number of Liberal Party self-defense leagues and adopted a Marxist philosophy.
- A general secretariat and six other senior commanders govern FARC; it is organized as a military organization, including specialized groups, such as urban fighting units.
- The Patriotic Union was created to act as the political wing of FARC but turned against the FARC tactics, and thus was all but eradicated after a time.
- Since its inception, FARC has received considerable assistance from Cuba, but this has recently has been reduced to medical aid, safe havens, and political consultation. Some weapons and other assistance have been received through Venezuela and other sources in South America.

Area of operations:

- Colombia, but has carried out kidnappings and other criminal acts in neighboring countries.

Aims/goals:

- Destabilization of the Colombian government.

Strengths:

- Estimated to be between 9,000 and 12,000 fighters with a substantial support apparatus.

Weapons/tactics/capabilities:

- FARC has carried out bombings, assassinations, kidnapping, hijackings, and mortar attacks. In addition, the group carries out conventional military actions against the Colombian military political targets; has also been linked to narcotics trafficking.
- Although FARC has entered into a number peace agreements, each has failed to produce any lasting solutions.

Major actions:

- Ongoing military campaign against the Colombian government that over the years has cost thousands of lives.

42. Revolutionary Organization 17

A.k.a.:

- Epanastatki Organosi 17 Noemvri, 17 November.

Organization:

- This radical leftist group was formed in 1975 to commemorate the 1973 student uprising protesting military rule.

Area of operations:

- Athens metropolitan area.

Aims/goals:

- Wants end of U.S. forces in Greece, removal of Turkish military units from Cyprus, and for Greece to end its relationship with NATO.

Strengths:

- Believed to consist of a very small number of active members.

Weapons/tactics/capabilities:

- Small arms and explosives to construct IEDs.
- 17 November has directed its attacks at senior U.S. officials and Greek public figures.
- It is not known whether or not the group is receiving any external aid.

Major actions:
  • June 2002: Made a failed bomb attack at the port of Athens that resulted in the arrest of 17 members of the terrorist group, including several key members.

43. Revolutionary People's Liberation Party/Front (DHKP/C)

A.k.a.:
  • Dev Sol, Dev Sol Armed Revolutionary Units, Dev Sol Silahli Devrimci Birlikleri, Dev Sol SDB, Devrimci Halk Kurtulus Partisi-Cephesi, Devrimci Sol, Revolutionary Left.

Organization:
  • This Turkish terrorist group was formed in 1978 as a splinter group of Dev Genc or Revolutionary Youth, taking the name Dev Sol. Infighting caused a rift and it changed its name, with the "party" handling political issues and the "front" carrying on with the terrorist operations.
  • The DHKP/C is suspected of maintaining offices or training facilities in the United Kingdom as well as Syria.

Area of operations:
  • Throughout Turkey but especially in the urban areas of Istanbul, Ankara, Izmir, and Adana.

Aims/goals:
  • The DHKP/C has a Marxist-Leninist philosophy and is profoundly anti-United States, as well as the Turkish government.
  • Hopes to establish a socialist state and demands a revamping of the Turkish prison system.

Strengths:
  • Very small, but has a substantial support group throughout Europe.

Weapons/tactics/capabilities:
  • Small arms and explosives.
  • The group is funded through extortion activities and legitimate donations from supporters in Europe.
  • Since the 1980s, the group has targeted Turkish security and military personnel, and later began attacking U.S. military and diplomatic targets.
  • Police raids on safe houses in both Belgium and Turkey netted a cache of weapons, and bomb-making materials and documents, as well as propaganda material. The raids resulted in the arrest of a number of DHKP/C members.

Major actions:

- July 2005: The group failed in a suicide bombing attempt against the Turkish Ministry of Justice building.
- June 2004: Suspected in a bombing of a bus at Istanbul University where 4 were killed and 21 injured.
- During the Gulf War, the group assassinated two U.S. military contractors and bombed more than 20 U.S. and NATO military targets inside Turkey.
- In 1996 assassinated a prominent Turkish businessman and two others.

44. Revolutionary Struggle (RS)

A.k.a.:

- Revolutionary Cells, ELA, Epanastatiki Pirines, Epanastatikos Laikos Agonas, June 78, Liberation Struggle, Organization of Revolutionary Internationalist Solidarity, Popular Revolutionary Struggle, Revolutionary People's Struggle, Revolutionary Popular Struggle.

Organization:

- An offshoot of the old ELA, first emerging in 2003.

Area of operations:

- Greece, especially in the Athens metro area.

Aims/goals:

- A leftist organization that is antiestablishment, anti-US/NATO/EU, and particularly against international capitalism and global trade.

Strengths:

- Unknown but believed to be fairly small.

Weapons/tactics/capabilities:

- In light of the critical financial status of the Greek government, the group has resumed active terrorist activities.
- Small arms and explosives; use of small IEDs and arson.
- The ELA carries out low-level bombing and arson attacks, usually against U.S. and European targets in the Athens area. Its attacks are usually accompanied by warning calls.

Major actions:

- April 2010: A police raid on a RS safe house netted a number of arrests and a cache of 430 pounds of explosives.
- 2007: An attack against the U.S. Embassy in Athens.
- December 2005: Bomb attack against the Greek government's finance building.

45. Shining Path (SL)

A.k.a.:

- Tupac Amaru, Sendero Luminoso, Ejercito Guerrillero Popular (People's Guerrilla Army) (EGP), Ejercito Popular de Liberacion (People's Liberation Army) (EPL), Partido Comunista del Peru (Communist Party of Peru) (PCP), Partido Comunista del Peru en el Sendaro Luminoso de Jose Carlos Mariategui (Communist Party of Peru on the Shining Path of Jose Carlos Mariategui), Socorro Popular del Peru (People Aid of Peru) (SPP).

Organization:

- Formed in the late 1960s by a former university professor, Abimael Guzman, based upon his belief in a militant Maoist doctrine. Since its beginnings the Shining Path gained the reputation of being the most ruthless terrorist group in the western hemisphere.
- Over the years the Peruvian government has declared that the Shining Path had been eliminated as a threat on a number of occasions, only to have it resurface stronger.

Area of operations:

- Throughout Peru, but especially in the rural areas of the Huallaga Valley, Ene River, and Apurimac Valley.

Aims/goals:

- The overthrow of the legitimate government of Peru, replacing it with a communist-orientated, peasant-controlled régime.

Strengths:

- Actual strength is unknown, but believed to be about 200 to 400 active fighters.
- There is no evidence that the Shining Path receives any external aid at this time.

Weapons/tactics/capabilities:

- SL has carried a protracted campaign of bombings, ambushes of Peruvian military and police units, as well as selective assassinations.
- Suspected that funds for the group are gotten through the trafficking of cocaine and the collection of "revolutionary taxes."

Major actions:

- October 2008: The group ambushed a military convoy in southern Peru and killed 13 soldiers, wounding a number more. It was their most successful action in a number of years.

- March 2002: Exploded a car bomb in front of the U.S. Embassy that killed 9 people only a short time prior to a visit by President Bush.
- 1983: Blew up several major transmission lines that caused a blackout in Lima.

46. United Self-Defense Forces of Colombia (AUC)

A.k.a.:
- Autodefensas Unidas de Colombia.

Organization:
- A paramilitary umbrella organization that was formed in April 1997, but over a period of time the AUC gave up its paramilitary operations in favor of the lucrative drug trade.

Area of operations:
- Operated for the most part in northwest Colombia.

Aims/goals:
- Originally formed to defend against leftist guerrillas, especially those of FARC.

Strengths:
- By 2007, AUC was all but dismantled, and many of its top leadership were under arrest and jailed in maximum-security facilities.

Weapons/tactics/capabilities:
- Except for a small cell, the military arm of AUC has virtually been dismantled. The Colombian government has declared that the AUC no longer exists, but in its wake some 20-odd criminal organizations were spawned.

Major actions:
- The AUC had in the past committed assassination of suspected insurgent supporters and engaging military units.

Index

I